Financing Sport

Titles in the Sport Management Library

Financing Sport

— THIRD EDITION —

Dennis R. Howard, PhD
University of Oregon

John L. Crompton, PhD
Texas A&M University

A Division of the International Center
for Performance Excellence
West Virginia University
262 Coliseum, WVU-CPASS
PO Box 6116
Morgantown, WV 26506-6116

Library of Congress Card Catalog Number: 2013948954

ISBN: 978-1-935412-42-7

Cover Design: Bellerophon Productions

Cover Photos: Stadium and runner images courtesy of BigStock Photo; tickets image courtesy of Joe DiFazio; money and calculator images courtesy of Dreamstime

Typesetter: Bellerophon Productions

Production Editors: Matt Brann and Rachel Tibbs

Copyeditor: Rachel Tibbs

Proofreader: Maria denBoer

Indexer: David denBoer

Printed by Sheridan Books, Inc.

10 9 8 7 6 5 4 3 2 1

FiT Publishing
A Division of the International Center for Performance Excellence
West Virginia University
262 Coliseum, WVU-CPASS
PO Box 6116
Morgantown, WV 26506-6116
800.477.4348 (toll free)
304.293.6888 (phone)
304.293.6658 (fax)
Email: fitcustomerservice@mail.wvu.edu
Website: www.fitpublishing.com

The foundation for our 40-year friendship has been our wonderful wives, Linda and Liz. Words cannot do justice to the enormous gratitude we have for their continuous love and support. We are truly two lucky guys.

—DH & JC

Contents

Detailed Contents

Acknowledgments

A project of this magnitude cannot be completed without the support of many individuals. We would like to acknowledge the many individuals whose support, advice, and commentary were invaluable to the preparation of this book.

Steve Acampa, Boston Celtics

David Bruce, Major League Soccer

Mary Burger, Texas A&M University

Mike DeMartini, Colorado College Athletics

Tim Dobyns, Row 27 Sports Marketing

Cindy Ferguson, University of Oregon

Ben Foster, University of Oregon, IT Consultant

Blake Holmes, Phoenix Suns

Erik Johannes, FC Dallas

Katy Lenn, University of Oregon Library

Matthew Maxson, University of Oregon

Kelsey Philpott, GMR Marketing

Paul Swangard, Warsaw Sports Marketing Center, University of Oregon

Nyea Sturman, Orlando Magic

Jenny Swaim, University of Oregon

Matt Van Wyen, Adidas

Introduction

In our view, the Great Recession has had a profound and lasting effect on the sports industry. The deep and punishing economic downturn began in December 2007 and technically ended in June 2009. However, it's clear the recession's impacts will be felt long into the future. The recovery has been lackluster with consumer demand, the housing sector, and bank lending all remaining weak into 2013. Some economists express concerns that our economy may never fully recover.[1] Whether this proves to be true or not, it is clear that sport managers are operating in a much more challenging economic environment than ever before. The impact of the Great Recession on most American families has been grim. More than three years after the recession was declared officially over, the net worth of the average U.S. household remained 20% under pre-recession levels. Given the declining financial condition of most American families, it is not surprising to find households reducing their spending, particularly on discretionary or entertainment options outside the home.[2] As will be discussed throughout the book, these changes in consumer spending have had and will continue to have a significant impact on the sports industry. Given the transformational impacts of the Great Recession, we believe it is important that its causes and long-term effects be fully understood by current and aspiring sport industry managers. Therefore, we have included this prologue to provide context for our frequent reference to the Great Recession throughout this new edition.

THE BOOM YEARS: THE 1990s AND EARLY MILLENNIUM YEARS

When the second edition of *Financing Sport* was published, the U.S. economy was in great shape. In fact, for most of the period from February 1991 through October 2007 the U.S. enjoyed unprecedented prosperity. The economy flourished in the 1990s, benefiting from the longest sustained period of economic growth in U.S. history.[1] The previous edition offered numerous examples of how the sports industry benefited from what we referred to as the '90s Boom. By the late 1990s, the economy was growing at a record rate and unemployment was at an all-time low.

The sports industry thrived during this period. The momentum of the 1990s allowed most sports leagues and properties to weather the brief economic recession in 2001. Overall industry growth, while expanding at a slower rate than in the '90s, continued largely unabated through most of 2007. Some of the notable features of this period of unprecedented growth included:

- **Sports Facility Construction Boom**
  Construction spending on new arenas and stadiums for major league professional sports teams was almost $16 billion during the 1995–2003 period (using the value of

the dollar in 2003). During the 1990s, over 160 new major and minor league ballparks, arenas, and auto racetracks were built in the United States and Canada.[2] New facility construction continued at a substantial pace through 2007, with 29 new stadiums and arenas coming on line for major league franchises between 2000 and 2007. At an average cost of $407 million per facility, the aggregate cost of new sports venue development over the first seven years of the new millennium totaled $11.8 billion (see Chapter 4 for a detailed cost breakdown of every major sport facility built between 1990 and 2012).

- **Proliferation of Professional Sports Leagues and Teams**
  In the 1990s, almost 180 new professional sport teams came into existence in North America, together with 13 new leagues (e.g., the XFL, National Rookie League, West Coast Hockey League). The total inventory of professional teams at all levels grew to more than 800. Unanticipated by analysts was the spectacular expansion of minor league hockey in the Sun Belt states and the emergence of women's sports leagues (e.g., Women's National Basketball Association, Women's United Soccer Association).

- **Increased Corporate Investment in Sport**
  Corporate investment in sport more than tripled from 1990 to reach $8 billion in 2000. By 2007, total corporate spending on sport in North America had increased to more than $20 billion. The three most common ways in which companies align with sports properties are corporate sponsorships, naming rights, and premium seating.

  - *Corporate sponsorships.* In 2000, companies in the United States and Canada spent $5.92 billion sponsoring sporting events and teams.[3] By 2008, total sponsorship spending on sport in North America had almost doubled to $11.28 billion.[4] By the mid-2000s, over 5,000 companies were partnered with sports organizations. The most common form of sponsorship occurs when a company pays a fee to have its company name or logo associated with a sports property such as the Professional Golf Association's (PGA) *Wells Fargo Championship* or the Women's Tennis Association's (WTA) *Pilot Pen Open.* Through sponsorships, companies attempt to capitalize on the appeal of the event to enhance the visibility and image of their brands in order to increase sales.

  - *Naming rights.* One of the most prominent manifestations of corporate America's alignment with sport has been the number of naming-rights deals since the mid-1990s. In 1990, only a handful of professional teams played in corporately named venues. In 2001, 82 major league teams played in arenas or stadiums named for a company brand or product.[5] When the growing number of Major League Soccer teams occupying new corporately-named venues is included, the total number of major league franchises currently playing in company-branded facilities has grown to 108 in the U.S. and Canada. By 2010, in the U.S. alone, over 250 sports venues at all levels—including racing tracks, minor league ballparks and arenas, and collegiate stadiums—were corporately named.[6] Some companies have made multiple naming rights investments. For example, Toyota is the naming rights holder at eight separate sports venues, ranging from the Toyota Speedway in Irwindale,

CA to Toyota Stadium in Georgetown, KY. With the proliferation of branded sports facilities has come a significant increase in the fees companies pay for naming rights. In the 1980s, the biggest naming rights deal was the $18.75 million entitlement of the Target Center in Minneapolis. Early in 2001, the $300 million barrier was broken when Reliant Energy Company paid $300 million over 30 years to name the home of the NFL's Houston Texans Reliant Stadium. In late 2006, Citigroup Inc. agreed to pay the owners of the New York Mets $400 million over 20 years for the naming rights to the team's new ballpark, Citi Field. Chapter 11 examines the benefits companies seek from naming partnerships with sports organizations and provides an in-depth examination of the essential features of naming rights contracts.

❍ *Premium seating.* By the mid-1990s, it was calculated that 114 teams in the four major leagues realized close to $1 billion from luxury suite revenues.[7] By 2007, NFL stadiums contained 4,354 suites, selling at an average of $100,000 per suite per season. Called *sky boxes* or *executive suites*, these amenity-laden suites are used by companies to entertain key clients or to reward high-performing employees. The great majority (over 75%) of these suite tenants are corporations with earnings that exceed $100 million annually. In addition to occupying the vast majority of suites, corporations reputedly purchase 50–60% of the most expensive season tickets sold in NHL and NBA arenas. It is evident, then, that overall corporate investment in sport properties at all levels grew substantially in this boom period.

- **Annual Sporting Goods Sales Steadily Climbed to a Record $90 Billion by 2007**
Table A shows that sporting good sales grew steadily over an extended period. The decade of the 1990s was a period of robust increases, with annual growth rates averaging a healthy 5%. By 2000, total expenditures for all sporting goods (e.g., footwear, apparel, equipment) and recreational transport (e.g., pleasure boats, bicycles, recreational vehicles, snowmobiles) approached $75 billion, an increase of almost 50% from the start of the 1980s. Solid growth continued through the mid-2000s, reaching a record level in 2007 of $91.4 billion. But, as shown in Table A, sporting good sales abruptly plummeted in 2008, dropping nearly 13% from the all-time high of 2007. By the end of 2009, overall sporting good sales had fallen 27% in just two years to $72 billion. The cause of the steep decline was a deep and prolonged economic downturn that ravaged the nation's economy. As will be seen in the next section, *all* sectors of the sports industry were adversely impacted by the unprecedented economic collapse that became known as the Great Recession. While the U.S. economy began to show signs of recovery in 2010 as reflected in Table A's projected improvement in sporting good sales, regaining the economic momentum of the pre-recession years has proven difficult. Persistently high rates of unemployment, a struggling housing market, and declining household income—all lingering effects of the Great Recession—have dramatically altered the economic landscape in which sport enterprises operate. The causes and impacts of the Great Recession and their implications for the sports industry are discussed at length in the next section.

Table A. Sporting Goods Sales by Product Category: 1990–2010

[In millions of dollars (50,725 represents $50,725,000), based on sample survey of 80,000 households in 1990 and 100,000 beginning in 2000]

Selected Product Category	1990	2000	2004	2005	2006	2007	2008	2009	2010 Proj.
Sales, all products	**50,725**	**74,442**	**85,811**	**88,434**	**90,472**	**91,423**	**79,632**	**72,055**	**75,666**
Annual percent change	(NA)	4.6	7.6	3.1	2.3	1.1	−12.9	−9.5	6.8
Athletic and sport clothing	*10,130*	*11,030*	*11,201*	*10,898*	*10,580*	*10,834*	*10,113*	*9,246*	*9,665*
Athletic and sport footwear	*11,654*	*13,026*	*14,752*	*15,719*	*16,910*	*17,524*	*17,190*	*17,069*	*17,282*
Aerobic shoes	611	292	237	261	262	280	260	223	216
Basketball shoes	918	786	877	878	964	892	718	741	735
Cross training shoes	679	1,528	1,327	1,437	1,516	1,584	1,626	1,531	1,527
Golf shoes	226	226	230	259	232	244	239	202	195
Gym shoes, sneakers	2,536	1,871	2,221	2,314	2,434	2,699	2,639	2,539	2,539
Jogging and running shoes	1,110	1,638	1,989	2,157	2,260	2,193	2,301	2,363	2,423
Tennis shoes	740	533	508	528	505	452	467	396	380
Walking shoes	2,950	3,317	3,496	3,673	4,091	4,197	4,204	4,416	4,543
Athletic and sport equipment	*14,349*	*21,608*	*23,328*	*23,735*	*24,497*	*25,061*	*24,862*	*24,421*	*24,568*
Archery	265	259	332	372	396	396	394	379	383
Baseball and softball	217	319	352	372	388	401	396	374	378
Billiards and indoor games	192	516	622	572	574	531	396	312	300
Camping	1,072	1,354	1,531	1,447	1,526	1,453	1,461	1,496	1,526
Exercise	1,824	3,610	5,074	5,177	5,239	5,500	5,328	5,301	5,345
Fishing tackle	1,910	2,030	2,026	2,139	2,218	2,247	2,067	1,859	1,861
Golf	2,514	3,805	3,198	3,466	3,669	3,772	3,495	2,836	2,864
Hunting and firearms	2,202	2,274	3,175	3,563	3,732	3,942	4,548	5,199	5,165
Optics	438	729	859	887	1,014	1,019	1,024	1,070	1,091
Skin diving and scuba	294	355	351	358	369	376	373	343	350
Snow skiing	475	495	452	643	501	531	482	502	516
Tennis	333	383	362	397	418	440	387	368	364
Recreational Transport	*14,502*	*28,779*	*36,531*	*38,082*	*38,485*	*38,003*	*28,226*	*20,120*	*24,151*
Bicycles and supplies	2,423	5,131	4,898	5,343	5,161	5,393	5,285	4,471	5,200
Pleasure boats, motors	7,644	13,224	16,054	17,634	17,907	17,473	13,679	9,097	10,781
Recreational vehicles	4,113	9,529	14,753	14,366	14,732	14,505	8,758	6,118	7,648
Snowmobiles	322	894	826	739	685	632	544	435	522

Source: National Sporting Goods Association, Mt. Prospect, IL., The Sporting Goods Market in 2010.

See http://www.nsga.org/i4a/pages/index.cfm?pageid=869\

THE GREAT RECESSION

The period of sustained economic growth came to an abrupt halt in November 2007, when the U.S. economy began what became known as the Great Recession. While officially declared over by June 2009, the impacts of this severe downturn have endured far beyond that date.

In order for the reader to more fully appreciate the challenges facing the sports industry as the economy struggles to recover from the devastating consequences of the 2007–2009 recession, a brief explanation of factors that led to the economic collapse is provided. There were a number of factors at work. In an effort to accelerate recovery during the previous 2001 recession, the Federal Reserve began to systematically cut interest rates. By December 2001, the federal funds rate (the interest rate banks charge each other for short-term loans) had been reduced to 1.75%, an almost 300% reduction from the 6.5% rate that prevailed in May of 2000. The falling interest rates made more affordable loans possible to millions of potential homeowners. As demand for housing increased, banks began extending mortgages to owners who traditionally would not have qualified for home loans. These so-called "subprime" mortgages were issued to borrowers with much lower credit ratings than historically had been required. Many receiving these subprime loans already carried extensive debt, often with a history of late or missed payments. Banks, anxious to fully exploit the housing boom, charged these high-risk borrowers a significantly higher rate of interest. Nonetheless, the more relaxed lending standards allowed millions of families to buy new or more expensive homes, further fueling the hyper-inflated housing market.

New home construction and housing prices reached a peak in late 2005. The housing boom began to wane in 2006, as a growing number of homeowners—mostly those with subprime loans—were unable to pay their mortgages. As more and more homes were put up for sale, market prices declined and new housing construction slowed. By 2007, the housing bubble had burst. Across the nation, homes sales and prices plummeted, falling a record 13% in the month of March 2007 alone.[8] Home foreclosures escalated dramatically. Homeowners no longer able to pay their mortgages and unable to sell their homes for anywhere near the price they originally paid were forced to give up their homes. As market values

The Stock market plunged during the Great Recession. Courtesy of BigStockPhoto

declined, many homeowners found themselves in a negative equity situation, commonly referred to as being "under water," where the homeowner owed more on the mortgage than the home was worth. By the end of 2009, 24% of all residential properties in the U.S. were under water.[9]

In the first quarter of 2008, foreclosure rates hit a record high.[10] The growing mortgage crisis hit major financial institutions very hard as mortgage-backed securities took heavy losses, a $250 billion decline in the first quarter of 2008 alone. Lehman Brothers, the 4th largest U.S. investment bank at that time, filed for bankruptcy in September 2008. Lehman had sold more mortgage-backed securities than any other firm. As the real estate market collapsed, losses mounted and the company's stock value plunged. Unable to recover, Lehman Brothers was forced to close its doors. Other venerable Wall Street giants, like Bear Stearns and Merrill Lynch, teetered on the edge of failure during the crisis (they were bought at "fire sale" prices by J.P. Morgan Chase and Bank of America, respectively). During 2008, 15 banks failed in the U.S., while many others were rescued by the federal government. As the financial crisis deepened, the stock market plunged. In one day in early October 2008, the Dow Jones Industrial Average (DJIA) fell 1,874 points or 18%. By March 2009, the DJIA had dropped to 6,969 from its peak of 14,164 in October 2007, a decline of 54%, representing a loss of over $11.2 trillion in just 17 months.[11] Even those families who had not invested directly in the stock market suffered serious losses as the value of their savings and retirement accounts plummeted with the crash of the market.

Grim Consequences for Many American Families

The struggling stock market reflected severe problems for the entire U.S. economy. By late 2008, official unemployment rates had risen to 10.8%. The U.S. Labor Department estimated that 8.4 million jobs were lost from late 2007 through early 2009. When *under*employed (part-time workers who can't find full employment) and the discouraged (those who were unsuccessful in finding work and stopped looking) are accounted for, the *real* or effective unemployment rate reached 16.4% at the height of the recession.[12] By contrast, the real jobless rate in May 2000 was 7.1%.

As jobless rates rose, household income fell. According to U.S. Census data, middle-class families in real dollar terms earned less in 2008 than they did at the start of the decade. Median household income in 2000 was $52,500. In 2008, when adjusted for inflation, it was down to $50,303.[13] Low-income Americans suffered even more. In 2000, 11.3% of the U.S. population was living below the poverty line. By the end of 2008, that number had grown to 13.2%.

A tally of some of the more grim statistics of the Great Recession illustrate the dire consequences. In a span of just 19 months, the recession had plunged 2.6 million more Americans into poverty, wiped out household income gains of an entire decade, and pushed unemployment numbers to the highest levels since the Great Depression.[14]

Not surprisingly, in such an unstable economic environment, many households curtailed spending. In 2009, consumer spending for all retail goods dropped more than 5%.[15] Significantly, for the sports industry, household expenditures on entertainment outside the home declined substantially. According to the Bureau of Labor Statistics, average annual spending on entertainment fell from $2,835 per household in 2008 to $2,693 in 2009, a 5.3% drop.[16]*

Still Digging Out

The U.S. economy showed signs of recovery by the end of 2009. Manufacturing productivity grew five straight months over the last half of 2009. Investors pushed stock market prices up substantially by the start of 2010. The Dow Jones Industrial Average rose from a low of 6,625 in March 2009 to 10,600 in January 2010, a jump in value of 60%. Even more gratifying was the stock market's steady growth over the next 24 months.

For many American households, the adverse impacts of the economic slump have endured well beyond the official end of the Great Recession in June 2009. A study released in late 2011 reported that between June 2009 and June 2011, inflation-adjusted median household income fell 6.7%, to $49,909.[21] The report attributed the continued decline in income to the fact that many people who lost jobs in the recession have taken significant pay cuts—an average of 17.5%—to find full-time employment again. In addition, the report found that two years after the end of the Great Recession, the duration of unemployment (the average length of time a person was out of work) increased to 40.5 weeks, the longest in 60 years. By late 2012, chronic or long-term unemployment persisted at levels not seen since the Great Depression of the 1930s. As of October 2012, three years after the Great Recession was declared over, 4.9 million Americans

Exhibit A
ONLY FEW BENEFIT FROM RECORD STOCK MARKET IN EARLY 2013

By March 2013, the Dow Jones average reached record highs, clearing 14,200 for the first time in history, completely erasing the markets 54% loss between 2007 and 2009. While the stock market gains represented progress in the nation's recovery, many economists pointed out that the U.S. economy was far from a full recovery and that most Americans realized little or no benefit from the bullish stock market. The real median wage still remained 8% below what it was in 2000.[17] Median household incomes fell 4.6% between June 2009 and June 2012, after adjusting for inflation. And, unemployment rates in early 2013 remain persistently high at 7.8%, 23.5 million Americans remained out of work or under-employed.[17] Former Secretary of Labor, Robert Reich, asserted that 90% of the economic gains achieved during the economic upsurge "went to richest 1% of Americans. The bottom 99% has continued to lose ground."[17] In fact, stock ownership remains concentrated among the very wealthy, with just 10% of the richest American families owning 85% of the stock market wealth.[19] In contrast, while 52% of American households report owning stock, "most families have a very small stake," with only 32% owning more than $10,000 of stock and 25% more than $25,000.[20] Given the concentration of holdings, it is not surprising to find that so few benefited from the record stock market in early 2013.

---

*An excellent explanation of the causes of the Great Recession is provided in an article written by Manoj Singh, "The 2007–08 Financial Crisis in Review" at the following website: www.investopedia.com/arti cles/economics/09/financial-crisis-review.asp

had been unemployed for more than 6 months and 3.6 million had been out of work for more than a year.[22]

As a result, most economists believe it will be a slow recovery. According to Nobel Laureate Paul Krugman, "We're digging out of a very deep hole." He projected that even if the economy were to grow 4% per year—which most economists believe would be an excellent accomplishment—reclaiming the more than 8 million jobs lost during the Great Recession will take years. "It's going to take a long time—2015—to get to [an unemployment rate of] 6%" (p. A9).[23]

It is clear that the adverse symptoms of a struggling economy will continue for the next several years. The next section will examine what this likely economic forecast means for the sports industry. One irrefutable consequence of the severe economic downturn of recent years is that sports are not immune to the negative impacts of a struggling economy. This new reality shattered the prevailing, widely held belief, going all the way back to the Great Depression, that the sports industry in North America was recession proof.[24]

SPORTS: NO LONGER RECESSION PROOF

The persistent conventional wisdom has been that, while in hard times the average consumer will forego certain discretionary income purchases, attending and/or watching sporting events will always remain a "basic need" because of fans' intense connections to their favorite teams. Indeed, some pundits expressed the view that avid fans remained even more devoted during tough economic times, using games as a way to escape life's harsh realities.[25] This view was based on the evidence of the last four decades, when the sports industry managed to weather a series of recessions occurring in 1970, 1974–75, 1980, 1982, 1990–91 and 2001.[26]

The severity and duration of the 2007–2009 Great Recession destroyed the notion that sports are impervious to a prolonged economic slump. As a column in *The New Yorker* pointed out, "In the old days, when you used to be able to go to Yankee Stadium for three dollars and fifty cents to buy a box seat, that kind of assumption [sports are recession proof] held . . . But, today, a box seat isn't three fifty, you pay twelve hundred and fifty dollars for the best box seat" (p. 2).[27] While the magnitude of increase may be a bit extreme in this example, the cost of attending professional sporting events across the country has grown exponentially over the past two decades.

The full price of attending a professional sports event has more than doubled since 1990 in real dollar terms.[28] In 1991, the average cost of a ticket to a Major League Baseball (MLB) game was less than $5.00. In 2011, that same ticket price had jumped to almost $27. And, among the major league sports, baseball is by far the best "bargain." In that same year, the average cost of a ticket to a National Football League (NFL) game was $77, followed by the National Hockey League (NHL) at $54.25 and the National Basketball League (NBA) at $47.66 per ticket.

But, of course, buying a ticket is only part of the cost of attending a big league game. When you include parking, food and beverage, etc., the full cost grows substantially. The complete price associated with attending a single game for a family of four *on aver-*

age exceeded $300 in 2010–11.[28] That accounts for 38% of an average household's *weekly* earnings. According to the 2010 U.S. Census, the median weekly earnings of a full-time wage and salary worker over 25 years of age in 2010 was $788.[29]

As always, average increases hide some extremely egregious cases. In a *New York Times* article, headlined "Gouge City," a prominent columnist reported:

> Long time ticket holders, the loyal of the loyal, are being billed for 100% increases or more just to hold on to the same seats they had for a decade or three. He gave examples including: "A seat at the Rangers on their Stanley Cup year of 1994 was $50, the price reached triple digits three years later, the seat in 2010 was $240. In 2011, it was increased to $715." The fan who held this seat and was subjected to these price increases observed: "The Garden (Madison Square Garden) is writing off its longtime fans in favor of corporate patrons. It's pretty evident that the Garden cares less whether we purchase its seats as long as someone does. That's plain to see in my section, where very few of the old guard are left, as they've been swept away like a Lundqvist clear. Like Seventh Avenue, loyalty is not a two-way street in this neighborhood.[30] (pp. 5, 8)

For many households, affordability, particularly in difficult economic times, is a serious issue. While it's certainly possible for fans to take advantage of cost-saving measures (purchase less expensive tickets [many teams are offering aggressive discounts], take public transportation, etc.), the full cost of attendance for many middle-class families still requires significant investment of scarce family resources. Even if a bargain-minded family of four could cut the cost of attending to half the average, or $150, that amount still consumes almost 20% of an average worker's weekly earnings. This has led many analysts to assert that most middle-income fans have been priced out of attending major league games.[31] Roger Angell, a celebrated baseball writer, proclaimed that "going to a ball game has become a perk of the rich" (pp. 8–9).[32] While Angell's assertion may be a bit extreme, it does appear that the relentless rise in the cost of tickets and ancillary costs over the past two decades makes contemporary sport much more vulnerable to economic downturns. When a family is struggling to make a house payment, it's hard to imagine them spending hundreds of dollars to attend a game, no matter what level of emotional attachment they might feel for their favorite team.

It's not surprising, then, to see professional sports leagues suffer attendance declines during the Great Recession. Table B shows that total attendance dropped for three of the four major leagues from 2007 to 2011. Major League Baseball suffered the greatest losses. Even with a modest uptick during the 2011 season, total attendance was well below pre-recession levels, with more than six million *fewer* fans attending games in 2011 than 2007 (the 2007 MLB season ended before the effects of the Great Recession were widely felt). Most troubling for baseball is that as recently as the 2011 season, one third of MLB franchises were barely able to sell 60% of their available seating inventory (four teams sold less than 50%). The lingering effects of the Great Recession are particularly apparent for teams that perform poorly. All four of the MLB teams with the lowest attendance were at or near the bottom of the standings in their respective divisions in 2010.

NASCAR reported attendance was down by 10% at a majority of race tracks on the Sprint Cup circuit in 2010.[33] Minor league baseball's 15 leagues and 176 teams also showed a modest but persistent decline in gross attendance from 2007 through 2010, down overall by 3.3%.[34]

The NBA and NFL also experienced attendance declines during the recession years, and by 2011 had still not reached pre-recession season attendance totals. The NFL's attendance was down 400,000 and the NBA's was down 540,000 over the 5-year time span. Again, it is disconcerting to see the dip continue beyond the end of the 2007–2009 recession. It is quite possible that the losses reflect the difficult times still facing many American families. A number of analysts attribute the persistent declines in major league attendance to more than just the high price of attendance. The advent of high-definition television and its ability to enhance the in-home viewing experience has created a cheaper and, for many, hassle-free alternative to live attendance. According to Eric Grubman, executive vice president of NFL Ventures and Business Operations, "The product [high-definition television] is really exceptional at home. That makes it easier, if you're having a tough time making ends meet, to not go to the stadium" (pp. 1A–2A).[35] According to the Leichtman Research Group, by 2012, 69% of U.S. households owned at least one HDTV, up from 17% in 2006.[36]

The Great Recession not only dampened fan spending on sport, the severe economic downturn also significantly curtailed corporate investment in sports properties at all levels. The decline in corporate support has been particularly painful during the 2007–2009 downturn. Since the prosperous 1990s, sports leagues and teams became increasingly dependent on corporations who spent lavishly on luxury suites, advertising and signage, naming rights agreements and the purchase of high-priced season ticket packages. Several years ago, it was estimated that corporations spent an estimated $20 billion a year on U.S. sports properties, accounting for no less than 25% of the gross annual revenues generated by major league sports teams.[24] As one team senior executive expressed, "corporate support has become the lifeblood of sports organizations" (p. 23).[24]

However, during the economic downturn, corporate spending on sports marketing dropped markedly. According to a leading sports economist, Andrew Zimbalist, by 2009, "[corporate] sponsorships, naming rights, advertising deals are going away or dis-

Table B. Attendance for Major U.S. Sports Leagues, 2007–2011 (in millions)

	2007	2008	2009	2010	2011	Diff.	% Diff '07–'11
MLB	79.50	78.59	73.39	73.05	73.45	−6.05	−8.2
NFL	17.52	17.33	17.15	17.00	17.12	−0.40	−2.3
NBA	21.84	21.40	21.39	21.09	21.30	−0.54	−2.5
NHL	20.86	21.29	21.49	20.91	20.93	+0.07	+0.4

Source: ESPN Attendance Reports: 2007, 2008, 2009, 2010, and 2011.

appearing" (p. 2).[37] This has been particularly true for several sectors of the economy that were hardest hit. Major U.S. automobile companies, such as General Motors and Chrysler, entered bankruptcy and had to be rescued by the federal government. Similarly, giant financial service and insurance firms devastated by the collapse of the housing market, such as the Bank of America, Citigroup and AIG, received billions of dollars in federal assistance in early 2009. All of these firms had been major investors in sports businesses. Sensitive to both their difficult financial positions and under intense public scrutiny as a result of the federal "bailout," these companies dramatically reduced their spending on sport during 2008 and 2009. For example, General Motors ended its long-standing partnership with the U.S. Olympic Committee, terminated numerous sponsorship agreements with NASCAR racing teams and the PGA and (after airing 11 advertisements during the 2008 Super Bowl) did not buy a single Super Bowl advertisement in 2009. As we'll see later in this chapter, General Motors, along with many other major companies, began reinvesting in sports marketing in 2010 as the economy improved. Indeed, GM returned in a big way to the Super Bowl in 2011, airing eight Chevrolet commercials during the game, a substantial investment given that the commercial air time averaged about $3 million per 30-second commercial unit during the telecast.

Like leaders in most other segments of the economy, sports executives were surprised by the severity of the 2007–2009 economic downturn. As economist Andrew Zimbalist pointed out, it wasn't only people in the sports sector who were caught off guard. "People in the financial sector certainly didn't see the collapse coming. You'd hardly expect David Stern and Bud Selig and Roger Goodell and so on to anticipate something that the country's leading economists and finance gurus didn't anticipate" (p. C5).[38] As the adverse impacts of the Great Recession became evident, leagues and teams made some difficult and painful decisions. In early October 2008, nearly a year into the recession, the NBA became the first major American sports league to announce layoffs, cutting 80 jobs, or about 9% of its U.S. workforce. In making the announcement, Commissioner Stern attributed the staff reductions to the "global economic slowdown." In December 2008, Commissioner Goodell issued a statement indicating that the NFL would be laying-off 168 employees, or 15% of its workforce, and that he would be taking a 20% salary cut (about $2 million!). Shortly thereafter, Major League Baseball Advanced Media, a league subsidiary responsible for running the sport's highly successful Internet division, laid off close to 5% of its workers. Similarly, NASCAR announced it would be releasing about 70 of its full-time employees. Amateur sports also suffered. In early 2009, the United States Olympic Committee cut 15% of its staff.

Job cuts occurring at the league level were indications of trends across the sports industry. Those announcing substantial workforce reductions, included NASCAR's Dale Earnhardt Racing (116 employees), the NBA Charlotte Bobcats (35 employees), and the NFL Washington Redskins (20 employees). To alleviate the financial crisis facing many of its teams, in February 2009 the NBA announced that it had arranged a $200 million dollar loan for up to 15 franchises struggling to cover operational losses.

In addition to making painful cost-cutting decisions, many sports organizations offered a number of price incentives to fans in an effort to sustain attendance. Increasingly unnerved by job security fears and declining home values, many adopted a more cautious approach to spending, particularly for what they considered to be discretionary or non-essential purchases. For many, the cost of attending a sporting event was seen as a luxury. In response to declining attendance, many teams initiated deep discount programs and promotional giveaways.

As Kotler asserted, "In a recession the goal is survival, not profits." Given the considerable evidence that winning back lost customers is difficult and expensive, a sensible approach during difficult economic conditions is to adjust prices to accommodate consumers' changing price expectations and willingness to pay.[39] Thus, prior to the 2009 MLB season, hoping to retain 11,000 season ticket customers up for renewal, the San Francisco Giants slashed prices for a significant portion of their season-ticket holders. Team president, Larry Baer, said, "Our ticket holders want some acknowledgement from the Giants that times are tough. We're sending a signal to our fans we'll work with them to make this work out" (p. D8).[40]

Some teams went to extraordinary lengths to induce fans to buy season tickets. The NHL St. Louis Blues, a team that had been struggling for years, offered a half-price-due-up-front deal on season ticket packages, with one unique caveat: The other half of the ticket price would only have to be paid IF the Blues made the playoffs. In fact, the team did not get into the playoffs that season. However, despite finishing close to the bottom of the standings, the special promotion would have to be termed a success from a fan support standpoint, as the Blues virtually sold out their arena for the entire season, averaging 19,950 fans per home game.[41] The NBA Minnesota Timberwolves went a step further. The team offered a "No Risk Pledge" season ticket plan that guaranteed full refunds to customers who lost their jobs in 2009.

A number of teams offered, for the first time, installment payment plans to season ticket holders, including the Los Angeles Lakers and Portland Trailblazers. The New Jersey Nets went even further, offering a deferred payment program. The team offered a full season ticket package that allowed consumers to attend games for the first two months of the season without having to pay until January, after almost 40% of the home games had been played.

According to Dave Checketts, the then-owner of the St. Louis Blues, one of many teams offering "interest free" installment payment plans to fans, "In the short term, we're going to end up looking more like car dealers than sport franchises" (p. 32).[42] It's clear that Mr. Checkett's characterization of sport franchises will apply for years to come. The slow economic recovery will require teams to remain price sensitive. Many of the ticket price discounts and special promotions that were considered a necessity during the Great Recession have become standard pricing tactics for teams during the post-recession recovery period. Sports organizations hoping to retain and grow their fan bases will continue to offer "budget-friendly " price incentives that consumers have come to expect. Installment and/or deferred ticket payment plans, money-back guarantees and special promotions like the NBA Miami Heat's prize to an early renewing season-ticket holder—the team paid up to $5,000 of the lucky winner's property taxes—have become standard practice.

LOOKING AHEAD

The golden era of unparalleled growth and optimism that characterized the '90s and most of the 2000s has given way to a future that is less certain. For the foreseeable future, successful managers will have to find ways to deal with a difficult economy. An economy characterized by persistently high unemployment, shrinking household income and conservative spending by most companies. Competition will be ferocious for the finite buying power and discretionary time of sport fans, who have more entertainment choices than ever before, both inside and outside of the home. At the same time, the cost of operating sports franchises and major college sports programs have skyrocketed over the past 10 to 15 years. Helping managers to effectively cope with the reality of plateauing revenues and rising costs is the essential thrust of the 3rd edition of our book.

ORGANIZATION OF THE BOOK

Although the focus of the book is on the two most visible segments of the sport industry, intercollegiate and professional sports, the methods and strategies of revenue acquisition discussed in its chapters can be adapted to a wide range of public and private sport organizations. Throughout the book, numerous references and examples are drawn from a variety of sport settings.

Sport organizations are likely to acquire financial resources from three generic sources, which are shown in Table C: the public sector, the private sector, and the sport enterprise.

The public sector has traditionally assumed a significant role in the financing of sport organizations. Although government support may be axiomatic in the collegiate context, some are surprised to find it is so pervasive in the professional sports area. Consider the following:

> Modern professional sport in the United States exists as we know it as a result of the public policies of federal, state, and local governments. Without favorable tax treatment of the professional sports industry, antitrust exemptions for the NFL-AFL merger and Major League Baseball, and the broad antitrust exemption for the packaging of telecast and broadcast rights to league games, the economics and business operations of professional sports leagues would be dramatically different.

Table C. Sources of Revenue for Sports Organizations		
Private Sector Sources	**Public Sources**	**Sports Enterprise Sources**
Investment capital	General ("hard") taxes	Tickets, concessions
Corporate sponsorships	Selective ("soft") taxes	PSLs
Donations	Grants, subsidies	Naming rights
	Tax abatements	Premium seating
		Licensed merchandise
		Media rights fees

Similarly, without the public financing of playing facilities, below-market rents for the facilities, tax exemptions, and other forms of subsidies provided by local and state governments, the economics and business operations of professional sports would be significantly different. This is just as true of those sports organizations and events that are not considered to be major league (i.e., the secondary sports market) as it is for the major league sports and premier sporting events.[43]

At the local government level, cities and counties have a long tradition of committing substantial tax monies in support of sport from youth programs to the construction and operation of stadiums and arenas for professional teams. However, in the past decade the sports landscape has been transformed by the commercial alignment of private companies with sports organizations in the form of event sponsorships (e. g., the Nokia Sugar Bowl) and stadium naming agreements (e. g., MetLife Stadium) that were valued at $9 billion per year by 2010. Finally, sports properties can generate substantial revenue directly from their own operations through the sale of admission tickets, concessions, licensed merchandise, and media rights. Over the past decade, prices for attending sports events have risen at unprecedented rates. Ticket prices to major league sporting events have almost doubled since the early 2000s. High-revenue-yielding premium seating options (club seats, luxury suites) displaced less expensive seating in all stadiums and arenas built over the past two decades. PSLs (permanent seat licenses), COIs (contractually obligated income streams), and a number of other revenue-enhancing innovations have become standard features throughout professional and collegiate sport in North America.

Before examining the major sources of revenue available to sport managers, Section I of the new edition lays the foundation for the book. Chapter 1 examines the many challenges and opportunities facing the sports industry in a post-recession economy. The chapter spotlights several emerging concerns such as the explosive growth of televised sports and its potentially adverse impact on live attendance, the narrowing demographics of sports attendance as leagues and teams become increasingly dependent on more affluent fans, and the increased pressure on sport managers to do more with less. The chapter concludes with an examination of how one sports property has effectively used social media as a prominent element of its business model to reach target markets.

Chapters 2 and 3 provide a comprehensive overview of the two most visible segments of organized sport, professional sports and intercollegiate athletics. Chapter 2 focuses on the many challenges facing collegiate athletic programs, including spiraling costs, increased competition, and flat or declining revenues. Issues related to Title IX compliance and the law's substantial financial implications are covered in detail. Chapter 3 provides an in-depth examination of the collective bargaining agreements of each of the major professional leagues and their implications for team financial performance. The intent of this introductory chapter is to furnish readers with insights into the many financial challenges and opportunities facing the thousands of sports teams operating in the United States and Canada at the major and minor league levels. Actual and hypothetical team profit and loss statements are included to illustrate the revenue and cost structure of team operations. Chapter 4 examines trends in the cost and number of new sports facilities built over the past two decades and discusses "who should pay" for the development of these new venues. Should sport facilities be financed primarily from public tax sources, or should teams and/or private owners pay their own way? The sources of momentum undergirding the large public investment in sport facilities are analyzed, and the contentious issues of opportunity costs and equity that invariably accompany public subsidy decisions are discussed.

Section II of the book focuses on economic rationales for public investment in major sport venues and events. Invariably, studies are undertaken to measure the magnitude of economic benefits purported to accrue from public investment in sport facilities. These are central to debates about the justification of tax-based subsidies that invariably arise when sports projects are proposed. Chapter 5 focuses on the principles of economic impact analysis and highlights errors commonly made in these analyses—sometimes inadvertently, but often deliberately to inflate the impact. Chapter 6 points out that economic impacts are only one side of the economic ledger, and they have to be weighed against the costs associated with new projects. Project proponents of new stadiums and arenas usually omit, and often suppress, cost information that should be central to making informed decisions. The importance of including such economic factors as opportunity and displacement costs and foregone property is highlighted. Total community benefits from sport projects are not confined to direct economic impacts, they also embrace the structural and social capital associated with them. As skepticism has grown toward the purported economic benefits of major sport facilities and events, advocates have redirected their justifications toward these less measurable benefits. Chapter 7 discusses the merits of the structural capital legacy case, which refers to built sport facilities, complementary development associated with them, and physical infrastructure improvements that they may stimulate. Chapter 8 evaluates the potential contribution of new facilities or events to social capital, which is concerned with the relationships that bind people together to accomplish collective community goals. How such projects might enhance a community's "brand equity" is described, that is awareness of its identity and desired image that cause it to "stand out in the crowd." Chapter 8 goes on to evaluate sport's potential for attracting businesses and tourists to give residents improved employment opportunities and income levels, how it may build community pride and self-esteem, and its potential for strengthening community bonding and social cohesion.

Section III covers the many capital funding options available from both public and private sector sources. When managers seek public sector funding, it is important that they have some understanding of the alternative options available for acquiring these tax dollars. Thus, Chapter 9 provides an overview of the basic sources of taxation. Content includes a discussion of how various property and sales taxes are administered by governments and the manner in which they have been used to finance sport facility development. The chapter concludes with a review of the various kinds of tax-exempt and taxable bonds used to underwrite stadium and arena construction projects. Chapter 10 describes how government agencies and sports organizations can creatively combine public and private sources of capital to produce opportunities that neither could achieve alone. The chapter examines the principles that underlie funding partnerships between sports properties and public sector authorities. Numerous examples of successful joint venture arrangements are provided to illustrate how managers can leverage partnerships with other entities.

Section IV of the book focuses on the financial resources that accrue directly from the operation of sport enterprises. Chapter 11 focuses on the three most prominent facility-related income sources: premium seating, permanent seat licenses (PSLs) and naming rights. These three income streams have transformed the sports landscape at all levels over the past 20 years. The almost $40 billion investment in new sports venue construction since the early 1990s is almost entirely attributable to the ability of professional and collegiate sports properties to sell this inventory at ever-increasing prices. The chapter provides an in-depth examination of current and best practices related to the sale and administration of premium seating, seat licenses and naming rights. The three remaining chapters in the section are contributed by leading experts in each topic area. We have invited leading authorities to write a chapter drawing on their extensive background and "firing line" experience in three specialty areas: ticket operations, media sales and licensing. Gregg Olson, Executive Vice President for Finance, with the Portland Trailblazers, is the principal author of Chapter 12, "Ticket Sales and Operations." The chapter content reflects his 20 year experience as the chief financial officer with three different professional sport franchises. Chapter 13, "Commercializing Media Rights," is contributed by Lee H. Berke, President and CEO of LHB Sports and Entertainment. Mr. Berke is the leading consultant for the creation of regional sports networks and was the co-author of the original YES Network business plan. Rick Van Brimmer, the Director of Trademark Licensing at The Ohio State University, contributed Chapter 14, "Sale of Licensed Merchandise." He is responsible for the strategic brand management of Ohio State's $9 billion apparel licensing program at Ohio State and is the only two-time President of the American Collegiate Licensing Association.

References

1. Reich, R. (2010). *After-shock: The next economy and America's future* . New York, NY: Alfred A. Knopf.
2. Howard, D. & Crompton, D. (2004). *Financing sport* (2nd ed.). Morgantown, WV: Fitness Information Technology.
3. *IEG Sponsorship Report.* (2000, December 20). p. 1.
4. *IEG Sponsorship Report.* (2011, February 9), p. 3.
5. *Team Marketing Report.* (2000, May). pp. 7–8.
6. SportsBusiness Journal. (2011, September 19–25). *Naming rights.*
7. Grinstead, J. (2010). *Revenues from Sports Venues: 2010 Pro Edition.* Nashville, TN: Mediaventures; Mansur, L. (2010). Revenues from Sports Venues: 2010 College Edition, Nash-ville, TN: Mediaventures; *Wikipedia: List of sports venues with sole naming rights*, March 2011.
8. U.S. National Association of Realtors Statistics: *1968–2008 Median Home Prices.* Retrieved from www.scribd.com
9. Glink, I. (2010, February 23). *Underwater with your mortgage? So are a growing number of home-owners.* Retrieved from Moneywatch.com
10. Realty Trac. (2008, April 13). *U.S. foreclosure activity increases 23 percent in first quarter.* Press Release, p. 1.
11. Paradis, T. (2009, October 10). The statistics of the Great Recession. *Huffington Post.* Retrieved from huffingtonpost.com
12. *U.S. Department of Labor Report*, May 2009.

13. Serwer, A. (2009, November 24). The '00s: Goodbye (at last) to the decade from hell. *Time*. Retrieved from www.time.com/time/print out/0,8816,19142834.html

14. Morello, C., & Keating, D. (2009, September 11). Recession has thrust millions into poverty, census statistics show, *Washington Post*.

15. Economic and Social Research Institute (2009, August). ESRI white paper: 2009 methodology statement—Consumer spending.

16. Bureau of Labor Statistics (2009, October 5). Consumer spending—2009, BLS Economic News Release.

17. Reich, R. (2013, March 5). Why there's a bull market for stocks and bear market for workers. *Huffington Post*. Retrieved from http://robert reich.org/post/44639598939

18. Wagner, D. (2013, March 5). 5 reasons the Dow Jones record high means nothing to average Americans. *KSHB*. Retrieved from http:// www .kshb.com/dpp/money/business_news/dow-jones -sets-new-record-high——but-so-what

19. Plumer, G. (2013 (March 11). Who benefits from a stock-markt boom? *Washington Post*. Retrieved from http://www.washingtonpost .com/blogs/wonkblog/wp/2013/03/11/graph-of -the-day-who-actually-benefits-from-a-stock-mar ket-boom/

20. The wealth divide: The growing gap in the United States between the rich and the rest. An Interview with Edward Wolff. *The Multinational Monitor*, 24(5). http://multinational monitor.org/mm2003/03may/may03interviews wolff.html

21. Pear, R. (2011, October 9). Recession officially over, U.S. incomes kept falling. *New York Times*. Retrieved from http://nytimes.com/2011/10 /10/us/recesssion-officially-over-us-incomes-kept -falling.html

22. Krugman, P. (2012, December 9). Unemployment issue is real tragedy, outrage. *Eugene Register Guard*, p. G3

23. Krugman, P. (2011, January 4). Economic good news could be bad news of jobs. *Eugene Register Guard*, p. A9.

24. Howard, D., & Burton, R. (2002, March/April). Sports marketing in a recession: It's a brand new game. *International Journal of Sports Marketing & Sponsorship*, p. 23.

25. Holmes, B. (2009, December 3). This time around sports aren't recession proof. *Los Angeles Times*. Retrieved from http://articles.latimes .com/2009/dec/30/sports/la-sp-economy30-2009 dec30

26. Kaplan, D. (1998, October 19–25). Is sports recession-proof? *SportsBusiness Journal*, pp. 1, 37; Howard, D., & Burton, R. (2002, April/May). Sports marketing in a recession: It's a brand new game. *International Journal of Sports Marketing & Sponsorship*, p. 25.

27. Zenilman, A. (2009, August 5). The sports recession. *The New Yorker*, p. 2.

28. Team Marketing Report (September 2011), p. 9.

29. Bureau of Labor Statistics (2011, January 20). Usual weekly earnings of wage and salary workers, fourth quarter 2010. *BLS News Release*.

30. Vecsey, G. (2011, April 6). Gasps from the grandstands after the invoice arrives. The *New York Times*, pp. 5, 8.

31. Zimbalist, A. (2001, March 12–18). History—and leading economic indicators—best guides to future. *SportsBusiness Journal*, pp. 1, 30.

32. Angell, R. (1998, June 17). Comment: Rudy awakening. *The New Yorker*, pp. 8–9.

33. Ryan, N. (2010, May 7). Lower prices, promotions don't stop NASCAR attendance drop in 2010. *USA Today*, p. 6C.

34. Kronheim, D. (2011). 2010 Minor League Baseball attendance analysis. *Number Tamer*. Retrieved from numbertamer.com

35. McCarthy, M. (2010, September 1). Attendance likely to fall for third straight season in 2010, to lowest level since 1998. *USA Today*, pp. 1–2A.

36. *Broadcast Engineering* (2012, June 17). U.S. HDTV households top two-thirds, says Leichtman Research Group. Retrieved from http:www //broadcastengineering.com/news/us_hdtv_two -thirds_research_01172012/

37. Jaffe, M. (2009, March 5). Is the sports business recession-proof? *ABC News*. Retrieved from abcnews.go.com/Business/Economy/t/story?id +7010282&pages=1

38. Zenilman, A. (2009, August 5). The sports recession. *The New Yorker*, p. 2.

39. Kotler, P. (2000). Plan for the recession. *Kotler Marketing Group*. Retrieved from www.kotler marketing

40. Schulman, H. (2008, December 8). Giants lowering ticket prices. *San Francisco Chronicle*, p. D8.

41. Daidone, A. (2010). *Recession-busting sports tickets deals*. Retrieved from Investopedia.com

42. Lefton, T. (2008, December 22). Top Executives: Throw Out the Playbook for '09. *Sports Business Journal*, p. 32.

43. Johnson, A.T. (1993). Rethinking the sport-city relationship: In search of partnership. *Journal of Sport Management*, 7, 61–70.

Section I
Sport Finance Trends and Challenges

1

Operating in the New Economic Reality

INTRODUCTION

It is clear that the post-recession economy poses serious challenges for the managers of sport enterprises. Paradoxically, consumers have more choices than ever before, but fewer discretionary dollars available to spend on entertainment options. The competition for sports fans' time and disposable income is ferocious. This chapter highlights many key changes that confront sports managers in this challenging environment. One emerging issue addressed in the chapter is the rapid proliferation of televised sport and its impact on live attendance. Sports fans now have access to a growing host of national and regional cable networks dedicated to providing 24/7 sports programming. The ubiquitous content presents a growing dilemma to the owners and operators of sports leagues and teams. Will fans reach a point where the quality and convenience of home viewing is preferable to going to the arena or stadium? There is already some evidence that fans are substituting live sport on TV for the live experience in the ballpark

Sport is operating in a new economic reality. Courtesy of Dreamstime

or arena. Consider America's most popular sports league. In 2012, the NFL's average television rating was up 15% compared to 2007. In contrast, over the same five year period, live game attendance steadily declined with almost 5% fewer fans attending in 2012.[1] While it is likely that more fans are choosing to forego the in-stadium or arena experience for the comfort and convenience of their living room television, it is clear that a contributing factor, if not the primary cause of eroding attendance for a growing number of fans, is the high cost of attendance. The lingering effects of the recession have made it increasingly difficult for many households to afford the cost of attending major professional and college sporting events. Evidence suggests that the high prices required to attend major league games has meant that only the most affluent American households can afford to attend on a regular basis. The chapter addresses the issue of price as an increasing barrier to live attendance and the growing likelihood of an ever-shrinking pool of prospective season-ticket holders representing as few as 15% to 20% of the households in a given marketplace. Again, consider the NFL. "Fans simply can't afford to go to games. If you take a family of four and you get an average seat—between the parking and making the day for the kids a good experience [with concession items] you are spending about $600, which is the price you'd pay for a good TV back home" (para. 6).[1] While franchise operators face the challenge of producing more revenue to meet ever-increasing operational costs (e.g., player salaries, venue debt obligations, etc.), they must recognize that fewer households may be able to afford the price of attending major sporting events. The impact of affordability on live attendance has become a heightened concern with the explosive growth of televised sport. It raises the serious question of whether even die-hard fans will be willing to spend hundreds of dollars to go to the ballpark when they can watch the same game for "free" on their 50-inch HD television? Successful managers will find creative ways to reduce price as a barrier to attendance to ensure access to as many fans as possible. The chapter also examines the challenges and opportunities resulting from the rapid globalization of sport. Major sports properties around the globe, led by the English Premier League, are aggressively pursuing efforts to expand their international presence through television, live exhibitions and licensing agreements. The NBA has led the charge in this country to penetrate markets in both Asia and Europe. Finally, the chapter examines how the Ultimate Fighting Championship (UFC) used social media to become the dominant sports property in what has become the world's fastest growing sport over the last decade, Mixed Martial Arts.

OPERATING IN A NEW ECONOMIC REALITY

While the economic recovery has been slow, real signs of life appeared in 2012 The Dow Jones Industrial Average's continuing climb, a rise in factory output, and the decline in the rate of job layoffs over the first quarter of the year were all encouraging signs. All of these positive trends continued into 2013. Even the housing market showed signs of recovery, with sales of existing homes edging up about 3%.[2] And as the general economy improved, so did the fortunes of most sports properties.

Corporate spending on sport has rebounded from a very down year in 2009. According to the *IEG Sponsorship Report*, investment by North American companies in sport grew a modest 3.4% in 2010, followed by an accelerated rate of 6.1% in 2011.[3] The four major leagues have been the primary beneficiaries of this expanded corporate investment. Since 2009, the four major sports leagues have seen sponsorship revenue increase by more than $400 million to a total of $2.46 billion in 2011.

Attendance at sporting events also showed a slight uptick into 2012. Major League Baseball attendance was up 4% from 2011, averaging 31,516 league-wide. While encouraging, MLB attendance remains below the pre-recession high of 32,785 in 2007. NFL attendance was essentially flat, with just a 0.3% increase. Significantly, nine NFL teams were down 6% or more from 2011 attendance levels. Both the NBA and NHL reported modest overall attendance gains for the 2010–11 season, with both leagues up just 1% over 2009–10. Although neither league has returned to pre-recession attendance levels, an encouraging sign is that almost two-thirds of the teams in each league showed an increase or, at least, no decline in average home attendance during the 2010–11 season. Unfortunately, there are a handful of teams in both leagues that continue to struggle at the gate. Attendance woes have plagued many of the NHL's so-called "Sun Belt" teams for years. Hockey franchises in a number of markets, such as Atlanta, Anaheim, and Phoenix, have perennially drawn an average of 3,000 to 5,000 fewer fans per home game than the league average. At the end of the 2011 season, the NHL franchise in Atlanta, the Thrashers, relocated to Winnipeg, Canada (now the Winnipeg Jets) due to dwindling attendance. There is a strong possibility that the Phoenix Coyotes will be the next Sun Belt team to relocate. Despite advancing to the Western Conference Finals, the team was dead last in attendance, averaging slightly more than 12,000 per home game during the 2011–12 season. According to the former owner of the Coyotes, the team has never made money in the Phoenix market, losing $30 million annually.[4] The NHL bought the team out of bankruptcy for $140 million in 2009 and had been trying to sell the franchise to ownership groups who would honor the team's existing lease with the City of Glendale. AZ. The inability of the league to find a qualified local buyer into 2013, has increased the probability of the team relocating to new markets in suburban Toronto, Quebec City and, possibly, to a new arena proposed in downtown Seattle.

The same was true for a number of NBA teams, where traditionally well-supported franchises, such as the Philadelphia 76ers and Sacramento Kings have suffered major attendance losses over several seasons as both teams fell toward the bottom of the standings. The economic downturn was devastating for the NBA's Detroit Pistons. In Detroit, the epicenter of the hard-hit automobile industry, the Great Recession resulted in unemployment close to a staggering 30%—one out of two auto workers was out of work in 2009.[5] Consequently, the Detroit Pistons' attendance fell from 1st in 2007–08 to 29th overall in 2011–12. Despite the continued woes of the Pistons and about half a dozen other teams in each league, it appears that live attendance in most North American markets has begun to increase in both the NBA and NHL.

While signs of recovery are apparent, it's clear that sports businesses are still operating in a rough economic environment. Many families continue to confront substantial financial challenges caused by persistently high levels of unemployment and an unsettled housing market, and many households are still deeply in debt. Consequently, consumers facing an uncertain economic future will be inclined to spend less and save more. This tendency to "hunker down" has repercussions for sports properties, across all levels of professional sport and for "Big Time" intercollegiate athletic programs. As many households constrain spending on consumer products, the effects are felt by the many companies manufacturing these products. The next section examines some of the most challenging issues that this new economic landscape presents the owners and operators of sports businesses.

FEROCIOUS COMPETITION FOR CONSUMERS' TIME AND MONEY

Competing for a fair share of consumers' disposable income in a post-recessionary economy will be a formidable challenge for sports enterprises. The challenge is pretty straightforward. People have a finite amount of discretionary income and an almost infinite number of choices on which to spend those limited dollars. As mentioned earlier in this chapter, in recent years, US families spent approximately $2,700 to $2,800 a year on entertainment outside the home, which is about 5% of their gross annual household income. Economists project no significant growth in entertainment spending into the foreseeable future. Meanwhile, the range of discretionary spending options appear limitless. *Business Week* referred to it as an "entertainment glut."[6]

The rapid expansion of movie theaters (one new IMAX Theater opened each week in 2011), theme parks, and a myriad number of other well-established "entertainment" outlets such as restaurants, museums, and shopping malls, all compete for consumers' discrete time and money. Add to that robust mix the many alluring sport-related options from bowling, to golf, to sports and fitness clubs, to the explosive growth of sports bars, and it's easy to see that consumers have an abundance of choices as to how they can spend their time and money outside the home.

That's *if* people are willing to leave their homes. There are more compelling home entertainment options available than ever before. Technology breakthroughs from high-definition to emerging 3D television, video on demand and increasingly interactive gaming options have resulted in the home entertainment sector growing in popularity. By 2010, both young (18–30 years) as well as more middle-aged (31–44 years) adults were found to spend more time on the Web than watching television. Both groups spent a total of 26 hours a week on average either online or with TV.[7]

According to another time study, when you add up all the in-home discretionary activities in which adults engage, Americans spend almost 5 hours each day watching TV or rented videos, surfing the Web, listening to music, playing video games, and/or reading for pleasure.[8] It is not surprising, then, to see that in 2010, spending on home entertainment exceeded a record $20 billion in the US.[9]

THE IMPACT OF TELEVISION ON LIVE ATTENDANCE

Sports fans have never had more opportunity to view their favorite sports team and/or sport on television. According to Nielsen, American viewers in 2012 could see more than 43,700 hours of live sporting events on broadcast and cable television.[10] By 2012, 26 national cable networks dedicated to sport had been established.

Table 1.1 provides a list of the networks and the year in which each first began broadcasting. Each of these networks provides year-round, "24–7" coverage focused on sports content. The Entertainment Sports Programming Network (ESPN) was the first cable network to devote its entire programming to a single

Is the explosive growth of TV negatively affecting live attendance? Courtesy of iStockphoto.com

subject. The pioneering network's initial broadcast in September, 1979 reached about one million homes, and featured a slow-pitch softball world series game between the Milwaukee Schlitzes and the Kentucky Bourbons. From that modest beginning, ESPN has become the leading destination for American sports fans, now reaching over 100 million homes. The original network has spun off five additional domestic ESPN-branded television broadcast outlets, which provide in-depth news, commentary and live event programming across multiple platforms.

The enormous success of ESPN inspired the launch of sport-specific networks in the mid-1990s, led by the Golf Channel (1995) and SPEED TV (1996), both of which now reach about 80 million US households. The proliferation of specialized sports networks is a relatively recent phenomenon, with two-thirds of the cable networks established within the last decade. Now viewers are provided in-depth coverage of their favorite sport across multiple outlets—most of which receive limited coverage on the major networks (ABC, CBS, FOX and NBC) such as outdoor sports (e.g., Outdoor Channel, Pursuit, WFN), motorsports (e.g., Fuel, SPEED)* and thoroughbred racing. (e.g., Horse Racing TV, TVG network).

For the home viewer, not only are there more sports than ever available on television, but technology has enhanced the viewing experience. According to the Consumer Electronics Association, over two-thirds of US households now own at least one high-definition television, an increase of 17% over 2009. The impact of HDTV on sports viewing is significant. Nielsen reports that sports viewing ratings are 21% higher on

---

*In August 2013, Fox Sports changed the name of SPEED TV to Fox Sports 1 and sports media analysts expect Fox to rebrand Fuel as Fox Sports 2 sometime in 2014.

Table 1.1. National Cable Sports Networks Distribution

Network (Year Established)	(# TV households)	Programming Focus
ESPN (1979)	101.5 MM	Comprehensive sports coverage
ESPN2 (1993)	99.5	2nd outlet for ESPN's mainstream coverage
Golf Channel (1995)	83.1	Golf news, commentary and tournament coverage
SPEED TV (1996)	77.2	Motorsports news, commentary and race coverage
ESPNews (1996)	75.3	24-hour-a-day sports news
Versus (2006)*	75.1	Comprehensive sports coverage
Big Ten Network (2007)	75.0	College sports exclusive to Big 10
ESPNU (2005)	72.5	College sports news, commentary, live events
NFL Network (2003)	56.8	NFL league-produced news, commentary, live coverage
MLB Network (2009)	55.2	MLB league-produced news, commentary, live coverage
NBA TV (1999)	54.0	NBA league-produced news, commentary, live coverage
NHL Network (2007)	40.0	NHL league-produced news, commentary, live coverage
ESPN Classic (1997)	39.7	Re-runs of classic sporting events, live coverage of poker, bowling, documentaries
Fox College Sports (2002)		College sports on 3 regional networks, live events
Soccer Channel (2005)	37.0	Live matches (MLS, Premier), news, commentary
Outdoor Channel (1994)	35.0	Hunting, Fishing
TVG Network (1999)	31.0	Horse Racing, Online betting
Tennis Channel (2003)	28.0	Live matches, news, commentary
Fuel TV (2003)	26.0	Adrenaline sports: Moto, skateboarding, surfing, snowboarding
Sportsman Channel (2003)	25.0	Hunting, Fishing,
Pursuit Channel (2008)	24.0	Hunting, Fishing
CBS College Sports Network (2002)	21.0	Live men's and women's college sports, news, commentary
World Fishing Network (2005)	20.0	Recreational and Sport Fishing
Horse Racing TV (2003)	19.0	Horse Racing and Online Betting
Fox Deportes (2010)	18.0	Sports programming in Spanish
Gol TV (2003)	9.0	Bilingual (English & Spanish) soccer matches, news, commentary
ESPN Deportes (2004)	5.2	(Hispanic Hshlds) Sports programming in Spanish

*Re-branded as NBC Sports Network in 2012, with 77.9 million viewers.

Source: Don Walker, The top sports networks? You might be surprised. The Business of Sports, JSOnline, 12/3/10, http//www.jsonline.com/blogs/sports/111275439.html

HD TVs.[11] Industry analysts are optimistic that 3D television will soon become the next "killer app." According to Bryan Burns, VP of Business Development for ESPN, "3D is a renaissance that will be fueled not by movies, but by live sports. . . ." (para. 2).[12]

While most of the viewing occurs in private households, the growing popularity of "sports" bars attests to the enormous popularity of televised sports outside the home. It is estimated that more than 6,000 sports bars exist across North America with HDTV technology.[13] This is an affordable option for fans who want to share the experience of watching their favorite team in the company of other sports enthusiasts.

Given the explosive growth of televised sport, the key issue facing leagues and teams is whether this abundance of in-home viewing opportunities is having (or will have) an adverse impact on live attendance at sporting events. For several years, researchers have examined whether television encourages or detracts from stadium or arena attendance. Some of the early work in both the US and England in the mid-1980s and 1990s indicated that watching sport on television had a positive or stimulative effect on live attendance. Much like advertising, the exposure provided by television encouraged people to witness live sports action in stadiums and arenas.[14] However, other studies reported a contrary result, showing that as television viewing increased, stadium attendance decreased. Andreff and Szymanski referred to this as a "substitution effect" (p. 179).[14] They concluded that a sports fan's decision to substitute watching a game on TV rather than attending in person will be influenced by a number of factors, including price of attendance, (household) income, and a number of "opportunity costs" associated with attending. Factors such as travel time, convenience, accessibility, and the quality of available seating opportunities all enter into a consumer's decision to substitute the comforts of home for the live experience.

The potential adverse impact of televised sport on live attendance has probably never been greater for several reasons. First, there is more content than ever before, creating considerably more opportunities for fans to substitute a televised broadcast for a live experience. Second, given the financial constraints facing many households, watching the game on television may be the only feasible option. The prospect of attending the game, even if live attendance were the preferred option, diminishes for many families when the average cost of attending a major league game for a party of four reaches $300 and beyond. Television becomes not only the cheaper alternative but, in fact, the *only* viewing option for these households. Finally, watching the game at home may be appealing for many fans because it eliminates the "hassle" associated with driving, parking, and in some cases, poor weather conditions.

While for many fans, there will never be a true substitute for the live, in-stadium experience, television may be an increasingly attractive alternative for a growing segment of the population. The quality of the viewing experience, enhanced by high-definition or even 3D transmission, and further augmented by replays and expert commentary, suggests that the potential for consumers to exercise the "substitute effect" has never been as compelling. As one New York Giants fan noted, "I can buy a huge HDTV for well less than the cost of one season ticket and never have to leave the comfort of my home. Forget driving, parking and $9 beer" (pp. 5, 8).[15]

Even those who may be able to afford to attend games in person may find the enhanced quality of the television broadcast a superior viewing alternative. The surge in home entertainment spending, led by the rapid adoption of high-definition television, has to be recognized as a prime competitor for consumers' scarce time and money.

TV Ratings Up, Attendance Down

The fact that more people are watching sport on television may more than compensate for any adverse impact television coverage may have on live attendance at sporting events. For some sports leagues, the ability to sell the broadcast rights to league games is the single largest source of annual income, more than offsetting any losses in gate receipts. Also, the relative contribution of television broadcast rights fees has grown substantially for most major sports properties over the past several decades. The NFL leads the way. In 2010, 43% of the total gross revenues generated by the league, over $3 billion, came from the sale of broadcast rights to major television networks. The recent renewal of the league's television broadcast agreements ensure that the NFL will generate close to $7 billion in annual revenues starting in 2014.

As Table 1.2 shows, the NFL is not the only entity receiving significant broadcast rights fees from television networks. Major national television networks committed over $30 billion to the four major professional sports leagues in North America between 2010 and 2013. The NHL's new 10-year, $2 billion deal with NBC more than doubles the value of the league's previous national broadcast agreement. In addition, Fox Sports has an 8-year contract with NASCAR through the 2014 racing season in which the network will pay the premier motorsports organization $4.5 billion for the exclusive right to air the Daytona 500 and 12 additional Sprint Cup series races each year. CBS and Turner Sports reached a nearly $11 billion agreement with the NCAA to broadcast the men's national basketball tournament from 2012 to 2024.

The reason networks have been willing to pay such large rights fees to broadcast live sports events is that sport programming delivers large audiences. In 2010, 11 of the 13 television programs (85%) that drew more than 30 million viewers were sports related. By comparison, in 2004–05, fewer than half the shows attracting 30 million or more viewers were sports programs.[16] The 2012 Super Bowl between the New England Patriots and the New York Giants was the most watched show in history, averaging 111.3 million viewers throughout the broadcast. It was this record audience that persuaded advertisers to pay up to $3.5 million to air a 30-second commercial during the game. During this period, ratings for sports telecasts were up across the board, with many properties attracting substantially larger viewing audiences. Sizeable gains were realized by the NFL, NBA, NHL, college football and basketball, and by the telecast of the 2010 Kentucky Derby (most watched horse race since 1989).

Emergence of Regional Sports Networks

With almost 44,000 hours of air time to fill, major network and cable channel operators are anxious to find compelling sport programming opportunities. As a result, sports leagues and individual teams have never had as much opportunity to exploit the abun-

Table 1.2. Television Broadcast Rights Fees for Major Sports Properties		
League/ Property	**Value of Rights Fee (network partner)**	**Length of Current Agreement(s)**
NFL	$20.4 billion (CBS, NBC, ESPN, Fox); $ 4.0 billion (Direct TV [satellite] $15.2 billion (ESPN) $27.8 billion (CBS, NBC, Fox)	through 2013; 2009–2014 2014–2021 2014–2022
MLB	$5.3 billion (Fox, ESPN, TBS); $700 million (Direct TV [satellite])	2007–2013; 2007–2013
NBA	$7.44 billion (ESPN/ABC, TNT)	2008/09–2015/16
NHL	$ 2.84 billion (NBC, TSN, CBC)	2005/06–2010/11
NASCAR	$4.48 billion (Fox, SPEED, TNT, ABC/ESPN)	2007–2014
NCAA Basketball Tournament	$10. 8 billion (CBS, TSN)	2011–2024

dance of programming opportunities. An increasing number are partnering with major cable distributors, like Fox and Comcast, to broadcast live games as well as specialized programming to fans in their local or regional market. These entities, known as Regional Sports Networks (RSNs), provide another layer of specialized or targeted sports programming. RSNs have proven to be very popular. There are now more than 40 regional sports networks in North America. A majority of RSNs are joint or multiple ventures involving two or more teams in a local market. For example, the New England Sports Network (NESN) is co-owned by the Boston Red Sox (MLB) and the Boston Bruins of the NHL. NESN also features minor league baseball, regional college sports and sports talk shows to viewers in six New England states. RSNs are very profitable, with margins estimated at 30–40% derived from average fees of $2 a month per subscriber. Media analyst company SNL Kagan reported that the New York Yankees' YES network took in $417.1 million in total revenues in 2009. Kagan reported that total revenues for the 36 regional networks in the US were up 6.6% in 2009, reaching $4.6 billion.[17] The variety of ways sports properties can produce, distribute and sell broadcast rights is discussed in detail in Chapter 13.

TV's Complex Relationship with Sport

Television's relationship with sport is two-edged. On one hand, it appears that home viewing competes with live gate ticket sales. Yet, at the same time, televised sports' growing popularity provides a lucrative source of revenue for many sport leagues and franchises.

This complex relationship is exemplified by the San Diego Padres' 2010 season. In the midst of a torrid pennant race over the last month of the season, the Padres played 12 home games against attractive opponents, including 3 games with their heated rivals,

the Los Angeles Dodgers. Despite the excitement of the pennant race, the average attendance (21,500) barely filled half the stadium's available capacity. Yet, over that same
period of time, the Padres' television ratings were up substantially. In fact, one Dodger
game drew a 9.2 rating, the highest of the season. Club officials attributed poor in-
stadium attendance to a number of factors, such as the struggling local economy and
the abundance of entertainment options in the San Diego market. However, a local
analyst provided an alternative explanation: "Why pay for tickets that cost as much as
$61, plus $8 beers, $5 hot dogs and $10 for parking when you can watch the games on
your big screen, high-definition TV with your feet propped up in the comfort of your
own living room."[18]

Does the Padre experience provide a window to the future? An interesting question
confronts the owners and operators of sports teams: Will the San Diego Padres' experience become a prevalent pattern across sports and markets in the years to come? Will
getting fans off their couches and out to stadiums and/or arenas become an increasingly
difficult challenge?

CUTTING THROUGH THE CLUTTER

Current trends suggest that for many consumers television will likely become an increasingly attractive alternative to live attendance. Yet, the challenge facing owners and
operators of sport franchises extends beyond the growing appeal of television to finding
ways to make attending live sporting events compelling in such a crowded entertainment market. To effectively compete will demand more creativity and flexibility in the
delivery of the sport experience. Teams will have to be more price conscious, offering
more affordable, budget-sensitive opportunities to prospective attendees. Increasingly,
fans will be presented with special discounts like the Charlotte Bobcats "Pay-The-Pick"
promotion described in Exhibit 1.1. Recent pricing tactics, including early or pre-
payment discounts, installment and/or deferred payment plans and, even, money-back
guarantees are likely to become standard practice. Emerging techniques like dynamic or
variable pricing also will become more prominent. Extensive coverage of traditional and
more recent pricing strategies and tactics is provided in Chapter 12.

In addition to ameliorating price barriers, teams will have to work harder at reinforc-
ing the benefits of live, in-person attendance. The unique affinity fans have with their
favorite teams is an important predictor of attendance.[19] Fan loyalty-building programs
such as regular newsletters and personal (email, tweets) communications; direct access
for members (e.g., chat rooms with coaches and players; regular pre- or post-game
meetings (e.g., chalk talks) with coaches or team executives; and special autograph signings opportunities with players, all correlate positively with increased attendance.

This underscores the need for teams to develop programs that enhance fans' identification with the team in which "their relationship with the team becomes a significant
part of their lives" (p. 322).[19] Multiple benefits result when fans feel a greater sense of
attachment with their favorite team. In addition to increased attendance, these fans display diminished price sensitivity and an increased propensity to seek out and patronize
team sponsors. All of which are crucial to the financial viability of a sports organization.

<table>
<tr><td colspan="2" align="center">Exhibit 1.1</td></tr>
<tr><td colspan="2" align="center">Bobcat Tickets for a Buck</td></tr>
<tr>
<td>

Immediately following the 2011–12 season, the NBA's Charlotte Bobcats offered their fans the opportunity to purchase a 2012–13 full-season ticket package for as little as $1 per game. The special promotion discount was pegged to the team's draft selection position. If the team was awarded the 1st pick, seats would be offered as cheaply as $1 per game or $43 for the season. At the end of the 2011–12 season, in which the team finished with the worst winning percentage (.106) in the history of the NBA, actual attendance had fallen to less than 14,000 per game (less than 70% of capacity). With the worst record, the Bobcats were guaranteed one of the top four picks in the draft, with a 25% chance of winning the first selection. The team's actual draft selection pick would be determined by a lottery held by the league at the end of May. The team placed 500 upper-deck tickets for

</td>
<td>

sale in the "Pay the Pick" promotion. The special promotion offered fans the opportunity to buy up to four seats for a little as $1 (#1 pick) to a maximum of $4 per game, if the team's pick fell to four. Even that worst case scenario at $172 resulted in a substantial savings, as the traditional price for these tickets ran $344.

The special promotion proved to be very successful. According to team president, Fred Whitfield, "The demand for the 'Pay-The-Pick' promotion surpassed anything we had hoped for." The original 500 seats sold out in less than a week. As a result, Whitfield increased the number of seats made available at the special discount price. In fact, the Bobcats received the second pick in the draft lottery, which meant fans responding to the special promotion were charged just $2 per seat per game or a total of $86 for the full season.

</td>
</tr>
</table>

Sources: *Sports Business News* (May 3, 2012); *Bobcats.com* (May 29, 2012). "Bobcats to Sell Limited Number of "Pay-The-Pick" Seats at Lottery Open House.

GROWING DEPENDENCE ON AFFLUENT HOUSEHOLDS: $100K AND UP

Earlier in the chapter, it was noted that a family of four now can expect to pay an average of $300 for the experience of attending a major league game. However, rising expenses are not limited to big league sports. The cost of attending a college football game between major conference opponents has risen dramatically as well. In 2010, the *Portland Oregonian* newspaper conducted a survey of single-game ticket prices for all 63 schools comprising the Bowl Championship Series (BCS).[20] The survey found that even in the midst of the Great Recession, in 2008 and 2009, the price of single-game tickets to "high-demand" games rose significantly over the two-year period, up 12–16% on average across the six major conferences represented in the BCS. The average face value of a high-demand ticket in the Big Ten conference was $84.17 (compared to the average NFL ticket price of $77.34 in 2011). Further, as Chapter 11 details, a ticket's face value doesn't reflect the true cost of entrance to a college football game. Many major football programs require mandatory "donations" for the privilege of purchasing the ticket. Many of these donations exceed $1,000 on top of the actual cost of the ticket.

NASCAR tickets also tend to be high end. A survey of NASCAR tracks found an average ticket price of $88.16 and noted that, while some bargains were available such as $25 general admission tickets at Phoenix and $39 at Lowe's Motor Speedway in Charlotte, "it was difficult to find much for less than $50," with many of the better seats selling on average for $91 (para. 3).[21]

It's not only sports organizations that charge high ticket prices. The Metropolitan Opera in New York City, while scrapping a plan to raise prices 8% because of the struggling economy, still charged $100 per ticket for opera goers sitting in the Orchestra section. That may seem like a bargain to those attending popular Broadway shows where ticket prices run on average $135 per person.

Thinning Fan Base

Given the rising cost of attendance, it is not surprising to find data that document the increasingly narrow demographics of those attending big-league games. Growing empirical evidence indicates that for some time middle-income and blue-collar fans, the traditional bedrock consumers of professional sports, have been pushed out of stadiums and arenas and replaced by more affluent spectators. A study reported in *American Demographics* found that adults with household incomes of $75,000 or more were 72% more likely than average wage earners to attend Major League Baseball games.[22] This finding was given credence by the *Washington Post*, which found that the household income of Washington, D.C. area residents attending Baltimore Orioles games averaged $87,500—almost $35,000, or 65%, more than the median household income of those residing in the Baltimore-D.C. area.[23]

It appears that major professional sports teams have become increasingly dependent on more affluent fans. This is particularly evident with NFL and NBA teams, where almost two-thirds of season-ticket holders report aggregate household incomes in excess of $100,000. One prominent NBA team reported that 24% of its full-season equivalent season ticket accounts reported annual household incomes of $250,000 and above.*

Let's examine the income profile of major league season ticket holders in a larger context. According to the most recent Census data, only 5.6% of individual income earners and 17.8% of all American households had incomes of more than $100,000. The proportion of households in the $250,000 plus income segment narrows significantly, to only 1.5% of all US homes. Recall that the median household income is approximately $50,000, which means that half the population in the US live on $50,000 or less. It is revealing to note that for all nine teams (three each from the NFL, NBA and MLB) sharing income data, 75% of season-ticket holders (STHs) reported household incomes of $50,000 and above. For several teams, fewer than 10% of the STH accounts were in the under $50,000 per year segment. Not surprisingly, the median household income across all of the teams for STHs was $93,000. When the income profile of American households is compared with the income profile of season-ticket holders of this sample of teams, it appears that many teams have become dependent on the most affluent households in their markets. It is evident that gate receipts are sus-

---

*We were able to obtain income data on season ticket holders from nine different teams across three of the major leagues. A number of teams were reluctant and eventually declined to share socio-demographic data (e.g., income, age, race) of any kind. Those teams that shared season-ticket customer profile information (not individual account data) provided the data on the condition that we would not divulge their team name.

tained by a finite number of affluent fans who have the capacity and willingness to purchase the expensive tickets and amenities demanded by teams.

The owners and operators of major sports properties must recognize that they rely on a very narrow segment of households, about 15% of all American households. Reliance on such a narrow range of consumers is precarious because these affluent consumers are likely to be the primary focus of every other entertainment provider in the marketplace. Cruise lines, resort operators, live theater, orchestras, and more are all competing for these consumers' disposable dollars.

CAN'T GO BACK TO THE "GOOD OLD DAYS"

It's naïve to think that sports leagues and teams can return to the "good old days." That simply by slashing prices, not charging for parking, and selling Cracker Jacks for 25 cents, those bedrock "blue collar" fans will return to stadiums and arenas. Such an approach is no longer workable because the costs of operating a major sports franchise have skyrocketed over the past several decades. As Chapter 4 describes, the cost of building new stadiums and arenas has more than doubled and player salaries across all of the major leagues have more than quadrupled on average since 1980.

In 1960, it cost one of the authors' family of four a total of $12.50 (including the cost of a 25-cent program) to attend a San Francisco 49ers game. Back then, the average player salary was $15,000. The 49ers realized a grand total of $85,000 from television revenues that season. Today, the same experience would cost a family of four around $440.00—the average cost of a ticket to a 49er game in 2012 was $83.54.[24] However, the average salary of a player on the 49er's roster amounted to $1.93 million (total payroll costs came to $106.2 million). During the 2011 season, the team received $95.8 million as its share of the NFL's national television broadcast agreement.* While the basic nature of the game has changed very little in 50 years, the scale of costs associated with amenity-laden stadiums (exemplified by the Dallas Cowboys $1.2 billion venue) and inflated payrolls (median team payroll for an NFL franchise in 2010 was $104.8 million), mean the costs associated with producing NFL football experiences have grown exponentially.

Consequently, franchise operators are under pressure to produce more and more revenues to meet their ever-growing annual operating expenses. Using the NFL to illustrate this point, in 2001, annual operating expenses for an NFL franchise averaged $117 million. By 2010, the average cost of running an NFL team had climbed to over $250 million, more than doubling in the 10-year period. A similar pattern of increase is found in the other major leagues.

Increasingly, teams have required fans to bear the brunt of paying for the lavish new sports venues and accelerating player salaries. Modern sport venues are characterized by the addition of an array of premium seating options, including luxury suites and a

---

*According to *Forbes*, the NFL's new nine-year television agreements with Fox, NBC, CBS and ESPN will be worth nearly $7 billion a year. Starting in 2014, every NFL team will receive around $200 million annually before the start of each season.

range of amenity-laden individual seating options such as club and terrace seats. All of these come with a substantially higher price tag. As will be shown in Chapter 11, it is common for these preferred seating options to sell for thousands of dollars per season. In addition, many teams have imposed a substantial up-front payment requirement (commonly called a PSL, or permanent seat license) to give fans the "right" to purchase tickets to these desired seat locations. Often PSLs cost thousands of dollars (on top of the actual cost of the tickets). It is not surprising, then, to see the income profile of regular season ticket holders to all major professional sport franchises skew so dramatically toward the high end of the household income continuum. Owners are depending on their affluent fan base to cover the rising costs associated with operating their franchises.

Is this "revenue model" sustainable? Can operators of major sports properties, including big-time collegiate athletic programs, continue to depend on approximately 15% of the households in their markets to pay the premium rates necessary to cover a significant share of their operational costs? For better or worse, most franchises are well along this path, increasingly reliant on highly affluent fans and corporations. But, this dependence on such a narrow segment of the population places teams in a vulnerable position.

While major sports properties will continue to rely on high income fans to purchase their more expensive, high-yield seating inventory, teams will also need to create opportunities for less affluent fans to enjoy the live sport experience. Earlier in this chapter we discussed the critical importance of sports organizations adopting a price-sensitive approach in order to attract a broader fan base and create opportunities for younger, less affluent fans to attend on a regular basis. Chapter 12 reviews ticketing programs that have proven to be highly effective in attracting youth, young professionals, and families to attend major league sporting events. Exposing the next generation of sports fans to the unique benefits of a live, in-venue experience, will be key to vibrant attendance in the future.

DOING MORE WITH LESS

Never before have sport managers faced as many complex challenges as those that confront them today. They face the daunting challenge of growing traditional revenue sources—tax support, media revenues, and in many cases, gate receipts—at the same time that costs are rapidly escalating. Maintaining programs even at current levels requires that sport managers learn to do more with less. At the beginning of the new millennium, only a handful of major league teams and only 48 of the 900-plus NCAA programs operated without a deficit.[25] As will be seen in the next two chapters, a majority of both professional teams and collegiate athletic programs struggle to break even financially.

The fiscal challenge has caused managers to look beyond traditional financing concepts and strategies and to supplement them with new imaginative approaches. It is the basic theme of this text that managers of sport organizations are required to seek out scarce resources from a wide range of possible sources and to use their marketing and financing skills to ensure that the scarce resources acquired are allocated in such a way that they yield optimum social and economic benefits. These are exactly the requirements of an entrepreneur. Indeed, we view the contemporary sport manager as an entrepreneur. Increasingly, effectiveness in professional, collegiate, and other forms of amateur sport will be dependent upon managers' abilities to aggressively seek out resources for their organizations. A major emphasis of this book is on providing readers with an in-depth understanding of the many traditional and innovative revenue acquisition methods available to sports organizations. It is the authors' belief that managers who are confident in their understanding of when and how to use a combination of these financing options will be in the best position to sustain and enhance the viability of their sports organizations.

The following quotation caught the authors' attention. It is extracted from a piece written in a national newspaper by a well-known commentator:

> Out of the clubs which form the League, it would probably be over the mark to say that one-sixth are beginning this season with a balance on the right side of their accounts. One result is that they are anxious to offer lower wages to their players. In spite of that some players are keeping up the prices happily.
>
> My point is that football is being ruined by being a commercial speculation. Local team spirit is being shattered by the purchases of players from outside, and is being replaced by merely mercenary ambitions on the part of the players.
>
> A large proportion of the clubs are so hard up that they can never hope to buy good enough players to rise to the top. . . . We have developed, on the one hand, into a ring of financiers, who have captured sport for its value in the market, and, on the other hand, into a raucous, grasping multitude, who are good enough at pushing through the turnstiles, or bellowing at a player, or even battering a referee, but who have no notion of taking any decent exercise for themselves at any time.[26]

There are many in North America who would concur with the sentiments expressed by the writer and advocate that such flimsy foundations make the contraction of professional sports inevitable and perhaps desirable. However, the article appeared in *The Daily Telegraph*, an English national newspaper; its context was the English Premier League; and it was published in September 1900! The writer was bemoaning the transfer of a player from one club to another for $500 and a team spending $6,000 on a new ground. In 2009, an English Premier League player was transferred for a fee of over $125 million, a bid of $160 million for another player was rejected as insufficient, and the new Wembley soccer stadium cost well over $1 billion. A large proportion of the clubs in 1900 were "so hard up that they could never hope to buy good enough players,"[26] but 90% of them are still in business 112 years later. Clearly, sports managers have responded to the challenge to find new revenues in the past, and the authors are confident they will do so in the future.

THE EMERGENCE OF MIXED MARTIAL ARTS

Exhibit 1.2 provides an in-depth description of the rapid emergence of arguably the fastest growing sport in the world, Mixed Martial Arts (MMA). At the center of the

Exhibit 1.2

Emergence of Mixed Martial Arts: Effective Use of Social Media

In 2010, the Ultimate Fighting Championship (UFC) eclipsed $400 million in revenue on the strength of 50 million fans worldwide purchasing 300,000 tickets and 9 million pay-per-view (PPV) copies to 26 events in five different countries. It was the fourth consecutive year of double digit growth for the fledging mixed martial arts (MMA) promotion that has quickly taken the sports world by storm. The UFC's edgy, if not exceptionally violent, form of combat is packaged in a manner that resonates strongly with today's male 18–34 demographic that craves non-stop action and instant gratification. This need for instant gratification is perhaps what has most allowed the UFC to pioneer the use of social media in its marketing efforts. The way the UFC leverages Twitter, Facebook and YouTube to more effectively engage its fans and drive greater consumption across all channels—attendance, PPV, merchandise, etc.—is truly a case study worthy of investigation.

What Is MMA?

Mixed martial arts, commonly referred to as MMA, is a combat sport combining several interdisciplinary fighting styles including boxing, wrestling, jiu-jitsu, muay thai, karate, judo and many others. The sport is contested inside of a square ring or multi-sided cage, officiated by one referee and scored by three judges over 3 or 5 five-minute rounds. MMA is not a no-holds-barred or tough man contest, but rather a rapidly growing combat sport governed by a strict set of Unified Rules, pre- and post-fight medicals, drug tests and heavy government oversight.

What Is UFC?

The Ultimate Fighting Championship (UFC) is the world's premier MMA fight league. Based out of Las Vegas, Nevada, the UFC promotes over 20 events per year in markets all over the world. Over 250 fighters compete in seven different weight classes on a myriad of different types of events—televised shows in small 10,000 person coliseums to 55,000 person major attractions held in domed stadiums and broadcast on PPV to millions.

It is important to note that MMA and UFC are not synonymous. The UFC is to MMA as the NBA is to basketball. However, many casual observers miss this distinction because the UFC popularized the sport of MMA in the United States.

UFC Business Brief

The fact that the UFC has become synonymous with MMA throughout the United States serves as a testament to its success since the turn of the millennium. Zuffa LLC., a group owned by Lorenzo Fertitta, Frank Ferttita Jr. and Dana White, purchased the UFC for $2 million in 2001. The group invested $40 million into the company before hitting the black at the end of 2005, largely due to the success of its breakout reality TV show, *The Ultimate Fighter*. The UFC's business then exploded: going from approximately $180 million in revenue at the end of 2006 to approximately $400 million in revenue in 2010. Moreover, Zuffa has also witnessed incredible appreciation in the value of the UFC—selling a 10% stake of the promotion to Flash Entertainment, an investment arm of the Abu Dhabi government, for $125 million in 2009.

How does the UFC make its money?—by selling live UFC events via private telecasts. The "pay-per-view" (PPV) concept, first popularized by boxing in the 1980s (Muhammed Ali vs. Joe Frazier in the "Thrilla in Manilla"), has become a profitable distribution model for the UFC. UFC events sell to individual subscribers from $49.99 to $54.99 (high definition). In 2010, the UFC broke its PPV sales record for the third year in a row by selling slightly under nine million PPV copies (or between $225 million to $250 million). Nearly 60% of the company's revenue comes from PPV sales. The remaining revenue is derived from ticket sales, television rights fees, sponsorship fees, licensing royalties and merchandise sales. This ratio has largely remained constant over the last half decade, but as the UFC continues to diversify its revenue streams, it is likely that television and sponsorship will become a more vital component of the business model. To see evidence of this, look no further than the seven-year, $700 million television deal the UFC signed with FOX Sports in November 2011.

Exhibit 1.2 *(Continued)*

Emergence of Mixed Martial Arts: Effective Use of Social Media

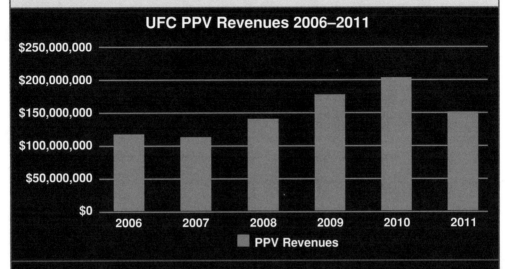

UFC PPV Revenues 2006–2011

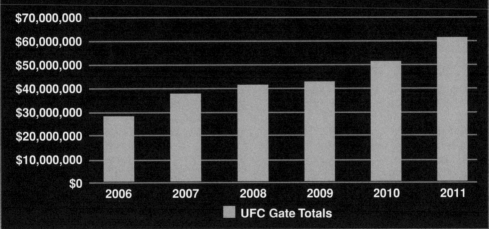

UFC Gate Totals 2006–2011

BEST PRACTICES IN SOCIAL MEDIA

Everything the UFC does from a marketing perspective is designed to drive fans toward its PPVs. Social media is no different. Twitter, Facebook and YouTube have provided the UFC with a mechanism to disseminate news, information and content; promote individual fighters; coordinate contests and giveaways; and, engage fans in candid conversations. These use-cases all serve to build interest in the PPV events that ultimately generate the lion's share of company revenue.

Twitter

The UFC began to adopt the use of Twitter as a marketing tool in early 2009. What began as slight and inconsistent experimentation has slowly developed into a coherent strategy with a corresponding set of tactics. Twitter is now a major component of the UFC's larger integrated marketing strategy.

Twitter is only as effective as the number of people a company can reach and engage with its messaging. Thus, the foundation of the UFC's Twitter strategy is a strong base of followers generated from across a number of dif-

Exhibit 1.2 *(Continued)*

Emergence of Mixed Martial Arts: Effective Use of Social Media

ferent Twitter accounts. The UFC does not just rely upon its brand account, but also those of UFC president Dana White, broadcast analyst Joe Rogan and many of the fighters that fans follow and regularly read. The UFC sees this base as so important that it became the first North American professional sports property to create quarterly bonuses for its athletes to incent Twitter usage.

The UFC uses Twitter primarily as an information, news and content distributor. Dana White will frequently tweet about new events, start times and broadcast information. Fighters often take to Twitter to announce their next bout or talk trash about his opponent. However, the growing base and popularity of these accounts has also allowed the UFC to stretch its strategy across other tactics.

Perhaps one of the more innovative ways the UFC has leveraged its Twitter base is through contest and giveaway coordination. The week of a fight is a very important promotional period for the UFC. Twitter allows the UFC to generate a significant amount of local buzz by providing information on contests and giveaways across the host city. Dana White and other UFC personalities leverage their sizable Twitter accounts to tweet contest details for followers to use in what equates to a scavenger hunt called #Hunt4UFC.

The benefit of Dana White's having over 1.7 million followers or Anderson Silva having over 900,000 followers is that small, seemingly innocuous, tweets can literally generate hundreds of people on-site within minutes. Twitter is essentially the UFC's mobile crowd tool.

This type of give and take is what allows the UFC to be so successful on Twitter. Instead of one-way information dissemination, the UFC engages fans in a conversation or interactive contest in which they are rewarded for participation. The end result is a very active and loyal group of followers that are not only motivated to consume social media content, but also more interested in purchasing PPV content and driving the UFC cash cow.

Facebook

Facebook has also become a major destination for UFC fans. The company posts event information, updates on fighters, and pictures from various UFC events (e.g., fights, weigh-ins, autograph signings, expos, etc.) on its page. UFC fans are also given an opportunity to tag themselves in pictures or comment on wall posts. However, it is the way the UFC leverages some of Facebook's more advanced features that makes for a superb case study.

In 2010, the UFC began to push the Facebook envelope by exploring some of its more advanced features and corresponding technologies like streaming video, gaming applications and contest registration. The UFC leveraged its partnership with Neu Lion Technologies to provide live, streaming fight coverage of previously untelevised undercard bouts. In concert with videogame developer, THQ, the UFC developed a Facebook application that allowed fans to train their own fighter and then battle other fans for MMA supremacy. The UFC also worked with various corporate partners like Bud Light and Harley Davidson to direct fans to branded Facebook contest pages where fans were given an opportunity to win exciting prizes like VIP UFC event packages. The only requirement of UFC fans to gain access to this new and advanced content was a simple "Like" of the UFC fan page.

Advanced Facebook content has provided the UFC with a new way to engage its fans, drive product consumption and ultimately increase affinity for the brand. The results? Staggering. In less than 18 months after advanced content rollout, the UFC nearly doubled its following on Facebook from four million to seven million people (i.e., the number of page "Likes") and enjoyed over 900,000 active monthly users on its gaming application. The growth is impressive, yet so too is the size of the audience. Facebook is not just an engagement tool, but also a customer database and relationship management system. Hence, the new and advanced Facebook content also helps the UFC to learn more about the tastes and preferences of a large portion of its fan base in order to improve the effectiveness of its traditional marketing messages and tweak the product itself.

Exhibit 1.2 *(Continued)*

Emergence of Mixed Martial Arts: Effective Use of Social Media

YouTube

YouTube is probably more properly defined as new media, as opposed to social media. Nevertheless, the way the UFC uses YouTube within its social media platform certainly deserves recognition and exploration in this vignette.

Similar to Facebook, YouTube is a major destination for UFC fans. The company uses the popular video-hosting website as a way to share in-depth and behind-the-scenes content that is more difficult to showcase through its television broadcast partnerships. YouTube is the home to an expected bevy of event trailers, highlight clips, interviews and special access shows. But what really takes the cake—and has proven incredibly successful for the UFC over the last five years—are the Dana White fight week video logs (vlogs). Dana White is a fascinating blend of imposing fight promoter, give-you-the-short-off-his back best friend, and clever prankster. All of which combine to produce a rather engaging series of videos that document his daily activities as he goes about the business of promoting his billion dollar fight company—the narrative akin to marrying MTV's "Cribs" and HBO's "Entourage" in reality video blog format. It practically sings success.

How successful, you ask? Twitter and Facebook help drive upwards of a million visitors to the UFC YouTube channel each week (most to see the video logs); that's upwards of one million engagements with the brand help to build awareness, influence consumption and increase affinity.

Explaining the UFC's Success

The UFC has been able to successfully navigate the social media space and implement numerous effective marketing strategies because of its commitment to experimentation, demand from a tech savvy and social media-crazy fan base, and a flexible brand positioning that allows the company to push the envelope. UFC's commitment to the idea of "going where the fans are" has meant traversing the relatively unknown realm of social media through means of trial and error. Here, the company has stumbled upon a way to better engage fans, disseminate news, share ideas and receive feedback on what it could do better. It has given fans a voice that they have never had before—certainly not with any other sports league. The result of this experimentation has meant an 18–34 year old, tech savvy and gadget heavy demographic with one serious need for instant gratification gobbling up all the fight clips, news and other information the UFC can muster.

However, there is no denying the UFC has distinct advantage over other sports leagues and properties in the sense that its edgy and progressive brand provides it with the flexibility to pursue marketing strategies that others cannot. The UFC is expected to be "as real as it gets" which means it can afford to take risks like incentivizing its fighters to use Twitter. What has it got to lose? By contrast, the NFL is a $9 billion/year enterprise that very much depends upon its conservative brand in order to continue signing hundred-plus million dollar contracts with equally conservative television networks and Fortune 500 companies. Sadly, fans are not likely to see Roger Goodell haphazardly tweeting with disgruntled fans or racing down the interstate in his brand new Ferrari any time soon.

Conclusion

Much of The UFC's success in the social media space is attributed to its willingness to experiment with a variety of tools and tactics. While other leagues have shied away from the transparency of social media, the UFC has embraced it—making the league more authentic and accessible. Fans feel like an actual part of the UFC community because their favorite athletes are more likely to interact directly with them. Even though the UFC doesn't have the largest fan base on some of the social media platforms, its rate of growth and activity of followers reinforces the fact that The UFC is an example of best practice in this space.

This vignette was provided by Kelsey Philpott, Account Executive with GMR Marketing, who has worked with various MMA organizations in marketing and public relations since 2008.

sport's meteoric rise is the Ultimate Fighting Championship (UFC), the largest MMA promotion company in the world. In less than a decade, UFC events have migrated from relatively obscure cable television productions in North America to coverage on mainstream media networks across the globe. In 2012, UFC telecast events on Fox in the US, ESPN in the United Kingdom, and delivered pay-per-view events to 150 countries in 22 different languages. The exhibit describes how UFC has shrewdly used social media as a prominent element of its business model to reach its key target market, 18–34 year old males.

GLOBALIZATION

The magnitude of the transition of professional sports from being a local to a global product could not have been foreseen by anyone 20 years ago. In that sense, it is unbelievable. Indeed, there has been no transition of similar magnitude and speed in the history of sports. When the corporate owners of broadcast media joined forces with the corporate owners of sport teams in the early 1990s, the globalization of sports gathered momentum. This alliance made it possible for new sports, new formats of existing sports, or new leagues to "go global" quickly with strong support from media, sponsors, advertisers and sport promoters. The remarkable evolution of the Indian Premier League described in Exhibit 1.3 illustrates the extraordinary speed with which growth can occur. This cricket league was launched in 2008. Four years later it had become a $4 billion property.[27]

Three of the four major leagues in the US have a substantial proportion of international players on their rosters. The NBA is most prominent, reporting 84 international players from 38 countries, mostly European, on their 2010 rosters, with 28 of the 30 NBA teams featuring at least one foreign player. The NHL has players from 20 different countries on its teams. Out of the 856 players on MLB opening day rosters, 243 (28%) were born outside the US, but a large proportion of them have their roots in the same marrow geographic zone of Caribbean

Exhibit 1.3

Growth of the Indian Premier League

The Indian Premier League was founded in 2008 with eight team franchises based in India's major cities. It is a "made-for-television" venture featuring the 20-over version of cricket. This is the sport's shortest format, characterized by high-scoring action that can be completed in a five hour time period. The teams play a total of 74 games in a six-week spring season. Each year a two-day player auction is held, broadcast live on television. In a recent auction, 127 cricketers were sold for $62 million. Four players on each playing team of 11 can be foreign. The franchises have a salary cap of $9 million to control costs.

Each game typically is viewed by approximately 150 million Indians, but global broadcasting rights mean the total number of viewers is much greater. The Indian audience is dominated by young middle-class city dwellers, who are among India's most free-spending consumers. Remarkably, 45% of these viewers are female.

Franchise fees are increasing exponentially. When two new franchises were admitted for the 2011 season, their owners paid a combined total of $700 million. This was more than the founding eight franchises paid in total four years previously when the league was formed. The value of the property is now estimated to be around $4 billion.

Island countries. The NFL has very few international players, and most of them are kickers, because there are few opportunities to learn and play the sport outside the US.

These data suggest that the NBA has the most potential for penetrating international markets. Indeed, the league has suggested four strategies it could adopt to expand into Europe: (i) by entering into "alliances" with European clubs, several of which have contacted the NBA to explore this option; (ii) taking over an existing league; (iii) forming a new league comprising existing European teams, which would withdraw from their national competitions; or (iv) awarding franchises to a number of European cities which would become members of the NBA.[27]

The biggest long-term financial opportunities for all sports, but especially basketball, probably are in China where sport is increasingly entering the consciousness of the emergent middle class. After Yao Ming joined the Houston Rockets, the team's games were widely broadcast in China. Thus, when the Rockets played Milwaukee, who had Yi Jianlian on their team, the live game to watch two of the biggest names in Chinese sport was broadcast by 19 television stations, two websites, and a mobile phone company. The audience exceeded 200 million. The NBA commissioner commented, "I have seen the future, and it is Chinese" (para. 8).[28] Consequently, the NBA decided to open a branch office in Beijing and expand its administrative staff in Hong Kong, create a Chinese web site, launch a Chinese basketball magazine, and schedule and play exhibition, preseason games in Beijing, Shanghai, and in other large Asian cities.[29] Exhibit 1.4 illustrates that English Premier League soccer sees similar potential in the Chinese market.[29]

The NFL is the richest of all the world's sports leagues, but is challenged to create a global market. Basketball and soccer are relatively easy to play and understand, but American football is not. One NFL executive stated: "The NFL is not adaptable. This is a much harder product to sell on a global basis. As big as the NFL is in the United States, it's one-third the size of rugby on a global basis."[30] Recognition of the limited global potential of the US leagues, except for the NBA, was central in the decision of the owner of the Boston Red Sox to purchase Liverpool Football Club which is described in Exhibit 1.5.[31]

Nevertheless, the NFL is "making concerted efforts to establish ourselves, internationally, going after half-a-dozen key territories to create some level of foundation."[30] For example, they periodically play a game in London and the NFL commissioner has stated, "There's a great deal of interest in holding a Super Bowl in London so we'll be looking at that."[30] An analysis of starting line-ups of all matches in the English Premier League is shown in Table 1.3.[32] It shows that only 35.47% of players who started EPL fixtures in that season were English. In a European Champions League semi-final game between Chelsea and Liverpool—the first all-English semi-final in the competition's history—players from 18 different countries were on the two teams' 18 member game squads. The involvement of so many international players in the games helps foster interest in the EPL in their home countries and contributes to the league's remarkable global penetration. The EPL's chief executive observed:

Exhibit 1.4

A Globalization Vignette:
360 Million Watch a Routine Premier League Soccer Game

Everton Football Club is located in the city of Liverpool and the soccer club has played in the English Premier League for 100 years which is longer than any other team. In recent years it has tended to finish in the middle of the 20 team league. Despite the team's distinguished heritage and pedigree, the lack of recent success made obtaining shirt sponsorship challenging. Eventually they signed an agreement with Kejian which is a Chinese mobile phone company. Soccer fever had taken hold in China after the national team qualified for the World Cup for the first time in 2002. The team lost all three games it played, but China's youth were taking up soccer faster than any other sport and enthusiasm was high. As a condition of their multi-million dollar annual fee, Kejian acquired not only the shirt sponsorship, but also required that Everton include two players from the Chinese national team as members of their playing squad! In addition to generating awareness in England of their company, Kejian also wanted to win the affection of the tens of millions of soccer fans in China for helping two of their players break into one of the world's major soccer leagues for the first time. Thus, Li Tie and Li Wei Fung arrived at Everton!

The Everton coach was skeptical and unhappy that his front office had foisted onto him two players whom he had never seen or heard about. However, Li Tie was the best and most well-known player in China, while Li Wei Fung was also a member of the national team. Li Tie's autobiography sold 100,000 copies in China within two weeks of its release and he enjoyed "iconic status of a demigod." The Chinese sent media representatives to England to cover the players' progress. Li Tie turned out to be a fine player—good enough to play regularly in the Everton team.

Four months into the nine month, 38 game season, Everton played Manchester City, another team who at that time were regularly positioned in the middle of the Premier League. This would normally be considered a routine game arousing little interest beyond the fans of these two clubs. However, after seeing Everton's success with Li Tie, Manchester City signed Sun Jihai who was the second most well-known player on the Chinese team. A host of Chinese journalists made the 6,000 mile trip for the game and it was shown on CCTVS, the state-owned national sports channel. The game was watched by 360 million people!

Fortuitously, there was a large Chinese community in Liverpool. Liverpool is twinned with Shanghai while its Chinatown is the oldest in Europe, dating back to the late 19th century. Just as the shipping industry first induced Chinese sailors to settle around the city's busy docks, so soccer became the city's new Sino-British link. Tens of millions of Chinese became fans of Everton! Everton immediately became the biggest player in the rapidly emerging Chinese soccer market, which has potential for generating substantial sales from sales of replica uniforms and club paraphernalia.

For the Manchester City game, Kejian flew dozens of Chinese executives to the game where they enjoyed the hospitality of both the company and the club. The club has sold a dozen luxury suites to companies which do business with China. One of these companies' CEOs said, "One of the first things Chinese business people say to me when they come over is can I get them tickets to the Everton soccer game? My box is always full."

There were 191 million mobile phones in circulation in China but most young people wanted Nokias, while Kejian was seen as a bit uncool! Li Tie and the association with top-flight soccer changed all that. Kejian now has the image of being cool and the phone to buy in China, and the company has gained valuable exposure to new markets in Europe.

Only the American leagues do better on a commercial basis than us, but they have a population of 300 million and we are only 60 million. They are interested in how we have done so well internationally. We have one big advantage—we play football, the global game. I don't have to show countries what football is, with exhibition matches to explain the rules.[30]

To further penetrate global markets, the EPL's chief executive promoted a plan for an international series of matches. This would involve expanding the number of games in the 20-team league from 38 (each opponent is played home and away in a season) to 39 with the extra match played abroad. This would lead to 10 overseas games, played in cities around the world. The CEO argued:

We believe that an international round of matches will enhance the strength of the Premier League as a competition; create extra interest in all 20 Premier League

Exhibit 1.5

Why the Fenway Group Bought the English Premier League's Liverpool Football Club

The Fenway Group, owners of the Boston Red Sox, had no knowledge of soccer—not even of some of its basic rules—when they purchased Liverpool F.C. for $320 million. Indeed, the principal owner acknowledged that while he was a lifelong American sports fan, he knew "virtually nothing" of Liverpool or the EPL before buying the club. However, when the club's prospects were explained to him, "A number of parallels emerged with the situation that existed in Boston when we arrived." He noted that the Red Sox and Liverpool were both historically successful clubs which had lost their dominance, and both had beloved old grounds not up to modern money-making standards. He believed Fenway could apply the same strategies at Liverpool as they had to winning effect in Boston, and also make an ambitious move into international sport.

There was more to it than just wanting to win. Central to Fenway's fascination was English football's, and Liverpool's, huge worldwide support, compared to the US-restricted following for American sports. Several Fenway executives recounted with awe that the Super Bowl, American sport's most prestigious event, is watched by around 20 million viewers outside the U.S., whereas Liverpool's 3–1 defeat of Manchester United in an EPL game attracted an estimated 500 million global audience.

Fenway became aware of the large sponsorship revenues from international companies which the American owners of Manchester United had obtained for that club and believed Liverpool had similar unexploited potential. They found it attractive that EPL clubs keep the money they make from such worldwide sponsorship, whereas MLB teams' income is taxed and shared and Fenway resented the amount of money the Red Sox had to share with smaller teams. Fenway were convinced that buying Liverpool was better value than US sports teams with their "limited global potential." Their spokesperson explained Liverpool's appeal: "So much internet clutter competes for mindshare now. Big sports clubs are one of the few things which can cut through and capture mindshare. We have one of the greatest baseball teams, but its ability is geographically limited. The Liverpool numbers blew us away. We believe there is a significant amount of monetization we can do, on a worldwide basis, which is not occurring now."

Table 1.3. The Number of Games Started by Each Nationality in the English Premier League, 2010–11 Season (Top 20 Nationalities)

Premier League	Number of Games
England	2,965
France	558
Ireland	452
Scotland	348
Wales	280
Spain	266
Netherlands	215
USA	180
Ivory Coast	172
Brazil	168
Argentina	159
Nigeria	144
Northern Ireland	139
Serbia	125
Portuga	121
Sweden	117
Belgium	116
Ghana	108
Cameroon	104
Senegal	99

clubs at home and abroad; and allow increased investment in talent development and acquisition, facilities, as well as our football development and community programmes.[30]

Cities would bid for the right to host the games which would be held on consecutive days. Cities would also be required to auction the television rights for the games. Commercially, the opportunities for the EPL would be enormous. The extra game in foreign lands would please the multinational companies seeking global audiences which are major EPL team sponsors. Indeed, the league's title sponsor, Barclays, "welcomed the proposal because it meets our desire to increase our global reach as a brand."[30] It was estimated that over a three year period, the sponsorship and television income would be around $400 million.[33] The strategy would complement the annual preseason tours that most EPL clubs now embark on to tap into burgeoning markets such as south-east Asia, the Middle East and the US.

The strategy did not win sufficient support to move forward, but as one commentator observed, "What seemed like a whimsical idea a few years ago can now be seen as possible. If there is a business rationale for doing it there will be opportunities to play games outside of Europe."[30]

The globalization of sport inevitably is resulting in globalization of the financing of sport. The English Premier League is perhaps the primary illustration of this trend. Table 1.4 shows that in 2011, 10 of the 20 teams in the EPL were owned primarily by non-UK residents. The owners were from the US (Arsenal, Aston Villa, Liverpool, Manchester United and Sunderland), India (Blackburn), Russia (Chelsea), Malaysia (Queens Park Rangers), Egypt (Fulham) and Kuwait (Manchester City).

The personal net worths of the owners of Chelsea and Manchester City are $21.7 billion and $37.0 billion, respectively. The unprecedented magnitude of their investments in these two teams is so massive that it is inconceivable they could expect a com-

	Table 1.4. English Premier League: Clubs, Owners, Net Worth and Sources of Wealth		
List of English Premier League Clubs, Owners, their estimate net worth in British Pound Sterling (BSP) and their sources of wealth. [net worth in US dollars December 31, 2012]			
CLUBS	**OWNER(S)**	**ESTIMATED COMBINED NET WORTH (BPS) [US$]**	**SOURCE OF WEALTH**
Arsenal	Stan Kroenke (US)	1.6b. [$2.59b]	Property & Sports Franchises
Aston Villa	Randy Lerner (US)	0.6b. [$0.97b]	Banking & Investment
Blackburn Rovers	Venky's (India) Limited	0.7b. [$1.14b]	Poultry, Farming & Pharmaceutical
Bolton Wonderers	Eddie Davies (England)	0.65m. [$1.05b]	Domestic Appliances
Chelsea	Roman Abramovich (Russia)	13.4b. [$21.7b]	Oil & Industry
Everton	Bill Kenwright (England)	10m [$16.2m]	Theatre Production
Fulham	Mohamed Al-Fayed (Egypt)	1.2b. [$1.95b]	Retail
Liverpool	Fenway Sports Group (US)	2.1b. [$3.41]	Fenway Sports-Investment
Manchester City	Mansour bin Zayed Al Nahyan (UAE)	22.8b [$37.0b]	Oil & Industry, Investment
Manchester United	Malcolm Glazer (US)	1.6b. [$2.59b]	Food Processing, Sport Teams & Real Estate
Newcastle United	Mike Ashley (English)	1.5b. [$2.44b]	Sports Goods
Norwich City	Delia Smith & Michael Wynn-Jones (England & Whales)	0.5b. [$0.81b]	Food Industry Publishing Poultry
Queens Park Rangers	Tony Fernandes (Malaysia)	0.3b. [$0.49b]	Airlines
Stoke City	Peter Coates (England)	0.4b [$0.65b]	Betting
Sunderland	Ellis Short (US)	1.3b. [$2.11b]	Private Equity & Hospitality
Swansea	Mel Nurse (Wales)	20m [$32m	Property
Tottenham Hotspur	Joe Lewis (English)	1.9b. [$3.09b]	Foreign
Wigan Athletic	Dave Whelan (English)	0.2b. [$0.32b]	Retail
Wolverhampton	Steve Morgan (English)	0.4b. [$0.65b]	Property
West Bromwich Albion	Jeremy Peace (English)	40m. [$65m]	Industrial

mercial return on it. Hence, their dominant motive for ownership appears to be personal gratification and the thrill of being involved with major sporting occasions. In contrast, most of the other owners appear to regard their ownership as a business investment with the expectation of a commercial return.

Companies are looking to be involved with events that have a strong mass appeal world-wide, which makes EPL games highly desirable. As one executive noted: "Businesses, whether they are US multinationals, UK or Asian based, are not talking about borders, that's the game changer here. It's a global opportunity."[30]

SUMMARY

Sport managers now and for years to come will be operating in a very challenging environment. The adverse impacts of the Great Recession will continue to affect how American families consume sport. Economic recovery has been slow and many US households continue to be affected by persistently high underemployment, a soft housing market and stagnant household income. Consequently, economists predict no increase in the amount of money US families will spend on entertainment outside the home into the foreseeable future. Competing for a fair share of consumers' limited discretionary income in a glutted entertainment market will be a formidable challenge. Spurred by advances in technology, spending on home entertainment has hit an all-time high. Sports fans can now consume sport on a variety of high quality platforms, including HD and 3D television, video on demand, and through interactive gaming options—without ever having to leave their homes. And, Americans have more opportunity to watch live sport on television than ever before. By 2012, 26 national cable networks and over 40 regional sports networks, all providing 24/7 coverage, contributed to the almost 44,000 hours of live sports programming on broadcast and cable television. The explosive growth of televised sports and its impact on live attendance is emerging as a serious issue. There is a growing concern that increasingly sports fan will substitute the enhanced quality, affordability and convenience of the in-home viewing experience for attending games in person. The proliferation of live televised sports coverage poses a dilemma. In effect, many teams may be competing with themselves. Finding the right balance between the increased exposure and revenue streams afforded by TV without cannibalizing live attendance will be a growing challenge for sport managers.

There is evidence that fewer households are able to afford the cost of attending major professional and college sporting events. The complete price of attending a major league game for a family of four on average exceeded $300 in 2012, accounting for almost 40% of an average household's median weekly income. The average face value of a ticket to attend a major college football game now exceeds $80. It's not surprising, then, to find that the economic profile of those attending big league sporting events is narrowing to an increasingly smaller, more affluent segment of the U.S. population. Income data provided by several teams indicate that the preponderance of season ticket holders come from a very narrow segment of households, about 15% of all American households. Does this growing dependence by major sports properties on such a relatively small proportion of consumers place teams in a vulnerable position? Whether the current "revenue model"? which relies on so few to contribute so much—is sustainable, will be tested over the next several years. Ameliorating price barriers by offering more affordable, budget-sensitive opportunities (e.g., deferred payment plans, special discounts, loyalty reward programs) will be crucial to expanding live attendance opportunities for more American households.

Finding creative ways to do more with fewer resources will be another challenge facing managers of sports organizations. With professional sport franchises facing squeezed operating margins and only a handful of college athletic programs operating in the "black," managers are under increasing pressure to aggressively find new revenue sources, as well as to preserve existing ones, to sustain the financial viability of their organizations. Allocating these finite resources to ensure optimum economic and social benefits will be crucial to the success of contemporary sport managers.

The globalization of sport continues at a rapid pace from ownership to the internationalization of team rosters. Within the past decade, North American sports leagues have aggressively initiated efforts to penetrate international markets. At the forefront of this effort has been the NBA which established a strong presence in China and developed strategic partnerships with European basketball clubs. The NBA's long-term vision would be to award franchises and to ultimately establish NBA-branded companion leagues in both Asia and Europe. The English Premier League (EPL) has also invested considerable effort at penetrating global markets. The fact that almost two-thirds of the players on EPL rosters come from countries other than England has played a key role in the league's successful global penetration. Underscoring the EPL's globalization is that by 2011, half the teams in the EPL were owned wholly or in part by non-UK residents, with owners from the US, Egypt, Russia, Kuwait, and India.

The chapter concludes with an examination on the fastest growing sport in the world, Mixed Martial Arts (MMA). The section focuses on the growth of MMA's preeminent organization, the Ultimate Fighting Championship (UFC), and its shrewd use of social media to move from relative obscurity to world-wide prominence.

References

1. Green, M. (2012, December 23). Why rising ticket prices and technology lead NFL fans to stay home. *Daily Beast.* Retrieved from http://www.thedailybeast.com/articles/2012/12/23/why-rising-ticket-prices-and-technology-are-leading-nfl-fans-to-stay-home.html

2. Kiplinger's economic outlooks. (2012, January 23). *Kiplinger.* Retrieved from http://www.kiplinger.com/businessresource/economic_outlook/#housing

3. IEG sponsorship report. (2011, February 9), p. 3.

4. Reichard, K. (2013, February 1). Phoenix Coyotes sale falls through. Arena Digest.com. Retrieved from http://arenadigest.com/phoenix_coyotes_sale_falls_through

5. Panic in Detroit: Unemployment stands at 50%. (2009, December 25). *Pakalert Press.* Retrieved from http://www.pakalertpress.com/2009/12/25/panic-in-detroit-unemployment-stands-at-50/

6. Stevens, L., & Grover, R. (1998, February 16). The entertainment glut. *Business Week*, p. 88.

7. Morrissey, F. (2010, December 13). Time spent on Internet is equal to TV. *Adweek.* Retrieved from http://www.adweek.com/news/technology/forester-time-spent-internet-equal-tv-104018

8. Bureau of Labor Statistics. (2010, June 22). Economic news release, American time use survey—2009 results. Retrieved from http://www.bls.gov

9. U.S. home entertainment spending hits $20

billion. (2010, January 7). *Digital TV News.* Retrieved from http://www.digitaltvnews.net/content/?p=12326

10. Networks air over 43,000 hours of sports coverage in 2009. (2010, January 21). *Nielsenwire.* Retrieved from http://blog.nielsen.com/nielsenwire/media_entertainment/networks-air-over-43000-hours-of-sports-event-coverage-in-2009/

11. HD TVs now the majority, but HD viewing lags behind. (2010, November 8). *Nielsenwire.* Retrieved from http://blog.nielsen.com/nielsenwire/media_entertainment/hd-tvs-now-the-majority-but-hd-viewing-lags-behind/

12. Davis, J. (2010, November 30). Sports the killer app for 3D? *Runco.com.* Retrieved from http://www.runco.com/_blog/This_Minute_at_Runco/post/Sports_the_Killer_App_for_3D/

13. Kayye, G. (2005, April 7). The digital transition: A sports bar's worst nightmare. *Creative Mac.* Retrieved from http://creativemac.com/article/The-Digital-Transition:-A-Sports-Bars-Worst-Nightmare-31687

14. Andreff, W., & Szymanski, S. (2006). *Handbook on the economics of sport.* Cheltenham, UK: Edward Elgar Publisher.

15. Vecsey, G. (2011, April 6). Gasps from the grandstands after the invoice arrives. *The New York Times*, pp. 5, 8.

16. Gregory, S. (2010, August 14). Why sports ratings are surging on TV. *Time.* Retrieved from http://www.time.com/time/printout/0,8816,2010746,00.html

17. Seidman, R. (2010, June 16). SNL Kagan data shows revenue up 6.6% at regional sports networks in 2009. *TV by the Numbers.* Retrieved from http://tvbythenumbers.zap2it.com/2010/06/16/snl-kagan-data-shows-revenue-up-6-6-at-regional-sports-networks-in-2009/54370

18. Norcross, D. (2010, September 8). Padre ticket sales show little pennant fever. *U-T San Diego News.* Retrieved from http://www.utsandiego.com/news/2010/sep/08/turnstiles-show-padres-fans-seem-immune-pennant-fe/

19. Pritchard, M., & Negro, C. (2001). Sport loyalty programs and their impact on fan relationships. *International Journal of Sports Marketing & Sponsorship*, *3*, 317–338.

20. Bachman, R. (2010, August 14). Despite recession, prices to nation's top games cost fans more than ever. *Portland Oregonian*, p. C3

21. Caraviello, D. (2008, October 25). NASCAR ticket prices can be a source of contention. *NASCAR.* Retrieved from http://cgi.nascar.com/2008/news/opinion/10/25/inside.line.dcaraviello.ticket.prices/index.html

22. Dortch, S. (1996, April). The future of baseball. *American Demographics*, pp. 22–28.

23. Fehr, S. (1997, October 31). Pricey new sports venues help make Washington no. 1 for high price tickets. *Washington Post*, p. C5.

24. 2011 MLB fan cost index—Team marketing report. (2011, April). *Teammarketing.com.* Retrieved from https://www.teammarketing.com/public/files/2011_mlb_fci.pdf

25. Lopiano, D. (2001, June 11–17). Division I cranks up the sports 'arms race.' *SportsBusiness Journal*, p. 33.

26. Boon, G., & James, D. (2002). *Annual review of football finance: Season 2000–2001.* London, UK: Deloitte & Touche Sport.

27. Whittell, I. (2002, March 12). NBA declares intention to expand into Europe. *London Times*, p. 39.

28. Oliver, B. (2007, November 18). 21st century sport: New world order. *The Observer.* Retrieved from http://www.guardian.co.uk/sport/blog/2007/nov/18/21stcenturysportnewworldo

29. Kay, O. (2002, August 24). All quiet on Western front for pioneer Li. *The Times.*

30. Oliver, B., & Gillis, R. (2007, October 28). Games without frontiers. *The Observer.* Retrieved from http://www.guardian.co.uk/sport/2007/oct/28/news.sport1

31. Conn, D. (2011, October 17). John W. Henry turns from Red Sox to red shirts for the global gains. *The Guardian.* Retrieved from http://www.guardian.co.uk/football/blog/2011/oct/13/john-w-henry-liverpool-boston

32. Foreign players in the Premier League 2010/2011. (2011, July 26). *Spirit of Mirko.* Retrieved from http://spiritofmirko.com/2011/07/26/foreign-players-in-the-premier-league-20102011/

33. Kelso, P. (2008, February 14). Scudamore's grand plan comes apart at the seams. *The Guardian.* Retrieved from http://www.guardian.co.uk/football/2008/feb/15/newsstory.premierleague

2

Challenges Facing College Sports

THE FINANCIAL STATUS OF INTERCOLLEGIATE ATHLETICS

The Organization of College Sports

Over the last two decades, college athletics has become an increasingly prominent part of the sports landscape in America. By 2012, 1,378 US colleges and universities operated comprehensive varsity sports programs, spending more than $9 billion a year on intercollegiate athletics.[1] Close to 80% of these programs (1,098) are members of the National Collegiate Athletic Association (NCAA) which is the primary regulatory body for college athletics. The organization provides a vehicle by which members create and enforce rules governing eligibility, recruiting, financial aid and playing and practice seasons. The NCAA conducts championships in 33 men's and women's sports. Its primary stated purpose is to ensure fair competition and to enhance the student-athlete experience. The National Association of Intercollegiate Athletics (NAIA) provides similar governance and oversight for smaller colleges and universities across the US. In 2011, the NAIA had 290 member institutions. In Canada, the national governing body for collegiate sport is Canadian Interuniversity Sport (CIS; formerly, the Canadian Intercollegiate Athletic Union). CIS has 54 member colleges and universities that compete in nine national championships.

As shown in Table 2.1, the 1,098 schools affiliated with the NCAA are separated into three divisions. Division I is the highest level, and includes the leading conferences and high-profile independent schools (e.g., Notre Dame), whose members commit millions of dollars annually to sustaining high-profile athletic programs. Division I has 347 member institutions. Division II provides an intermediate level of competi-

Table 2.1. NCAA Membership by Division	
Division	Number of Members
IA (FBS)	121
IAA (FCS)	125
I (without football)	101
II	308
III	443

tion for affiliated members. The 308 active members of Division II are typically regional institutions with smaller enrollments (average enrollment around 4,500). Very few athletes competing at the Division II level receive full grants-in-aid ("full rides"). Many, however, will receive partial athletic scholarships and/or some level of financial support from the institution.

Division III of the NCAA represents schools that offer varsity sports as essentially an extracurricular activity for students. The 443 schools competing at the Division III level de-emphasize the commercial aspects of college athletics. Member schools are not allowed to provide athletic scholarships and may not establish private endowment funds for the express purpose of supporting athletics.

The NCAA has imposed minimum requirements for admission to each of the three divisions. Eligibility requirements are the most demanding for Division I. In order to qualify for inclusion at this top level, member institutions must sponsor a minimum of 14 varsity sports, at least seven for men and seven for women (or six for men and eight for women). In 2007, the NCAA adopted a new classification scheme for Division I schools playing football. Athletic departments with large-scale investments in football (highly paid coaching staffs, elaborate facilities) were placed in the Football Bowl Subdivision (FBS; formerly known as the Division I-A) and schools with a less intensive financial commitment to football were assigned to the Football Championship Subdivision (FCS; formerly known as Division I-AA). To meet the threshold for inclusion and continuation as a FBS member, schools must meet a minimum attendance requirement of 15,000 in actual or paid home attendance per game every other year. FCS schools are exempt from a minimum attendance requirement. However, all "D1" level schools must comply with minimum grants-in-aid or scholarship requirements for each sport. For football, FBS members are allowed to offer a maximum of 85 scholarships of which no fewer than 90% must be awarded in any given season. The threshold for FCS subdivision schools is considerably lower. The NCAA allows FCS schools to offer 63 scholarships to football players. However, FCS programs are afforded greater flexibility in awarding grants-in-aid to athletes playing football. Unlike FBS schools, which can offer only full scholarships to individual players, FCS programs are allowed to offer partial grants-in-aid. Therefore, most FCS football programs divide their 63 scholarships among 85 players to fill out a complete roster. To maintain their FCS status, no fewer than 76.5 players must receive some form of scholarship support.

Eligibility standards for Division II and III NCAA members are far less stringent. Both divisions require schools to sponsor a minimum of 10 varsity sports, at least five sports for men and five for women. While Division II programs may offer athletic scholarships, the NCAA imposes much stricter limits on the number of scholarships awarded to teams in almost every sport. For example, Division II football programs are allowed to give a maximum of 36 full scholarships compared to 85 full scholarships at the Division I level. While the discrepancy between Division I and II programs is not nearly as dramatic as for football, Table 2.2 shows Division II athletic departments offer fewer scholarships to men and women in every sport except women's rowing and ice hockey, and men's and women's tennis.

Table 2.2. Scholarship Limits by Sport for Men and Women By NCAA Divisions

Sport	Max. # of Scholarships			
	Div. I		Div. II	
	Men's	Women's	Men's	Women's
Archery	0	5	0	9.0
Baseball	11.7	0	9.0	0
Badminton	0	6	0	10.0
Basketball	13.0	15.0	10.0	10.0
Bowling	0	5.0	0	5.0
Cross County/Track and Field	12.6	18.0	12.6	12.6
Equestrian	0	15.0	0	15.0
Fencing	4.5	5.0	4.5	4.5
Field Hockey	0	12.0	0	6.3

Football
  FBS (Div. 1–A)
  FCS (Div. 1AA)
	
	85
	63
		
		0
		0
			36	0

Golf	4.5	6.0	3.6	5.4
Gymnastics	6.3	12.0	5.4	6.0
Handball	0	0	0	12.0
Ice Hockey	18.0	18.0	13.5	18.0
Lacrosse	12.6	12.0	10.8	9.9
Rifle	3.6	0	3.6	7.2
Rowing	0	20.0	0	20.0
Skiing	6.3	7.0	6.3	6.3
Soccer	9.9	12.0	9.0	9.9
Softball	0	12.0	0	7.2
Squash	0	12.0	9.0	7.2
Swimming and Diving	9.9	14.0	8.1	9.0
Synchronized Swimming	0	5.0	0	5.0
Team Handball	0	10.0	0	12.0
Tennis	4.5	8.0	4.5	6.0
Volleyball	4.5	12.0	4.5	8.0
Water Polo	4.5	8.0	4.5	8.0
Wrestling	9.9	0	9.0	0
TOTAl	221.31	249.0	163.9	229.5

1. The total number for FCS athletic programs is 199.3

Source: NCAA Sports Sponsorship and Participation Rates Report, 1981–82—2009–10

Participation Patterns for Men and Women

Closer examination of Table 2.2 reveals that across all varsity sports at the Division I level, there are potentially more athletic scholarships available to women than men. A comparison of individual sports at both the Division I and II levels shows that with few exceptions, women have been allocated more grants-in-aid than for the equivalent men's team. For D1 programs, the uneven pattern is true for basketball (women 15, men 13), track and field (women 18, men 12.6), gymnastics (women 12, men 6.3), soccer (women 12, men 9.9), swimming and diving (women 14, men 9.9) and volleyball (women 12, men 4.5). In large part, the disproportionate allocation of scholarships is a result football, a sport exclusive to men, receiving *four times* as many scholarships as any single women's sports team. The 20 grants-in-aid awarded female rowing programs are dwarfed by the 85 full rides available to FBS football teams. No other sport comes close to the number of scholarships provided for football. Consequently, under the NCAA's existing allocation arrangement, the only way institutions can come close to achieving mandated federal gender equity standards is to provide disproportionally more scholarships to women across a wide range of other sports.

Table 2.3 identifies the complete list of varsity sports sponsored by the NCAA at the Division I level. The inventory provides a breakdown of the number of teams, number of athletes and average squad size for each men's and women's sport. The NCAA recognizes 23 individual and team sports for women and 19 for men. Five sports are classified as Coed Sports, in which men and women participate jointly: equestrian, fencing, riflery, sailing, and skiing. In addition, the NCAA created a category called "Emerging Sports." In an effort to provide women with greater participation opportunities, in 1994 the NCAA established a Gender-Equity Task Force for the purpose of identifying sports that had the potential to become classified as championship sports. In order to gain championship status, a minimum of 40 athletic departments must have varsity teams competing in the sport. Of the nine sports on the original emerging sports list, five (bowling, ice hockey, rowing, water polo and squash) have become NCAA-recognized championship sports. Rugby, sand volleyball and equestrian are making progress toward becoming championship sports. Importantly, schools are permitted to count emerging sports toward meeting the minimum NCAA eligibility requirement for Division I and II status.

No collegiate athletic program comes close to offering the full menu of participation opportunities. Indeed, only a handful offer more than 30 sports for men and women—most notably Ohio State and Stanford, which sponsor 36 and 35 teams, respectively. The vast majority of athletic programs offer a much more limited number of options. In 2010, the average Division I athletic department sponsored 19 teams, 9 for men and 10 for women. Division II institutions offer a more restricted number of participation opportunities, sponsoring on average approximately 14 sports teams (6.7 for men and 7.6 for women). At the Division III level, athletic programs sponsored an average of 17 teams, eight for men and nine for women. The more active profile at the Division III level corresponds to the division's emphasis on student participation in sport as an important extracurricular activity. In addition, it reflects the division's financial reality.

Sport	Men			Women		
	# of Teams	# of Athletes	# Avg. Squad	# of Teams	# of Athletes	# Avg. Squad
Archery	0	0	N/A	0	0	N/A
Badminton	0	0	N/A	0	0	N/A
Baseball	294	9,964	33.9	N/A	N/A	N/A
Basketball	333	5,182	15.5	332	4,766	14.4
Bowling	0	0	N/A	30	266	8.9
Cross Country	306	4,796	15.7	331	5,752	17.4
Equestrian	0	0	N/A	18	739	41.1
Fencing	20	374	18.7	23	399	17.3
Football	238	26,325	110.6	N/A	N/A	N/A
FBS	120	14,319	119.3	–	–	–
FCS	118	12,006	101.7	–	–	–
Golf	291	2,973	10.2	245	2,112	8.6
Gymnastics	16	311	19.4	63	1,054	16.7
Ice Hockey	58	1,605	27.7	35	793	22.7
Lacrosse	58	2,685	46.3	89	2,444	27.5
Rifle	20	142	7.1	23	137	6.0
Rowing	28	1,303	46.5	86	3,221	60.7
Rugby	0	0	N/A	1	19	19.0
Sailing	10	241	24.1	0	0	N/A
Skiing	12	191	15.9	13	203	15.6
Soccer	197	5,579	28.3	313	8,302	26.5
Softball	N/A	N/A	N/A	279	5,539	19.9
Squash	10	154	15.4	9	119	13.2
Swimming/Diving	138	3,877	28.1	194	5,392	27.8
Synchronized Swimming	0	0	N/A	0	0	N/A
Tennis	258	2,639	10.2	313	2,905	9.3
Track, Indoor	252	9,578	38.7	303	11,816	39.0
Track, Outdoor	270	10,812	40.0	310	11,934	38.5
Volleyball	23	471	20.5	319	4,752	14.9
Water Polo	22	586	26.6	32	734	22.9
Wrestling	82	2,567	31.3	N/A	N/A	N/A
TOTAL	2,938	92,535		3,439	77,129	

Table 2.3. Sports Participation by Gender. Division I

Source: *NCAA Sponsorship and Participation Rates Report: 1981–82 to 2009–10*

The exemption from having to underwrite the cost of expensive athletic scholarships means Division III programs are better able to afford to offer a broader variety of varsity sports.

Tables 2.2 and 2.3 show that women are offered a broader range of sports in which to participate and a slightly greater number of potential athletic scholarships at the Division I level than men. Despite these advantages, the overall participation of males exceeds that of female student athletes. Of the nearly 170,000 students participating in Division I level sports in 2010, 54.5% or 92,535 were men, compared to 77,129 women.[2] The proportion of male to female student athletes is even higher at the Division II level, with 59.2% of the participants being male. According to the NCAA, in 2010, the average member institution had 406 student-athletes, 232 male and 174 female.

There are a number of reasons why more men than women participate in intercollegiate athletics. A core factor is that women were not afforded the same opportunities to compete in college sport until much later than men. Women's sports did not become a part of the NCAA until 1982. For the first 70 years of its existence, the NCAA provided opportunities for only male athletes. In fact, the NCAA initially opposed the passage of Title IX, the landmark legislation that would require equal treatment in athletics for women (a section on the impact of Title IX is included later in this chapter). Prior to the adoption of Title IX, the NCAA feared that elevating the status of women would threaten its control and dominance over intercollegiate athletics.[3] With the passage of the law, and subsequent growth of women's sports, the NCAA opportunistically determined that offering membership to institutions sponsoring women's sports was in the organization's best interests. Not surprisingly, since the NCAA's inclusion of women's sports in late 1982, female participation rates have increased dramatically. The total number of women participating in NCAA-sponsored sports has almost tripled over the last three decades, growing from 74,239 in 1982–83 to 186,460 in 2009–10.[2]

While women have made substantial progress, they still have some catching up to do. The total number of men competing in NCAA sports across all three divisions grew to 249,307 in 2009–10. An examination of average squad sizes reveals some interesting differences in current levels of participation between men and women (see Table 2.3). A comparison of Division I sports in which both men and women compete shows that in almost every case a greater number of men participate in the sport than women. Surprisingly, even in several sports where women receive a higher number of scholarships, the average squad size was larger for men than for women. Despite the increased opportunities for financial support, in the average number of women on varsity rosters for basketball, golf, soccer and gymnastics is fewer than men. Some suggest the larger squad size for men is primarily a function of supply and demand. There are considerably more boys participating in high school sports than girls. During the 2009–10 school year, 4.6 million boys and 3.2 million girls participated in high school sports. Substantial differences exist in the number of boys and girls competing in sports like basketball (boys 540,207, girls 439,550), track and field (boys 572,123, girls 469,177) and golf (boys 157,756, girls 70,872). While more boys than girls are playing soccer (boys 391,839, girls 356,116) and competing in cross country (boys 239,608, girls 201,968), the margin of difference has closed considerably over the past five years, with girls making substantial gains. By 2010, girls had eclipsed boys in two sports: tennis (girls 182,395, boys 162,755) and swimming and diving (girls 158,419, boys 131,376). The participation figures do give credence to the claim that greater roster sizes in several sports are attributable to there being more highly skilled male athletes available to compete at the collegiate level. Many of whom are willing to "walk on" or participate as members of a varsity squad without any financial assistance.

GRIM FINANCIAL REALITIES

The cost of intercollegiate athletics has grown enormously over the past several decades. During the last decade alone, the average annual operating budget of a Division I, Football Bowl Subdivision program more than doubled from $21.9 million in 2000 to $46.7 million in 2010.[5]

Despite the tremendous increase in investment, the overall financial state of intercollegiate athletics is grim. In 1999, the executive director of the NCAA asserted, "You can probably count on your two hands the number of athletic departments that actually have a surplus" (p. 157).[6] Over a decade later, his claim still accurately depicts the overall economic condition of collegiate sport. The NCAA's annual report on revenues and expenses showed that in 2010, only 22 of the 120 FBS-level programs generated a net surplus.* More than 80% of the largest athletic programs are losing money, and smaller colleges at the Division III and NAIA levels are experiencing even greater financial pressures, with close to 100% relying heavily on institutional subsidies to operate on even a breakeven basis.[7]

The extent to which athletic departments are struggling financially at all levels is evident in Table 2.4 (overleaf), which reveals that in 2010 all three divisions fell far short of financial self sufficiency. In fact, the median operating deficit for a FBS program was $9.44 million. This figure represents the net difference between total generated revenues (e.g., ticket sales, NCAA and conference distributions, media rights, private donations and other sources excluding institutional or governmental support or student fees), less total operating expenses. Even with considerably less investment, median operating deficits are even greater at the FCS (formerly known as Division IAA) level, with losses averaging $9.79 million. For several decades, the NCAA has been collecting revenue and expense data from athletic departments in all three divisions.# A detailed breakdown of the financial condition and performance of college athletic programs is reported annually.

---

*A closer examination of available data shows that in fact only eight FBS schools are "truly" financially self-sufficient. Fourteen of the 22 programs showing net revenues in the NCAA reports received some level of "allocated support" (e.g., student activity fees, direct general fund appropriation). The eight wholly financially-independent "public" university athletic programs are: LSU, Texas A&M, Purdue, Nebraska, Texas, Oklahoma, Penn State and Ohio State.

#While the NCAA Revenues and Expenses reports go all the way back to 1969, 2004 is considered the baseline year for trend analysis. In 2004, substantial changes were made in the manner in which data were both collected and reported. Therefore, meaningful comparisons from year to year are only possible dating back to 2004.

Table 2.4. Median (and Range) 2010 Revenues and Expenses

For Division I Institutions by Subdivision

	FBS	FCS
Generated Revenues	$35,336,000 ($3.8 million to $143.5 million)	$3,289,000 ($279,000 to $14.4 million)
Total Revenues	$48,298,000 ($9.5 million to $143.5 million)	$13,189,000 ($3.1 million to $40.2 million)
Total Expenses	$46,688,000 ($10.7 million to $130 million)	$13,091, 000 ($3.2 million to $39.2 million)
Net Revenues*	($9,446,000) ($36.7 million to $41.9 million)	($9,789,000) ($25.3 million to $1.9 million)

* Amounts do not add up evenly due to use of median values.

Source: *NCAA Division I Intercollegiate Athletics Programs Report: Revenues & Expenses, 2004–2010*, Tables 2.3 and 4.5

An examination of the most current NCAA financial data for Division IA (FBS) programs shows that overall revenues have grown at a healthy rate. As shown in Table 2.5, from 2004 to 2010, average total revenues increased 71% from $28.2 million to $48.3 million. Over the same period, overall Division IA expenditures grew 61% from $29.9 million to $46.7 million. The trend toward greater financial self sufficiency is a recent development. It has only been since 2008 that revenues outpaced expenditures for three consecutive years. In fact, 2010 was the first and only year in which total revenues exceeded total expenditures for Division IA programs—by a healthy margin of $1.6

Table 2.5. Revenue and Expenditure Trends: 2004–2010. Division I Athletic Programs

Division I-A (FBS)							
	2004	2005	2006	2007	2008	2009	2010
Total Revenues	$28,214	$32,849	$35,400	$37,566	$41,088	$45,698	$48,298
% Change	–	+16.4%	+7.7%	+6.1%	+9.4%	+11.2%	+5.7%
Total Expenditures	$29,991	$31,128	$35,756	$39,192	$41,363	$45,887	$46,688
% Change	–	+3.7%	+14.9%	+9.1%	+5.5%	+10.9%	+1.7%
Division I-AA (FCS)							
	2004	2005	2006	2007	2008	2009	2010
Total Revenues	$7,700	$9,007	$9,642	$10,527	$12,080	$12,111	$13,189
% Change	–	+17.0%	+0.6%	+0.9%	+14.8%	+0.3%	+8.9%
Total Expenditures	$7,810	$8,665	$9,485	$10,041	$12,115	$12,019	$13,091
% Change	–	+10.9%	+10.7%	+11.3%	+14.9%	0.8%	+8.9%

Source: *NCAA Division I Intercollegiate Athletics Programs Revenues & Expenses Report: 2004–2010*

million. Ostensibly, this finding is promising. However, a closer inspection of the NCAA data reveals a very different circumstance for most FBS institutions. As indicated previously, fewer than 20% of all Division IA athletic departments reported positive net revenues in 2010. The median net *surplus* for those 22 institutions averaged $7.4 million, compared with the median net *deficit* of $11.3 million for the remaining FBS schools. And, the gap between the relatively few highest performing programs and the rest of the FBS is widening. In one year alone, the difference in net revenues between those schools producing a surplus and those who were not grew more than 20% from $15.6 million in 2009 to $19 million in 2010.

Table 2.6 (overleaf) illustrates the huge gap between the few "haves" (those schools largely restricted to the first quartile) and the large majority of programs composing the other three quartiles (each quartile representing approximately 30 D1 programs). The disparity in "total generated revenues" (ticket sales, NCAA and conference distributions, contributions, media rights, and other sources excluding institutional and government support and student fees) between schools in the first (highest) and fourth (lowest) quartiles is enormous at $80 million. But what may be even more disconcerting is the $41-million gap between first and second quartile schools.

The inability of all but a few athletic departments to operate on a financially self-sufficient basis has meant that most universities subsidize a significant portion of the costs of operating their athletic programs. The growing dependence of athletic departments on institutional support is a serious concern. Institutional support includes funds that are directly transferred from general university sources to the athletic department. These sources may include direct appropriations from the university's general fund, student fees and, in some cases, indirect support in which the institution underwrites all or a portion of maintenance, utility and insurance expenses. In fewer than 15 years, the level of institutional support necessary to sustain intercollegiate athletic programs at all levels has increased dramatically. In 1999, Division IA programs received on average $1.94 million annually in institutional support, amounting to approximately 9% of total operating revenues.[8] Over the past decade, the average amount of institutional subsidy for Division IA programs has grown steadily, from $5.3 million in 2003, to $7.0 million in 2006 to $9.8 million annually, in 2010. The almost $10 million in institutional support accounted for more than 20% of total revenues generated by all Division IA athletic programs in 2010. However, Table 2.6 again shows the summary figure to be misleading. While schools in the first quartile received no institutional subsidies, the level of support increased dramatically from the second through fourth quartiles, from a fairly modest 16% in the second quartile to a dominant 66% for athletic programs in the fourth quartile. At the Division I-AA or FCS level, the reliance on institutional subsidies across the board is much greater. In 2010, the $8.02 million in institutional support provided on average to Division I-AA athletic departments accounted for 66% of the total revenues generated by FCS programs.

The pattern of increasing dependence on institutional support is troubling in light of the difficult financial challenges facing higher education in recent years. In 2010, *U.S. News and World Report* proclaimed that the Great Recession's toll on higher education

Table 2.6. Sources of Revenue by Quartile. Division I—FBS Fiscal Year 2010. Median Values*

	First Quartile	Second Quartile	Third Quartile	Fourth Quartile
Generated Revenues				
Total ticket sales	24,418,000	12,704,000	6,258,000	1,113,000
NCAA & conference distributions	19,334,000	9,914,000	3,661,000	1,233,000
Guarantees and options	412,000	623,000	615,000	1,085,000
Cash contributions from alumni, others	23,616,000	10,942,000	5,304,000	1,423,000
Third party support	0	0	0	0
Concessions/ programs/novelties	1,831,000	1,453,000	631,000	136,000
Broadcast rights	1,665,000	83,000	53,000	0
Royalties/advertising/ sponsorship	6,534,000	4,197,000	1,399,000	590,000
Sports camps	557,000	12,000	15,000	157,000
Endowment/investment income	1,667,000	653,000	187,000	60,000
Miscellaneous	2,137,000	788,000	645,000	250,000
Total generated revenues	**86,942,000**	**45,404,000**	**23,072,000**	**6,836,000**
Allocated Revenues				
Direct institutional support	0	4,924,000	3,822,000	4,730,000
Indirect institutional support	0	122,000	365,000	728,000
Student fees	0	1,583,000	1,714,000	4,891,000
Direct government support	0	0	0	0
Total allocated revenues	**3,380,000**	**9,446,000**	**11,409,000**	**13,615,000**
Total all revenues	**89,236,000**	**57,841,000**	**36,586,000**	**20,567,000**

*Amounts may not add up to totals shown.

Source: *NCAA Division I Intercollegiate Athletic Programs Report: Revenues & Expenses, 2004–2010* Table 3.8

has been "devastating."[9] Public, or state-supported institutions, which account for 75% of the total student enrollment in four-year colleges and universities, have been hit the hardest. The prolonged economic downturn of the late 2000s resulted in state legislatures across the country slashing higher education budgets. In 2010 alone, state support for colleges and universities in the U.S. fell an estimated 5% or $4.5 billion.[9] In several states, cuts have been particularly severe. In recent years, California, Pennsylvania, Louisiana, and Arizona—to name just a few—have all made double-digit reductions in higher education funding. The effect of deep budget cuts on many campuses has meant faculty pay cuts, furloughs and even layoffs, as well as the elimination of academic programs and substantial increases in student tuition and fees. For example, the University of California, Berkeley, in response to a $500 million or 16.4% reduction in state general fund support, increased undergraduate tuition by more than 20% in 2011.

Athletic programs have not been immune to the serious financial difficulties facing their institutions. When examined over an extended period of time, the NCAA financial data show significant increases in overall institutional support. However, that pattern has recently begun to change. In the last few years, the amount of direct institutional support has declined. In a short span of time, from 2008 to 2010, the median annual amount of money directly transferred from the institution's general fund to the athletic department decreased by $630,000 on average for all Division IA (FBS) programs and by $864,000 on average for all Division IAA (FCS) programs. While the magnitude of reduction has not reached a serious level for most athletic programs, the prospect for continued declines in institutional support does raise serious concerns. As institutions continue to struggle with a deteriorating financial environment, athletic programs will be under increased scrutiny.

The negative impacts are already evident at a number of institutions. In those states hardest hit by budget shortfalls, many athletic programs have experienced substantial reductions in the amount of direct support they have received from their university's general fund. In response to their massive budget cut of $500 million in 2011–12, the University of California at Berkeley announced the elimination of five varsity sports (women's lacrosse and gymnastics, baseball, men's gymnastics, and the demotion of men's rugby to club sport status). The "Cal" athletic program had been operating at a deficit for well over a decade.[10] In the 2009–10 fiscal year, the athletic department accrued an operating loss of $12.09 million (on $57.24 million in generated revenues and $69.35 million in expenses). This substantial deficit represented a persistent and growing pattern of losses. For more than a decade, the Cal athletic department reported losses ranging from $9 to $13 million.[11] Each year, losses had been covered by funds transferred from the university's general fund. At a time when the university was struggling to preserve core academic programs, providing athletic subsidies at that level became untenable. Pressure from both faculty and students resulted in central administration dramatically reducing the level of subvention when the athletic director announced the decision to eliminate five of 29 varsity sports. At the same time the athletic director announced the cuts, she also left the door open for their future reinstatement by stating that that if private supporters could raise $25 million (sufficient to ensure the long-term financial stability of each sport), all five teams could be restored. In less than 4 months, backers were able to raise $13 million in private donations. Despite falling far short of the target, the university announced that three of the five teams (all except baseball and men's gymnastics) would be reinstated. Shortly thereafter, the school announced that it would restore baseball as a result of a successful fundraising campaign which raised almost $10 million to preserve varsity baseball at Cal. The university's decision to cut, then restore, athletic teams prompted a heated debate on campus that questioned the athletic department's receiving millions of dollars in university subsidies at a time when the rest of the university was suffering through program cuts, mandated furloughs, and a record tuition increase. Although all but one of the varsity sports was reinstated due to private fundraising efforts, the university adopted a plan that would limit the university's annual contribution to athletics to $5 million a year by 2014.[12]

While philanthropy was used to compensate for declining institutional support at UC Berkeley, increases in student fee support have been used to "rescue" or preserve sports on other campuses facing severe budget pressures. For example, faced with the elimination of football, the students at St. Cloud State University approved a $1.74 increase in athletic fees per credit hour for three years starting in 2012.[13] The new athletic fee generates $1.3 million in additional funding for the athletic program. Without the additional student support, football at the Division II institution would have been eliminated as part of the university's efforts to cope with a 10% reduction in state-appropriated funds. Along with football (a $500,000 saving), the university president proposed cuts that would eliminate dozens of academic programs and nearly 80 faculty positions. In making his original recommendation, the president stated, "I cannot lay off tenured faculty and leave sports untouched" (para. 5).[14] Only the students' willingness to pay a special fee in support of football sustained the program for at least three additional years. Similar efforts to offset declining institutional support through increased student fees have not been as successful as the experience at St. Cloud State.

Students at several universities have voted down proposals to increase funding for sports. They rejected athletic fee increases at the University of California at Davis and Irvine, the University of New Orleans, California State Northridge, California State Fullerton and Long Beach State. Consequently, varsity sports teams were eliminated at all of these institutions. UC Davis dropped four sports (women's rowing, men's wrestling, men's indoor track, and men's swimming and diving); UC Irvine eliminated five teams (men's and women's swimming and diving, men's and women's crew, and co-ed sailing); and the University of New Orleans, facing a $1.4 million cut in athletics funding, cut four varsity sports (men's and women's swimming and diving, and men's and women's track and field). Following the failed student referendum and cuts in varsity sports, the University of New Orleans petitioned the NCAA to be reclassified as a Division II program because the school could no longer meet the Division I eligibility standard of sponsoring a minimum of 14 varsity sports teams.[15]

On a number of campuses, students are not given the opportunity to vote on whether they would devote a portion of their incidental fees to support athletics. According to *USA Today*, during the 2008–09 school year, students were charged $795 million to support sports programs at 222 Division I public institutions.[16] The amount accounts for 23% of the total fees paid annually by in-state students. Not surprisingly, the charge to students is substantial, exceeding $1,000 per school year at many institutions.* In most cases, the mandatory athletics fee has been imposed by the institution's state board of higher education. The *USA Today* investigation discovered that most students (and their parents) were unaware of the scope of dedicated athletic fees, as many universities were found not to disclose their athletic charges on their billing statements. When queried about the lack of transparency, a spokesperson at one institution responded: At Virginia Military Institute, the athletics fee figure is "buried in our budget," said Col. Stewart MacInnis. "I had to go dig it out myself. It's not where anybody would go look for it. You've identified a weak spot" (para. 17).[16]

Pressure is mounting for increased accountability in the disclosure of all required student tuition and fees. In 2011, more rigorous enforcement of the Higher Education Opportunity Act of 2008 will require schools to report annually the largest increases in fees over the last three years by department. In June 2011, the Knight Commission on Intercollegiate Athletics recommended that institutions make student fees transparent as a way of reforming athletic spending. According to the co-chair, "I think that (transparency) is a way to bring pressure to bear—and a beginning to put a hold on, to tamp down, the rate of increase (of spending) in intercollegiate athletics" ("A Matter of Transparency" section, para. 6).[16]

Although increased accountability in the reporting of athletic fees is likely, it is evident that athletic programs struggling to keep up with the growing costs will seek to rely on student fees as a prominent resource. The University of Hawaii is a prime example. For a number of years, the university's athletic program had been accruing annual operating losses at a rate of $1.5 to $ 2 million a year. Unable to defray the continuing deficits from generated income sources (ticket sales, donations, television), the state board of regents voted to impose a student fee of $50 per semester. The dedicated athletic fee is projected to add $1.8 million per year to the athletic department budget. The regents' decision was made despite strong resistance from student advocacy groups. In response to the vigorous opposition, the Associate Athletic Director, stated: "Athletics is by no means the most important part (of the institution) . . . but, a strong, successful athletic program is a very important connection with alumni, donors and leaders in the state, and it magnifies the university not only in Hawaii, but beyond the state. That's the visibility that the athletics program can provide" ("Absolutely Getting Nothing" section, para. 11).[16]

In response to the difficult budget environment, intercollegiate athletic departments, particularly at the Division I level, have placed great emphasis on growing revenues. As shown in Table 2.7, programs at both the FBS and FCS level have succeeded in expanding revenues. From 2004 to 2010, top-tier, FBS programs have increased total generated revenues, on average, from $22.86 million to $35.34 million, or 55%. Generated revenues include income produced independently by the athletic department through ticket sales, donor contributions, conference and NCAA distributions, etc. While

---

*A study conducted by *The Virginian-Pilot* found that 7 universities in Virginia charged each student more than $1,000 athletics fee for the 2009–10 school year. Longwood University led the way with a $2,009 per year student fee, followed by Norfolk State at $1,379, William and Mary at $1,324 and VMI at $1,298.[17]

Table 2.7. Total Generated Revenues 2004–2010. Division I Median Values				
	2004	**2006**	**2008**	**2010**
Division IA (FBS)	$22,864,000	$26,432,000	$30,494,000	$35,336,000
Division IAA (FCS)	$2,078,000	$2,345,000	$2,978,000	$3,289,000
Source: NCAA Division I Intercollegiate Athletics Programs Revenues & ExpensesReport: 2004–2010				

smaller, FCS division programs have also demonstrated solid revenue growth, the increase of $1.2 million is modest when compared to the larger schools' $12.5 improvement over the same period of time.

The substantial difference in income generation is largely attributable to football. In 2010, according to the NCAA, football accounted for 45% of the total revenues generated by FBS athletic programs. An FBS football program generated approximately $16.2 million in 2010, almost doubling the median amount of $8.3 million produced in 2004. In comparison, at the Division I-AA or FBS level, football plays a much smaller role, accounting for 24% of total revenues.

Major football programs, in preeminent conferences like the Southeastern Conference, Big 12, and Big 10, typically generate in excess of $70 million. No other sport comes close to producing that magnitude of income. In 2010, the median total revenue generated by a Division IA men's basketball program was $4.78 million. Only a relatively few men's basketball programs are capable of producing revenues that approach $20 million per year.

It is likely that the NCAA figures understate the real contribution of football to overall athletic department revenues. When you take into account that a considerable portion of the total cash contributions made by "donors" to major athletic programs are specifically tied to the purchase of premium seating options for football, the impact on overall ticket sales is much greater than reported by the NCAA. The NCAA data only attributes "total ticket sales" to the face value of tickets actually sold by member schools. Not included in their tabulation is the revenue associated with mandatory "donations" imposed by the athletic department in order for fans to purchase the best seats in the stadium. These required premium seating charges can be as high as $2,500 per seat (in addition to the actual cost of the ticket). The millions of dollars in revenue produced by these premium seating (sometimes referred to as seat license) programs are typically accounted for in revenue summaries as part of the general "donations" or cash contributions, separate from ticket sales. Consequently, their real impact on total football revenues is underrepresented. If donations or private contributions via preferred seating were accurately attributed to football, as well as income from corporate sponsorships and broadcast rights fees, it is likely that football at many schools contributes more than two-thirds of the athletic department's total revenues. For example, football at the University of Texas accounts for an estimated 80% of the athletic department's total revenues. According to *Forbes*, the Texas Longhorns football program amassed a whopping

$93.9 million in gross revenues and cleared a $69 million profit during the 2010 season.[18] And, in the case of the Longhorns, the rich will get richer. In 2011, Texas established a partnership with ESPN to launch a new television network, the "Longhorn Network"—the very first network to feature sports programming from a single athletic department. The lucrative partnership will provide the Texas athletic program with over $12 million a year in new revenues over 15 years.

By 2012, the UT athletic budget had grown to a record $153.5 million, up 18% from $129.9 million in 2010.[19] A hundred miles to the east, at Texas A&M University, the athletic director proclaimed, "Football pays for everything" (p. 47).[20] The revenue disparity between football and the rest of the school's sports programs is enormous. "Every other sport except men's basketball hemorrhaged red ink" (p. 47).[20] Fortunately, football at A&M turned a $25.3 million surplus in 2011.[18]

Big-time football programs at places like Texas and Texas A&M are able to exploit growing fan passion for college football. A recent report indicates single game prices to the most sought-after college football games have soared, increasing 30% in three years, to an average of $65.[21] The nation's highest priced ticket in 2011 was $125 for Oklahoma at Oklahoma State. In 2008, the cost of a ticket to a premium game at the University of Washington could be purchased for $30. In 2011—after season records of 0–12, 5–7 and 7–6—the cost to see Oregon play at Husky Stadium was $80, a 167% increase.[21]

However, for every top-tier football program turning a major profit from growing television and ticket sales revenues, there are three to four other schools struggling to make ends meet. Many of these institutions continue to invest heavily in football as it is often the only sport able to generate a surplus. But, in most cases, the "profit" realized is modest. Oregon State University is a good example. Its football program has enjoyed unprecedented success over the past decade, appearing in eight post-season bowl games and setting new attendance records. In 2010, the football program generated total revenues of $19 million, netting an operating surplus of $7 million.[27] According to the school's athletic director, football accounts for about 70% of the department's total revenues. "Football and to a lesser extent (men's) basketball finance the rest of the athletics department" (p. 3).[22]

Football is the financial linchpin of big-time college athletic programs. Courtesy of BigStock Photo

Despite football's success, the surplus it generates is not sufficient to fully cover the cost of fielding 16 other varsity sports. In 2010, Oregon State's athletic program reported a deficit of $5.9 million.[23] Unfortunately, Oregon State's financial situation more closely reflects the reality of most athletic departments competing at the highest levels of NCAA football. Recall that only 22 Division I athletic programs reported making a "profit" in 2010. As will be shown in greater detail in the next section, the rising costs associated with sustaining top-tier football programs consumes enormous financial resources, making it increasingly challenging for many programs to produce even a modest return. According to NCAA data, about half the FBS football programs (51) operated at a deficit, while only four programs at the FCS level realized a profit.

The Cost Control Struggle

Controlling rapidly rising costs is one of the most serious challenges facing the majority of intercollegiate athletic programs. In the relatively short period between 2004 and 2010, the median operating budget for a Division IA (FBS) athletic department increased from $28.9 million to nearly $47 million. What makes cost containment so challenging is that two of the major expenditure growth categories are largely beyond the control of the athletic department.

At most institutions, the university charges the athletic program the cost of student-athletes' scholarships or grants-in-aid. The athletic department must pay all or defray a significant portion of every scholarship athlete's tuition and fees. For the past two decades, tuition costs have soared at more than twice the rate of inflation. Since 2000, the cost of attending a college or university in the US has more than doubled.[24] The impact on athletic programs is considerable. For example, between 2005 and 2010 the cost of supporting varsity athletes on grants-in-aid at the University of Alabama increased from $6.5 million to $11.5 million, or more than 75%.[25] The escalating costs borne by the University of Alabama athletic department are not unusual. With more than 300 athletes on scholarship at many Division IA programs, double-digit tuition increases contribute significantly to rising operating costs.

Complying with federally mandated gender equity standards requires substantial investment in women's sports. Although Title IX addresses decades of unequal opportunities for women in sport, the law imposes a considerable financial obligation on athletic departments (a detailed discussion of the history and compliance requirements of Title IX is provided later in this chapter). Division I programs are required by the NCAA to offer no fewer than seven varsity sports for women; the minimum number for men is six. In fact, most Division IA departments offer more women's sports than required. On average, FBS programs sponsor 10 female varsity sports teams. To conform to NCAA membership requirements, athletic departments at the Division II and III levels must offer at least five women's sports.

When the cost of funding a varsity sport is considered, the challenge facing athletic departments becomes evident. As shown in Table 2.8, the median cost of fielding a women's sport at the Division IA level ranges from over $2 million per year for basket-

Table 2.8. Total Generated Revenues and Expenses by Sport. Division I—FBS. Fiscal Year 2010. Median Values*#

Sport	Men's Programs			Women's Programs		
	Generated Revenue	Expenses	Net Revenue	Generated Revenues	Expenses	Net Revenue
Baseball	338,000	1,292,000	(588,000)	N/A	N/A	N/A
Basketball	4,776,000	4,003,000	788,000	277,000	2,168,000	(1.168,000)
Crew	N/A	N/A	N/A	105,000	1,104,000	(860,000)
Equestrian	N/A	N/A	N/A	79,000	910,000	(854,000)
Fencing	30,000	175,000	(80,000)	45,000	244,000	(96,000)
Field Hockey	N/A	N/A	N/A	68,000	817,000	(714,000)
Football	16,210,000	12,367,000	3,148,000	N/A	N/A	N/A
Golf	68,000	382,000	(228,000)	48,000	427,000	(274,000)
Gymnastics	61,000	573,000	(290,000)	70,000	824,000	(547,000)
Ice Hockey	919,000	2,155,000	(333,000)	120,000	1,174,000	(1,016,000)
Lacrosse	548,000	1,162,000	(460,000)	157,000	814,000	(390,000)
Rifle	–	28,000	(28,000)	31,000	41,000	(9,000)
Skiing	43,000	379,000	(190,000)	43,000	311,000	(173,000)
Soccer	132,000	811,000	(510,000)	67,000	873,000	(529,000)
Softball	N/A	N/A	N/A	66,000	819,000	(582,000)
Swimming	58,000	625,000	(448,000)	47,000	742,000	(463,000)
Tennis	45,000	448,000	(290,000)	27,000	479,000	(337,000)
Track/X Country	70,000	798,000	(485,000)	52,000	941,000	(596,000)
Volleyball	162,000	628,000	(350,000)	78,000	927,000	(595,000)
Water Polo	168,000	539,000	(335,000)	35,000	611,000	(485,000)
Wrestling	140,000	719,000	(373,000)	N/A	N/A	N/A

*Net revenues enclosed in parenthesis are negative amounts

#Amounts may not add up evenly due to use of median values

Source: *NCAA Division I Intercollegiate Athletic Programs Revenues & Expenses Report: 2004–2010,* Table 3.11

ball to $244,000 for fencing. The total cost of meeting the minimum NCAA requirement of seven varsity sports for women is likely to exceed $8 million per year.

As recently as 2010, not one of the 120 Division IA women's sports programs generated a surplus. In fact, the median net loss for all women's programs totaled $6.3 million, up almost 50% from a median deficit of $2.03 million in 2004. Table 2.8 shows that some women's sports are hemorrhaging red ink at alarming levels. Both basketball and ice hockey reported annual median deficits in excess of $1 million.

These significant losses impose considerable pressure on athletic departments. Sustaining women's sports requires substantial and growing subsidies. At the Division IA level, revenue derived from women's sports has increased significantly over the last several years, up 70% from a total of $516,000 in 2004 to $876,000 in 2010. Nevertheless, the relative contribution of women's sports to total athletic department revenues has remained very modest. The $876,000 produced by all women's sports teams accounts for only 2% of the total revenues of over $35 million generated by typical Division IA athletic programs.

It is important to point out that it's not only women's sports that lose money. Among the men's varsity sports offered at the Division I level, only football and basketball produce a consistent surplus. Table 2.8 shows that the overall profit margin for football was approximately $3.15 million.* While this represents a healthy surplus, when you consider that all other sports, except men's basketball, lose money—on average, more than $400,000 per sport—it is easy to understand why so many athletic programs are struggling financially and are dependent on institutional support.

While athletic departments may not be able to fully control costs associated with tuition increases and complying with the requirements of maintaining a comprehensive sports program for female students, a significant portion of the growing annual operating budget is entirely a function of institutional priorities (or what the NCAA calls "market-driven" forces). Driven by competitive market forces (or the fear of losing a competitive advantage) and, in some cases, hyper-competitive alumni and donors, some (mostly big-time) athletic programs continue to invest in sport even in the face of painful institutional budget cuts. The University of Florida spends close to $100 million annually on its sports program. From 2007 through 2010, in response to a $150 million reduction in state support, the institution laid off 139 faculty and staff. Over that same time period, the athletic department budget increased 6% to $94.9 million. In defending the university's spending priorities, President Bernard Machen stated, "If we are going to be competitive in something, we want to win at it—whether it is in pediatrics or women's gymnastics. It is important to our supporters, both financial and among our community. It is part of our culture. We want people to know that [the University of] Florida is a place for winners."[26]

One area where many athletic programs have spent lavishly to maintain a competitive advantage is on coaches' salaries. Salary inflation has been particularly evident for head football coaches. Over a relatively short time span, median total compensation (salary plus benefits) for Division IA head football coaches has more than doubled, from $582,000 in 2004 to $1,640,000 in 2012. According to a *USA Today* study, by 2012, 44 top-level football coaches were making more than $2 million per season, two with salaries in excess of $5 million.[27] In many cases, the guaranteed portion of the con-

---

*The largest net revenue reported for a football program was more than $93 million. As noted earlier in the chapter, only a relatively few elite programs are capable of achieving a high level of financial success. NCAA data show that over the last decade, slightly more than half (about 55%) of the 120 schools playing Division IA football operated at a surplus. In 2010, 51 FBS football programs reported operating losses in excess of $2 million. At the FCS level, only 4% of the football programs reported positive net operating revenues.

tract was augmented by generous bonus provisions. For example, the contract for Coach Mack Brown at the University of Texas-Austin provides $850,000 in potential bonuses on top of the $5.35 million in guaranteed compensation. Among the various performance bonuses, Coach Brown would receive $250,000 if Texas wins the Big 12 Conference championship and an additional $100,000 if the football team achieves a graduation rate of 75%.

While not as dramatic, Division I programs have also invested heavily in men's basketball coaching salaries. The *USA Today* study identified one men's head basketball coach making at least $2 million in 2007. By 2012, 15 schools were paying their head men's basketball coaches more than $2 million, including three making more than $4 million.[28] From 2006 to 2010, the median total compensation for head men's basketball coaches increased a healthy 57% from $612,000 to $962,000. Interestingly, head women's basketball coaches at the Division I level are paid considerably less than their male counterparts. From 2006 to 2010, head women's basketball coaches' median total compensation grew about 45% from $241,000 to $348,000.

The rapidly escalating cost of head coaches' salaries represents just a portion of the overall investment major programs are making in their coaching staffs, particularly for football and men's basketball. The NCAA allows Division IA or FBS football programs to hire nine full-time coaching assistants. *USA Today* reported that the average pay for assistant football coaches at FBS schools at nearly $201,000 in 2012.[29] The same report found that the nine assistants at Clemson University earned an average of more than $465,000, eclipsing LSU's average football staff pay of $445,000. According to NCAA data, by 2010, the median cost for the entire football coaching staff of an FBS program totaled $3.5 million.*

The contract of head football coach Chip Kelly at the University of Oregon demonstrates the level of investment major football programs are willing to make to retain talented coaches.# Originally hired in 2009 at a salary of $1.8 million, Kelly quickly achieved unprecedented success. In his first two seasons, he accumulated a 19–3 win/loss record, culminating in Oregon playing Auburn in the BCS national championship game in January 2011. With more than three years remaining on his current contract, the University of Oregon signed Coach Kelly to a six-year, $20.5 million contract extension, binding him to the school through the 2015 season. Table 2.9 illustrates the dramatic increase in guaranteed compensation over the length of Kelly's contract. The increase from $2.4 million in 2010–11 to $4.0 million in 2014–15 represents a 67% increase over the first 5 years of the new agreement (a 122% increase over the last year

---

*To provide some perspective, according to a salary survey conducted by the *Chronicle of Higher Education* in 2010–11, the average salary for full professors at public doctoral degree universities in was $118,054. The same study found the average total compensation package for presidents of public doctoral degree granting institutions to be $388,995. According to Charles Clotfelter in his book, *Big Time Sports in America*, between 1985 and 2010 the average salary of head football coaches rose more than 750% (adjusted for inflation) compared to 32% for full professors and 90% for university presidents.

#In January 2013, Chip Kelly accepted the head coaching position with the NFL Philadelphia Eagles, receiving a five-year deal worth $32.5 million. Kelly's first-year salary of $6.5 million represents a $3-million increase over what he would have received had he stayed at Oregon for the 2013 season.

Table 2.9. Chip Kelly's Oregon Contract		
Season	**Guaranteed**	**Buyout**
2010–11	$2.4 million	$4 million
2011–12	$2.8 million	$3.75 million
2012–13	$3.5 million	$3.5 million
2013–14	$3.8 million	$2.5 million
2014–15	$4.0 million	$2 million

Source: K. Goe (2010, September 28). Oregon coach Chip Kelly signs six-year, $20.5 million contract, The Oregonian, D3

of the previous contract). University of Oregon Athletic Director, Rob Mullens, in explaining his rationale for Coach Kelly's generous contract extension stated, "He was on everybody's radar as a superstar. We wanted to make sure he was here for a long time" (p. D1).[30]

As coaches' salaries continue to climb, so do the concerns of most university presidents. The Knight Commission on Intercollegiate Athletics, an organization lobbying for more institutional control of college athletics, released a survey in which six of seven presidents of FBS schools expressed the belief that total compensation for football and basketball coaches was excessive.[31] Despite the growing concern, Knight Commission members believe that finding ways to curb soaring coaches' salaries will be a daunting challenge, a sentiment echoed by Jim Delany, long time commissioner of the Big Ten Conference. Commenting on the challenge facing university presidents, Delany stated, "Cutting costs, especially at the national conference level, is heavy lifting . . . Unless you're prepared to deal with boosters, board members, power coaches and the public, and I'm talking about a conflict-rich environment, don't take it on."[31]

Long-time college athletics reform advocate Andrew Zimbalist offered a concrete recommendation for curbing coaches' salaries. Zimbalist advocates that the NCAA impose a limit on coaches' compensation packages. Zimbalist argues that placing a limit of "say $400,000"on coaches' salaries "would not affect the quality of coaching or the level of intercollegiate competition one iota" (p. 119).[32] In his view, if a cap were imposed, the next best alternative for FBS-level coaches would be extremely limited (there are only 32 head coaching positions in the National Football League). While there are strong economic and ethical reasons to cap coaches' salaries, any attempt to limit compensation would likely be construed as a violation of the Sherman Antitrust Act. In order to regulate coaches' salaries, the NCAA would have to seek a partial antitrust exemption. Even Zimbalist believes this action to be a long shot, commenting, "Most (university presidents) appear to be skeptical about seeking an antitrust exemption from the U.S. Congress. There is an unspecified fear that if colleges invite government into their business, then Congress will seek greater control and regulation over it" (p. 119).[32]

While it is unlikely that any meaningful structural reforms will be adopted to constrain the soaring costs of coaches' salaries, many athletic departments faced with shrinking budget resources have implemented cost-cutting measures in other areas. These practices include reducing travel expenses, shortening the length of the season for non-revenue sports, and eliminating the practice of lodging teams in local hotels prior to home games. The cost of transporting athletes, coaches and equipment to away competitions can be very high. Median travel expenses for Division I athletic programs in 2010 exceeded $3 million. In an effort to pare mounting travel costs at the University of Kansas, even the perennial national power men's basketball team took more trips by bus than plane in recent seasons. Colorado State cut more than $160,000 from its budget, mostly by trimming marketing and facility operation costs. The University of Nevada at Las Vegas no longer provides insurance for non-scholarship or "walk-on" athletes. And Florida International University's athletic department eliminated support for the cheerleading squad and marching band.[33]

Despite these rather modest efforts to moderate spending, some are dubious that much, if any, progress will be made in achieving real savings. The athletic director at the University of Texas asserted, "There's a tendency in college athletics, like Congress, to spend if you have it" (p. 34).[34] The tendency of athletic departments to rapidly consume available resources was underscored in the remarks of a senior administrator of a major Division I program, whose department completed a $90-million stadium expansion the previous year. When asked about the disposition of the millions in incremental revenues generated from the 12,000 additional seats and 15 new suites, the official commented:

> Athletics is an insatiable activity. It's amazing, our expenses have caught up with our revenues faster that we thought they would. When we did forecasts of how much our new football stadium expansion would bring, we thought we'd have lots of additional revenue. The biggest surprise of all is that expenses are just about driven up to whatever your revenues reach. These revenues are just consumed. Every coach steps up with new demands, whether it's new equipment or for more recruiting. (T. Larson, personal communication, April 5, 2007)

Television to the Rescue

A recent development that has provided significant relief is the investing of billions of dollars by television networks in collegiate sport. A tally of all the major conference television contracts listed in Table 2.10 adds up to a nearly $16-billion commitment. When you add the nearly $11-billion agreement CBS and Turner Broadcasting (TBS) agreed to pay the NCAA for the rights to the Division I men's basketball championship tournament, TV's massive and dominant impact on college sports is evident. Television rights fees have become the lifeblood of the NCAA itself. More than 95% of the national organization's annual operating revenues come from a portion of the $740 million CBS pays a year for the rights to air every game in the tournament known as March Madness.

The hundreds of millions of dollars that flow to major conferences shown in Table 2.10 have become an increasingly crucial component of each athletic department's

Table 2.10. Television Contracts for Major Athletic Conferences

Conference	Network	Total Amount	Annual Payout Per School	Length of Contract	Ends
Southeastern Conference (SEC)	ESPN CBS	$2.25 billion $825 million	$19.5 million	15 years 15 years	2023–24 2023–24
Big Ten	Big Ten Network ABC/ESPN CBS	$2.8 billion $1.0 billion $72 million	$25.7 million	25 years 10 years 10 years	2031–32 2016 2016–17
PAC 12	ESPN Fox	$2.7 billion (split)	$20.8 million	12 years	2023–24
Atlantic Coast Conference (ACC)	ESPN	$3.6 billion	$17.1 million	15 years	2026–27
Big 12	ESPN Fox Sports Net	$2.6 billion	$ 20 million	13 years	2024–25
Big East	ABC/ESPN	$200 million	Not available	6 years	2013

annual budget. For example, under the Atlantic Coast Conference's (ACC) $3.6 billion, 15-year deal with ESPN, the conference receives $240 million per year. The ACC conference office in turn distributes approximately $17.1 million to each of the 12 conference affiliates.

Though substantial, the ACC's annual payout pales in comparison to the agreement the PAC 12 Conference signed with Fox and ESPN in 2011. The almost $3-billion deal guarantees that each school will receive an equal annual rights fee share of almost $21 million. The annual payout is a major windfall, particularly for those conference schools that had struggled for years with budget deficits. For example, athletic programs at Cal, Oregon State, and Washington State all saw their deficits disappear as a result of the conference's television partnership.

While the conference television agreements listed in Table 2.10 have had a profound effect on the financial status of the 65 schools affiliated with the six major football conferences (ACC, Big East, Big 10, Big 12, PAC 12, and SEC), the lucrative deals have served to further accentuate the gap between the power-conference schools and smaller Division I programs. For example, schools like Hawaii and Miami of Ohio, who belong to less prestigious conferences, the Mountain West and MAC, respectively, are at a huge disadvantage. The current Mountain West Conference television agreement pays each member school $1.1 million, $20 million less than their FBS counterparts affiliated with the PAC 12.

THE IMPACT OF TITLE IX

In an environment of rising costs, athletic administrators now are also required to confront the substantial financial implications of complying with Title IX. A series of dramatic events in the early 1990s required colleges to make a serious commitment to addressing the gender equity issue. For almost two decades after the passage of Title IX of the Education Amendments Act in 1972, many college athletic programs paid only lip service to the notion of equal treatment of sexes. Then, beginning in 1991, in quick succession, three developments gave Title IX great momentum:

- A Supreme Court ruling in the Georgia case, *Franklin v. Gwinnett Public Schools*, for the first time permitted stiff monetary penalties for Title IX violations.
- The Office of Civil Rights identified "discrimination on the basis of sex in athletic programs" as a priority in its overall enforcement strategy.
- The Big Ten Council of Presidents adopted a resolution requiring conference schools to achieve a ratio of at least 40% female athletes to 60% male athletes by August, 1997.

Although some schools and conferences had taken proactive actions on their own, real across-the-board progress in the 1990s emerged as a result of more rigorous enforcement of compliance standards by the U.S. Department of Education's Office of Civil Rights. The basic requirements set forth by the Office of Civil Rights require schools to meet *one* of three criteria, often referred to as the three-prong test of compliance:

Title IX requires college athletic programs to make a substantial financial investment in women's sports. Courtesy of Dreamstime

1. Prong One—The *substantial proportionality test* requires that women athletes receive participation opportunities and resources proportionate to the women in the student body at large. To be in full compliance with this test, a school must either (a) offer varsity sport participation opportunities to women within an allowable difference of no more than 5% of the proportion of women in the general student population; or (b) allocate scholarship monies to women athletes within 1% of the proportionate to the percentage of female student athletes in the athletic department.

For example, on a campus in which women represented 53% of the total undergraduate enrollment, to be in full compliance with the first provision of the proportionality test, no fewer than 48% of the athletes would be women,

OR

2. Prong Two—The *continued improvement* test requires that the university demonstrate a consistent history of expanding and improving women's sports programs,

OR

3. Prong Three—The *accommodation of interest* test requires the university's athletic department is fully and effectively accommodating the interests and abilities of its female student athletes.

In order to meet any one of these tests, athletic departments have responded in one or a combination of three ways: (a) by securing more money in order to add more women's sports; (b) by redistributing resources from men's to women's programs; and (c) by cutting existing men's sports. To date, roster capping and the elimination of men's programs have been the most common approaches used by departments to comply with Title IX.

During the 1990s, every men's non-revenue sport, with the exception of golf, lacrosse, and track, lost teams or participants. Over 400 men's athletic teams have been abolished in order to meet Title IX. Between 1992 and 1997, 3.4 men's positions on college teams were cut for every woman's spot created.[35] Coaches from those men's sports that have been affected the most severely such as swimming, wrestling, and gymnastics have unsuccessfully lobbied Congress to eliminate the proportionality test. A spokesperson for the U.S. Track Coaches Association stated, "The intent of Title IX is not to have discrimination, and clearly there is" (p. C4).[36] However, the Executive Director of the Women's Sports Foundation argues that the coaches are attacking the wrong target: "The problem is financial—football and basketball expenses have gone up faster than revenues. Instead of forcing the big budgets to take a smaller piece of the pie, they cut minor men's sports and then blame Title IX" (p. 33).[37] She points out that substantial new revenue is being injected into athletic departments, but it "is being used to fuel the arms race being fought in college football and men's basketball. NCAA research shows that of every three new dollars going into college athletic programs over the last five years, two go to men's sports and only one to women's sports" (p. 33).[37] Her position is that schools should be required to retain all men's sports programs while they bring women's sports into compliance with Title IX.

Although football in particular is for many big schools the major source of revenue, it is also by a significant margin the most expensive sports program to operate. Substantial savings could be realized by cutting back the funds allocated to football. For example, as much as $600,000 to $900,000 in savings a year could result from cutting the number of grants-in-aid or scholarships awarded by Division IA football programs from 85 to 60, but such proposals have been met with aggressive resistance from coaches and many senior athletic department officials, who believe a significant reduction would seriously diminish the quality and, thereby, the marketability of collegiate football. As one senior NCAA official declared in a personal conversation with one of the authors,

"It (further cuts) would be akin to killing the Golden Goose." Although the impact of any reduction is unclear, it appears unlikely that cuts in the number of scholarships for football at the Division IA level will be made.

Despite the controversy, the courts have repeatedly reaffirmed the legality of the Title IX's compliance standards. In 2011, a federal appeals court upheld, for a second time, James Madison University's decision to eliminate seven men's teams and three women's teams to achieve gender balance. At the time of the university's decision to eliminate 10 sports, women represented 51% of all athletes but made up 61% of the overall student population. The appeals court ruled that the university's effort to meet the "substantial proportionality" test was appropriate and did not constitute "intentional discrimination" (para. 8, 10).[38]

Although the courts have provided the legal authority for advancing the interests of women athletes, managers of college athletics have to assume moral responsibility for ensuring an equitable balance between men's and women's sports opportunities on college campuses. Finding new revenues and implementing cost-containment strategies to achieve the goal of gender equity are major fiscal challenges facing sport administrators. The courts have decreed that there will be no compromise on the issue of gender equity, so these are challenges that must be met aggressively.

SUMMARY

By 2012, almost 1,400 colleges and universities sponsored comprehensive varsity sports programs. The total cost of intercollegiate athletics exceeds $9 billion annually. The dominant regulating body for college athletics is the National Collegiate Athletic Association (NCAA) with over 1,000 member schools. The primary purpose of the NCAA is to ensure fair competition and to enhance the student-athlete experience by enforcing rules governing eligibility, financial aid, recruiting, and playing and practice sessions.

The NCAA separates member schools into three classifications: Division I, Division II, and Division III. The total number of students participating in varsity sports at all three levels in 2010 was 435,767. While the number of women participants has tripled from 74,329 in 1982–83 to 186,460 in 2009–10, men at 249,307 account for 57% of all varsity competitors. The eligibility standards for membership in Division I are the most stringent. Division I athletic programs are subdivided into the Football Bowl Subdivision or FBS (formerly known as Division IA) and the Football Championship Subdivision or FCS (formerly known as Division IAA). While Division I membership requires athletic programs to sponsor a minimum of 14 varsity sports (at least 8 for women), FBS schools are required to make a far greater financial investment in football. Schools competing at the FBS level must provide a maximum of 85 full scholarships for football, while FCS football programs are allowed to provide a maximum of 63 scholarships. Division II schools offer an intermediate level of competition with much less stringent membership requirements. They must sponsor a minimum of 10 varsity sports and, while schools may offer athletic scholarships, the maximum limits for most sports are much lower than for Division I programs (e.g., 36 scholarships for football). At the Division III level, sports are offered as essentially extra-curricular activities for students.

While competition among Division III schools can be intense (the NCAA sponsors national championships for all varsity sports), the financial investment for athletic programs at this level is considerably lower as member schools are not allowed to offer athletic scholarships.

Data provided by the NCAA reveal that only a small number of major athletic departments are able to pay their own way. Over 80% of FBS programs operated at a loss in 2010. As a result, the vast majority of intercollegiate athletic programs depend on substantial institutional support in the form of subsidies from their universities' general funds, student fees and/or, in the case of public universities, direct appropriations from state government. The amount of institutional support has grown substantially over the past decade. By 2010, on average, almost $10 million or 30% of the total revenues generated by FBS athletic programs came from institutional sources. The dependence level for FCS schools is far greater, with institutional support accounting for 66% of the total revenues generated by Division IAA programs. The growing reliance on institutional subsidies is troubling given the difficult financial challenges facing higher education in general. With many colleges and universities still under severe budget pressure, resulting in the elimination of faculty and programs, diverting monies from academics to athletics has come under increasing scrutiny. In fact, over the past few years, the amount of direct institutional support directed to athletics has declined. From 2008 to 2010, the median amount of money directly transferred from an institution's general fund to the athletic department has decreased by $630,000 on average for all Division IA (FBS) programs and by $864,000 for all Division IAA (FCS) programs. Consequently, athletic administrators are under increased pressure to grow revenues. From 2004 to 2010, top-tier FBS schools have increased total generated revenues on average 55% from $22.8 million to $35.3 million. FCS programs also demonstrated solid growth, with generated revenues increasing 58% from $2.1 million to $3.3 million. At the FBS level, football is the dominant revenue producer. When premium seating charges (often classified as a charitable donation), corporate sponsorships and broadcast revenues are added to ticket sales, football accounts for more than two-thirds of all revenues generated at schools with nationally prominent football programs.

Despite the abundant revenues produced by the relatively small number of big-time football programs, the surplus generated at most FBS schools is relatively modest. The heavy investment required to field a competitive football program (over $12 million at the FBS level), reduces the average "profit margin" to just over $3 million. Given that with very few exceptions, all women's and all but one other men's varsity sport (men's basketball) lose money at the Division I level, it is not surprising to find that only 22 Division IA athletic programs reported making a profit in 2010.

Controlling rapidly rising costs is a serious challenge for intercollegiate athletic programs at all levels. Between 2004 and 2010, the median operating budget for a Division IA (FBS) athletic department increased 63% from $28.9 million to nearly $47 million. Containing costs is an increasingly challenging issue because two of the major expenditure categories are largely beyond the control of athletic departments. Universities charge athletic departments the full cost of grants-in-aid or scholarships awarded to student athletes. Over the past decade tuition and fees at US colleges and universities have more than doubled, adding millions of dollars in operating costs to athletic department budgets. Complying with the federally-mandated gender equity program, commonly referred to at Title IX, also requires significant investment in women's sports. The NCAA requires Division I departments to offer no fewer than eight varsity sports for women (FBS programs, on average, offer 10 women's sports). At a median cost of around $800,000 for each women's varsity sport, the NCAA reported that Division IA programs ran cumulative deficits exceeding $6 million on average to deliver a full range of women's sports programs in 2010. The NCAA data revealed that men's programs, other than football and men's basketball, lost, on average, $400,000 per sport.

Athletic programs have spent lavishly to achieve a competitive advantage. One area of significant investment has been coaches' salaries, particularly for high revenue sports such as football and basketball. Salaries for head football coaches at the FBS level have more than doubled from $582,000 in 2004 to $1,383,000 in 2010. While many schools have trimmed operational costs related to such activities as travel and recruiting, the overall impact of these cost curtailment efforts have been relatively modest. As one athletic director at a prominent FBS school asserted, "There's a tendency in college sports, like Congress, to spend if you have it."

The recent influx of television monies has provided some relief for hard-pressed athletic departments. Television networks have committed nearly 16 billion to major sports conferences for the rights to broadcast regular and championship games through the next decade. While the substantial rights fees represent a windfall for schools in the six major conferences, they further accentuate the gap between those Division I programs affiliated with less prestigious conferences, which receive much less generous television support.

The chapter concludes with a discussion of the requirements for complying with Title IX and the financial implications of this federal law that mandates athletic departments to address gender equity. The Office of Civil Rights requires schools to meet one of three criteria: 1) the substantial proportionality test, which specifies women athletes receive proportional participation opportunities (within 5%) and scholarship support (within 1%) relative to the proportion of women in the general student body; 2) the continued improvement test, which demonstrates consistent expansion of the women's varsity sports programs; or 3) the accommodation of interest test, which shows that the athletic department is fully accommodating the varsity sport participation interests of its female students. Athletic departments have used a number of tactics to comply with Title IX requirements. To date, eliminating men's sports and roster capping—limiting the number of men on team rosters—have been the most common approaches used. Despite a number of challenges, the courts have consistently reaffirmed the legality of Title IX's compliance standards.

The current reality of college athletics is far from its popular perception as a "cash cow" for higher education. Spiraling costs, increased competition, and flat or declining revenues have all combined to place intercollegiate sports programs under severe financial pressure. A large majority are operating at a deficit. Grappling with budget issues—revenue generation and cost containment—will be a key issue confronting collegiate sport managers for the foreseeable future.

References

1. Compiled from membership directories provided by the National Collegiate Athletic Association and the National Association of Intercollegiate Athletics, December 2012.

2. NCAA sports sponsorship and participation rates report, 1981–82–2009–10, p. 8. Indianapolis: IN: National Collegiate Athletic Association.

3. Bell, R. (2007). A history of women in sport prior to Title IX. *The Sport Journal, 10*, 2.

4. High school sports participation increases for 21st consecutive year. National Federation of State High School Associations, news release, September 2010.

5. Fulks, D. (2011). *Revenues and expenses of Division I intercollegiate athletic programs, 2004–2010.* Indianapolis, IN: National Collegiate Athletic Association.

6. Zimbalist, A. (1999). *Unpaid professionals: Commercialism and conflict in big-time college sports.* Princeton, NJ: Princeton Press.

7. Fulks, D. (2005). *Revenues and expenses of Division III intercollegiate athletic programs, 2004.* Indianapolis, IN: National Collegiate Athletic Association.

8. Fulks, D. (2000). *Revenues and expenses of Division I and II intercollegiate athletic programs, financing trends and relationships—1999.* Indianapolis, IN: National Collegiate Athletic Association.

9. Clark, K. (2010, September 10). The Great Recession's toll on higher education. *U.S. News & World Report.* Retrieved from http://www.usnews.com/education/articles/2010/09/10/the-great-recessions-toll-on-higher-education

10. Upton, J., & Gillum, J. (2010, April 2). What NCAA schools spend on athletics. *USA Today.* Retrieved from http://www.usatoday.com/sports/college/ncaa-finances.htm

11. Report of the Chancellor's Committee on Intercollegiate Athletics. (2010, July 6.) University of California, Berkeley.

12. Asimov, N. (2011, June 19). Budget plan bans taxpayer funds for UC athletics. *San Francisco Chronicle*, D1.

13. St. Cloud students give football a reprieve. (2010, November 19). *Star Tribune.* Retrieved from http://www.startribune.com/sports/gophers/109066119.html

14. Post, T. (2010, August 18). College sports not immune from budget cuts. *MPRnews.* Retrieved from http://minnesota.publicradio.org/display/web/2010/08/18/st-cloud-university-cuts

15. Young, L. (2009, May 23). Budget cuts endanger UNO's athletic program. *New York Times Student Journal Institute.* Retrieved from http://nola09.nytimes-institute.com

16. Berkowitz, S., Upton, J., McCarthy, M., & Gillum, J. (2010, October 6). How student fees boost college sports amid rising budgets. *USA Today.* Retrieved from http://www.usatoday.com/sports/college/2010-09-21-student-fees-boost-college-sports_N.htm

17. Tucker, K. (2011, May 29). As athletics costs grow, students are paying more. *The Virginian-Pilot, 1*, 10.

18. Dosh, K. (2011, March 20). Who's making money in Big 12 football? *Forbes.* Retrieved from http://www.forbes.com/sites/sportsmoney/2011/03/20/whos-making-money-in-big-12-football

19. Smith, M. (2011, August 22). Athletic budgets continue to climb. *SportsBusiness Journal.* Retrieved from http://www.sportsbusinessdaily.com/Journal/Issues/2011/08/22/In-Depth/Budgets.aspx

20. Burke, P. (1999, March). Inside Aggie Inc. *Texas Monthly*, pp. 46–50.

21. Bachman, R. (2011, August 26). College football ticket prices to top games rise 30 percent despite economy. *Oregon Live.* Retrieved from http://www.oregonlive.com/pac-12/index.ssf/2011/08/college_football_ticket_prices_to_top_games_rise_30_percent_despite_economy.html

22. Jacklet, B. (2010, September). Money ball: Oregon colleges follow the cash to football. *Oregon Business.* Retrieved from http://www.oregonbusiness.com/articles/90-september-2010/3994-oregon-college-football-industry

23. Graves, B. (2010, March 3). Oregon State University and University of Oregon report sports finances in the red. *The Oregonian.* Retrieved from http://www.oregonlive.com/education/in

dex.ssf/2010/03/oregon_state_university_and_un.html

24. Wang, P. (2009, April 13). Is college still worth the price? *CNNMoney.* Retrieved from http://cnn.com/2009.04/13/pf/college_price.moneymag/

25. Schnaars, C., Upton, J., Mosemak, J., & DeRamus, K. (2012, May 16). NCAA college athletics department finances database. *USA Today.* Retrieved from http://www.usatoday.com/sports/college/ncaa-finances.htm

26. Drape, & Thomas, K. (2010, September 3). An arms race, with no shortage of muscle. *Sarasota Herald-Tribune.* Retrieved from http://www.heraldtribune.com/article/20100903/ARTICLE/9031047?p=2&tc=pg

27. Berkowitz, S. & Upton, J. (2013, February 12). Pay rises yet again for college football's new coaching hires. *USA Today.* Retrieved from http://www.usatoday.com/story/sports/ncaaf/2013/02/11/college-football-coach-salary-changes-ncaa/1907359/

28. Schnaars, C., & DeRamus, K. (2012, March 28). College basketball coaches' salaries, 2011–12. *USA Today.* Retrieved from http://www.usatoday.com/sports/college/mensbasketball/story/2012–03–28/ncaa-coaches-salary-database/53827374/1

29. Berkowitz, S., & Upton, J. (2012, December 18). College football assistants seeing salary surge. *USA Today.* Retrieved from http://www.usatoday.com/story/sports/ncaaf/2012/12/18/assistant-coaches-salaries-bowl-subdivision/1777719/

30. Goe, K. (2010, September 28). Oregon coach Chip Kelly signs six-year, $20.5 million contract. *The Oregonian,* p. D1.

31. Survey reveals alarm on college sports spending. (2009, October 27). *Indy.com.* Retrieved from http://www.indy.com

32. Zimbalist, A. (2010). Dollar dilemmas during the downturn: A financial crossroads for college sports. *Journal of Intercollegiate Sport, 3,* 119.

33. Schalbach, M. (2009, July 13). Programs struggle to balance budget. *ESPN.com.* Retrieved from http://sports.espn.go.com/espn/print?id+4314195&type=story

34. Krupa, G., & Dunnavant, K. (1989, January 2). The struggle with the downside. *Sports Inc.,* 33–38.

35. Will, G. D. (2002, May 27). A train wreck called Title IX. *Newsweek, 139,* 82.

36. Gardman, A. (2000, September 7). Coaches lobby for Title IX changes. *USA Today,* p. C4.

37. Lopiano, D. (2001, June 11–17). Division I cranks up sports "arms race." *SportsBusiness Journal,* 33.

38. Sander, K. (2011, March 8). James Madison U.'s elimination of 10 sports teams was legal, appeals court affirms. *The Chronicle of Higher Education.* Retrieved from http://chronicle.com/article/James-Madison-Us-Elimination/126655/

3

Challenges Facing Professional Sports

GROWTH OF PROFESSIONAL SPORTS

Major Leagues

The 1990s was a period of substantial growth for professional sports at all levels. The number of teams in the Big 4 major leagues grew from 103 franchises in 1989 to 122 franchises by 2001. During that time, the National Hockey League (NHL) added eight expansion teams, Major League Baseball (MLB) added four, the National Football League (NFL) added three, and the National Basketball Association (NBA) added five teams. In addition, several new leagues were launched in the 1990s with aspirations of becoming prominent national properties, most notably Major League Soccer (MLS) and the Women's National Basketball Association (WNBA).

By 2001, each of the Big 4 leagues had reached a saturation point, having established franchises in nearly every city capable of sustaining a major sports property. A few markets remain available for certain leagues. For example, Los Angeles has not had an NFL team since the Rams abandoned LA for a new stadium in St. Louis in 1995. While the NFL would welcome a franchise in the country's 3rd largest television market, the lack of a modern, "NFL-ready" stadium has prevented a team from filling this attractive void. Several proposals for a new stadium in the Los Angeles market have been introduced over the past decade. While none to date have managed to secure the necessary financial and/or political support, many analysts are convinced that the NFL will have a team playing in a new stadium in the LA area not later than 2015.

In the case of the NHL, rather than adding more teams, over the next several years it appears that the league will be returning a number of franchises to Canada. Throughout the 1990s, in order to expand the NHL's presence in the U.S. and to boost television ratings, Commissioner Bettman embarked on an aggressive expansion strategy—commonly referred to as the "Southern growth strategy"—which resulted in NHL teams being established in San Jose, CA (1991), Tampa Bay, FL (1992), Dallas, TX (1993), Sunrise, FL (1993), Anaheim, CA (1993), Phoenix, AZ (1996, from Winnipeg), Raleigh, NC (1997) and Nashville, TN (1998). Recent developments indicate that the league's southern strategy may be failing as several franchises in Sun Belt cities have not generated sufficient fan support to remain financially viable. In June 2011, the NHL Board of Governors approved the relocation of the Atlanta (Thrashers) franchise to Winnipeg, Canada. In 12 seasons in Atlanta, the Thrashers had only one playoff appearance. The team's poor performance contributed to dwindling attendance—over their last three seasons in Atlanta, the team sold out the arena for only one game (conversely, the new Winnipeg team sold out its full season ticket inventory within 17 minutes!). Consequently, the need to relocate the team was inevitable. The Atlanta Thrashers' (now the Jets) move to Winnipeg could be followed by two additional Southern U.S. city NHL franchises relocating to Canadian cities in Quebec and southern Ontario.[1]

At the current time, neither the NBA nor MLB have announced any expansion plans, so apart from the relocation of existing franchises restricted primarily to the NHL, it appears that the Big 4 will retain their current complement of 123 teams into the foreseeable future.

The only major league property to see substantial growth in the first decade of this century has been Major League Soccer. Since its inaugural season in 1996, MLS has grown from 10 to 19 teams and has established a presence in almost all major markets in the U.S. (16 teams) and Canada (3 teams). A key factor in propelling the expansion of the MLS has been the league's success in developing of soccer-specific stadiums. Fourteen teams now play in venues built specifically to accommodate MLS soccer matches. The movement to fully loaded soccer stadiums was led by the Columbus Crew, the first MLS franchise to build a soccer-specific stadium in 1999. However, the state-of-the-art model facility is the Los Angeles Galaxy's Home Depot Center in Carson, CA. The $150-million, 27,000-seat stadium, capped by a stunning translucent

Keeping arenas full is a growing challenge. Courtesy of BigStockPhoto

roof, was constructed in 2003. The rationale for the new facility was explained in the following terms:

> Why does a stadium in sunny SoCal need a roof over the seats? (To magnify the noise, of course.) Why does it hold only 27,000? (So a seat becomes a rare and precious thing, and demand increases.) For that matter, why does Major League Soccer, which has never made money, need its own stadiums? So that it can inch toward the black. By controlling its own revenue streams, the Galaxy this year cleared the first operating profit in league history, a modest $250,000. (p. 66)[2]

These new facilities include all the amenities found in NFL stadiums (luxury suites, video screens, etc.) but are sized to meet the specific requirements of MLS teams. Rather than playing in stadiums built for football, the playing surfaces meet international (FIFA) field standards—110–120 yards (100–110m) long by 70–80 yards (64–75m) wide—and the seating capacities realistically reflect attendance demand for professional soccer in North America, ranging from 18,500 to 27,000. Ten of these new soccer-specific venues have been built since 2007.

Minor Leagues

The most spectacular growth in professional team sports, however, has occurred at the secondary, or minor league level. As shown in Table 3.1, over 500 minor league teams in 40 separate leagues currently operate in North America. The purpose of the minor leagues across all sports is to provide opportunities for player development. Typically, minor league franchises are located in smaller markets (from Anchorage, Alaska to Portland, Maine) and play in substantially smaller venues (3,000 to 8,000 seat arenas for hockey and basketball; 2,500 to 5,000 for baseball). For the most part, the minor leagues are organized on a hierarchical basis, with each successive level representing a step toward the major leagues. With 241 teams in the U.S., Canada and Mexico, baseball has the most developed minor league system. Young players normally begin at either the Rookie (lowest classification) or Class A-Short Season level with aspirations of advancing to Class A-Advanced, and on to Class AA and eventually to Class AAA, the final step before reaching the major leagues. With few exceptions, minor league teams are independently owned businesses. However, particularly in baseball, many are directly affiliated with a major league team. Under this arrangement, the "parent" or major league team assigns players under contract to its minor league affiliates and pays their salaries with the hope that several will advance through the minor leagues to eventually play on the major league roster.

Minor league baseball has grown substantially over the past two decades. New ballparks, better marketing and promotions, and good entertainment provided at family-affordable prices have all contributed to healthy growth. Table 3.2 shows that overall minor league attendance has more than doubled since 1989. During this period, 72 additional franchises were established. Importantly, minor league baseball demonstrated remarkable resilience during the Great Recession of 2007–2009. In 2008, when the U.S. economy was struggling, attendance reached an all-time high, eclipsing 50 million.

Table 3.1. Listing of the Minor Leagues in North America
Name of League and (# of Teams)

Baseball	
AAA International (14) Pacific Coast (16) Mexican (16) *AA* Eastern (12) Southern (10) Texas (8) *A* California (10) Carolina (8)	Florida State (12) Midwest (16) South Atlantic (14) New York-Penn (14) Northwest (8) Appalachian (10) Arizona (13) Pioneer (8) Independent Leagues (60)
Football	
Arena Football League (18) United Football League (4)	Canadian Football League (8)
Hockey	
American Hockey League (30) ECHL (23) Western Hockey League (22) Ontario Hockey League (20) Central Hockey League (10)	United States Hockey League (16) Southern Professional League (9) Federal Hockey League (6) Quebec Major Junior League (18) Ligue Nord-Americaine de Hockey (7)
Basketball	
NBA Development League (16)	
Soccer	
Major Indoor Soccer League (8) United Soccer Leagues (12)	Professional Arena Soccer League—Pro (16) North American Soccer League (9)
Lacrosse	
Major League Lacrosse (8) National Lacrosse League (10)	National Arena Lacrosse League (6)

The President of Minor League Baseball attributes this success to the fact that "Minor League Baseball continues to lead the way in providing affordable family entertainment in these tough economic times" (para. 3).[3] There is empirical support for his assertion. A survey of 160 teams by Minor League Baseball in 2009 found that the average price for an adult ticket was $7 or less in 75% of minor league baseball stadiums and that a family of four could enjoy a night at the ballpark for around $50.[4] The cost of attending a *major* league baseball game for that same hypothetical family of four would have been four times greater according to *Team Marketing Report*.[4] In 2009, according to TMR's Fan Cost Index, the average cost of attending a major league baseball game for a party of four, including tickets, food and beverage, and parking, totaled $197.

Table 3.2. Minor League Baseball Attendance: 2010 vs. 1989		
League	2010 (# teams)	1989 (# teams)
International	6,942,740 (14)	2,613,347 (8)
Pacific Coast	7,032,545 (16)	2,554,417 (10)
Mexican	2,714,995 (16)	1,975,723 (14)
Eastern	3,996,241 (12)	1,272,812 (8)
Southern	2,209,830 (10)	1,687,884 (10)
Texas	2,942,930 (8)	1,511,610 (8)
California	1,566,501 (10)	933,883 (10)
Carolina	1,810,537 (8)	1,006,738 (8)
Florida State	1,182,581 (12)	957,344 (14)
Midwest	4,184,843 (16)	1,716,443 (14)
South Atlantic	3,223,655 (14)	1,060,964 (12)
New York-Penn	1,829,755 (14)	714,561 (14)
Northwest	885,025 (8)	636,187 (8)
Appalachian	289,929 (10)	311,510 (10)
Pioneer	650,389 (8)	483,168 (8)
NAPBL Total	41,432,456 (176)	23,103,593 (164)
Independent Lgs	8,105,046 (60)	0 (0)
GRAND TOTAL	49,537,502	23,103,593

New ballparks have been another significant factor in the growth of minor league baseball. Since 1998, 166 minor league ballparks have been built or substantially renovated—127 between 1995 and 1999; and 85 since 2000.[5] These new, modernized venues have stimulated attendance by further enhancing the fan experience at minor league ballparks across the U.S. and Canada.

While minor league hockey has generally prospered over the last two decades, it has experienced considerably more instability than minor league baseball. In 2013, 10 leagues and 161 minor league hockey teams (including Juniors) were operating in the U.S. and Canada. Unlike baseball, with its long tradition as America's pastime, hockey (Canada's national sport) was new to many cities across the U.S. Following the NHL's southern strategy, in the late 1990s through 2005, minor league hockey franchises were established in new arenas in small to medium-sized markets throughout the Deep South (e.g., Biloxi, MS; Lafayette, LA; Macon, GA) and in Texas, Oklahoma and Kansas (e.g., Amarillo, TX; Tulsa, OK; Wichita, KS). Like the NHL, the results were mixed. Several franchises continue to thrive (e.g., Florida Everblades, Gwinnett Gladiators, Charlotte Checkers), while many failed (e.g., Bossier-Shreveport, LA; Lubbock, TX; New Mexico

Scorpions). Most of the now-defunct minor league hockey franchises failed because of their inability to generate sufficient fan support. In many cases, market indifference was aggravated by struggling local economies during the difficult years from 2007 through 2009. During this period, scores of teams either shut down or relocated and six leagues ceased operations.

Despite these struggles in general, minor league hockey has proven to be resilient and a number of franchises have flourished in non-traditional markets such as San Antonio, Texas. Presently, all 10 of the existing minor hockey leagues in the U.S. and Canada, after several years of consolidation and franchise realignment, are in sound financial condition.

Professional basketball at the secondary or minor league level has had considerably less success than both baseball and hockey. Of the 11 leagues operating at some point during the past decade, seven no longer exist. The enormous popularity of college basketball has made it difficult for minor league basketball to succeed in most secondary markets in the U.S. More than 32 million fans attended men's college basketball games during the 2011–12 season. Teams playing in the Big 10, Atlantic Coast, Southeastern, Big 12 and Big East conferences averaged over 10,000 fans per game. Most basketball fans view collegiate basketball as the primary talent development source for the NBA. Consequently, only one largely post-collegiate minor basketball league, The NBA Development League or NBA D-League (NBDL), has remained viable in a growing number of secondary cities across the U.S. The NBA established the NBDL in 2001 as a full-fledged minor league to groom not only young players but front office staff and game officials for eventual entry into the parent league. The league provides NBA teams with the opportunity to assign young, untested players to a professional league where they can enhance their skills. The NBA D-League has proven to be a true developmental pipeline to the NBA. During the 2012–13 season, close to one-third of the players on NBA rosters had spent time in the D-League.

The NBA Development League has increased from its eight original franchises in 2001 (all located in the southeastern U.S.) to 16 teams by the start of the 2012–13 season. The league is gradually moving to an ownership model similar to minor league baseball. D-League officials expect that the new single-affiliation model, in which teams partner with a single "parent" team, will become the prevalent operating structure over the next few years. Recently, the D-League's Rio Grande Vipers affiliated with the NBA Houston Rockets. Under this arrangement, the Rockets will be responsible for basketball operations (selecting and paying for players on the Vipers' roster as well as for the coaching staff), while the locally based ownership oversees the team's business operations (ticket sales, marketing and promotions, food and beverage concession, etc).

In January 2010, the NBA D-League signed its first national television agreement with Versus (which became the NBC Sports Nework in 2012). The cable television network agreed to carry 10 regular season and 6 post-season games during the 2010–11 season, as well as 25 hours of specialized programming highlighting the league's top players and coaches.

Much like basketball, minor league football has struggled to remain viable in secondary markets in North America. Over the past two decades, there have been two notable failed attempts to establish new professional football leagues. The most spectacular failure was the short-lived XFL, which lasted just one season. The league was founded by Vince McMahon, the chairman of the WWE (formerly known as the World Wrestling Federation) in 2001. The new league was conceived as an offseason (spring-summer) complement to the NFL. To further differentiate the new league from the NFL, Mr. McMahon promoted the new league with the hype of professional wrestling (e.g., games featured trash-talking public address announcers, scantily-clad cheerleaders, and provocative team names . . . Rage, Hitmen, Maniax). Despite the hype, public interest in the XFL waned quickly. Beset by negative media, which ridiculed both the poor quality of play and the wrestlemania atmosphere, the league folded after its first and only season. The World Football League of America lasted just two seasons. This 10-team league, comprised of teams in North America (e.g., Montreal, Orlando, Birmingham) and Europe (Barcelona, London), began play in 1991. However, the WLAF never found an audience, particularly in the U.S., and shut down operation at the end of the 1992 season.

Interestingly, the only professional football league other than the NFL to succeed in the U.S. has been an indoor version of the game called arena football. Inspired by indoor soccer, arena football is a hybrid version of the outdoor game with similar scoring, rules and the basics of blocking and tackling. The major difference is that it is played indoors, on a surface half the size of a regulation football field, surrounded by padded dasherboards, similar to hockey. The result is a game called the "50-Yard Indoor War" or the "Brawl Inside the Wall."[6] The Arena Football League (AFL) was established in 1987. From its modest beginning, with just four teams, the AFL quickly grew to 16 teams by the late 1990s. Expansion accelerated in the early 2000s with the creation of a second arena league, af2. The new "developmental league," intended to prepare players to adapt to the new rules and pace of play of arena football, targeted smaller cities and venues in markets like Albany, GA and Des Moines, IA. The af2 quickly grew to 25 teams. By 2002, there were close to 50 indoor football teams playing under the auspices of the Arena Football League.

Despite what looked to be a bright future for the AFL well into the mid-2000s, the Great Recession had a devastating impact on the league. The league's rapid expansion into some indifferent markets, combined with the absence of effective cost controls, left many teams vulnerable when the economy tumbled. In December 2008, at the lowest depth of the recession, the league announced it would suspend operations indefinitely. Shortly thereafter the AFL declared bankruptcy and ceased operations. However, early in 2010, as the economy showed signs of recovery, the formation of the new Arena Football One league was announced, spearheaded by many long-term owners and officials of the recently dissolved arena league. The new league began play with 15 teams in the spring of 2010 and expanded to 18 teams for the 2011 season. A key distinguishing feature of the reconstituted league was that it would operate under a "single entity" operating model. Under the arrangement, all players and coaches would be considered employees of the league, allowing for centralized control over payroll, the league's single largest operating expense. In a single-entity organization, individual team operators own a stake in the AFL and share the profits (and losses) of the organization on a league-wide basis. While team operators under this model may not realize the full returns of independent ownership (where all the profits accrue to the team owner), the single entity offers the benefits of shared risk (we're all in this together) and greater cost certainty (league-imposed salary limits). The founders of the reconstituted AFL believe the new single-entity structure is the "blueprint for success," a model that will ensure a stable financial future for the league (para. 4).[7]

Minor league sports across the board appear to have settled into a stable state following the recession years of the late 2000s. During the depths of the Great Recession, almost all minor leagues faced serious financial challenges as many of their teams struggled to survive the tough economic conditions. As we've seen, many teams and leagues were casualties of this difficult time. However, the period of widespread consolidation and/or contraction has greatly diminished in recent years. Minor league baseball, in particular, is now in a very solid position. The recently signed extension of the Professional Baseball Agreement (PBA) assures that Major League Baseball will field at least 160 minor league teams through 2020. Under the PBA, major league teams (often referred to as the "parent club") underwrite the entire cost of players and coaches (salaries and benefits) as well as furnish all of the equipment for each of their minor league affiliate teams. Minor league teams are responsible for paying all of the in-season operational costs such as team travel, ballpark maintenance, and game-day expenses. The generous subsidy furnished by major league teams has proven essential to the continued stability of minor league baseball. While the period of exuberant growth—particularly for minor league hockey and basketball—is past, the current complement of secondary or developmental leagues and teams across all sports in North America has reached a steady state. The existing mix of leagues shown in Table 3.1 should largely remain intact into the foreseeable future.

The Status of Women's Professional Sports Leagues

The promise of women's sport finding prominence in the highly competitive U.S. sports marketplace became evident in 1999 at the Women's Soccer World Cup. The United States national team triumphed over China in a dramatic penalty-kick shootout. With an estimated 36.6 million U.S. viewers, the championship final was the most watched soccer match in the history of U.S. network television, and the crowd of 90,185 at the Rose Bowl was the largest ever for a women's sporting event.* However, since that event, women's sports have not been able to capture the same level of widespread public enthusiasm for an on-going, domestic sports league. In the late 1990s and early 2000s, four new women's professional leagues were established in basketball (Women's National Basketball Association, WNBA; and the now-defunct American Basketball League, ABL), soccer (Women's United Soccer Association, WUSA), and softball (Women's Professional Softball League, WPSL). Unfortunately, only one of those leagues, the WNBA, is still in existence.

---

*By comparison, the combined viewership on ESPN and ABC of the live and taped telecasts of the U.S. men's soccer World Cup quarter-final game against Germany in 2002 was 6.8 million viewers, even though this was the best ever performance by a men's U.S. team in the World Cup.

Hoping to capitalize on the unprecedented popularity of women's basketball following the gold medal performance of the women's team, the formation of two new women's leagues was announced shortly after the 1996 Summer Olympic Games. The first league to launch was the 8-team American Basketball League, which began play late in the fall of 1996. The ABL started with great promise, as the league managed to sign almost the entire roster of the undefeated gold medal team.

The Women's National Basketball Association's inaugural season began the summer of 1997. The WNBA was conceived and bankrolled entirely by the NBA in an effort to showcase women's basketball talent in NBA arenas during the offseason. The summer league (34-game regular season schedule) allowed the NBA to extend its brand while filling arenas that otherwise would have been vacant during the summer months. The original eight WNBA teams were owned and operated by individual NBA franchises in key markets around the U.S. (e.g., New York, Los Angeles, Houston). The huge advantages of the NBA-affiliated league soon overwhelmed the ABL. After just two seasons, faced with mounting operational losses, the ABL ceased operations in 1998. The WNBA's ability to access the marketing muscle of the parent league, tap into existing corporate sponsorships, and play in some of the best arenas in the U.S. provided a strong foundation for the league to grow to 16 teams by 2001. Despite widespread interest and initial growth, the WNBA has struggled financially from its inception. According to a number of sources, the league has operated at a loss every season.[8] In 2002, the NBA made the decision to no longer subsidize the WNBA and to allow private (non-NBA franchise operators) ownership parties to purchase franchises. This decision caused two struggling NBA owned/operated franchises in Portland and Miami to fold and the Orlando Magic owned franchise to be sold to a private party and relocated to Connecticut. Currently, five WNBA teams are privately owned and operated, three of which are playing in non-NBA arenas (Tulsa, Connecticut, and Seattle).

The WNBA, like other sports leagues, was not immune to the adverse impacts of the Great Recession. From 2007 through 2009, three franchises (Charlotte, Sacramento, and Houston) ceased operations due largely to the poor economy, and the Detroit team relocated to Tulsa to hopefully benefit from a more robust local economy. Despite these struggles, the WNBA has managed to endure. The current 12-team WNBA emerged in sound financial condition by 2010. Regular season attendance has stabilized at an average of 7,500 per game. An encouraging sign is the substantial rise in playoff attendance over the past few years, with averages eclipsing 10,000 in both 2010 and 2011. In 2007, the league signed an 8-year broadcast agreement with ESPN. Significantly, this was the first television deal signed by a women's professional league that provided an annual rights fee, reputedly worth millions, to the league. While the league has struggled to find a significant television audience during the regular season (regular season telecasts of WNBA games on NBA.TV averaged 50,000 viewers during the 2011 season), the highly promoted 2011 WNBA All-Star game showed a notable boost in viewership, earning a 0.54 rating and 756,000 viewers, up 76% from the previous year.[9]

The prospects for professional women's soccer in North America improved dramatically with the announcement that a new league would be launched in 2013. The new

8-team league, called the National Women's Soccer League, is the third attempt to form a top-notch women's soccer league in the U.S. The two previous efforts ended in failure. The first professional league, called WUSA, despite the star power of World Cup and Olympic champions Mia Hamm and Brandy Chastain, lasted just three seasons. WUSA shut down in 2003 after losing close to $100 million in its short existence. In an effort to revive women's professional soccer, a second league was initiated in 2009. The Women's Professional Soccer league (WPS), like its predecessor, folded after three seasons. The WPS, like WUSA, was unable to generate enough fan interest; attendance averaged less than 3,000. Nor did it have adequate corporate support and a television audience sufficient to sustain its operations.

Will the third time be the charm? Will women's professional soccer finally succeed? According to the U.S. Soccer Federation President, the new women's league is built on an economically sustainable model.[10] What makes the new model unique is the significant financial contribution of the Canadian and Mexican soccer federations along with U.S. Soccer. The three federations will subsidize a substantial portion of the new league's operating expenses. U.S. Soccer promised to pay the salaries of 24 players—3 per team—all members of its national team. The Canadians will pay for up to 16 national team players and the Mexicans a minimum of 12 national players. To further reduce the financial burdens of the new league, U.S. Soccer has committed to underwriting the administrative costs of the league's national office. Optimism for the new league is based on the belief that the financial safety net furnished by the three federations—something WPS and WUSA never had—provides a sustainable foundation for the new league.

While the WNBA and the National Women's Soccer League can look forward with optimism, the future for women's professional softball is much more problematic. Women's fast pitch softball has also found it difficult to establish a commercially viable professional league. Suffering from the same issues of poor attendance and limited corporate and media support, softball's first professional league, the Women's Professional Softball League (WPSL), lasted just four seasons, ceasing operations in 2001. However, much like women's soccer, a determined group of core supporters resurrected a professional league for women in 2004, establishing the National Pro Fastpitch league (NPF). While modest in scope and scale—just four teams in three markets—NPF has managed to create a sustainable business model. The league has established a team salary cap of just $150,000, with individual player salaries ranging from $4,000 to $25,000 for the 3-month season.[11] The relatively modest operational costs have allowed teams to continue operating with the hope that they can build both greater fan and corporate support over time. While it is highly unlikely that the NPF will ever become a prominent part of the sports landscape in North America, its future as a niche sport, appealing to a small but avid fan base, appears promising.

Will women's professional sports ever achieve significance in the crowded North American sports marketplace? Using recent history as an indicator, it is difficult to be optimistic. Even the most well-established women's sports property, the Ladies Professional Golf Association (LPGA), has faced significant challenges in recent years. Founded in 1950, the LPGA governs the worldwide professional golf tour for women. The elite tour experienced remarkable growth in the 1990s. During this decade of unprecedented economic growth, corporate support for the women's golf tour more than doubled, with sponsor-supported prize money increasing from $17.1 million in 1990 to $36.2 million for the 2000 season.[12] The LPGA tour grew more modestly through the first half of the 2000s, but was severely impacted by the economic downturn that began in 2007. In a span of three years, the number of sponsored tour events dropped from a high of 35 in 2007 to 24 in 2010. Total prize money declined from a high of $54 million in 2007 to $41.4 million in 2010. Companies facing difficult economic challenges were hard-pressed to commit the $2 to $4 million required to become the title sponsor of an LPGA event. In 2008 alone, six corporate partners severed their relationship with the LPGA, some breaching long-term contracts as tour sponsors. Fortunately, during the depths of this difficult period, the LPGA signed a 10-year broadcast rights agreement with the Golf Channel. The deal, reputed to be worth as much as $4 million per year, gives the Golf Channel rights to broadcast a broad range of domestic and international tournaments as well as exclusive rights to the Solheim Cup. The agreement, which began in 2010, has had a transformational effect on women's professional golf.

Previous LPGA television agreements had been strictly time-buy arrangements. Rather than being paid a fee by networks, the LPGA actually paid the networks for the coverage time, in effect "renting" space on the network to broadcast their events. The LPGA then attempted to recoup the cost of buying the air time by selling advertising during the broadcast. The new agreement provides the LPGA—for the first time—with a stable, long-term income stream. In fact, the partnership with the Golf Channel establishes the LPGA as the only stand-alone women's professional sports association in the U.S. to receive a rights fee agreement for domestic broadcast coverage.[13] The agreement could not have come at a better time as the LPGA continues to struggle with the defection of many longtime corporate partners. By 2012, there were signs that the ladies' golf tour was beginning to rebound. The number of sponsored tournament events grew slightly to 27, and, significantly, corporate-sponsored prize money increased to almost $47 million for the 2012 season (up from $41.4 million in 2010).

The experience of the LPGA is emblematic of the challenges facing women's professional sport in the U.S. It's clear that as a nation we have not embraced women's professional sports to anywhere near the degree fans and corporations support men's professional sports. Golf is an exemplar of the huge gap between men's and women's sports. The elite men's tour, the Professional Golf Association (PGA) Tour, added seven new corporate sponsors in 2011, bringing total prize money to $288 million—6.5 times more than the total purse for the women. And the men's tour schedule reflects the overall strength of the PGA with almost twice the number of sponsored events (45) as the LPGA. Further evidence of the massive disparity is found in the respective television deals signed by each tour. Whereas the LPGA signed a 10-year deal with the Golf Channel for an estimated $40 million—the single largest rights fee ever signed by women's sports property—the PGA Tour is currently in a six-year deal with two major networks, CBS and NBC, worth $2.95 billion.[14] As Christine Brennan points out, "Men's sports have a huge head start" (para. 9).[15] Will women's sports be able to close the gap? Given the already crowded sports marketplace and the constraints imposed by a fragile economy, where belt-tightening rather than spending is the norm, prospects for women to close the gap are not promising. Meanwhile, the experience of the LPGA, WNBA, WPS (Women's Professional Soccer) and the NPF (National Pro Fastpitch) indicates that women's sports properties will continue to struggle to find a secure niche in a cluttered sports marketplace.

Finding and connecting with consumers in any given market who are most appreciative of, and responsive to, women's sports will be crucial to establishing a sustainable market presence. Demonstrating that women's sports enable companies to meaningfully reach audiences different from those who watch traditional men's sports will be key in securing adequate corporate support. Finally, controlling costs in order to ensure the delivery of affordable and accessible entertainment will help to further differentiate women's sports from much of its more established male competition.

Other Successful Sports Properties

Growth over the past 15 to 20 years has not been confined only to team or league sports. Indeed, the fastest-growing sports property of the 1990s was NASCAR. Ticket sales for the stock car circuit in the 1990s increased by 91%, and television ratings increased over 40% from 1996 to 1999.[16] The latter achievement is most notable because this growth occurred during a period when overall TV viewing for other sports properties, even the NFL, declined. By 2000, NASCAR had supplanted the NHL as the fourth-largest major sport in terms of gross revenues, which were projected to exceed $3.4 billion by 2006.[17] While NASCAR was hard hit by the Great Recession, it appears that this preeminent auto racing circuit has rebounded strongly. In large part, NASCAR's ability to recover so quickly was the result of a long-term television deal signed prior to the onset of the recession. In 2005, NASCAR signed an 8-year contract with multiple networks (Fox, ABC/ESPN, TNT) for $4.48 billion. The NASCAR package was more than twice the value of the current NHL television deal. In 2011, the racing circuit's average broadcast rating of 5.0 was topped only by the NFL. During the 2011 season, Fox averaged a 3-year high of 8.6 million viewers, up 9% over 2010.[16a] It was the largest one-year audience increase in over a decade. Significantly, viewership of the hard-to-reach 18–34 year old male demographic was up 20% over 2010. The ratings boost resulted in NASCAR signing a new TV deal with Fox for a sizeable increase. The 8-year extension will pay NASCAR $2.4 billion for the first 13 races of the 2015 to 2022 seasons, a 36% increase over Fox's current 8-year, $1.76 billion agreement. The negotiating window for the remaining 23 races on the annual NASCAR schedule opens in the summer of 2013. At that time, the other two broadcast partners, TNT and ESPN have first rights to extend their partnerships with ESPN through 2022.* In late 2012, ESPN declared it would be an aggressive bidder or those rights, signaling that along with Fox's record

*From 2007 through 2014, TNT and ESPN committed $2.74 billion to share the rights to televise the 23 NASCAR races. TNT was given exclusive rights to air six midseason races and ESPN the "Chase for the Sprint Cup" races at the end of the season.

payment, NASCAR's total TV rights package from 2014 to 2022 could reach as much as $6 billion.

Another sports property that has become a big financial success in recent years is the U.S. Open Tennis Championships, arguably the single most profitable sporting event in North America. In 2011, the U.S. Open generated total revenues of $215 million. America's preeminent tennis tournament sold more than 700,000 tickets (average first round tickets cost $104) and secured sponsor revenues in excess of $60 million. According to the U.S. Tennis Association, the median income for Open attendees is $150,000, which attracts long-time Open sponsors like Mercedes-Benz, Tiffany, and JPMorgan Chase. *Forbes* estimates that the tournament produces annual net operating profits of around $100 million. The profit margin of almost 50% is remarkable when compared to any other sports property. As will be shown later in the chapter, the average operating margin for major league sports teams is well under 10%.

THE ECONOMIC REALITY OF PROFESSIONAL SPORTS

In 2012 the estimated total market value of the 122 franchises across the four major leagues in the United States and Canada was approximately $74 billion, more than double their market value in 2000 and quadruple that of 1990. In addition, the cumulative revenues generated by teams in the big four leagues in 2012 totaled $24.6 billion, a more than 150% increase over total revenues realized by all teams in 2000. When you consider the difficult economy over the last few years of the previous decade, the magnitude of growth is impressive. The relative economic valuation of each league is shown in Exhibit 3.1.

While the overall growth profile of major league sports has been impressive, it is clear that some leagues have done much better than others. A closer inspection shows that a surprising number of teams across all of the leagues have struggled financially. Consider the following data:

- During the 2011–12 season, 18 NHL teams operated in the red.
- Several small-market MLB teams "survive" on revenue sharing.
- During the 2010–11 season, the NBA claims to have lost $300 million.
- In 2011, the wealthiest eight teams in the NFL generated an average net operating profit of $89.5 million, while the bottom eight teams realized an average net profit of just $12.5 million.

Forbes's annual estimates of team finances in each of the four largest major leagues indicate that the overall profit margins are relatively modest. Table 3.3 provides figures on the net operating profit of each league by dividing the average net operating income of each league by average gross revenues. Overall, the NFL is clearly the top financial performer with a healthy net profit of almost 12%. The NBA comes closest to the NFL with a solid profit margin of 9.2%. The enhanced financial performance of NBA franchises is largely attributable to the new CBA, which reduced player costs from 57% to 50%. The positive impact of the agreement was immediate, with profit margins on average increasing almost 30% in the first year of the new CBA. *Forbes* estimated the

Exhibit 3.1
Current Status of Major Sports Leagues in North America

Major League Baseball	**National Football League**
Founded: National League in 1876, American League in 1901, *Teams:* 30, Commissioner: Bud Selig *Gross Revenues:* $7.5 billion *Net Worth:* $18.15 billion	*Founded:* 1920, *Teams:* 32, *Commissioner:* Roger Goodell, *Gross Revenues:* $9.7 billion *Net Worth:* $35.2 billion
National Hockey League	**National Basketball Association**
Founded: 1917, *Teams:* 30, *Commissioner:* Gary Bettman, *Gross Revenues:* $3.4 billion *Net Worth:* $8.46 billion	*Founded:* 1946, *Teams:* 30, *Commissioner:* David Stern (succeeded by Adam Silver on February 1, 2014) *Gross Revenues:* $4.0 billion *Net Worth:* $11.79 billion

average net operating profit for Major League Baseball franchises at 8.1%. The league-wide net profits for the NHL were considerably lower at an average of 5.6%.

Table 3.3 illustrates the huge discrepancy in gross revenues among the leagues. The average NFL franchise in 2012 realized more than $276 million in total revenues, almost $73 million more than the average MLB team, and more than twice as much as NBA and NHL franchises. The NFL's substantial advantage is attributable largely to the generous television rights fees received annually from its network partners. CBS, NBC, ESPN, Fox and DirecTV have committed to pay the NFL an average of $4 billion a year to televise league games through 2013. Under this arrangement, *Forbes* estimated that each NFL franchise received $125 million from national television broadcast fees. This amount alone exceeds the entire annual revenues for the average NHL franchise. Although the disparity is not nearly as dramatic, the gap in broadcast revenues between the NFL and both the NBA and MLB is substantial. The NBA recently signed an 8-year agreement with ESPN and ABC and TNT worth $7.4 billion. In 2012, Major League Baseball entered into a new deal with ESPN, Fox and Turner Sports worth a combined $21.4 billion. The agreement ensures the league will receive an average of $1.55 billion each year from 2014 through 2021. When the NBA and MLB league offices pass through the new broadcast revenues to individual teams starting in 2014, each team in the NBA will receive an estimated annual payment of $30 million, while each MLB team will receive an annual common share of TV revenues of around $52 million.

Table 3.3. 2011–12 Profit Margins by League				
	NFL	**MLB**	**NBA**	**NHL**
Gross Revenues (per team	$276 MM	$203 MM	$123 MM	$94 MM
Net Oper. Income (per team)	$32.6 MM	$16.4 MM	$11.3 MM	5.3 MM
Net Profit (EBITDA)	11.7%	8.1%	9.2%	5.6%

Over the next decade, the financial gap between the NFL and the three other major leagues will widen even further. In December 2011, the NFL announced a 9-year extension of its broadcast package with Fox, NBC, ESPN and CBS that is expected to pay the league 60% more than its existing agreement. Assuming no change in DirecTV payment of $1 billion per year, starting in 2014, the league's broadcast partners have committed to paying the league an annual rights fee in excess of $6 billion. This means that every NFL franchise will receive an average of $200 million each year through 2022 *before* one ticket, beer or jersey is sold. Chapter 13 provides a detailed breakdown and analysis of the television broadcast rights agreements for each league.

Team Financial Statements

Examination of available team financial documents provides revealing insights into the economic health and financial performance of a number of major league franchises. As private companies, with the exception of the community-owned Green Bay Packers, major league teams are under no obligation to disclose financial performance information. In fact, most leagues and teams do not reveal any detailed figures on how much they make or spend annually.

Fortunately, over the years some individual team records have become publicly available, providing a realistic glimpse into the financial condition of franchises in several leagues. In the case of the Cleveland Indians, complete financial disclosure was required when then-owner Richard Jacobs took the team "public" in December 1998. In an effort to raise capital, Jacobs initiated the first-ever initial public offering or IPO, in which he offered the general public the opportunity to buy newly issued stock shares in his baseball team. The IPO made 4.6 million shares (about 47% of the outstanding shares) of the Cleveland Indians Baseball Company available at an offering price of $15 per share. The public's response, in the words of one analyst, was a "home run." In the first 24 hours, all available shares were sold at an average price of $14, generating $64 million for Mr. Jacobs and the Indians. Mr. Jacobs paid $45 million for the team when he purchased the Indians in 1986. The exuberant public response came on the heels of the team's unprecedented success. In the three years prior to the issuance of the IPO, the team won three American League Central Division championships and two American League championships. During each of those three years, the team sold out all available tickets prior to the start of each season. In 1997, the Indians played 18 of 19 potential post-season games, losing only to the Florida Marlins in the seventh and deciding game of the World Series. Prior to issuing stock shares to the public, the Cleveland Indians were required to file a full financial disclosure document with the Securities and Exchange Commission (SEC). The prospectus included audited financial statements. One of these summary documents is represented in Table 3.4. A close inspection of the highlighted 1997 year-end column itemizing revenues and expenses reveals that even at the height of success, the Indians realized a relatively modest net operating profit of $8.3 million, or 5.9%. What is most revealing about the financial performance of the Indians during the 1997 season is that 83% of those profits were contributed from one source: post-season play. As highlighted in Table 3.4, the 18 games played

Table 3.4. Cleveland Indians Baseball Company, Inc. Initial Public Offering Prospectus. Summary of Financial Data. Year Ended December 31

Income From Statement Data Revenues	1995	1996	1997
Net ticket sales	$32,267,000	$45,658,000	$49,279,000
Local radio and television	9,667,000	13,631,000	17,014,000
Concessions and catering	11,827,000	14,726,000	14,095,000
Private suite and club seat rental	5,635,000	7,035,000	8,704,000
Advertising and promotion	5,742,000	6,891,000	8,754,000
Merchandise	15,024,000	14,683,000	17,449,000
Major Leagues Central Fund	12,369,000	15,505,000	15,505,000
Other	2,979,000	3,002,000	3,365,000
Post-season	9,888,000	1,933,000	13,051,000
Benefit (provision) for revenue sharing	(2,056,000)	(5,731,000)	(7,186,000)
Total revenues	**97,651,000**	**114,197,000**	**140,030,000**
Operating Expenses			
Major league team	38,904,000	53,420,000	66,125,000
Player development	8,298,000	8,735,000	11,146,000
Ballpark operations	9,071,000	10,389,000	10,965,000
Cost of merchandise sold	9,224,000	11,629,000	12,982,000
Administrative and general	9,769,000	9,275,000	10,292,000
Major Leagues Central Fund	1,498,000	4,146,000	4,938,000
Advertising and promotion	3,805,000	2,960,000	3,584,000
Post-season	5,457,000	1,309,000	6,252,000
Amortization of signing bonuses and player contracts	3,242,000	3,212,000	3,630,000
Depreciation and amortization	1,361,000	1,326,000	1,629,000
Total operating expenses	**90,629,000**	**106,464,000**	**131,813,000**
Operating income (loss)	7,022,000	7,733,000	8,217,000
Other income (expense):			
Interest income	1,658,000	3,855,000	4,672,000
Interest expense	(2,005,000)	(2,045,000)	(2,301,000)
Gain (loss) on player transactions	71,000	616,000	2,696,000
League expansion proceeds	—	—	9,268,000
Income (loss) before provision for income taxes	6,746,000	10,159,000	22,570,000
Net income (loss)	**6,746,000**	**$10,159,000**	**22,570,000**

after the regular season, culminating in game seven of the World Series, accounted for $6.25 million of the Indians' overall net income of $8.21 million. Because of the full disclosure mandated by the SEC, the following excerpt appeared in the public offering prospectus filed by the Cleveland Indians:

> Management believes that the Indians' local revenue potential has already been realized, and that future increases in net income are likely to be substantially less than in the past five years. Without the contribution of post-season playoff revenues, the team would not have produced a profit in 1997 (p.8).[16b]

So, one of the most successful teams in major league baseball, a franchise that presold over 3 million tickets, revealed that only their successful appearance in postseason playoffs allowed them to turn a modest profit. Despite that public declaration, the Indians' IPO was a great success, allowing the owner to raise over $60 million literally overnight. Interestingly, Jacobs sold the team 18 months after the IPO for $320 million. The case of the Cleveland Indians illustrates a critical point about the financial returns related to owning a professional sports franchise. As will be discussed later in this chapter, historically real gains from team ownership are realized through franchise appreciation. It's when owners sell their teams that they achieve an enormous return on investment. For example, Jacobs bought the Indians for $45 million and 13 years later sold the team for $320 million. Over most of the time he owned the franchise, the team lost money every year. Even at the peak of its success, annual returns were not spectacular. So, when examining the investment prospects of team ownership, it's important to look beyond *annual* performance and focus on the substantial franchise appreciation benefits that result when teams are sold to new owners.

Important insights into the financial performance of a number of other baseball clubs became available through the unauthorized posting of the audited financial statements of six major league teams. In August 2010, *Deadspin.com* posted the complete financials of the Florida Marlins, Seattle Mariners, Pittsburgh Pirates, Texas Rangers, Los Angeles Angels, and Tampa Bay Rays. The leaked documents provided detailed information on key revenue sources, operations expenses and certified bottom-line or operating income figures for all six clubs. For the first time ever, the exact amount of monies teams receive or pay under MLB's revenue sharing plan was revealed. Under the existing revenue sharing program, monies are redistributed from the league's highest revenue earning teams like the New York Yankees (the team contributed an estimated $76 million to revenue sharing in 2010) to MLB's lowest earners like the Kansas City Royals. In 2010, $404 million was transferred from the league's wealthiest teams to less fortunate franchises.

The consolidated income statement for the Florida Marlins (renamed the Miami Marlins in 2012) posted by Deadspin.com is shown in Table 3.5. The financial statement covers two operational years, 2008 and 2009. In both years, the Marlins turned a profit. In fact, 2008 was a particularly profitable year for the club. The net income of $39.2 million represents a profit margin of 28% on gross revenues of $139.6 million.

A close inspection of revenues shows that the single largest source of income in both

2008 and 2009 was provided by MLB revenue sharing—$47.9 million and $43.9 million, respectively. That contribution alone accounted for over a third (34.4%) of the team's total revenues. Obviously, without the substantial transfer of funds from the league's more affluent clubs, the Marlins would have operated at a loss in 2009. In fact,

Table 3.5. Florida Marlins. Consolidated Statement of Operations. Year Ended October 31		
Revenues	**2009**	**2008**
Home game ticket revenue	$21,529,000	$20,958,000
Concession and novelties	2,582,000	2,268,000
Advertising and publications	1,546,000	1,706,000
Sponsorship revenue	3,343,000	4,348,000
Parking revenue	450,000	434,000
Local radio and television broadcasting	16,716,000	15,900,000
Other revenue	382,000	1,199,000
Major League Baseball Revenue Sharing Plan	43,973,000	47,982,000
Major League Baseball Central Fund	31,592,000	31,298,000
Major League Baseball Properties—Royalties	7,620,000	8,623,000
Equity gain from investment in Major League Baseball Advanced Media L.P.	2,908,000	2,940,000
Equity gain from investment in MLB Network	836,000	—
Total Revenues	**133,531,000**	**139,647,000**
Operating Expenses		
Major League Players' Compensation	43,002,000	29,739,000
Operations and administration—baseball	24,806,000	23,646,000
Amateur players signing bonuses	5,218,000	6,324,000
Stadium and ticket office	7,847,000	7,715,000
Sales and marketing	8,858,000	9,808,000
Sponsorship and promotion expense	1,236,000	1,735,000
Local radio and television broadcasting	747,000	630,000
Administration expenses	10,766,000	10,090,000
Management fee—related party	2,800,000	2,600,000
Major League Baseball expenses	5,146,000	6,495,000
Operating expenses from joint venture	1,762,000	—
Ballpark related expenses	10,666,000	—
Total Operating Expenses	**122,854,000**	**100,433,000**
Operating income (before amortization and depreciation)	**12,677,000**	**39,214,000**

locally-derived revenues (e.g., from ticket sales, local TV and broadcasting) totaled less than $47 million in 2009, well below the team's cumulative operating costs of just over $122 million. Note that the second highest source of revenue also came from an external source, the MLB's Central Fund. The Central Fund includes monies collected from national television and radio broadcast contracts, the Internet, and MLB licensing agreements. A share of these monies is then allocated by Major League Baseball to each team. In 2009, the Marlins' share was $31.6 million.

Of the six teams whose financial records were posted on *Deadspin.com*, three were revenue sharing recipients and three were contributors or payers. Along with the Marlins, the Pittsburgh Pirates and Tampa Bay Rays were substantial beneficiaries of revenue sharing at $39 million and $35 million, respectively. Conversely, the Texas Rangers contributed $23 million to revenue sharing, followed by the Los Angeles Angels and Seattle Mariners at a little over $16 million each.

The only stipulation for the use of revenue sharing funds is that the money should be spent on making the team more competitive. While there is no direct requirement that teams receiving revenue sharing monies must invest in higher player salaries or in player development (e.g., upgrading scouting and minor league operations), the intent is for the funds to be spent on enhancing team performance. In the case of the Marlins, an examination of revenues and expenses in Table 3.5 shows that the team did invest a considerable portion of revenue sharing monies as intended. From 2008 to 2009, the club increased player salaries from $29.7 million to $43 million and invested almost $10.7 million in "ballpark-related expenses." The latter entry accounts for the Marlins' ongoing efforts to build a new, baseball-only ballpark in downtown Miami. For years, the team shared a facility with the NFL's Miami Dolphins, a stadium originally built for football and poorly suited for baseball.

While the Marlins' financial documents provide evidence for the proponents of revenue sharing, a close look at the Pirates' figures provides fuel for critics of the program who assert that some clubs abuse revenue sharing by padding their profits instead of applying the funds to make their teams more competitive.[18] Recall that in 2009, the Pirates received a revenue sharing payment of $39 million. The following year, the club increased players' salaries a miniscule $170,000 from $50.8 million to $51 million and spent approximately $2 million more on enhancing their minor league operations. The most striking and controversial discovery, however, was that the Pirates directed $20.4 million to the team's ownership group to pay a portion of the income taxes they incurred as a result of their ownership interest in the team.

Aside from the controversy around the use of revenue-sharing monies by some clubs like the Pirates, the *Deadspin.com* posting provides further evidence of the relatively modest annual operating margins realized by many major league baseball franchises. The profit margins produced by high revenue teams were far from robust. In fact, the Seattle Mariners, who generated $70 million more in gross revenues than the Pirates in 2008, reported a net operating loss of $7.6 million, while the Pirates produced a sizeable profit of $14.4 million. Of course, in the Pirates' case, the profit margin was attributable entirely to MLB's generous revenue sharing program.

Table 3.6. Green Bay Packers Statement of Income

	2009	2010
Operating Income		
National Income		
Television	$94,484,631	$95,762,500
Road games	16,175,953	16,024,404
Other NFL income	36,600,000	45,838,620
Total *National* Revenue	$147,260,584	$157,625,524
Local Income		
Home games (net)	$31,097,266	$31,137,552
Private box income	12,827,613	12,897,690
Marketing/pro shop revenue	43,717,750	43,024,293
Other—local media, concessions, parking (net)	13,167,973	13,304,388
Total *Local* Revenue	$100,810,602	$100,363,923
Total Operating Income	**$248,071,186**	**$257,989,447**
Operating Expenses		
Player costs	$138,697,272	$160,839,497
General and administrative	31,693,990	32,326,139
Team expenses	26,934,103	25,642,062
Sales and marketing	23,334,394	21,956,462
Other expenses	7,160,551	7,435,016
Total Operating Expenses	**$227,820,310**	**$248,199,176**
Profit from Operations	**$20,250,876**	**$9,790,271**

The Green Bay Packers operate under a unique ownership model in that they are the only community-owned franchise in professional sports. The unusual ownership arrangement dates back to 1923. Unlike most publicly traded companies, the Packers' articles of incorporation stipulate that the stock price cannot appreciate in value and no dividends will be paid. Shares of stock do include voting rights, and the over 100,000 shareholders elect a board of directors to oversee the operations of the team. As a "public" company, the Packers are the only major league sports team to release an annual financial statement (see Table 3.6). These financials provide a revealing picture of how this small-market team benefits from the league's huge television deals and its passionate fan base. The Packers' income statement serves as a proxy for the 31 other NFL teams.

Controlling Player Costs

The fundamental problem for many teams is that although revenues are rising, costs are increasing at a more accelerated rate. Table 3.7 provides clear evidence of this pattern for the Green Bay Packers. The analysis compares changes in key revenue and expenditure categories between 2004 and 2011. The figures show that despite robust increases in revenues, up $103 million or 58%, expenses increased at an even more accelerated pace, up almost $123 million or 80.5%. As a result, the Packers show a significant decline in net operating income, down 41.4% over the eight-year period. The table reveals that rising player costs were the single greatest contributor to the diminished operating

Table 3.7. Revealing Comparison: Packers' P&L			
	2004	**2011**	**Diff. %**
National revenues	$99.8 million	$165.6 million	+ 65.9%
Local revenues	$79.2 million	$120.8 million	+ 52.5%
Total operating income	$179.2 million	$282.4 million	+ 57.6%
Player costs	$96.0 million	$165.8 million	+ 72.7%
Total operating expenditures	$149.9 million	$270.6 million	+ 80.5%
Net operating income	$29.2 million	$17.1 million	− 41.4%

profits of the Packers. Over the comparison period, player salaries increased more than 70% from $96 million in 2004 to $165.8 million in 2011.

The level of salary inflation exhibited by the Green Bay Packers is emblematic of player payroll growth throughout the major league sports. As shown in Table 3.8, average player salaries have more than doubled in every major league over the past 15 years. Major League Baseball and the National Basketball Association have led the way. Individual salaries in MLB have jumped from an average of $1.18 million to almost $3.3 million in 2010, while NBA player salaries have grown astronomically from $2.3 million to over $5.8 million.

The single greatest operational expense for major league teams is player costs. Player payroll costs represent about two-thirds of the total operational expenses incurred by teams. The deputy commissioner of the NBA declared, "We have an economic system that we think is out of whack" (p. 81)[19] This declaration was not a revelation to those who owned or operated those franchises. The owners are ultimately responsible for paying the players' salaries, but the chairman of the Chicago White Sox and Chicago Bulls expressed frustration at the lack of constraint demonstrated by fellow owners by commenting, "In paying ballplayers, we are at the mercy of our *dumbest* competitor"(p. 81).[19]

Each of the four major leagues has attempted, with varying degrees of success, to bring spiraling salaries under some form of control. The varying systems, involving hard and soft salary caps, free agency constraints, and luxury taxes, have all been designed to act as a "drag" on the rapid inflation of player salaries. In every instance, however, own-

Table 3.8. Salary Increases by League: 1996–2011				
Year	**MLB**	**NFL**	**NBA**	**NHL**
2010–11	$3,297,828	$1,870,998	$5,850,000	$2,400,000
2007–08	$2,930,000	$1,700,000	$5,356,000	$1,508,760
2004–05	$2,452,368	$1,411,000	$3,936,421	$1,640,000
2001–02	$2,236,487	$1,392,000	$3,000,000	$1,385,000
1995–96	$1,176,967	$751,000	$2,300,000	$1,073,670
Increase	180%	149%	154%	123%

ers' efforts to impose a constraint on roster costs have met with fierce resistance from the collective bargaining unit or players' association representing the interests of players in each of the leagues. Every league endured at least one labor conflict over the past decade. Major League Baseball has led the way with six lockouts or strikes since 1972.

As recently as 2011, both the NFL and NBA experienced protracted labor disputes with their players. In March 2011, NFL owners imposed a lockout on players which lasted over 4 months. A lockout effectively closes down the league. Players are prevented from accessing team facilities, trainers, and coaches. Teams are not allowed to sign, trade, or contact players. And, importantly, players receive no salary or compensation benefits during the lockout. The lockout was precipitated by the inability of both sides to agree on the essential terms of a new collective bargaining agreement. Among the many contested issues obstructing a new NFL agreement were owners' demands for an extended, 18-game regular-season schedule (currently 16), the imposition of a rookie wage scale, and a significant reduction in the amount of league-wide revenues to be received by players. A settlement was reached just prior to the start of the 2011 football season (the details of the new agreement are provided in the following section).

Salary reduction was at the heart of the NBA bargaining dispute. NBA team owners claimed that the league in total had lost $300 million during the previous season. Initially, the owners proposed to reduce player salaries by 40% through the imposition of a hard salary cap. The NBA Players Association rejected the owners' proposal to strengthen the existing salary cap structure. On July 1, 2011, the owners imposed a lockout, the fourth in the history of the league. The previous lockout was not settled until well after the start of the 1998–99 NBA season, resulting in a shortened 50-game season. The most recent lockout, which placed the 2011–12 season at risk, was settled on December 8, 2011, resulting in another shortened regular season of 66 games.

The labor struggles of the NBA and NFL appeared to have a moderating effect on Major League Baseball. Anxious to avoid a contentious labor dispute, MLB players and owners agreed to a new 5-year labor agreement in November of 2011. In signing the new deal, Commissioner Selig acknowledged that MLB was conscious of avoiding the labor problems of the NFL and NBA, claiming, "We've learned from our past experiences and look forward to 21 consecutive years of labor peace."

Many analysts believed the National Hockey League would also reach an amicable agreement when their CBA expired at the end of the 2011–12 season. When the previous CBA ended in 2004, the league and players struggled to reach an agreement resulting in the cancellation of the entire 2004–05 season. There was reason to be optimistic when the CBA expired on September 15, 2012, that the NHL would avoid another protracted labor dispute. The league had just completed its most successful season, generating a record $3.3 billion in revenues. In addition, the NHL signed the biggest TV deal in its history, a $2 billion, 10-year contract with NBC Sports, guaranteeing the league $200 million a year through 2020–21. Unfortunately, the negotiations between the NHL and the NHL Players Association quickly turned contentious with the owners imposing a lockout on September 17, 2012. Similar to the NFL and NBA, owners of NHL franchises demanded substantial salary concessions from players. The lockout lasted 3½ months, taking the league to the brink of cancelling the entire 2012–13 season. On January 15, 2013, a new 10-year CBA was ratified. The lengthy lockout resulted in the NHL playing a shortened regular season of 48 games in 2013. As will be discussed in greater detail later in this chapter, the owners were successful in substantially reducing player's share of league revenues.

With the settlement of the NHL lockout, it appears that for most of the decade ahead, all four major leagues should be operating in a relatively stable labor environment. The collective bargaining agreements currently in place should remain essentially the same, at least into the foreseeable future.

The following sections provide an overview of the current state of each of the major leagues with respect to their ability to control or constrain player salaries.

National Football League

On July 28, 2011, the NFL owners and players signed a 10-year agreement, ending the longest work stoppage in league history and the first since the 1987 players strike. The new collective bargaining agreement (CBA) ensures labor peace through 2020. Central to the new CBA is a revenue sharing arrangement in which the owners will receive approximately 52% and the players 48% of the league's annual revenues. Under the previous contract, the revenue distribution was closer to 50–50. While the players agreed to a smaller share, the new agreement stipulates that the amount of revenue available for distribution will be significantly larger. The new revenue model will be based on a split of "all revenues." In the old model, teams could deduct certain expenses as cost credits from shared revenues. In the last year of the previous collective bargaining agreement, expense credits reached more than $1.1 billion. Under the new revenue sharing arrangement, no expense deductions will be allowed; the players' share will be allocated from all of the revenues generated annually by the league. This is a critical feature of the new agreement because total league revenues are expected to rise from $9.3 billion in 2010 to as much as $20 billion by the end of the decade.

The CBA retains a maximum team salary cap provision. During the first year of the agreement, the players and owners agreed to a salary cap of $142.4 million. Under this arrangement, teams were limited to spending $120.375 million on player salaries and bonuses, and up to $22.025 million on player benefits (e.g., health insurance, pension, etc.). At the start of the 2012 season, the salary cap was determined on the basis of a more explicit revenue sharing plan in which the players will receive:

- 55% of national media revenue (rights fees from national TV broadcast contracts with ESPN, ABC, Fox, and CBS)
- 45% of NFL Ventures revenue (accounted for $1.8 billion in league revenues in 2010 from licensing royalties, sponsorship sales, satellite TV and radio, and international business)
- 40% of local team revenue (ticket sales, advertising, concessions, parking, etc.)

The CBA anticipates that the team salary cap will rise significantly over the 10-year agreement. To further protect the players' share, the agreement includes a minimum salary guarantee or "floor" in which each team must commit to spending no less than 89% of the salary cap in any given year.

One major concession owners were able to achieve in the current CBA is a new rookie compensation system that dramatically reduces the growth rate of guaranteed payments to first-round draft choices. Guaranteed payments in the form of signing bonuses to first-round picks had increased 223% from 2000 to 2010, totaling over $3.5 billion. Owners had become increasingly resistant to making substantial payments to untried rookies, particularly in the wake of notable failures like JaMarcus Russell, to whom the Oakland Raiders paid $32 million as the first overall pick in the 2007 NFL draft. Russell was released in 2009 with the lowest rating among quarterbacks in the league. The new rookie system sets limits based on an average of veteran salaries at the drafted player's respective position. For the first 10 picks, salaries will be based on the average of the top 10 veteran salaries at their respective positions, and for players selected 11 through 32, rookies will be paid an average of the top 3 to 25 salaries at their respective positions. The new rookie system has had a major impact. For example, quarterback Cam Newton, the first player chosen in the 2011 draft, received less than half the amount granted the first overall pick in the 2010 draft. Under the old contract, with no restrictions on rookie pay, Sam Bradford signed a 6-year, $78 million contract, with a $50 million guarantee. Newton's deal was for 4 years at $22 million. While the contract amount was fully guaranteed, the example clearly illustrates that owners achieved their goal of dramatically reducing rookie pay.

Shortly after the original CBA was established in 1994, players found a way to circumvent the so-called hard cap. The first player to exploit the loophole was Deion Sanders, whose agent proposed in 1995 that Sanders receive a significant portion of his new contract in the form of an up-front signing bonus. Rather than paying out his salary in annual increments over the length of the contract, none of which would be guaranteed beyond each season, the new contract stipulated that Deion Sanders would receive over half the full value of the contract at signing, and that the value of the signing bonus would not apply against the salary cap because the new CBA did not contain language that counted signing bonuses as part of the designated team salary cap. The new contract threatened to undermine the salary cap provision of the new CBA. The league moved quickly to achieve a compromise in order to preserve some degree of protection against salary inflation. The compromise allows teams to pay players substantial up-front signing bonuses, but count only a small portion of the bonus payment toward their cap. Teams are allowed to prorate the amount of the bonus over the length of the player's contract. So hypothetically, let's say Deion Sanders signed a $50 million deal with the Dallas Cowboys for 5 years. Under the compromise that was reached between the league and the NFL Players Association, no more than 20% of the total value of the contract could be designated as a signing bonus in a given year. Therefore, in this example, the signing bonus would be limited to $10 million. Sanders would receive that amount when he signed his contract. For cap purposes, however, the $10 million bonus would be prorated over the 5-year contract in equal amounts of $2 million per year

($10 million/5 years = $2 million per year). The team would only have to count $2 million of the actual $10 million paid to Deion against the salary cap in the first year of his contract.

Table 3.9 shows how a typical NFL contract is structured. Normally, the contract includes three basic compensation elements. The first is the base salary or the actual amount paid for a given work period (typically a complete season). The second includes various bonuses granted the player, which could include a signing bonus, a roster bonus (paid if a player makes the team roster) and/or a workout bonus (paid if a player attends off-season team workouts). The third compensation component includes performance-based bonuses referred to as either Likely To Be Earned (LTBE) bonuses. These pay incentives are based on historical performance metrics for each player. For example, a contract that rewarded perennial All-Pro quarterback Aaron Rogers of the Green Bay Packers $100,000 for being named to the All-Pro team in any given year of a contract would be treated as a Likely To Be Earned incentive. However, a $100,000 bonus that would be earned if he scored 10 rushing touchdowns in a season would be an example of a Not Likely to Be Earned incentive (since Rogers had never scored more than 5 running or rushing touchdowns in any season over the length of his career). The distinction is important for salary cap purposes because only the LTBEs are counted as part of the annual team salary cap calculation. In the case of Aaron Rogers, the entire $100,000 Pro Bowl incentive would count against the Green Bay Packers salary cap.

For the hypothetical contract depicted in Table 3.9, the total value comes to $50.5 million dollars over the 5-year contract period. The largest portion, the $40 million base salary, is paid out in progressively larger annual installment payments. This represents a typical NFL contract in which a disproportionate share of the base—in this case, $22 million—is paid over the last two years of the contract. These so-called "backloaded" contracts are common because NFL contracts are not guaranteed. A multi-year contract is valid in only those years the player is on the team's roster. By deferring a significant portion of the overall contract value, the team is protecting itself if it believes in several years the player is not worth the contractually stipulated salary. In that case, it

Table 3.9. Sample NFL Player Contract			
Player signed a $50.5 million, 5-year contract which includes a $10 million signing bonus and annual performance incentives (LTBEs)			
	Base Salary	**Signing Bonus**	**LTBE**	**Total Annual Payment**
Year 1	$4,500,000	$10,000,000	$100,000	$14,600,000
Year 2	$5,850,000	—	$100,000	$5,950,000
Year 3	$7,650,000	—	$100,000	$7,750,000
Year 4	$9,750,000	—	$100,000	$9,850,000
Year 5	$12,250,000	—	$100,000	$12,350,000
Total	**$40,000,000**	**$10,000,000**	**$500,000**	**$50,500,000**

could decide to release or not re-sign the player or restructure the contract at a more manageable, or cap-friendly, level.

In this example, in the first year of the contract, the team would only have to count the pro-rated share of the player's signing bonus, or $2 million; along with the base, $4,500,000; and LTBE, $100,000 payment as part of the team's salary cap. The total obligation for this player against the cap would be $6,600,000.

As shown in Table 3.9, the actual amount paid the player during the first year of the contract, however, would be $14,600,000. Therefore, it is easy to see how an NFL team's annual payroll can exceed the salary cap in a given season. For example, in 2009, the Green Bay Packers reported spending $140 million on team payroll, which was $20 million more than the NFL's salary cap in a year.

What allows teams the ability to maintain salary expenditures well above the cap is that the league has flourished over the last several decades. The robust revenues realized from the league's national television broadcast agreements have produced double-digit growth even through the recession period. In addition, the league's underlying economic structure has created substantial financial parity among NFL franchises. The NFL has the greatest amount of revenue-sharing among its owners, where as much as two-thirds of the total revenues generated by the league are shared among its 32 teams. Revenues from national television broadcast contracts, which escalated from $2.0 billion in 2000, to $2.8 billion in 2005, to over $3 billion by 2010, are shared equally among teams, amounting to almost $100 million per team annually.

The result of the extensive revenue sharing in the NFL is that it is the healthiest of the major sports leagues in North America. The 2011 CBA provides an equitable distribution of league revenues between teams and players for the end of this decade, ensuring labor peace and a prosperous future for the league.

National Basketball Association

After a bitter 5-month lockout which threatened cancellation of the 2011–12 season, the NBA and its players reached a 10-year agreement on December 8, 2011. The contentious dispute between the league and players—the 4th NBA labor stoppage since 1995—was brought about by the owners' intent to make fundamental changes in the CBA to offset reported annual losses of $300 million over the last several years of the previous agreement. Owners wanted to impose strict controls on player payrolls, shorten player contracts, and close the widening payroll gap between high-spending large market teams and financially challenged teams in smaller markets.* The owners' starting negotiating position proposed a hard salary cap, an elimination of guaranteed contracts—both features similar to the NFL model—and a much more punitive penalty on high-spending teams. The first two provisions were intended to reduce players' share of

---

*During the 2010–11 season, the Los Angeles Lakers payroll, including the luxury tax penalty, totaled $116.6 million, compared to the $42 million team payroll for the Sacramento Kings—a discrepancy of $75 million. Analysis conducted by the *NY Times* demonstrated the substantial competitive advantage of high payroll teams. During the 2010–11 season, the top 10 spending teams averaged 50 wins, the bottom 10 just 32. From 2005 through 2011, every NBA champion has been among the 10 highest spending teams.

Table 3.10. Major Features of NBA Collective Bargaining Agreement, 2012–2021. (Compared to Previous CBA, 2006–2011)

Feature	Current CBA	Previous CBA
BRI split	49–51%	57%
Luxury tax threshold	$70 million	$70.31 million
Luxury tax rates	Same $1-for-$1 penalty for first two years; starting in Year 3, $1.50 for first $5 million over, up to $3.75 for every dollar over $20 million	$1-for-$1 penalty
Contract lengths	Bird Exception contracts 5 years max; all others 4 years max	Bird contracts 6 years max; all others 5 years max
Annual increases	7.5% for "Bird players;" 4.5% for others	10.5% for "Bird" players; 8% for others
Escrow tax	10% withheld from player checks	8% withheld in 2011
Min. team payroll	85% of salary cap for first two years; 90% after	75% of salary cap

league revenues from 57% to 47% or lower. With each percentage point equivalent to around $35 million, the stakes were high. The reduction from 57% to 47% represented a $350 million redistribution of the NBA's almost $4 billion in gross annual revenues.

The players, represented by the National Basketball Players Association, resisted efforts to reduce their share of league revenues, particularly the owners' proposal to "harden" the league's salary cap. Players wanted to maintain a soft cap with a number of so-called exceptions that would allow teams to continue to pay well above any specified team salary limit.

A compromise, reached more than a month after the scheduled start of the 2011–12 season, resulted in a new 10-year labor agreement.* The terms of the new CBA show that the owners were successful in achieving many concessions and most of their goals, while the players were able to preserve a soft cap system. Table 3.10 provides a summary of the key features of the current CBA, comparing the most important elements of the current agreement with the previous 6-year contract. Under the current agreement, players' share of Basketball-Related Income (BRI) will be no less than 49% and no greater than 51%, with the salary cap pegged at a 50/50 split of BRI. BRI is the term used in the collective bargaining agreement to represent gross league revenues. BRI includes almost every revenue stream generated by teams and income received by the league from entities such as NBA Properties and NBA Media Ventures.

---

*The 2011–12 regular season was shortened to 66 games (from 82), starting on Christmas Day. The 10-year agreement provides a mutual opt-out provision after 6 years, allowing either side to reopen negotiations for a new CBA after the 2016–17 season.

Exhibit 3.2

Major Income Sources Constituting Basketball-Related Income (BRI)

- Ticket sales (regular season, exhibition, playoff)
- National Television Broadcast Rights contracts (ABC, ESPN, TNT)
- Local (team) Television Broadcast Rights (e.g., LA Lakers-Time Warner)
- Concession, novelty and program sales
- Parking
- Proceeds from team sponsorships
- Arena club revenues
- 40% of proceeds from arena signage
- 40% of proceeds from luxury suites
- 45–50% of proceeds from arena naming rights
- Proceeds from other premium seat licenses

Ehibit 3.2 provides an itemized summary of the income sources that contribute to BRI. The NBA and NBPA (Players Association) jointly released an audited statement at the end of the 2010–11 basketball season showing the BRI had increased 4.8% from $3.643 billion in 2009–10 to $3.817 billion in 2010–11. Under the previous agreement, in which players received 57% of the BRI, total player compensation reached $2.176 billion. As shown in Table 3.9, the new CBA reduces players' share to around 50%. Assuming the same amount of BRI, under the new agreement the total compensation distributed to players would fall to $1.908 billion, a reduction of $268 million.

Not only did owners achieve substantial payroll savings with the reduced revenue sharing split, but they also received a number of other important concessions from players. The most important changes were in shortening the length of contracts, reducing annual salary increases, imposing a much harsher luxury tax on high-spending teams and their owners, and increasing the escrow tax on player pay checks.

Length of Contract and Annual Increases. While the owners failed in their attempt to eliminate or severely curtail guaranteed contracts, they were able to reduce standard contracts from a maximum of five to four years. The one major exception pertained to a carryover provision called the "Bird Exception," named for former Boston Celtics star Larry Bird.* The Bird Exception is the most prominent among a number of exceptions in the CBA that allows teams to sign players even if by adding their salaries the team's payroll exceeds the salary cap. The Bird provision allows teams to re-sign one veteran up to the player's maximum salary, even if the amount pushes the team's total annual payroll beyond the salary cap. The intent of the rule is to ensure that teams are provided a substantial advantage in being able to retain their star players. To be eligible for "Bird rights," a player must be an active member of a team's roster for a minimum of three years. A player receiving the exception is entitled to the maximum salary allowed by the

---

*The NBA first adopted the salary cap in 1983 ($3.6 million!). The original intent was to impose a hard cap on player salaries. However, the year prior to the institution of the salary cap, Larry Bird, had signed a then-historic contract with the Celtics. When added to the overall team payroll, the $12.6 million, 7-year agreement placed the Celtics well over the salary cap threshold. The exception was created to allow Bird to remain on the Celtics roster.

Table 3.11. Maximum NBA Player Salaries		
# of Years	Defined Max Salary	2013–14
1–6	$9,000,000 or 25% of cap	$13,701,250
7–9	$11,000,000 or 30% of cap	$16,441,500
10+	$14,000,000 or 35% of cap	$19,181,750

CBA as well as a longer guaranteed contract (5 years) at a higher rate of annual increase (7.5% per year) than non-Bird players. A player can only receive these benefits if he re-signs with his current team. The following example demonstrates the powerful financial incentive for a player to re-sign under this special exception.

Let's assume, in a hypothetical example, that the Bird-designated player is a 5-year veteran, completing his first contract. A player completing five years of service in the league would fall into the first level of maximum salaries specified in the current CBA as shown in Table 3.11. The maximum amount players can make is dependent on the number of years they have played. Players with one to six years of service are eligible to receive a maximum annual salary of either $9 million or 25% of the current salary cap, whichever is greater. The salary cap for the 2012–13 season was $58.7 million. Those players with ten or more years in the league are capable of making more than $19 million in a single season.

In our example, the 5-year veteran could receive a maximum salary of $13.7 million. Table 3.12 shows the substantial economic benefits this player would receive by taking advantage of the Bird Exception provisions by re-signing with his current team as compared to signing as a free agent with another team. The total value of the Bird rights contract, at $95 million, is worth $25 million *more* than the maximum value of a non-Bird contract. The extra year and 3% greater annual increase when compounded over the length of the agreement creates a considerable "home team" advantage.

Not only does the Bird Exception provide a powerful incentive for star players to stay with their current teams, the significant reduction in the maximum allowa-

Table 3.12. Comparing Value of Bird vs. Non-Bird Contracts		
	"Bird" @7.5%/yr	"Non-Bird" @4.5%/yr
Year 1	$16.44 million	$16.44 million
Year 2	$17.67 million	$17.18 million
Year 3	$18.99 million	$17.95 million
Year 4	$20.42 million	$18.76 million
Year 5	$21.95 million	(4-year maximum)
Total	$95.47 million	$70.33 million

ble annual raise provided to players in the current CBA has saved teams millions in reduced payroll expenses. As shown in Table 3.10, owners were able to reduce the maximum annual rate of player salary increases for Bird players from 10.5% to 7.5% and from 8% to 4.5% for non-Bird players. Under the current agreement, the 3% difference for Bird players alone allows teams to realize savings of millions. As shown in Table 3.11, the maximum value of a current Bird contract is $94.75 million. Under the previous CBA, the maximum worth of a Bird Exception contract, at an annual rate of increase of 10.5% over 6 years, totaled $127.7 million. The combination of reduced annual raises and shorter contracts provided for in the current CBA has substantially improved the ability of NBA teams to responsibly manage payroll growth over the next decade.

Other Salary Cap Exceptions. The CBA does contain a number of provisions, like the Bird Exception, that allow teams to spend well above the salary cap. Listed below are brief summaries of the other primary exceptions available to teams:

Early Bird Exception. This exception allows teams to exceed the salary cap to re-sign players who have been on their rosters for two or fewer seasons. A team may re-sign its own free agents for up to either the NBA league average or 175% of their previous season's salary, whichever is greater.

Mid-Level Exception (MLE). The MLE can be used by teams over the salary cap to sign one or multiple free agents. Historically, the mid-level exception has been set to the average NBA salary. Under the current CBA, the MLE distinguishes between teams under the luxury tax threshold—discussed in the next section—that do not pay a payroll tax and high-salaried teams that pay the tax. Non-taxpaying teams are allowed to sign free agents starting at $5 million (growing at 3% annually), for up to 4 years, while taxpaying teams are restricted to offering free agents a maximum salary starting at $3 million (growing 3% annually) for 3 years. The provision is designed to benefit those teams that manage to stay beneath the luxury tax threshold by forcing players signing with taxpaying teams to make a significant financial sacrifice. An additional MLE was included in the current CBA, referred to as the Mid-Level Exception for Room Teams. This provision allows team with "room" (current payroll is under the salary cap) to use their available cap room plus an additional $2.5 million to sign one or more free agents.

Bi-annual Exception. Can only be used by non-taxpaying teams. Teams over the salary cap but not paying the luxury tax may use this exception every other year at a starting amount of $1.9 million, growing at 3% annually.

Disabled Player Exception. Enables a team that is over the cap to sign a replacement for a player who suffered a season-ending injury. The maximum salary of the replacement player is the lesser of 50% of the disabled player's salary or the amount of the Non-Taxpayers Mid-Level Exception.

The CBA provides a number of additional exceptions, including the Minimum Salary Exception, the Traded Player Exception, the Rookie Exception, and the

Non-Bird Exception (see Larry Coon's *NBA Salary Cap FAQ* for details of each of these exceptions at www.cbafaq.com).

Luxury Tax. Given all of the options to exceed the salary cap, it should come as no surprise that most NBA teams have payrolls well above the cap. In fact, over the last decade, it has not been unusual to find as many as two-thirds of the NBA teams exceeding the cap in a given season. Big-market teams have typically been the big spenders. The Los Angeles Lakers have led the way in recent years with total player payrolls consistently over $90 million.

In an effort to constrain or deter high-spending teams and their owners from profligate spending, the 2005 CBA introduced for the first time a luxury tax provision. The intent of the new rule was to penalize those teams spending well above the salary cap. Under the original luxury tax, teams exceeding a designated "tax threshold" were forced to pay a penalty to the league of one dollar for every dollar they were over the tax level. The tax threshold is established at 61% of Basketball-Related Income (less the total cost of player benefits divided by the number of teams). The tax level was set at $70.37 million during the 2012–13 season. Nine teams, led by the LA Lakers at $93.5 million, exceeded the tax threshold that season. The tax bill paid by the Lakers totaled $23.13 million. When added to the actual salary costs, the total effective payroll expense borne by the Lakers that season exceeded $116 million.

The current CBA includes a luxury tax with an even more punitive financial penalty for teams spending above the tax threshold. Beginning with the 2013–14 season, teams must pay a progressively steeper tax for every dollar they spend above the luxury tax threshold (still pegged at 61% of BRI). The new tax structure will work as shown in Table 3.13. The much harsher penalty of this incremental tax is apparent when applied to the Lakers. Under the current system, the $23 million tax the team paid in 2012–13 would more than double during the 2013–14 to almost $57 million, an increase of $34 million.

Not only do teams have to pay a stiff price for exceeding the luxury tax threshold, the CBA rules also stipulate that taxpaying teams will not receive any of the tax monies collected by the league. Teams *under* the tax level split half of the tax

Table 3.13. Luxury Tax Penalties	
Amount Over Tax Threshold	**Amount Over Tax Threshold**
$1 million–$5 million	$1.50 for every dollar over
$5 million–$10 million	$1.75 for every dollar over
$10 million–$15 million	$2.50 for every dollar over
$15 million–$20 million	$3.25 for every dollar over
Over $20 million	$3.75 for every dollar over

monies, with the other half going to the NBA. The league has broad discretion to allocate its share of collected tax funds in support of "league purposes." In recent years, the tax share distributed to non-taxpaying teams has amounted to over $5 million per season.

Small-market teams in places like Oklahoma City, Memphis and Sacramento are hopeful that the more punitive luxury tax system will discourage higher revenue teams in Los Angeles, New York and Chicago from spending well above the cap to monopolize the free agent market. As a result, it will provide small- and midsize-market teams with greater opportunities to re-sign and keep players in order to stay competitive with big-market clubs.

Escrow Tax. In order to ensure that players do not receive more than 50% of total league revenues, the CBA imposes a 10% tax on player salaries and benefits. This tax is referred to as the "escrow tax." Every pay period, 10% of each player's paycheck is withheld and deposited in an escrow account maintained by the NBA. At the end of each season, the total amount in player wages and benefits deposited in the escrow account is compared against total league-wide revenues or BRI. If the percentage of compensation falls below the 50% escrow tax threshold, all the money held in escrow is refunded to the players. However, if the total salary and benefits exceed 50%, the "overage" amount is returned to the owners.

Historically, the escrow tax has resulted in significant gains for the owners. From 2005 to 2010, player salaries exceeded the escrow tax threshold every season. Over those five seasons, nearly $937 million was withheld from player paychecks and placed in the league's escrow account. Of the total amount, 92% or $860 million was returned to owners. In effect, the escrow tax resulted in the players giving back about 9% of the full value of their contracted compensation over those 5 seasons.

Minimum Team Salary. One area of the current CBA in which players achieved significant gains was in establishing a higher minimum team payroll. By raising the salary floor, each team is required to spend more on player salaries. Under the current agreement, teams must spend up to at least 85% of the cap in 2011–12 and 2012–13, and up to at least 90% throughout the remaining (up to 8) years of the CBA. With the salary cap set at $58.04 million for the 2011–12 and 2012–13 seasons, the minimum team salary is $49.3 million. This new salary floor represents a substantial increase over the team minimum in the previous CBA, which was set at 75% of the cap or $43.5 million. With the cap projected to grow at approximately 4% per year over the length of the 10-year CBA, the jump to 90% in 2013–14 assures a significant increase in the salary floor for years to come.

It is clear that the current CBA places substantially greater constraints on salary inflation in the NBA than ever before. High spending teams and owners bear a much more serious financial burden, especially for those teams spending above the luxury tax threshold. Not only are taxpaying teams paying a substantially greater penalty for spending above the tax level, but they are allowed fewer, and smaller, salary exceptions under the current labor contract. Smaller market teams should benefit from the spending restrictions placed on big market franchises because the CBA rewards players who re-sign with their current teams or with non-taxpaying teams.

Major League Baseball

Major League Baseball is the only major league that does not have a salary cap. The powerful MLB Players Association has repeatedly rebuffed baseball owners' efforts to establish a maximum team payroll. Consequently, baseball players' salaries have grown at a faster pace than any of the other sports leagues. Over the last two decades, the average salary of a MLB player has more than doubled, increasing from $1.18 million in 1994 to $3.44 million in 2012.

For most of the last 50 years, baseball has had a difficult labor history. In the period from 1970 through 1995 alone, it suffered eight work stoppages. A CBA settlement in 2002 represented the first time since 1970 that players and owners accepted a new labor agreement without a strike or lockout—and that agreement was reached just hours before a strike deadline. In 1994, negotiations broke down between the owners and the MLB Players Association, resulting in a 7-month strike that led to cancellation of the 1994 World Series and a shortened 1995 season.

Although the 2002 agreement did not institute a salary cap, the new labor pact significantly altered the economic structure of MLB. The settlement substantially increased revenue sharing among teams and imposed a luxury tax on payrolls of high-spending teams. The current CBA, which is signed through 2016, extends both of these provisions.

> **Revenue Sharing.** The original revenue sharing plan, adopted in the 2002 CBA, required each team to contribute 34% of its local net revenues to a pool that is redistributed equally to all 30 MLB teams. Local team revenues include income derived from ticket sales, television and radio broadcast agreements, concessions, and parking. As a result of the growing concerns raised by large market teams, who were required to transfer millions annually to low revenue clubs, the 2006 CBA reduced each team's revenue sharing contribution to 31% of locally generated revenues. The 31% contribution rate was extended in the latest agreement through 2016. The adoption of a broad revenue sharing program was crucial to preserving the economic viability and competitiveness of many small market teams. Unlike the NFL, which for decades has shared a majority of revenues generated at the national level, MLB teams historically depended primarily on revenues raised in their own markets from local team revenues. As a result, by the late 1990s, the revenue disparity between small and large market teams had become a serious issue. In 2001, the New York Yankees generated over $242 million in gross revenues, compared to the Minnesota Twins' $56 million and the Kansas City Royals' $63.7 million—disparities of $186 million and $178.3 million, respectively. The Yankees' payroll that year was $135 million, compared to the Royals'

$47 million. A "blue ribbon" panel commissioned by MLB concluded that "large and growing disparities exist that are causing problems of chronic competitive imbalance. Year after year, too many clubs know in spring training that they have no realistic prospect of reaching postseason play" (para. 3).[20] The panel's recommendation that MLB establish a meaningful revenue transfer system was instrumental to the adoption of revenue sharing in the 2002 agreement.

Under the current revenue-sharing plan, all teams contribute 31% of their local net revenues (less expenses such as stadium depreciation and sales costs) into a pool from which shares are disproportionately allocated to teams based on their relative revenues. Teams pay or receive the difference between their local revenue figure and the league average. In 2010, $404 million was transferred from the revenue sharing pool to low-revenue teams, down slightly from the $433 million transferred in 2009.[21]

In the wake of the 2010 disclosures from *Deadspin.com*, which revealed that several teams profited, literally, as a result of receiving substantial revenue sharing payments from other teams, the new CBA adopted in 2012 established new rules for teams receiving revenue-sharing monies. No longer can teams spend their distribution on enhancing front office salaries or on paying down team debt. The new agreement stipulates that teams report specifically on how they spend their revenue-sharing dollars to improve the team. New guidelines require that team payrolls of revenue sharing recipients be at least 25% larger than the amount they received. A team receiving a revenue-sharing payment of $40 million would have to spend a minimum of $50 million on team salaries the next season. For the first time, teams receiving revenue sharing distributions in 2013 will have to submit an explicit report accounting for how they spent their revenue-sharing dollars to improve the performance of their major league roster.

While the revenue redistribution has allowed several small market teams to achieve profitability, it's hard to make a case that revenue sharing has constrained salary inflation. In fact, the case can be made that revenue sharing has allowed low revenue teams to spend more on player compensation. A review of the Marlins' financials supports that point of view. From 2008 to 2009, the team directed a significant share of the revenue sharing monies received to enhance team performance. The team increased player development and payroll expenditures in 2009 by close to $15 million (a 44% increase). In addition, $10.5 million was directed to developing and promoting a new ballpark, which opened in 2012.

Luxury Tax. The only mechanism in place specifically intended to reduce salary expenditures in MLB is the Competitive Balance Tax (CBT), or as it is more commonly known, the Luxury Tax. The CBT was adopted as part of the 2002 collective bargaining agreement. The intent of the tax was to discourage exorbitant payroll spending by high-revenue teams by imposing a tax on teams whose payrolls exceeded pre-designated payroll thresholds.

While owners initially proposed as much as a 50% tax on low payroll thresholds (e.g., $98 million), the Players Association forced the adoption of much lower tax rates on substantially higher threshold levels. The first luxury tax threshold established for the 2003 season was $117 million. In the 2006 agreement, owners were successful in establishing progressively higher thresholds each year, so that by the 2011 season, the tax penalty threshold was $178 million.

Table 3.14. Major League Baseball Luxury Tax Rates	
Threshold Violations	
First time over	17.5%
Second time over	30.0%
Third time over	40.0%
Fourth time over	50.0%

In the current CBA, the luxury tax remained at $178 million for the 2012 and 2013 seasons. The threshold rises to $189 million for the 2014–2016 seasons.

The tax penalty imposed on MLB teams exceeding the tax threshold is much less severe than the NBA's luxury tax sanctions. While NBA teams must pay from $1.50 to $3.50 for every dollar over the limit, MLB teams pay only a fraction or percentage of every dollar spent on player salaries beyond the threshold. The tax rates imposed on teams exceeding the thresholds increase by the number of times a team violates the threshold, according to the following terms (see Table 3.14):

Under this arrangement, a team with a payroll of $188 million in 2012, whose payroll surpassed the payroll threshold of $178 million for the first time would pay a luxury tax of $1,750,000. The team would pay 17.5% on every dollar it spent beyond the $178 million threshold, or $10 million (17.5% × $10 million = $1.75 million). A team with the same payroll who was a second-time offender would pay a luxury tax penalty of $3,000,000 (30% × $10 million = $3.0 million). Ironically, the monies collected from the tax are not redistributed back to smaller market teams to promote competitive balance. Instead, the money is placed in an Industry Growth Fund earmarked for player benefits and a fund dedicated to developing players in countries lacking organized baseball.

Since the luxury tax was first imposed, only one team, the New York Yankees, has consistently paid the tax. According to *BizofBaseball.com*, the Yankees have paid close to $220 million in luxury tax penalties since the tax was first established.[22] As a result, some pundits have referred to the CBT as the Yankee Tax. In fact, only four teams have ever exceeded the payroll threshold: the Boston Red Sox, the Los Angeles Angels of Anaheim, the Detroit Tigers, and the Yankees.

There is little evidence that the luxury tax serves as a serious deterrent to salary inflation. Allegedly, the Philadelphia Phillies made a decision during the 2011 season to *not* sign a high-priced free agent player because the additional salary would have placed the team over the payroll threshold. In reality, most MLB team payrolls are so far below the payroll threshold that the luxury tax has little or no relevance. With no salary cap in sight, and an ineffectual luxury tax deterrent, it appears that baseball will have to rely on revenue sharing as the one mechanism that will moderate the league's potential competitive imbalance problem between large and small market teams. The expectation is that MLB salary inflation will continue to set the pace for major league sports in North America.

National Hockey League

The NHL ended a bitter 113-day lockout in early January 2013. The protracted labor dispute brought the league to the brink of cancelling the entire 2012–13 season. By the time the new agreement was reached, the league had already lost 510 games scheduled for the 2012–13 season as well as the New Year's Day Winter Classic and the All-Star Game. As a result, the NHL was able to offer only a shortened, 48-game regular season (rather than the full 82-game schedule), with Stanley Cup playoffs games stretching through the end of June 2013.

The central issues in the NHL labor dispute, much like the NBA and NFL, were economic. The owners claimed despite the league generating record revenues of $3.3 billion, many NHL teams were losing money. *Forbes* estimated that almost half of the league's teams were operating in the red in 2012.[23] Consequently, the league's bargaining position was driven by the owners' efforts to reclaim a larger share of the league revenues. Two of the most contentious issues focused on revenue sharing between the players and owners and the terms of individual player contracts.

Revenue Sharing: Under the terms of the previous agreement, players received 57% of league revenues or Hockey Related Revenues (HRR). HRR is based on the NBA's Basketball Related Income (BRI) concept. While the revenue streams constituting BRI and HRR are not exactly the same, similar to the NBA, hockey related revenues encompass income generated from the production of regular season and play-off games and NHL-related events, including ticket sales, concessions, radio and television broadcast fees, corporate sponsorships, club and suite sales and leases, and parking. In 2011–12, hockey related revenues totaled $3.3 billion, of which the players received 57% or $1.89 billion.

The league's initial proposal to the NHL Players Association was to reduce the players share to 43%. Eventually, both parties settled on a 50/50 revenue split, essentially the same revenue distribution arrangement reached by the NFL and NBA. In the end, NHL players, like those in the NBA and NFL, made substantial concessions with respect to their share of league-wide revenues. The reduction of the players' share of league revenues from 57% to 50%, using the 2011–12 HRR total of $3.3 billion, would result in players' forfeiting approximately $230 million. In 2013–14, the first full season under the new CBA, the salary cap for each NHL team was $64.3 million, well under the $70.2 million cap that had been projected for the 2013–14 season prior to the lockout. However, under the new agreement, the 2013–14 salary cap of $64.3 million is just a "reset point" in that future caps will be based on a 50–50 split of hockey-related revenues. Similar to the NFL and NBA agreements, players are assuming that over time, as league revenues grow, the larger pool of income will more than offset their reduced share of HRR. There is no question that the new agreement provides substantial financial benefit to team owners. According to one analyst, "reducing the share given to players by seven percentage points enriches the owners by roughly $230 million a year" (para. 6).[24] Assuming a modest annual growth rate of 3%, the owners will realize a total of $2.7 billion in additional HRR revenues over the entire 10-year agreement.

The new CBA also established a minimum team payroll (aka the "floor") of $44 million for the shortened 2013 and 2013–14 seasons (considerably lower than the $48.3 million floor in 2011–12). Beginning in 2014–15, the floor will be reset every year at 70% of the salary cap. Minimum player salaries begin at the 2011–12 level of $525,000 but are scheduled to progressively rise to $750,000 by 2021–22.

Individual Player Contract Terms: Under the previous CBA, there were no limits on the length of player contracts. It was a loophole that was fully exploited by teams to circumvent the team salary cap. General managers anxious to sign attractive free agents could sign players to long-term, so-called "back diving" contracts. These were deals that provided players with lots of money upfront and relatively very little in the final few years of the contract. For example, the Minnesota Wild signed two of the top free agents at the end of the 2012 season to identical 13 year, $98 million contracts, for an average annual salary of $7.54 million. The annual average is significant because it serves as the basis for determining what portion of the player's salary is counted against the team's salary cap. The actual contract stipulated that both players would receive $12 million in years 1 and 2 of the agreement, with their annual salary payment progressively declining to $1 million in years 12 and 13. For these two players, then, the team's cap hit over the duration of their contracts—the amount counted against the cap—would be $15.04 million (2 × $7.54 million) every year. In fact, the team would be paying these players $48 million ($24 million each) over just the first two years of the contract. The ability of teams to artificially deflate their salary cap hit by issuing long-term contracts became a contentious issue in the NHL negotiations, particularly for teams that were struggling financially. Owners of struggling franchises couldn't compete against wealthier, high-spending teams facing no serious salary cap penalties for signing free agents to expensive long-term contracts. Consequently, the NHL owners initially proposed limiting the maximum length of player contracts to five years for free agents and seven years for those players already under contract who are re-signed. The final settlement allows teams to sign new players for a maximum of seven years and to re-sign their own players for up to eight-years. To curtail the growing practice of outlandish front-loaded contracts or back diving, the owners demanded and won the inclusion of a variance rule which stipulates that a player's salary may not increase or decrease by more than 35% year-to-year, and by no more than 50% over the length of the contract. Thus, if a player makes $5 million his first year, he can make no less than $3.25 million the second year, and at no point during his contract is the player allowed to make less than $2.5 million. The provision will eliminate "cheat" contracts and create more flexibility for teams to spread their limited salary cap dollars to other deserving players on their rosters.

The NHL Players Association was able to win a significant concession from league owners. The new agreement requires the league to make $300 million in transition payments to compensate players who signed contracts prior to the new CBA. The provision is intended to "make whole" those players who would suffer substantial salary losses under the new agreement that immediately reduced players' share of HRR from 57% to 50%. The provision ensures players receive at least most of the salaries they were promised. The transition payments made over the first three years of the agreement ensure that players share of revenues will exceed 50% for the first several years of the new 10-year CBA.

The length of the new CBA is significant for a league that has struggled through three difficult labor disputes over the last 18 years. A 301-day lockout in 2004–05 resulted in the NHL's canceling the entire season—the first and only professional league in North America to ever to do so. While the players initially rejected the league's proposal for a 10-year CBA, preferring a 5-year deal, ultimately the players association recognized the need for long-term stability. A concession granted by the league was the inclusion of an opt-out clause that allows either party to terminate the CBA after Year 8. The new deal ensures labor peace between NHL owners and players at least through the 2019–20 season.

CREATIVE ACCOUNTING

Although league officials and team owners consistently report that their franchises are losing a lot of money, the actual extent and magnitude of these claims are difficult to substantiate because with the exception of the Green Bay Packers, all teams are privately owned. Ownership in most cases is mainly in the hands of private individuals, families, or closely held corporations, all of which are under no legal obligation to disclose detailed financial information about their team's operations. Financial experts and players association representatives have repeatedly challenged the authenticity of the owners' claims of financial distress, claiming that creative accounting procedures used by the owners made the teams' financial positions look much worse than they really were.

Baseball teams have been described as "physical embodiments of tax accountants' minds."[25] There are four main legal accounting maneuvers used by team owners to make it appear they are losing money from their investment in the team rather than making money.[26] The result of these strategies is that owners increase their personal wealth from their investments, while submitting financial reports to the Internal Revenue Service showing their team's incurred losses.

First, owners and their dependents may receive salaries or fees from their teams. For example, in a court case it was revealed that the owner of the Philadelphia Eagles paid himself an annual salary of $7 million. Thus, the owner was making $7 million a year more on his investment than he appeared to be. The team may also purchase services from other companies controlled by an owner, for example, legal, public relations, or information technology services. To the extent that these services are either superfluous or charge more than market rate, the added costs to the franchise are merely revenues retained by the owner via another vehicle.[26]

An owner who controls the team, the stadium, and the team's broadcast and television outlets, or some combination of these, has multiple opportunities to create accounting losses by shifting revenues among the entities. They can be shifted at the owner's discretion to whichever entity best suits the purpose at hand. For example, in a carefully documented case, a former owner of the Florida Marlins claimed the team lost $30 million when winning the World Series in 1997. However, revenues from luxury suites, premium seats, naming rights, parking, signage, merchandising and concessions were all attributed to the stadium that he also owned, not to the team. The estimated revenues from these sources were $36 million. In addition, the value of the media outlet increased by $40 million in that year as a result of the team's success. Hence, the reality was that the team's activities resulted in a net gain to the owner of $46 million, rather than the $30 million loss he reported.[27]

The third accounting maneuver stems from the type of corporate structure used by the franchises. Many of them are subchapter S corporations.[26] These are limited to having no more than 75 shareholders, and these corporations do not directly pay income taxes. Rather, the income gains or losses and taxes are computed at the corporate level, but they are passed through to the shareholders and reported by the shareholders on their individual 1040 federal income tax forms according to their proportional share of the ownership. The advantages of this arrangement are illustrated in the following example:

A partnership of 10 owners contributed equally to the purchase of a professional franchise for $200 million. In a given year, the team reported an annual operating loss of $30 million. Owner A, who was a member of the partnership, had a taxable income of $2 million in that year. He filed a joint tax return with his spouse and so was required to pay $638,000 in federal income taxes on his earned income. However, he also received $3 million in losses as his one-tenth share of the subchapter S corporation's losses. When this is included in his tax return, his $2 million taxable income falls to zero. Thus, he saves $638,000 that he would otherwise have had to pay to the federal government in income taxes. Further, he can carry forward the additional $1 million in losses to the following year and use it to offset his taxable income in that year.

Roster Depreciation Allowance

A former president of the Toronto Blue Jays reputedly stated, "Under generally accepted accounting principles, I can turn a $4 million profit into a $2 million loss, and I can get every national accounting firm to agree with me" (p. 62).[27] This was a reference to the roster depreciation (RDA) allowance provided to the owners of professional sports teams. RDA allows owners to substantially reduce their tax obligations on earned income, producing extraordinary savings.

All credit for the unique and generous tax benefit afforded the owners of sports teams goes to Bill Veeck ("Veeck as in Wreck"). Mr. Veeck was a longtime owner of major league baseball franchises including the St. Louis Browns, the Cleveland Indians and the Chicago White Sox. In the mid-1950s, as then-owner of the Cleveland Indians, Veeck convinced his good friend, the commissioner of the Internal Revenue Service Midwest district, that the player roster of a professional baseball team is like a piece of machinery or building that wears out over time, so like these items, the roster should be depreciable over time.[26] As a result, the IRS granted Veeck a special provision called the "Veeck Tax Provision." Under this arrangement, Mr. Veeck, and (eventually) all other owners of sports teams, were allowed to claim half of what they paid to purchase a team as depreciation on player contracts. Specifically, owners could assign 50% of the franchise purchase price to player contracts. Then, for tax purposes, the roster could be treated as a declining or "wasting" asset, depreciating the value of the contract over a 5-year period. The original Veeck provision was also referred to as the "50/5" rule because owners were allowed to write off half the value of the team at purchase over the first five years of ownership.

As if the 50/5 rule wasn't generous enough, in 2004 the special tax benefit granted to owners of sports franchises was expanded. In the last session of the 2004 Congress, a rider was attached to a massive export tax bill focused on multinational corporations. The new rule contained in a single sentence of the 633-page bill allows owners to depreciate the full value of their franchises. Under the expanded tax shelter, sports team owners were allowed to write off the entire value of the purchase price over a 15-year period. The new and current depreciation allowance is referred to as the "100/15" rule.

The following example clarifies how an owner can take advantage of this tax sheltering provision:

Suppose someone buys an MLB team for $600 million. The new owner assigns 100% of the purchase price to player contracts (the maximum allowed under the law), and then depreciates the contracts over 15 years at $40 million per year. Assume that gross revenues for the team are $220 million per year, and that costs, exclusive of player contract depreciation, are $200 million. Then, for the first 15 years of operation of the team, the books of the team will look like this:

Revenue . . . . $220 million
Less Costs. . . . . $200 million
Net Operating Income . . . . $20 million
Less Depreciation . . . . $40 million
Pretax profits . . . . ($20 million)

The depreciation of $40 million is simply a bookkeeping entry with no actual cash expended to cover this expense, so a $20 million profit is transformed by legitimate accounting procedures to a $20 million pretax loss. In actuality, however, the owner will have revenues of $20 million in his or her pocket.

In addition to pocketing a substantial profit, owners can also apply the pretax loss of $20 million to reduce their tax obligations from other sources of taxable income. The following illustration, based on an actual transaction, demonstrates the substantial tax shelter benefits provided by the RDA provision. In 2008, Stephen Ross purchased a 95% share of the NFL Miami Dolphins for $1.1 billion, including a 95% share of Land Shark (now Sun Life) Stadium. During the 2009 season, the Dolphins lost money. As shown below, net operating income plunged to minus $7.7 million.

Miami Dolphins' Finances 2009
Total Operating Income . . . . $247.0 million
Total Operating Expenses . . . . $254.7 million
Operating Profit (Loss) . . . . ($7.7) million

Let's assume that when Mr. Ross purchased the team, he elected to organize his owner-ship interest in the team as an S Corporation. The S Corporation ownership structure is commonly used because it provides substantial tax benefits, and it provides owners with limited liability protection from creditors. With an S Corporation, the income, deductions and tax credits produced by the company flow or pass through to the indi-vidual owners or shareholders, who then claim them on their own individual tax returns. Therefore, it would be possible for Mr. Ross to claim a total of $81 million in losses attributable to his ownership interest in the Dolphins. These losses would include the $7.7 million net operating loss as well as the $73.3 million deprecation allowed to owners of sports franchises. Recall that Mr. Ross purchased the team for $1.1 billion. Under the RDA provision, he is allowed to depreciate or write off 100% of the pur-chase price over 15 years. In this case, he could claim a depreciation allowance of $73.3 million in 2009 ($1.1 billion/15 = $73.3 million).

The Internal Revenue Service (IRS) allows S Corporation business owners to deduct losses from other earned income. It would be fair to presume that Mr. Ross, as a multi-billionaire, would have substantial income from his numerous other business interests (*Forbes* estimated his net worth in 2009 to be $3.4 billion). It would be possible, then, for him to apply all of the $81 million loss from the Dolphins against these other earn-ings. Assuming Mr. Ross is in the 35% tax bracket (the highest tax bracket in 2009), it would be possible for him to realize over $28 million in tax savings directly attributable to his ownership of the Miami Dolphins (35% × $81 million = $28.3 million). The $28.3 million represents the tax savings on $81 million *less* in taxable income at the 35% tax rate.

FRANCHISE APPRECIATION

In addition to the special tax benefits they receive, owners of sports teams have been able to count on steep increases in the market value of their teams. Franchise values have skyrocketed over the past 20 years. Some owners have seen their team investments grow to unimaginable levels. Jerry Jones, who purchased the Dallas Cowboys football team in 1989 for $150 million, owns a franchise that *Forbes* estimates to be worth $2.1 *billion* if the team were to be sold today. While not all owners have enjoyed the impres-sive growth of the Cowboys, Figure 3.1 shows that team values have increased substan-tially across all of the leagues. On a league-wide basis, teams have appreciated at very healthy rates, with the NFL leading the way with a *compound annual* growth rate of 8.4% from 2000 to 2012. The average value of an NFL franchise in 2012 was $1.1 bil-lion. Major League Baseball team values also grew at a robust rate over the same period, increasing at an average of 8.3% annually. By 2012, the average MLB team was esti-mated to be worth $605 million. Not surprisingly, the New York Yankees led the way at an estimated value of $1.85 billion. Although, on average, values for NBA and NHL teams are not as high, both of these leagues have experienced solid rates of annual growth, at 6.6% and 5.5%, respectively. In 2013, the New York Knicks surpassed the Los Angeles Lakers as the most expensive team in the NBA. *Forbes* estimated the Knicks to be worth $1.1 billion, with the Lakers close behind at $1.0 billion. The Toronto

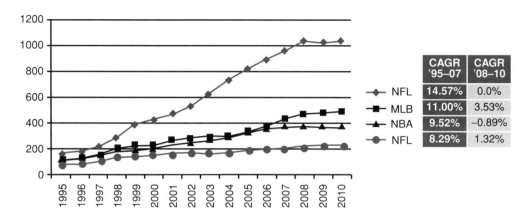

Figure 3.1. Historic Franchise Value 1995–2010 (in millions).

Maple Leafs franchise was ranked as the most highly valued team in the NHL. *Forbes* estimated the market value of the Maple Leafs at $1.0 billion, based on the club's robust 2011–12 operating revenues of $200 million.

As shown in Figure 3.1, the Great Recession had a significant impact on franchise values. Trend lines for all four major leagues flattened dramatically between 2008 and 2010, as teams struggled to sell tickets and corporate sponsorships in a down economy. Even many teams in the NFL—the league that many considered to be recession proof—declined. In 2010, for the first time since tracking the league's financials, analysts at *Forbes* reduced the values of 21 of the NFL's 32 teams.[28] The overall value of NFL teams fell 2% over the 2009 season, dropping from an average of $1.04 billion the previous year to $1.02 billion. Although the estimated losses per franchise were fairly modest, team values slipped because the bad economy reduced demand and resulted in less non-broadcasting revenue for many teams. Some teams were particularly hard hit. The Jacksonville Jaguars' season-ticket base dropped from 42,000 to 25,000 from 2008 to 2009, as the northern Florida area struggled to cope with a devastating housing market collapse.

By 2011, it was evident that the NFL had recaptured its upward momentum. During that year, *Forbes* analysts upgraded the value of 23 teams, resulting in a return to near-record average team values of almost $1.04 billion. The league's recovery was even more impressive in 2012, with 31 of 32 franchises gaining value, resulting in average values of $1.1 billion, an all-time high.* According to *Forbes*, in 2012, 20 NFL franchises were worth more than $1 billion. The significant spike in team values was largely attributable to the new TV package signed in late 2011 with Fox, NBC, CBS and ESPN that increased the NFL's annual broadcast revenues (starting in 2014) by 63%, guaranteeing each team an additional $75 million per year (to about $200 million) through 2021.

Similar to the NFL, the other three major leagues also gained considerable post-recession momentum. Major League Baseball posted the most impressive gain over the

---

*The only NFL team not upgraded by *Forbes* in 2012 was the Cincinnati Bengals, who showed no appreciation from 2011 to 2012. The club's value remained at $871 million for both years.

two year span, with average franchise values growing 23% from 2010 to 2012. Not far behind baseball was the National Hockey League, with Forbes analysts raising the average value of an NHL franchise to a record $282 million, 18% above 2011 average valuation. While not as dramatic, the average NBA franchise appreciated a healthy 7.1%. The NBA's more modest growth rate was largely the result of the "momentum-killing lockout" discussed earlier in this chapter.*

Also similar to the NFL, massive increases in TV rights fees were primarily responsible for the robust franchise appreciation growth across MLB, NBA and the NHL. The NBA's current deal with its broadcast partners, TNT and Disney's ESPN/ABC, pays the league an average of $930 million per year through 2021, with each club receiving an equal share of more than $30 million. MLB teams receive an even larger amount of money each year from the league's $12.4 billion national TV deal. In addition to the more than $50 million distributed by MLB to each team, all 30 teams have sold the broadcast rights to cable television channels in their own local markets. The aggregate rights of cable TV deals established by individual teams were estimated to worth $923 million in 2012.[30] In January 2013, the Los Angeles Dodgers announced a deal with Time Warner Cable to create a new TV channel in the Los Angeles market that analysts predict will pay the team more than $7 billion over 25 years.[31] The value of the agreement is more than double what Major League Baseball thought the rights were worth when the team was sold out of bankruptcy in 2012.

The NHL's national broadcast deal with NBC Sports, which more than doubled the television revenues, contributed to the league generating $3.4 billion in total revenues for the 2011–12 season. On the basis of the league's record-setting performance, *Forbes* analysts increased NHL franchise values to an all-time high in 2012. However, due to the league's protracted labor dispute, which placed the entire 2012–13 season at risk of cancellation, it is very likely that the market values of NHL teams will fall and take several years to recover to 2012 levels.

DRIVERS OF FRANCHISE VALUES

The key to determining the relative value of a franchise is its revenue-generating capability. The more overall income a team can produce, the higher its value. Experienced market analysts Mitchell Ziets and David Haber provide an informative analysis of the factors that determine the income-producing capacity of a team.[32] Specifically, they identify a number of key drivers of franchise values. We have organized these drivers into four primary categories:

1. **Local Market Conditions:** Ziets and Haber state that *market size* is the most important driver. As would be expected, the greater the population, the larger the potential fan base to purchase tickets as well as to watch games on local TV. Further, the bigger the marketplace, the greater the number of corporations with the

---

*Any concerns about the NBA's labor stoppage having an adverse impact on the 2012–13 season quickly dissipated. According to the *SportsBusiness Journal*, prior to the start of the new season the league sold more than 50,000 *new* full-season tickets and total full-season ticket packages eclipsed 250,000.[29]

capacity to purchase sponsorships and premium seating. While a positive correlation between size of market and franchise values was found for MLB, NBA and NHL teams, market size was found to be much less of a determining factor for NFL franchises. The fact that the NFL shares so much of its ample revenues makes NFL teams less dependent on fans and companies in their local markets. That's why the Green Bay Packers, despite playing in the smallest market of all major league franchises (the 2010 Green Bay metro population was 306,000, compared to Chicago's 9.8 million), was ranked as the 9th most valuable franchise in the NFL at $1.09 billion by *Forbes* in 2011.

One factor that moderates the impact of market size on a team's revenue potential is the number of other teams sharing the same market. For example, Phoenix, AZ, is the 14th largest metropolitan area in the U.S. with 4.2 million people. Phoenix is also the home to four major league franchises and a major college athletic program at Arizona State University. The four teams compete ferociously for the finite time and money of fans and for the support of local corporations. Each franchise plays in a modern venue, full of the latest premium seating options (e.g., luxury suites, club seats, loge boxes). Cumulatively, the four professional teams and Arizona State offer 409 suites and almost 14,000 club seats. The price of a suite per season in the four professional team venues averages over $100,000 (ranging from $65,000 to $150,000), with club seats averaging well over $5,000 per season (ranging from $1,000 to $11,000).[33]

The challenge of selling this high-priced inventory in such a competitive marketplace is illustrated by the *2010 Dun & Bradstreet's Business Rankings*, which report there were only 136 companies located in the Phoenix metro area that generated in excess of $100 million in annual sales. Additionally, only 12 *Fortune 1000* firms are headquartered in the Phoenix area and only four of the largest 250 law firms in the U.S. This is significant in that a survey found that a prominent characteristic of companies that leased luxury suites in professional sports venues was annual sales *in excess of $100 million*.[34] Given that the total number of suites (409) exceeds the primary prospect pool (approximately 375 firms), it should come as no surprise that not one of the four major league teams in the crowded Phoenix marketplace has been able to sell or lease all of its suite inventory.

In contrast, the San Antonio Spurs, while operating in a market less than half the size of the Phoenix metro area, is the only major sports franchise located in the San Antonio market and has no major collegiate competition. The team offers 54 suites, priced from $125,000 to $295,000 per season. *Dun & Bradstreet's Business Rankings* identifies 168 companies with over $100 million in annual sales located in the San Antonio market. While the primary prospect pool is much smaller overall than it is in Phoenix, the suite-to-corporate prospect ratio in San Antonio—at 3 to 1—is considerably more favorable. As a result, the Spurs have been able to sell almost all of their most expensive suite inventory to corporate partners. In this case, the benefits of literally being "the only game in town" clearly outweigh the advantages of operating in a much larger but more cluttered marketplace.

2. **League-wide Economics:** As mentioned earlier, the extent to which leagues share revenues can be a significant determinant of an individual team's income-generating capability. The substantially higher average team values for NFL franchises is driven largely by the massive television rights fees received by the league. In 2014, the league's national television broadcast partners will pay the league more than $6 billion for the rights to telecast NFL games. Each team's share amounts to close to $200 million While the NHL's 10-year, $1.9 billion agreement with NBC more than doubled the league's national broadcast rights fee, the amount shared with individual teams, approximately $6 million a year, is quite modest when compared to the NFL. The significant difference is one major reason that NFL teams on average are valued at $800 million more than NHL franchises.

As we saw earlier in examining the financials of several Major League Baseball teams, the generous revenue-sharing program adopted by MLB results in a number of smaller market and revenue teams receiving as much as $30 to $40 million per year. It is largely because of this revenue sharing arrangement that the Pittsburgh Pirates, ranked last among all MLB teams in *Forbes* 2011 franchise valuations at $304 million, was still worth considerably more than the NHL's Pittsburgh Penguins. The Penguins were ranked as the 9th most valuable franchise in the NHL by *Forbes*. Despite playing in a new $321 million arena and producing a franchise record of $92 million in revenues in 2010, the Penguins still generated almost $70 million *less* in total revenues than the Pirates. Of the $145 million in total revenues reported by the Pirates on their income statement, $51.7 million came from revenues distributed by Major League Baseball, including $39 million from revenue sharing, $8.9 million from the league's Central Fund and $3.8 million from MLB Properties. Clearly, without this generous league support, the value of the Pirates franchise would be substantially diminished.

3. **Individual Team's Venue Economics:** As Ziets and Haber point out, a team's stadium or arena situation is a large driver of value. Typically, the newer the facility the greater its revenue-generating capacity. Modern sports venues have been built for the express purpose of maximizing income-producing opportunities. Sports venues built since the late-1990s are fully loaded with premium seating options, including expensive club seats, loge boxes, and corporate suites. The average NFL stadium contains 140 luxury suites and 7,000 club seats. Robert Kraft, the owner of the New England Patriots, realizes an estimated $45 to $50 million a year from just the sale of 80 suites (from $85,000 to $305,000/year) and 6,000 club seats (from $3,750 to $6,000/year). New facilities also stimulate greater in-venue spending by providing more varied and accessible points of sale for concessions and merchandise sales. The impact of playing in a new venue is evidenced by the fact that all 10 of the NFL's highest valued teams play in modern, fully loaded stadiums, while 7 of the league's 10 lowest valued teams play in venues more than 20 years old, several in facilities over 30 years of age.

Perhaps the single best example of the new facility effect on franchise value is the Minnesota Twins baseball team. In 2010, the Twins moved from the aging Humphrey Dome, which they shared for almost 20 years with the NFL Vikings, into a new $440 million downtown stadium. The first year in their new baseball-only ballpark, the Twins sold 3.2 million tickets, setting an all-time attendance record. The team generated an additional $51 million in revenue their initial year in the new venue. The move to the new stadium had a transformational impact on the financial condition of the ballclub. In 2009, while playing in the old domed stadium, *Forbes* estimated the team's value at $358 million on an estimated $158 million in annual revenues. The first year in their new ballpark, the team generated an estimated $213 million in total revenues. The substantial boost led analysts to reappraise the value of the team in 2011 at $490 million. In just two seasons, the value of the team increased 37%, a jump almost entirely attributable to the team's occupancy of their new downtown stadium.

4. **Lease Agreement:** Finally, a key driver—often overlooked—in determining team value is the franchise's lease agreement. Very few teams actually own or control the venues they play in. In most cases, teams are tenants in stadiums and arenas and their use of the facility and claim on various venue revenue streams is dependent on the lease agreement they sign with the leaseholder, typically a local government such as a city or county or local stadium authority. The variation in lease agreements from city to city and team to team is considerable. In some cases, teams pay little or no rent for use of the stadium and claim almost all of the revenues. Several teams are the beneficiaries of these so-called "sweetheart" leases. The NFL Baltimore Ravens are a prime example. In an effort to entice an existing NFL franchise to relocate to Baltimore to occupy a brand new, state-of-the-art football stadium, the Maryland Stadium Authority offered rent-free occupancy to any team accepting its invitation. In addition to charging no rent, the new tenant was promised a lease agreement that would guarantee the team would receive 100% of all stadium revenues, including suite leases, ticket sales, parking, signage and concessions. The ownership of the then-Cleveland Browns accepted the State of Maryland's generous offer and in 1996 moved the franchise to Baltimore and changed the team name to the Baltimore Ravens. In 1998, the Ravens played their first game in the new stadium. Just one year later, a new Cleveland Browns franchise played its first game in a brand new, publicly financed stadium in downtown Cleveland.

Stung by the loss of their beloved Browns, the voters overwhelmingly approved the construction of a $283 million stadium in 1997. The NFL awarded Cleveland a new expansion franchise in 1998, which reclaimed the historic franchise name of the Browns. The new franchise was rewarded with a very favorable lease agreement by the local stadium authority. The Browns annual rental fee was a nominal $250,000 per season. And, similar to the Ravens, the team received all revenues produced by the stadium. These generous stadium lease agreements are in strict contrast to the lease currently in place in San Francisco. The San Francisco 49ers play in the oldest venue currently in use in the NFL. The team plays in Candlestick Park, originally built in 1960 for the baseball Giants. The stadium is owned by the City of San Francisco and the 49ers have been a tenant in the venue since 1971. Under the current lease agreement, rent is based on a percentage of gross ticket sales. The lease stipulated that the 49ers would pay 10% of gross ticket sales PLUS the greater of $7,500 per suite or 15% of gross suite revenues. Given that the team has averaged 550,000 paid attendance over the past several years with an average ticket price of approximately $73, estimated gross ticket sales total approximately $40 million. So, the lease agreement requires the 49ers to pay 10% or $4 million of that amount as part of their rent obligation. In addition, Candlestick Park includes 93 luxury suites, of which the team must pay a minimum rental rate of $7,500 per suite, for a total of $697,500. So, at the very least, the 49ers must pay $4.7 million to the City of San Francisco in annual rent to play in Candlestick.

In addition, the lease stipulates that the team will receive just 58% of gross parking revenues, 85% of gross suite revenues and 100% of gross concession revenues, up to $4.5 million, and 85% thereafter. The restricted revenues combined with the significantly higher rental fee place the 49ers at a significant disadvantage when compared to Baltimore and Cleveland. The difference is striking! The Browns and Ravens enjoy at least a $5 million advantage over the 49ers on just the basis of their more favorable stadium lease agreements. This advantage is reflected in the team valuations. *Forbes* places the value of the Ravens, even though they are playing in a considerably smaller market, at $1.09 billion, almost $200 million more than the 49ers at $990 million. The combination of playing in a new stadium with a sweetheart lease resulted in the Ravens generating almost $30 million more in revenues than the 49ers during the 2010 season.

While the value of teams may vary considerably on the basis of the four drivers discussed above, it is important to recognize that with very few exceptions, the owners of professional sports teams realize significant returns on their investments over time. According to one analyst, the fact that there are only 122 major league teams provides owners with a unique advantage:

Sports teams are like da Vincis: They're worthy investments because they're prestigious and rare. More worthy, in fact, because they offer benefits other rare commodities don't. If you own a team, you can pay yourself, your family or your pals big consulting fees or annual salaries ($7.5 million in the case of one NFL owner). You can also charge personal expenses—say, flying the team jet—to the club. And, there are tax benefits. As Mavs owner Mark Cuban puts it: "You can balance potential tax payments with the tax loss of your team." (p. 93)[35]

SUMMARY

The four most established major professional sports leagues, the NFL, MLB, NBA and NHL, have almost reached a saturation point in North America at 122 franchises. Few markets remain that have the necessary requirements (large fan base, strong corporate community) to support a major league franchise. While expansion into new markets was a common pattern across all leagues over the past several decades, in the years ahead franchise movement in the four "big leagues" will be largely restricted to the relocation of existing teams. There's a high probability that an NFL team will move one of its current franchises into the long-vacant Los Angeles market, if one of several new stadium proposals is successful.* And it's quite likely that at least one other NHL franchise will follow the Winnipeg Jets, which recently vacated Atlanta, to another city in Canada. Major League Soccer is the one major league property still pursuing an aggressive expansion program. The league's impressive growth has been anchored by its development of 14 "soccer-specific" stadiums.

However, the most spectacular growth of professional sport has occurred at the secondary or minor league level. Currently, more than 500 teams in 40 separate leagues operate in North America. Baseball has the most well developed minor league system with 241 teams playing in the U.S. and Canada. Positioned as a family affordable entertainment option (average price of a adult ticket in 2010 was $7), total minor league baseball attendance has climbed to nearly 50 million per year. Minor league franchises across other sports have not flourished to the same degree as baseball. Reaction to the introduction of hockey in small to medium U.S. markets, especially in the southern or "Sunbelt" region, has been mixed. Particularly hard hit during the Great Recession, six minor league hockey leagues ceased operations from 2007 to 2009. The ten remaining minor hockey leagues (161 teams) in the U.S. and Canada are in sound financial condition. Minor league basketball and football leagues have struggled to remain viable. With multiple failures across both sports over the past 20 years, only the NBA's Development League (NDBL) and an indoor version of football, the Arena Football League (AFL) have managed to endure. Women's professional sports leagues have struggled as well. It's clear that American fans have not embraced women's sports to the same degree as men's professional sports. Of the four new women's sports leagues launched in the late 1990s, only the Women's National Basketball League (WNBA) is still in existence. Start-up leagues in soccer (WUSA, WPS), softball (WPSL) and basketball (ABL) all failed. The Ladies Professional Golf Association (LPGA) illustrates the significant gap between men's and women's professional sports. The LPGA's current television deal with the Golf Channel is reputed to be worth $40 million over 10 years, while the men's tour (PGA) signed a 6-year agreement worth $2.95 billion.

The estimated aggregated value of franchises in the four major leagues in North America is $71.5 billion, more than double their market value in 2000. Over the past decade,

---

*In June 2012, NFL Commissioner Goodell established the ground rules for a franchise's potential move to Los Angeles. While expressing satisfaction with the league's current 32-team roster, the commissioner left the door open for adding one or two expansion teams, indicating the new stadium should be capable of hosting two franchises.

aggregate annual revenues more than doubled to $25 billion in 2012. The NFL is the most profitable of the four largest professional leagues by a substantial margin. In 2012, the average NFL team's net operating income topped $41 million, more than twice as much as teams in the nearest league, Major League Baseball (MLB) at $15 million. The NFL's substantial advantage is attributable largely to the generous television rights fees received annually from its network partners, which guarantee that each team will receive approximately $200 million per season through 2021. Other than the NFL (its teams on average posted net profits of almost 15%), net profit margins for teams across the other major leagues are relatively modest, most falling in a range from 4 to 7%).

A major challenge facing teams in all professional sports leagues is controlling rapidly rising player costs. Player salaries have more than doubled in every league over the past 15 years. Each league has attempted, with varying degrees of success, to implement mechanisms for slowing salary inflation. The most common methods have been to establish a ceiling on the total amount a team can pay its players (salary cap) and/or to impose a tax on high spending teams (luxury tax). Players have fiercely resisted team owners' efforts to curb salaries. As a result, every league has endured at least one protracted labor dispute—either a lockout or strike—over the past decade.

In 2011, the NFL and NBA, followed by the NHL in 2012–13, settled contentious conflicts with their player associations, which brought all three leagues to the brink of cancelling their upcoming seasons. The new bargaining agreements reached between the players and owners resulted in each league strengthening its ability to constrain salary growth. The new NFL agreement reduced players' share of overall league-wide revenues from 50% to 48% and instituted a new rookie compensation system, which dramatically reduces the growth rate of salary paid to untried rookies. Despite the "concessions" made by players, it is anticipated that the fortunes of NFL players will continue to rise, as overall league revenues are projected to more than double from $9.3 billion in 2010 to $20 billion by the end of the decade.

While NBA owners were not successful in imposing a hard salary cap or in eliminating guaranteed contracts, they were able to achieve a significant reduction in the players' share of league revenues (Basketball-Related Income or BRI) from 57% to around 50%. In addition, the new NBA collective bargaining agreement (CBA) triples the luxury tax penalty on teams spending well above the salary tax threshold (61% of BRI) as well as increases the escrow tax imposed on players from 8 to 10%. The new NBA labor agreement places substantially greater constraints on salary inflation than ever before. The current NFL, NBA and NHL collective bargaining agreements are 10-year contracts, ensuring labor stability through the 2020–21 season. MLB players and owners reached an amicable 5-year agreement in late 2011. It appears that for the remainder of this decade all four major leagues should be operating in a relatively stable and peaceful labor environment.

Owners of professional sports teams are provided generous tax shelter benefits. For decades, the Internal Revenue Service (IRS) has allowed team owners to substantially reduce their income tax obligations through a roster depreciation allowance (RDA). The RDA provision is unique in that the tax shelter is extended only to the owners of professional sports teams. Credit for the special provision is attributable to Bill Veeck who, while as the owner of the Cleveland Indians in the 1950s, convinced the IRS that he should be allowed to depreciate the value of his player roster similar to a manufacturer depreciating the wear and tear on machinery over time. Over time, this special depreciation allowance has been extended to the owners of all sports teams. In 2004, the U.S. Congress expanded the special tax benefit granted team owners to what is called the "100/15 rule," which allows owners to "write off" or depreciate the total purchase value of their teams over the first 15 years of ownership. Under the 100/15 rule, an owner who purchases a team for $600 million can claim a depreciation allowance of $40 million per year for the next 15 years. Since the RDA is simply a bookkeeping entry (no actual cash is expended), it allows owners to claim that their teams are losing money when in fact their teams are producing sizeable profits.

The special tax benefits received by owners have contributed to the substantial increase in the value of professional sports teams. Franchise values have skyrocketed over the past several decades. Not surprisingly, the NFL has enjoyed the most impressive growth, at an annual rate of increase of 8.4% from 2000 to 2012. In 2012, the average value of an NFL franchise was $1.1 billion. The value of a sports franchise is determined largely by the team's ability to generate income. Analysts have identified four "key drivers" for determining the value of sport franchises, including: *local market conditions* (e.g., size of population, relative affluence, number of sizeable companies), *league-wide economics* (e.g., size of league's national television broadcast agreement, provisions for league-wide revenue sharing), *individual team's venue economics* (e.g., the revenue-generating capability of the team's venue such as the size of the premium seating inventory) and the *lease agreement*. The latter takes into account that most teams are tenants in the venues in which they play and their claims on venue income streams (e.g., percentage of luxury suite revenues) depend on the terms of the lease agreement. While the value of teams may vary considerably on the basis of the four drivers, with very few exceptions, the owners of sports teams realize substantial returns. The very limited opportunity to own a prestigious major league franchise makes them highly attractive ownership investments.

References

1. Mann, B. (2011, June 8). NHL's "Southern strategy" of moving Canadian teams is a failure. *HuffPost Canada*. Retrieved from http://www.huffingtonpost.ca/bill-mann/nhls-southern-strategy-of_b_872848.html

2. Wahl, G. (2003, December 12). A site to behold. *Sports Illustrated, 99*(12), 66.

3. Minor League Baseball. (2009, March 9). Bargains found at Minor League ballparks. *MiLB.com*. Retrieved from http://www.milb.com/gen/articles/printer_friendly/milb/press/y2009/m03/d09/c521509.jsp

4. Team marketing report. (2009, April). 2009 MLB Fan Cost Index, Chicago, IL.

5. Compiled from examination of "List of Minor League Baseball leagues and teams," provided by *Wikipedia*, http://en.wikipedia.org/wiki/List_of_Minor_League_Baseball_leagues_and_teams

6. Fitzgerald, B. (2000, July 25). Arena football dreams bigger than the field. *San Jose Mercury News*.

7. Jewkes, W. (2010, February 18). Arena Football League: AFL will return this season with 15 teams. *Deseret News*. Retrieved from http://

www.deseretnews.com/article/700010256/Arena
-Football-League-AFL-will-return-this-season-
with-15-teams.html?pg=all

8. Albers, J. (2011, September 24). Profitability
remains on WNBA's to-do list. *Chicago Sun-
Times.* Retrieved from http://www.suntimes
.com/sports/basketball/sky/5761833-419/profi
tability-remains-on-wnbas-to-do-list.html?print
=true

9. Costa B. (2011, July 29). Ratings roundup: Live
poker scores for ESPN; WNBA all-star game
most watched since '07. *Sports Video Group.*
http://sportsvideo.org/main/blog/2011/07/29/
ratings-roundup-live-poker-scores-for-espn-nba
-all-star-game-most-watched-since-07li-nba-all
psve/

10. Evans, S. (2012, November 21). Update 1—
Soccer—New women's soccer league launched
in U.S. *Yahoo! Sports.* Retrieved from http://
sports.yahoo.com

11. Janes, C. (2011, June 9). Pro softball players go
to bat for league. *USA Today.* Retrieved from
http://usatoday30.usatoday.com/sports/2011–0
6–08-Softball-players-choose-npf_n.htm

12. Williams, L. (2000, August 10). LPGA at 50:
Progress but still not parity. *New York Times,*
p. D4.

13. Kelly, B. (2009, February 11). LPGA, Golf
Channel strike 10-year deal. *About.com.* Retrieved from http://golf.about.com/b/2009/02
/11/lpga-golf-channel-strike-10-year-deal.htm

14. Smith, M., & Ourland, J. (2011, January 17–
23). Teeing up PGA Tour TV talks. *SportsBusiness Journal,* p. 1.

15. RCS interviews Christine Brennan. (2012, May
18). *Real Clear Sports.* Retrieved from http://
www.realclearsports.com/lists/christine_brennan
_interview/rcs_interviews_christine_brennan
.html

16. Poole, M. (2000, August 7–13). NASCAR faces
questions, not crisis, as market determines future. *SportsBusiness Journal,* p. 13.

16a. Mickle, T. (2011, June 14). Fox's TV ratings rise
after three-year decline. *SportingNews.* Retrieved
from http://aol.sportingnews.com/nascar/story
/2011–06-14/foxs-tv-ratings-rise-after-three-year
-decline

16b. Cleveland Indians Baseball Company Prospectus. Prepared by McDonald & Company for
IPO stock offering of 4,000,000 shares, May
20, 1998.

17. King, B. (1999, November 15–22). NASCAR
goes prime time. *SportsBusiness Journal,* pp. 1, 11.

18. Larry@IIATMS. (2010, August 30). Secrets and
lies (part 2 of why revenue sharing is dead). *It's
About the Money & The Yankee Analysts.* Retrieved from http://itsaboutthemoney.net/ar
chives/2010/08/30/secrets-and-lies-part-2-of-why
-revenue-sharing-is-dead/

19. Howard, D. (1999). The changing fanscape of
big-league sports. *Journal of Sport Management,
13*(1), 78–91.

20. Jacobsen, D. (2008, July 14). MLB's revenue-
sharing formula. *BNET.* Retrieved from http://
www.bnet.com/article/mlbs-revenue-sharing-for
mula/210897

21. Lackey, P. (2010, December 22). MLB revenue
sharing dips slightly in 2010. *FanHouse.* Retrieved from http://www.aolnews.com/2010/12
/22/mlb-revenue-sharing-down-slightly-in-2010/

22. Brown, M. (2012, December 18). After adjustments, Yankees 2012 luxury tax bill exceeds
$19.3 million. *The Biz of Baseball.* Retrieved
from http://bizofbaseball.com

23. Ozanian, M., Badenhausen, K. & Settimi, C.
(2012, November 28). The business of hockey:
NHL team values. *Forbes.* Retrieved from
forbes.com

24. Keller, T. (2013, January 8). Tony Keller: The
winners and losers in the new NHL deal. *National Post.* http://fullcomment.nationalpost
.com/2013/01/08/tony-keller-the-winners-and
-losers-in-the-new-nhl-deal/

25. Whitford, D. (1993). *Playing hardball: The high-
stakes battle for baseball's new franchises.* New
York, NY: Doubleday.

26. Fort, R. D. (2002). *Sports economics.* Upper Saddle River, NJ: Prentice Hall.

27. Zimbalist, A. (1992). *Baseball and billions.* New
York, NY: Basic Books.

28. Badenhausen, K., Ozanian, M., & Settimi, C.
(2010, August 25). The most valuable NFL
teams. Forbes. Retrieved from http://www
.forbes.com

29. Lombardo, J. (2012, October 22–28). NBA season-ticket sales heat up the box office. *Sports-
Business Journal,* pp. 1, 22.

30. Ozanian, M. (2012, March 21). The business
of baseball 2012. Forbes. Retrieved from http://
www.forbes.com/sites/mikeozanian/2012/03/21
/the-business-of-baseball-2012/

31. Nakashima, R. & Blum, R. (2013, January 28).
Dodgers TV deal: L.A. club inks $7 billion
Time Warner Cable, MLB to determine revenue-
sharing impact. *Huffington Post.* Retrieved from
http://www.huffingtonpost.com/2013/01/28

/dodgers-tv-deal-time-warner-mlb_n_2570677
.html

32. Ziets, M., & Haber, D. (2008). The financial valuation of sports franchises. In B. Humphreys & D. Howard (Eds.), *The business of sports, volume 2: Economic perspectives on sport* (pp. 107–124). Westport, CT: Praeger Publishers.

33. Grinstead, J. (2011, February 21). *2011 revenues from sports venues.* Nashville, TN: Mediaventures

34. Howard, D. (1999). The changing fanscape of big-league sports. *Journal of Sport Management, 13*(1), 78–91.

35. Keating, P. (2002, January 7). Artful dodging. *ESPN The Magazine,* p. 93.

4

Trends in Sport Facility Financing

Investments in professional sport facilities have increased exponentially over the past two decades, and their rate of growth is unprecedented. This chapter commences with an analysis of trends in the number and cost of new stadiums and arenas constructed for franchises in the four major leagues in North America, and of the relative contributions to those projects made by the public sector and by the franchises. This is followed by a discussion of the factors that have contributed to the trend of increasing private sector investments in these facilities in recent decades. The primary sources of momentum undergirding the public sector investment in facilities for professional teams are reviewed and a framework which explains the rationale for public subsidy is presented. The chapter concludes with a review of facility financing trends in the minor leagues and colleges.

THE SPORTS FACILITY BOOM

During the 1990s, the sports industry was a beneficiary of the longest sustained period of economic prosperity in U.S. history. Economic growth provided the necessary condition for unprecedented investment in new sport facilities. Construction spending on new arenas and stadiums for teams in the four major sports leagues exceeded $14 billion (at the value of the dollar in 2013) from 1990 to 1999. During the 1990s, over 160 new major and minor league ballparks, arenas, stadiums and racetracks were built in the U.S. and Canada.[1]

This aggressive growth period ushered in a new generation of sport facilities that were filled with elaborate amenities and seating options designed to create new revenue opportunities: luxury suites, club seats, elaborate concessions, and even bars, restaurants and apartments with a view of the field. These special features were almost nonexistent in the relatively bland, multipurpose facilities built in the 1970s and 1980s. Exhibit 4.1 lists the common features included in a modern, fully loaded, state-of-the-art facility built since 1990. It has been suggested: "These structures are monuments to the centrality of sport in American culture and to how wealth is expressed through sports" (p. 1).[2] In business terms, sports have undergone what is known as "Disneyfication":

Exhibit 4.1

Elements in a "State-of-the-Art" Facility

(1) **Luxury Suites:** The more the merrier—with fifty to seventy-five being the absolute minimum. These suites should also annually generate at least $75,000 to $100,000.

(2) **Preferred or Club Seating:** At least 500 to 2,500 seats that have an additional fee associated with the purchase of these seats. These seats give the team more revenue and the patron additional benefits.

(3) **Stadium Arena Club or Restaurant:** This can offer benefits to either the preferred seat patrons or to the team's whole fan base. Ideally, such facilities should also be accessible on non-game days.

(4) **Novelty Shops:** The old days of mere concession stand selling small trinkets are passé. New facilities must have a number of small shops dedicated to a variety of specialized items. For example, Chicago's United Center has a store called "Fandemonium" which sells everything from T-shirts, to special Harley Davidson motorcycles, to golf carts decorated in the colors of the Chicago Bulls and Blackhawks.

(5) **Hall of Fame:** While these shops do no directly generate revenue, they can make fans "wax nostalgic" which can encourage them to buy vintage caps, jerseys, etc. . . .

(6) **Concession Stands:** The days of the typical cold hot dog and flat beer are also long gone. New facilities must offer a variety of dietary and beverage choices. Vegetarian and foreign cuisine are also requirements of any facility. Some facilities offer special "kids-only" stands which offer mini-servings and special kid items such as peanut butter and jelly sandwiches. Also, there need to be large numbers of points of sale with televisions at each stand, so fans do not miss a single play.

(7) **Auxiliary Developments (Microbreweries, Hotels, Theaters, Etc. . . .):** The hottest trend in sports facilities now is to incorporate either entertainment options designed to lure the fan to the sports complex, even on non-game days. For example, the Sandlot Brewery at Coors Field generates over 1,000 barrels of beer a year while Toronto's Skydome lures numerous patrons to its hotel and Hard Rock Café.

(8) **Automated Teller Machines:** With such a variety of spending options, a state of the art facility will want to give its patrons a number of ways to access their money. It should also go without saying that all stands and stores will accept credit cards as well and every major league sports facility has an ATM on site.

(9) **Wide Concourses for Signage:** Wide Concourses allow for the inclusion of more revenue generators and allow fans to move about freely. Of course, they also allow for the inclusion of another popular revenue generator, signage.

(10) **Restrooms:** With all of these concessions stands, there is a need for restrooms designed to aid in the fans' comfort. Again, the more the merrier as fan comfort is a key concern. Baby changing tables in the women's and men's bathrooms are also a plus. Of course, advertising can be installed here as well.

(11) **Other Signage:** The inclusion of advertising along the outfield walls and base lines is also a requirement. Of course, it should be done in a tasteful manner that does not detract from the game on the field.

(12) **Scoreboard With Replay Capability:** In this "instant replay" conscious world, a large scoreboard that can offer visual replays of highlights from the current game and other games from around the country as necessary. Permanent scoreboard offering out-of-town scores is also a requirement.

(13) **A Large Number of Comfortable Seats:** Depending on the sport, a minimum number of easily accessible, comfortable seats need to be in the facility.

(14) **Adequate On-site Parking:** Such parking should be safe and close to the facility if at all possible. Thus, allowing the team to control these revenues for itself.

(15) **Corporate Name:** All new facilities will have to have a corporate name, and account for such revenues through additional taxpayer dollars, in order to be considered state of the art.

(16) **Administrative Offices:** Finally, a facility should have sufficient office space to allow the team to conduct its day-to-day operations comfortably and economically (i.e., rent free).

Source: Greenburg, M. & Gray, J.T. (1996). *The Stadium Game*. Marquette University Law School: National Sports Law Institute, pp. 17–19.

What is meant by this term is drawn from comments alleged to have been made by Walt Disney when he viewed all the development of hotels, restaurants and other theme parks surrounding Disneyland in Anaheim in California. He declared that if he ever built another theme or amusement park it would be a Disney World sufficiently large enough to capture all of the facilities in which tourists spend money (hotels, restaurants, golf courses, and other parks for additional days of entertainment). Building multiple theme parks and including other tourist amenities such as golf courses, hotels, restaurants and convention centers in the midst of Disney World accomplished this. (p. 222)[2]

The Palace of Auburn Hills, home of the NBA Detroit Pistons, played a pivotal role in the emergence of the modern, fully loaded sports venue. When it became fully operational in 1989, it was the first facility to underwrite all of the venue construction costs from the sale of premium seating. The owner of the Pistons built the Palace for the relatively low cost of $70 million and self-financed the new facility by pre-selling 180 luxury suites and 2,000 club seats. Both the number and quality of these premium seating options were unprecedented. In the late 1980s, most arenas had only a small inventory of suites. Indeed, two other major arenas built at the same time as the Palace, the Charlotte Coliseum and Miami Arena, contained only 12 and 16 luxury suites, respectively. The large inventory of suites and club seats at the Palace generated $18 million in annual revenues. The $13 million derived from luxury-suite sales alone serviced the facility's annual construction debt payments.

In contrast, the NBA Hornets, occupants of the newly constructed Charlotte Coliseum, received just $989,000 in revenues in 1989 from the 12 suites available. Despite having the largest seating capacity in the NBA, with 24,000 seats, the absence of meaningful premium seating made it difficult for the Hornets to remain financially competitive with Detroit and other franchises occupying more luxurious buildings. As early as 1991, analysts declared the Charlotte Coliseum economically obsolete.[3] By 2005, barely 15 years after its opening, the Charlotte Coliseum was closed when the NBA Hornets left Charlotte for New Orleans. In 2007, the building was razed to make way for a new $265-million publicly financed arena which would become the home for the new NBA franchise, the Charlotte Bobcats. This arena, unlike the "old" Coliseum it replaced, was fully loaded with 51 luxury suites and 2,300 club seats.

The success of the Detroit Pistons' arena precipitated what might be called a "Palace Revolution." The Palace was the first to demonstrate the income-generating capability of a fully loaded sports venue. Its success prompted owners across all leagues to seek their own sport "palaces" incorporating the latest technology (fiber optics), a wide array of revenue-generating amenities, and enhancement of more basic service elements such as increased number and improved quality of restrooms. Thus, by the year 2000, the average NBA arena contained 82 suites and 2,152 club seats.[4]

The Palace pioneered the revolution, but subsequent arenas have taken the return on investment capability of facilities to higher levels. The substantial income-generating ability of a contemporary arena is exemplified by the Staples Center. While the Palace at Auburn Hills generates gross revenues of $40 million per year, the $400 million Staples Center, which began operating a decade later, produced more than $120 million in venue-generated revenues during its first year of operation.[5] Home to three major league teams (NBA's Lakers and Clippers; NHL's Kings) as well as the WNBA's Sparks and an arena football league team, the venue is guaranteed at least 156 dates per year from the regular league games alone. Including playoff games and the numerous concert and cultural events the arena hosts annually, the Staples Center typically books approximately 250 events.

The revenue-generating capacity of these new buildings sustained demand for new facility construction from 2000 through 2010 when 41 new or substantially renovated major sports facilities were built in North America. The total capital investment for that decade's generation of venues exceeded $21 billion. Table 4.1 provides a summary of the number and cost of all new arenas and stadiums built for teams in the four major leagues during the past two decades. The total price tag for the 92 buildings is $36.27 billion.

Measurement Challenges

Before analyzing the trends and implications of sport facility development over the past two decades, measurement issues need to be discussed. It has been pointed out that determining the cost of sport facilities is not straightforward. There are a number of "conundrums and pitfalls" (p.235)[6] that make it difficult to accurately assess the true expense of building arenas and stadiums.

The first concern is the huge gap that often exists between initial and final cost estimates. Commonly, the initial pre-construction estimates are significantly lower than the final built-out costs. Cost overruns often exceed the initial publicly announced price by more than 30%. The construction of what is now called Safeco Field, the home of the MLB Seattle Mariners, provides an example of how final costs can far outstrip the original pre-construction estimate. King County officials initially announced that the new downtown ballpark would cost $384.5 million. But once construction commenced, the contractors encountered weather-related, design and engineering problems, all of which put the project months behind schedule. Cost overruns mounted at a staggering rate. Shortly after the facility opened, the Washington State Public Facilities Board issued a report stating the total construction costs reached $534 million ($719 million in 2013 dollars), almost $150 million more than the original publicly announced estimate.

Many cost estimates consider only construction costs, failing to include other major project expenditures.[4] A detailed discussion of these ancillary and often nuanced costs is provided in Chapter 6, but in order to accurately interpret the trend tables in this chapter, a brief overview of some of the cost issues is given here. These additional costs may include the cost, or the opportunity cost, of land; the cost of infrastructure such as enhanced roads, utilities, or parking; and the cost of relocating existing residents or businesses to other sites. The authors cross-referenced a broad spectrum of industry and academic sources to derive total capital investment costs for each facility, including building construction, land and related infrastructure.*

There are other nuances. For example, the decision as to whether to count PSLs and ticket surcharges as public or private contributions is largely an arbitrary one. Thus, to make a public contribution seem smaller, a team and city could mutually agree to a fixed ticket surcharge but could stipulate that ticket buyers would pay this "tax" to the team rather than to the city.[7]

In some cases, the true or full cost of a new sports venue has been uncovered by diligent investigative reporting. Since franchise owners are not required to disclose the amount they invest in development and construction of new facilities, many of the real costs remain hidden. In the case of Reliant Stadium, built in 2002 as the new home of the Houston Texans, the publicly stated cost of the new venue was $367 million. However, a 2004 investigation by the *Houston Chronicle* found that the $367 million figure represented only the amount of bonds issued by the city of Houston. A more detailed breakdown provided by the *Chronicle* found the full construction costs amounted to $500 million. The publicly reported costs omitted a $93 million contribution from the Houston Texans ($50 million from Texas fans purchasing personal seat licenses), $22.5 million in loans from Harris County, a $7.5 million upfront payment from the venue concessionaire, and a nearly $10 million contribution from Rodeo Houston and the Harris County Sports & Convention Corporation. The uncovering of the full development costs brought the final price tag for Reliant Stadium (including an estimated $100 million for the prime development land which was also effectively donated by Harris County and omitted from official numbers) to $600 million, well above the publicly announced figure of $367 million.

The use of public tax-supported subsidies for the new generation of sport venues is controversial. Table 4.1 identifies the amount and proportion of *total public investment* in all sports facilities built for teams in the four major leagues in the last two decades. This enables changes in the relative contribution of public and private funding sources to be identified over this 20-year period.

Tables 4.2 and 4.3 show the amount of public money used to subsidize the development of every facility built from 1990 through 2010, and the proportion of the total cost contributed by the public and private sectors. Given the complexities of public-private development partnerships, (and sometimes the lack of complete transparency), it can be challenging to determine the exact level of contribution. It has been noted: "Details and nuances invariably escape the grasp of even the most careful analysis" (p. 238).[6] As a result, public subsidies for sport facilities are often underestimated because land, infrastructure, operational costs (maintenance, rent) and foregone property taxes are routinely ignored or undervalued.[8] The estimates do not include ongoing public subsidies related to the operation of facilities such as abated property taxes, "sweetheart" lease agreements and the extension of free municipal services such as police, fire

---

*The analysis is limited to capital costs. No attempt is made to include ongoing annual expenses related to maintenance and capital improvements. The focus is strictly on capturing the full cost of developing the facility.

and utilities. While many governments offer generous operational benefits to teams who lease their facilities in the form of free or reduced rent and maintenance expenses, these operational subsidies are highly variable and difficult to estimate. Therefore, the calculations in Tables 4.2 and 4.3 reflect only the amount of government support related to facility *development* costs.

Table 4.1. Total Capital Investment and Public Share of Major League Sport Facilities, 1990–2010 (In Millions, 2013 U.S. dollars)

ALL FACILITIES						
	1990–94	1995–99	1990–99	2000–2004	2005–2010	2000–10
No. Opened	16	35	51	26	15	41
Total Capital Investment	$3,977	$10,454	$14,431	$11,067	$10,774	$21,841
Average Capital Cost	$249	$299	$283	$426	$718	$532
Total Public Investment	$2,785	$5,540	$8,325	$6,615	$5,003	$11,648
Average Public Cost	$174	$158	$163	$254	$336	$284
% Public Contribution	70	53	58	60	47	53
STADIUMS						
	1990–94	1995–99	1990–99	2000–2004	2005–2010	2000–10
No. Opened	7	14	21	18	11	29
Total Capital Investment	$1,986	$4,960	$6,892	$8,856	$9,258	$18,114
Average Capital Cost	$284	$350	$328	$492	$842	$625
Total Public Investment	$1,896	$3,312	$5,208	$5,220	$4,058	$9,278
Average Public Cost	$271	$237	$248	$290	$369	$320
% Public Contribution	96	67	76	59	44	51
ARENAS						
	1990–94	1995–99	1990–99	2000–2004	2005–2010	2000–10
No. Opened	9	21	30	8	4	12
Total Capital Investment	$1,991	$5,548	$7,539	$2,211	$1,516	$3,727
Average Capital Cost	$221	$264	$251	$276	$379	$311
Total Public Investment	$889	$2,228	$3,187	$1,395	$975	$2,370
Average Public Cost	$99	$106	$104	$174	$244	$198
% Public Contribution	45	40	42	63	64	64

Note: Includes capital costs (building, land, infrastructure) and majority facility renovations of over $100 million (Madison Square Garden, Oracle Arena, Everbank Field, 0.co Coliseum, Angel Stadium, Arvest Bank Stadium, Lambeau Field, Soldier Field and Arrowhead Stadium)

Sources: Zimbalist, A. and J. Long (2008). Facility Finance: Measurement, Trends and Analysis, In *The Business of Sport*, Vol. 2 (Eds., B. Humphreys & D. Howard), pp. 235–252; J. Long (2002). Full Count: The Real Cost of Public Funding for Major League Sports Facilities and Why Some Cities Pay More to Play, Ph.D. dissertation, Harvard University; Grinstead J. (2011). *Revenues from Sports Venues, 2011 Pro Edition,* Nashville: Mediaventures; National Sports Law Institute of Marquette University Law School (2011). *Sports Facility Reports, Vol. 12* and numerous media sources, including newspapers, blogs and magazines.

Description of the Trend Tables

Tables 4.1, 4.2 and 4.3 provide a comprehensive inventory of "Big Four" league facilities built between 1990 and 2012. Table 4.1 lists the new arenas and stadiums (including major renovations of over $100 million), and the total and average cost of each new type of facility in five- and ten-year intervals. Tables 4.2 and 4.3 chronologically list stadiums and arenas constructed from 1990 through 2012 in the four major leagues. They show that 107 of the 122 major league teams play in 94 facilities built during that time period. To account for inflation over the past two decades, the original cost figures shown in column 4 have been converted into present-value May 2013 dollars.

The U.S. Bureau of Census identifies a number of organizations that track inflation in specific spheres of the economy and annually develops indexes that adjust for it. The most reputable construction cost index (CCI) is produced by *Engineering News Record*, a trade magazine published by McGraw-Hill. The CCI is a national average that is shown in column 5. It was used to convert the original costs in column 4 to May 2013 dollars. Thus, the present-value figures in column 6 allow for meaningful trend comparisons because all costs have been adjusted for inflation over the 24-year period. For example, the Target Center, which was built in 1990 for $125 million, would have cost $185.1 million to construct in 2013 due to the increased cost of construction materials and labor.

Column 7 reports the dollar amount with which each facility was subsidized by public resources. Column 8 shows the value of the public contribution in May 2013 dollars, taking into account inflation over the past two decades. Columns 9 and 10 show the proportion of each facility's cost that was contributed by the public and private sectors.

Examination of Table 4.1 reveals that facility costs increased dramatically from 1990 to 2010. The average cost of developing new arenas and stadiums almost tripled, from $249 million in the early 1990s to $718 million in the 2005–2010 period. While most of this cost is attributable to the new luxury features demanded by the teams, it also reflects a shift toward in-town, more expensive locations. In earlier years, owners had pushed for sites close to major highways with room for extensive surface parking. However, in more recent years central cities have seen these facilities become the focus of their downtown growth strategies and insisted on downtown locations.[9]

The extraordinary cost increases are most evident in new stadiums. In 2009 and 2010, several new stadium projects were completed for which total development costs exceeded $1 billion. In 2009, both the New York Yankees and Dallas Cowboys opened new facilities that for the very first time exceeded the billion dollar threshold. The "New" Yankee Stadium, located across the street from the old or former Yankee Stadium, opened in April 2009 at a cost of $1.3 billion. At the time of its opening, it was the most expensive sports facility ever built in North America (at the time, second in the world only to the New Wembley Stadium which opened in London in 2007 with an estimated price tag of $1.5 billion). The Cowboys' new stadium, which opened in May of 2009, cost $1.2 billion. Both stadiums offer unmatched amenity features. The

Table 4.2. Historical and Inflation Adjusted Costs for STADIUMS 1990–2012 (May 2013 Prices)

Current Name Of Facility	Tenant(s)	Year Opened	Original Develop. Cost (millions $)
Tropicana Field	Tampa Bay Rays (MLB)	1990	$138.0
Cellular Field	Chicago White Sox (MLB)	1991	$167.0
Georgia Dome	Atlanta Falcons (NFL)	1992	$214.0
Camden Yards	Baltimore Orioles (MLB)	1992	$171.5
Alamo Dome	San Antonio Spurs (NBA) 1993–2002	1993	$195.0
Rangers Park	Texas Rangers (MLB)	1994	$191.0
Progressive Field	Cleveland Indians (MLB)	1994	$282.0
Coors Field	Colorado Rockies (MLB)	1995	$215.0
EverBank Field[a]	Jacksonville Jaguars (NFL)	1995	$130.0
Edward Jones Dome	St. Louis Rams (NFL)	1995	$280.0
Bank of America Stadium	Carolina Panthers (NFL)	1996	$248.0
O.co Coliseum[b]	Oakland Raiders (NFL)/A's (MLB)	1997	$197.0
FedEx Field	Washington Redskins (NFL)	1997	$251.0
Turner Field	Atlanta Braves (MLB)	1997	$248.0
MT&T Bank Stadium	Baltimore Ravens (NFL)	1998	$223.0
Chase Field	Arizona Diamondbacks (MLB)	1998	$354.0
Raymond James Stadium	Tampa Bay Buccaneers (NFL)	1998	$169.0
Angel Stadium of Anaheim[c]	Los Angeles Angels (MLB)	1998	$121.0
LP Field	Tennessee Titans (NFL)	1999	$272.0
Cleveland Browns Stadium	Cleveland Browns (NFL)	1999	$314.0
Safeco Field	Seattle Mariners (MLB)	1999	$534.0
Comerica Park	Detroit Tigers (MLB)	2000	$361.0
Minute Maid Park	Houston Astros (MLB)	2000	$266.0
AT&T Park	San Francisco Giants (MLB)	2000	$330.0
Paul Brown Stadium	Cincinnati Bengals (NFL)	2000	$458.0
Sports Authority Field at Mile High	Denver Broncos (NFL)	2001	$364.0
Miller Park	Milwaukee Brewers (MLB)	2001	$394.0
PNC Park	Pittsburgh Pirates (MLB)	2001	$262.0
Heinz Field	Pittsburgh Steelers (NFL)	2001	$281.0
Gillette Stadium	New England Patriots (NFL)	2002	$355.0
CenturyLink Field	Seattle Seahawks (NFL)	2002	$360.0
Ford Field	Detroit Lions (NFL)	2002	$430.0
Reliant Stadium	Houston Texans (NFL)	2002	$367.0
Great American Ballpark	Cincinnati Reds (MLB)	2003	$334.0
Lincoln Financial Field	Philadelphia Eagles (NFL)	2003	$512.0
Soldier Field[d]	Chicago Bears (NFL)	2003	$587.0
Lambeau Field[e]	Green Bay Packers (NFL)	2003	$295.0
Citizens Bank Park	Philadelphia Phillies (MLB)	2004	$346.0
Petco Park[f]	San Diego Padres (MLB)	2004	$457.0
Busch Stadium	St. Louis Cardinals (MLB)	2006	$365.0
University of Phoenix Stadium	Arizona Cardinals (NFL)	2006	$455.0
Nationals Park	Washington Nationals (MLB)	2008	$693.0
Lucas Oil Stadium	Indianapolis Colts (NFL)	2008	$750.0

Table 4.2. Historical and Inflation Adjusted Costs for STADIUMS 1990–2012 (May 2013 Prices)

CC Index	Present Value	Original Public Contrib. (millions $)	Present Value of Public Contrib.	% Public	% Private
4732	$207.4	$138.0	$207.4	100	0
4835	$249.1	$167.0	$249.1	100	0
4985	$315.9	$214.0	$315.9	100	0
4985	$253.2	$162.0	$239.1	95	5
5210	$283.2	$195.0	$283.2	100	0
5408	$273.5	$160.0	$229.1	84	16
5408	$403.7	$260.0	$327.2	92	8
5471	$306.4	$162.0	$230.9	75	25
5471	$185.3	$117.0	$166.7	90	10
5471	$394.6	$280.0	$394.6	100	0
5620	$344.2	$62.0	$86.0	25	75
5826	$273.3	$197.0	$273.3	100	0
5826	$348.3	$70.5	$97.8	28	72
5826	$341.7	$14.0	$27.8	6	94
5920	$307.3	$202.0	$278.3	91	9
5920	$487.8	$253.0	$348.6	71	29
5920	$232.9	$169.0	$232.9	100	0
5920	$166.7	$33.0	$45.9	27	73
6059	$370.8	$220.0	$299.9	81	19
6059	$421.1	$241.0	$328.6	77	23
6059	$718.9	$372.0	$500.8	70	30
6221	$486.0	$115.0	$154.8	32	68
6221	$358.1	$215.0	$289.4	81	19
6221	$444.3	$47.8	$62.2	14	86
6221	$616.6	$408.0	$549.1	89	11
6334	$485.7	$266.0	$354.9	73	27
6334	$525.7	$310.0	$413.7	79	21
6334	$349.6	$239.0	$318.9	91	9
6334	$375.0	$205.0	$273.5	73	27
6538	$466.1	$70.0	$91.9	20	80
6538	$472.7	$300.0	$393.9	83	17
6538	$564.6	$219.0	$287.5	51	49
6538	$481.9	$252.0	$330.9	69	31
6695	$433.0	$280.0	$363.0	84	16
6695	$648.0	$200.0	$259.3	40	60
6695	$761.0	$200.0	$259.3	34	64
6695	$382.5	$169.0	$219.1	57	43
7115	$433.3	$174.0	$217.9	50	50
7115	$572.3	$304.0	$380.7	67	33
7751	$432.7	$45.0	$53.3	13	87
7751	$539.4	$346.0	$410.2	76	24
8309	$780.9	$693.0	$780.9	100	0
8309	$845.1	$620.0	$698.6	83	17

Table 4.2. (cont.) Historical and Inflation Adjusted Costs for STADIUMS 1990–2012 (May 2013 Prices)			
Current Name Of Facility	Tenant(s)	Year Opened	Original Develop. Cost (millions $)
Citi Field	New York Mets (MLB)	2009	$860.0
Yankee Stadium	New York Yankees (MLB)	2009	$1300.0
Arvest Bank Stadium	Kansas City Royals (MLB)	2009	$250.0
Cowboys Stadium	Dallas Cowboys (NFL)	2009	$1200
Target Field	Minnesota Twins (MLB)	2010	$545.0
Arrowhead Stadium[g]	Kansas City Chiefs (NFL)	2010	$375.0
MetLife Stadium	New York Giants (NFL)/Jets (NFL)	2010	$1600.0
Miami Ballpark	Miami Marlins	2012	$525.0
Total Facility Cost			$20,591.5
Average Facility Cost			$403.8

[a] In 1995, $130 million was spent renovating the Jackson Municipal Stadium. Financing was provided through bonds issued by the City repaid from lodging taxes and ticket surcharges. The Jaguars contributed $13 million.
[b] Alameda County and the City of Oakland issued $197 million in bonds to cover the cost of expanding and renovating the Oakland-Alameda Coliseum when the Raiders returned to Oakland for Los Angeles for the 1997 NFL season.
[c] The Angels completed a $117 million renovation of Angel Stadium in 1998. Walt Disney Company committed $89 million and the City of Anaheim contributed $30 million.
[d] The Illinois legislature approved a $587 million renovation of Soldier Field of which $387 was funded by bonds supported by a hotel tax. The Chicago Bears contributed $200 million, $100 million from the NFL's G-3 loan program and $100 million from seat license sales.

New Yankee Stadium contains 60 luxury suites, a martini bar and a steakhouse. The Cowboys' lavish furnishings throughout the new stadium resemble those of a 5-star hotel.

In 2010, the NFL New York Jets and Giants moved into MetLife Stadium, which at the time of occupancy claimed the title of most expensive sport facility ever built at a total cost of $1.6 billion. While other billion-dollar stadiums are currently under construction for the NFL San Francisco 49ers and Minnesota Vikings, it may be some time before the current record stadium expense is surpassed. The construction of lavish new facilities in recent years has raised the average cost of new stadiums to unprecedented levels. As shown in Table 4.1, the average cost of a stadium almost tripled from $284 million in the early 1990s to $842 million in the 2005–2010 period.

While not as dramatic, the average cost of a new arena has climbed substantially, from $221 to $379 million over the 20 year period. The most expensive new arena built to date is the Barclays Center in Brooklyn which is home to the NBA Nets and NHL Islanders (beginning in 2015). The lavish sports and entertainment center contains 101 luxury suites, four bars and lounges and two exclusive clubs. The 2013 present value of the building was $647 million. However, the massive renovation of Madison Square Garden in 2013 set a new threshold for arena investment at an estimated cost of $995 million.

The Evolution of Facility Funding

There is a long tradition in the U.S. of local governments assuming a substantial role in the financing, construction and operation of sport facilities. Some of the nation's most

		Table 4.2. (cont.) Historical and Inflation Adjusted Costs for STADIUMS 1990–2012 (May 2013 Prices)			
CC Index	Present Value	Original Public Contrib. (millions $)	Present Value of Public Contrib.	% Public	% Private
8574	$945.1	$164.0	$180.2	19	81
8574	$1428.7	$220.0	$241.8	17	83
8574	$274.7	$250.0	$274.7	100	0
8574	$1318.8	$325.0	$357.2	27	73
8865	$582.3	$392.0	$418.8	72	28
8865	$400.7	$250.0	$267.1	67	33
8865	$1709.5	$0.0	$0.0	0	100
	$533.3	$525.0	$376.0	70	30
	$25,540.1	$11,337.3	$14,486.9		
	$500.8	$222.3	$284.1	57	43

[e] Brown County voters passed a $295 million referendum to renovate Lambeau Field. The stadium expansion and improvements were paid from a 0.5 county sales tax.

[f] According to most estimates, the final cost of the Petco Project was $456.8 million. The Padres share of stadium development was $153 million. The remaining $303 million came from the City of San Diego ($220 million bond issue), $21 million from the San Diego Unified Port District and $58 million from the City's redevelopment agency.

[g] In 2006, Jackson County voters approved a bond issue to issue $850 million in debt to renovate both Arrowhead and Kauffman Stadiums. The cost of renovating Arrowhead Stadium totaled $375 million, of which the County paid $250 million and the Chiefs $125 million.

iconic stadiums such as the Los Angeles Coliseum (1923) and Chicago's Soldier Field (1929) were built entirely from public funds with the intention of hosting the Olympic Games.[10] There were two major events that spurred widespread public subsidy in the early years of professional sports:

> The Depression and World War II drained the resources of major league baseball, leaving no money to build new stadiums or refurbish aging ballparks. After World War II, private stadium development became more daunting, as urban land prices rose rapidly, large parcels became more difficult to assemble, and land requirements increased because of the need to provide parking.[11]

During the 1950s, cities began to compete for teams by offering them new, publicly financed venues in which to play. Only six new stadiums and arenas were built in the 1950s, all publicly funded, but the pace accelerated thereafter and 25 new facilities opened in the 1960s, 17 of which were publicly funded and owned. In the 1950–1970 period, the number of major league stadiums and arenas increased from 32 to 52, and 60% were publicly owned.[9]

This period may be termed the *Civic Development Era*. It marks the beginning of a period in which the norm was for governments to finance and construct facilities for the franchises. Local governments became landlords of the facilities in which professional sport franchises were primary tenants. The lease specified the annual rent payment the team would pay and the extent to which the two parties would share venue revenues such as those derived from parking and concessions. Facilities built during this era were basic, lacking amenities. This bare bones approach made sense because the

Table 4.3. Historical and Inflation Adjusted Costs for ARENAS 1990–2012 (May 2013 Prices)

Current Name Of Facility	Tenant(s)	Year Opened	Original Develop. Cost (millions $)
Target Center	Minnesota Timberwolves (NBA)	1990	$125.0
Energy Solutions Arena	Utah Jazz (NBA)	1991	$102.6
Madison Square Garden[a]	New York Knicks (NBA)/Rangers (NHL)	1991	$200.0
US Airways Center	Phoenix Suns (NBA)	1992	$90.0
Honda Center	Anaheim Ducks (NHL)	1993	$120.0
HP Pavilion	San Jose Sharks (NHL)	1993	$168.0
Scott Trade Center	St. Louis Blues (NHL)	1994	$171.5
Quicken Loans Arena	Cleveland Cavaliers (NBA)	1994	$183.0
United Center	Chicago Bulls (NBA)/Blackhawks (NBA)	1994	$205.0
Rogers Arena	Vancouver Canucks (NHL)	1995	$144.5[a]
TD Garden	Boston Celtics (NBA)/Bruins (NHL	1995	$160.0
Scotiabank Place	Ottawa Senators (NBA)	1996	$145.0[a]
Bridgestone Arena	Nashville Predators (NBA)	1996	$144.0
HSBC Arena	Buffalo Sabres (NHL)	1996	$127.5
Le Centre Bell	Montreal Canadiens (NHL)	1996	$161.0[a]
Rose Garden	Portland Trailblazers (NBA)	1996	$262.0
Wells Fargo Center	Philadelphia 76ers (NBA)/Flyers (NHL)	1996	$217.5
St. Pete Times Forum	Tampa Bay Lightening (NHL)	1996	$161.8
Oracle Arena[b]	Golden State Warriors (NBA)	1997	$121.0
Verizon Center	Washington Wizards (NBA)/Caps (NHL)	1997	$260.0
Bank Atlantic Center	Florida Panthers (NHL)	1998	$212.0
Air Canada Center	Toronto Raptors (NBA)/Maple Leafs	1999	$208.6[a]
American Airlines Arena	Miami Heat (NBA)	1999	$250.0
Conseco Fieldhouse	Indiana Pacers (NBA)	1999	$183.0
Pepsi Center	Denver Nuggets (NBA)/Avalanche (NHL)	1999	$170.0
Philips Arena	Atlanta Hawks (NBA)	1999	$213.0
RBC Center	Carolina Hurricanes (NHL)	1999	$158.0
New Orleans Arena	New Orleans Pelicans (NBA)	1999	$110.0
MTS Centre	Winnipeg Jets (NHL)	1999	$133.5[a]
Staples Center	L.A. Lakers (NBA), Clippers (NBA)/Kings	1999	$400.0
Nationwide Arena	Columbus Blue Jackets (NHL)	2000	$150.0
Xcel Energy Center	Minnesota Wild (NHL)	2000	$130.0
American Airlines Center	Dallas Mavericks (NBA)/Stars (NHL)	2001	$427.0
AT&T Center	San Antonio Spurs (NBA)	2002	$186.0
Chesapeake Energy Arena	Oklahoma City (NBA)	2002	$89.0
Toyota Center	Houston Rockets (NBA)	2003	$235.0
Jobing.com Arena	Phoenix Coyotes (NHL)	2003	$220.0
Fed Ex Forum	Memphis Grizzlies (NBA)	2004	$250.0
Time Warner Cable Arena	Charlotte Bobcats (NBA)	2005	$265.0
Prudential Center	New Jersey Nets (NBA)/Devils (NHL)	2007	$375.0
Amway Center	Orlando Magic (NBA)	2010	$380.0
Consol Energy Center	Pittsburgh Penguins (NHL)	2010	$321.0
Barclays Center	Brooklyn Nets (NBA)	2012	$637.0
Total Facility Cost			$9,952.5
Average Facility Cost			$226.2

[a]Costs adjusted to reflect U.S.-Canada dollar exchange rates at time of facility opening[a] $200 million in renovations completed in 1991.

Table 4.3. Historical and Inflation Adjusted Costs for ARENAS 1990–2012 (May 2013 Prices)

CC Index	Present Value	Original Public Contrib. (millions $)	Present Value of Public Contrib.	% Public	% Private
4732	$187.8	$75.7	$113.8	60	40
4835	$153.1	$24.6	$37.0	24	76
4835	$298.4	$0.0	$0.0	0	100
4985	$132.9	$35.0	$51.7	39	61
5210	$174.3	$120.0	$174.3	100	0
5210	$244.0	$136.0	$197.5	81	19
5408	$245.5	$34.5	$49.4	20	80
5408	$262.0	$155.0	$221.9	85	15
5408	$293.5	$30.0	$43.0	15	85
5471	$205.9	$144.5	$205.9	100	0
5471	$228.0	$160.0	$228.0	0	100
5620	$204.4	$0.0	$0.0	0	100
5620	$203.0	$144.0	$203.0	100	0
5620	$179.7	$53.7	$75.7	42	58
5620	$226.9	$0.0	$0.0	0	100
5620	$369.3	$35.0	$49.3	13	87
5620	$306.5	$32.0	$45.1	15	85
5620	$228.0	$102.0	$143.8	63	37
5826	$167.9	$24.2	$34.1	20	80
5826	$360.8	$60.0	$83.3	23	77
5920	$292.1	$184.7	$254.5	87	13
6059	$370.5	$0.0	$0.0	0	100
6059	$340.8	$37.0	$50.4	15	85
6059	$249.5	$79.0	$107.7	43	57
6059	$231.8	$8.8	$12.0	5	95
6059	$290.4	$184.0	$250.8	86	14
6059	$215.4	$134.0	$182.7	85	15
6059	$150.0	$110.0	$150.0	100	0
6059	$182.0	$40.5	$55.21	30	70
6059	$554.3	$70.5	$96.1	18	82
6221	$201.9	$0.0	$0.0	0	100
6221	$175.0	$95.0	$127.9	73	27
6334	$569.8	$125.0	$166.8	29	71
6538	$244.2	$146.5	$192.3	79	21
6538	$116.9	$89.0	$116.9	100	0
6695	$304.7	$235.0	$304.7	100	0
6695	$285.2	$180.0	$233.4	82	18
7115	$313.1	$202.0	$253.0	81	18
7446	$322.6	$265.0	$322.6	100	0
7856	$440.4	$210.0	$246.6	56	44
8805	$408.0	$330.0	$354.7	87	13
8805	$345.0	$47.6	$51.2	15	85
9362	$647.3	$231.0	$234.7	36	64
	$12,909.7	$4370.8	$6,716.9		
	$284.4	$99.3	$152.6	44	56

[b]The City of Oakland and Alameda County issued $140 million in bonds to cover the cost of renovating the Oakland arena. The Golden State Warriors guaranteed the bonds and repaid 80% of the debt service and the city and county paid 20% of the debt obligation

public authorities who owned and operated the venues possessed "little drive for profitability."[8] Interest in professional sports in this era was confined primarily to the Northeast and upper Midwest, because that is where most of the franchises were located and there was little widespread television interest.

The trend of local governments assuming primary fiscal and operational control of sport venues reached its zenith in the *Public Subsidy Era*.[12] During this period, which stretched from 1970 to 1984, the popularity of professional sports grew substantially. Growth occurred in the number of franchises, in venue attendance, and in television viewing. The value of franchises increased exponentially. Funding expectations were set by the precedents of the Civic Development Era, so funding was widely perceived to be the exclusive responsibility of public entities primarily using either general obligation bonds or revenue bonds redeemed by some form of sales tax. Eighteen of the twenty-two major sports facilities constructed in this period were 100% funded by governments, and two of the remaining four were over 90% subsidized.[12]

The high level of subsidies that characterized the Public Subsidy era coincided with the most active period of expansion and relocation of professional teams ever to occur in North America, which transformed major league sports teams from a regional phenomenon to a national phenomenon. Before this shift, enacted either through migration or expansion of sport teams to Sunbelt cities, major league teams were almost entirely confined to major cities in the Northeast and upper Midwest. The advent of jet travel and the emergent growth and prosperity of cities in the Sunbelt made it profitable for the leagues to place teams in those enthusiastic and untapped markets.

Representatives of western and southern cities were willing to provide fully subsidized playing facilities as an inducement for teams to relocate or expand. Precipitated by the move in the 1950s of the MLB Braves, Dodgers, and Giants from Boston and New York City to Milwaukee, Los Angeles, and San Francisco, respectively, there was an ongoing emergence of teams in southern and western cities. In almost every instance, local and state governments eager to attract a team provided generous venue arrangements to team owners. Government generosity resulted in public subsidies reaching an all-time high during this period. From 1970 through the mid-1980s, local and state governments contributed 93% of the development costs for major sport venues built in the United States and Canada.[12]

However, government's role in the development of new sports facilities began to change in the mid-1980s. This period from 1985 to 1994 may be termed as the *Transitional Era*.[12] It was a period in which governments assumed a progressively diminishing proportionate role in the financing of major new sport facilities. The leagues were attracting much larger television contracts, so teams' revenues expanded. In addition, two attempts were made to curb governments' ability to convey largesse to the teams. First, the Deficit Reduction Act of 1984 prohibited the use of tax-exempt bonds to finance luxury boxes. Second, the Tax Reform Act of 1986 prohibited the use of tax-exempt bonds to finance sport facilities if more than 10% of a facility's revenues came from a single tenant such as a professional sport team. These two acts are discussed in more detail in Chapter 9.

The intent of these acts was to discourage cities and states from issuing tax-exempt bonds, which had been the traditional source of government financing for professional sport facilities. Historically, tax-exempt interest rates are generally 2% lower than rates for taxable bonds. It was anticipated by the sponsors of these new laws that they would force governments to issue taxable bonds for these purposes and, thus, discourage public-sector financing of facilities for professional teams. An interest rate difference of 2% on $200 million in borrowed capital over 20 years could add $20 million to the overall project cost. It was thought that the increased cost would make it more difficult for government agencies, both fiscally and politically, to assume the entire cost of financing major sport venues.

In some instances this anticipated outcome may have occurred, but for the most part cities found ways to circumvent the act's intention. Many responded by offering more generous leases that required the franchises to pay less than 10% of a facility's debt charges, thus enabling tax-exempt bonds still to be issued. Others responded by making upfront payments for concession rights and lowering their sales revenue from other sources to recompense the share of government entities for some of the increase in debt charges that they absorbed as a result of the act: "Thus, the 1986 act incentivized teams to substitute lower rent (and stadium revenue-sharing) for higher initial contributions to facility capital costs. Other things being equal then, the act would lower the public share in capital costs, but have no impact on the public share in total cost" (p. 246).[6] The result was more complex financing structures.

During this transitional period, the first public-private partnerships, or joint ventures, of government agencies and team owners emerged. These projects were characterized by teams contributing a substantial, albeit minority, share of the venue's development costs. The development of more luxurious, fully loaded venues in the early 1990s demonstrated to governments and their taxpaying electorates that new facilities, especially arenas, had the capability of generating revenues sufficient to pay a considerable share of the construction costs.

Notable public-private partnerships of this period were the Target Center in Minneapolis, the HP Pavilion in San Jose, and the Gund Arena (now Quicken Loans Arena) and Jacobs Field (now Progressive Field) in Cleveland. The shared-cost model became an acceptable development formula for both parties. Government officials who were anxious to find a solution for accommodating a franchise's demand for new facilities found public-private partnerships effective in ameliorating taxpayer resistance to expensive public subsidies. Teams, on the other hand, were willing to make a significant upfront contribution with the expectation they would realize greater financial returns from the incremental income produced by the new, fully loaded facility.

Typically, during this period, the public-private development agreements between teams and local government entities were accompanied by lease agreements that were generous to the franchises, guaranteeing them a majority, if not all, of the revenues from luxury suites, concessions, parking, and sponsor agreements. Although joint ventures became prevalent during the early 1990s, a number of major projects at that time, particularly stadiums, were still completely underwritten with public monies. Both

St. Louis and Baltimore, for example, each anxious to lure NFL teams back to their cities, provided fully subsidized, state-of-the-art facilities to induce teams from Los Angeles and Cleveland, respectively, to relocate to their communities.

The remarkable growth in the popularity of professional sports during this era was accompanied by the desire of corporations to be associated with them. This was manifested in their willingness to pay high prices for luxury boxes and associated amenities: "The corporate customer is relatively price-insensitive, but he demands his creature comforts" (p. 74).[13] By the year 2000, 60% of season tickets in the NBA and NFL were corporate purchases, so corporate support provided impetus for the franchises to transition from basic multipurpose facilities into elaborate single-sport facilities.

The "Fully Loaded (Private-public) Era," which took off in the mid-1990s and continues to be the primary model for sport facility development, has been an era of extraordinary proliferation in which 78 major new or substantially renovated facilities were completed. This represents approximately 67% of the total inventory of major league franchise facilities currently in use. In most cases, facilities from which teams moved were not physically obsolete; rather, they were commercially obsolete. The dominant characteristics of this era were the escalation in facility costs, which accompanied the owners' accelerated demands for elaborate facilities, and the ability of these fully loaded venues to generate substantial revenues. Most of these facilities are financed through private-public partnerships.

In contrast to those facilities constructed during the Transitional Era, partnerships in the Fully Loaded Era between local government entities and teams usually required teams to contribute a substantial portion of the new facility development costs. The increased contributions from franchises reflected the growing unwillingness of taxpayers to wholly fund these projects with tax monies. As shown in Table 4.2, of the 43 stadiums built from 1995 through 2010, 38 (88%) were financed, in part, from team resources. A similar profile is evident for arenas (Table 4.3), with 33 of the 39 (85%) built over the same period receiving some level of financial support, often substantial, from the franchise or franchises occupying the new facility. Indeed, in almost half of these new fully loaded arenas, teams were responsible for contributing over 50% of the total development costs.

While teams' contributing to new facility construction has become the norm, public subsidies have remained the dominant source of new facility development capital. Table 4.1 shows that while the public sector's overall share of sport facility financing diminished substantially over the past two decades from 70% to 43%, in 2011 dollars the average amount per facility invested by government *increased* from $173 million to $300 million.

Because of the accelerating cost of new stadiums and arenas, both governments and teams have found more creative and expedient ways to raise capital to pay for their respective shares of escalating investment costs. Many teams have replicated tactics originally used in the construction of the Palace at Auburn Hills. These owners have pledged a portion of the income generated from the sale of premium seating inventory to cover their share of construction costs. A popular variation has been the sale of personal seat licenses (PSLs) in which fans are required to pay a one-time, upfront fee (often several thousand dollars) for the right to purchase season tickets in the new venue. The primary intent of team owners in applying these methods is to transfer a significant share of their development obligation to the team's most avid fans, rather than committing their own financial resources. Owners have consistently exploited the passion of a team's fans to generate most, if not all, of a franchise's contribution to financing a new venue. All of these income-producing tactics are discussed in Chapter 11.

During the Fully Loaded Era, governments have also shifted their approach to financing their contribution. Since the mid-1990s, they have moved from their traditional reliance on general taxes to an almost complete dependence on selective taxes. (These taxes are discussed in detail in Chapter 9.) Historically, cities and counties funded sports facilities by levying a property or sales tax on all local residents. These taxes are commonly referred to as general taxes because the burden of payment falls on all, or a significant proportion of, taxpayers in a jurisdiction and are therefore politically difficult to enact. Selective taxes include hotel-motel or "bed" taxes, a "jock" tax that taxes professional athletes for the games they play in a particular jurisdiction, a tax on "sin" products such as alcohol and cigarettes, and car rental taxes. In these cases, the burden is borne by a select, relatively small number of taxpayers in a jurisdiction. Bed and car rental taxes have become popular because of a perception that they transfer the burden of payment to out-of-area visitors. For each of these visitors, a tax is imposed as part of their lodging or car rental bill. The monies collected are earmarked to pay all or a portion of the public sector's share for a new arena or stadium. Consequently, selective taxes have become popular with both politicians and voters who are pleased to shift the lion's share of the tax burden to tourist and business visitors.

The prominence of selective tax financing is most evident in the NFL. Of the 20 new or substantially renovated football stadiums that opened between 1995 and 2010, all but 2 were financed primarily from public sources. For 14 of the 18 publicly subsidized stadiums, the main contribution came from selective tax sources, most commonly in the form of hotel-motel or car rental taxes. Overall, since 1995, selective taxes have been used to subsidize the construction of 43 new major arenas and stadiums across the country. Given their popularity, it is likely that a mix of bed, car rental, jock and sin taxes will continue to provide the bases for government support for sport facility development into the foreseeable future.

The trend toward fully loaded facilities elsewhere in the world has been relatively slow because no other nation has governments that provide funds for professional sport teams. Elsewhere, teams are required to raise their own resources to renovate or construct new stadiums. The contrast, for example, between the U.S. leagues and the English soccer leagues is marked. Of the 92 teams in the Premier League (20 teams) and three professional leagues below it (72 teams), 26 have relocated to new stadiums since 1990.[14] The primary stimulus, however, was safety rather than increased commercialization. Following the trampling deaths of 96 Liverpool supporters at a game at Hillsborough Stadium in Sheffield in 1989, all grounds were required to remove their traditional standing room areas and become seat-only stadiums. While such changes were regarded as transformational, facilities remained sparse and minimalistic by U.S. standards.

Only two teams, Manchester United and Arsenal in the Premier League have stadiums that could be considered fully loaded. Manchester United's stadium seats 76,000 and provides 8,500 corporate hospitality seats with accompanying restaurants and other amenities. These seats contribute over one-third of the team's game day revenues. At Arsenal's Highbury Stadium, its home for over 90 years, the season's game day revenues in 2005/2006 were £31 million. In the following season when the team moved to its new home, Emirates Stadium, the executive tier of 6,743 seats alone in the 60,000 seat stadium brought in the same amount and the total game day revenues for the season increased to £75 million.[15]

WHO PAYS AND HOW MUCH?

Tables 4.2 and 4.3 show that when expressed in 2013 dollars, total investment since 1990 in the stadiums and arenas being used by major league teams through 2010 was $36.27 billion—$25.01 billion for stadiums and $11.26 billion for arenas. Of this $36.27 billion, $32.29 billion (89%) was invested between 1995 and 2010.

It was noted earlier that the public sector's *share* of facility costs has declined over the past decades. However, a review of the trends specific to stadiums and arenas reveals a contrast in the relative contribution of public and private resources (Table 4.1). With respect to stadiums, the *proportional share* of public support has diminished dramatically. In the early 1990s, taxpayers paid 96% of the cost of developing new stadiums. By the 2005–2010 period, the portion of government subsidies for stadiums had fallen to an average of 44% of total investment costs. Despite this fall in proportional payment, the *amount of money* continued to increase, reflecting the increased cost of Fully Loaded Era facilities.

Conversely, both the *proportion* and *amount* of public sector subsidies for arenas climbed substantially over the last decade. Indeed, the significant increase in government support represents reversal of the funding pattern evident in the 1990s. During the 1990s, the public's share of arena construction costs marginally declined, but both the share and magnitude of public investment in arenas accelerated rapidly from 2000 through 2010. On average, almost two-thirds of total development costs of the 12 arenas built during this period were provided from public tax resources.

Cost Sharing Trends for Arenas

This increase in the public share of arena development costs over the past decade is surprising. In 1989, the Palace at Auburn Hills demonstrated that arenas financed entirely from private sources could operate profitably. Thus, in the decade of the 1990s the public's share of the costs decreased to 42%. This reflected the arenas' ability to generate substantial income from hosting 200 to 300 events a year. Their versatility allows arena operators to utilize the facility for a wide range of events from family shows to concerts, allowing teams to capture additional revenues. In contrast, stadiums, particularly outdoor, football-only, and baseball-only venues have much more limited capability to host supplementary events due to both size and weather constraints.

This is particularly true when the venue's primary, or anchor, tenant is an NFL football team. Most NFL franchises will play two preseason games and eight regular-season games in their home stadium. In a successful season, a team may play one or two postseason playoff games at home. Thus, the best-case scenario is that an NFL team will occupy its home venue on 12 dates a year. This makes it challenging to produce substantial revenues, even if the football dates are supplemented with occasional concerts. Thus even in the largest stadium, FedEx Field, home of the traditionally well-supported Washington Redskins, a standard 10-game season can accommodate only slightly over 800,000 spectators. The Staples Center, by comparison, from its three primary tenants alone (Lakers, Clippers, Kings) typically hosts over 250 events and attracts over 4 million patrons in a year. Not surprisingly, the Staples Center generates more than three times the number of tickets sold, hot dogs consumed, and cars parked when compared to the most well-attended NFL venue.

On the surface, at least, the more recent trend toward increased taxpayer subsidy for new arenas is counter to reasonable expectation. Given the demonstrated capability of modern arenas built during the Fully Loaded Era to generate robust income streams across hundreds of events on a year-round basis, the need for public subsidies would appear to be questionable. Yet, in only three of the arenas built since 2000 has private financing accounted for a majority of the development costs. Indeed, three of the new arenas built in this period were financed entirely from public resources.

What accounts for this significant shift toward increased public support? A primary explanation is that unlike the 1990s, where ten arenas were developed for joint NBA/NHL team use, eleven of the thirteen arenas built between 2000 and 2012 were occupied by only one major league tenant—seven solo NBA arenas and four solo NHL arenas. The only joint-use facilities were the American Airlines Center in Dallas, which accommodates both the NBA Dallas Mavericks and the NHL Dallas Stars and the Barclays Center in Brooklyn home to both the NBA Nets and NHL Islanders.*

Table 4.3 shows that the difference in proportion of public and private financing in single versus joint tenancy facilities is considerable. On average, for the 10 joint-use arenas built during the 1990s, 71% of the development costs were provided from private sources. In contrast, over that same time period, 20 arenas were built for a single major league tenant, either an NBA or NHL franchise and the average private share for these arenas fell to slightly over 50%. Thus, the fundamental reason for the significant reduction in private investment is that it is much easier to generate revenue from arenas with more than one anchor tenant. With two major rent-paying tenants, and the guarantee of double the number of "lit nights" (no fewer than 82 regular season games for joint NBA-NHL tenancy), private arena operators can generate more revenue. Hence, the public's contribution to the development of joint tenant arenas tends to be much smaller.

---

*The New York Islanders announced in October 2012 their intention to relocate from the suburban Nassau Coliseum to the Barclays Center for the start of the 2015 NHL season.

There are multiple reasons why so many single-team arenas were built in the 2000–2010 period, but at least half of them were built in smaller, so-called second-tier cities, such as Oklahoma City, Memphis, Columbus, San Antonio and Orlando.* Market size limitations with respect to population, number of TV households, and the number of large companies in these communities make it unrealistic for these smaller metropolitan areas to sustain more than one major league franchise. Thus, in each of these cities, arenas were built either to attract a new (first time) team or to retain an existing franchise. Attractive downtown arenas were built in Oklahoma City and Memphis to entice established but financially struggling franchises to relocate to the new fully loaded venues. Oklahoma City lured the NBA Sonics from Seattle, and Memphis the NBA Grizzlies from Vancouver. In each case, the cities offered the franchise owners favorable lease terms and the prospect of monopolizing (e.g., "owning") the local professional sport market. In the case of San Antonio and Orlando, new arenas were built in order to retain popular, well-established NBA franchises seeking more modern, upgraded facilities that would allow the teams to generate more income.

Strong public sentiment existed in all of these communities for subsidizing new arenas to attract or retain a franchise. In Oklahoma City, voters approved a one-cent sales tax by a 62% to 38% margin, committing $117 million to making the city arena NBA-ready as well as to building a separate practice facility. In Orlando, San Antonio and Memphis, selective taxes primarily hotel-motel and car rental taxes, were adopted with little public resistance. In the case of Charlotte, a new $265 million arena was built entirely with public funds without a referendum (an earlier referendum to finance an arena was soundly defeated by voters). Despite organized public opposition, the mayor and city council of Charlotte committed tourist development tax funds to finance the new arena so a new replacement NBA franchise could return to the city.[#]

Cost Sharing Trends for Stadiums

Unlike the trend line for arenas, the public sector's share of development costs for stadiums declined substantially over the same period. The proportionate contribution of private capital to new stadium development increased appreciably from an average of 24% in the 1990s to 49% for all stadiums built from 2000 to 2010. The decline in public share was progressive from 76% in the 1990s, through 59% for stadiums opened between 2000 and 2004, to 44% over the last half of the decade. However, the averages are somewhat deceptive. A close inspection of the 12 new or renovated stadiums built between 2005 and 2012 shows a bipolar distribution. At seven of the venues, tax resources

---

*While there is no precise definition for Second-Tier Cities (STCs), there is a general consensus among urban planners that STCs are cities with populations between 350,000 and two million. They are spatially distinct areas, separate and different from sprawling Consolidated Metropolitan Statistical Areas (CMSAs) like New York-New Jersey (21 million) and Dallas-Fort Worth (5.2 million).

[#]In 2002, the Hornets franchise left Charlotte for New Orleans, claiming that without a new arena the team could not remain economically viable. A 2001 referendum for a new downtown arena was defeated by a 57% to 43% margin. Shortly following the departure of the Hornets, the NBA awarded Charlotte the rights to a new NBA expansion franchise. The new owner, Robert Johnson, was successful in negotiating a new arena deal with the City of Charlotte. In 2005, the team played its first game in the new Charlotte Bobcats Arenas (later named the Time Warner Cable Arena).

provided from 67% to 100% of the total development costs, while at the other five buildings public funding from private sources ranged from 0% to 27% of overall costs.

In the case of baseball stadiums, a contributing factor to the increased private share was the revenue sharing plan agreed in baseball's 2002 labor agreement. This required teams to pay an average of forty cents on each new dollar of revenue into a pool to aid lower-revenue teams. The tax was levied on gross revenue, not net, so no deductions were allowed on expenses. However, there was one exception: stadium operations costs, which were defined to include payments on stadium construction bonds.[16]

Nevertheless, it is difficult to suggest a generalizable explanation to the divergent funding profile shown by the data. Each project was different in terms of the extent of public sector participation. In the case of three franchises receiving large public subsidies, the Minnesota Twins (72%), the Arizona Cardinals (76%), the Indianapolis Colts (86%) efforts to secure significant public tax support had been a longstanding in their communities.

The financing of the Twins' new downtown ballpark provides insight into the role and influence of professional sports in local and state politics. The team for almost two decades had lobbied for a new stadium. They struggled through most of the 1990s and were identified as a potential target for "contraction" by the baseball commissioner in 2001. The threat of losing the team galvanized both the state legislature and, the governor to support a new stadium initiative. Ultimately, an agreement was reached between the Twins and Hennepin County by which the team would pay about 30% (approximately $125 million) of the stadium costs, with the remainder accruing from imposition of a county-wide 0.15% sales tax. At the time, Minnesota state law required that a county seeking to impose a sales tax must bring the issue before the voters. However, after Hennepin County Commissioners voted 4–3 to support the sales tax for the new stadium, the state legislature passed a bill suspending the referendum requirement which allowed the County to implement the new sales tax without voter approval. The sales tax was projected to provide a $392 million subsidy for the $545 million stadium, which opened in 2010.

The substantial public subsidies used to finance construction of new stadiums in Indianapolis and in the Phoenix area (Glendale) are derived from a mix of tourism-development taxes in both jurisdictions. Voters in Maricopa County, Arizona, approved (by the small margin of 51.9% for and 48.1% against) the adoption of increases on car rental (3.25%) and hotel-motel (1%) taxes. Voters in Marion County, Indiana, approved a combination of selective taxes, including a lodging, car rental, admission (ticket surcharge) and restaurant tax to provide a significant share of the public's almost $700 million contribution to the cost of Lucas Oil Stadium. The county commissioners in eight other counties surrounding Indianapolis approved a 1% restaurant tax similar to Marion County's to help underwrite the cost of the new downtown stadium (more details on these taxes are provided in Chapter 9).

When the new Nationals Park in Washington, D.C. was considered, there was strong sentiment to bring major league baseball back to the nation's capitol. An earlier franchise owner faced with declining attendance and an aging ballpark, had moved the team from Washington D.C. to Minnesota in 1961. Since that time, a number of stadium initiatives had been proposed in Northern Virginia but none could generate sufficient political or financial support. However, in 2004 Major League Baseball entered an agreement with the District of Columbia to relocate the Montreal Expos to Washington D.C., pending the approval of a public financing package that would build a new 41,888 seat ballpark. Led by the mayor, a financing plan was adopted in which the District agreed to finance stadium construction from the collection of in-stadium taxes on tickets, concessions and merchandise. In addition, a new tax was imposed on businesses with gross receipts of $3 million or more per year. While highly controversial, the new publicly-financed stadium opened in 2008 with a brand new franchise, the Washington Nationals, as its anchor tenant.

Often agreements are made on the basis of the "local idiosyncrasies of politicians, the personalities of team owners, the relationship between politicians and team owners, the fiscal situation and real estate market" (p. 248).[6] For example, it has been suggested that had avid Yankee fan Rudi Guiliani remained as New York City mayor, instead of being replaced by the more fiscally conservative Michael Bloomberg, it is highly likely that both the Yankees as well as the Mets would have received significantly greater public subsidies for their new ballparks.[6]

While that may be true, both teams did receive hundreds of millions of dollars in public support from New York City and the state of New York in the form of direct subsidies, tax breaks and infrastructure improvements. Although both the Yankees and Mets assumed primary responsibility for the construction costs of their stadiums, public authorities provided each team with huge tax benefits. According to the city's Budget Office, the city facilitated the Yankees being able to issue $943 million and the Mets $547 million in tax-exempt bonds.[17] In addition, the city exempted both teams from paying property taxes on the facilities. The ability to issue tax-exempt bonds to finance stadium construction substantially reduced their capital borrowing costs, resulting in hundreds of millions of dollars in savings. An estimate provided by the Tax Foundation indicated that the lower borrowing costs would save the Yankees between $231 million and $471 million over the 30-year borrowing period.[17] These substantial indirect subsidies are not reflected in the "Public Contribution" figures shown in Table 4.2 ($180.2 million for the Mets and $241.8 for the Yankees), which account for only direct government contributions to land, construction and infrastructure costs (e.g., the State of New York contribution of $70 million to build parking garages adjacent to the New Yankee Stadium). If these indirect subsidies were taken into account, the full impact of the government's contribution would far exceed the less than 20% shares shown in Table 4.2.

The home of the NFL Jets and Giants, MetLife Stadium, which opened in 2010, is an anomaly. It is the only fully, privately-funded stadium that has been built over the last two decades. The ability of the two teams to essentially self-finance the most expensive sport facility ever built, at $1.6 billion, is a function of several factors. First, the stadium was built in the largest market in the U.S., the headquarters of more Fortune 500 companies than any other city in America. Both teams had large, passionate fan bases. As a result, the teams could afford to build the second largest stadium in the country (seating capacity of 82,556), with an unusually large proportion of expensive premium seating (10,005 club seats, 218 luxury suites). In addition, both teams initiated aggressive personal seat license (PSL) programs, hoping to realize no less than $150 million each from pre-selling the rights to purchase season tickets to their most avid fans.*

In addition to the club's pledge of stadium revenues toward construction costs, the teams received a $300 million loan from the NFL to help finance the construction of the new venue. Shortly after the stadium opened, the teams announced that MetLife, one of the world's largest insurance companies, headquartered in New York City, had signed the richest naming rights deal in NFL history, worth $400 million. The company agreed to pay the teams $17 to $20 million per year over a 25-year period for a total of $400 million for the naming rights to the new stadium. The lucrative corporate support combined with substantial league assistance and the ability to generate robust income from the sale of expensive seating inventory in the new venue, allowed the ownerships of the Jets and Giants to wholly self-finance their new building.

FACTORS CONTRIBUTING TO INCREASED TEAM/OWNER INVESTMENT IN MAJOR LEAGUE FACILITIES

The review of facility financing trends indicated that, overall, the public sector continues to pay the greatest share of facility development costs. However, with the construction of the progressively more extravagant venues built over the last decade the financial contributions from *both* the public and private sectors have increased. Despite the continued prominent role of government subsidies in sport facility development, it seems likely that teams and owners will be expected to pay a substantial, and, in many cases, majority share of the costs of new venues in the years ahead.

The two examples in Exhibit 4.2 illustrate the pattern evident in new stadium construction financing in the most recent era, where the relative share of public support fell substantially. While teams still seek substantial public subsidies, the reality is that most major league franchise operators are required to pay an increasing share of the development costs. As the costs of new stadiums climb, teams and their owners are contributing significantly more. The illustration in Exhibit 4.3 suggests that this pattern is true for arenas as well.

A number of factors account for the shift towards franchise owners paying a greater proportion of facility costs. A primary impetus that has been recognized throughout the chapter has been the enhanced revenue streams accruing to the franchises from the sale of luxury suites, premium seating, seat licenses, concessions and corporate sponsorships. In addition, over the past decade, franchises have received substantially increased annual revenues from broadcast rights, merchandising, licensing, and gate receipts. These exponentially increased revenue streams have resulted in a widespread perception that franchises have the financial capacity to make substantial investments in the facilities they use.

---

*The Jets' actual sale of PSLs fell far short of projections. The specifics of both the Jets and Giants PSL programs are covered in detail in Chapter 11).

Exhibit 4.2

A Tale of Two Teams

In 2011, the San Francisco 49ers and the Minnesota Vikings were playing in the two oldest stadiums in the NFL. Since 1971, the 49ers played in Candlestick Park, which was originally built in 1960 for the San Francisco Giants baseball team. In 1982, the Vikings began playing in the Metrodome, the second oldest facility in the NFL. For years, (in the case of the 49ers, decades), both teams had sought new, modern stadiums. Twenty-eight of the 32 teams the 49ers and Vikings were competing against were playing in new or significantly renovated venues that opened during the Fully-Loaded era. This placed both teams at a significant financial disadvantage. *Forbes* ranked the Vikings (#31) and the 49ers (#27) near the bottom in revenues. The Vikings' reported operational revenues in 2011 of $227 million were nearly $50 million less than the league average and $170 million lower than the league-leading Dallas Cowboys which generated $406 million in gross revenues in 2011.[18] Even though the 49ers were playing in a larger venue, the lack of amenities and premium seating options in Candlestick Park placed the team far behind most of its competitors in the NFL.

Both teams' efforts to build a new facility were directed at securing substantial public funding. In 1997, San Francisco voters approved $100 million in city spending to build a new stadium. While hoping for greater public financial assistance, the team realized that the $100 million subsidy was as far as the residents of San Francisco were willing to go in helping to build a new stadium. After several years of contentious negotiations, the team and city were unable to reach an agreement on both an appropriate site and a financing plan.

In 2006, 49er ownership announced they were shifting their efforts to build a new stadium to Santa Clara, an affluent community located in Silicon Valley, 40 miles south of San Francisco. Two years of negotiations produced an agreement to build a 68,500-seat stadium adjacent to the Great America theme park. In 2010, Santa Clara residents approved, by a 58% to 42% margin, a proposal to approve the construction of new stadium. However, while authorizing the 49ers and the city to raise $937 million for stadium construction, the ballot measure specified that no city general funds and no new taxes could be used for the project. The city council established an independent authority, the Santa Clara Stadium Authority (on which all council members served), to serve as the city's agent in working with the 49ers to arrange financing for the new stadium. In 2011, the Stadium Authority agreed to borrow $850 million from Goldman Sachs, Bank of America and U.S. Bank. The construction loan agreement specifies that the 49ers will be largely responsible for repayment over a 25 year period, with income derived from a combination of a sur-charge on ticket sales, annual rent payments and the sale of naming rights. The team agreed to pay $30 million annually in rent for use of the stadium. The city agreed to contribute approximately $130 million from existing reserves and the pledge of existing hotel tax revenues. In February 2010, the NFL owners approved a loan to the 49ers of $200 million to be applied solely to their share of construction costs. The loan is from the league's new G-4 program which was adopted shortly after the new CBA was approved. The team will be responsible for approximately 87% of the total development costs. It is projected that the 49ers' financial commitment will exceed $800 million. Early in 2012, the team announced it would implement a seat license program requiring an upfront payment for the right to purchase 9,000 club seats at prices ranging from $20,000 to $80,000 each. The cost of tickets to those 9,000 premium seats is projected to range from $325 to $375 per *game*.

The Minnesota Vikings enjoy widespread fan support throughout the state. One out of every two Minnesotans follows the team each Sunday on either TV, radio or in person. The Vikings averaged a 66–69% TV share over the 2010 and 2011 seasons, meaning that over two-thirds of the televisions turned on were tuned into the game.[19] Despite the widespread support, playing in one the oldest and smallest venues in the NFL severely constrained the team's revenue generating capacity. As a result, the Vikings sought a public-private partnership to build a new stadium with one or more government entities, similar to the deal achieved by the Minnesota Twins. In 2010, the MLB Twins moved into a $545 million downtown ballpark, of which $392 million or 70% of the venue's full development cost was provided by Hennepin County taxpayers in the form of a sales tax.

In March 2012, a preliminary agreement was reached to build a $975 million stadium near the Metrodome. The agreement stipulated a pledge of $427 million from the Vikings, a $398 million commitment from the state and $150 million contribution from the city toward the building's construction. The combined pledge of state and local funds amounts to 56% of the total projected construction costs. While this represents a smaller percentage of overall support than the 70% public contribution received by the Twins, the total pledge of $548 million is greater than the public funds invested in the downtown ballpark. While the Vikings received considerably more government assistance, their $427 million contribution represents the 5th largest team contribution ever made. The magnitude of the Vikings' financial pledge to stadium construction follows only the San Francisco 49ers, the New York Giants and Jets and the Dallas Cowboys. All of these venues were built since 2009 and, in each case, the team/owner contribution exceeded $500 million.

Sources: Badenhausen, K., Ozanian, M. & Settimi, C. (2011, September 11). The business of football. *Forbes*. Retrieved from http://www.forbes.com/lists/2011/30/nfl-variations-11_land.html; Minnesota facts. New Minnesota Stadium (n.d.). *Vikings.com*. Retrieved from http://www.vikings.com/stadium/new-stadium/facts.html

Exhibit 4.3

Barclays Center Arena

The new 18,000-seat arena was originally conceived to be the "anchor" of a $4.9 billion development, a residential and business complex, called Atlantic Yards in Brooklyn, New York. The project was spearheaded by a real estate developer who owned the New Jersey Nets and planned to move the NBA team into the new arena. However, at the time of its opening in September 2012, the Barclays Center was the only completed building on the Atlantic Yards site. The Great Recession and slow recovery of the economy hampered the project's progress and resulted in the development of a "smaller and simpler" version of the arena than was originally planned.

In 2010, the Nets were sold, but the new owner agreed to move the team into the Barclays Center as the Brooklyn Nets. Even in its scaled-down state, the Barclay's Center is the most expensive arena built in North America. The estimated cost of the new building is $637 million. As shown in Table 4-3, the public sector's contribution of $231 million amounted to about one-third of the arena's overall development costs. Most of the state and city's funding was directed to infrastructure improvements, including streets and mass transit. The team's owner assumed primary responsibility for underwriting the $511 million debt on the new venue. Barclays Bank purchased the naming rights to the arena for a reputed $400 million, over 20 years. In addition, the owner's investment will be supported by the revenues from the 104 luxury suites. The initial offering price for the 9 best suites was $540,000 per season, while the rest of the suites were offered at an average of $264,550.

Source: Brooklyn Nets news update (2011, October 24). *InsideHoops.com*. Retrieved from http://www.insidehoops.com/brooklyn-nets.html

A second contributing factor to enhanced private sector investment in facilities is the progressive trend over the past 25 years requiring the private sector to invest more in all public services and amenities from which they accrue benefits. In 1976, the portion of the gross national product accounted for by government fell for the first time in 50 years. This auspicious trend break marked the beginning of the tax revolt movement.[18] It spread widely and quickly across the United States, so by the end of the millennium only six states were not constrained by some sort of statutorily mandated tax limitation.[19] These statutory provisions were reinforced by the political actions of elected representatives who recognized that aspiration to, and survival in, office depended on them demonstrating frugality to the electorate.

In response to the revised political reality of having reduced tax funds available, governments have engaged in "load shedding" which is designed to shift costs over to the private sector that had previously been absorbed by the public sector. Hence, the shift to the private sector paying a higher proportion of sport facility costs is consistent with the broad movement of government entities tending to adopt this *modus operandi* in all services with which they are involved.

A third factor is assistance given to individual owners by the leagues. In the late 1990s, both the NFL and MLB introduced subsidy programs to assist team contributions to new stadiums. Thus, the NFL provides league grants up to $200 million to this end. MLB uses a complex formula, but it has been estimated, for example, that MLB effectively contributed $280 million to the Yankees new stadium which represented approximately 26% of the team's total investment in it.[6]

Figure 4.1. The Growing Controversy Over Who Pays for New Sports Facilities.
Source: Houston Chronicle, Thursday, August 31, 2000

A fourth factor that has contributed to the shift to more private investment is the increased public contentiousness of the merits associated with subsidizing major league facilities. The cartoon in Figure 4.1 captures the atmosphere that prevailed in Houston when authorization was sought from taxpayers to subsidize a new arena.

The Equity Issue

Invariably, equity concerns are a central element in the contentiousness of public spending on facilities for professional sport teams. Equity is concerned with fairness. When allocating public resources, equity revolves around the question "Who gets what?" or, in normative terms, "Who ought to get what?"

In the context of professional sports, two dimensions of equity emerge. The first dimension is relatively narrow and focused. It relates to who wins and who loses among the specific demographic groups located in the area where a major new facility is constructed. A city is not a unitary entity that is impacted uniformly by a major public construction project. Such projects have a "tendency to displace groups of citizens located in the poorer sections of cities," either through mandatory relocation or more insidiously by substantial increases in housing and real estate values that may follow public improvements of the area (p. 29).[20] The people most impacted by such displacement typically are those who are least able to organize and finance community resistance to such proposals. Although the context is a mega-event rather than a major sports facility, the findings reported in a study of the potential impacts of the Sydney Olympics on low-income housing illustrate this dimension of the equity issue:

It concluded that previous mega-events often had a detrimental effect on low-income people who are disadvantaged by a localized boom in rent and real estate prices, thereby creating dislocation in extreme cases. The same rise in prices is considered beneficial to homeowners and developers. Past events have also shown that this has led to public and private lower-cost housing developments being pushed out of preferred areas as a result of increased land and construction costs. In the case of the Barcelona Games the market price of old and new housing rose in the six years preceding the Games by 240% and 287%, respectively.[21]

In Australia, past mega-events have led to:

- increased rental fees;
- increased conversion of boarding houses to tourist accommodation;
- accelerating gentrification of certain suburbs near where major events are held; and
- a tendency for low income renters to be forced out of their homes. (p. 174)[21]

The second critical dimension of the equity issue is the financial nexus between who pays for and who benefits from major new facilities. Labor strife in professional sports has been characterized as a battle between "the haves and the have mores," but much of the dispute between the owners and players is over the allocation of "a revenue pool built by the tax dollars of citizens who can only dream of million-dollar salaries" (p. 11).[22] It has been noted that, "While public subsidies in the presence of monopoly should be used to increase supply, in the majority of new professional baseball stadiums, as well as in several new NFL stadiums, subsidies have been used to reduce supply [by making new stadiums smaller than those they replace] and raise prices resulting in windfall profits for teams at public expense" (p. 206).[7]

In essence, the public subsidies transfer income from ordinary people to highly paid owners, executives, and players. It is this perversion of fairness, obvious inequity, and irrationality that is galling to many. The Mayor of Houston opposed providing a publicly provided stadium for the NFL Houston Oilers because he had "this terrific hard time with the idea that the average guys are called on to pay for this out of the taxes on their house, and then can't afford to buy a ticket."[23] Ironically, his successor supported a new stadium after the Oilers left the city, but he used selective rather than general taxes to fund it.

The transferring of money from middle-class and blue-collar workers to an immensely profitable entertainment business offends the sensibilities. One commentator suggested that there should be an adaptation of Winston Churchill's legendary remark after the air battle for Britain, "Never have so many owed so much to so few" to "Never have so few received so much from so many" (p. 70).[24] This transfer is particularly galling given that sports team owners are among the richest men in the world. According to *Forbes* magazine, 16 billionaires hold a primary ownership interest of teams in the NFL, while among all the four major leagues at least 27 owners are billionaires.[25]

Figure 3.1 in Chapter 3 showed that professional sport team owners achieve a remarkable return on their investment. However, a substantial proportion of this return is attributable to the leagues' cartel status and teams' consequent ability to leverage large public subsidies for their businesses. This is illustrated in Exhibit 4.4 and in the following vignette:

MLB, which is a corporation jointly owned by the team owners, bought the Montreal Expos for $240 million in 2002. The franchise had lost public support in Montreal and was losing money. Four years later, the team was sold for $450 million to owners who moved the franchise to Washington D.C. What caused the team to appreciate in value by 87.5% over four years?

Before selling the franchise, MLB required the city to agree to spend $693 million on a new stadium for the team. The MLB team owners shared the $210 million profit from this transaction that was essentially created by a subsidy that was $243 million greater than the purchase price the owners paid for the team! The owners "received a transfer of wealth from the taxpayer just by moving a failing team to a city willing to lavish [much] more than a half billion taxpayer dollars on a new stadium" (p. 65).[25]

Exhibit 4.4

An Illustration of Taxpayers Creating Wealth for Professional Sport Team Owners

In 1989 George W. Bush, whose father was President at the time, borrowed $600,000 to buy a 1.8% share and become general managing partner in the partnership he had assembled to purchase the Texas Rangers MLB team for $86 million. The previous owner was a long-time family friend. Mr. Bush "was the figure head of a Rangers ownership group made up of his father's friends and allies" (p. 41).[31] After the purchase, the partnership gave Bush an extra 10% stake on the grounds that "his name" offered a measure of "celebrity" to the purchase.

Bush promptly threatened to move the Rangers from Arlington if the city failed to build and pay for a new stadium for the team. The new stadium required about 17 acres of land, but the Bush partnership wanted more than 200 acres to develop a whole entertainment zone including hotels and restaurants. When some landowners refused to sell, the partnership persuaded the city to use eminent domain to acquire the land at a price substantially below what it would have yielded in free market transactions. A journalist commented, "Never before had a municipal authority in Texas been given license to seize the property of a private citizen for the benefit of other private citizens" (p. 42).[31]

The city provided the funds and built the stadium. The husband of U.S. Senator Kay Bailey Hutchinson who represented the city's interests in the transaction and was recognized as "the leading authority on Texas municipal bond finance" said the total value of the subsidy was $202.5 million (p. 80).[25] Bush sold his stake in the partnership in 1998. On his tax return, which he made public, he reported a long-term capital gain of almost $16.9 million from the Rangers sale, representing a 2,800% return on his investment. Commentators observed, the owners of the Rangers got the stadium "without putting down a penny of their own money" (p. 43).[31] and "Every dollar that Bush and the other investors pocketed when they sold the team came from the taxpayers" (p. 81).[25]

When Bush announced his plans to run for governor a journalist wrote: "He didn't blush when he proclaimed that his campaign theme would demand self-reliance and personal responsibility rather than dependence on government" (p. 43).[34] In 1998, Bush declared, "It has been a win-win for everyone" (p. 82).[25]

To many ordinary taxpayers, public subsidies seem unnecessary. There is a disconnect between the everyday lives of taxpayers and the economics of professional sports. They are out of kilter. The average player annual salaries on the NBA, NFL, MLB and NHL in 2011–12 were $5.15 million, $1.98 million, $3.34 million and $2.40 million, respectively,[26] while the median household income in the U.S. was $51,413.[27] Players are paid too much. Owners' franchise values and profits are too high. Tickets are unaffordable. Given these factors, the notion that public subsidy is needed seems ludicrous. On the subject of ticket prices one sports writer observed:

> What goes unsaid in the campaigns to get public money approved is the facilities are largely for *new* fans—wealthier individuals and corporations that can afford the seats in these often, ironically, smaller stadiums and arenas. Cheap seats remain at these facilities, but not that many and not as close to the action as they used to be. The net effect is long-time fans and middle-income families are increasingly driven from the games, replaced by corporations that can buy larger blocks of tickets and use them as tax writeoffs.[28]

The irritation of many taxpayers with public subsidy was epitomized by the acronym formulated by opponents to a new stadium for the NFL's Chicago Bears: STINCS (This Stadium Tax Is Nothing but Corporate Subsidy).[29] If public subsidy were not there, then the teams would have to compensate for its unavailability by using more of their revenues to repay the annual facility debt charges. This would leave less money available to remunerate players, owners, and executives whose salaries appear outrageously excessive to ordinary people. Without public subsidies, these individuals would still receive very large salaries, but the obviously inequitable transfer of resources from ordinary taxpayer to multi-millionaire players and owners would cease.

The principle of the inequity described here is not unique to professional sports; rather, it is generic across all types of businesses. In recent years, it has entered the lexicon as *corporate welfare*, which has been defined as

> any action by local, state or federal government that gives a corporation or an entire industry a benefit not offered to others. It can be an outright subsidy, a grant, real estate, a low-interest loan, or a government service. It can also be a tax break—a credit, exemption, deferral or deduction, or a tax rate lower than the one others pay.[30]

All of the subsidy elements cited in this definition have been given to professional sports franchises, but they are only one of many beneficiaries. Nevertheless, "they are the true welfare kings. No industry receives as high a percentage of corporate welfare while keeping its books hidden in shadows" (p. 24).[31] Corporate welfare has a long history in the United States—perhaps starting with the tax abatement Alexander Hamilton received from the state of New Jersey or the major land grants given by the federal government to the railroads.[22] However, public subsidies did not become widespread or egregious until the economic downturn of the late 1970s and 1980s when government entities, desperate to counter unemployment, competed with ever-growing subsidies to persuade companies to remain or to relocate to their communities.[22] It is estimated that a corporate welfare bureaucracy of 11,000 organizations and agencies now exists with access to city halls, statehouses, the Capitol, and the White House.[32] Today, it is unlikely that any business would locate in any community without receiving a package of subsidy elements from the community. Hence, the subsidy question confronting elected officials in the context of sport facilities is also asked of them by all other sections of the private economy. In the concluding comments of an unprecedented four-part series of articles on corporate welfare in which professional sports was never discussed, *Time Magazine* asked

> What's a Mayor to Do? A major employer wants to expand or build anew. Rather than simply doing so, the corporation stirs up a bidding war to see which city and state will pony up the most cash, loans and tax breaks in the form of economic incentives. If you're the mayor and the facility means jobs and income for your town, do you play hardball and risk losing the plan and the jobs? Or do you give in and hand out tax money, only to face a never-ending string of similar demands from others? Right now it's not much of a debate: the mayors cave.[30]

It is ironic that at the same time federal and state legislatures and both political parties have engaged in prolonged debates about ways to reduce welfare payments for individuals, they have substantially increased their contributions to corporate welfare. People who seek public assistance are frequently disdained, but this assistance is lavished on the wealthy owners of professional sport teams. Welfare is perceived to be morally corroding when recipients forego employment for public assistance but, schizophrenically, this corruption is not perceived to extend to professional franchises.

Although it is pervasive in all sections of the private economy, proposals to subsidize sport facilities invariably arouse more passion than corporate welfare offered to other types of businesses. There are two main reasons for this. First, the scale of the largesse is likely to be greater. Instead of $10–20 million for a new manufacturing plant, Table 4.1 shows that the subsidy for a stadium is likely to be $300 million. Second, the newsworthiness of professional sports, the high visibility of the beneficiaries, and their extraordinary levels of remuneration all ensure that a subsidy proposal will receive extensive publicity.

FACTORS CONTRIBUTING TO CONTINUING PUBLIC SUBSIDIES

Although the proportion of private sector investment in major league facilities has consistently increased, the data in Tables 4.1 show that the public sector's contributions are both substantial and increasing. In the 1960s, 1970s, and 1980s, the momentum for investment in major league facilities emanated primarily from two sources. First, the unique cartel-like status of the professional leagues allowed them to collaborate to restrict the supply of teams. This enables franchise owners to threaten to relocate, which provides them with substantial leverage to obtain public investment either from a threatened government entity or from a receptive new host jurisdiction. A second traditional source of momentum has been the community power structure in which those who control "the system" often have a vested interest in new facilities. Third, in the Fully-Loaded Era (post-1994), the shift from the use of general to selective taxes allowed elected officials in local governments to continue to commit significant public monies to new facility construction. The role of each of these sources of momentum is reviewed in the following subsections of the chapter.

Owner Leverage

The baseball, football, basketball, and hockey leagues within which franchises play are unique in that they are exempt from normal antitrust rules that prohibit barriers to competition. The Sherman Antitrust Act of 1890 prohibited restraint of trade and all attempts to monopolize any part of an industry. However, it has generally been judged not to apply to professional sports. Essentially, the courts have viewed leagues as single entities, like McDonald's, with multiple franchise outlets, and the owners have the right to locate their "outlets" (teams) and dictate their terms of trade as they wish. Opponents have failed to make the case that teams should be considered independent business entities and, as such, be required to desist from restraining trade through collaboration. In *North American Soccer League v. NFL*, Supreme Court Justice William Rehnquist observed:

> The NFL owners are joint venturers who produce a product, professional football, which competes with other sports and other forms of entertainment in the entertainment marketplace. Although individual NFL teams compete on the playing field, they rarely compete in the marketplace. . . . The league competes as a unit against other forms of entertainment (p. 37).[33]

The leagues are effectively unregulated cartels and individual teams resemble unregulated local monopolies.[7] A cartel is a group of firms that organize together to control production, sales, and wages within an industry. In addition to controlling the number of franchises, the leagues effectively operate as cartels in three major ways:

1. They restrict inter-team competition for players by controlling the rights of workers (players) through player drafts, contracts, and trades, thereby reducing competitive bidding among teams for player services.
2. They act in concert to admit or deny new teams, and they control the location and relocation of teams.
3. They control the rights to the broadcast of games and create rules that enable teams to exercise control over their local broadcast territories (i.e., the sale of home games not included on the national broadcast package and the right to protect the local listener/viewer market from infringement by broadcasts from other teams in the league).

The leagues have used their cartel-like power to limit expansion. In effect, leagues are able to specify not only how many teams will exist, but also where they will play.[22] Historically, the number of cities seeking franchises has outnumbered the available supply of teams. Major league sports appear to be a culturally unique experience for an influential segment of the U.S. population, in that they cannot be replaced by other forms of entertainment. The imbalance of supply and demand creates a competitive environment that leads cities to escalate their offers of public inducements as they attempt to outbid one another for franchises. It has been noted that "teams manipulate cities by selling them against each other in a scramble for the limited number of major league teams. While the cities fight each other, the teams sit back and wait for the best conditions and terms."[34] If Major League Baseball, for example, had 40 or 50 teams rather than 28, then much of the leverage used to garner public subsidies would be removed.

The leverage potential of owners was first demonstrated and exploited by the shocking decision to move the Dodgers from Brooklyn to Los Angeles that is described in Exhibit 4.5.[35,36] Franchise owners in subsequent decades have consistently demonstrated their readiness to take advantage of this leverage potential. Since 1950, there have been 50 franchise relocations in the four major leagues: MLB, 11; NFL, 9; NBA, 20; and NHL, 10. The moves of the Raiders from Oakland to Los Angeles and the Colts from Baltimore to Indianapolis were illustrative of relocations that occurred despite long histories of sellouts and financial and playing success.[37]

This leverage trend reached its zenith in 1995 when it was estimated that 49 of the 113 major league franchises were considering a move unless they obtained a new arena or stadium or a more favorable deal from the government entity that owned their building.[38] Clearly, this was a factor in explaining the extraordinary proliferation of new facilities that were built between 1995 and 2004.

Expansion of the number of teams in a major league is a careful balancing act. From the owner's perspective, more teams means more competition for star players, which leads to higher salaries; fewer big-draw games played between traditional rivals; a smaller proportion of television revenues; a decrease in the value of their franchise as more become available; and a diminution in the quality of play and, hence, in the entertainment value of the product.[39]

Multiple franchises in a city may offer leverage potential for improvement since whenever a public subsidy concession is made to one franchise, then inevitably it will become an expectation for the others. Thus, when Cleveland developed new facilities for its baseball and basketball franchises but failed to do this for football, the owner of the NFL franchise moved it to Baltimore commenting, "I wanted and was promised equal treatment and it wasn't forthcoming" (p. 257).[23]

Owner leverage also extends to the movement of franchises in the minor leagues, where parent clubs are continually pressuring their minor league affiliates to relocate if another community will provide improved playing facilities, better player accommodations, or more fans in front of whom to play. It is noted later in the chapter that this leverage in baseball was accentuated in 1990 by Attachment 58.

The leverage exerted by franchises stems not only from the fiscal packages offered by other cities, but also from the sunk costs incurred by their current host cities. It has been noted that "[t]he fundamental fact of life concerning stadiums and arenas is that once they are built, they are fixed in place, while the teams that use them are potentially mobile. This puts an enormous bargaining advantage in the hands of teams playing in

Exhibit 4.5

The Dodgers Move From Brooklyn to Los Angeles

No professional sports franchise had been as closely identified with its host city as the Dodgers were with Brooklyn. The club was by a wide margin the most important institution in the borough and for all Americans it symbolized the character, culture, and ethnic diversity of Brooklyn, whose population was outnumbered by only four other cities. "The Dodgers were more than a business. They represented a cultural totem, a tangible symbol of the community and its values" (p. 18).

In the early 1950s the Dodgers were the most profitable franchise in baseball, drawing huge crowds and enjoying the most lucrative media contracts in the sport. The Dodgers were financially more prosperous than any other team in the major leagues, including the New York Yankees, but the team's owner was concerned about the future economic viability of the franchise. He wanted the city to help him replace the deteriorating and undersized 35,000-seat Ebbets Field, one of the smallest in the league. The neighborhood was becoming unsafe and less accessible to Long Island automobile commuters, and the owner wanted a new site in a better neighborhood more accessible to subway lines and with better parking facilities. As more middle-class fans moved to the suburbs, the automobile was becoming the prime mode of transportation to ball games.

Negotiations with the city for a new and more accessible ballpark failed because of the city's multilayered decision-making process, growing public suspicion about the value of public works, conflicting political pressures, and a conviction that the owner would never leave Brooklyn for parts unknown. To the city's chagrin, the owner turned his attention to Los Angeles. By the fall of 1956 the mayor of Los Angeles was urging him to move to the coast and recommending Chavez Ravine, a large, nearly vacant area adjacent to the downtown and near three freeways, as a possible location. The Dodgers' owner saw Los Angeles as a huge unexploited territory ripe for developing, with millions of potential fans living within driving distance and even more possible customers for pay-television broadcasts.

In November 1957 the owner agreed to trade Wrigley Field, the playing field of the minor league L.A. Angels, that he had recently acquired from the Wrigley family to the city in return for a 300-acre site in Chavez Ravine and pledges by the city and county to spend up to $5 million for public improvements, including access roads to the freeways. There was a lot of public opposition to this sweetheart deal because the city land had an estimated commercial value of $18 million, was the only decent-sized vacant public lot near downtown, and was required by law to be used for a public purpose. In many people's minds this meant public housing which was a controversial issue since there was a segment of the community who regarded this as "creeping socialism" aimed at benefiting Mexican Americans.

This was an outstanding business decision for the owner and a great coup for Los Angeles which got a major league team and a tax-generating property, but it was a devastating blow to Brooklyn from which the city never got over. A referendum held to approve the contract got a lot of support from local boosters, Hollywood stars, and the print media, and passed by 24,000 votes out of a record 667,000 ballots. The owner had hoped that the city would further assist him by building a new ballpark, but it refused to, based on the community's traditional hostility to bond issues and the sharp divisions created by the trade of Chavez Ravine.

Source: Adapted from Reiss, S. A. (1989). *City games: The evolution of American urban society and the rise of sports.* Urbana, IL: University of Illinois Press, pp. 236–237.

publicly owned stadiums. Teams can exploit their threat of leaving a city to wring out of the manager of the stadium rental agreements that leave the city pretty much holding the bag" (p. 172).[40]

A possible corollary of this observation is that the larger the equity investment made by franchises in facilities, the less likely they are to relocate. Such facilities are likely to be difficult or impossible to sell, so relocation may mean teams would lose their equity investments in facilities. Hence, the increased share of building costs from franchise funds which is characteristic of recent facility construction may enhance franchise stability in the coming years.

Since 2005, franchise relocation has slowed dramatically. Two main factors have contributed to this. First, all four major leagues currently have 30 to 32 franchises. Most owners believe this is an optimal size. Other than the NFL, which desires to re-establish a franchise in the long vacated Los Angeles market, none of the leagues is considering expansion at the time of writing. Second, by 2000, almost all of the cities in the U.S. and Canada with the population, affluence and corporate support sufficient to sustain a professional sports franchise were already supporting one or more teams.

All three of the most recent relocations—the NHL Atlanta Thashers became the Winnipeg Jets in 2011, the Seattle Sonics became the Oklahoma City Thunder in 2008, and the Montreal Expos became the Washington Nationals in 2005—were the result of failing attendance and apathetic fan support. The prospect of moving a struggling franchise to a new venue under generous lease terms, coupled with the opportunity to take advantage of an excited fan base, were driving factors in each of these relocation decisions.

In the case of the Seattle Supersonics, the threat of the franchise being sold to an owner who planned to move the team to Oklahoma City was not enough to stimulate either the political leadership at any level of government (city, county or state) or prominent business leaders to mount a serious effort to resist the team's impending departure. The lack of a strong response was attributable to two factors. First, in 2008, the significant adverse impacts of the Great Recession had become evident. The willingness to commit substantial public financial support to the team was further eroded by the State of Washington and King County having committed close to a billion dollars in public subsidies to build two new facilities for the MLB Seattle Mariners and the NFL Seattle Seahawks within the past decade. The Sonics played in the smallest arena in the NBA and had lost an estimated $30 million during their last season in the city. When the new ownership moved the team to Oklahoma City, they were given a "sweetheart" lease agreement (nominal rent and access to almost 100% of arena revenues) in a new fully-loaded arena, and the opportunity to "own the market" as the only major league franchise in the State of Oklahoma.

The potential for owners to exercise the kind of leverage they have in the past has diminished greatly. As the cartoon in Figure 4.2 suggests, Los Angeles remains the only major vacant market for the NFL. In recent years, NFL franchise owners in San Diego, Minnesota and Oakland have played the "LA card," either directly stating or implying their intentions to relocate the team to Los Angeles, if they could not reach an acceptable new stadium deal in their current city. In early 2012, the San Diego Chargers

TANK McNAMARA   **BY JEFF MILLAR & BILL HINDS**

Figure 4.2.

announced they would not relocate to Los Angeles for the start of the 2012 season. In a joint statement with the City of San Diego, the Chargers committed to continue "to explore publicly acceptable ways to build a Super Bowl-quality stadium . . . in downtown San Diego."[41] The threat of departure was very real, however, as the Chargers had negotiated an escape clause in their existing lease at Qualcomm Stadium that provided a three-month window every year during which they could negotiate with other cities and relocate without the threat of a lawsuit from the city. Whether the team can use this provision, and the very real prospect of relocating to Los Angeles, as leverage to induce favorable public support for a new stadium, is difficult to predict. After 10 years of trying to find a new stadium solution in San Diego, the prospects for the team relocating to Los Angeles appear high if a new stadium deal in San Diego were not approved by the end of 2013.

The extent to which the threat of relocating to Los Angeles played a role in the Minnesota Vikings ultimately receiving significant public subsidies for their new stadium is impossible to identify, because the improving economy and regional popularity of the team were strong factors in the decision. However, the threat was consistently referenced in media reports relating to the new stadium debate.

The Community Power Structure

Franchises, and the construction of stadiums and arenas that accompany them, tend to be enthusiastically recruited by a community's powerful vested interests, such as banks; real estate developers; elements of the tourism industry like restaurants and hotels; legal firms; insurance companies; construction firms; and potential suppliers of merchandise, equipment and other services and materials. Consider, for example, the role of bond lawyers who are hired by a government entity as consultants to develop the legal documentation associated with issuing bonds. They have been called, "The civic power brokers no one elected" (p. 114).[16] If a major bond issue of the magnitude required to fund a stadium or arena is approved, their fee is likely to exceed $1 million.[16]

Major league sports exemplify the classic interest-group dynamic whereby economic benefits are conferred on a numerically small set of actors, whereas the costs are widely distributed among the general public. Thus, team owners and other proponents are likely to have both the incentive and the resources to invest heavily in a pro-team publicity campaign soliciting public support for a proposed subsidy, whereas opponents are unlikely to have either the incentive or access to similar resources. Professional sports offer a classic illustration of the application of organized-interest perspective, which states that organized interests

> seek special benefits, subsidies, privileges, and protections from the government. The costs of these concentrated benefits are usually dispersed to all taxpayers, none of who individually bears enough added cost to merit spending time, energy, or money to organize a group to oppose the benefit. Thus the interest group system concentrates benefits to the few and disperses costs to the many. The system favors small, well-organized, homogeneous interests that seek the expansion of government activity at the expense of larger, but less well-organized citizen-taxpayers.[10]

The difference in incentive between supporters and opponents of new facilities is explained by the distribution of benefits and costs that accrue from a new facility. Substantial financial benefits accrue to team owners and a select number of others, motivating them to become politically active. In contrast, the cost to ordinary residents is likely to be $25–50 each per year in additional taxes, which may be too small to motivate them to engage in active opposition.[16]

Similarly, the resources available to community elites and owners are likely to be substantial. The actions of the owner of the Seattle Seahawks are illustrative. The owner needed to expedite the placement of a football stadium referendum on the Washington state ballot before his option to buy the Seahawks expired. He offered the state $4.2 million to avoid the time-consuming signature-gathering phase that is usually required to authorize a proposal on the state ballot. The state legislature accepted and agreed to schedule the vote as a special referendum for which the owner agreed to meet the costs. A special election made it likely that all those supporting the stadium would vote, while those who were ambivalent would not bother voting. In a regular general election the advocates would probably have constituted a smaller proportion of the total electorate. The owner then spent a further $5 million in 6 weeks on a public relations campaign to persuade the public to vote positively, which they did.[16] The opposition spent only $160,000.

The vast disparity in campaign support between supporters of new sports facilities and those in opposition is common. While advocacy groups are well funded and have well-established organizations with a meticulously planned campaign strategy, opponents typically are unorganized, inadequately funded, and grassroots in nature. The organizations are usually of an ad hoc nature and often represent a hastily created coalition of social liberals and anti-tax libertarians. Opposition groups typically lack the

Exhibit 4.6

Anatomy of a Stadium Referendum Campaign

The residents of Hamilton County, Ohio, ratified a 0.5% sales tax increase which raised $540 million to build two new stadia in Cincinnati for use by the Bengals football and Reds baseball franchises. Before the referendum campaign launched by the supporters of this proposal, a telephone poll of 750 Cincinnati residents contacted by Louis Harris and Associates for the Cincinnati Enquirer found little support for public financing: Nearly 60% opposed the construction of a new stadium for the Reds and Bengals, with 17% favoring such a project; 17% supported the construction of two new stadia and just 19% supported a tax increase to pay for such projects. Despite this initial lack of support, the prostadia interests were able to launch a campaign which resulted in 61% supporting a tax increase to build two stadia.

The prostadia coalition commissioned an economic impact study that said the construction of two stadia would bring about a one-time economic benefit to the county of $1.13 billion; the annual economic impact of the Reds and Bengals operating in the new stadia would be $296 million; the new stadia would support 6,883 jobs; and about half of the sales tax increase would be paid by non-Hamilton County residents. Those opposing the stadium also released an economic impact study which challenged the validity of these findings.

The principal means by which those pro and con the issue communicated with the public was the media. The difference between the two campaigns' resources was enormous. The pro-tax group had the support of major corporations and businesses, while the anti-tax group had no large underwriter. One side raised small contributions by passing the hat, whereas the other side had the Cincinnati Business Committee assigning four- and five-figure contribution quotas to individual firms. The campaign managers of the prostadia campaign raised more than $1.1 million, whereas the opposition group spent less than $30,000. The pro-tax side received substantial contributions from the Bengals ($300,000), Cincinnati-headquartered Procter & Gamble ($77,000), the Northern Kentucky Chamber of Commerce ($35,000), the Cincinnati Area Board of Realtors ($30,000), and home-based companies Kroger ($23,000), Cincinnati Bell ($16,000), and Cincinnati Gas & Electric ($13,000) whose parent company recently purchased the naming rights (Cinergy Field) of the former Riverfront stadium. The following table gives a breakdown of the 42 major ($5,000 or more) contributors' economic interests. They account for 73% of the funds raised. An examination of contributions between $1,000 and $4,999 identifies another $90,000 from 45 additional contributors with similar interests. (continued)

Economic Interests of Major Contributors ($5,000 or more)		
Category	n	Amount($)
Sports Franchise	1	300,000
Manufacturers	6	108,000
Wholesale and retail	4	73,500
Local economic development	3	70,000
Insurance	5	67,500
Services	6	58,000
Financial services and banking	6	53,000
Real estate	3	40,000
Trade associations	3	25,000
Hotel and restaurant	3	18,000
Miscellaneous business	2	15,000
Total		828,000

Exhibit 4.6 *(Continued)*

Anatomy of a Stadium Referendum Campaign

Those who stood to gain the most from public funding of the sports stadia were prominent in financially supporting the Issue 1 campaign. The Cincinnati Bengals made by far the largest single contribution. Real estate interests with a stake in the development of downtown and riverfront properties, financial institutions that stood to profit by the sale of bonds, and flagship corporations with an interest in protecting the overall business climate of the city as well as their roles as civic leaders were conspicuous in their generosity to the pro-tax campaign. Although the prostadia coalition had many smaller contributors, over 80% of its million dollar campaign was raised from fewer than 100 businesses. After the election, the owner of the *Reds* wrote a $41,000 check to retire the organization's campaign debt.

The prostadia organization also benefited from its association with established local organized institutions such as the Cincinnati Business Community, the Greater Cincinnati Chamber of Commerce, the Northern Kentucky Chamber of Commerce, and the leading spokespersons for City Council and County Commission. With its abundant resources it was able to hire professional campaign management and consulting services. On the other hand, the opposing group was a much more heterogeneous collection of people who operated with the double disadvantage of volunteer leadership and woefully inadequate resources. Their spokesman explained that "without money we could not take advantage of the volunteers" available.

The pro-tax group had all the trappings of a modern campaign for major public office, and the anti-tax group almost none. They had a take-no-prisoners approach to the referendum. Its goal was to "set the terms of the debate, shut them down at every opportunity, marginalize the opposition" while maintaining "complete credibility at all times." The television and radio campaign was impressive in magnitude, as were the major efforts made in direct mail, telephone contact, and yard signs. The campaign benefitted from professional consulting, daily tracking phone polls, and a major "Voter ID/Get-Out-the-Vote" effort.

The telemarketing effort (i.e., voter identification) was one of the most impressive and effective aspects of the prostadia campaign. With a "scope that was unprecedented" for Ohio politics, paid staffers called hundreds of thousands of registered primary voters to determine their stance on Issue I. "Pro" voters received an offer of a yard sign and a chance to volunteer. "Neutral" voters were probed as to what would move them. These undecided voters received follow-up informational mail and an extensive phone call by volunteers about their reservations in the closing weeks of the campaign.

The labor force to make the thousands of follow-up calls, to erect an estimated 10,000 yard signs, and to mount the election day push came from hundreds of young sports fans who were there from the beginning of the campaign. Many had been solicited from Bengals' season ticket holders and were regarded as the campaign's most important resource.

The pro campaign was also fueled by the cheerleading boosterism of the local media, including sports talk radio. The leading opposition spokesman complained that the media was not evenhanded, especially in the final weeks of the campaign. He called the one-sidedness of local radio superstation WLW ("The Big One" and "The Home of the Reds/Bengals") "shameless."

Despite heavy rain on election day, a record 49.5% of eligible voters participated in the election and the issue passed easily with 61% approval.

Source: Brown, C. & Paul, D.M. (1999). Local organized interests and the 1996 Cincinnati sports stadia tax referendum. *Journal of Sports and Social Issues, 23*(2), 218–237.

organization and focus of the proponents.[42] A review of 40 referendums for professional sport facilities revealed that advocates outspent opponents by an average of 73 to 1.[43]

Exhibit 4.6 describes how the community power structure in Hamilton County, Ohio, was able to move from having only 19% of voters support a tax increase to pay for new facilities for the Cincinnati Bengals (NFL) and Reds (MLB) to winning a referendum on the issue with 61% approval.[43]

Elected leaders may be able to reciprocate the support they receive from the business elite and consolidate their own political position through the subtle patronage of key supporters that large scale projects sometimes foster. This latter role was identified by a commentator in Detroit, who after ten years of watching the city's politicians maneuver to build a new baseball stadium concluded:

> The local politicians, particularly the mayor and the county executive, know that they get far more mileage out of having a big new project than out of a renovation. They have the ability to say who gets the contracts, whose land is used, which developers are employed, which bond attorneys do it—and all of those people are the people who contribute to their war chests. That is why expensive projects like new stadiums win out over small-scale ones. . . . Not because they are intrinsically better for the city, or better for the team or anything. There is a political interest in doing it. (p. 104)[16]

Major projects such as shopping malls, business parks, airports, professional sports facilities, and the like are favored by some elected officials because they believe the projects will be perceived as highly visible, tangible evidence confirming that a community is "moving forward." It is anticipated voters will view such projects as bold initiatives that are manifestations of elected officials' leadership ability. Some politicians, especially mayors and governors, have built careers around the development of major sport facilities. Politicians recognize the popularity of professional sports and, regardless of their personal views of the merits of a case, are likely to look for ways to facilitate an association with such projects to enhance their own popularity. Decisions relating to subsidies for sports franchises ultimately are invariably based on a political rather than economic benefit-cost calculus, even though the latter may be the public overt manifestation of the issue. The notion of there being a "political premium" was egregiously exemplified by the pricing of seats at the Washington Nationals' stadium:

> The most expensive seats are not, as one might imagine, the closest to the action on the field. Instead, they are the seats that are in the sight lines of television cameras. Getting on television is valuable to politicians trying to implant a memory of their faces in the same way that shampoo bottles come in distinctive shapes, as visual clues to encourage purchases without thinking. Also, being seen with powerful officials has value for the rich and their lobbyists.[25]

From a political perspective, whether a sports facility performs as projected in the pro forma financial statements often is not of central concern to officials. It is likely to be many years after the project was authorized before any negative financial outcomes emerge, by which time it is likely that those who authorized it are no longer in office. Further, if the financial targets are not met, the community may still have a professional franchise and facility of which it can be proud. In contrast, if public investment in a business park or a shopping mall fails, there are no redeeming community benefits.

In a referendum campaign, paid and free media access are the principal means by which those who are pro and con the issue communicate with the voters.[45] The local media are likely to be strongly supportive of public subsidy for major league facilities because of the added news and sports interest a franchise brings:

> Sports editors and writers freely acknowledge the symbiosis that exists between the news media and pro sports. Newspapers create excitement among fans, who drive up ticket sales. And while pro teams themselves don't create a lot of advertising, a thriving franchise attracts readers to the paper who might not otherwise pick it up. In Seattle, press runs of newspapers the day after a game are increased by anywhere from 10 to 20%, depending on which team played and whether it won or lost. (p. 111)[16]

The impetus for media support may extend beyond this mutual symbiosis. In some cases, media owners may have a vested interest in government investment. An egregious example of this occurred in the 1970s when the publisher of the *Minneapolis Star Tribune* raised $10.5 million to help city officials buy land for the Metrodome and in exchange received the right to develop 200 acres of land surrounding the site. The staff of the *Star Tribute* paid for a full-page advertisement in the newspaper, disassociating themselves from the paper's Metrodome coverage. In recent years, the *Tribune's* owners continued to make donations to the team's lobbying arm that is campaigning for a new stadium. If it is built, the paper's owners are likely to profit greatly from the parking lots that would rise on the property it acquired in the original Metrodome transaction.[16]

There has been one notable exception to local media support and, ironically, it well illustrates the media's power to influence professional sport decisions:

> The potential influence of a less sycophantic media was apparent in Pittsburgh, where the city's 'second' mainstream newspaper (*The Pittsburgh Tribune*) was as critical of publicly financed stadiums as the 'first' paper (*The Pittsburgh Post-Gazette*) was supportive. In addition, the libertarian publisher of this paper, Richard Scaife, owned his own think tank, the Allegheny Institute on Public Policy, which generated scores of position papers critical of publicly financed stadiums. These reports, of course, were picked up and legitimated by the *Tribune* where they had a very important impact on Pittsburgh's new stadium initiative. In fact, in almost unprecedented fashion, stadium advocates were crushed in a referendum seeking to raise local taxes for these two new ballparks and had to completely rethink their strategy (which was ultimately successful). The *Tribune's* hostility certainly contributed to this surprising electoral defeat. Perhaps other referendums in other cities would have unfolded differently had the local media not been economic and political bedfellows of pro-stadium forces (p. 207).[44]

The elite business and political interests in a community who control much of its decision making have a number of incentives to work enthusiastically to invest public funds in a major league facility. This coalition controls "the system," that is, the financial, knowledge, information dissemination, and legal resources needed to bring a major project to fruition. Their control over political decisions enables them to dictate the timing of referendums, evaluate the vehicles that may be used to avoid referendums, the size of the jurisdiction that should fund it (city, region, state), the revision and resubmission of proposals that failed, the nature of the partnership, and a myriad of other details. Their ability to set and control the agenda provides elite interests with an overwhelming advantage.

The actions of the elite are legitimized by fans who want a sports franchise in their community and who are likely to be vociferous in their advocacy. The word "fan" is short for "fanatic." Such people are likely to be sufficiently myopic in their focus that they do not care if the project means their fellow taxpayers, a majority of whom are not fans, will have to pay for it also. The political and economic power of supporters and the difficulty of forming and sustaining organized opposition without resources make it challenging for those who oppose such projects to be heard. Further, although those supporting investment of public funds in a franchise base their arguments on *particular* benefits that they believe will emerge, those opposed are often able to base their case only on the less convincing grounds that *general* benefits will accrue to the city if these resources are allocated elsewhere. Thus, the opposition's case often lacks the focus and conviction that supporters are able to inject into the debate:

> Citizens can make the argument that sports and stadiums are poor development tools and that $200 million can be better spent on education, police, or housing programs; but such arguments often carry little weight, because the results of such spending are undramatic and recipients of the services are unorganized and sometimes even hostile. There is no guarantee that spending the money on education, for example, would markedly improve schools; the money, after all, would not transform the system but would go to the same bureaucracy and neighborhoods, without alleviating the problems of poverty and alienation they are experiencing. Why then, bother to shift the $200 million from the stadium project to the education system? (p. 60)[45]

The influence of the community power structure is apparent in the results achieved. Over the last two decades, 28 of the 35 bond referendums for major league sports facilities were passed (20 of 24 in the '90s and 8 of 11 in the following decade).*

There are two other facets of referenda worth noting. First, a team's goal is to extract from government the maximum amount a majority of voters will approve. Hence, if 65% of voters approve a referendum, then the franchise owners are likely to conclude that they requested too little. If they are successful in receiving the maximum amount of tax funding, then the approval vote should resemble 51% to 49%!

The second facet to note is the bias inherent in the process to ratchet up the quality of facility that is approved. Invariably, advocates specify a facility incorporating elements which make it superior to, and more expensive than, any similar amenity in 2011 were targeted at tourist visitors. Twenty of the referendums were based on tax the coun-

---

*Four facility initiatives that failed to receive a favorable vote were eventually funded without a public vote. And, in each instance, the level of funding was substantially higher than the amount rejected by voters in the earlier referendum. Voters in Charlotte (new arena), Seattle (new ballpark), Pittsburgh (new ballpark and stadium) and Houston (new arena) voted NO on funding facility projects that were later funded through direct state legislative or local government approval.

try. The only options in a referendum available to voters are approval or disapproval. There are likely to be many voters who would prefer to approve a fully loaded facility that was not the biggest and best in the nation and that cost somewhat less. However they do not have that option. Hence, they reluctantly vote for the new 'Taj Mahal' because to vote against it risks losing the franchise.[46]

The Shift From General to Selective Taxes

Beginning in the mid-90s, there was a movement from general to selective taxes. Thus, two-thirds of the sport venue tax initiatives brought to voters between 1995 and 2011 were targeted at tourist visitors. Twenty of the referendums were based on tax monies captured from transient taxes imposed on people staying in hotels or motels and/or renting vehicles in each of the jurisdictions. The popularity of these selective taxes was reinforced by their exceptionally high rate of passage. Only one of the facility proposals based on them was rejected. This politically-palatable approach to providing public subsidies is a primary reason local governments (cities and counties) continue to contribute significantly to the development of new sports facilities.

THE RATIONAL FOR PUBLIC SUBSIDY

Economists have developed a useful framework for examining the rationale for public subsidy. Too often, "the squeaky wheel gets the grease." That is, those who are most powerful, vociferous, and persistent win the case through emotional rhetoric, rather than on rational grounds. In an effort to counter this, the economists' framework classifies all types of goods and services into one of three categories: private, merit, or public. The debate about whether or not there should be public subsidy and, if so, at what level, revolves around the classification of the good or service. The differences among the categories are summarized in Figure 4.3.

If a project exhibits the characteristics of a *private* service, its benefits accrue exclusively to the franchise and spectators at the games. If there are no benefits received by

Type of Good Continuum		
PUBLIC GOOD	MERIT GOOD	PRIVATE GOOD
Who benefits?		
All people	Franchise owners benefit most, but all members of the community benefit somewhat	Franchise owners
Who pays?		
The community	Franchise owners pay partial costs	Franchise owners

Figure 4.3. Differences Between Goods with Public, Merit, and Private Characteristics.

the general community, then it is reasonable to expect the franchise to pay all the costs and there should be no public subsidy. At the other end of the continuum, a *public* service is perceived by a community as contributing health, knowledge, safety, or welfare benefits to all residents in the community. Because all residents benefit, it is equitable that they should all pay through the tax system so public subsidy would be appropriate.

Many projects lie between the pole anchors of the public-private continuum. Such projects are called *merit* services. These are private goods that have been endowed with the public interest, and this appears to represent how most communities currently conceptualize major league sport facilities. That is, part of their benefit is perceived to be received by the franchise owner and spectators at the game, but part is perceived as accruing to the community in general. In this case, it is not reasonable to expect franchise owners to pay all the costs because spillover benefits are received by the whole community. Thus, franchise owners should be subsidized to the extent that benefits to the whole community are perceived to occur.

An important point in understanding this public-merit-private classification is that the decisions as to where a sports facility project should be located along the continuum shown in Figure 4.3 are defined through political processes. Hence, this position may ebb and flow with changes in the cultural mores and values of a community, and it is likely that sport projects will be defined differently in different communities depending on a community's perceptions of the extent of spillover benefits. Franchises typically stress the spillover benefits that will accrue to the community in order to persuade elected officials and taxpayers that their facilities are public goods that should be at least partially paid for through tax revenues. In contrast, the efforts of subsidy opponents are directed to arguing that there are no general community benefits and to shifting perceptions of a project to the private end of the continuum so franchises will have to pay the full cost. The actual point on the continuum at which a particular project is located, and thus the magnitude of public subsidy, will depend on the persuasive power and political strength of the two sides.

The primary argument offered by proponents of subsidy invariably is that major sport facilities produce substantial economic benefits for the community. Hence, it is common practice for the supporters of new venues to procure the services of a nationally known consulting firm to demonstrate the substantial economic benefits that a new sports facility will provide for a community or region. The supporters are often an organized confederation of powerful vested interests (a community's powerful elite who were described earlier in the chapter). They commission the economic impact study either from their own resources or by applying pressure to elected officials to underwrite such a study. The standard operating procedure is for the consulting firm to produce an economic impact study that purports to scientifically document the economic contributions of the project. Typically, the results of their analysis are presented as objective evidence that the economic benefits (jobs, widespread income dissemination, tax revenues, etc.) produced by the new sports venue clearly outweigh the cost of public investment.

Despite a broad consensus that the benefits claimed by economic impact studies are frequently outrageously exaggerated, the vested interests that commissioned the study use the exaggerated figures to create a public impression that the new facility is a good community investment. They again draw on their considerable resources, both monetary and political, to ensure the study's findings receive widespread visibility in the local area. Because of the crucial role of economic impact studies in the public debate of who should pay, Chapter 5 is devoted to an in-depth discussion of how these studies are conducted.

The criticism provided by academics who analyze, research and write about these economic impact studies has resulted in facility advocates emphasizing improved infrastructure and downtown development, and/or social capital accruing to all residents rather than economic impact. These claims are addressed in detail in Chapters 7 and 8.

TRENDS IN THE MINOR LEAGUES

The trend for dramatic investment increases in facilities extends beyond the major leagues to the minor leagues and collegiate facilities. The investment increases have been particularly pronounced in minor league baseball, where 125 new stadiums have opened over the last two decades. Two stimuli have driven these increases. First, there has been a resurgence of interest in the minor leagues. Minor league baseball has led the way. Over the past 20 years, minor league baseball attendance has increased substantially. Fans are attracted by the relatively low prices and the new fan-friendly features of the new stadiums such as playgrounds or grassy areas, basketball or volleyball courts, and videogame rooms, where children can play if they get antsy. During the 1989 season, total attendance at minor league baseball games was approximately 23 million. Two decades later, that number had grown to approximately 50 million, an increase of more than 117% (Table 3.2 in Chapter 3). These attendance increases have spawned an urge for bigger and better stadiums.

A second cause of major new investment was stimulated by Major League Baseball's incorporating Attachment 58 (A-58) to the 1990 Professional Baseball Agreement. A58 specified minor league facility standards and compliance inspection procedures. It listed a comprehensive set of stadium specifications aimed at substantially raising the standards of these amenities, and minor league teams were required to comply with them.[47] Existing stadiums were given until 1995 to meet these standards, which required most existing minor league stadiums to invest in substantial renovations or to rebuild. If teams failed to meet the new standards, then those franchises would lose their major league affiliation and their player development contracts, which are key to the financial success of minor league teams. Effectively, the teams would no longer be viable enterprises in these stadiums.

The A58 specifications had been carefully negotiated between MLB and the minor league franchise owners. The minor league owners accepted them with enthusiasm. Approximately 95% of the 220 minor league baseball teams play in publicly funded stadiums in the United States and Canada.[48] Thus, minor league owners saw this as an opportunity to pressure their host communities to invest in upgrading or replacing stadiums. If communities failed to do so, then the franchise would relocate elsewhere. Hence, most of the investment in minor league stadiums has been by local governments. The impact of A58 on new stadium development was profound. Since 1998,

166 minor league ballparks have been built or substantially renovated, 127 since 1995 and 85 of these since 2000.[49] The consensus among minor league officials is that A58 has, indeed, substantially improved the financial condition of many minor league teams.[47]

For six weeks each spring baseball teams head to Florida or Arizona where they spend two weeks practicing, and the following month they play an exhibition season known as the Grapefruit League in Florida and the Cactus League in Arizona. Municipalities compete to host teams and since stadium leases expire at staggered intervals, each year there are battles to host the teams. This competition has enabled the teams to be gifted elaborate facilities by local governments, without making any contribution to them. The following cases are typical:

- In 2010, Florida's Lee County had a large budget deficit. The county cut millions of dollars from its EMS budget, instituted employee pay cuts and furloughs, and took $75 million from its "rainy day" reserve fund. At the same time the county decided to sell $81 million in bonds to fund a new baseball stadium where the Boston Red Sox would play 18 exhibition games a year. The Red Sox were being courted by other cities even though the existing stadium in Lee County was built in 1992. Indeed, $17.5 million of bonds on that facility remained outstanding. The Red Sox MLB franchise, valued at $870 million contributed nothing to the new stadium.
- The Cleveland Indians trained from 1993 to 2008 at Winter Haven, Florida. The team paid no rent and kept the bulk of revenue from ticket sales, concessions, parking and advertising, while the city paid all the operational costs which amounted to $800,000 annually. Goodyear, Arizona, "stole" the team from Winter Haven by building the Indians a $108 million, 8,000 seat facility, designed by HOK, the premier architect of athletic venues. Winter Haven's sales tax revenue fell by $133,000 the year after the team departed, which was 16% of the cost of operating the stadium. The Winter Haven stadium was demolished and a commercial development built on the site.[50]

Supporters justify such expenditures as investments on economic development that have two dimensions. First is the spending from outside visitors attracted to a community by spring training. In Chapter 5, we suggest that most of this is likely to be illusionary, and the Winter Haven experience appears to confirm this outcome. Second, the publicity the cities receive "can result in businesses investing in the community."[50] Again, in Chapter 8, it is pointed out that this is mostly wishful thinking and aspirational, rather than supported by any empirical evidence.

TREND IN COLLEGES

At the collegiate level, it is more difficult to find aggregate data on investments in stadiums and arenas. Obviously, college teams do not threaten to relocate to new sites, which means that a major stimulus for constructing new facilities is removed. Further, most college stadiums have been renovated and/or expanded rather than rebuilt. However, anecdotal information suggests there has been a marked increase not only in the number of arenas built on college campuses, but also in their scale and the quality of amenities contained within them.

The best student athletes and the best coaches are attracted to institutions that have the best facilities. Because success is so strongly influenced by quality of facilities, as some colleges upgrade others are forced to match them or accept that they will attract only second-tier athletes and coaches. This process has sometimes been called "the 'arms race' of athletic facilities." The "arms race" has been fueled by the substantial increase in funds major colleges have received from football bowl payouts, football television fees, and the billion-dollar television fees for the NCAA Men's Division I basketball tournament. It was further enhanced in the late 1990s by the extraordinary gains in the stock market, which led to an escalation in donations from supporters.

The stadium "arms race" has continued unabated through the first decade of the new millennium. In 2001, at least 43 of the 117 teams playing Division 1-A football were in the process of upgrading facilities. The institutions leading the way in facility improvements, especially stadiums, at the beginning of the 2000s were Ohio State, $350 million (of which $210 million was for the stadium renovation); Penn State, $93.5 million; and Florida, $50 million.[51] Investment in stadium improvements focused on creating new revenue streams. Texas A&M spent $55 million on closing the north end of its football stadium, adding 10,000 seats and skyboxes. The trend toward incorporating more expensive premium seating inventory has accelerated in recent years. In 2010, the University of Michigan invested $226 million to add 83 luxury suites and 3,200 club seats to Michigan Stadium. By the start of the 2011 season, all the suites had been leased for three years from $55,000 to $85,000 per year, and close to 3,000 of the club seats at a cost of $1,500 to $4,000. The gross revenues realized from the addition of this premium seating inventory yield over $13 million per season for the Michigan athletic program. The University of North Carolina spent $70 million in 2011 adding a five-story structure in the east end of its football stadium. The "Blue Zone" contained 20 luxury suites, two amenity-laden club rooms supporting 2,300 premium seats and a separate level with 224 loge seats.

New or substantial stadium renovation projects currently under construction at the time of writing all focus on expensive seating inventory. The $250 million renovation of the University of Washington football stadium is due for completion in 2013. The enhanced facility will include 27 luxury suites, 2,550 south side club seats, 756 Don James Center seats, and 40 patio suites. This new premium inventory will accommodate approximately 4,000 fans, accounting for about 6% of the total seating capacity of 70,000. Fans occupying these seats, while accounting for only 6% of the total attendance, will produce over $12 million per year in incremental revenues. The University of California at Berkeley recently completed major renovation costing $321 million. The renovated stadium will feature three different club rooms each targeted to service 3,000 donors who commit from $40,000 to $225,000 to Cal's Endowment Seating Program (ESP). Fans purchasing these expensive seats have the option of paying for them over a 30-year period. Those purchasing the best and most expensive ESP seats, University Club Seats at $225,000 per seat, would be allowed to pay a 30-year annual fee of $15,421 (under that payment plan the full price comes to $462,630). The university anticipated raising $300 million from their premium seating program over the 30-year period.

Major college sports programs are following the same path as professional franchises. Fully-loaded venues are replacing the traditional, bleacher-only, concrete bowls that dominated the college landscape through the 1980s. New facility construction and expansion is driven by the inclusion of expensive seating and amenity features for which avid fans are expected to underwrite the capital improvements by purchasing the premium inventory.

SUMMARY

During the 1950s and 1960s, the Civic Development Era, professional sport franchises were primarily confined to the Northeast and upper Midwest, and facilities were constructed for them by government entities. Government entities continued to be the almost exclusive provider of facilities in the Public Subsidy Era (1970–1984) when professional sports franchises expanded to reach a national rather than a regional audience. The Transitional (Public-Private Partnership) Era from 1985–1994 was characterized by more complex financing arrangements for facilities to which franchises now contributed and a transition from bland multipurpose facilities into elaborate, fully loaded, single-sport facilities. The Fully Loaded (Private-Public Partnership) Era (post 1994) has been an era of extraordinary proliferation. Currently, over 80% of major league sport teams are playing in venues built during this time. The era has been characterized by a marked escalation in building costs. The capital cost of a stadium built between 2005 and 2010 averaged $842 million, almost three times more than a stadium built during the first half of the 1990s (measured in 2013 dollars). The average cost of an arena increased from an average of $221 million in the early 1990s to $379 million by the late 2000s.

More than $38 billion has been spent on sport facility construction since 1990. Courtesy of stock.xchang

The total investment in the stadiums and arenas completed from 1990 to 2013 exceeded $38 billion.

The public sector's contribution to sport facility development has been considerable. Government subsidies for stadiums and arenas built between 1990 and 2010 totaled $20 billion, accounting for 54% of the total capital investment. While the public's *share* of overall costs has steadily declined over the past two decades, the actual *amount* of public funds committed to new sport facilities has increased. The overall proportion of public support declined from

70% in the early 1990s to 47% in the 2005–2010 period. Over the same time period, however, the *actual* contribution by government entities increased on average from $174 million to $336 million in 2013 dollars. The increase reflects the much higher cost of recent facilities, with the average capital cost of new stadiums and arenas increasing from $249 million to $718 million between the 1990–1994 and 2005–2010 time periods. more than that of venues built during the previous decade.

While state and local governments continue to pay a substantial portion of the cost of new facilities, teams and owners are paying an increasingly larger share of the full costs. The average investment from franchise sources has more than doubled over the last decade from an average of $110 million in the 1990s to more than $250 million for facilities built from 2000 to 2010. Four factors were identified as contributing to the shift towards franchise owners' paying a greater proportion of facility costs. First, the enhanced revenue streams from the sale of luxury suites, premium seating, seat licenses, and corporate sponsorships. As will be shown in Chapter 11, the sale of this expensive inventory can increase stadium revenues by at least $30 million per season, providing teams with the capacity to contribute more to the cost of developing new venues. Second, the general trend over the past 25 years requiring the private sector in all segments of the economy to invest more in all public amenities and services from which they accrue benefits.

A third factor is the assistance given to individual owners by the leagues. The final stimulus for greater private investment reflects the reality that when proposals emerge to commit public resources to constructing facilities for professional sports franchises, such proposals are invariably contentious. The commitment of private sector funds is likely to alleviate some of the contentiousness. Equity is frequently a factor in contentiousness. Equity is concerned with the fairness of transferring income from ordinary people to highly paid players, owners, and executives. Although this type of corporate welfare is pervasive across all sections of the private economy, it arouses especially high passions in this context because of the relatively high subsidies involved and the newsworthiness of professional sports.

Three primary factors account for the substantial contributions made by the public sector. First, owners have leverage to persuade host communities to build new facilities deriving from the leagues' being exempt from normal antitrust rules. This enables the leagues to ensure that demand always exceeds supply, which encourages cities to escalate their offers of public inducements as they attempt to outbid one another for franchises.

Second, the elite business and political interests in a community who control much of the decision making have a vested self-interest to enthusiastically support public subsidies of facilities. This coalition of business leaders, elected officials, and the media controls "the system," that is, the financial, knowledge and legal resources needed to bring a major project to fruition. Third, the ability of elected officials to shift primary responsibility for the public's share on to non-residents has had a profound impact on voter support for expensive sport facilities. Selective taxes, most commonly in the form of hotel-motel and car rental taxes, are targeted at tourist visitors, who cannot vote in local referenda on the question of whether to impose these tourismdevelopment taxes. Consequently, the passage rate for facility financing plans based on selective taxes is extraordinarily high.

The minor leagues have similarly benefited from government investment. In minor league baseball 125 new stadiums have opened in the past two decades and almost all of them were funded primarily by local governments with only minimal investment by the franchises. At the collegiate level, an "arms race" of athletic facilities has occurred with most major colleges investing in large-scale renovations to add the luxury suites and premium seats that are the norm in the professional leagues. These are underwritten by avid fans who purchase the inventory.

Economists classify all types of goods into one of three categories: private, merit, and public goods. The debate about whether or not there should be public subsidy, and if so at what level, revolves around the classification of the good. This offers a useful framework for examining the rationale for public subsidy of a sports facility. To justify such subsidies, a project has to demonstrate there are benefits to the community as a whole, beyond those that accrue to the franchise owner and spectators at the games.

References

1. Howard, D. R. (1999). The changing fanscape for big-league sports: Implications for sport managers. *Journal of Sport Management, 13*(1), 78–91.

2. Rich, W. C. (2000). *The economics and politics of sport facilities.* Westport, CT: Quorum.

3. Simonich, M. (2003, July 18). A pyramid scheme in Memphis: 12-year old arena consigned to oblivion at early age. *Pittsburgh Post-Gazette,* A1, A9.

4. The making of the $213 billion sports business industry. (1999, December 20–26). *SportsBusiness Journal,* 24–25.

5. Noll, R. G., & Zimbalist, A. (1997). Build the stadium—create the jobs! In R. G. Noll & A. Zimbalist (Eds.), *Sports, jobs and taxes* (pp. 1–54). Washington, D.C.: The Brookings Institution.

6. Zimbalist, A., & Long, J. G. (2008). Facility finance: Measurement, trends and analysis. In B. Humphreys & D. R. Howard (Eds.), *The business of sports, Volume 2* (pp. 235–252). Westport, CT: Praeger Publishers.

7. Baade, R. A., & Matheson, V. A. (2006). Have public finance principles been shut out in financing new stadiums for the NFL? *Public Finance and Management, 6*(8), 284–320.

8. Long, J. G. (2002). Full count: The real cost of public funding for major leagues sports facilities, Ph.D. dissertation, Harvard University, Massachusetts.

9. Altshaler, A., & Luberoff, D. (2003). *Mega projects: The changing politics of urban public investment.* Washington D.C.: The Brookings Institution.

10. Siegfried, J., & Zimbalist, A. (2000). The economics of sports facilities and their communities. *Journal of Economic Perspectives, 14*(3), 95–114.

11. Danielson, M.N. (1997). *Home team: Professional sports and the American metropolis.* Princeton, NJ: Princeton University Press.

12. Crompton, J. L., Howard, D. R., & Var, T. (2003). Financing major league facilities: Status, evolution and conflicting forces. *Journal of Sport Management, 17*(2), 156–184.

13. Swift, E. M. (2000, May 15). Hey fans: Sit on it! *Sports Illustrated,* 70–85.

14. Walters, G. (2011). The implementation of a stakeholder management strategy during stadium development: A case study of Arsenal Football Club and the Emirates Stadium. *Managing Leisure, 16,* 49–64.

15. Gibson, O. (2006, March 16). Home improvement funded by corporate cash. *The Guardian.* Retrieved from http://www.guardian.co.uk/football/2006/mar/16/sport.comment1

16. DeMause, N., & Cagan, J. (2008). *Field of schemes: How the great stadium swindle turns public money into private profit.* Lincoln, NE: University of Nebraska Press.

17. Greaves, T., & Henchman, J. (2009, April 6). From the house that Ruth built to the house the IRS built: New York City and New York Yankees abuse PILOTs to finance new stadium. *The Tax Foundation.* Retrieved from http://taxfoundation.org/article/house-ruth-built-house-irs-built

18. Crompton, J. L. (1999). *Financing and acquiring park and recreation resources.* Champaign, IL: Human Kinetics.

19. O'Sullivan, A. (2001) Limits on property taxation: The United States' experience. In W. E. Oates (Ed.), *Property taxation and local government finance* (pp. 177–207). Cambridge, MA: Lincoln Institute of Land Policy.

20. Wilkinson, J. (1994). *The Olympic Games: Past history and present expectations.* Sydney, Australia: NSW Parliamentary Library.

21. Hall, C. M. (2001). Imaging, tourism and sports event fever. In C. Gralton & I. F. Henry (Eds.), *Sport in the city* (pp. 166–184). New York, NY: Routledge.

22. Rosentraub, M. S. (1997). *Major league losers: The real cost of sports and who's paying for it.* New York, NY: Basic Books.

23. Danielson, M. N. (1997). *Home team: Professional sports and the American metropolis.* Princeton, NJ: Princeton University Press.

24. Will, G. E. (1996, January 22). Modell sacks Maryland. *Newsweek,* 70.

25. Johnson, D. C. (2007). *Free lunch.* New York, NY: Longman.

26. Dorish, J. (2011, November 12). Average salaries on the NBA, NFL, MLB and NHL. *Yahoo! Sports.* Retrieved from http://sports.yahoo.com/nba/news?slug=ycn-10423863

27. Davidson, P. (2012, February 9). U.S. median household income up 4% at end of 2011. *USA Today.* Retrieved from http://usatoday30.usatoday.com/money/economy/story/2012–02–09/income-rising/53033322/1

28. Farrey, T. (1998, September 16). New stadiums, new fans. *ESPN.* Retrieved from ESPN.com

29. Baade, R. A., & Sanderson, A. R. (1997a). Bearing down in Chicago: Location, location, location. In R. G. Noll & A. Zimbalist (Eds.), *Sports jobs and taxes* (pp. 324–354). Washington, D.C.: Brookings Institution.

30. Barlett, D. L., & Steele, J. B. (1998a, November 9). Corporate welfare. *Time, 151,* 36–54.

31. Zirin, D. (2010) *Bad sports: How owners are ruining the games we love.* New York, NY: Scribner.

32. Barlett, D. L., & Steele, J. B. (1998b, November 30). Five ways out. *Time, 151,* 66–67.

33. *Professional Sports: The challenges facing the future of the industry,* Committee on the Judiciary United States Senate, 104th Congress, 2nd session, January 23, 1966. J-104-61.

34. Sullivan, N. J. (2001). *The diamond in the Bronx: Yankee stadium and the politics of New York.* New York, NY: Oxford University Press.

35. Reiss, S. A. (2000). Historical perspectives on sports and public policy. In W. C. Rich (Ed.), *The economics and politics of sport facilities* (pp. 13–52). Westport, CT: Quorum.

36. Sullivan, N. J. (1987). *The Dodgers move west.* New York, NY: Oxford University Press.

37. Quirk , J.P. & Fort, R.D. (1999). *Hard ball: The abuse of power in pro sports teams.* Princeton, NJ: Princeton University Press.

38. The holdouts. (1995, July 23). *Dallas Morning News,* Section J, p. 1.

39. Whitford, D. (1993). *Playing handball: The high-stakes battle for baseball's new franchises.* New York, NY: Doubleday.

40. Quirk, J. P., & Fort, R. D. (1992). *Pay dirt: The business of professional team sports.* Princeton, NJ: Princeton University Press.

41. Mayor, Chargers issue statement. (2012, January 9). *San Diego Chargers News.* Retrieved from http://www.chargers.com/news/article-1/Mayor-Chargers-issue-statement/4a3401f9-bdcd-4f68-9f86-8282613877f7

42. Brown, C., & Paul, D. M. (1999). Local organized interests and the 1996 Cincinnati sports stadia tax referendum. *Journal of Sport and Social Issues, 23*(2), 218–237.

43. Brown, C., & Paul, D. M. (2002). The political scorecard of professional sports facility referendums in the United States, 1984–2000. *Journal of Sport & Social Issues, 26*(3), 248–267.

44. Delaney, K. J., & Eckstein, P. (2003). The devil is in the details: Neutralizing critical studies of publicly subsidized stadiums. *Critical Sociology, 29*(2), 189–210.

45. Euchner, C. C. (1993). *Playing the field: Why sports teams move and cities fight to keep them.* Baltimore, MD: The Johns Hopkins University Press.

46. Fort, F. D. (2002). *Sport economics.* Upper Saddle River, NJ: Prentice Hall.

47. Baade, R. A., & Sanderson, A. R. (1997b). Minor league teams and communities. In R. G. Noll & A. Zimbalist (Eds.), *Sports, jobs, and taxes* (pp. 452–493). Washington, D.C.: Brookings Institution.

48. Johnson, A. T. (1993). *Minor league baseball and local economic development.* Urbana, IL: University of Illinois Press.

49. Ballparkdigest.com

50. Holywell, R. (2011, March 21). The economics of baseball's spring training. *Governing.*

51. Menninger, B. (1999, May 3–9). Byproduct of success: Money. *SportsBusiness Journal,* 21 & 30–31.

Section II
Economic Rationales for Public Investments in Sport Venues and Events

5

Principles of Economic Impact Analysis

I n 1776, political economist Adam Smith, who is widely cited as the father of modern economics and capitalism, recognized that a legitimate role of government is to provide

> those public institutions and those public works, which, though they may be in the highest degree advantageous to a great society, are, however, of such a nature, that the profit could never repay the expense to any individual or small number of individuals, and which it therefore cannot be expected that any individual or small number of individuals should erect or maintain. (p. 224)[1]

This undergirds the primary argument for the substantial public subsidization which was illustrated in Chapter 4. That argument invariably focuses on the economic benefits that advocates propose will be generated by public investment in sports facilities or events, but which cannot be captured directly by the public-sector entity that invests in them. It may require the public sector to assist in financing an event or facility and incurring losses associated with it in order to generate benefits to the local economy.

Economic impact refers to the net economic change in the income of host residents that results from spending by visitors from outside the community. There is always likely to be public debate about the merits of investing substantial public dollars into relatively discretionary projects such as major sports facilities and events, and invariably economic impacts will be a central element in the debate. Thus, after an initial explanation of the conceptual rationale for economic analysis, much of this chapter is devoted to explaining the principles upon which the legitimacy and validity of economic impact studies depend.

The goal in this chapter is to provide information that will equip sport managers to better understand, interpret, and possibly undertake, economic impact studies that are done with integrity, and to recognize the fallacies in mischievous studies presented by others. Too many of the studies we have reviewed, especially those commissioned by proponents of new sports facilities and events, produce mischievous numbers that consistently exaggerate the real economic impact, often by a factor of 10 or 15. We demonstrate how this occurs by reviewing common mistakes and deliberate distortions that abuse the integrity of economic impact analyses.*

The conceptual rationale for economic impact studies is sound, and their function in highlighting the sport field's contributions to community residents' prosperity is legitimate. However, this legitimacy is predicated on the studies' being undertaken with integrity. Because the motivation undergirding them usually is to demonstrate the legitimacy of a project's economic case, the temptation to engage in mischievous practices designed to enhance and exaggerate that case is substantial. In some cases, these practices are the result of ignorance and are inadvertent, but too often they are deliberate and enacted with intent to mislead and distort.

Ultimately, doing ethical work is a personal rather than an institutional responsibility. The only practical countermeasure to unethical procedures is to alert people to them and point out their potential adverse implications on public policy decisions. Doing so, it is hoped, will ferment a societal backlash against those who engage in such malfeasance, which will shame them into desisting. The intent here is to arm sport managers with sufficient knowledge of basic principles such that they will be able to identify studies which are ethically challenged and distance themselves from those studies.

THE RATIONALE FOR ECONOMIC IMPACT ANALYSIS

Sports teams and events are business investments both for the individual entrepreneur or sports entity that organizes and promotes them, and for the communities that subsidize and host them. Civic leaders anticipate that sports events will attract visitors from outside their jurisdiction whose expenditures will infuse new wealth into the community. City officials are eager to promote economic development as a means of generating local tax revenues and providing jobs. A sports stadium, franchise, or large event is a high-profile project that gives widespread visibility to a city's economic development efforts, and elected officials frequently commission a study to identify the economic gains that can be tied to the project. While entrepreneurs and sports organizations have directly measurable bottom lines that evaluate their fiscal performance, communities that are being asked to subsidize projects with public funds need to assess benefits in a broader context.

Figure 5.1 illustrates the conceptual reasoning for commissioning economic impact studies. It shows that residents and visitors in a community "give" funds to the city council in the form of taxes. The city council uses a proportion of these funds to subsidize production of a sport event or development of a facility. The facility or event attracts nonresident visitors who spend money in the local community both inside and outside of the events and facilities that they visit. This new money from outside the community creates income and jobs for residents. This completes the virtuous cycle of economic development. Community residents, aided by visitors' bed and sales taxes, are responsible for providing the initial funds, and residents receive a return on their invest-

---

*A "hands-on" guide detailing a step-by-step process for how to conduct an economic impact study has been written by one of the authors and is available at no cost to interested readers at http://agrilifecdn.tamu.edu/cromptonrpts/files /2011/06/Crompton_Economic_Impact_1.pdf

The economic justification for new sports facilities is highly controversial. Courtesy of Dreamstime

ment in the form of new jobs and more household income.

Figure 5.1 shows that a proportion of the tax funds invested in a sport agency's programs and facilities may serve as seed money that could leverage economic gains for the community. In some cases, if public sector resources are not used to financially underwrite the cost of constructing facilities or staging events, then the consequent economic benefits to the local community will not accrue. In some situations, private enterprises are unlikely to commit funds to organizing sport events, because none of those individual businesses is likely to capture a large enough proportion of the money spent by participants to obtain a satisfactory return on their investment.

The traditional financial balance sheet assumes that the cycle shown in Figure 5.1 starts and ends with the city council, rather than with a community's residents. This leads to a narrow definition of economic impact because it includes only the taxes and revenues that accrue to local government from the event or facility. That narrow definition focuses on income accruing to the city council from lease fees, admission revenues,

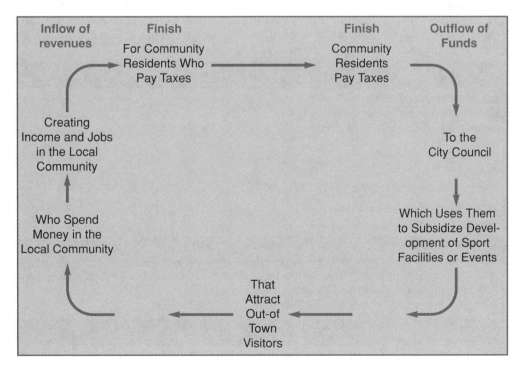

Figure 5.1. The Conceptual Rationale for Commissioning Economic Impact Studies.

bed taxes, increased sales tax revenues, and the like. However, this approach is conceptually flawed because the money invested does not belong to the council; it belongs to the city's residents. Although it is efficient for a resident's investment to be funneled through the council, the return that residents receive is what is important, not merely the proportion of the total return that filters back to the council. The purpose of economic impact studies is to measure the economic return to residents.

The difference between the financial and economic approaches is illustrated in Table 5.1. The city's park and recreation department's financial balance sheet shows a net loss of $38,347 from the tournament. However, if the agency used an economic balance sheet, then it would show a net return of $2.0 million, $3.69 million, or $1.12 million depending on whether economic impact was reported in terms of direct expenditures, sales impact, or impact on personal incomes. (These figures were calculated by taking the gross amounts shown and subtracting from them the $38,347 net cost to the city for hosting the event.)

The capital cost of the softball complex was approximately $12 million, which means that if the personal income measurement of economic impact was used (the reasons for

Table 5.1. A Comparison of the Financial and Economic Returns to a City from an Amateur Softball Association Girls 18 & Under Class A National Softball Championship Tournament

Context

1,810 players on 133 teams participated in the tournament. All were from out of town. Because it was an elimination tournament, the length of time the teams stayed in the community varied from 4 to 7 nights. 697 players' parents were interviewed.

Financial Data	$
Income: Entry fees $300 × 133	39,900
Gate Admission fees	74,843
Concessions/Souvenirs % of gross	32,395
Hotel rebate	4,650
Social fee	5,683
Programs	1,440
Total	158,911
Tournament costs and staff time	197,258
Net loss	(38,347)

Economic Data

Total expenditures in the local area by the 1,810 players and their family/friends: $2,039,000.
Economic impact on sales: $3,731,000.
Economic impact on income: $1,162,000.

Return on Investment

For each dollar invested, residents' income increased by $30.30 ($1,162,000/38,347). The facility cost $12 million to build, so the payback period to residents is approximately 10 tournaments of this size.

preferring this measurement are given later in the chapter during the discussion of multipliers), then the investment would pay for itself after approximately 10 similar tournaments. These data demonstrate the potential contribution of sport events to a community's economy. How many other investments is a jurisdiction likely to have that pay for themselves in three to four years (assuming three to four similar tournaments per year) and continue to contribute $3 to $4 million to residents annually for the next 20 years?

A STUDY'S SPONSORS EXPECT TO GET WHAT THEY PAY FOR

Community officials commission economic impact analyses in response to citizens' demands that they be accountable for demonstrating the efficacy of tax-dollar investments. The public wants to be assured that government is making a "profit" in return for any subsidization it is giving to sport projects that are justified on economic development grounds. Similarly, when such studies are commissioned by sport organizations, it is usually with the expectation that their results will reinforce the case for allocating public dollars to a project. In these circumstances, there is a temptation to manipulate the procedures to strengthen the case. It has been noted that:

> The buyers of event studies are event promoters seeking subsidies and the government agencies that wish to support them, and the audience is composed of taxpayers and government representatives. These studies are seldom criticized and seldom published where they might be subjected to scholarly review. With a rationally ignorant audience and concentrated special interest support, bias is likely. (p. 63)[2]

Thus, the motives of a study's sponsor invariably dictate the study's outcome. The point was well illustrated in the contentious debate in the city of Arlington, Texas, that revolved around the investment of public funds for a new football stadium for the NFL Dallas Cowboys. Economic impact studies were commissioned by four different factions in this debate. The four consulting entities hired to do the work all had a long track record of doing economic impact studies and had substantial national visibility. The results are summarized below, with the sponsors and authors of the reports shown in the parentheses:

1. "The stadium would generate $238 million a year in economic impact in Arlington and $416 million a year in Tarrant County." (p. 2)[3]
2. "A new Cowboys Stadium would bring in $346 million a year to Dallas County." (p. 1)[4]
3. "The City of Irving, if a new stadium were built, would see an annual economic impact of approximately $51 million." (p. 10)[5]
4. "The best outcome Arlington can expect is that it will lose $290.5 million as a result of the building of a new stadium for the Cowboys . . . The loss for Arlington could be as high as $325.3 million." (p. 1)[6]

The difference in estimates between Study 4 and the other three reports is substantially greater than it appears at first glance because Study 4 used as its time frame the projected 30-year life of the stadium, whereas the other three studies reported only an annual amount. If the annual amounts given in Studies 1, 2, and 3 are extrapolated to the same 30-year-life time frame using the same 5% and 10% discount rates to calculate net present value that were adopted in Study 4, the projected benefits to Arlington or Irving during the 30-year period would be as shown in Table 5.2.

It seems likely that the motives of the study sponsors at least partially explain the results. The Arlington city council supported a public investment of $325 million, which was half of the stadium's projected cost. Supporters of the project spent $10 million on the referendum campaign, of which the Cowboys contributed $6 million, whereas the project's opponents raised just under $45,000.[7] A prominent feature of the brochure advocating support for the project, which was widely distributed to Arlington households, was the supposed high economic return. The brochure proclaimed, "The new Dallas Cowboys stadium is a big win for Arlington's economy," and touted that the stadium would generate "billions in economic impact" (p. 2).[8] In the nearby city of Irving, which is where the existing Cowboys stadium was located, a property development company was interested in selling land to Irving for the stadium. Hence, the large economic impact number emerging from Study 2 would be similarly advantageous to that company.

The City of Irving was in danger of losing the Cowboys, which likely would have generated negative vibrations from at least some sections of the community toward elected officials. Thus, a relatively low figure would serve to minimize the negative political fallout. However, Irving still had aspirations to negotiate with the Cowboys and was willing to offer $80 million of public investment if Arlington voters rejected the referendum proposition. Thus, a level of economic impact that would justify the $80 million tax subsidy was desirable. The $51 million figure in Study 3 appears to offer a reasonable balance between those somewhat dichotomous scenarios.

Study 4 adopted procedures that would be supported by most economists. By commissioning as their consultants respected academics who feature prominently in the sport economic impact literature, those opposed to the study could anticipate receiving a low or negative economic impact outcome.

Consultants supposedly are hired to provide independent evidence, but in many cases, that evidence is manipulated or selectively presented to tell clients what they want to

Table 5.2. Projected Benefits to Interested Communities with Annual Amounts Extrapolated to a 30-year Time Frame Using Net Present Value Discount Rates of 5% and 10%

	5%	10%
Study 1, $238 million per year for Arlington for 30 years	$3.7 billion	$2.2 billion
$416 million per year in Tarrant County for 30 years	$6.4 billion	$3.9 billion
Study 2, $346 million per year in Dallas County for 30 years	$5.3 billion	$3.3 billion
Study 3, $51 million per year in Irving for 30 years	$748 million	$481 million

hear, "and what they want to hear is that their event or team or whatever is going to generate a lot of money" (p. 33).[9] A consulting organization that fails to deliver the economic impact numbers that its client expects is unlikely to receive either repeat business from that client or new commissions from others. Clients expect to get what they pay for!

Some of the consulting companies that are hired to do economic impact studies are related to, and share the names of, firms with respected national and international reputations for their work as accountants in auditing organizations' financial statements. By hiring consulting firms with nationally respected names, sponsors also are buying the aura of respect and integrity that accompanies the consultant's name, anticipating that this will enhance the credibility and public and political acceptance of the results, and quell any questioning of the procedures used.

How might such consultants retain and protect their reputations when they use inappropriate procedures to give clients the large-dollar impact number that sponsors usually are seeking? Two strategies are used widely. First, extensive qualifiers are likely to be inserted into the report. Consider the following extract from a report undertaken by a well-known national consulting organization:

> We have not audited or verified any information provided to us and as such will take no responsibility for the accuracy of the information which was provided by third parties . . . Some assumptions inevitably will not materialize and unanticipated events and circumstances may occur; therefore actual results achieved during the analysis period may vary from those described in the report, and the variations may be material. (p. 12)[10]

Ostensibly, this is a reasonable caveat for any consultant to include but, unfortunately, it also provides license for thoroughly unreasonable assumptions and obviously biased analyses to be adopted. This seems especially likely to happen when the information is provided to consultants by the study's sponsors which, as in this case, frequently occurs. It is difficult to reconcile such uncritical acceptance of information and assumptions with typical claims that "the scope of services for this analysis entailed an independent evaluation of the economic and fiscal impacts" of a project (p. 8).[3]

A second strategy for protecting consultants' reputations often is found in the cover letter accompanying a final report, as the following extract illustrates:

> It should be noted that the analysis utilizes assumptions that were developed based on our market analysis, surveys with comparable arenas, hypothetical lease terms, and *conditions and assumptions provided by the City and the developer.* [11]

And in a study of the economic impact of the San Francisco 49ers moving to a new stadium in Santa Clara:

> The analysis contained in the report is based on information provided by the San Francisco 49ers, the City of Santa Clara, Santa Clara County and the State of California. The company does not make any representations or warranties as to the accuracy or completeness of the information provided to us. Information pro-

vided to us has not been audited or verified and has been assumed to be correct.[12]

Thus, the consultants offer no critique of the legitimacy of the assumptions given to them by the project's strongest advocates, but merely accept the assumptions as a given irrespective of how outrageous they may be.

These explicit qualifying statements invariably receive no visibility in the ensuing publicity announcing the report's results, as advocates tout only the outrageously high numbers that typically emerge. These qualifiers provide the loophole that enables consultants to make unreasonable assumptions, engage in doubtful procedures, and announce mischievous results. It was not surprising, then, that one investigator who tried to gain access to a threshold number of these economic impact reports to evaluate their integrity reported that they were "cited time and again by the local media and the respective lobby groups keen to sway public opinion, and then they disappeared" (p. 22).[13]

Most research projects are predicated on a search for the truth, but the goal in economic impact studies is less auspicious; the goal is to legitimize a position. Usually, they are undertaken to justify a public expenditure in quantitative dollar terms with the expectation that the results will reinforce the case for sustaining or increasing resources allocated to the service. In these circumstances, there is a temptation to manipulate the procedures to strengthen the case.

Ostensibly, the people hired to conduct economic impact studies appear to be both expert and neutral. However, "they are in truth the exact equivalent of an expert witness in a lawsuit who comes to testify in support of the side that is paying the expert's bill. An expert whose testimony harms his employer's case doesn't get much repeat business" (p. 7).[14] The same commentator suggests, "The fees for the study are like a religious tithe paid to a priest to come bless some endeavor" (p. 7).[14] This type of cynical comment about the integrity of economic studies is becoming increasingly pervasive. The cynicism is provoked by extravagant claims for the impact of visitor spending that many of these studies have made.

THE FUNDAMENTAL PRINCIPLES
OF ECONOMIC IMPACT STUDIES

The economic impact of visitor spending typically is estimated by some variation of the following simple formula:[15]

Economic Impact of Visitor Spending = Number of Visitors * Average Spending per Visitor * Multiplier

This formula suggests four distinct steps:

1. Define who qualifies as a "visitor."
2. Estimate the number of visitors attracted to the community by the sport event or facility.
3. Estimate the average level of spending of visitors in the local area.
4. Determine the ripple effects of this new money through the community by applying appropriate multipliers.

Community events can produce meaningful economic impacts. Courtesy of BigStockPhoto

In this section, each of these elements is discussed. The first three stages are the most important. The key to producing a credible estimate of economic impact is an accurate measure of visitor spending, since any errors in this measure are compounded when these data are used in stage 4 to estimate indirect expenditures.

Because economic impact studies produce quantifiable outcomes and sometimes use complex procedures, often there is a presumption in the minds of bottom line-oriented audiences who are unfamiliar with the technique that the analyses are "scientific" and, hence, the outputs are objective and unequivocal. This is fallacious. The quantifiable outcomes offer a misleading guise of statistical sophistication. Economic impact analysis is an inexact process and output numbers should be regarded as a "best guess" rather than as being inviolably accurate. Indeed, if the same event was studied by five individuals who were knowledgeable about the procedures and who strove to honor key assumptions, then it is probable that there would be five different results.

There are multiple points in an analysis where underlying assumptions have to be made that will substantially impact the final result. Unfortunately, this means there is a temptation to adopt inappropriate procedures and assumptions to generate high economic impact numbers that will better justify a project. Sometimes such errors are the result of a genuine lack of understanding of economic impact analysis and the procedures used in it, but in other instances they are committed deliberately and mischievously to generate large numbers and mislead stakeholders.

Reviewing the stream of mischievous studies masquerading under the rubric of economic impact, one is reminded of Macbeth's lament in Act V, Scene V: "It is a tale told by an idiot, full of sound and fury, signifying nothing" (p. 86).[16] However, the tales are not told by idiots; they are, for the most part, told by knowledgeable consultants who recognize that the general public and elected officials (audiences they are targeting) are frequently deficient in economic literacy.

Accurate Participation Numbers

If a reasonably accurate count of the number of participants is not feasible, then it is probably a waste of resources to proceed with an economic impact study. This is because reasonably accurate measurements of economic impact depend on reasonably accurate counts of visitors, since the impact estimates are derived by extrapolating from a sample or from secondary sources to a total visitation count. At gated venues that charge an admission and at tournaments where there is a list of participants, accurate counts are likely to be available from ticket sales, turnstile counts, or highway counters. However, many venues are not gated, do not charge admission, and do not have a list of participants. In these cases, attendance counts are frequently guesstimates made by the organizers who sometimes are tempted to exaggerate them. An example is given in Exhibit 5.1.[17]

Exclusion of Local Residents and Local Sources of Funds

Economic impact attributable to a sport opportunity relates only to new money injected into an economy by visitors, vendors, media, sponsors, external government entities, and banks and investors from outside the community. Only the spending of those visitors who reside outside the jurisdiction and whose primary motivation for visiting is to attend the event, or who stay longer and spend more time there because of the event, should be included in an economic impact study.

Consider what economists call the *broken-window fallacy*. Let's say hooligans toss a brick through a bakery window. The baker must spend money to have the window repaired. This will boost the glassmaker's income, which will add to another merchant's income, which will add to another merchant's income, and so on. The chain of spending will multiply, generating higher income and employment. But there's a catch. If the

---

Exhibit 5.1

Attendance Hyperbole at the London Marathon

A figure of one million is often used by the media as an estimate of the number of spectators who watch the annual London marathon race. For example, it is consistently used by the BBC which provides live television coverage of the event. However, for this to be the case, spectators would need to be approximately five deep either side of the course along the entire 26.2 miles. On close examination of the television coverage this was clearly not the case. Even in the most populated areas, crowds rarely reached such levels. In addition, because of the excellent transport system in London, spectators were found to travel to different parts of the course (using the tube or bus) once the runners had gone by, which led to double counting. The Metropolitan Police Force estimated spectators at nearer 500,000, but even this figure appeared to be optimistic based on close scrutiny of BBC television coverage. Based on the analysis of that coverage and the propensity for spectators to move around the course, 300,000 was the spectator attendance estimate used by a research team estimating the economic impact of the London marathon.

baker hadn't spent his money on window repair, he could have spent it on a new suit. Then the tailor would have new income and so on down the line. The broken window didn't create net new spending. It simply diverted spending from somewhere else, impeding economic activity that otherwise would have occurred.

Expenditures by those who reside in the community do not contribute to an event's economic impact because these expenditures represent a recycling of money that already existed. There is no new economic growth, only a transfer of resources between sectors of the local economy. It is probable that if local residents had not spent their money at the sport event, then they would have disposed of it either now or later by purchasing other goods and services in the community. Thus, an analysis of the impact of professional sport franchises on incomes and employment in the amusement and recreation sector of those local economies which hosted franchises reported a small positive effect. However, this was offset by decreases in other sectors of the economy, suggesting that franchises do not create employment or income; rather, they simply shift consumption from one sector to another.[18]

Fifty dollars spent by a local family at a sport event is likely to be fifty fewer dollars spent on other purchases elsewhere in the community. This switched spending offers no net economic stimulus to the community. Hence, it should not be included when estimating economic impact. Exhibit 5.2 elaborates on this issue,[19] while the letter reproduced in Exhibit 5.3 vividly indicates the potential adverse impact of major sport facilities on neighboring businesses.

Many assume that because a sport organization is spending money in a community, it is *de facto* strengthening the community's economy. That assumption is erroneous because the government must tax Peter to pay Paul. Consider a hypothetical situation in which all funds paid to a city's sport employees are withdrawn and the employees terminated. There may be three alternate uses for the funds:

Exhibit 5.2

Elaboration of the Concept of Substitute or Recycled Expenditures

How much more food do people eat because of the presence of a team? In other words, if a family eats dinner near the stadium or arena before a game, where did they not eat their dinner that night? If they would have eaten at a restaurant near their home, then the consumption of food as part of the sporting event is merely a transfer of expenditures from a restaurant near their home to one near the stadium or arena. This change of location for the expenditure certainly creates an impact in both areas—more spending near the facility and less in the neighborhood. But from the economy's perspective there is no growth or increase in spending levels, merely a transfer. Further, if the family would have eaten at home instead of at a restaurant, then the transfer of expenditures takes place between the supermarket and the restaurant, with consumption declining at the supermarket while restaurant sales increase. Again, there is economic impact in the sense that the restaurant may gain while the supermarket suffers, but the overall change in the community or city is not one of growth, but merely a transfer of activity from one vendor to another.

Exhibit 5.3

Downtown Eateries Lose on Game Days

In discussing the possibility of a new home for the Colts or a direct subsidy for the team, many have been making the assumption that a new arena would mean a huge windfall for Downtown restaurants. A decision to give millions of dollars of public money to the team should be based on facts, and suggesting that a new dome or payments to the team can be subsidized from some financial benefit they bring to our industry is pure fiction. If the team is a benefit to the entire population, then the voters should pay the taxes directly and our customers should not be targeted.

Former Mayor Stephen Goldsmith first promoted this myth over many local restaurateurs' objections as justification for building Conseco Fieldhouse, when one of the prime motivators for any new sports facility is to enhance food and beverage sales for the facility itself by increasing sales opportunities. Those include wide hallways, broader menu options and various other amenities. Net per-person sales from event customers have substantially increased in the new fieldhouse and the market share has decreased for neighboring restaurants.

That was also a primary reason for 7 p.m. start times; people do not have time to eat park and claim seats. They most often eat inside the facility because of timing issues.

A recent survey of Downtown restaurant association members shows the majority experience a net decrease on fieldhouse event nights and a whopping 80% experience a chilling effect on even non-event nights as suburbanites fear that an event might be going on Downtown and parking prices will be absurdly high. This same phenomenon exists at the RCA Dome now.

Few of Sunday's football crowds eat Downtown before a noon game and most go directly home afterward. There are some Downtown restaurants that that don't even bother opening on football Sundays.

A new football arena will exert every effort to take what little outside food and beverage sales exist and transfer that income to the team. There is little, if any, significant net contribution to the annual sales for the majority of Downtown restaurants from football, even though our customers are taxed 1% of our sales to pay for these facilities every day of the year, whether they use them or not.

The primary effect on the local economy from football is that parking companies reap a huge windfall when they inflate their rates by 1,000% or more during events. They again are the primary outside beneficiaries, certainly not restaurants.

If a better Downtown is the focus, then that money is better spent on the many substantive real improvements, rather than paying for the bragging rights that we have an NFL team. I would be remiss in not pointing out that the restaurant industry fills 300% more downtown seats annually than the Colts, Pacers and Indians combined. And we do that every night of the year without being subsidized by public money and not just a handful of Sunday afternoons and a few select evenings.

(The writer, Ted Bulthaup, owns Hollywood Bar & Filmworks in Indianapolis)

Letter to the *Indianapolis Star*. September 24, 2002. Reproduced from S.R. Sandy, R.S. Slaone, N. Rosentraub (2004). *The Economics of Sport: An international perspective.* New York: Palgrave, McMillan.

1. All sport staff could be reassigned to dig holes for the first six months of the year and to fill them up again for the second six months. The operational money from their former sport work will be used to acquire and service the equipment needed to perform these tasks efficiently.

2. The staff and operating resources formerly allocated to sport could all be redirected to improving streets.

3. Taxpayers and users could be allowed to retain the taxes and user fees that were formerly used to fund the sport employees.

In all three cases, the impact on the local economy of removing funds from sport would be zero, because those funds would be spent elsewhere in the community. The spending has merely been switched. The only net loss to the economy would be any lost spending from out-of-town visitors who came for sporting events.

For major sports events, the most important non-local spectators may be those watching television because media sponsorship fees associated with the event, which flow back into the community, are likely to be a function of the number of television viewers the event attracts.

When the economic impact of team sport events is estimated, the notion of reciprocal spending has to be considered. Ostensibly, expenditures made by visiting team athletes, coaches, cheerleaders, band members, and their family supporters should be included because they are from outside the local area. However, they probably should be excluded because these expenditures are likely to be reciprocated when the home team visits opponents. Hence, the gain to the local economy provided by these visitors is offset by the loss to the local economy when the home team spend equivalent money on their road games.[20]

Exhibit 5.4

Estimated Economic, Fiscal and Jobs Impact During the Period of Constructing the Metrodome Next Facility

Direct Spending	$734,000,000
Total Output	$1,351,000,000
Personal Earnings	$577,000,000
Employment (1)	13,400
Tax Revenues:	
Personal Income	$20,800,000
State Sales(2)	11,810,000
Other Sales(2)	580,000
Total Tax Revenues	$33,190,000

(1) Includes full and part-time jobs supported by the economic activity generated by the project.

(2) Includes sales taxes on indirect spending generated by construction. Does not include sales taxes in direct construction expenditures, which are assumed to be tax-exempt.

The report's authors state: "As shown, the $734 million of construction spending taking place in the State of Minnesota is estimated to generate approximately $1.4 billion in total output during the construction period. This level of economic activity is estimated to support 13,400 jobs with total personal earnings of approximately $577 million. These jobs and related earnings represent construction jobs as well as jobs supported in other industries as a result of construction-related spending. A total of $33.2 million in personal income taxes are estimated to be generated by the construction project."

It was anticipated that these funds would originate from the State of Minnesota and the Vikings team. They would not be new funds entering the state's economy, so the economic impact of constructing the facility is likely to be zero, not $1.4 billion!

Sometimes expenditures on capital projects are assumed to generate economic impacts. An example of this is shown in Exhibit 5.4.[21] However, if these capital facilities are designed to serve primarily local residents and if they are being paid for by property taxes, then these are substitutable expenditures that have no economic impact.

Studies of new sports stadium impacts frequently include the economic impact accruing from construction. If the economic impact area of interest is the city and the facility is being constructed with city funds, then this investment is a substitute expenditure, not new money coming into the city. Either the money would have been spent by the city on another project, or it would not have been collected from taxpayers, who would then have spent it themselves—most probably somewhere within the city. Any employment benefits from these projects are likely to be offset by an equal number of employment losses elsewhere in the system. Thus, city funds should be excluded from an economic impact analysis.

Federal funds, such as Community Development Block Grants, which are awarded to communities on a formula basis that mainly reflects level of poverty, have been used in some communities to partially fund sport stadiums. However, they should not be included in an economic impact analysis because they could have been allocated to a variety of alternative community projects. The sport project was not responsible for attracting them. Similarly, if federal or state funds were already designated to a city but were accelerated to facilitate building a new facility, then they also should be excluded from consideration. For example, a previously approved Federal Transportation Administration grant to improve the public transportation system in Atlanta was moved up six years due to the awarding of the Olympic Games to the city. This grant should not be included and considered new money because it would have been forthcoming regardless of the Games.[22] However, if the money is coming from state or federal sources and would not have been granted to the city for other projects, then it can legitimately be considered as having an economic impact on the city.[19]

Spurious Rationales

The widespread admonition from economists to disregard locals' expenditures is frequently ignored in consultants' studies because when expenditures by local residents are omitted, the economic impact numbers become too small to be politically useful. Thus, a review of economic impact studies of proposed facilities for professional sports teams reported that 13 of the 19 studies erroneously included spending by locals as part of the economic impact estimate.[13] This is consistent with the findings of an earlier review undertaken by one of the authors of this book.[23] The result of these egregious procedures is to massively overstate the benefits attributable to a team. For example, an internationally known consulting firm, commissioned to undertake an analysis of economic benefits associated with the operations of the Green Bay Packers, reported that the team had an annual impact of $144 million on Brown County. They blatantly and explicitly acknowledged breaking the fundamental principle of excluding local spending by stating that the spending and related benefits estimated in this report represent total annual spending and benefits occurring in Brown County as a result of the Green Bay Packers. It should be noted that no attempt has been made to estimate the portion of this spending and related benefits that is new to the area.[24]

When the San Diego Padres were lobbying for public funds for a new baseball stadium (which eventually became PETCO Park), the study they commissioned from an internationally renowned firm predicted that "the Ballpark and its surrounding development should generate about $588.5 million" per year in expenditures and support 5,268 jobs. A one-sentence note buried in the report says: "The substitution effect is difficult to accurately quantify and has not been included in this analysis." Thus, the economic impact report used by the Padres to lobby San Diego citizens to approve a referendum for public funds was admittedly egregiously misleading.[25]

Another well-known national consulting firm used the phrase "gross economic impact" to convey that they included local spending (as opposed to "net" which would indicate only new money from non-locals). They brazenly stated: "A gross expenditures and economic multiplier approach was used in conducting this study, which is the most widely accepted approach in conducting these types of studies" (p. 6).[26] This statement is mischievous and disingenuous. It is the most widely *used* approach by consultants who are intent on producing a high economic impact number for their clients, but it is not "widely accepted" by anyone other than other consultants doing similar mischievous studies for similar client groups. Indeed, the authors are unaware of any reputable economist who has endorsed such a procedure.

Sometimes consultants acknowledge the inappropriateness of including local residents, then go on mischievously to provide a spurious rationale that they surely know is fallacious and appears to be designed to obfuscate and confuse the reader. For example, another study completed by a well-known national firm rationalized its decision to incorporate local expenditures with this spurious reasoning:

> The substitution effect refers to the economic phenomenon whereby new or additional spending leads to reduced spending *within other sectors* of that economy, immediately or over time . . . We are not aware of a reliable method for determining the amount and impact of the substitution effect resulting from various economic activities. Previous attempts to quantify the substitution effect have yielded unreliable results. The substitution effect is difficult to accurately quantify and has not been included in this analysis. (p. 86)[26]

This verbiage was adopted almost verbatim by another major consulting company commissioned to advise on a different project for a different client in the same geographic area:

> The substitution effect refers to the economic phenomenon whereby new or additional spending leads to reduced spending within other sectors of that economy over time . . . We are not aware of a reliable method for quantifying the amount of substitution resulting from various economic activities. Previous attempts to

quantify the substitution effect have yielded unreliable results. Although the substitution effect is difficult to quantify, it is reasonable to assume that much of the economic activity generated by the proposed stadium and franchise would be *new* to the City of Arlington and to Tarrant County. (p. 15)[3]

Au contraire, the reasonable assumption is that much of this economic activity would *not* be new to the city and county!

It was noted at the beginning of this chapter that *economic impact* refers to the net economic change in the income of host residents that results from spending by visitors from outside the community. Recognizing this, some agencies, organizations and their consultants, who seek a high number for political purposes, have changed the terminology from *economic impact* to *economic activity, total annual spending, gross economic impact, economic surge, gross economic output, gross economic value, total contribution to the economy, economic significance,* or some other analogous phrase that facilitates the incorporation of local residents' expenditures into their analyses.

Non-economists are unlikely to differentiate the nuances and to falsely consider these other phrases as synonyms of *economic impact*. When their procedures are challenged by economists, they are likely to declare, "But we didn't measure economic impact, we measured economic activity (or whatever)." The following example is indicative of the verbiage used in such studies:

> A study estimating the "contribution of the golf course industry to the state economy" concluded: "Our findings indicate that the state's golf courses and related activities (pro shops, restaurants and bars, and clubhouses) were estimated to contribute 16,334 full-time-equivalent jobs and $379.8 million in income. This indicates that the golf course industry is an important component of the state's tourism sector and a significant contributor to the state's economy." (p. 19)[27]

Two Caveats

Conceptually, there are two types of situations in which it may be appropriate to include the expenditures of some or all local residents in an economic study. First, if there is evidence to suggest that a sport event keeps some residents at home who would otherwise leave the area for a trip, these local expenditures legitimately could be considered an economic impact because money has been retained in the host community that otherwise would have been spent outside it. This may be termed *deflected impact*. It is deflected in the sense that instead of leaving town to go to a sporting event, these individuals now spend their money in the local community.

Examples of deflected income occur when communities host championship tournaments, because local teams that qualified for the tournament would probably have traveled to participate in it if it had been held elsewhere. Their spending elsewhere would have been a loss to the local economy. In this case, it is probably appropriate to recognize their local spending as a net gain to the economy that would not have occurred if the community was not hosting the tournament. Ostensibly, expenditures by these teams are likely to be considered as being relatively small because their participants likely live in the community and most probably sleep and eat at home. Thus, it would appear that excluding these participants from an economic impact analysis is likely to have no meaningful influence on the reported results.

However, their expenditures would be different if they had traveled to another community for the tournament. Indeed, it is likely they would resemble those of visiting teams to the community's tournament, rather than their actual local expenditures. Consider the following case:

> When local participants in the Cincinnati Flying Pig marathon and half-marathon races were surveyed and asked the likelihood that they would have participated in an out-of-town race had the local races not taken place, 1,545 (38%) reported they were "sure" they would do so while another 22% stated they were "unsure" and 40% responded they would not do so. When the local participants were asked to estimate how much they would spend at that out-of-town replacement race, the averages for marathoners and half-marathoners were $615 and $418 respectively. These amounts were similar to the expenditures reported by non-local participants in the Cincinnati races.[28]

In cases such as this where there is a clear rationale and/or empirical evidence to support that substantial expenditures were deflected from outside the local area into the local economy, then they should be included as part of the local economic impact. In the Cincinnati study, the deflected impact from those who were "sure" they would have gone to an out-of-town replacement race amounted to $800,000. If this had not been included, the races' overall economic impact would have been underestimated by 25%.[28] Similarly, when Texas A&M University decided to undertake a $450 million renovation and expansion of its football stadium, it was possible that its games would have to be played in Houston for a season while the work was being done. The university is located in College Station-Bryan. The community's tourism agency commissioned a study to estimate the economic loss to the community if the games were moved. The losses were of two types. First, the $15 million per game ($105 million per season) of direct expenditures in the community by out-of-town visitors would be lost. Second, there would be leakage out of the local economy by residents of the College Station-Bryan area who travelled to the games. This deflected income amounted to $16 million for the season and was appropriately included in the economic impact analysis.[29]

A further nuance related to deflected impact is that the expenditure categories of the deflected funds will be different. That is, instead of spending on hotels and restaurants in another community, the money is likely to go to groceries, local entertainment and other general purchase categories in the local area.

Unfortunately, consultants sometimes use this deflected impact caveat indiscriminately and mischievously implement it in all situations, whereas it is likely to apply only to a minority of competitive athletic contests. Evidence of deflected impact is very difficult to collect. In most cases, the evidence is likely to be tenuous, and the deflected impact is likely to be minimal, so the accepted convention by economists is to disregard it unless there is a strong rationale or empirical evidence to the contrary.

The second situation in which local residents' expenditures are included is when a study is intended to be a significance analysis rather than an economic impact analysis. A significance analysis is "a measure of the importance or significance of the project/program (rather than impacts) within the local economy as it shows the size and nature of economic activity associated with recreation/tourism activity in the area" (Attributing Impacts section, para. 3).[15] Unlike a legitimate economic impact study, it offers no useful information that would inform the trade-offs involved in decisions regarding how best to invest public funds. Its only *raison d'être* appears to be to enhance the sport sector's political profile.

A significance analysis is a legitimate economic procedure, but it becomes mischievous when the differences between it and an economic impact study are ignored, blurred, or not made explicit. For example, the consultants' heading in the illustration in Exhibit 5.4 refers to "Estimated Economic . . . Impact." However, in the accompanying narrative justifying their mischievous $1.4 billion number for impact on the state of the facility's construction, they subtly change the wording to "economic activity." A significance analysis offers a resolution to the conundrum confronting consultants with ethical reservations about bidding on mischievous economic impact studies. They have to make a living, and if they do not bid on the study it will still be commissioned from a competitor, so their acting with integrity does not change anything. A solution is to state explicitly, unambiguously, and prominently that the study is not an economic impact study but is a significance analysis. For example, the author of a study on the economic significance of amateur sport in Edmonton, at the beginning of his report, prominently stated:

> A crucial distinction between an economic significance study and an economic-impact study is that the former does not attempt to determine what would happen if the amateur sport and active recreation sector of the economy were to disappear altogether. Instead the purpose is to calculate the "amateur sport and active recreation gross municipal product" within the city of Edmonton for a specified year (p. 6).[30]

The author's appropriate allusion is that if the sector he is measuring were to disappear, the impact on the city's economy would be minimal because people would likely spend their funds on substitute activities. The gross municipal product of this sector of the city's economy was estimated at $500 million, of which $125 million was government funding. These data offer no useful information for guiding policy. Their only utility is to provide advocates with a large, albeit meaningless, number that can be used to raise the sector's political profile and to imply that more government investment in facilities for these activities is justified. However, the consultant was able to retain his integrity while accepting the commission.

Exclusion of Time Switchers and Casuals

Expenditures from out-of-town visitors should be net of "time-switchers" and "casuals." Some non-local participants may have been planning a visit to the community for some time, but changed the timing of their visit to coincide with a sporting event. The spending in the community of these *time-switchers* should not be attributed to the event since it would have occurred without the event, albeit at a different time of the year. For example, when the FIFA World Cup was held in South Africa, it was estimated that four-fifths of all World Cup-goers were time-switchers who would have gone to South Africa at some point anyway, but timed their visit to coincide with the World Cup.[31]

Time-switching is likely to be the most prominent at events held in major cities or resort destinations. Irrespective of an event, it is likely that more people plan to visit these places than other locations, so *ipso facto* there will be more time-switchers.

For major events, it is possible that prices in the community may be raised during the event, so the expenditures of time-switcher visitors may be higher at that time than if they had visited at a different time of the year. However, most economists are likely to advocate that this increment be disregarded in the analysis because of the difficulty of accurately assessing the magnitude of the increase across all sectors of the local economy. Rather, it should be recognized in the accompanying narrative as one factor contributing to the analyses' measurements being conservative.

Casuals are visitors who are already in the community, attracted by other features, and who elect to go to the event instead of doing something else. For example, San Antonio is a popular convention destination because of its climate and the ambiance of the River Walk, where the convention center and major hotels are located. If conference attendees go to an NBA basketball game in the city, their economic impact should not be attributable to the game because without it the likely scenario is that these visitors would have spent a similar amount of money at, for example, a restaurant on the River Walk. The game was not what brought them to San Antonio.

Expenditures by time-switchers and casuals would have occurred without the event, so income generated by their expenditures should not be attributed to it. However, if visitors who qualify as members of these two groups stay in the jurisdiction for more days than they would have done if the event had not been held, then their expenditures on those extra days should be included in the economic impact analysis.

Some non-local visitors to sports events are likely to be partial casuals. That is, the event may be only one of multiple attractions that persuaded them to visit the area. Without it they would not have come, but at the same time without the other attractions they would not have come. This situation was shown to prevail, for example, in a survey of spectators to games of the twelve teams that played spring training games in the Cactus League in the Phoenix/Tucson areas in Arizona.[32] The results are shown in Table 5.3. The consultant's pro-rated out-of-area attendees' economic impact attributable to the Cactus League as follows:

- If out-of-area attendees indicated the Cactus League was *PRIMARY* in their decision, 100% of their expenditures were included.
- If out-of-area attendees indicated the Cactus League was *MAJOR* in their decision, 75% of their expenditures were included.
- If out-of-area attendees indicated the Cactus League was *MINOR* in their decision, 25% of their expenditures were included.

Table 5.3. Importance of Spring Training on the Visitation Decision (of Out-of-Area Visitors)

"How important was attending spring training games in your decision to visit metro (Phoenix/Tucson)—was it your primary reason, a major reason, a minor reason or not a reason?"

	Primary	Major	Minor	Not a Reason
Chicago Cubs	64	20	14	2
San Francisco Giants	78	9	9	3
Seattle Mariners	68	18	13	1
Los Angeles Angels	77	12	6	6
San Diego Padres	73	16	12	0
Arizona Diamondbacks	54	21	14	11
Oakland Athletics	73	14	10	3
Texas Rangers	54	27	12	6
Chicago White Sox	51	11	19	20
Kansas City Royals	64	20	12	4
Milwaukee Brewers	73	17	8	1
Colorado Rockies	66	15	15	4

A more sophisticated procedure for pro-rating the spending of these partial casuals is described in Exhibit 5.5.

Time-switchers and casuals can usually be disregarded when the event is a sports tournament whose economic impact is almost all contributed by the participants and family or friends traveling with them. If a city hosts a softball tournament, for example, it is unlikely that any players on the teams that enter will be time-switchers or casuals. Their reason for visiting the community is exclusively associated with the team's tournament involvement. However, if much of an event's impact is generated by spectators rather than participants, or if it is the impact of a facility rather than an event that is being measured, then there may be substantial numbers of time-switchers and casuals.

USE AND ABUSE OF MULTIPLIERS

There is widespread recognition among elected officials and sport professionals that when visitors inject new money into a local community, it spreads through its economy like ripples in a pool after a stone has been thrown into it. The concept of the new money being spent and re-spent, so its initial impact is multiplied, is easy to grasp. However, the operationalization of multipliers is complex, and relatively few elected officials or sport professionals have an understanding of the nuances and limitations of multipliers. This has resulted in gross abuses in their calculation, presentation, and interpretation.

Exhibit 5.5

Measuring the Influence of a Sport Event in Visitors' Decisions to Go to a Destination

Circle the number below that indicates how important this event was in your decision to visit [city] on this trip, where 0 indicates it had no influence and you would	have come to the area anyway and 10 indicates that this event is the only reason for visiting [city] today.

0	1	2	3	4	5	6	7	8	9	10

None: I would have come to the event anyway	**Half of my reason for coming to the area**	**My only reason for coming to the area**

The proportion of spending that is attributable to the facility or event is based on responses to this question. For example, if a respondent reports that the facility/event had "0" influence on the decision to visit the community, then the economic impact would be zero. If he or she indicated a score of 6, then 60% of the spending in the community would be attributable to the event.	It is recognized that such estimates of proportionality are subjective and subject to errors. However, they are likely to be more accurate than the standard assumption that 100% of visitors' expenditures are attributable to the events. This process distinguishes between general economic impact from visitors to a community and the economic impacts attributable to a specific sport event or facility.

Given the complexities associated with multipliers, the wisest course of action for sport professionals is to focus their economic impact efforts on obtaining a good estimate of visitor spending and not attempt to use multipliers. This will remove the high probability that the multipliers applied to the spending data will be flawed. If multipliers are used, then sport professionals could adopt one of two options. The preferred option is to seek out technical assistance from experts who understand the nuances of multipliers. If this is not possible, the following guidelines are for making "best guesstimates":

> For sales multipliers, use 1.2 for small rural areas, 1.4 for larger rural areas, 1.5 for moderate size communities, and 1.7 for state or metro area analyses. To convert to full-time equivalent jobs and to income, national tourism average ratios for direct effects could be used (i.e., 20 jobs per $1 million in sales or 16 jobs per $1 million of visitor spending). The income ratio is approximately 35% relative to sales and 28% relative to spending. These ratios are averages. They will vary by sector, and job ratios are higher in rural areas and smaller in large metro regions.[33]

Notwithstanding this advice, for a variety of reasons there will be occasions when it will not be followed. Further, there will be times when elected officials and sport professionals will receive studies done by others who include multipliers that they will be required to evaluate. Hence, this section is intended to facilitate a better understanding of them.

The Multiplier Concept

The multiplier concept recognizes that when visitors to a facility or event spend money in a community, their initial direct expenditure stimulates economic activity and creates additional business turnover, personal income, employment, and government revenue in the host community. One person's spending becomes income for others, who in turn spend a portion of that new income, which creates income for others, and so on. The concept is based on recognition that the industries constituting an economy are interdependent. That is, each business will purchase goods and services produced by other establishments within the local economy. Thus, expenditures by visitors from outside the local economy will affect not only the business at which the initial expenditure is made, but also the suppliers of that business, the suppliers' suppliers, and so on.

Multipliers are derived from input-output tables that disaggregate an economy into industrial sectors and examine the flow of goods and services among them. The IMPLAN input-output model, which is perhaps the most widely used, has 440 industrial sectors. In essence, an input-output model is an elaborate accounting system that keeps track of the transactions and flow of new money throughout an economy. The process enables a separate multiplier to be applied for each of the industrial sectors affected by the initial direct expenditure.

The multiplier process is diagrammed in Figure 5.2. To illustrate the process, the figure assumes that visitors spend their money at four different types of establishments in a community. Their initial injection of money constitutes the direct economic impact on the community. Figure 5.2 shows the six different ways in which each of the establishments receiving the initial funds could disburse the money it receives. They are:

1. To other private sector businesses in the same jurisdiction (local inter-industry purchases) to restock inventories to provide for future sales; to maintain buildings, fittings, and equipment; to pay insurance premiums; and for a myriad of other purposes.
2. To employees or shareholders who reside within the community in the form of salaries and wages or dividends, which constitutes personal income to them (local household income).
3. To local governments as sales taxes, property taxes, and license fees (local government revenue).
4. To private sector businesses located outside the local jurisdiction (non-local inter-industry purchases).
5. To employees or stakeholders who reside outside the community in the form of salaries and wages or dividends which constitute personal income to them (non-local household income).
6. To non-local (e.g., state and federal) governments as sales taxes or taxes on profits.

The latter three categories of spending illustrate that the host city is part of a larger economy. The money in these categories leaks out of the community's economic system to pay taxes to, or buy labor, goods and services from, entities outside the community.

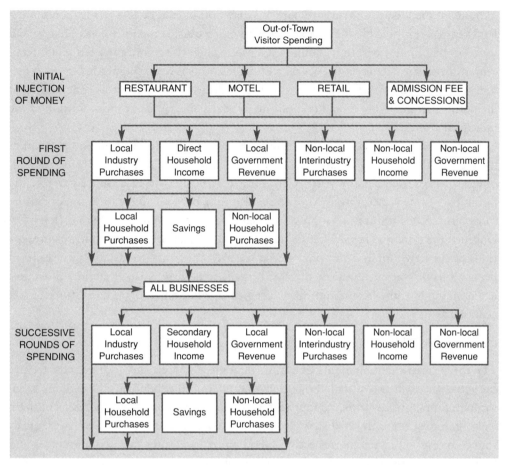

Figure 5.2. The Multiplier Effect of Visitor Spending at a Sports Event.

Only those dollars remaining within the host community after leakage has taken place constitute an economic gain to the community. The amount of the initial expenditures that remains in the jurisdiction from local inter-industry purchases, local household income, and local government revenue is subsequently spent in one of the six ways previously listed and thereby sets in motion a further chain of economic activity.

Because local government revenue from taxes and fees is likely to be immediately expended back into the local economy for services the local government provides, this money is considered to remain a source of local stimulus. However, some of the direct household income received by local residents may not be spent in the local economy. Rather, some of it may be saved, in which case it contributes nothing further to local economic stimulus (Figure 5.2). As far as the community is concerned, saving the household income received is similar to spending it outside the community. The effect is the same in that the economic stimulus potential is lost. Figure 5.2 also shows potential leakage from some household income being spent outside the local jurisdiction on non-local household purchases.

Some of the leakage shown in Figure 5.2 may not, in fact, be lost to the community. For example, it is possible that employees who reside outside the jurisdiction may spend some of their money within its boundaries, especially if the community is a major retail center for the area. This return of leaked funds is not shown in Figure 5.7 for two reasons. First, it is likely to be relatively small in most cases; second, it was concluded that including it in the figure would complicate rather than expedite communication of the multiplier principle.

One of the unknowns is the time it takes for new money to be spent and re-spent as it circulates through an economy. Does it take a year for the full impact to be realized, or less, or does it take many years? Certainly, there is likely to be a time lag before the full impact of new spending is complete and it may have relatively little impact in the short term. A key feature in people's understanding of the multiplier that is often overlooked is the potential for substantial leakage at each cycle of the multiplier as proportions of the new money go to pay salaries or taxes or to buy goods and services from people or entities located outside the city. It needs to be emphasized that only those dollars remaining in the host community after leakage has taken place constitute the net economic gain.

Constituent Elements of a Multiplier

The three constituent elements of a multiplier are direct effects, indirect effects, and induced effects. It was noted above that visitors' initial expenditures are likely to go through numerous iterations as they seep through the economy, with portions of them leaking out each round until they decline to a negligible amount. These subsequent rounds of economic activity reflecting spending by local inter-industry purchases and local government revenues are termed *indirect impacts*.

The proportion of household income that is spent locally on goods and services is termed an *induced impact*, which is defined as the increase in economic activity generated by local consumption due to increases in employee compensation, proprietary income, and other property income. The *indirect* and *induced* effects together are frequently called *secondary impacts*. In summary, the three elements that contribute to the total impact of a given initial injection of expenditures from out-of-town visitors are:

Direct Effects: Direct effects are the first-round effects of visitor spending, that is, how much the restaurateurs, hoteliers, and others who received the initial dollars spend on goods and services from other industries in the local economy and pay employees, self-employed individuals, and shareholders who live in the jurisdiction. It is important to note that there is a difference between direct effects and visitors' initial spending. Multiplier models appropriately recognize that spending includes cost of goods sold, so they measure direct effects by subtracting the cost of goods sold from visitor spending. Only about 80% of visitor spending in the local area is typically captured by the local economy as direct sales. The other 20% goes to cover the cost of goods sold at retail that are not made locally.

Indirect Effects: Indirect effects are the ripple effects of additional rounds of recir-

Table 5.4. Average Multiplier Coefficients Across Six Visitor-Related Sectors in a Texas City of 90,000 Population[a]								
Sales			Personal Income			Jobs		
Direct	Direct + Indirect	Direct + Indirect + Induced	Direct	Direct + Indirect	Direct + Indirect + Induced	Direct	Direct + Indirect	Direct + Indirect + Induced
0.8	1.06	1.24	0.29	0.37	0.58	18.71	22.36	31.07

[a] The direct effects were estimated to be 80% of total visitor spending (this capture rate removes the cost of sales and ensures only the incremental increase in value of products that occur in the community is included).

culating the direct effects dollars by local businesses and local governments.

Induced Effects: Induced effects are the other ripple effects generated by the direct and indirect effects, caused by employees of impacted businesses spending some of their salaries and wages in other businesses in the city.

Sometimes critics in a community argue that the only beneficiaries of visitor spending in the community are businesses and their employees who are the direct recipients of that spending. Indirect expenditures expand this to other businesses that trade with the initial business recipients, while induced income effects are "the tide which raises all boats." These effects disseminate the "new money" widely throughout the community.

The three different effects are illustrated in Table 5.4. For example, the middle column of this table shows that each dollar spent in this city generated 29 cents in direct personal income, another 8 cents in indirect personal income, and an additional 21 cents in induced income.

Operationalization of the Multiplier

The term *multiplier* should more accurately be termed a *multiplier coefficient*. A sales multiplier coefficient is calculated by the following formula:

$$\frac{\text{Direct sales} + \text{Indirect sales} + \text{Induced sales}}{\text{Direct sales}}$$

Interpolating the numbers from Table 5.4 to the formula indicates that the sales multiplier is 1.55.

$$\frac{1.24}{.80} = 1.55$$

Thus, every $1 of visitor spending, or 80 cents of direct effects, would generate $1.55 in sales in the economy.

Similarly, a personal income multiplier would use the following formula:

$$\frac{\text{Direct income} + \text{Indirect income} + \text{Induced income}}{\text{Direct sales}}$$

Again, interpolating the numbers from Table 5.4 to the formula indicates that the total personal income coefficient is .72

$$.29 + .08 + .21 = \frac{.58}{.80} = .72$$

The personal income coefficient indicates that for every 80 cents of direct effects, or $1 of total spending, injected by visitors into the economy of this city, 72 cents of personal income accrues to residents in the form of employee wages and salaries and proprietary income.

Sometimes studies replace the *direct effects of visitor expenditures* denominator with *direct effects on income*. If very high multipliers are reported, for example an income multiplier higher than 1, then it is probably because this type of ratio formula has been used. Over three decades ago, one of the pioneers of economic impact analysis in this field advocated "general abandonment of the 'ratio' multiplier approach and the consequent removal of the confusion which its use creates. It is difficult to envisage how or why such an inappropriate approach has gained such wide usage . . . It has no basis in economic theory and it provides misleading policy prescriptions" (p. 518).[34]

One reason it is used by some, even though it is confusing, is because it results in some multipliers, especially personal income multipliers, being larger numbers. For example, if the personal income data from Table 5.4 are interpolated using "direct effect on income" as the formula's denominator, then the multiplier is shown to be 2.0 (.58/.29) instead of .72. This could mischievously be interpreted to mean that for every $1 of visitor expenditure (80 cents of direct effects), $2 in income is generated. This is inaccurate. It really means that $1 in secondary income is generated for every $1 of direct income.

Influence of a Community's Size and Business Structure on Multipliers

The magnitude of a multiplier is likely to be substantially influenced by the structure of the host community. Structure refers to the degree to which businesses where visitors spend their money engage in trade with other businesses within the impact area of interest, rather than with enterprises outside the defined geographical area. Communities near major trading centers, where the trading centers are located outside the local economy, will have smaller multipliers due to leakage than do similar communities that contain their own major trading centers.

Many sport events are held in metroplex areas composed of multiple cities. In these instances, it is especially difficult for the particular city in which they take place (and which may be asked to provide public subsidies for them) to capture most of the economic impact. It has been noted that:

> The integrated nature of regions makes it difficult for any city to capture the benefits from the intraregional changes in consumers' spending associated with a team's location. The presence of a team in a particular city moves discretionary spending into that locality. However, in the absence of local taxes (sales or in-

come) that permit an investor city to exclusively retain revenue, the benefits from fans' spending quickly disperses within the region in proportion to existing distributions of labor and business. (p. 278)[35]

The nexus to trade centers is a key element in assessing the likely economic consequences of sport franchises moving from downtown to suburban facilities. In such cases, much of the economic impact may remain in the downtown area where the business infrastructure is located. A referendum was held in Dallas on a financial package the city proposed to invest in a new arena for the city's NBA and NHL franchises, subsequently called the American Airlines Center. If the referendum failed, then it was likely that the franchises would emulate the NFL Dallas Cowboys and move to the suburbs. Opponents to the public subsidy package argued that the city would lose little from the teams' move to the suburbs:

> Whether the arena is built in the city or the suburbs, it will have just about the same economic impact on Dallas and the metropolitan area. That's because most of the jobs generated by a new arena—from Dallas Mavericks T-shirt production to french-fry and hamburger-bun distribution—will probably stay in the same place no matter where the stadium is, so long as it remains in the Metroplex. "What does Dallas care?" says one local economist. "Those hot dogs will get made at the same hot-dog factory whether the teams play in Arlington or Dallas." (p. 4)[36]

As a general rule, a smaller community tends not to have the business interdependencies within its economy that facilitate retention of monies spent during the first round of expenditures. Hence, much of the expenditure would be re-spent outside the local region, leading to a relatively low local economic multiplier. Larger, more diverse economies have higher multipliers than do smaller communities because they are able to retain a larger portion of each successive round of spending. Thus, conventional wisdom posits that the larger the defined area's economic base, the smaller the leakage that is likely to occur and the larger is likely to be the value added from the original expenditures. In Figure 5.3, the multiplier for the city is likely to be smaller than that for the county, which will probably be smaller than that for the region, which in turn will be smaller than the multiplier for a statewide economy.

The magnitude of economic impact is strongly influenced by two factors that tend to be countervailing forces: the extent of leakage and the number of non-residents participating. Leakage is likely to be smaller, and hence the multiplier larger, as size of the geographical area increases. However, as geographical area size increases, the proportion of visitors who come from outside that area is likely to decrease. A *small city* event is likely to attract a large proportion of its visitors (say 90%) from outside its boundaries, but it will have large leakage and a small income multiplier (say .2). In contrast, if the economic impact of that event on the *state's* economy is measured, then it is likely that the proportion of visitors attracted to it from outside the state is low (say 5%), but leakage will be small, yielding a higher income multiplier (say .8). An egregious tactic sometimes used by mischievous studies to boost the purported economic impact is to use a

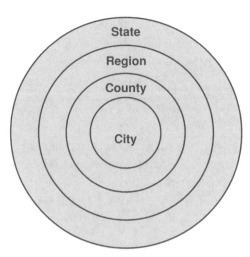

Figure 5.3. Size of Multiplier is Likely to Reflect Size of Geographic Area.

regional multiplier to estimate the impact of spending on the much smaller area of a community within the region.

Table 5.5 reports the income multiplier coefficients used to estimate the economic impact of sport events held in three cities: College Station, Texas (population 90,000); Des Moines, Iowa (200,000); and San Antonio, Texas (936,000). This table illustrates two points.

First, as the size of the cities increases, the multipliers become larger. It was noted earlier that larger communities are more likely to have greater interdependencies among businesses, so there is less leakage out of their economies.

Second, the coefficients are different for each category of expenditure that is listed. The multiplier is greater for some categories of spending than for others. The magnitude of the total spending and re-spending that will be retained in the local economy will depend on the categories of expenditure. For example, in College Station, a $1 ex-

Table 5.5. Personal Income Multiplier Coefficients in Three Cities of Different Sizes			
	College Station (90,000)	**Des Moines** (200,000)	**San Antonio** (936,000)
Restaurants, Bars, Nighclubs	.55	.78	1.26
Admission Fees	.62	.81	1.07
Groceries	.52	.71	1.08
Retail Shopping	.63	.94	1.12
Lodging Expenses	.51	.71	1.05
Automobile Gas and Oil	.44	.62	.69
Airfares, Rental Cars, Taxis	.38	.49	.81

penditure by visitors in retail shopping yielded 63 cents in personal income to residents, while $1 spent on commercial transportation yielded 38 cents in personal income. This is because most expenditures on commercial transportation (primarily airfares and to a lesser extent rental cars) are paid directly to companies based outside the community whose operating personnel and suppliers also are primarily from outside the community. In contrast, most personnel and service suppliers to retail stores come from inside the city, so they are more extensively linked to other elements of the local economy.

A region's normal business structure is likely to change when it hosts a mega event. This means that the use of standard models (e.g., IMPLAN and RIMS II) to calculate multipliers is especially suspect because the inter-industry relationships within a region are based on the region's normal economic patterns. The scale of mega events make it likely that they will create a different pattern and that if standard models are used, their multipliers will be much too high because:

> Expenditures in industries dominated by nationally owned chains such as large hotels, rental car agencies, and airlines, and to a lesser extent motels, restaurants, and general retailers may rise significantly due to a mega-event, but local incomes will not increase substantially. Since the benefits accrue to non-local capital owners leading to higher than normal leakages of income, the money generated from these events is unlikely to recirculate through the economy, and any multipliers applied are, therefore, probably inflated. (p. 69)[37]

In the specific case of hotels, for example, room rates may be increased by two, three or four times their normal amounts during a mega event, but the wages paid to hotel staff remain unchanged. Since the hotel owners are likely to reside outside the community, a much greater proportion of the hotel's income from visitors is likely to leak out of the community in a mega event, so the multiplier will be much smaller.[37]

The dominant economic role of those who own mega event properties contribute to this distortion. Thus, the NFL takes over the facility hosting the Super Bowl and controls all money from the event (ticket sales, television, sponsorship, etc.), which then goes to the league, not the host team or community, so there is extraordinary leakage. When the Rugby World Cup was held in France, the leakage level was similarly extraordinarily high because the International Rugby Board (IRB), which is headquartered in Ireland, collected all the commercial income from the event (sponsorship, television rights, VIP seats and executive boxes worth $200 million). Much of this money came from French businesses and represented leakage outside the national economy, much of which would not have occurred if France had not been hosting the event. For example, French television companies paid $60 million for broadcasting rights to the IRB.[38] Clearly, application of a standard multiplier in these cases exaggerates the impact substantially.

Interpreting Sales and Income Multipliers

Three different types of economic impact measures are commonly reported: sales, personal income, and employment. A *sales* or *output measure* reports the direct, indirect, and induced effect of an extra unit of spending by a sport visitor on economic activity within a host community. It relates visitor expenditure to the increase in business turnover that it creates. Sales output is a rather esoteric measure with very limited practical value. It may be of some interest to economists interested in researching industry interdependencies or to business proprietors interested in sales impacts, but it does not offer insights that are useful for guiding public policy decisions.

The *personal income measure* of economic impact reports the direct, indirect, and induced effect of an extra unit of visitor spending on the changes that result in level of personal income in the host community. In contrast to the sales output indicator, the income measure has substantial practical implications for stakeholders because it enables them to relate the economic benefits received by residents to the costs they invested. The income coefficient reports the income per dollar of direct sales that accrues to residents and includes employee compensation and proprietor income. Figure 5.1 and Table 5.1 showed that the ratio of the economic benefits residents receive in return for costs they invested in an event, tournament, or facility provide the fundamental rationale for undertaking economic impact analysis.

Table 5.4 reported the sales output, personal income, and employment (jobs) multipliers for a selected city. The formula that used these data earlier in this chapter to calculate sales and income multipliers illustrated that the values of *sales* indicators are substantially higher than those of *personal income* measures. For example, the formulas indicated that on average, each $1 expenditure by visitors (80 cents in direct effects) will generate 72 cents in personal income for residents of the city, but sales or business activity in the city is likely to rise by $1.55. If analysts do not clearly define which economic impact measure is being discussed, then there is a danger that inaccurate, exaggerated, spurious inferences will be drawn from the data.

In an analysis of a sport event or facility, sales measures of economic impact are not of interest to local residents. The point of interest is the impact of visitors' expenditures on residents' personal incomes. Most government officials and taxpayers are likely to be interested only in knowing how much extra income residents will receive from the injection of funds from visitors. Their interest in value of sales per se is likely to be small because it does not directly impact residents' standard of living. Further, the use of sales indicators may give a false impression of the true impacts of visitor spending because the highest effects on personal income are not necessarily generated from the highest increase in sales, and the income effect may not be uniform across income classes.

The conceptual model shown at the beginning of the chapter in Figure 5.1, which illustrates the rationale for economic impact studies, specifies that their purpose is to compare how much money residents invest in a sport event or facility with how much income they receive from it. The notion of sales transactions does not appear anywhere in the model and, from the perspective of residents and elected officials, it is irrelevant to the analysis.

Nevertheless, because sales measures of economic impact are generally two or three times larger than personal income indicators, sponsors of economic impact studies invariably report economic impact in terms of sales outputs rather than personal income.

The higher numbers appear to better justify the public investment that is being advocated, but they are meaningless for this purpose. They mislead rather than inform those charged with using this information to guide public policy. The use of sales rather than income multipliers probably means that inaccurate, exaggerated, spurious inferences will be drawn from the data, as most stakeholders are uninformed as to the differences between sales and personal income measures.

Interpreting Employment Multipliers

An *employment multiplier coefficient* measures the direct, indirect, and induced effect of an extra unit of visitor spending on employment in the host community. Employment multipliers are expressed in terms of number of jobs per million dollars in direct sales. Table 5.4 showed the average employment coefficients across six industries. It indicates that for every $1 million in direct sales in those six industries by visitors from outside the area, 31 jobs would be created: approximately 19 direct jobs, 3 indirect jobs (22.36–18.71), and 9 induced jobs (31.07–22.36).

The State of Maryland committed $200 million for a stadium to attract the NFL Cleveland Browns to play in Baltimore and become the Baltimore Ravens. Findings from the economic impact study commissioned by the state were widely publicized in order to justify this investment of public funds. The study concluded that a Baltimore football team would bring the equivalent of 1,170 full-time jobs to the local economy, even though the team would have only 71 full-time employees, including the 50-man player roster.[39] Given that the team plays only 10 home games a year, the contention that it would beget 1,170 full-time equivalent jobs seems intuitively unreasonable. Part of this big number was attributable to the inclusion of locals, casuals, and time switchers in the calculation of monetary economic impact; but there are three other important caveats regarding estimates of employment that were ignored in the study and that should always be considered.

First, estimates include both full-time and part-time jobs, and do not distinguish between them. This was illustrated in Exhibit 5.4 where the report authors' footnote states their impact "includes full and part-time jobs." However, their subsequent report narrative simply refers to 13,400 jobs, so both many in the media and unalert readers of the report are likely to erroneously conclude these are all full-time jobs. The employment measurement does not identify the number of hours worked in each job or the proportion of jobs that are full- and part-time. However, it seems reasonable to posit that local businesses are unlikely to hire additional full-time employees in response to additional demands created by a tournament or event because the extra business demands will last only for a few days. In these situations, the number of employees is not likely to increase. Rather, it is the number of hours that existing employees work that will increase. Existing employees may be requested to work overtime or released from other duties to accommodate this temporary peak demand. At best, only a few very short-term additional employees may be hired. Hence, it is improbable that anything like 1,170 full-time jobs would be created by the Baltimore Ravens NFL team, or that

31 jobs will be created in City A if an extra $1 million expenditure attributable to an event is forthcoming (Exhibit 5.4). The few jobs that do emerge will probably be short-term and part-time jobs. However, decision makers easily may be misled into assuming these are full-time positions.

These types of employment adjustments were reported in interviews with managers in transportation and restaurant businesses immediately after the Adelaide Grand Prix.[40,41] It was found that companies in both types of businesses accommodated their labor requirements by increasing the hours of existing employees, although some restaurant establishments indicated they hired casuals to supplement this action. It was concluded: "There were virtually no new permanent jobs in the transport area generated as a result of the Grand Prix. In fact several companies had organized the increased work load in such a way that they did not pay overtime although this was not possible for all the extra work" (p. 81).[40]

A second caveat is that the employment estimates assume all existing employees are fully occupied, so an increase in sport visitor spending will require an increase in level of employment. In the context of a hotel's front desk, for example, the employment estimator assumes that the existing staff would be unable to handle additional guests checking in for overnight stays associated with a tournament. However, in most cases, they are sufficiently underworked to do this, so additional staff would not be needed. In these situations, the employment coefficient is exaggerated. Further, it has been noted that even after businesses have fully used their existing capacity:

> Expansion is likely to depend on the businesses' longer-term expectation about whether the additional spending is temporary or permanent. In either case, the additional hiring may be delayed for a significant time. This will slow each cycle of expansion and possibly stretch the total expansion out over a lengthy period. (p. 116)[42]

A third potentially misleading dimension of employment estimates is that they imply all new jobs will be filled by residents from within the community. However, it is possible that some proportion of them will be filled by commuters or temporary employees from outside the community. If the work requires specialized skills or the host community enjoys high employment, then labor is likely to come from elsewhere. In these cases, it would obviously be inappropriate to conclude that all the jobs benefit the community's residents. A well-publicized notorious example of work requiring specialist skills occurred during the 2006 World Soccer Cup in Germany where it was reported that the country's brothels imported an estimated 40,000 sex workers to accommodate anticipated demand![43]

The first and second caveats suggest that the employment multiplier coefficient is an inappropriate output measure for reporting the economic impact of short-term events such as sport tournaments. It becomes appropriate only when the focus is on those sport facilities where there is a consistent flow of visitors from outside the area to the facility making it likely that full-time jobs are likely to be created.

ILLUSTRATIONS OF THE IMPLICATIONS OF ABUSING THE FUNDAMENTAL PRINCIPLES OF ECONOMIC IMPACT ANALYSIS

The analysis reported in Exhibit 5.6 illustrates the impact of different assumptions. It describes the State of Connecticut's failed efforts to attract the New England Patriots to the state. Central to the governor's case for spending hundreds of millions of dollars to induce the Patriots to move to the city of Hartford was the positive impact the NFL team would have on the state's economy. The consultants reported an economic impact of a new stadium for the NFL franchise at $170.3 million per year, but the authors' analysis of their report indicated widespread abuse of basic principles. When these were followed, the authors projected the economic impact to be $13.3 million.

The magnitude of distortion that occurs when the principles of economic impact analysis and multipliers are abused was vividly illustrated to one of the authors when he reported to a city's events board the results of an economic impact study of a festival incorporating more than 60 events, including a number of sport tournaments, during a three-week period in a large city. This study estimated the economic impact on residents' incomes to be approximately $16 million. The data that were reported are shown in Table 5.6.[44]

At the conclusion of the presentation, some board members quickly challenged the results, arguing that they were much too low. They observed that two weeks previously, the city council had heard a similar presentation from the convention and visitors bureau relating to a professional rodeo event the city hosted annually. The council members were informed that the economic impact of the three-day professional rodeo event was almost $30 million. The conundrum confronting the events board was posed in the

Table 5.6. The Spurious Measures of "Economic Impact" That Resulted When Time-Switchers and Casuals Were Included and Sales Multipliers Used

Items	Personal Income	Number of Jobs Created*
Restaurants, Bars, Nighclubs	5,088,151	328
Admission Fees	874,005	67
Groceries	753,562	28
Retail Shopping	3,012,571	193
Lodging Expenses	4,449,879	256
Automobile Gas and Oil	502,541	25
Airfares, Rental Cars, Taxis	1,319,433	54
Other Expenses	139,305	9
TOTAL	16,139,447	960

*This figure refers to both full-time and part-time jobs. It assumes the local economy is operating at full capacity and that there is no slack to absorb additional demand created by these events.

Exhibit 5.6

Anatomy of a Mischievous Economic Impact Study

THE DEAL

On January 12, 1999, Governor John Rowland signed a bill authorizing $374 million in state spending for a new stadium for the New England Patriots. The development agreement obligated the State of Connecticut to pay for a riverfront stadium in downtown Hartford which would serve as the new home of the NFL Patriots. Robert Kraft, the owner of the New England team, had agreed to relocate his team from the Boston-area pending approval of the new stadium.

In addition to providing a new 68,000-seat stadium rent-free, the state promised to pay Kraft as much as $175 million in cash over the first 10 years if he failed to sell out the stadium's 125 luxury suites and 6000 club seats. The taxpayers of Connecticut would pay to build new highway ramps and thousands of parking places to accommodate stadium traffic. The agreement also promised that the state would pay as much as $200 million for improvements and renovations over the least period.

A BREAK-EVEN PROJECT?

From the inception of the idea of bringing an NFL team to the capitol city, Governor Rowland was an enthusiastic supporter of the stadium project. Several months prior to signing the stadium bill the governor authorized the hiring of an internationally known consulting firm to determine the economic impacts that a proposed new stadium would have with the New England Patriots as the primary tenant. The firm had a long track record of completing fiscal and economic analyses for proposed professional sport franchises.

The final draft of the firm's economic impact analysis, issued in November 1998, concluded that the stadium would more than pay for itself in 30 years. In fact, the analysts predicted that the cumulative economic benefits from direct and indirect spending and increased tax revenues would produce a $3.2 million *profit* by the time the stadium bonds were paid off over 30 years. At a news conference to announce the study's findings, Governor Rowland pronounced that the sta-

dium would "create jobs, act as a catalyst for more development and pay for itself."

In reaching the conclusion that the proposed stadium would be economically viable, the consulting firm applied commonly accepted techniques for conducting economic impact analyses. However, careful evaluation of several assumptions underlying the analysis clearly demonstrate how mischievous economic data are generated. The following figures, drawn directly from the consulting firm's report, illustrate the extent to which the conclusions greatly exaggerate the economic benefits attributed to the $375 stadium project.

1. Assumptions Inflate Direct Spending Estimates

Direct spending in 2001, the first year in which the stadium was projected to open (and the base year for all subsequent calculations), including both gross revenue spending at the stadium ($100 million) and attendee spending outside of the stadium ($7 million) was projected at $107 million. This direct spending figure was based on the following assumptions:

Assumption #1: The Patriots would sell 95% of their regular ticket inventory at an escalating average price of $50 to $63 for the first five years.

Facts: Achieving that performance standard would exceed the sales record of every new NFL franchise established in the 1990s. The Carolina Panthers over the first four years sold 87.3% of their regular season ticket inventory. The St. Louis Rams sold less than 90% of their available inventory in years 2 and 3 in their new stadium. In the fifth year of operation, the play-off bound Jacksonville Jaguars, sold 92% of their seating capacity. From 1996 through the 2000 season, an NFL team, on average, sold 92% of its ticket inventory.

Assumption #2: The Patriots would sell 100% of their 6000 club seats at $4,250 each for the first five years.

Exhibit 5.6 *(Continued)*

Anatomy of a Mischievous Economic Impact Study

Facts: During the 1998 season, the first year in their new stadium (what is now named, FedEx Field), the historically popular Washington Redskins were unable to sell 8,000 club seats. According to the Association of Luxury Suite Directors (ALSD), in 1999 the NFL overall sold 92% of the league's available club seat inventory. The average club seat price used by the consulting firm was almost two thousand dollars *above* the league wide average which the ALSD reported was $2,500. [As part of the agreement the State agreed to make up the difference if the club seats failed to bring in $20 million annually!]

Assumption #3: The Patriots would generate a concession sales per capita of $18.50 to $20.52 over the first five years of playing in the stadium.

Facts: Concession revenues, the income generated from the sale of food service items and souvenirs, are commonly tabulated on the basis of per capita sales— the total amount of concessions sold divided by the number of patrons. The consulting firm projected that the average attendee to a Patriots game would spend around $20 per visit on hot dogs, beer, souvenir pennants, etc. According to the leading authority on concession spending at sports venues, the per cap projection used by the Hartford stadium consultants was 33% above the NFL average. The Bigelow Companies reported that the amount spent on concessions at NFL venues averaged around $15.00 during the 2000 season.

2. Failure to Exclude "Local" Resident Spending

Assumption #4: The consultant claimed that "90% of the total spending ($107 million in 2001) would be incremental." They assumed that $9 of every $10 spent on attending Patriots games, amounting to $97 million in 2001, would be "export" dollars or new money entering into the Connecticut economy.

Facts: In their market analysis the consultants acknowledged that most of the attendees would come from the Greater Hartford area, and most of the rest from within the state of Connecticut. A more reasonable assumption would be that 20% of the fans attending Patriots games would be traveling from outside the state, resulting in an estimate that 20% of the direct spending would be new or incremental money.

3. Use of Inappropriate Multiplier

Assumption #5: To account for the "total output" of economic activity (direct, indirect and induced) that would result from on-going stadium operations, the consultants applied a sales or output multiplier of 1.75. This allowed the analysts to claim that the total economic impact of the new stadium would be $170.3 million in 2001, growing to $200.6 by 2005.

1.75 (sales multiplier) × $97,083,000
(direct "incremental spending)
= $170.3 million (total output)

Facts: Inviolable principle #3 in this chapter emphasizes that sales measure are inappropriate and income multipliers should be used. Residents are only interested in how much extra income they will receive from the injection of visitors' funds. Sales *per se* do not impact residents' standard of living.

4. Distorted Employment Claims

Assumption #6: By 2005, stadium construction and spending prompted by the operation of the stadium would create 3,240 FTE (full-time equivalent) jobs in the state.

Facts: The projected number of jobs was derived from the fallacious direct expenditure and "non-locals" data identified above. The report also fails to acknowledge that virtually all of the jobs which would emanate from the stadium project are likely to be part-time or seasonal, not full-time, with pay at close to minimum wage levels.

Exhibit 5.6 *(Continued)*

Anatomy of a Mischievous Economic Impact Study

IMPACT OF ALTERNATIVE ASSUMPTIONS If more reasonable assumptions are substituted for those on which the consultants based their economic impact, the results are quantumly different. Consider the following:

We believe this is likely to be a much more accurate estimate of the economic impact of the new stadium on the residents of Connecticut in 2001 than the consultants' estimate of $170.3 million!

1. Direct Spending:	Consultant	Revised
Consultant		
IF 90% (not 95%) of regular tickets were sold	$43,715,367	$46,144,000
IF 92% (not 100%) of club seats sold at $2500 (not $4250)	$13,800,000	$25,500,000
IF concession per cap were $15.00 (not $18.50)	$11,670,000	$14,393,000
	$69,185,367	$86,037,000

Using these three sources of direct spending, the revised assumptions reduce the consultants' estimate by almost $17 million in just 2001! The consultants' other sources of direct spending in the stadium are parking, novelties and advertising. If their assumptions in these three areas and the outside stadium estimates remain unchanged, the total direct spending falls to $88.6 million from $107 million.

2. **Incremental Spending Impact**

IF out-of-state attendees are projected to be 20% of the total attendance (rather than 90%) then the estimate of new direct or "incremental" spending would be $17.7 million (.2 × $88.6 million).

Remember that the key to economic impact is the infusion of new dollars from outside the local economy. It is fair to assume that a great majority of direct spending would be from local Hartford-area residents who would most likely be substituting their spending at Patriots games for other entertainment options in the local community. In any event, their spending would not be adding new dollars to the state's economy. Thus, the true economic impact related to the new stadium would be far less than projected by the consultants.

3. **Personal Income Multiplier**

IF an average personal income multiplier of .75 were used, rather than the 1.75 sales multiplier used by the consultants, the economic impact would be (.75 × $17.7 million): $13.3 million

AFTERWARD DENOUEMONT

Governor Rowland's enthusiastic support for the new stadium had never once been mentioned in his recent re-election campaign, presumable because it would have been controversial. Thus, when he announced the deal, it awakened public outrage that a huge amount of money was to be given to a professional franchise with minimum public input.

The opportunity cost of the funds became a prominent issue: "The low income housing allowance is being cut again for the third year in a row. A report just came out that thirty to thirty-five schools in Hartford alone are not up to safety codes. They have leaky roofs, no heat: kids are wearing coats all day to school. Where's the priorities here."[a] Subsequently, environmental problems emerged with the site adding substantial additional cost. Further, the NFL did not want to leave the Boston media market, the sixth largest in the country, so it offered Kraft low interest guaranteed loans up to $150 million to pay up to half the cost of a new stadium.

All of these issues caused Kraft to accept an inferior offer from the state of Massachusetts which required him to use his funds to build a new stadium at Foxboro with the state's contributions limited to $70 million for roads and sewers.

---

[a] DeMause, N & Cagan, J. (2008). *Field of schemes: How the great stadium swindle turns public money into private profit.* Lincoln, Nebraska: University of Nebraska Press

following terms: How can we possibly accept that this festival lasting for 3 weeks and embracing more than 60 events had a smaller economic impact than a 3-day rodeo? The city council provides a substantially larger budget to us to stage the festival than they allocate to the convention and visitors bureau to host the professional rodeo event. When they compare the festival data which have been presented to us with those from the rodeo, there is a real possibility that the festival budget will be cut, because the festival costs much more to stage and its economic impact on the city is barely half that of the rodeo.

When a copy of the rodeo economic impact study was reviewed, it quickly became apparent that it abused four fundamental principles. The study included local residents, included time-switchers and casuals, used sales output as the measure of economic impact, and implied full-time jobs resulted from the visitors' expenditures. The author's response in his subsequent presentation to the city council was to replicate the presentation made to the events board, but then to extend it by referring to the rodeo study and showing the results if those erroneous assumptions were applied to the festival.

The data in Table 5.7 include time-switchers, casuals, and sales multipliers. Respondents were asked questions that showed 27% of non-local participants were time-switchers who would have visited the city if the festival had not been held, but the festival influenced their decision to come at that time. Another 43% were casuals who would have come to the city at that time, irrespective of the event. They went to the festival because it was an attractive entertainment option while they were in the community. By inappropriately including those individuals in the analysis and by focusing attention on sales rather than personal income multipliers, the "economic impact" was claimed to be $125 million (as compared to $16 million in Table 5.6).

Table 5.7. The Spurious Measures of "Economic Impact" That Resulted When Time-Switchers and Casuals Were Included and Sales Multipliers Used

Items	Total Sales	Personal Income	Number of Jobs Created*
Restaurants, Bars, Nighclubs	37,859,887	16,737,554	1078
Admission Fees	7,837,688	2,875,055	222
Groceries	4,555,057	2,478,865	91
Retail Shopping	23,545,491	9,909,880	635
Lodging Expenses	35,124,109	14,637,961	843
Automobile Gas and Oil	4,744,930	1,653,118	84
Airfares, Rental Cars, Taxis	10,710,664	4,340,311	179
Other Expenses	1,088,768	458,243	29
TOTAL	125,466,594	53,090,987	3,161

*This figure refers to both full-time and part-time jobs. It assumes the local economy is operating at full capacity and that there is no slack to absorb additional demand created by these events.

Table 5.8 is the most egregious exaggeration of "economic impact" because it inappropriately includes local residents in the analysis; it prominently displays economic activity in terms of value of sales; it includes time-switchers and casuals; and it displays total jobs created, failing to note (as in the original rodeo study) that they are a combination of part-time and full-time jobs and that they are unlikely to be sustained because the festival will not provide a consistent flow of visitors throughout the year. Indeed, even if the mischievous job totals are ignored, the results in Table 5.8 are a measure of the festival's economic significance, *not* of its economic impact.

This illustration demonstrates the wide range of numbers that purport to measure economic impact that may be presented to stakeholders from the same set of primary data. If a press conference was held in City X to report the festival's economic impact, the organizers could, at one extreme, announce that the sales output from economic activity associated with the festival was more than $321 million and that it generated 8,258 jobs, implying that they were full-time, permanent positions (Table 5.8). At the other extreme, they could announce that the economic impact of the festival on personal income was approximately $16 million and while the analysis showed that it generated 960 part-time or full-time jobs, there were some assumptions which make it likely that this number is unreasonably optimistic (Exhibit 5.6).

The media, general public, city council, and other relevant publics are unlikely to be aware of the underlying assumptions, subtleties, and potential error sources associated with economic impact studies. Their lack of sophistication and the apparent objectivity conveyed by the numbers make it tempting for advocates to act unethically.

Clearly, there is an ethical conundrum. Acting ethically when others do not could critically damage the event's standing. If the correct $16 million figure for City X is pre-

Table 5.8. The Spurious Measures of "Economic Impact" That Resulted When Local Residents, Time-Switchers, and Casuals Were Included and Sales Multipliers Used

Items	Total Sales	Personal Income	Number of Jobs Created*
Restaurants, Bars, Nightclubs	109,196,634	48,238,234	3110
Admission Fees	38,691,412	14,200,095	1095
Groceries	20,163,133	10,987,611	402
Retail Shopping	66,934,134	28,159,101	1805
Lodging Expenses	47,872,258	19,922,456	1148
Automobile Gas and Oil	14,727,339	5,123,586	259
Airfares, Rental Cars, Taxis	22,146,640	9,126,217	370
Other Expenses	1,874,950	1,076,825	69
TOTAL	321,606,500	136,834,125	8,258

*This figure refers to both full-time and part-time jobs. It assumes the local economy is operating at full capacity and that there is no slack to absorb additional demand created by these events.

sented, the festival's economic contribution is likely to appear relatively insignificant compared to other events that announce the equivalent of the $321 million figure as their estimated "economic impact." The relatively small impact of the festival is likely to translate into commensurately less political and resource support for it from decision makers and perhaps, ultimately, even withdrawal of appropriations for it.

Alternatively, some may rationalize that it is justifiable to use the same set of mischievous measures to compare the economic contributions of events because others have used them, even though the results of all of them are grossly misleading. If such a position is accepted, then abuses incorporated into one economic impact analysis become contagious. When precedent has been established in one study, others are likely to feel compelled to knowingly perpetuate the abuse by incorporating the misleading procedures into their own analyses. If they fail to do so, then the economic impact attributed to their event or facility is perceived to be lower than that reported by others and thus less worthy of public investment.

To resolve this ethical conundrum, it is recommended that all three measures—personal income, sales, and jobs—be reported so like measures can be compared to like, but that the limitations of the sales and jobs measures be emphasized and the principles of legitimate economic impact studies clarified.

Despite growing skepticism of the mischievous results emanating from advocacy studies, they are likely to continue to be commissioned as long as they contribute to two ends, the first of which is to provide political cover for elected officials supporting the public subsidies, and the second to persuade at least a small number of people to vote in favor of a subsidy in a referendum. For example, in a community where 54% of voters are either undecided about the issue or opposed to a subsidy and 46% are in favor, a mischievous economic impact study that misleads only 5% of the voters can change the outcome. It has been pointed out that "if bogus studies can sway only a relatively few people, the interests that benefit from facility construction (the sports team, local contractors, construction unions, real estate operators, bankers) are motivated to produce them" (p. 85).[45] These powerful interests are able to raise substantial funds to promulgate the mischievous numbers in promotional campaigns so they become firmly entrenched without substantial challenge from opponents who lack those resources. Thus, in the days before a referendum on spending almost $300 million of public funds for a new stadium for the San Diego Padres, the pro-proposition campaign spent almost $3 million, which came from the Padres, MLB, local television stations, the construction industry and the stadium caterer. In contrast, the anti-stadium group raised $26,000. They were outspent by 111 to 1 and the referendum passed 60% to 40%.[25]

> When San Francisco and the state of Washington held referenda on whether to subsidize a new NFL football stadium, both referenda won by tiny margins. In San Francisco, proponents outspent opponents by 25 to 1, while in Washington the spending ratio was an amazing 80 to 1! If as few as 2% of voters were misled by the incorrect claims about the economic effects of the stadium proposals in these campaigns, the bogus studies determined the outcome in these elections.

With the campaign spending so unequal, such an outcome surely is not implausible. (p. 85)[45]

MISCHIEVOUSLY EXPANDING THE PROJECT SCOPE

Some sport projects receive support from government entities because they position themselves as catalysts for enhancing the tax base through stimulating regeneration of a dilapidated area or, in the case of green-fields sites, for encouraging ancillary development around them. This position then is used to justify studies that expand the project's scope to measure the economic impact associated with the whole area rather than being confined to the specific sport project. For example, a study titled "Evaluation of the Proposed Dallas Arena" was commissioned to assess the economic impact of a multi-purpose downtown arena for the NBA team in Dallas. The city's voters were being asked to approve a $125 million investment in it.

However, the report staked out a wider brief than the arena:

In addition to the multi-purpose downtown arena previously described in this report, the developer has indicated that, subject to future market demand, they [sic] would develop a variety of real estate properties in the downtown Dallas area over a 15 year period. The project components are anticipated to include the following uses: office, retail (both specialty and entertainment), residential and hotel . . . For the purposes of this analysis, the economic and fiscal impacts have been based on stabilized operations of the *completed development*. (pp. 80, 81)[11]

The supposed "economic and fiscal impact study" metamorphosed in the narrative to a study of "gross economic output." It embraced the egregious practices of including locals' and casuals' expenditures, counting city investments in capital projects as new money, applying sales multipliers to these, and so on. However, in addition, it included the speculative other developments in the calculations. This enabled it to conclude:

The total cumulative gross economic output generated within the City by the construction of the proposed project is estimated to be approximately $708.7 million. This economic activity supports a cumulative total of 8,078 gross FTE jobs and $288.6 million in employee compensation over the construction period. (p. 88)[11]

Of the $708.7 million, $210.7 million (30%) was attributable to the arena and $498 million (70%) to the "other developments." A similar strategy was used to derive annual impacts:

The total gross economic output within the City generated by the operation of the proposed project is anticipated to be approximately $648.5 million annually. The economic activity supports a cumulative total of 8,089 gross FTE employment and $209.5 million in employee compensation. (p. 94)[11]

The arena accounted for $236 million (36%) and the "other developments" $412.4 million (64%). Hence, the influence of the inappropriate procedures used to derive the arena's "economic/fiscal impact analysis" (the description used by the consultants in the cover letter accompanying the report) was magnified considerably by the mischievous inclusion of the highly speculative "other developments." The voters approved the city's investment of $125 million, and presumably, some of them were influenced by these misleading economic data. However, seven years after the study was completed and five years after the arena opened, none of the other developments had either materialized or been planned, causing the city's mayor at that time to observe angrily:

> They show all the pretty watercolors of the private development that they will build once the arena opens and then nothing ever happens. They tell us they're going to have stores, including a Wolford, where they sell French panty hose for fifty dollars a pair. Well, I talked to Wolford in New York, and you couldn't get a Wolford next door to a basketball arena at any price. The mixed use complex has never gotten off the drawing board. (p. 105)[46]

Nevertheless, the arena's advocates had achieved their goal.

The City of Arlington paid $160 million of the $191 million total cost of the new Ballpark at Arlington to accommodate the Texas Rangers baseball team. Again, a major element contributing to the projected economic impact was to be the associated proximate development that the ball field would stimulate. The synergy proved to be mythical. Ten years later, the mayor of Dallas observed:

> Walk over to the Ballpark and see there is nothing happening. The area just south of the Ballpark is a blighted neighborhood with the highest crime rate in the city. All the promised offices, high-rises and retail shops that were supposed to line a river walk and border a man-made lake never materialized. Similar promises were made to Irving when Texas Stadium was built with local sales tax revenue [the total cost of the stadium was met by the city]. What you see today is a parking lot that stretches to the horizon. (p. 80)[46]

THE MAGNITUDE OF ECONOMIC IMPACT FROM SPORT PROJECTS

Although the results from economic impact studies are situational specific (that is, every situation is different), their extensive use in the past couple of decades enables some general conclusions to be made. The study contexts can be assigned to one of three categories: (i) professional sport franchises; (ii) mega sports events; and (iii) community sports tournaments. The material in this section is subsumed under these three headings.

Professional Sport Franchises

Most professional sport franchises are located in major metropolitan areas. The structural integration of these economies suggests that much of the visitor income received by franchises is likely to remain in these communities. However, this may be fallacious for two reasons. First, much of a team's ownership business and practice operations may be located outside the city. It is plausible, for example, that a good portion of owners' incomes derived from the operation of a sports team will leave the host cities. Second, athletes who typically receive approximately half the money accruing to a franchise are not average people. They may reside for most of the year in a different community and spend most of their dollars there. The following observation was made some years ago, but the principle remains valid:

> The biggest single expenditure of teams—player salaries—gets taken to the players' posh homes outside the local area. When I attend a game at Fenway Park, I am helping the economy of Boston less than that of Katy, Texas, where Red Sox pitcher Roger Clemens takes his $15 million salary. Even the skimpy wages of concessionaires and beer vendors tend to leave the city, according to reliable surveys. (p. 31)[19]

Given that their peak earnings time frame is relatively short, professional athletes may save more money than the average person does. Their wealth may result in the purchase of more luxury items that are not produced in the local economy. Their high incomes mean they pay a higher share of their income in income-related taxes that leak out of the local economy, and so they have proportionately less disposable income to spend locally. Almost all players and owners pay the top federal marginal tax rate of 35% and an additional 1.45% Medicare tax, so over 36% of their incomes leak directly to Washington, DC.

Further, in Chapter 9 it is pointed out that income taxes are levied on players' salaries in most of the states and in many of the cities where they play their games. Outcomes such as these mean a large leakage occurs, and because multipliers are based on the usual spending patterns of the proverbial "average person," the multiplier for athletes is likely to be much smaller than the average multiplier used in standard software packages designed to calculate economic impact. If players do take money from the economy in these ways, then the spending on tickets that occurs by local people may result in a net loss to the economy, because if the community members had spent this money at small, locally owned businesses such as bowling centers or restaurants, more of it would have stayed in the local economy.

In contrast to this generalization, there is evidence that in some cases, revenues franchises receive from out-of-town visitors and other external sources such as television may tend to stay in the local area. For example, it was reported that 70% of expenditures by the Atlanta Falcons were made locally: "79% of the players and staff of the team live here all year; 39 of 58 players and 46 of 50 staff members live in Atlanta. Most field personnel are local residents, printing is local, the team uses Atlanta banks as well as an Atlanta based airline, and the team is locally owned" (p. 15).[47] Thus, much of the visitors' revenues received by the Falcons was re-spent inside the local region, leading to a relatively high economic multiplier.

The findings of those who have independently evaluated the economic impact resulting from large public subsidies by local communities for sports team facilities, free from the pressures of a commissioning sponsor, are not encouraging. The findings from a series of such studies conducted in a variety of contexts by different investigators in the past twenty years consistently report that there is no statistical relationship between sport facility construction and economic development or job creation.[48–56]

These findings have for almost three decades led respected authorities in this field to conclude: "The overwhelming consensus of opinion in these studies is that the local economic effect of a sports facility is between nonexistent and extremely modest. If stadiums do not contribute to any increase in local economic activity, they cannot cause a significant increase in revenues from local taxes" (p. 15).[48] Another report concluded: "The statistical evidence . . . indicates that professional sports as a golden goose ranks among the most enduring and greatest sports myths" (p. 313).[39] The analyst went on to observe:

> The NFL seems an especially poor investment for a city. The teams play only eight regular season and two exhibition games at home each year. And the new stadiums are uniquely ill-suited for other purposes. Researchers at the University of California at Los Angeles even claimed that the sports industry had actually grown in L.A. after the Rams and Raiders bolted. Other sports, including a slew of minor league ones, flourished with the diminished competition. (p. 315)[39]

Teams typically employ 70–130 people in their front offices and hire approximately 1,000–1,500 part-timers for unskilled, low-wage day-of-game jobs. Firms with annual budgets of this magnitude are valued in the development of any region's economy, but these gross revenues are relatively small when viewed in the context of the overall economic activity in even the smaller major league cities.[18] Table 5.9 shows that in no county in the United States does the proportion of jobs classified by the North American Industrial Classification System as *professional sports or managers* exceed four-tenths of 1% of all jobs in the county.[57] To provide a sense of perspective, consider that the economic significance of sports in the local economy of Dallas is about the same as the coin-operated laundry and interior design businesses. Car rental and leasing businesses in the city, for example, generate almost 10 times as much in annual receipts.[58] In the broader context of spectators, consider that Americans spend nearly three times as much money on flowers, seeds, and potted plants as they do on all spectator sports! "Sports may attract a great deal of attention, but they are not an economic engine, they will not generate a lot of jobs and they will not revitalize a city's economy" (p. 451).[19] Indeed, it has been suggested that "the construction of sports stadiums and the creation of professional sports franchises have served as a reflection of economic development rather than a means to it" (p. 4).[59]

County (State)	%
Summit (OH)	.35
Fulton (GA)	.32
Baltimore (MD)	.26
Oakland (MI)	.24
Bronx (NY)	.19
Erie (NY)	.19
Queens (NY)	.18
Cook (IL)	.16
Marion (IN)	.16
St. Louis (city)	.16
Suffolk (MA	.16
Philadelphia (PA)	.13
Salt Lake City	.11
Hennepin (MN)	.10

Table 5.9. U.S. Counties with the Highest Level of Professional Sports Employment When Expressed as a Percentage of All Jobs

The consensus of discouraging findings in the scientific literature regarding the economic impact of sports stadiums and arenas appears gradually to be diffusing to the popular media, which are increasingly urging reduction of public funding to support sport facilities despite the media's symbiotic relationship with sport. Typical is the editorial in the *Toronto Globe Mail* that concluded, "There is no sound argument for the construction of publicly funded sports stadiums. Period. End of story. You can look it up."[60] The evidence relating to the economic impact of sports venues has been summarized as follows:

1. Sports teams themselves are small to medium-sized firms. They are clearly vibrant, even vital components of any city's economy, but no more so in economic terms than many, many other firms. By themselves, sports teams are not economic engines; they have too few employees and involve too few direct dollars to be a driving force.

2. The professional sports sector, even in areas with multiple teams, is a very small portion of any region's economy. In no county do professional team sports account for as much as 1% of the county's payroll or private sector jobs.

3. A substantial portion of the spending that takes place at arenas and ballparks, and at restaurants and retail outlets near or in these facilities, is merely a transfer of economic activity within the market area. Some studies have shown that as much as four-fifths of the spending would occur in the absence of the team.

4. The majority of revenue collected by the team is used to pay players. However, players tend to save more money than do other people, and they tend to spend money in their "home" communities. More than half the funds spent by fans being used to pay players will not be respent in the local economy. (p. 167)[19]

A belief in the preeminence of the economic value of sport franchises percolates through to the minor leagues. Thus, when city managers were asked to identify the benefits that their communities derived from minor league professional baseball 85% cited economic impact, whereas other benefits were much less frequently mentioned.[58]

Justifying public subsidy of minor league teams on the basis of their economic impact is particularly tenuous, because their impact is likely to be analogous only to that of a small local business. For example, a minor league baseball team's gross operating budget, with few exceptions, ranges from approximately $250,000 to $2 million, depending on the level of the league in which the team plays. This compares to the $7 million in gross sales reported by the average grocery store, which also employs more people on a year-round basis.[61] The lack of economic impact is apparent from the following data, which were derived from an analysis of minor league baseball teams:

A team employs 5 to 20 individuals beyond its 21 to 26 players and coaches. Some of these employees, if not most, will be employed on a seasonal basis and paid on a commission basis. Players receive a minimum salary of $700 a month during the playing season only (April to August). Workers behind the concession stands and vendors may be volunteers or work on a part-time basis. The profits of a team with no local owners likely will be invested elsewhere. Visiting teams stay at a hotel in the community, thus increasing that establishment's revenue, but not necessarily increasing employment there. The low per diem given to players (from $5.50 to $14.00) makes it unlikely they have a major impact on the restaurant and bar business. There are two to three umpires per game, a small number of fans occasionally may follow the visiting team to town and stay one night (in many cases they can return home the same night), and scouts and personnel from the parent club visit the community on an irregular basis. (p. 317)[61]

Mega Sports Events

Ostensibly, the influx of large numbers of out-of-town spectators, participants, media personnel and sponsors for mega events is an obvious indicator to all stakeholders that such events will have substantial economic impact on their host areas. This is invariably reinforced by the owners of mega events who frequently cite consultants' reports showing large economic impacts. A review of booster studies commissioned by the NFL, MLB and the NCAA reported: "The NFL typically claims an economic impact from the Super Bowl of around $300 to $400 million, MLB attaches a $75 million benefit to the All-Star Game and up to almost $250 million for the World Series, and the estimated effect of the NCAA Men's Basketball Final Four ranges from $30 million to $110 million" (p. 81).[62]

These huge, purportedly positive, mega event economic benefits serve two purposes for the property owners. First, they are used to encourage cities to bid for the events and to accept the substantial costs associated with staging them. These costs are discussed in the next chapter. Second, they are used as leverage by the professional leagues to encourage cities to expand public funds to finance new arenas and stadiums for the leagues' owners. The promise is that if cities build the new facilities, then they will be selected to host these events in them. For example, over a fifteen-year period, thirteen of the MLB All-Star Games were hosted in stadiums built in the previous five years.[63]

Unfortunately, large economic gains from mega events are usually illusory. When the actual performance of economies is measured over the duration of a mega event after it is completed, the evidence invariably shows that little or no economic impact occurred.

Studies have been published in the scientific literature relating to the economic impact of the Final Four NCAA Basketball Championships, the soccer World Cup, NFL Super Bowls, MLB All-Star Games, and the Atlanta Olympic Games. They consistently report that these mega events have minimal impact on host communities.

A study of the NCAA men's and women's Final Four Basketball Tournaments' impacts on host cities over periods of 30 and 18 years, respectively, concluded: "The evidence presented suggests that the Final Four for Men and Women boost the local economy by not much if at all . . . The evidence indicates that the economic impact of the Final Four will more likely be the equivalent of a financial 'airball' than an economic 'slam dunk'" (p. 129).[64]

Investigations of the soccer World Cup reported no economic impact on the host nations.[65] For example, when it was held in the United States, investigators concluded: "The evidence suggests that a $4 billion economic impact for the U.S. projected by Cup boosters probably did not materialize. On the contrary, the evidence indicates a far greater likelihood that the World Cup had an overall negative impact on the average host city and the US economy overall" (p. 351).[64]

A study of the impact of six Super Bowls held in Miami (3), Tampa (2), and Phoenix caused the author to conclude: "The results are shocking. For each of the six events studied in three different locations, there is no measurable impact on spending associated with the event" (Porter, 1999, p. 61). For one of these Miami Super Bowls, the NFL had claimed taxable sales in South Florida increased by more than $670 million. However, other investigators concluded that the NFL exaggerated the impact of the Miami Super Bowl by approximately a factor of 10 even when using assumptions that favored identifying a strong economic impact.[67]

An investigation of MLB's All-Star Game in three California cities that hosted it reported that those cities suffered an average drop in taxable sales of approximately $30 million in the quarter in which the game took place.[61] Finally, a study of gate arrivals at the Atlanta airport compared the summer months of the 1996 Atlanta Olympic Games with the same months in 1995 and 1997 and found the numbers were identical.[68]

All of these studies used an *ex post*, i.e. after the event, approach. They reviewed the revenues that occurred in the host community during the time frame of the mega event and reported that in almost all cases there was no increase. The consistency of these findings essentially provides a benchmark that requires future economic impact studies of mega events to address the question, What is it that makes a large impact likely or possible, when evaluations of similar past events have consistently shown little or no economic impact?

A major reason for the lack of economic impact is likely to be that the revenues these events generated for the most part displaced existing revenues in the host area rather than adding to them. This issue of displacement costs is discussed in the following chapter. Another contributing factor is that whenever mega events are held, it is likely that a region's multiplier may fall in comparison to normal times, leading to an overestimate of the true impact of these events on the local economy that *ex ante* studies reveal:

> Hotels, for example, routinely double or triple their room rates during mega-events, but the wages paid to hotel workers remain unchanged. In fact, workers may be expected to simply work harder during times of high demand without any additional monetary compensation. The return to capital (as a percentage of revenues) rises while the return of labor falls as a hotel's revenue increases without a corresponding increase in costs. Because capital income is more mobile than labor income, one might expect a fall in the multiplier effect during the mega-events because of these increased leakages. (p. 111)[69]

This leakage effect is reinforced by what has been termed *VIP leakage*. As the size of sport events increases, the more likely it is that the catering, sport personalities and entertainment will be provided by external companies and individuals, rather than local sources.[22]

Community Sports Tournaments

Almost all cities have athletic facilities, which are invariably used periodically to host sports tournaments. Indeed, some cities have invested amounts exceeding $20 million into high-quality major athletic complexes with the explicit intent that they should attract tournaments and contribute to economic development. Table 5.10 summarizes the results of economic impact studies undertaken at 14 sports tournaments hosted by the city of College Station, Texas.

The city adhered to the admonition "to focus economic impact efforts on obtaining a good estimate of visitor spending and not attempt to use multipliers." Further, no assessments of displacement or other costs are included in the table. In all cases, the data were collected on site in personal interviews. However, for junior events, the participants' parents/coaches were interviewed rather than the athletes because they were responsible for making the expenditures. The following points, which are likely to be reasonably generalizable to all community sports tournaments, emerged.

- The proportion of participants who were from the local area was less than 5% in every tournament and in some it was zero.
- Economic impact is likely to be a function of both number of non-local partici-

Table 5.10. Expenditures at 14 Sports Tournaments

Overnight stay (mode)	Number of non-local participants	Number of non-local participants surveyed	Per day per non-local participant expenditure		Per night per non-local participant expenditure		Total expenditures per non-local participant		Total expenditures of all non-local participants in the local area	
			Mean	Median	Mean	Median	Mean	Median	Mean	Median
3	132	27	$209.36	$200.00	$267.17	$245.00	$1,002.25	$900.00	$132,297.00	$118,800.00
1	313	51	$59.56	$40.00	$171.89	$144.50	$110.86	$85.00	$34,699.18	$26,605.00
1	3741	397	$85.46	$67.50	$173.53	$135.63	$181.31	$136.25	$678,280.71	$509,711.25
1	677	80	$132.30	$106.25	$373.20	$322.50	$270.75	$222.50	$183,297.75	$150,632.50
2	1344	114	$109.91	$105.93	$182.03	$167.50	$326.44	$312.50	$438,735.36	$420,000.00
4	850	149	$143.69	$141.43	$190.58	$188.33	$783.44	$755.00	$665,924.00	$641,750.00
2	123	49	$84.96	$76.67	$130.18	$118.75	$222.80	$217.50	$27,404.40	$26,752.50
1	640	87	$90.24	$92.50	$193.87	$190.00	$180.48	$185.00	$115,507.20	$118,400.00
2	534	128	$108.42	$106.34	$189.74	$187.23	$271.01	$264.89	$144,719.34	$141,451.26
2	976	186	$106.04	$101.67	$159.05	$152.50	$318.11	$305.00	$310,475.36	297,680.00
6	1810	689	$160.85	N/A	$187.66	N/A	$1,125.97	N/A	$2,038,005.70	N/A
5	222	105	$72.20	N/A	N/A	N/A	$433.18	N/A	$139,487.00	N/A
2	171	97	$47.71	N/A	N/A	N/A	$245.57	N/A	$41,993.00	N/A
1	94	51	$157.88	N/A	N/A	N/A	$157.88	N/A	$14,641.00	N/A
N/A	11627	2210	N/A		N/A	N/A	N/A	N/A	N/A	N/A

pants *and* length of stay. Thus, the largest expenditures in Table 5.10 were at events 11 and 6 where the modal lengths of stay were 6 and 4 nights, respectively.

- If an overnight stay is not required, then the economic impact on the community is likely to be small. Some participants in some of the events in Table 5.10 elected to commute and their spending was much lower. This accounts for the big difference between per day and per night expenditures, for example in events 2 and 3.

- The importance of an overnight stay exemplifies the retailing principle that the longer people remain in the area, the more they are likely to spend. Increasing visitors' average length of stay is the most efficient way to increase the economic impact of a sport event on the community. Host agencies should vigorously promote attractions that may persuade participants to stay additional days in the local area.

- Both mean and median expenditures were calculated. Generally, the median is preferred, especially in small samples, because a few extreme values can distort the mean.

SUMMARY

The primary argument for the substantial public subsidies that are invested in many sport facilities and events invariably focuses on the economic benefits that are purported to emanate from them. Economic impact studies provide a broad framework that enables an estimate to be made of the amount of income that a community's residents receive as a result of the investment of those residents' tax dollars in sport facilities or events.

Economic impact is defined as the net economic change in the income of host residents that results from spending attributed to a sport event or facility by visitors from outside the community. Economic impact studies are not value-free tools, because their results are dependent upon the assumptions that guide the analysis—assumptions that invariably agree with those of the study sponsor. Most economic impact studies are commissioned by sponsors who seek numbers that will support their advocacy position. Unfortunately, this often leads those undertaking the studies to adopt procedures and underlying assumptions that substantially bias the results in a direction desired by the sponsors. Indeed, most of these reports should be viewed as political documents designed to support an advocacy position, rather than as legitimate studies of economic impact.

There are five principles whose inviolability is central to the integrity of economic impact analysis. First, if a reasonably accurate count of the number of participants is not feasible, then it is probably a waste of resources to proceed with an economic impact study. Second, only the expenditures of visitors to a sport event should be considered. Those by residents who live within the defined impact area should not be included in the analysis because such expenditures represent only a recycling of money that already exists there.

Third, expenditures by time-switchers who were planning to visit the community for other reasons but scheduled their visit to coincide with the event, and casuals who attended the sport event but were in the community for other purposes and whose visit was not influenced by the event, should be excluded from an economic impact analysis. Only the net increment of those expenditures attributable to increased length of stay because of the sport event should be included.

Multiplier coefficients measure the extent to which initial visitor expenditures ripple through a local economy, creating additional business, turnover, personal income and employment in the host community. The three most widely used multiplier coefficients are those for sales, income, and employment. The fourth inviolable principle is that household-income multipliers should be used for assessing economic impact and not sales multipliers, because the point of interest for policy decisions is the impact of the sales on household income and employment. This is commonly abused. Sales outputs tend to be inappropriately used as *the* multiplier in economic analyses of sport events because they are substantially higher than income multipliers.

The geographic area within which economic impact is to be assessed will be specified by those commissioning the study. The larger the area's economic base, the smaller the leakage that is likely to occur and the larger the multiplier is likely to be. However, this gain is offset because as geographical area size increases, the proportion of visitors who come from outside that area is likely to decrease.

The fifth inviolable principle requires that measures of employment output be carefully interpreted and reported. These measures typically do not differentiate between full-time and part-time jobs, and in the context of sport events many are likely to be short-term, part-time positions. Further, these measures assume that all existing employees are fully occupied so there is no spare capacity in the system, and that all new jobs emerging will be filled by residents from within the community. Both of these assumptions are often challengeable.

Sometimes, the scope of a sport project is expanded beyond the facility of interest to include an assumption that it will stimulate substantial proximate ancillary growth around it. Making major economic policy decisions on such tenuous assumptions is inappropriate, because usually the ancillary development remains a mirage.

The consensus of impartial empirical studies is that both professional franchises and the development of major sport facilities to accommodate them, and mega sport events such as the Olympic Games, World Soccer Cup, Super Bowl, MLB All-Star game or Men's Final Four tournaments, generally have no discernible positive impact on a city's economy. In contrast, community sport tournaments frequently do have a meaningful economic impact. Reports commissioned by advocates indicating large positive economic impacts from major facilities and mega events invariably arrive at their conclusions by breaking at least some of the five inviolable principles. Despite a growing awareness that the results from these reports are frequently bogus, it is likely they will continue to be commissioned because they provide mischievous numbers for advocates to promulgate in promotion campaigns designed to convince residents to be supportive in referendums.

References

1. Smith, A. (1976). *An inquiry into the nature and cause of the wealth of nations, Volume 2.* E. Cannan (Ed.). Chicago, IL: University of Chicago Press. (Original work published 1776)

2. Porter, P. K. (1999). Mega-sports events as municipal investments: A critique of impact analysis. In J. Fizel, E. Gustafson & L. Hadley (Eds.), *Sports economics: Current research* (pp. 61–73). Westport, CT: Prager.

3. Economic Research Associates. (2004). *Economic and fiscal impacts for the proposed NFL Stadium in Arlington, Texas.* City of Arlington: ERA Project Number 15652.

4. Dickson, G., & Claunch S. (2004, October 2). Irving study supports stadium benefits. *Fort Worth Star-Telegram.*

5. Turnkey Sports. (2004). *Study of the economic and fiscal impacts for Texas stadium and a new Cowboys stadium.* Irving, TX: City of Irving.

6. Rosentraub, M. S., & Swindell D. (2004). *The economic value of a proposed football and multi-purpose stadium and the Dallas Cowboys for Arlington, Texas.* Cleveland, OH: Cleveland State University College of Urban Affairs.

7. Cohen, A. (2005, March). Ride on, Cowboys. *Athletic Business*, p. 9.

8. Shah, A., & Brown S.(2004, September 14). Seeing a stadium as salvation. *The Dallas Morning News*, p. 2.

9. Dunnavant, K. (1989, March 13). The impact of economics. *Sports Inc.*, pp. 31–33.

10. PwC & CSL International. (2000). *Analysis of economic benefits associated with the operations of the Green Bay Packers.* Green Bay, WI: Green Bay Area Chamber of Commerce.

11. Deloitte & Touche. (1997). Evaluation of the proposed Dallas Arena. Los Angeles, CA: Deloitte & Touche LLP.

12. CSL International. (2007). Economic and fiscal impacts of a new state-of-the art stadium in Santa Clara. San Francisco, CA: San Francisco 49ers.

13. Hudson, I. (2001). The use and misuse of economic impact analysis. *Journal of Sport and Social Issues, 25*(1), 20–39.

14. Curtis, G. (1993, September). Waterlogged. *Texas Monthly*, p. 7.

15. Stynes, D. J. (2001). Economic impact concepts. Retrieved from http://www.msu.edu/course/prr/840/econimpact/concepts.htm

16. Shakespeare, W. (1959). *The complete works of William Shakespeare.* London, UK: Oxford University Press.

17. Leisure Industries Research Center. (2001). An evaluation of the economic impact, place marketing effects and people's perceptions of Bristol at the 2001 IAAF World Half Marathon Championships. Sheffield, UK: LIRC.

18. Coates, D., & Humphreys, B. R. (2003). The effect of professional sports on earnings and employment in the services and retail sectors in US cities. *Regional Science and Urban Economics, 33*, 173–198.

19. Rosentraub, M. S. (1997). *Major league losers: The real cost of sports and who's paying for it.* New York, NY: Basic Books.

20. Chang, S., & Canode, S. (2002). Economic impact of a future college football program. *Journal of Sport Management, 16*, 239–246.

21. CSL International. (2009). *Economic and jobs impact of Metrodome next multipurpose facility.* Minneapolis, MN: Metropolitan Sports Facilities Commission.

22. Delpy, L., & Li, M. (1998). The art and science of conducting economic impact studies. *Journal of Vacation Marketing, 4*(3), 230–254.

23. Crompton, J. L. (1995). Economic impact analysis of sports facilities and events: Eleven sources of misapplication. *Journal of Sport Management, 9*, 14–35.

24. PwC & CSL International (2000). *Analysis of economic benefits associated with the operation of the Green Bay Packers.* Green Bay, WI: Green Bay Chamber of Commerce & Greater Green Bay Visitor & Convention Bureau.

25. Hitchcock, M. (2011). *Welcome to PETCO Park: Home of your Enron-by-the-sea Padres.* Berkeley, CA: University of California.

26. Deloitte & Touche. (1993). *Economic impact of a Major League Baseball franchise.* Unpublished consultant report.

27. Barkley, D. L., Henry, M. S., & Evatt, M. G. (1995). *Contribution of the golf course industry to the state economy: South Carolina, 1994.* Clemson, SC: Department of Agricultural and Applied Economics, Clemson University.

28. Cobb, S., & Olberding, D. J. (2007). The importance of import substitution in marathon economic impact analysis. *International Journal of Sport Finance, 2*(2), 108–121.

29. Oxford Economics. (2012). *The economic impact of Texas A&M University home football games.* College Station, TX: Convention and Visitors Bureau.

30. Berrett, T. (2001). *The economic significance of amateur sport and active recreation in Edmonton*

in 2000. Edmonton, Alberta: Caminata Consulting.

31. Schaerlaeckens, L. (2010). Why the World Cup won't make money. *ESPN Soccernet.* Retrieved from http://soccernet.espn.go.com

32. FMR Associates. (2007). *Cactus League attendee tracking survey.* Phoenix, AZ: Cactus League Baseball Association.

33. Stynes, D. J. (2010). Personal communication.

34. Archer, B. H. (1984). Economic impact: Misleading multiplier. *Annals of Tourism Research, 11*(3), 517–518.

35. Rosentraub, M. S. (2006). The local context of a sports strategy for economic development. *Economic Development Quarterly, 20*(3), 278–291.

36. Barta, P. (1998, January 14). As arena vote nears, economists say much of the debate is irrelevant. *Wall Street Journal,* Section T, p. 4.

37. Matheson, V. A. (2009). Economic multipliers and mega-event analysis. *International Journal of Sport Finance, 4,* 63–70.

38. Barget, E., & Gouget, J. J. (2010). Hosting mega-sporting events: Which decision-making role? *International Journal of Sport Finance, 5,* 141–162.

39. Morgan, J. (1997). *Glory for sale.* Baltimore, MD: Bancroft Press.

40. Arnold, A. (1986). The impact of the Grand Prix on the transport sector. In J. P. A. Burns, J. H. Hatch, & T. J. Mules (Eds.), *The Adelaide Grand Prix: The impact of a special event* (pp. 58–81). Adelaide, South Australia: The Centre for South Australian Economic Studies.

41. Bishop, G., & Haitch, J. (1986). The impact of the Grand Prix on the accommodation sector. In J. P. A. Burns, J. H. Hatch, & T. J. Mules (Eds.), *The Adelaide Grand Prix: The impact of a special event* (pp. 82–94). Adelaide, South Australia: The Centre for South Australian Economic Studies.

42. Power, T. M. (1998). *The economic pursuit of quality.* Armonk, NY: ME Sharpe.

43. Tavella, A. M. (2007). Sex trafficking and the 2006 World Cup in Germany: Concerns, actions and implications for future international sporting events. *Northwestern Journal of International Human Rights, 6*(1), 196–217.

44. Crompton, J. L., & McKay, S. L. (1994). Measuring the economic impact of festivals and events: Some myths, misapplications and ethical dilemmas. *Festival Management & Event Tourism, 2,* 33–43.

45. Noll, R. G., & Zimbalist, A. (1997). The economic impact of sports teams and facilities. In R. G. Noll & A. Zimbalist (Eds.), *Sports, jobs & taxes: The economic impact of sports teams and stadiums* (pp. 55–91). Washington, DC: The Brookings Institution.

46. Cartright, G. (2004, October). Arlington's team. *Texas Monthly,* pp. 78–80, 105.

47. Schaffer, W. A., & Davidson, L. S. (1984). *Economic impact of the Falcons on Atlanta.* Atlanta, GA: Georgia Institute of Technology.

48. Lipsitz, G. (1984). Sports stadia and urban development: A tale of three cities. *Journal of Sport and Social Issues, 8*(2), 1–18.

49. Baade, R. A., & Dye, R. F. (1990, Spring). The impact of stadiums and professional sports on metropolitan area development. *Growth and Change,* 1–14.

50. Rosentraub, M. (1994). Sport and downtown development strategy. *Journal of Urban Affairs, 16*(3), 228–239.

51. Baade, R. (1996). Professional sports as catalysts for metropolitan economic development. *Journal of Urban Affairs, 18*(1), 1–17.

52. Noll, R. G., & Zimbalist, A. (1997). Build the stadium—create the jobs. In R. G. Noll & A. Zimbalist (Eds.), *Sports, jobs & taxes. The economic impact of sports teams and stadiums* (pp. 1–54). Washington, DC: The Brookings Institute.

53. Jasina, J., & Rotthoff, K. W. (2008). The impact of a professional sports franchise on county employment and wages. *International Journal of Sports Finance, 3,* 210–227.

54. Walden, M. (1997, October/November). Don't play ball. *Carolina Journal,* p. 23.

55. Coates, D., & Humphreys, B. B. (1999). The growth effects of sport franchises, stadia and arenas. *Journal of Policy Analysis and Management, 18*(4), 601–624.

56. Miller, P. A. (2002). The economic impact of sports stadium construction: The case of the construction industry in St. Louis, MO. *Journal of Urban Affairs, 24*(2), 159–173.

57. Nunn, S., & Rosentraub, M. S. (1997). Sports wars: Suburbs and outer cities in a zero-sum game. *Journal of Sport & Social Issues, 21*(1), 65–82.

58. Euchner, C .C. (1995, July 23) A new arena: Fair play? Take a walk. *Dallas Morning News,* pp. J1, J10.

59. Baade, R .A., & Matheson, V. A. (2011). *Financing professional sports facilities.* Worcester, MA: College of Holy Cross Working Paper 12–02.

60. Emperor has no clothes. (1997, June 16). *Toronto Globe & Mail*. Retrieved from http://www.theglobeandmail.com/

61. Johnson, A. T. (1991). Local government, minor league baseball, and economic development strategies. *Economic Development Quarterly*, 5(4), 313–324.

62. Matheson, V. A. (2008). Mega-events: The effect of the world's biggest sporting event on local, regional, ad national economies. In B. R. Humphreys & D. R. Howard (Eds.), *The business of sports, Volume 1*. Westport, CT: Praeger.

63. Baade, R. A., & Matheson V .A. (2001). Home run or wild pitch? Assessing the economic impact of Major League Baseball's All Star Game. *Journal of Sports Economics*, 2(4), 307–327.

64. Baade, R. A., & Matheson, V. A. (2004). An economic slam dunk or March madness? Assessing the economic impact of the NCAA Basketball Tournament. In J. Fizel & R. Fort (Eds.), *Economics of college sports*. Westport, CT: Praeger, pp. 111–133.

65. Szymanski, S. (2002). The economic impact of the World Cup. *World Economics*, 3(1), 169–177.

66. Baade, R. A., & Matheson, V. A. (2004). The quest for the cup: Assessing the economic impact of the World Cup. *Regional Studies*, 38(4), 343–354.

67. Baade, R. A., & Matheson, V. A. (2000). An assessment of the economic impact of the American Football Championship, the Super Bowl, on host communities. *Reflets et perspectives de la vie économique*, 39(2–3), 35–46.

68. Porter, P. (1999). Mega-sports events as municipal investments: A critique of impact analysis. In J. Fizel, E. Gustafson, & L. Hadley (Eds.), *Sports economics: Current research* (pp. 61–74). Westport, CN: Praeger.

69. Baumann, R. W., Matheson, V. A., & Musoi, C. (2009) Bowling in Hawaii: Examining the effectiveness of sports based tourism strategies. *Journal of Sports Economics*, 10(1), 107–123.

6

Costs: The Rest of the Economic Impact Story

COSTS: THE REST OF THE ECONOMIC STORY

An economic impact study, even when it is done with integrity, represents only the economic benefits associated with a facility or event. However, if there is an increase in economic impact in a local economy, it is probable that there also will be an increase in costs associated with it. Thus, in order to ascertain whether the project is a good investment, its costs also have to be identified. These costs often are subtle and nuanced, so they remain "under the radar." Their inherent lack of visibility is reinforced by the likely lack of interest in articulating them among projects' advocates and boosters who typically only want to publicize the benefits. Hence, too often only positive economic benefits associated with sport are reported, and costs of negative impacts borne by a community are not considered. It has been suggested that "ignoring these costs is roughly equivalent to a certified public accountant omitting a balance sheet's liabilities and then touting the success of the company"(p. 1).[1] Clearly, if costs exceed the benefits then, even if there is a relatively high gross economic impact, the project likely would not be a good investment for the community.

Incorporating costs into a study changes it from an economic impact analysis to a benefit-cost analysis. While an economic impact analysis is designed to study the economic effect of additional spending attributable to a sport facility or event, a benefit-cost analysis is designed to identify the *net* return on the investment. For example, an investigation of the economic impact of a medium-sized sport event on a medium-sized city using both economic impact and benefit-cost analyses revealed very different results. Whereas the economic impact from non-local visitor spending showed the community benefitted by almost $1 million flowing into its economy, the benefit-cost analysis revealed a net loss to the community of $2.4 million.[2] An example of a benefit-cost analysis that was commissioned by the City of Indianapolis is summarized in Exhibit 6.1.

There is often an inadvertent or mischievous blurring of the distinction between economic impact and benefit-cost analyses. For example, with reference to the city's proposed $325 million investment on a new stadium for the Dallas Cowboys, the mayor of Arlington was quoted as saying the city "won't proceed unless an outside consultants'

Exhibit 6.1

Compiling a Benefit-Cost Analysis

In the mid-1970s, leaders in Indianapolis searched for new ways to bring vitality to the city. One key strategy that emerged was to make Indianapolis a national center for amateur sports. In 1992 a benefit-cost analysis was commissioned to evaluate the effectiveness of this strategy between 1977 and 1991. The analysis excluded non-monetary costs and the opportunity costs of using sites for sports facilities, but it offers a reasonably good model of how to use benefit-cost analysis to identify return on monetary investments in sport.

The monetary "social costs" of creating the amateur sports industry were estimated at $124 million at the time they occurred. Most of this cost ($112 million) consisted of investments in sports facilities. Also included were tax abatements, public safety services, and subsidies to organizations and facilities for operations. In 1991 dollars, the total investment amounted to $164 million. Pie chart A in figure A shows that over half of the investment came from philanthropic sources. These costs represent the amount of funds that would not have been invested in the local economy but for the amateur sports strategy.

Pie chart B shows the sectors of the Indianapolis economy that benefitted from the $1.05 billion attracted to the city by the amateur sports movement. This represents the aggregate spending by out-of-town visitors ($787 million) and expenditures by sports organizations and facilities from external sources ($213 million and $51 million, respectively). Since most of this money was in the form of visitor spending, it was not surprising that half of it went to hotels and restaurants.

Applying multipliers to the $1.05 billion direct economic impact yielded a total sales output impact of $1.89 billion. Pie chart C shows where these gross sales revenues eventually ended up. Over a third ($683 million) went as income to Indianapolis residents in the form of salaries and wages. A further breakdown of this $683 million revealed that while hotels and restaurants were the biggest winners in terms of direct economic impact, workers in other services industries actually ended up benefitting more (in total dollars) than those in the lodging or food services industries.

Table A summarizes the annual and total income and cost of investment flows. These investment and return figures can be converted into a rate of return once adjustments are made for the delays between the years in which the investment took place and the returns achieved. When adjustments for the timing are made, the rate of return on the investment is equivalent to an annual average rate of 64.1%, a figure that is substantially higher than that achieved in most business investments. In addition, this figure may be viewed as somewhat conservative because the amateur sports development strategy did not end in 1991. Returns from the investment will continue into the future.

Table A. Annual Income on Investment Costs in Indianapolis Generated by the Amateur Sports Strategy 1977–91 ($1991)

Year	Net Income	Investment	Year	Net Income	Investment
1977	960,000	1,000	1985	34,410,000	3,119,000
1978	1,440,000	7,800,000	1986	49,860,000	12,411,000
1979	3,770,000	2,088,000	1987	147,340,000	42,966,000
1980	4,260,000	6,035,000	1988	70,070,000	15,101,000
1981	3,380,000	14,793,000	1989	75,600,000	2,806,000
1982	47,150,000	26,079,000	1990	75,740,000	2,188,000
1983	46,050,000	25,131,000	1991	85,180,000	2,052,000
1984	38,700,000	1,445,000	Total	$683,910,000	$164,015,000

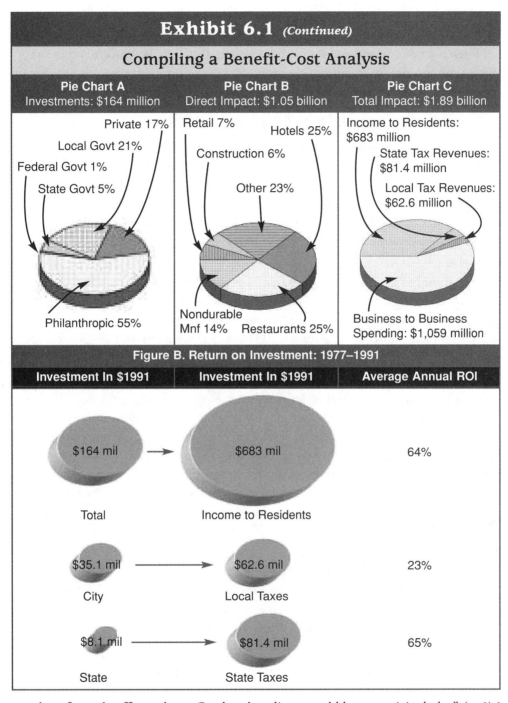

Exhibit 6.1 *(Continued)*

Compiling a Benefit-Cost Analysis

Pie Chart A
Investments: $164 million

Private 17%
Local Govt 21%
Federal Govt 1%
State Govt 5%

Philanthropic 55%

Pie Chart B
Direct Impact: $1.05 billion

Retail 7%
Hotels 25%
Construction 6%
Other 23%

Nondurable Mnf 14%   Restaurants 25%

Pie Chart C
Total Impact: $1.89 billion

Income to Residents: $683 million
State Tax Revenues: $81.4 million
Local Tax Revenues: $62.6 million

Business to Business Spending: $1,059 million

Figure B. Return on Investment: 1977–1991

Investment In $1991	Investment In $1991	Average Annual ROI
$164 mil Total	$683 mil Income to Residents	64%
$35.1 mil City	$62.6 mil Local Taxes	23%
$8.1 mil State	$81.4 mil State Taxes	65%

cost-benefit study affirms that a Cowboys' stadium would be a municipal plus" (p. 2).[3] The term *benefit-cost analysis* was used consistently to describe the study in the local media. However, the consultants' study made no reference to costs, focusing only on purported economic and fiscal benefits.[4]

In the authors' view, decision makers should use benefit-cost analyses when evaluating alternative investments, despite the difficulties associated with deriving accurate costs. Nine types of costs should be considered: (1) society-wide costs, (2) strategic underestimation of capital costs of facilities and overstatement of revenue streams, (3) interest costs, (4) land and infrastructure costs, (5) foregone property taxes, (6) operation and maintenance costs, (7) event costs, (8) displacement costs, and (9) opportunity costs. Each is discussed in this chapter.

SOCIETY-WIDE COSTS

Sport costs that are borne by society as a whole are manifested as special dispensations that allow private corporations to avoid paying taxes to the federal government. As one commentator noted, "Whenever the federal government allows deductions for one group and not for another—for homeowners but not for renters, say, or for sports franchises but not for other businesses—the subsidy may be hidden, but it's just as real as if Congress were doling out cash from the federal treasury" (p. 45).[5]

The most prominent society-wide cost stems from the use of tax-exempt bonds to assist private entities to construct sport facilities. Typically, they enable money to be borrowed at approximately 2% lower than taxable bonds. Thus, when the Yankee Stadium was built with $943 million of tax-exempt bonds, it meant the Yankees saved and the federal government (society) lost between $231 and $471 million over the 30-year life of the bonds.[6] A full discussion of tax-exempt bonds is forthcoming in Chapter 9. At this point, it is sufficient to acknowledge the hidden costs they inflict on society.

A second cost that society incurs derives from the rules relating to the depreciation of professional sport franchises. The key tax rule is called the roster depreciation allowance (RDA). This rule has been amended several times by both Congress and the IRS since Bill Veeck convinced the IRS of its appropriateness in 1946, but the current version dates from 2005. When a team is bought, like other businesses its owners can depreciate its tangible assets such as physical equipment, buildings, cars and office equipment. However, unlike other businesses, when a professional sports team is bought, this rule allows 100% of the "intangible assets" to be deducted from taxes over 15 years. It is known as the 100/15 rule.

Intangible assets include team members and their salaries, which the rule considers to be assets that are depreciating each year, and this number can be deducted from profits. However, only the contracts of the players who were on the team when it was purchased, not subsequent contracts, can be written off. Nevertheless, no other type of business in the U.S. is allowed to depreciate its human assets in this way.

Intangible asset value extends beyond team member contracts to include assets that derive from "league membership (territorial rights, revenue shares from attendance and television, and shares of future expansion fees), while others derive from their relationship with state and local hosts (revenues from tickets, parking, and concessions). Finally, there are 'other values' like related business opportunities, accounting costs that are actually profit-taking, and revenue-shifting tax advantages from joint ownership" (p. 2).[7]

This depreciation rule is special interest legislation that for no apparent reason, other than the political influence of franchise owners, treats sport businesses more favorably than all other businesses. Its egregiousness is further enhanced by two flaws in the conceptual rationale that underpins it:

> First, while some players may be in the declining end of their careers, still other players are appreciating in value; it is not at all clear that "the roster" itself depreciates . . . Second, the depreciation allowance surely involves double counting because the salaries and player development costs that create the asset are already treated as expenses at market-determined values. (p. 3)[7]

The 100/15 rule turns an actual profit on which franchise owners would have to pay taxes to federal and state governments to paper losses. Its impact was noted in the following observation by a vice president of the Toronto Blue Jays: "Anyone who quotes profits of a baseball club is missing the point. Under generally accepted accounting principles, I can turn a $4 million profit into a $2 million loss, and can get every major accounting firm to agree with me" (p. 42).[5]

This rule has created a lucrative tax shelter, especially for those who can use it to write off profits from other business on which they would otherwise have to pay taxes. Thus, when an owner sells a team 15 years after purchasing it, he or she not only reaps the capital gain from a team's appreciation in value, but also the tax shelter the 100/15 rule provides. For example, if the RDA at the time of purchase was valued at $300 million and the owner was at the highest marginal federal income tax rate of 35%, then the savings that otherwise would have been paid in federal income tax on his or her income would amount to $105 million.

A third cost to society stems from the tax rules pertaining to corporate entertainment expenses, which effectively mean that society subsidizes the luxury suites and club seats that overwhelmingly are purchased by corporations.

> When an average fan plunks down $25 for a ticket, the money comes straight out of his or her pocket, but when a corporation buys tickets, the finances work differently. Companies are able to claim sports as a business-entertainment deduction, on the theory that this is a perk they use to lure clients, wining and dining them in an attempt to land business deals. Because of this, so long as a company has profits to declare the deduction against, it can rest assured that the federal government will pick up the tab for a portion on the purchase price. Team owners can then safely charge more for their boxes, knowing that corporations will happily pay higher rates if the purchase is tax-deductible. (p. 49)[5]

In addition to these three major sources of tax subsidy, there are a number of other, less-obvious tax loopholes available to franchise owners:

> For one thing, they can deduct interest payments on loans they take out to buy the team; better still, owners can create dummy corporations to own their teams, lend *themselves* money, and then deduct the interest payments that the teams pay back to themselves. Team owners who have their own television stations—as fran-

chise prices soar, more and more teams find themselves owned by media con-
glomerates—can sell themselves their broadcast rights at bargain-basement prices,
creating yet another book loss. (p. 47)[5]

STRATEGIC UNDERESTIMATION OF CAPITAL COSTS AND OVERESTIMATION OF REVENUE STREAMS

The hosting of mega events invariably means large new construction projects will be
required. For example, Germany spent almost $2 billion building or rehabilitating
twelve stadiums when they hosted the soccer World Cup, of which at least 35% was
provided by the public purse.[8] Similarly, when they jointly hosted the World Cup,
South Korea built ten new stadiums costing $2.7 billion, while Japan built six new sta-
diums and refurbished four others at a cost of $4.6 billion.[9]

Advocates for hosting major sport events and facilities frequently underestimate or
publicly understate the costs associated with developing them. Some of this error may
arise from unforeseen contingencies such as increases in the costs of materials, but the
egregious magnitude of the errors in some cases suggests that they are often strategic
and deliberate with the intent of reducing negative political reactions that higher costs
are likely to arouse, which in turn might derail advocates' efforts to organize a host
community's bid for an event. Examples abound:

- The Barcelona Olympic Games' costs increased fivefold over the eight-year period preceding them.
- Athens initially projected its Games would cost $1.6 billion, but they cost close to $16 billion.

The integrity of economic impact analysis depends on the accurate measurement of
all costs. Courtesy of iStockPhoto

- Beijing projected costs of $1.6 billion but the actual cost exceeded $30 billion.
- The initial London Olympics bid for 2012 estimated costs to be $5 billion, but within two years this had escalated to $19 billion.
- The Manchester Commonwealth Games' cost was five times the original estimate.

Cost overruns of 30% or more on major league sport facilities are similarly common "because bells and whistles are often added after the original designs, political approval, [and] because of mistakes in the *a priori* cost consideration" (p. 236).[10]

Errors of this magnitude rarely occur when private enterprises develop projects with their own funds, because potential contingencies are carefully identified and their potential cost is incorporated into project budgets. Thus, investment decisions and evaluations of risk are made with full knowledge of a project's worst case scenario. Public sector investments in sport projects should require independent, third-party critical evaluations of both the cost estimates in a budget and the legitimacy of the assumptions on which they are based, and provision of worst case scenarios to ensure advocates are not engaging in deliberate strategic underbidding.

Voters sometimes are assured a facility will not raise their taxes because bonds will be paid off by the lottery, bed tax, etc. However, this assurance is predicated on assumptions about use levels of those products and revenues being realistic, whereas a strategic decision may have been made to make them overly optimistic in order to forestall opposition.

A common legacy associated with strategic underbidding to host mega events is huge debt payments and under-utilized infrastructure that results in large, ongoing operating losses. As the grandiosity of the facilities and infrastructure increases, so does the concomitant onerous burden on local taxpayers usually stretching out for 20 to 30 years. Beijing's Water Cube—the 17,000 seat state-of-the-art swimming center—was recognized as a technological and architectural wonder in its role as a centerpiece for the 2008 Summer Olympics. The facility is now used by the general public for free swimming, making it the world's most expensive lap pool.[11]

OMISSION OF INTEREST COSTS

Discussions of capital costs focus on the amount of money borrowed for the project, but this is not the total cost incurred by the community because it omits interest paid on the bonds. This is illustrated by two bond schedules shown in Chapter 9. Table 9.3 shows that a $10 million graduated serial bond issued for 20 years requires the community to pay an additional $8.9 million in interest payments, so the full cost is $18.9 million. Similarly, in Exhibit 9.6 the $13.87 million borrowed results in the agency paying an additional $15.4 million, so the real total is $29.21 million. When net present values are applied these costs would be substantially reduced, but the general point here is that interest costs in absolute or net present value terms are never discussed.

The Cincinnati Bengals' Paul Brown Stadium was funded with $400 million of public money. However, the interest charges of these bonds amounted to an additional $354 million and the city's agreement to pay for the stadium's maintenance for the

25-year period of the bonds amounts to $230 million. Hence, the real cost to the public is close to $1 billion rather than the advertised $400 million figure.[12]

LAND AND INFRASTRUCTURE COSTS

When major sport facilities are constructed, government entities often contribute not only to the cost of building the stadium or arena buildings, but also by providing land and infrastructure for the facilities. However, these latter two costs are rarely included in the publicity surrounding the government's contributions. This omission is a relatively recent phenomenon, dating from the 1980s and 1990s when land costs soared in urban areas. It has been estimated that on average, land costs associated with major league sport facilities approximate 25% of the construction cost of the building.[13] Again, the obvious overarching reason for governments not publicizing these costs is to reduce the negative reaction that inevitably arises among some stakeholders when major expenditures on sport facilities are contemplated. The following more nuanced explanation suggests why the omission of these costs in the public dialogue is not controversial:

> Land cost data are tricky because of the complexity of appraising these sites, and because both team owners and some government officials have an interest in suppressing public knowledge of the market value of the site should it be sold privately. Infrastructure costs are also less likely to be reported because it is difficult to disentangle benefits to the sport facility from those enjoyed by adjacent sites, especially when bundled with other high-profile civic improvements, and also because tax payers are less likely to question infrastructure spending because such projects continue to be perceived as a legitimate function of local governments. For these reasons, the tendency of subsidy advocates to obscure these costs is likely to continue. (p. 137)[14]

Assistance with land from governments may take two forms. First, it may involve a public entity assembling the land. Typically, in central urban areas the relatively large sites needed for major sport facilities will be in multiple ownership. Acquiring these multiple smaller sites has traditionally been easier for government entities than for a private developer, because they could use their powers of eminent domain to assemble the land. New York City used its eminent domain powers to put together a 22-acre site for a private developer, of which 8.5 acres was for the New York Nets to build their new arena at Atlantic Yards near downtown Brooklyn. The remaining acreage was designated for high-rise residential development. Those living in the areas contested the action, arguing that private property was being taken from law-abiding people and sold against their will to other private interests for the purpose of real estate development. It took almost four years, from 2006 to 2009, for the court cases emanating from the city's actions to be resolved.

Residents of the largely African American South Armour Square neighborhood in Chicago lost their fight to save 500 households from being moved in order to facilitate the construction of the Chicago White Sox's new Comiskey Park (now U.S. Cellular Field). Although they lost, they received $10 million in compensation beyond what was legally required in order to forestall lengthy, drawn-out court proceedings.[15] As laws have been passed to require public hearings, open meetings, full disclosure of studies and enhancement of government transparency, so the opportunities for opponents of major sport projects to delay them have increased. All of this drives up the costs for public entities.

Similarly, the city of Arlington used its eminent domain powers to assemble the land needed to build a new Dallas Cowboys Stadium. Using this authority it condemned over 150 homes, apartments and small businesses. One critical commentator observed:

> Arlington spent approximately $80 million in what was euphemistically called "land acquisition" but might more accurately have been dubbed "payment for stolen land." Numerous home and business owners took the city to court over its low-ball offers. One homeowner, offered $351,000 for a house and four acres of land, was eventually awarded $2.75 million, though most of her fellow litigants in the eminent domain cases lost their suits. The last resident to settle, Paul D. Jordan, told the *Dallas Morning News* that the area which the Cowboys demolished was "one of those rare neighborhoods that you don't often find that had a sense of community. I knew everyone around me on a first name basis . . . We were paying more taxes than [the Cowboys] will ever pay. That's such a lopsided, one-sided bad deal for anybody but Jerry Jones." Another Arlingtonion said, "All that we nice Christian folks in Arlington ended up doing is using eminent domain to take homes and businesses from our fellow citizens and agreeing to fork over millions in taxes that could have been used for other city services" (n.p.)[16]

The obvious angst and sense of outrage evident in these comments explain why in recent years the use of eminent domain has become more difficult as state legislatures and the courts have placed tighter parameters on eminent domain authority. As the Arlington case showed, it is likely to spawn court cases as impacted parties challenge either the eminent domain authority being used, or the compensation being offered. Thus, court costs sometimes are another hidden cost that governments may incur.

The more prominent role of governments with land is to lease land that they already own to a sport team for a nominal amount—often one dollar a year. If this is done for a 20-acre parcel whose value is $500,000 an acre, then the cost to the public purse is $10 million. In reference to a proposed stadium development in St. Louis it was observed:

> The downtown stadium will use land that would be owned by the city and that had potentially valuable alternative uses. The true economic cost of the stadium should include foregone property taxes that would have been paid if the land had been sold or leased for private development, and it should include foregone rents that could be earned from such alternative users. (p. SR8)[17]

There are numerous examples of land being donated for major league sport facilities. The MLB and NFL stadiums in Baltimore were reported as costing $106 million and $220 million, respectively. However, the land for the entire project was acquired for an additional $100 million that was paid for with public funds.[18] The value of the land for the Safeco Field in Seattle was estimated to be $35 million; at Charlotte's Ericsson Stadium (now Bank of America Stadium) it was $40 million; at Phillip's Arena in Atlanta the building cost was $131 million, but an additional land contribution by the city was valued at $62 million; and for the Staples Center in Los Angeles the city contributed nothing to the building cost, but spent over $70 million to acquire the land for it.[13] When the Yankees needed land to build a new stadium, New York City came forward with a 22-acre public park site valued at $13.5 million. In none of these cases was the land value included in the popular media reports of the projects' public cost.

Infrastructure assistance refers to government entities' taking responsibility for building roads, transit, sewers, and water and electricity connections. Taxpayers are less likely to question infrastructure costs than land or facility costs because in non-sports facility contexts, such spending is a normal and legitimate function of a local government. Again, these costs are usually omitted from publicity relating to a city's cost contributions. For example: "Washington's Verizon Center is often touted as a private facility, but in fact only the $216 million building was privately funded; an additional $64 million was spent on land and infrastructure by the District of Columbia, so that the public share of the development costs is really 23% [not 0%]" (p. 95).[13]

Other examples include Washington D.C.'s FedExField, which was reported as costing $180 million, all privately funded, when it was constructed. What was not reported was the over $70 million spent on road improvements and parking by the city.[19] Dallas widely publicized its public cap of $125 million for the American Airlines Center, but the city did not publicize that it also spent $30 million in infrastructure for the arena.[13] The cost of Sports Authority Field at Mile High in Denver was widely perceived to be $421 million, with the public's share amounting to $310 million. However, these numbers fail to recognize that Sports Authority Field was also the beneficiary of $74 million of infrastructure improvements paid for by public entities. In addition, the city gave the team the land for which the city had paid $14 million twenty-five years earlier—so its contemporary value was probably double or triple that amount.[13] The new Yankee stadium received $70 million from New York State to construct four parking structures at the stadium from which the state received no revenue, while the city's Metropolitan Transit Authority built a new commuter rail station for the Yankees at a public cost of $45 million.[5] In Milwaukee, the city ($18 million), county ($18 million) and state ($36 million) contributed a total of $72 million in infrastructure improvements for Miller Park, in addition to the $207 million the public paid towards the $285 million cost of the stadium.[13]

FORGONE PROPERTY TAXES

Many teams have negotiated with cities that they will not have to pay property taxes on the facility they occupy. In some instances, this occurs even when the facility is not publicly owned. It is justified on the basis that, irrespective of ownership, major league sport facilities are used for a public purpose. Over the life of a facility, forgone property taxes may be the largest cost contribution public bodies make to a project. For example, it has been estimated that property taxes foregone at PNC Park in Pittsburgh over a 30-year period will amount to $65 million in current dollars, while at the NFL Carolina Panthers' new stadium in Charlotte, North Carolina, the estimate was $61 million.[13]

In some instances, the tax forbearance has also extended to sales taxes. For example, the Yankees, Mets, and Nets facilities in New York City were all exempted from sales taxes on construction materials.[10]

OPERATION AND MAINTENANCE COSTS

It was noted earlier that a common legacy of many mega sport events has been a huge debt and much under-utilized infrastructure. This results in large ongoing operating losses subsequently being incurred by facilities constructed for a specific event, which have limited legacy use, and large ongoing debt costs that may stretch out for the next 20–50 years. These become a continuing cost for local taxpayers and represent a substantial long-term economic cost.[20]

Thus, the $4.6 billion Japan spent on developing soccer stadiums when it hosted the FIFA World Cup means that construction spending per game was nearly $150 million! Given that the average attendance at J-League games was 16,000, about one third of the capacity of most of the new stadiums, their taxpayers have incurred onerous long-term costs for a month-long party! The cost situation for its co-host South Korea, which invested $2.7 million in new stadiums, is perhaps even worse because professional soccer in that country generally draws only 3,000 people to a game.[9]

More obvious operation and maintenance costs may be classified as either onsite or offsite. Onsite costs include ongoing operating expenses such as utilities (electricity, gas, water, sewer, telephone, fiber optics), insurance and administration, and maintenance expenses such as the cost of repairs or supplies, cleaning, trash removal, landscaping, the cost of additional labor contracted to assist with an event, and the cost of the time invested in the project by a city's existing employees. In Table 5.1, for example, the costs incurred by the city parks and recreation department in hosting a softball tournament were tracked, recorded, and included in the analysis, so the economic impact net of onsite maintenance costs could be presented.

At facilities used by professional sport franchises, responsibility for operation and maintenance costs varies widely. They can be classified into two broad categories whereby either the franchise is almost exclusively responsible for them, or the public partner is required to pay all, or a substantial portion, of these costs. However, there are wide variations within both of these broad categories.

The NHL's Minnesota Wild's lease with the city of St. Paul is an example of a lease obligating the franchise to pay all maintenance and operation costs for the entire arena, including everything from concessions and concessions equipment, to groundskeeping and refurbishing the arena floor. The Wild also are responsible for all the trash removal, cleaning of interior driveways, maintenance of the arena exterior and roof, and preventative maintenance.[21]

Similarly, at Safeco Field the Seattle Mariners lease reads, "The Mariners are responsible for all labor, materials, and equipment involved with operating and maintaining the facility. This includes such things as: maintaining the electrical, plumbing and mechanical systems, groundskeeping, painting, removing trash, hiring security, and staffing the facility" (p. 240).[21] At Comerica Park, the Detroit Tigers are responsible for maintenance, repair and management of the facility, as well as game-day and event operations expenses. However, a capital improvement fund for future renovations is jointly funded by annual contributions of $300,000 from the team and $250,000 from the public, with both sides having to agree on disbursements from this fund.[21]

Although 46% of major league sport facilities receive at least some maintenance cost assistance from public entities,[13] these annual costs are rarely reported. In most of these instances, the public partner will be required to provide maintenance, game day expenses, security, utilities, operations, and capital improvements at no cost to the franchise. The only exception is typically the team areas, including luxury suites, club seats, locker rooms and club offices, which are the franchise's responsibility.[21]

Teams often recoup some of their upfront capital costs in lease negotiations with public landlords by persuading them to be responsible for maintenance costs and to provide other incentives, such as guarantees by the city to compensate the team for ticket sales that fall below a threshold. For example, the City of San Diego guaranteed the NFL Chargers attendance of at least 60,000 for every game, promising to purchase any unsold tickets under that amount. From 1995 until 2004, that deal cost the city $36.4 million.[22] These arrangements sometimes are termed *lease give backs*.[10]

Examples of teams receiving government maintenance assistance include the NBA Miami Heat, which receives an operating subsidy from the city of Miami of $6.4 million for annual operating expenses; the San Diego Padres, which receives $3.5 million annually from the city of San Diego; and the Milwaukee Brewers at Miller Park, which receives 64% of annual maintenance costs or $3.85 million (whichever is less), plus a $700,000 annual contribution to capital improvements. An example of game-day obligations of the public partner in these situations is the Tampa Bay Buccaneers' agreement, where Section 13(d) of the lease says:

> "The Authority shall provide for BSC's use, at the Authority's sole cost and expense, the Stadium and field ready on the date of each Buccaneer's NFL Game for the exhibition of the professional football games to be played by the Buccaneers with all facilities and equipment reasonably necessary for the operation and maintenance of the Stadium as a facility suitable for the performance of football games of NFL caliber, in accordance with the standards of the NFL." This includes game day personnel and services such as event coordinators, ticket takers, ushers, security guards, parking lot attendants, information attendants, and standby maintenance crews. (p. 243).[21]

Several attempts have been made to measure operating costs of facilities incurred by the public partner.[23–26] The most recent and most comprehensive analysis led to the following generalizable amounts. These are indicative of the kinds of maintenance assistance granted to teams receiving these subsidies:

For new MLB facilities, average annual maintenance expenses are estimated at $3 million per year, and if the facility has a roof, $4 million per year. For older MLB facilities, the estimated average is $2 million per year, and $3 million if it has a roof. For new NFL facilities, because they have fewer game days than any other facility type, it is estimated that average annual maintenance expenses are $2 million per year, $3 million if it has a roof. For older NFL stadiums, expenses are $1 million per year, or $2 million if it has a roof. If a stadium is used for both MLB and NFL teams, $1 million per year is added. For all arenas, I assume annual maintenance costs of $2 million per year, only slightly lower than stadiums because of its smaller capacity and fixed roof. (p. 132)[14]

When large numbers of visitors are attracted to a community, they are likely to create extra demands on its services and inflict social costs on community residents. Offsite operation costs borne by a community may include such elements as traffic congestion, increased sanitation facilities and public transportation, road accidents, vandalism, police and fire protection, environmental degradation, garbage collection, increased prices to local residents in retail and restaurant establishments, increased costs to other businesses seeking new workers if there is a shortage of labor supply, loss of access, and disruption of residents' lifestyles.

The annual cost to cities of providing police, firefighters, special insurance to cover facility-specific hazards, and other municipal services for a professional sport facility typically ranges from $2 to $5 million.[13] The variable costs borne by the host city of a Super Bowl are at least $1.5 million. Greece spent over $1.5 billion on security alone for the 2004 Summer Olympics,[8] while in 2012 the security bill for the London Games was approximately $1 billion.[27]

Translating some of the municipal costs into economic values is relatively easy (for example, costs of extra police or fire protection and offsite clean-up costs), but in other cases it is difficult. This difficulty is one reason why such costs are usually ignored. If some of these costs cannot be translated into economic values, they should at least be described, qualitatively assessed, and included in a presentation to a legislative body to be considered in an evaluation of an event's net benefits. An alternative approach is to monitor the level of residents' tolerance for these offsite costs during the event; a questionnaire instrument for this purpose has been developed.[28]

EVENT COSTS

Most elected officials and taxpayers are unaware of the magnitude of investments needed to support a major event. The costs are likely to be substantial and in many cases, sport organizations are expected to meet those costs from revenue streams associated with the event.

Table 6.1 shows a city's budget for hosting a Fast Pitch Softball National Tournament. The event attracted 160 teams, who spent more than $2 million in the community during the six days of the tournament. This large economic impact means that there is considerable competition among communities to host such events. The bid fees to the organizing associations who sanction the championships are substantial, as are the costs of hosting the event. Table 6.1 shows that the city's total investment was close to $300,000. It also shows the revenue streams that raised over $181,000. The net investment by the city was $118,000, and it yielded more than $2 million in direct economic impact to the community.

Organizations that control regional, national and international sport events, and the allocation of professional sport franchises, are essentially monopolies. They exploit this position by requiring potential hosts to bid against each other so they will maximize the amount of cost a community hosting the event or facility will voluntarily absorb. Typically, this means the owners of these properties will capture a large proportion of the revenues that come from marketing rights and broadcasting, while communities accept all the costs associated with their presentation. In recent years, these costs have grown substantially as the property owners have recognized the strength of their bargaining positions and consistently made the events more grandiose.

For example, the incremental increase in tourists coming to Hawaii for the NFL Pro Bowl was 5,600 visitors. The Hawaii Tourism Authority survey date suggests this translated into a $5.7 million impact in the state's economy. Since the state paid the NFL $5.3 million for the right to host the event, the NFL extracted almost the entire economic benefit to the host city, while leaving the city to pay all costs associated with the Pro Bowl.[29]

Conceptually, if the monopolist property owners succeed in fully leveraging their position, then they should be able to persuade host cities to absorb all event costs up to the point where they are $1 less than the estimated net economic impact. Thus, by definition, cities should not expect their investments in hosting these types of sport properties to yield a return. Inevitably, this situation makes it likely that in some instances host cities may suffer the winner's curse, which occurs when benefits are insufficient to cover the costs incurred.[30] The city that bids the most for the facility or event is the one with the most optimistic assessments of its benefits. Among a large set of bidders, the most

Hosting an event such as the NFL Pro Bowl is costly for the host city. Courtesy of U.S. Navy

Table 6.1. USA/ASA 16U Girl's Fast Pitch National Tournament Budget

TOURNAMENT EXPENSES

Products		Services	
Label machine—bracket boards	$236.93	Technical computer assistance	$500.00
Label tape—bracket boards	$159.92	Band—Opening Ceremonies	$2,000.00
Laminate—signs and information	$324.00	Meal for band	$51.41
Water hoses—food tent	$137.88	DJ—Opening Ceremonies	$350.00
Tablecloths—food tent	$137.79	Sound system—Opening Ceremonies	$800.00
Pens and markers—check in	$12.60	Air Jump Inc—bounce houses	$1,497.50
Tables/Water/Batteries—check in	$573.36	Banquet managers meeting	$11,820.84
Containers for PA system	$23.88	Catering BBQ—Opening Ceremonies	$28,500.00
Cone cups/Amplifiers/Microphones	$1,057.37	Concession services—Opening Ceremonies	$2,500.00
Cup holders for dugout water coolers	$403.69	Water & Sausage—Opening Ceremonies	$295.28
Ice chest for score keepers' water	$139.93	BVSUA—foor for umpires	$1,500.00
Ice chest for gate workers' water	$99.96	BVSUA—game fees	$28,950.00
Envelopes—team packets	$16.58	BVSUA—game fees additional	$9,360.00
Envelopes/Paper clips/Binders/Printing	$668.91	BVSUA—mileage for umpire travel	$4,500.00
Glue dots & adhesive putty—signs team check in	$25.21	Score keepers & announcers	$10,476.00
Mason jars—pool draw at managers' meeting	$13.99	Lodging for umpires—Econolodge	$21,347.50
Cleaning supplies—facility cleanup	$39.17	**Sub total**	**$124,448.53**
Sunscreen—for workers	$8.97	**ASA Assessment Fees & Reps**	
Label tape—bracket boards	$30.91	ASA Rep, Umpire UIC, Assistant UICs	$2,400.00
Tab dividers/Hole punch/Stapler/Etc.	$122.89	Bid Deposit	$1,000.00
Wristbands—tournament passes	$1,825.00	ASA Assessment Fees (Advance)	$20,000.00
Wristbands—daily passes	$55.40	**ASA Assessment Fees (Final)**	**$43,000.00**
Wristbands—daily passes	$67.30	**ASA District 30 Assessment Fees**	**$4,000.00**
Wristbands—Opening Ceremonies	$1,093.00	Sub total	$70,400.00
Decorations—Opening Ceremonies	$2,000.00	**Staff / Workers**	
40 x 40 tent—eating area	$1,105.00	**Tournament Prep Workers—Athletics**	
30 x 30 tent—service line	$665.00	**Full time**	**$462.16**
Assorted chips—Opening Ceremonies meal	$1,346.40	**Part time seasonal**	**$21,469.17**
Misc snacks—Opening Ceremonies workers	$67.75	**Overtime**	**$26,560.09**
Signs—Opening Ceremonies	$1,413.35	**FICA, etc**	**$6,122.92**
Binders—team packets & college roster books	$329.34	**Opening Ceremonies concert workers**	**$761.95**
Binders—team packets & college roster books	$918.16	**Field maintenance crew**	**$8,556.72**
Padfolios—gift to team managers & umpires	$1,768.00	Sub total	$63,933.01
Carabiner fan—gift to players	$3,090.00		
Mini bats—pool draw & umpire gift	$1,260.00	**TOURNAMENT REVENUE**	
Texas magnets—bracket draw	$387.00	**Entry Fees (160 teams at $350)**	$56,000.00
Tournament staff shirts—polos	$1,955.00	**Gate Fees**	$103,169.00
Check in staff shirts—polos	$1,320.00	**Souvenir Sales %**	$21,080.94
Maintenance staff work shirts	$1,717.50	**Programs**	$1,237.00
Softballs—tournament play	$1,541.70	**Total Revenue**	$181,486.94
Programs	$8,763.00		
Block ice—dugout water coolers	$689.50		
Trophies—individual and team	$1,588.77		
Powerade—umpires and staff	$940.40	Grand Total Cost	$299,351.25
Quench sports drink—umpires and staff	$95.76	Total Tournament Revenue	$181,486.94
Lunch—at Opening Ceremonies	$303.52	Profit/Loss	($117,864.31)
Water—Opening Ceremonies	$29.92		

optimistic one usually overestimates the value of the facility or event. Thus, it has been argued that since events like the Summer Olympic Games often are perceived to have a substantial political value, it is reasonable for host communities to be willing to accept negative returns on the economic investment and to view it as a premium paid for the intangible political return.[31]

The influence of this monopoly power is vividly illustrated by the recent history of the Olympic Games. In 1984, Los Angeles was the only bidder for the Games. Thus, it was able to counter the monopoly power of the International Olympic Committee (IOC) and emerge as the only economically profitable Olympic Games in recent times. By 1992 there were 22 bidders, and similarly large numbers of cities have been involved in subsequent years. This means the IOC is able to dictate the economic terms. IOC Rule 4 requires the host city to accept all the financial costs associated with the Games. Thus, while many of the revenue streams that made the Los Angeles Games profitable have been claimed by the IOC, host cities have incurred the substantial financial costs that have accompanied the expansion and higher presentation expectations engendered by each successive Olympic Games.

DISPLACEMENT COSTS

Displacement costs are revenues foregone by a community. People who would otherwise spend money there are unable or unwilling to do so because they are crowded out and displaced by visitors to a sport event. The displacement costs may emanate from four sources:

- *Leavers* are residents who leave the community or area at the time of the event, and thus reduce their expenditures in the community.
- *Avoiders* are visitors who stay away, but who would have come if the sport event had not been held. They do not come because they could not obtain accommodations, were unwilling to pay higher prices, or were not prepared to mingle with the crowds attracted by the event. There is always a risk that some of these avoiders who have come to a destination on a regular basis might prefer their new option and stay away in the future.
- *Place switchers* are those who forego visiting other potential vacation destinations in a region or country in order to go to the sport event.
- *Replacement* costs occur when new facilities displace existing facilities whose revenues are foregone.

Obviously, displacement costs associated with the first three sources are lowest when regular, non-event visitation associated with the ordinary economic life of a community is relatively low. Ironically, because smaller events are likely to be less disruptive to the prevailing economic life of a community, their displacement costs are likely to be relatively small so failure to address them is of relatively little consequence. Most communities have convention and visitor bureaus whose business is to see that the community's infrastructure is efficiently utilized. Their job is to seek out peripatetic sport events that will fill the spare capacity in "down times" and so minimize displacement costs and optimize the net economic impact.

Data for economic impact studies typically are collected at events by surveying visitors who are in the area for the event. Each visitor then is regarded as a source of new economic impact. However, if each visitor merely replaces another potential visitor who stayed away from the community because of the congestion associated with the sport event, then there is no new economic impact. It has been noted that

> the survey technique readily identifies and samples those who, but for the event, would not be in the area and declares their spending as net new spending. What the survey technique cannot identify and sample are those not in the area that, but for the event, would have been. If the foxes held their convention in the hen house, this survey technique would attribute positive impacts to the foxes and never notice that all the hens were gone. (p. 64)[32]

Thus, while surveys collect expenditure information on those attending an event, they provide no information on the spending behavior of those who have been displaced by it.

Leavers

Irrespective of the nature of a sport event, there is likely to be a continuum of diverse reactions to it among community residents ranging from embracement, through tolerance, to reluctant adjustment to it and, ultimately, withdrawal because of the lifestyle disruptions caused by large numbers of visitors. Leavers are those residents who withdraw.[33]

The reality of displacement costs at the micro level was starkly illustrated by retailers whose businesses were adversely affected by road closures needed to facilitate the IAAF World Half-Marathon Championships. A survey of businesses revealed that 21% thought staging the event had a positive effect on business, 29% thought the effect was negative, and the remainder indicated that it had no effect. The negative comments included:

- The half-marathon seriously diluted sales.
- It absolutely stinks . . . We might as well have closed. I do not support this in any way . . . Is there any chance of compensation for loss of trade?
- In business terms, Sunday was a disaster. (p. 30).[4]

The economic impact of the event on the city, measured by the direct spending of non-locals, was approximately $800,000. However, this did not include any allowance for offsetting the displacement costs of locals who did not make purchases because of the event.

Evidence of leavers was provided by a survey of Barcelona residents in which 16% of people interviewed six months prior to the Olympic Games stated they were considering taking vacations outside the Costa Brava region during the Games.[34] A similar survey before the Sydney Olympics showed that 30% of residents had no interest in the Games, and among those intending to leave Sydney over 60% indicated they would travel abroad.[34]

Avoiders

There is evidence to suggest that avoiders may also inflict substantial displacement costs on communities that host the Olympic Games. For example, 66% of Danish tourists avoided the Lillehammer region during the Winter Olympics there.[34] Similarly, the Utah Skier Survey found that 50% of nonresident skiers would stay away from Utah during the Winter Olympics because they anticipated there would be larger crowds and higher prices.[35] However, the extent to which leavers or avoiders represent an economic cost depends on how many of them are really pre- or post-event time switchers. That is, what proportion of them simply go to the destination or make a purchase at a different time, rather than not visit it or make a purchase at all?[36]

The NFL Super Bowl is promoted as a having a large economic impact on the host community. Thus, studies sponsored by the NFL on the economic impact of the 1999 Miami and 2000 Atlanta Super Bowls reported economic impacts on Miami and Georgia of $396 million and $292 million, respectively.[37] However, a study that compared January spending in Super Bowl host cities to spending in that month in those cities during a series of non-Super Bowl years before and after the event found only a minimal increase: "occupancy rates [in hotels in the area] rose only 1.24%, 2.29%, and 4.3% for the [three] Super Bowls, respectively" (p. 69).[32] The author concluded, "Super Bowl demand (the foxes) merely squeezed out normal demand (the hens)" (p. 70).[32]

Multiple reasons were suggested to explain these results. However, a primary reason was the displacement effect. The Super Bowls that were studied were held in the cities of Tampa, Miami, and Phoenix. Hotel rooms in January in these three Sunbelt cities are close to being fully booked when there is no Super Bowl event. Further, in most cases, a minimum number of nights' stay is required by hotels during a Super Bowl period, and many guests do not stay all the nights for which they are required to pay. Although the room is paid for, when a guest leaves early it is empty. Consequently, there is no ancillary spending impact from restaurants, shopping, and so on. In contrast, if the Super Bowl were not there, the room would be filled with a guest spending at these other businesses. If, however, those displaced were all associated with another event, it may be argued there is no displacement effect because without recruiting an event, the rooms would be empty.

Hotel prices during these three Super Bowls rose 11.26% in Tampa, 19.83% in Miami, and 4.40% in Phoenix. Hence, estimates of the Super Bowls' economic impacts should be limited to consideration of the incremental increases in occupancy rates and prices, rather than embracing all revenue, since most of the revenues reflected displaced visitor spending that would have occurred if the Super Bowls had not been held.

The avoiders displacement cost principle was illustrated by events at the Atlanta Olympic Games:

> To the surprise of all, the masses never came. Further, those that came did not spend the money expected of them. The tour buses sat empty and the area's attractions remained relatively unseen. The Olympic consumer proved a very different marketing customer from the ordinary tourist or business traveler: an unpre-

dictable hybrid—sports-mad, tight-fisted and uninterested in traditional tourist attractions. It has been estimated that on average, spectators at the Atlanta Games spent just $15 a day after accommodation and transport. Normal business travelers, by comparison, would spend $350 a day and ordinary tourists about $100 a day on a similar basis. (p. 243)[38]

Olympic guests had no interest in eating out, visiting attractions, or retail shopping because they spent so much time getting to venues and sitting through events that by the end of the day, they wanted to relax in front of the television. Consequently, they spent much less than the regular visitors to Atlanta, whom they displaced.

The 2008 Beijing Olympics fared no better since security restrictions and other concerns "virtually eliminated any boost in tourism from the Olympics. The number of visitors to Beijing in August 2008 as predicted by its tourism bureau was 450,000, about the same as last August" and total visitor arrivals for the whole year were significantly lower than the previous year (p. 110).[29]

When the soccer World Cup was hosted by South Korea and Japan, the number of foreign visitors was identical to the number during the same period in the previous year, suggesting there were a large number of avoiders.[39] Within the countries there were also displacement costs: "Some casinos and hotels had drop-offs as regular customers and business travelers avoided World Cup hassles" (p. 2).[40] At mega events, such as World Cups and Olympic Games, there may also be pre-avoiders. During the months or years prior to the event they are dissuaded from visiting because of the often massive amounts of new construction, renovation and infrastructure work in progress that disrupts access around the community.[36]

A study of the impact of the NCAA men and women's Final Four basketball tournaments in the host cities over periods of 30 and 18 years, respectively, reported that on average, the men's event (FFM) resulted in a reduction in real income as a consequence of the events of $44.38 million, while the women's event (FFW) generated a net gain in income of approximately $70 million. The discrepancy between these results is attributed by the authors to displacement:

> The FFW has tended to be held in cities that are not otherwise normally considered prime tourist or convention destinations, such as Norfolk, Virginia; Austin, Texas; and Knoxville, Tennessee. If these cities do not normally attract significant numbers of business or recreational travelers, the tournament will not crowd out these other visitors, leading to a smaller substitution effect. The FFM has more commonly been held in "destination" venues such as New Orleans or Seattle, cities that would be more likely to attract other visitor travel even in the absence of the sporting event. (p. 129)[41]

The NFL Pro Bowl is held each February in Honolulu. The Hawaiian Tourist Board reported that it attracted 27,000 visitors to the Islands. However, a check of daily passenger arrivals indicated that the boost in members over the Pro Bowl time period was 6,500. This suggests that over 20,000 potential regular tourists to Hawaii avoided the

Islands at that time. Further, it was found there was a statistically significant decline in visitors arriving during the seven days prior to the Pro Bowl. The researchers' explanation for this was:

> Because of its distant location, regular tourists often spend periods of at least 1 week in the state. If visitors cannot find hotel accommodations during the following weekend after their arrival due to a sporting event, they are unlikely to make the choice to arrive in the previous week in the first place. These events may be replacing regular visitors planning on staying an entire week with sports visitors staying only for the weekend of the event, an outcome that would certainly negatively affect the economy. (p. 119)[29]

An assessment of the likely impact of a proposed Formula One (F1) race in Austin, Texas, in 2012 assumed that 90% of the Austin area's hotels would be filled with F1 fans during much of the race week. That is about 27,000 rooms, which it was estimated would generate around $28 million of direct hotel-related economic impact attributable to Formula One. However, this estimate failed to consider both the compatibility of the rooms with the clientele's needs or existing advance bookings by other groups. F1 fans tend to like amenity-filled hotel rooms, and only 6,000 of Austin's rooms are in that category. Further, three large conventions were already scheduled in Austin during 2012 F1 week and their expected attendees had reserved approximately 3,000 of these rooms. Indeed, during the same week in the past three years without F1 races, average hotel occupancy in Austin ranged from 72% in 2008 to 65.5% in 2010.[42] Again, this study substantially exaggerated the economic impact because it failed to acknowledge the avoiders' displacement cost. All anticipated spending by F1 fans was attributed to the race's economic impact instead of only the increment that exceeded revenues from the displaced visitors.

Place Switchers

Evidence of place switchers emerged at the Barcelona Olympics when the adjacent Costa Brava vacation region lost part of its high summer seasonal demand because many vacationers shifted their focus to Barcelona. The place switcher issue was also highlighted in a survey of hotel activity in Sydney and other Australian state capital cities prior to and during the Olympic Games:

> As expected, survey results indicate the vast majority of Sydney hotels peaking at near 100% occupancies during the Games period from September 16–30. This represents an increase of 49% in occupancy levels relative to the first half of September. In contrast, other capital cities experienced significant demand shortfalls for the same period. For example, occupancies in Melbourne and Brisbane plummeted by 19% and 17% in the second half of September relative to the period from 1–15 September. Overall, with the exception of Sydney and Adelaide, all hotel markets in Australia experienced a decline in occupancy in September 2000 relative to September 1999 despite the Olympic Games, as reported in the Hotel

Industry Benchmark Survey. Hoteliers indicated that while international demand was strong, . . . domestic leisure travel traditionally taking place during the September school holiday period was displaced to Sydney for the Olympics. (p. 346)[39]

It was pointed out that "Sydney's gains may well have come at the expense of other Australian cities, and if the federal government subsidizes the games there must be a rationale for enriching Sydney at the expense of Melbourne and other regional cities" (p. 346).[39] This kind of displacement may result in synergies that enhance the competitiveness of host cities of such mega events so they become long-term centers of growth at the expense of other destinations in a region or country.[34]

An investigation of the economic impact of the soccer FIFA World Cup on the U.S. cities that hosted the event counterintuitively concluded that "the World Cup had an overall negative impact on the host city economies of $9.26 billion . . . [which] stands in stark contrast to the increase projected by the boosters of the event of 'conservatively' $4 billion" (pp. 348, 349).[39] The authors attributed most of this loss to displacement costs:

> The apparent negative impact of the Cup can be explained by the fact that matches are not held on consecutive days. The "crowding-out" effect due to perceptions relating to limited hotel rooms and high hotel prices, rowdy behavior of football fans and peak use of public goods such as highways and sidewalks may be substantial if the Cup matches take place over a period of weeks as opposed to days. For example, the high negative impact for New York may be attributable to the fact that World Cup matches diverted convention activity from New York for a period of three and a half weeks rather than just the seven days on which matches were scheduled. Furthermore, the net effect on the New York economy of the conventions or other tourists who went elsewhere would depend on the details relating to the spending patterns of soccer fans versus those of the lost visitors and convention attendees. Thus, the spending of residents of the host city may be altered to the detriment of the city's economy. Residents may not frequent areas in which the event occurs or the fans stay. Further, if the games are televised, some fans may stay inside to view the games rather than going out as they normally might. (p. 350)[39]

Replacement Costs

The final source of displacement costs is replacement. This occurs when an old facility is replaced by a new facility. For example, in the context of professional sports, economic impact studies undertaken on new facilities typically attribute all economic gains to the new facility. However, most of these already were accruing to the community from the old facility. Only the incremental gains uniquely attributable to the new facility constitute new economic income to the community. The remaining element of economic gains is merely displaced impact from the original facility.

The Metropolitan Sports Facilities Commission and the NFL Minnesota Vikings commissioned an "Economic and Jobs Impact" study of developing "Metrodome Next," which would be a reconstructed stadium on the existing Metrodome site in downtown

Table 6.2. Assumptions for Recurring Stadium Events at the Proposed New "Metrodome Next" Facility			
Event	**Annual Events**	**Average Attendance**	**Total Annual Attendance**
Vikings	10	63,000	630,000
Concerts	2	30,000	60,000
High School Football	4	20,000	80,000
High School Soccer	3	5,000	15,000
Flat Floor	10	3,000	30,000
HS/Amateur Baseball	75	250	18,750
College Football	4	2,000	8,000
Motorsports	3	40,000	120,000
Amateur Football/Soccer	25	250	6,250
Other Ticketed Events	3	12,000	36,000
Other Events	50	250	12,500
Concourse	100	175	17,500
Total	**289**		**1,034,000**

Minneapolis. Their study was based on the attendance estimates shown in Table 6.2.[43] However, as two Minnesota legislators pointed out, "We already have the Metrodome which is paid for and fully functional" (p. A13).[44] Presumably, a substantial proportion of the events and attendances listed in Table 6.2 already occur at the Metrodome. Thus, the only net increase in economic impact is that attributable to the *incremental increases* on events and attendances at the new facility compared to those in the existing Metrodome, *not* the total attendances shown in Table 6.2.

OPPORTUNITY COSTS

Opportunity costs are the benefits that would be forthcoming if the public resources committed to a sport project were (1) redirected to other public services, or (2) retained by the taxpayer. Sport managers may like to think that government investment in sport projects and programs will have a positive economic impact, but the key question is, compared to what? The issue of opportunity costs is the fundamental social issue associated with government investment in sport. The key question is not whether an investment in sports is likely to be a profitable investment for the community. Rather, it is whether more benefits would be generated from any number of other opportunities such as investment in a local college, public schools, transportation infrastructure, health programs, or incentives to attract other kinds of businesses to locate in the community.

Conceptually, for an investment of public money to be justified, it must meet the criterion of "highest and best use." That is, it should yield a return to residents that is at least equal to that which could be obtained from other ventures in which the government entity could invest. Opportunity cost is the value of the best alternative *not* taken when a decision to expend government money is made. Thus, "if an alternative generates $2 million of benefits net of subsidy, and a stadium generates $1.5 million net of subsidy, the stadium can be viewed as imposing a $0.5 million *loss* on taxpayers, not a $1.5 million *benefit*" (p. 15).[45] Consider the following situation confronting the city of Denver when they were seeking an MLB franchise:

> Politicians in Denver did not exactly drop their jaws in shock when a Brown, Bortz and Coddington study projected a $16.5 million annual impact were the city to get a Major League Baseball team. It was more like a yawn. "It's nice, but I can't say we were all that impressed," said a mayoral assistant. "We just finished approving a convention center that's going to generate $200 million." (p. 32)[47]

The difference in economic impacts of these two types of facilities is attributable to who uses them. Sport teams primarily entertain local residents, whereas convention centers attract nonresidents to the community. Ironically, it is the sport team that is likely to be more popular politically because its contribution to the host community's quality of life is likely to be more obvious to most residents. In the above example, the city invested in both enterprises. If resources had been available for only one of them and community politicians had selected the baseball option, the economic impact analysis would have been positive, so the city probably would have supported the baseball opportunity. From an economic perspective, however, this would have been an unwise investment of public dollars because the opportunity cost of not being able to invest in the convention center was not considered.

The issue was illustrated by a letter writer to the *Baltimore Sun* who made the following observations: "The city is full of ruined houses, the jails are overcrowded, the dome is falling off City Hall, there are potholes in the streets, crippled children can't get to school, taxes are going up and services are going down—but we're going to have a sports complex" (p. 50).[48] The conundrum of priorities for the use of public tax dollars was highlighted in Cleveland. The day before the city council approved a large injection of public funds to build a new football stadium, the Cleveland public school system announced it would cut $52 million over 2 years, laying off 160 teachers and eliminating interscholastic athletics from a school system that its superintendent described as "in the worst financial shape of any school district in the country" (p. 22).[5] This caused one commentator to conclude, "Crumbling schools, staggering African American infant mortality and lingering unemployment are the undiscussed realities behind Cleveland's stadium-enhanced renaissance" (p. 153).[5]

Similarly, when the New York City council voted by 39 to 5 to spend $76 million to build a minor league ballpark in Staten Island for a Yankee farm team. It was suggested: "The inevitable conclusion is that schoolchildren subsidize professional athletes and owners by playing under substandard conditions while professional playgrounds are maintained to the highest standards" (p. 181).[49] A journalist pointed out that "the city will spend more money on this palatial ballpark than has been spent for all public school sports for the last 10 years put together" (p. 176).[49] He characterized it as a "$76 million summer jobs program for Hal Steinbrenner (son of George, [former] owner of the Yankees) and 25 teenagers from Arizona and Florida."(p. 176).[40]

Given the immense fiscal crisis confronting governments, especially in the major cities, and the numerous social and infrastructure needs requiring additional funds, it is incongruous and unconscionable to some that scarce public resources should be committed to such an apparently discretionary and relatively frivolous use.

The efforts of the mayor of San Jose to persuade the city's residents to approve a referendum allocating $265 million of public finds to a new stadium in which the Giants would play were strenuously opposed by the CEO of a prominent major high-tech company in the city. He objected to

> subsidizing a multimillionaire [the ball-club owner] with a quarter-billion dollar asset. This is a terrible investment when we're losing jobs and we don't have enough teachers and police. [The owner's] no villain. He'd be a fool not to get the best deal he can. You look for suckers in these deals, which in today's world means government. (p. 52)[50]

Borrowing for sports facilities also reduces the bonding capacity that a jurisdiction has available for other projects it may wish to undertake:

> Financing a new stadium in Jacksonville delayed a planned expansion of port facilities which, in the view of a critic in the city council, meant trading an investment in "10,000 very high-paying longshoreman-type jobs" for a sports project that would create "3,000 seasonal minimum-wage jobs."(p. 276)[15]

It was noted earlier that the legacy of mega events too often includes stadiums and highly specialized facilities that continue to cost large sums to maintain and receive relatively little use. They are highly visible, expensive symbols of investments that could have provided a much higher level of sustained benefits if the money had been used differently. Thus, it is surely reasonable to ask if the $1.6 billion spent on new stadiums by South Africa as host of the FIFA World Cup, when one third of its population lives on less than $2 a day, would not have yielded a better economic return if it had been invested in schools and health care to produce a better educated and more healthy citizenry.

The opportunity cost issue is particularly galling among those residing in cities that authorized subsidies for facilities in the 1980s and then watched as franchises departed after a relatively short period for better facilities elsewhere. For example, the new arenas built for the NBA expansion teams in Miami and Charlotte in 1989 were abandoned by those teams in 1999 and 2005, respectively, and when the then-Vancouver Grizzlies moved to Memphis in 2001, it was contingent on Memphis constructing a replacement for the Pyramid—built way back in 1991.[5] Typically, the public subsidy was in the form of bonds repayable over a 20- or 30-year period. Thus, some of these communities continued to make annual multimillion-dollar debt payments on facilities that had become white elephants because they had no major league team. Meanwhile, there was no money available to rectify deteriorating schools, streets, and public services. This emphasizes that the risk on major sport facilities is carried exclusively by the public sector because it is the owner of a depreciating asset, which is another dimension of opportunity cost.

There are two important caveats relating to the source of funds that need to be inserted into this opportunity cost debate. First, while ostensibly it may be conceptually obvious that resources invested in sport projects have an opportunity cost, the political reality is often different. If those resources are not spent on the sport project, then the probable political alternative is to cancel increases in the proposed concomitant taxing source(s), rather than to proceed with them and allocate the funds to pressing community needs. A second caveat is that facility advocates seek funds for *capital* investments, whereas funding for such needs as hiring more teachers or police officers, or developing new health or welfare programs originates from cities' *operational* budgets. This means that choices between sport projects and social needs often are more rhetorical than real because capital and operating budgets are not directly substitutable. It is generally easier to persuade voters to commit tax funds for capital projects, especially if the source of funds is not property or sales taxes, than it is to persuade them (or their legislative representatives) to accept higher annual tax rates for operating budgets to attack social problems.

In addition to considering the opportunity cost of not investing government resources into other projects because these resources are being expended for sport, there are opportunity costs associated with taking taxes from residents and visitors because it is likely that those funds would have been spent in the community if the government had not taken them. Every dollar that local governments spend in an economy must first be taxed or borrowed. Hence, the money is merely redistributed from one group of people to another: "Removing water from one end of a swimming pool and pouring it in the other end will not raise the overall water level—no matter how large the bucket. Similarly, redistributing dollars from one part of the economy to another will not expand the economy, no matter how much is transferred" (p. A10).[51]

It is tempting to believe sport investment creates new income and jobs because economic impact studies report these benefits. What such studies do not report, however, is the income and jobs that would have been created elsewhere in the community with those same dollars if they had not been used for this purpose. When residents are taxed to support an event or facility, the negative multiplier effect of taxing residents is likely to offset any positive multiplier: "Everybody who pays a dollar in taxes to support the facility must reduce his or her spending. The diminished spending goes round and round, just like the positive multiplier effect. The studies supporting [sport] projects never mention that counter effect assuming that the cost of capital is free" (p. 18).[52]

The emphasis placed on multipliers in economic impact analysis may lead the unwary to suppose that there is some unique property conferred on income and employment generation resulting from sport events or facilities that is not shared by other sectors of the economy. The inclusion of opportunity cost in an analysis recognizes that this is not the case and that it is the comparative size of the multiplier that is important. Indeed, it has been pointed out that nonsports entertainment spending has a bigger ripple effect in the economy than sports-related entertainment spending. Therefore, the economic gains from sports-related spending will never be large enough to fully offset the economic loss from a decline in nonsports entertainment spending. This reduction in earnings for nonsports industries would lead to a reduction in the earnings of workers in nonsports-related occupational groups. (p. 4)[53]

Distribution Issues

Opportunity costs are not distributed evenly, so it is unfortunate that invariably it is only total economic benefits and costs that are measured, and their distribution is not considered. "Who benefits and who pays should be a standard part of any impact analysis . . . The 'big number' buries all of the assumptions and doesn't identify the winners and losers; thus, 'Everybody Wins.' In most cases, the winners are those who already have political or economic clout and the losers don't know the difference" (n.p.).[16]

Much of the emotional rhetoric surrounding public investments in professional sport projects stems not only from the realization that the economic return from sports is slight, but also that benefits accrue disproportionately to wealthier segments of the community. For example, the Camden Yards complex in Baltimore ultimately resulted in an expenditure of $400 million from the Maryland State Treasury when interest charges on the debt are included in the cost.[48] The project was funded by revenue bonds supported by a specially created sports lottery. Hence, the bulk of the funds came from poor Baltimoreans who were the lottery's best customers. That $400 million could have been spent on the city's considerable needs for education or drug treatment from which the economically disadvantaged would have been most likely to benefit. A further irony of the situation is that a disproportionate number of those who paid for the ballpark—the buyers of Maryland lottery tickets who are relatively poor—are the least able to enjoy the events that occur in it because ticket prices in the new stadium are so much higher than they were in the old stadium. Further, the City of Baltimore lost many of the 1,000 manufacturing jobs provided by the 26 companies that had existed on the Camden Yards site, as well as the property taxes that the food plants and other businesses on the site had generated.[48]

When employment measures of economic impact are announced, the implied intent often is to laud the new jobs that will accrue in the local economy. However, if the opportunity cost is considered, the number of new jobs created will inevitably be perceived as offering a relatively poor return in the public investment. In response to an advocacy group's study reporting that a new baseball stadium for the Minnesota twins would cost the city $310 million and generate the equivalent of 168 full-time jobs, one economist remarked that if the money were "dropped out of a helicopter over the Twin Cities, you would probably create eight to ten times as many jobs" (p. 36).[54] The following comment refers to the state of Maryland's commitment of $200 million to attract the Baltimore Ravens NFL team: "Without question, communities willing to put up $200 million to attract a new company can do better than a football team, which employs 71 workers and annually earns $80 million to $100 million . . . Using a pair of economic-impact studies, the Congressional Research Service estimated that each job created by the Ravens and their stadium will cost Maryland from $127,000 to $331,000. By contrast, the service said the state's 'sunny day' fund, used to help attract and retain conventional businesses, created jobs at an average cost of $6,250" (p. 315).[54]

If public funds for major sport facilities and events were invested in health, education, or productive industry, it is likely that the result would be a wider distribution of benefits.

> Most sports revenue goes to a relatively few players, managers, coaches and executives who earn extremely high salaries—all well above the earnings of people who work in the industries that are substitutes for sports. Most stadium employees work part time at very low wages and earn a small fraction of team revenues. Thus, substituting spending on sports for other recreational spending concentrates income, reduces the total number of jobs, and replaces full-time jobs with low-wage, part-time jobs. (p. 37)[55]

Thus, for example, if a baseball player's salary of $6 million were spread among 200 people earning $30,000, local dry cleaners, restaurants, and other businesses would be likely to do better and hire more workers.

Perhaps nowhere is the regressive nature of opportunity costs better illustrated than in the public subsidies for professional sport stadiums and arenas, in which forty-five individuals from the *Forbes* magazine list of the wealthiest 400 Americans (all with net assets exceeding $500 million) owned a direct interest in a team in one of the four major leagues. Indeed, a review of NFL teams in 2010 revealed that 16 of the 31 owners (excluding Green Bay's community-owned team) were billionaires.[16] The transferring of money from middle-class and blue-collar workers to an immensely profitable entertainment business is regressive and works to the disadvantage of those groups.

SUMMARY

Economic impact is too often erroneously equated with profitability. The numbers emerging from an economic impact study measure only economic benefits, and the costs and negative impacts on a community associated with a sport event invariably are not considered. Independent critiques of economic impact studies invariably show that the purported teams' facilities or mega events are generally small or nonexistent, despite the studies issued by boosters to the contrary. When the costs associated with these facilities and events are considered, then their viability invites even more skepticism.

It is in the interest of mega event property or sport facility owners to suppress cost information, but voters and decision makers need information on both sides of the equation to make informed decisions. In addition to the direct monetary costs incurred, consideration should be given to nine other types of costs: society wide costs; strategic underestimation of capital costs and overstatement of revenue streams; omission of interest costs; land and infrastructure costs; foregone property taxes; operation and maintenance costs; event costs; displacement costs; and opportunity costs.

Tax revenues the federal government foregoes by giving dispensations to special groups are costs borne by society as a whole, since others have to pay higher taxes to compensate for this largesse. Three are especially prominent in sport. First, the ability of private entities to access tax-exempt bonds issued by governments substantially reduces the cost of their capital projects. Second, when a franchise is purchased, a roster depreciation allowance is authorized. This views players' salaries as an asset that depreciates each year so this number can be deducted from profits before they are taxed. No other type of business in the U.S. is allowed to depreciate its human assets in this way. Third, corporate purchases of luxury suites and club seats can be deducted as an entertainment expense, which effectively means society subsidizes these purchases.

Strategic underestimation of capital costs occurs when a public entity bids to attract a major event or facility to a community, and to bolster public and political support it substantially underestimates the costs involved. Sometimes cost overruns may be inadvertently caused by unforeseeable contingencies, but in other cases their magnitude suggests they are strategic and deliberate.

Discussions of capital costs focus on the amount of money borrowed for the project, but this is not the total cost incurred by the community because it omits interest paid on the bonds over their 20- to30-year life. Similarly, when the costs of facilities are announced, they often exclude costs of associated land and infrastructure costs incurred by governments. The relatively large tracts of land needed for facilities often are acquired and paid for with public funds, and then donated to the projects. Similarly, public funds used to pay for new roads, transit, sewers, and water and electricity connections, frequently are omitted from the publicized cost of facilities.

Cities forego property taxes when teams negotiate that they will not have to pay them on the facility they occupy. In some instances, this occurs even when the facility is not publicly owned.

Operation and maintenance costs incurred by public entities may be both onsite and offsite. Onsite costs include some ongoing operating expenses such as utilities, insurance, and administration, and maintenance expenses such as the cost of labor needed to service a facility or event—cleaning, trash removal etc.—landscaping, and additional equipment and supplies. In some cases, this extends to guarantees by a city to compensate for low ticket sales. Offsite expenses are those inflicted on a community by large crowds such as traffic congestion, police and fire protection and vandalism.

An evaluation of the effect of omitting land and infrastructure costs, forgone property taxes, and operations and maintenance costs from the published public subsidies for all four of the major leagues' stadiums and arenas concluded:

> Whereas industry sources report an average facility cost of $203 million with an average public share of $125 million or 56%, I estimate that the average facility cost is $222 million, with an average public share of $175 million or 79%, an increase in public share of 23 percentage points. I estimate that the omission of land and infrastructure comprises $17 million or 8% of these unreported public costs, while net annual costs [forgone property taxes and annual operations and maintenance costs] make up the remaining $34 million or 15%. (p. 94)[13]

Elsewhere, the same researcher reported:

> I estimate the total value of the underreported public subsidy at $5 billion. More worrisome is that the gap between reported and actual costs is widening: For the 65 new facilities opened between 1990 and 2001, the average uncounted public cost increases to $71 million per facility, bringing the average public subsidy to $195 million based on a total development cost of $242 million. (p. 135)[14]

Most residents and elected officials are unaware of the costs involved in staging a major sport event. Since there is usually competition among communities to host such events, the organizations that control these properties often are able to pass through most of the associated costs while retaining many of the revenue streams.

Displacement costs occur when people who would otherwise spend money in a community are unable or unwilling to do so because they are "crowded out" and displaced by visitors to a sport event. They are comprised of leavers, who are residents who leave the community at the time of the event and thus reduce their expenditures in the community; avoiders, who are visitors who stay away, but who would have come if the sport event had not been held; and place switchers, who forgo visiting other potential vacation destinations in a region or country in order to go to the sport event. An alternative form of displacement is the replacement of an existing facility with a new amenity in the same community.

Opportunity costs are benefits that would be forthcoming if the public resources committed to a sport project were either redirected to other public services or retained by the taxpayer. When taxes are taken from residents to invest in a sport project, it is likely that those funds would have been spent in the community if the government had not taken them. This should be incorporated in an economic analysis because quality-of-life outcomes and the multiplier coefficient of these alternative investments may be as high as or higher than that associated with the sport investment. An investment in a sport project can only be a net benefit to society if the resources given up by individual taxpayers are used to produce greater benefits than they would produce in the absence of the project.

Four arguments are used to suggest that opportunity costs are likely to disadvantage lower-income residents most. First, if lottery profits are used as a funding source, they are invariably regressive. Second, the cost of jobs created by sport investments is high and they tend to be low paid. If governments used these resources to create jobs in other sections of the economy, more would be created. Third, the major beneficiaries of these public funds are likely to be relatively affluent event or team owners and athletes. Fourth, the high admission prices typically associated with new professional sport facilities or mega events effectively exclude lower-income residents.

References

1. LaFaive, M. D. (2009). Special events: Flawed report on film incentive provides distorted lens. Mackinac, MI: Mackinac Center for Public Policy.
2. Taks, M., Kesenne, S., Chalip, L., Green B. C., & Martyu S. (2011). Economic impact analysis versus cost benefit analysis; The case of a medium-sized sport event. *International Journal of Sport Finance, 6*(3), 187–203.
3. Shah, A., & Brown S. (2004, September 14). Seeing a stadium as salvation. *The Dallas Morning News*, p. 2.

4. Economic Research Associates (2004). *Economic and fiscal impacts for the proposed NFL Stadium in Arlington, Texas.* City of Arlington: ERA Project Number 15652.

5. DeMause, N., & Cagan, J. (2008). *Field of schemes: How the great stadium swindle turns public money into private profit.* Lincoln, NE: University of Nebraska Press.

6. Greaves, T., & Henchman, J. (2009). *From the house that Ruth built to the house the IRS built. Fiscal Fact #167.* Washington DC: The Tax Foundation.

7. Coulson, N. E., & Fort, R. (2010). Tax revisions of 2004 and pro sports team ownership. *Contemporary Economic Policy, 28*(4), 464–473.

8. Matheson, V. A. (2008). Mega-events: The effect of the world's biggest sporting event on local, regional, and national economies. In B. R. Humphreys & D. R. Howards (Eds.), *The business of sports, volume 1* (pp. 81–100). Westport, CT: Praeger.

9. Brooke, J. (2002, June 2). Soccer: Legacy of World Cup may be the stadiums left behind. *The New York Times.* Retrieved from http://www.nytimes.com/2002/06/02/sports/soccer-legacy-of-world-cup-may-be-the-stadiums-left-behind.html

10. Zimbalist, A., & Long, J. G. (2008). Facility finance: measurement, trends, and analysis. In B. R. Humphreys & D. R. Howard (Eds.), *The business of sports, volume 2* (pp. 235–252). Westport, CT: Praeger.

11. Baade, R. A., & Matheson, V. A. (2011). *Financing professional sports facilities.* Worcester, MA: College of Holy Cross Working Paper. 11–02.

12. Gessing, P. J. (2001). *Public funding of sports stadiums: Ballpark boondoggle.* Washington DC: National Taxpayers Union Foundation Policy Paper #133.

13. Long, J. G. (2002). *Full court. The real cost of public subsidies for major league sports facilities.* PhD dissertation. Cambridge, MA: Harvard University.

14. Long, J. G. (2005). The real cost of public funding for major league sports facilities. *Journal of Sports Economics, 6*(2), 119–143.

15. Danielson, M. N. (1997). *Home team: Professional sports and the American metropolis.* Princeton, NJ: Princeton University Press.

16. Bennett, J. T. (2011). *They play, you play: Why taxpayers build ballparks and stadiums for billionaire owners and millionaire players.* Prepublication manuscript.

17. Quirk, J. P. (1987, January 18). The Quirk study: A close look at the two proposals. *St. Louis Post-Dispatch*, Special Report 8.

18. Peterson, D. C. (1996). *Sports convention and entertainment facilities.* Washington DC: The Urban Land Institute.

19. Zimmerman, D. (1991). *The private use of tax-exempt bonds: Controlling public subsidy of private activities.* Washington DC: Urban Institute Press.

20. Mules, T., & Dwyer, L. (2005). Public sector support for sport tourism events: The role of cost-benefit analysis. *Sport in Society, 8*(2), 338–355.

21. Greenburg, M. J. (2001). *The stadium game.* Milwaukee, WI: Marquette University Press.

22. Hitchcock, M. (2011) *Welcome to PETCO Park: Home of your Enron-by-the-Sea Padres.* Berkeley, CA: University of California.

23. Okner, B. A. (1974). Taxation and sports enterprises. In R. Noll (Ed), *Government and the sports business* (pp. 325–349). Washington DC: The Brookings Institute.

24. Baim, D. (1994). The sports stadium as a municipal investment. Westport, CT: Greenwood Press.

25. Quirk, J., & Fort, R. D. (1997). *Pay dirt: The business of professional team sports.* Princeton, NJ: Princeton University Press.

26. Rosentraub, M. S. (1997). *Major league losers: The real cost of sports and who's paying for it.* New York, NY: Basic Books, Harper Collins.

27. Gibson, O. (2011, December 8). Lord Coe admits to financial concerns over London 2012 Olympic budget. *The Guardian*, p. 3.

28. Ap, J., & Crompton, J. L. (1998). Development and testing of a tourism impact scale. *Journal of Travel Research, 37*(2), 120–130.

29. Baumann, R. W., Matheson, V. A., & Muroi, C. (2009). Bowling in Hawaii: Examining the effectiveness of sports-based tourism strategies. *Journal of Sports Economics, 10*(1), 107–123.

30. Rosentraub, M. S. (2006). The local context of a sports strategy for economic development. *Economic Development Quarterly, 20*(3), 278–291.

31. Baade, R. A., & Matheson, V. A. (2002). Bidding for the Olympics: Fool's gold? In C. Barros, M. Ibrahim, & S. Szymanski (Eds.), *Transatlantic sport: The comparative economics of North American and European sports* (pp. 127–151). London, UK: Edward Elgar.

32. Porter, P. K. (1999). Mega-sports events as municipal investments: A critique of impact analysis. In J. Fizel, E. Gustafson, & L. Hadley (Eds.), *Sports economics: Current research* (pp. 61–73). Westport, CT: Praeger.

33. Ap, J., & Crompton, J. L. (1993). Residents' strategies for responding to tourism impacts. *Journal of Travel Research*, *32*(1), 47–49.

34. Preuss, H. (2004). *The economics of staging the Olympics: Hosting the Games 1972–2008*. Cheltenham, UK: Edward Elgar.

35. Governor's Office of Planning and Budgeting. (2002). *2002 Olympic Winter Games: Economic, demographic and fiscal impacts*. Salt Lake City, UT: Demographic and Economic Analysis Section.

36. Pruess, H. (2005). The economic impact of visitors at major multi-sport events. *European Sport Management Quarterly*, *5*(3), 281–301.

37. Williams, P. (2001, January 15–21). Economic impact of Super Bowls tough, if not impossible, to gauge. *SportsBusiness Journal*, pp. 21–22.

38. Ratnatunga, J., & Muthaly, S. K. (2000, September/October). Lessons from the Atlanta Olympics: Marketing and organizational considerations for Sydney 2000. *Sports Marketing & Sponsorship*, *2*(3), 239–257.

39. Baade, R. A., & Matheson, V. A. (2004a). The quest for the Cup: Assessing the economic impact of the World Cup. *Regional Studies 38*(4), 343–354.

40. World says sayonara till '06. (2002, July 1). *USA Today*, p. C2.

41. Baade, R. A., & Matheson, V. A. (2004b). An economic slam dunk or March madness? Assessing the economic impact of the NCAA Basketball Tournament. In J. Fizel & R. Fort (Eds.), *Economics of college sports* (pp. 111–133). Westport, CT: Praeger.

42. Dexheimer, E. (2011, June 26). Taking a closer look at economic benefits claimed for Austin's Formula One project. *Austin American Statesman*, p. 1.

43. CSL International. (2009). *Economic and job impact of Metrodome Next multipurpose facility*. Minneapolis, MN: Metropolitan Sports Facility Commission.

44. Drazeowski, S., & Lohmer, K. (2011, October 20). Two stadium issues: 'Whether?' and 'where?' *Star Tribune*, p. A13.

45. Zimmerman, D. (1996). *Tax-exempt bonds and the economies of professional sports stadiums*. Washington DC: Congressional Research Service, The Library of Congress.

47. Dunnavant, K. (1989, March 13). The impact of economics. *Sports Inc.*, pp. 31–33.

48. Richmond, P. (1993). *Ballpark: Camden Yards and the building of an American dream*. New York, NY: Simon and Shuster.

49. Sullivan, N. J. (2001). *The diamond in the Bronx: Yankee Stadium and the politics of New York*. New York, NY: Oxford University Press.

50. Fimrite, B. (1992, June 1). *Oh give me a home. . . . Sports Illustrated*, *76*, 50–52, 57.

51. Riedl, B. M. (2010, January 3). Government economic stimulus plan is giant shell game. *Bryan-College Station Eagle*, p. A10.

52. Keating, R. J. (1999). *Sports pork: The costly relationship between major league sports and government*. Washington DC: Cato Institute Policy Analysis #339.

53. Coates, D., & Humphreys, B. R. (2004). *Caught stealing: Debunking the economic case for D.C. baseball*. Washington DC: Cato Institute Briefing Paper #89.

54. Morgan, J. (1997). *Glory for sale*. Baltimore, MD: Bancroft Press.

55. Noll, R. G. (1997). Bread not circuses: Are new stadiums worth the cost? *The Brookings Review*, *15*(3), 35–39.

7

Alternate Justifications for Public Subsidy: Structural Capital

INTRODUCTION

The benefit principle of taxation requires that those who pay for a public investment should receive commensurate benefits from it. Chapters 5 and 6 demonstrated that in most cases the direct net economic gains accruing to the taxpaying public from major facilities are too small to justify public investment in them. However, those discussions provided only part of the context because total community benefits comprise not only direct economic benefits, but also enhanced structural and social capital. Thus, analyses of a community's return on its investment also have to include consideration of these two outcomes.

When public sector funds are used to pay for capital development and/or operating costs of a sport facility, they can be considered an *investment* if the sector receives economic impact from subsequent use of the sport facility, proximate infrastructure development it has stimulated, and social capital emanating from it, which together substantially offset the tax dollars spent. If this criterion is not met, then the public expenditures are a *subsidy* for the private partner.

Increased public skepticism with the contention that substantial direct economic returns accrue does not necessarily mean public funds should not be forthcoming, since project proponents have the opportunity to demonstrate that these additional structural and social capital benefits justify those expenditures. The key question is, what is the public legacy from this investment? Legacy refers to the sustainable gains that accrue to the people living within a jurisdiction who paid for the facilities. It suggests that rather than the goal being to meet a short-term end goal, new facilities should be viewed as a means to intentionally accomplish specified social goals.

Structural capital refers to the built sport facilities, complementary development associated with them, and physical infrastructure improvements that they stimulate. *Social capital* is concerned with society's social interactions and is defined as "the development of relationships of mutual reciprocity embedded in social networks that enable action . . . generate trust, establish expectations, and create norms" (p. 43).[1]

The two outcomes are interrelated. For example, improved infrastructure may contribute to binding people together. It is what happens as a result of the structural capital investment that determines the quality and quantity of social capital. Indeed, it has been suggested that structural and social capital are so integrated that differentiating between them is redundant and that social capital captures both constructs.

> Sport as social capital can be defined by separating the two concepts or words. The capital component involves the facilities constructed to host the events. The social dimension involves one set of outcomes or benefits from sporting events that increases the interactions between members of a society or between individuals and the social support for a governance system or a society . . . by their role in city planning and development [sport facilities] have a prima facie case leading to their classification as social capital. (p. 342)[2]

The two outcomes are addressed sequentially in this chapter and in Chapter 8 to simplify the exposition, but the planning of sport facilities should consider them holistically as an integrated package. For example, where rejuvenation or urban redevelopment is an intended outcome, physical structures may contribute, but it is the contributions they make to the social, economic and psychic needs of the people living there that are key to its success—i.e., social capital.

Political leaders are required to justify to their constituents the opportunity cost of their spending substantial public funds on sport facilities for professional franchises or mega events while critical social needs go unmet. Given that the claims of direct economic benefits have been widely exposed and acknowledged as specious, their responses are likely to focus on the structural capital the investment represents and its contribution to economic development. This emphasizes the potential catalytic effect of the facility in stimulating retail, commercial, and residential development.

The discussion in Chapter 4 pointed out that business elites are likely to have a vested interest in major facilities being developed. However, in contrast to political leaders, business leaders are often skeptical of economic development claims, recognizing that there are alternate projects in which the hundreds of millions of dollars invested would yield a higher return. Thus, their advocacy tends to focus on the structural and social capital benefits that may accrue from the project.

As the debate has shifted, it has been suggested that the hyperbole that characterized many of the economic impact analyses is now a feature of arguments proclaiming the structural and social capital benefits of major sport facilities.[3] This chapter focuses on structural capital, while Chapter 8 addresses social capital. The discussion in this chapter focuses primarily on major league franchises and mega events, but most of the principles apply to sport facilities and events in other contexts such as varsity athletics, intramurals, and city park and recreation agencies.

THE CONCEPT OF STRUCTURAL CAPITAL

In addition to their role in facilitating social capital, major sport facilities invariably are viewed as anchors for economic development. It was pointed out in Chapter 6 that because either they are publicly owned, or property taxes were waived or abated in negotiations with a private developer, most major sport facilities do not directly generate tax revenues for a city. However, they have become ubiquitous in the downtowns of US cities. The intent is they will serve as catalysts that stimulate proximate retail, commercial, and residential development.

While the building of major sport facilities affords cities an opportunity to steer development to a desired location and to jumpstart economic development there, some proportion of the new spending will be substitutable expenditures. That is, if the public amenities and private facilities were not built in the redevelopment location, either they would have been constructed elsewhere in the city, or the consumer expenditures made in them would have occurred elsewhere in the city. Indeed, rejuvenation of a district inevitably redirects dollars to it that were previously spent in other city outlets. Thus, it is the marginal economic impact reflecting the amount of new money entering the local economy that should be the criterion used to measure the economic success of a downtown rejuvenation project.

Further, rejuvenation inevitably is accompanied by gentrification. In Chapters 4 and 6, it was noted that major sport projects sometimes result in the displacement of poorer people living in the cities. There is a Machiavellian rationale related to image enhancement that supports these kinds of actions. Sport in cities traditionally has been associated with the urban working classes. It has been suggested that is "hardly the image that would be deemed to attract the 'right sort of people' to cities which already possess enduringly strong working-class reputations" (p. 131).[4] The increasing gentrification of sport effectively removes the working classes from the scene, replacing them with a more wealthy clientele. It is believed this is likely to attract more affluent entities from the business and tourism sectors which, in the eyes of some, contribute to upgrading and enhancing a city's image.

Low-income renters who typically are unskilled and unemployed workers, often recent immigrants and single parents with no ability to politically influence the process, are likely to be displaced as property values rise. What happens to them? Do they move to other areas of the city, migrate to other communities, or become homeless? The challenge of accommodating their needs remains.

Notwithstanding these reservations, advocates argue that expenditures on these sport facilities represent investments, not subsidies, because the proximate development will produce higher revenues for public jurisdictions from income taxes, sales taxes, and property taxes that will be sufficient to repay the initial public investment in the sport facility. The public sector intent is

> to create lively, convivial downtown spaces that promote a street-fair atmosphere as well as meet the needs of a button-down business environment for office and commercial space. The intention is that both sets of activities will generate the tax dollars needed to meet a city's social responsibilities while simultaneously reducing the inventory of dilapidated properties leading to the movement of residences and businesses away from the center city. (p. 60)[5]

THE PRINCIPLE OF CUMULATIVE ATTRACTION

In cities where this strategy is perceived to have been successful, the sport facilities were not isolated investments. Rather, they were part of an overall development plan that led to complementary downtown investments in entertainment, arts, and cultural centers. These cities have followed the principle of creating a threshold level of cumulative attraction. This recognizes that a given number of attractions will do more business and create more proximate development if they are located close to each other than if they are dispersed. The emergence of "urban entertainment destinations" has been identified as one of the most significant developments in transforming cities throughout the developed world.[6] The cumulative attraction principle states that in order to persuade people to go downtown so there is sufficient traffic for it to be viable for businesses to locate there, there has to be a critical mass of complementary attractions. This notion was an explicit reason for selecting the Camden Yards site for the pioneering Orioles' baseball park, which was a model others sought to emulate. "The basic rationale for selecting the site was that the presence of multiple attractions would induce more attendance both at Orioles' games and other downtown attractions than either could generate in the absence of the other" (p. 255).[7] It is untenable to believe that a single facility standing alone, such as an MLB ballpark, could induce substantial associated economic development given that it operates only for three hours a day, a few days a week, between May and September. There must be other reasons to visit the area when games are not being played.

It is widely acknowledged that "Indianapolis wrote the textbook on using sports and cultural facilities to revitalize its downtown area" (p. 94).[8] Exhibit 7.1 describes how the city's leadership, over a four-decade period, not only rebuilt a moribund downtown center, but also kept it vibrant and expanding with a second wave of capital projects to replace facilities built to initiate the rebuilding process.[8,9]

Baltimore and Cleveland are two other cities where public investment to create a threshold level of cumulative attraction is widely believed to have resulted in relatively successful downtown rejuvenation. At the Baltimore Inner Harbor area, in addition to the new MLB and NFL stadiums, the city contributed to building the $50 million PowerPlant Live!, a two-block entertainment complex, a convention center and a science center that also hosts the National Aquarium. Similarly, while Cleveland's redevelopment effort was highlighted by its investment in three new facilities at the Gateway Complex for NFL, MLB, and NBA franchises, the city also restored the five theaters for the performing arts that constitute Playhouse Square, built the Rock and Roll Hall of Fame and Museum, and constructed the Science Center and IMAX theater.

The principle of cumulative attraction has been similarly prominent in cities where minor league facilities have been a central element in successful downtown rejuvenation. For example:

- AT&T Bricktown Ballpark, home of the Oklahoma Redhawks, is the anchor of the city's entertainment district. It sits next to a canal where visitors can ride a wa-

Exhibit 7.1

The Renaissance of Indianapolis

Indianapolis is most often cited as the city which most effectively used sports as a central focus for rejuvenation. It was a model which officials in many other cities sought to emulate. The city was the eleventh largest city in the United States in 1980, but the only thing people thought of when Indianapolis was mentioned was its annual 500-mile auto race. The novelist Kurt Vonnegut who was a native son, when appearing on *The Tonight Show* famously commented that the city was a cemetery that came to life for one day each year for the Indianapolis 500 and then fell back comatose for the other 364! The city was derisively nicknamed "India-no-place" or "Naptown." Indeed, the principal of a consulting firm commissioned to conduct a national survey to understand the perception of the city's image, commenced his presentation to political leaders by saying, "Gentlemen, the good news is your city does not have a bad image. The bad news is it doesn't have a good image. In fact, to many people in the country, Indianapolis has no image at all." The city was simply unknown to many Americans.

The downtown core of the city was dirty and filled with vacant, dilapidated buildings. Like many other old industrial cities, Indianapolis' businesses and residents had moved away from the central business district. The Director of the Indianapolis Department of Metropolitan Development recalled that in the late 1970s, the emptiness of the city led to some interesting Sunday afternoon excursions for local Jaycees (escorted by police): "They were downtown with shotguns and bags, shooting pigeons. If you can imagine a downtown so desolate, there were roving guys with shotguns. We had nothing downtown. If our goal was to create a city nobody wanted to live in, we'd done it."[9]

To address this desolation, a plan was developed by elected officials, business leaders, and the major philanthropic institution in the city to collaborate and use sport as the central foundation upon which to build an amenity infrastructure for the downtown area, but it was to be accompanied by investment in other complementary live entertainment facilities. The city's central demographic location, both within the state of Indiana and in the United States, was perceived as an asset. The goal was to turn Indianapolis into the "Sports Capital of the U.S." It was anticipated that this would stimulate downtown redevelopment and provide a positive image and national identity for the city.

It was a comprehensive strategy. It commenced with recruitment of NBA and NFL franchises (Pacers and Colts) which with the existing Indianapolis 500 race provided a good foundation for implementing the vision. These were key anchors. When the city persuaded the Baltimore Colts franchise to relocate there, the Mayor of Indianapolis commented:

> "I was saying for eight years we were in the process of becoming major league; now we can say, I think without grandiose pomposity, that we are a major league city." On another occasion the Mayor reiterated this theme: "Yes sir, we're going all the way now. It's a wonderful thing for our community. It's a boost to the city's image nationally and to local morale as a symbol of major league status . . . We want people to sit up and say "By gosh, that city has a lot going for it."[9]

Successfully luring the Colts was a key to the success of Indianapolis' sports strategy. However, the sport plan was much more ambitious since it extended to amateur sports and attracting a continuous flow of major sporting events. The vision was to create a vibrant downtown area through sports which would encourage other companies and residents to move there. There were existing institutions there to build around: Indiana University Medical Center; the 27,000 enrollment Indiana University—Purdue University (IUPUI) campus; a large private-sector

Exhibit 7.1 *(Continued)*

The Renaissance of Indianapolis

employer (Lilly); government facilities employing thousands in state and local government; and the Hoosier Dome which was built for the NFL team, but also was part of the Indiana Convention Center.

To persuade amateur sports organizations to consider moving their headquarters to Indianapolis and locating their championship events there, the city built a new track and field stadium, tennis center, and state-of-the-art natatorium on the IUPUI campus; a velodrome; and championship standard facilities in other parts of the city for soccer, rowing, archery, ice skating and golf.

In the following decade, after the Colts arrived, two dozen sports-connected organizations, including one international and seven national sports governing bodies, established their headquarters in Indianapo-

lis: The Indianapolis sports movement captured widespread attention. It was complemented with investment in a number of cultural centers that were renovated or built to complement the sport facilities and ensure the downtown area was a year-round attraction. These included: The Indiana Theater, home of the Indiana Repertory Company; the Circle Theater for the Indianapolis Symphony; the Indianapolis Zoo and Botanical Gardens; the Eiteljong Museum of American Indian and Western Art; an IMAX theater; the County Public Library; and new homes for the Indiana Historical Society and the Indiana State Museum.

Between 1974 and 2008, nine major sports facilities were built. These are shown in the following table:[8]

Facility	Description	Opened	Replaced
Market Square Arena	Indoor arena for Indiana Pacers; capacity 16,530	1974	1999
Tennis Center	Seating capacity 10,000	1979	
Track and Field	Seating capacity 12,111	1982	
Natatorium	Championship pools; capacity 5,000	1982	
Hoosier Dome	Indoor stadium for Colts, other events, conventions; capacity 57,980	1984	2008
Fitness Center	Training and fitness center for all athletes	1988	
Victory Field	Minor League Baseball Park for Indianapolis Indians; capacity 15,000	1997	
Conesco Fieldhouse	Home for Indiana Pacers, other events; capacity 18,345	1999	
Lucas Oil Stadium	Domed stadium for Indianapolis Colts, NCAA Championships, other amateur sports events; conventions; events; capacity 63,000 (expandable to 70,000)	2009	

ter taxi. There is also plenty of shopping, as well as outdoor dining and nightclubs. The whole neighborhood has become a destination.

- Louisville Slugger Field in Kentucky is close not only to the baseball bat museum but also to the Fourth Street Live entertainment district, featuring a comedy club, music clubs and a Hard Rock Café. "People just pour over there after the game,"

Exhibit 7.1 *(Continued)*

The Renaissance of Indianapolis

The investments made in rebuilding downtown Indianapolis (in 2007 dollars) are listed below:[8]

These data show that the city's commitment was $2.54 billion, while the total investment in downtown Indianapolis during this period was $8.32 billion. Thus for every dollar the city invested, it leveraged $2.25 from other stakeholders. The city's success has been lauded by the national and international media which have carried a plethora of glowing reports about the city's transformation from "India-no-place" to "the state of the snowbelt," which was the title bestowed on it by an article in the *Wall Street Journal.*

Project Type	Public Sector		Nongovernmental		Total
	Local	*Nonlocal*	*Private*	*Nonprofit*	
Sports	998.2	88.8	329.6	191.9	1,708.5
Culture/ Entertainment	166.7	51.5	355.1	296.9	870.2
Commercial	1,323.3	977	2,224.9	8.8	4,534.0
Residential	49.2	112.6	380.4	3.7	545.9
Education		663.9			663.9
Total	2,537.4	1,993.8	3,290.0	501.3	8,322.5

said a Louisville Bats spokesman. "Most of the people who come here aren't coming to see the players. It's the attractions, the promotions" (p. B1).[10]

Indianapolis, Los Angeles, San Diego and Columbus, Ohio, have all been identified as cities in which sport projects have been an effective catalyst for urban redevelopment.[8] A key to their success was that these cities' investments were concentrated in a relatively small area and they built out from the middle. Revitalization is most likely if the core demographic area of redevelopment is relatively small, since this makes it easier to ensure that all buildings and land within the district are developed. This creates an image of success and vitality that contrasts with the previous dilapidated buildings, deterioration and dereliction. In contrast, if amenities are dispersed across a wide area, more resources are required to develop all properties in the district, so there is a risk the final outcome may be that each amenity "is an isolated island of activity in a larger sea of deteriorating properties" (p. 252).[8] In short, there is a danger that the legacy may be limited to a set of (perhaps) iconic buildings separated by a vacuum of windswept empty space, isolated from the city around them.

In addition to the tightly defined geographic district, two other conditions are key features of successful rejuvenations. First, catalyst investments must offer unique experiences. That is, the experiences cannot be replicated anywhere else in the metropolitan area, so there are no direct substitute options. Major sport facilities generally meet this criterion, as do other major entertainment, concert, theater or cultural facilities. Second, these facilities must have convenient parking options or proximate reliable public transportation so suburbanites can easily access them.[8]

CLUSTERING

Clustering is a form of cumulative attraction that occurs at a regional rather than a local level. It recognizes that there is a tendency for businesses in any industry to cluster in a particular region in industrial agglomerations because of the symbiotic and complementary relationships among them. Some sports, especially those where cutting-edge technology is paramount to their competitive viability, have stimulated such clusters.

For example, the British motorsports industry is clustered in a 50-mile radius around Oxfordshire. The region is known as Motor Sport Valley. The cluster employs over 30,000 people and is composed primarily of small and medium-sized firms, with only a handful employing more than 200 people. They constitute a "knowledge community" united by a common set of norms, values, and understanding.[11] The area produces vehicles and equipment for Formula One, Championship Auto Racing, Indy Racing League, and Rally cars.[12] The proximate location of these companies results in technological knowledge spillovers that enhance the chances of winning. An empirical study of clustering concluded, "One of the most important ways in which knowledge is spread within the motor sports industry is by the rapid and continual transfer of staff between the companies within the industry" (p. 128).[11] Indeed, on average, personnel move every 3.7 years, so there is a "churning of knowledge" (p. 194).[11]

When the America's Cup Challenge was held in Freemantle, Western Australia, it had the effect on the city of boosting development of both new marine related industries and non-marine related, high-technology businesses such as computer systems, advanced metals technology, and synthetic fibers. These products were prominently publicized in the Australian media during the prolonged period of years during which the media were preoccupied with the America's Cup. The frequent references to high-technology products and Freemantle created a nexus in many people's minds and stimulated such development in the area.[13]

The Indianapolis Motor Speedway (IMS), Indianapolis Raceway Park, Indianapolis Speedrome and other venues stimulated the emergence of over 400 motor sport related businesses, employing almost 9,000 people, to support the multiple CART, Indy Racing League, National Hot Rod Association, karting, and midget and sprint car teams that are based in the city. A major hub of these ancillary businesses is a four-block area south of the Indianapolis Speedway known as "Gasoline Alley," where an impressive array of suppliers, fabricators, chassis builders, and engine builders are located. An analysis of the Indianapolis cluster concluded, "The concentration of racing firms in the state enables both individuals and companies to enjoy the benefits of a highly skilled and mobile work force that moves from company to company as demand changes" (p. 8).[14] Proximity was viewed as critical because immediate, face-to-face feedback from the team of companies striving to improve the reliability or speed of a vehicle is required. Interestingly, the IMS was built with private investment; all subsequent improvements to the facility are privately funded, and it pays its full share of property taxes.

Perhaps the most renowned example of sport clustering is the array of ancillary business that have been spawned by the presence of NASCAR headquarters and teams in the Charlotte area of North Carolina. This is described in Exhibit 7.2.[12]

Exhibit 7.2

The Industrial Cluster Stimulated by NASCAR[12]

The cradle of stock car racing was the southeastern region of the United States. Most of the NASCAR races were staged within this region, Charlotte became the primary NASCAR team location because it was centrally located and, thus, minimized team transportation costs. During the past two decades, NASCAR expanded out of its traditional geographic regions and grew to be the second most popular sport watched on television in the United States. NASCAR's and the motor sports' industry's growth in North Carolina has been driven by six major factors: (a) the creation and growth of the NASCAR Craftsman Truck Series; (b) the rapid growth and increasing popularity of the NASCAR Busch Series; (c) the NASCAR television package which increased national exposure and built the NASCAR fan base; (d) the open-wheel sanctioning split, which shifted many fans to NASCAR sanctioned racing; (e) the construction and promotion of new tracks across the country hosting NASCAR sanctioned races; and (f) the rapid increase in the cost of major sponsorships for companies wishing to identify with NASCAR teams.

As the sport expanded, many southeastern races disappeared and were replaced by venues throughout the United States. As a result, Charlotte, North Carolina, no longer represents the geographic least-cost transportation center for the series. However, the Charlotte area remains home to most NASCAR teams because the region had developed a specialized labor pool, a well-developed supplier chain, an infrastructure in the form of race tracks and testing facilities, and a culture of stock car racing. These factors still provide the teams that are located in Charlotte with a significant cost advantage in obtaining highly qualified specialized labor, a specialized parts industry, access to testing facilities and knowledge spillovers. These combined factors continue to make the Charlotte region a least-cost location while enhancing chances of winning. At least 50 NASCAR teams have their home base there: "If you need it for racing, somebody makes it somewhere in town. The infrastructure is here to support racing. Parts suppliers, machine shops, coating companies. If you go any place else in the country and try to do this, you're going to be FedExing stuff back and forth every day" (p. 25).[15]

The North Carolina cluster includes race car construction, engine manufacturers and specialist supporters, but it is also comprised of racing-specific businesses that are not engaged in producing race cars or parts such as specialized sport marketing, souvenir manufacturing and retailing, television production, and other motorsports related activities. The cluster's aggregate annual direct expenditure in the North Carolina economy is $3.8 billion which represents over 1% of all direct spending in the state. The employment impact consisted of 14,300 direct jobs, with the primary employers being NASCAR teams (4,445 jobs), suppliers (2,050 jobs) and marketing sector (1,768 jobs).

Indicative of NASCAR's widespread indirect impact on the state is its role in the development of Concord Regional Airport. NASCAR, and the nearby Lowe's Motor Speedway, are primarily responsible for its development, since 40 planes belonging to race teams are based at the airport. Those planes purchase $4.5 million worth of airplane fuel a year at Concord airport. When the Speedway hosts its three annual Winston Cup events, the airport traffic grows much heavier with sponsors and fans bringing in their planes. The NASCAR connection has created a community asset, because without it the airport would not be a viable enterprise.[16]

REJUVENATION THROUGH MEGA EVENTS

Almost all mega event property owners include urban rejuvenation as a prime requirement in the bid specification documents that prospective host cities submit. For example, the London Games bid stated, "By staging the Games in this part of the city, the most enduring legacy of the Olympics will be the regeneration of an entire community for the direct benefit of everyone who lives there" (p. 318).[16a] They are given a major weighting among the host selection criteria because properties recognize that the costs of staging mega events are so high, they cannot be justified by prospective bidders to their constituencies as investments rather than subsidies without urban rejuvenation being a prominent outcome. The rejuvenation legacy is likely to comprise three elements: 1) rehabilitation of derelict land, decaying industrial sites, or contaminated areas; 2) a set of new and/or upgraded sports facilities; and 3) infrastructure improvements.

The *site locations* of some facilities at most Olympic Games since Munich in 1972 illustrate the first element.

- Munich 1972: Development of a 600-acre derelict site for the Olympic Park.
- Seoul 1988: Decontamination of the Hun River.
- Barcelona 1992: Development of a decaying industrial area, including 5 kilometers of derelict port that cut off the sea from the rest of the city.
- Atlanta 1996: Development of a city center contaminated site.
- Sydney 2000: Creation of the Olympic Park at Homebush, the city's largest brownfields site where the 600 acres was previously occupied by an armaments depot, a brickworks and an abattoir.
- Athens 2004: Development of the city's old airport site.
- London 2012: Regeneration of the industrially decayed and economically depressed Lea Valley East London district of Stratford. After 150 years of industrial abuse and dereliction, the river was polluted with raw sewage, and the soil was contaminated with arsenic, lead and a host of other pollutants.

Do the economic and social benefits of sports facilities justify taxpayer investment?
Courtesy of BigStockPhoto

The reality confronting most major cities is that the large acreages required for new sport facilities and ancillary parking are only available at affordable prices at these deteriorated sites. Their redevelopment is expensive, but the civic and ecological benefits from upgrading them may be perceived to be sufficient to justify the expense to constituents.

If *facilities* built for a mega event are planned with their future utilization as the primary consideration, then they can be an ongoing source of both positive economic impact and social capital. Exhibit 7.3 describes the comprehensive array of viable sport facilities that the English city of Manchester enjoyed as its legacy from hosting the Commonwealth Games. The key factors in its success were integration of the sport facilities with other amenities as part of the city's long term comprehensive plan, and a clear *a priori* vision of their post-Games role.

Exhibit 7.3

The Sport City Legacy of the Commonwealth Games in Manchester, England

Manchester's cotton mills were at the heart of the industrial revolution in the nineteenth and early twentieth centuries. These were supplemented by heavy engineering works and transport, chemical and other manufacturing plants. In the post WWII years, its industrial base eroded so in the last two decades of the twentieth century the city sought to reposition itself as a business and tourism destination. Manchester's successful bid to host the Commonwealth Games was part of its 25 year plan to rejuvenate the city. The Commonwealth Games ranks as the third largest sporting event in the world after the Olympics and World Cup, involving 72 countries in 17 sports.

The core strategy was development of an impressive array of publicly funded attractions and much was accomplished in the 1980s and 1990s. Its airport was expanded and emerged as a major European hub. It served the North and Midlands of England via a well-developed freeway system and excellent rail links. A 20,000 seat arena hosted an impressive number of concerts and an international convention center was built. The city art gallery received a $50 million renovation; new contemporary art galleries emerged; two live theaters were renovated; the Imperial War Museum of the North was opened; and the futuristic architecture of Urbis, the museum of the city, became a noted landmark.

In 1996, an IRA terrorist bomb devastated the city center. There were no fatalities, but over 200 people were injured and insurance pay outs for property damage exceeded $1.5 billion. However, from this adversity came a rebuilding investment of over $2 billion in the next four years creating a host of new stunning cultural and commercial structures that complemented the city-center's majestic Victorian architecture.

The city's intent was to use the Games to create its "Sportcity" which would complement the vibrant cultural amenities. Already it was home to the world's most famous soccer club, Manchester United, and its lesser known Premier League rival, Manchester City. (By 2012 Manchester City had been transformed from an "ordinary" Premier League team to join United as one of the world's top five soccer clubs). In addition, the city had constructed a world-class velodrome and established it as the National Cycling Center, which was the catalyst to establishing the United Kingdom as a major force in international cycling.

Most of the Sportcity facilities were located in East Manchester at Eastlands on a brownfield site which was designated an urban regeneration area, characterized by large numbers of derelict and abandoned houses. It comprised the following elements:

(continued overleaf)

Exhibit 7.3 *(Continued)*

The Sport City Legacy of the Commonwealth Games in Manchester, England

- The City of Manchester Stadium—Originally a 38,000 seater athletics stadium, it was converted into a soccer ground after the Commonwealth Games. It became the home of Manchester City FC and had an increased capacity of 48,000.

- The Regional Athletics Arena—A £3.5m 6,000 seater stadium constructed around the Commonwealth Games warm up track and training area. The arena was used for domestic and international track and field meetings. The stadium was also the base for the famous Sale Harriers track and field club.

- The National Squash Center—It had seven squash courts and world class facilities. The center was the new home of England Squash, the sport's national governing body.

- The National Tennis Center—consisting of six indoor courts, six outdoor courts and a junior court.

- A £32 million Aquatics Center—the only swimming complex in the UK to have two 50 meter pools. It is also the regional high performance center for elite swimmers.

- Bolton Arena, comprising indoor and outdoor tennis courts, a 400-meter athletics track, plus football, basketball and netball pitches. The arena is the Lawn Tennis Association's North West Regional Tennis Center. Its Sport Science and Performance Unit has state of the art sports science and sports performance testing facilities.

- The redeveloped Belle Vue Leisure Center, east of the city center. This facility boasts 2 water-based synthetic hockey pitches, 8 badminton courts and a cricket academy. It was designated as the Regional Performance Center for both hockey and badminton. Both the girls and boys Under 16's and Under 18's England hockey squads use Belle Vue as their training base.

- A £1 million lawn bowling complex was built at Heaton Park in North Manchester. The park has four top grade flat greens. The venue was conferred national status by the English Bowls Association and is home of the Manchester Commonwealth Bowling Club.

These facilities were designed for their post-Games purposes and have resulted in both substantial economic impact from the hosting of numerous national and international sports events, and social capital for the city's residents.

If *a priori* consideration for post-event use does not underpin the whole planning process, then the result is likely to be a herd of white elephants, which was the legacy of the Athens Olympic Games. This occurs because mega events are exceptional in terms of both their infrequency and the specialist and immediate demands they make on a host economy. They are alien to the host economy and are unlikely to be a natural fit with it, so changes have to be made to accommodate the events. There are limited uses for shooting ranges, velodromes, rowing centers, equestrian courses, and the array of other esoteric sport facilities that host communities commit to providing. Diverting substantial resources into constructing and operating a plethora of non-sustainable sport facilities, rather than more productive uses, means that mega events have the potential to disrupt rather than enhance the host community's long term economic growth.

In the case of mega events especially, the problem of over-building may be exacerbated by the substantial regional, state and federal funds often made available for developing facilities. These external entities may want the biggest, best, most ostentatious facilities in order to garner maximum prestige and political premium from the event, while the onerous post-event costs of operating them is usually borne exclusively by the cities.

The hubris that too often accompanies mega events was well illustrated by some of the new stadium construction in Japan when that country co-hosted the soccer World Cup:

- In Saitama, an hour north of Tokyo, the prefectural governor expanded the original seating capacity of its stadium by 50%, to 63,700, gambling that his suburb would win the championship game. Although $640 million was spent, the final game went to Yokohama.
- In Miyagi, a 49,000-seat stadium was built in a remote location accessible from the prefectural capital by taking two trains and a 10-minute bus ride. That showcase cost $585 million.
- In Oita, promoters boasted that the 43,000-seat Big Eye cost $464 million. Local tax critics noted that the J-League soccer games have been averaging only 3,000 fans.[16b]

Integration into an holistic plan involves considering not only the post-event capacity of facilities *per se*, but also its effect on existing facilities. If viability of the new facilities is accomplished by cannibalizing the use of pre-existing facilities, then there are no net economic, structural, or social capital gains. This was the conundrum confronting the two major stadiums built for the Sydney Games. It appeared their viability could only be achieved by pre-empting events at pre-existing stadiums in the metropolitan area, which were all newly built or extensively renovated in the previous decade and a half.[17]

In many cases, hosting a mega event enables cities to "fast track" *infrastructure improvements* that have long been talked about but not enacted. It focuses the attention of elected officials and creates a sense of urgency and priority. The commitment and media headlines inherent in mega events are dynamic forces for driving through projects that might otherwise languish in bureaucratic limbo. Thus, the London Chamber of Commerce opined, "The most enduring reason for bringing the Games to London is that it will create an impetus to raise the capital's transport infrastructure" (p. 21).[18] Invariably, the expedited timeframe is possible because additional resources originating outside the city from regional, state or federal governments are mobilized that otherwise would not be forthcoming.

There are real time constraints that are not postponable. If the infrastructure upgrades needed to accommodate the event are not completed, then the consequences are worldwide criticism; civic ridicule, disgrace, and humiliation; and a severely damaged image. Thus, things are accomplished that otherwise would not be completed or would be delayed. The external pressures solve internal urban conflicts. Inflexible positions among planners, politicians, business elites, and residents are resolved either by negotiated compromises, or by special legislation or regulation. The downside of the expedited timeframe is the potential for irreversible planning mistakes stemming from too little input or suppressing opposition to improvements, especially from less influential stakeholders.

The potential of mega events for upgrading infrastructure was well-illustrated by the Olympic Games in Barcelona, which are widely heralded as the Regeneration Games. The city used the Games to implement an imaginative, wide-ranging urban renewal plan that transformed its decaying industrial fabric.[19] The city was opened to the sea, and a run-down coastal area was rejuvenated to include a new marina, leisure facilities and attractive sandy beaches. There was major investment in new transportation systems, including construction of a coastal ring road, modernization of the port and airport, and restructuring of the city's rail network. Other major improvements included renovating the sewer system, building residential facilities that served as the Olympic Village, and upgrading the urban technology and communications systems, which was necessary in order to accommodate the world's media. Officials in Barcelona estimated that hosting the Games resulted in 50 years worth of infrastructure being collapsed into an eight-year period at a cost of $8 billion.[20]

Similarly, the substantial investment in telecommunications infrastructure for the Sydney Olympic Games was an enduring legacy for that city:

> The successful handling of the telecommunications aspects of the Sydney Games, not only provided a major boost to the international credibility of the technology providers (coordinated by the national telco—Telstra), but also provided Sydney with a long-term inheritance in the form of significant extensions and enhancements to the City's fiber optic network. Telstra's Millennium network included a total of 4,800 km of fiber optic cable, linking 105 locations but focused on a ring between the Sydney CBD and Olympic Park in the city's inner western suburbs. (p. 107)[21]

From an economist's perspective, the defining question in ascertaining the success of a mega event in stimulating rejuvenation is: Could these regeneration benefits have been secured at a cost less than (for example) the estimated $20 billion cost of hosting the Barcelona Olympics?

> If regeneration is needed, it should be worth doing irrespective of any investment in major sporting events and facilities. The relevant analysis should compare the costs and benefits of achieving regeneration in other ways, to establish which is likely to be the more cost-effective. (p. 68)[22]

INTEGRATION: A KEY TO EFFECTIVE REJUVENATION

The aspiration is that sport facilities will serve as "giant embers slowly kindling a fire" (p. 6).[23] However, a major sport facility can only be an effective catalyst for redevelopment if it is part of an integrated, coherent master plan rather than an *ad-hoc* initiative that, it is vaguely hoped, may stimulate private retail commercial or residential development nearby. It is widely recognized, for example, that a key factor in the success of the Barcelona Games was their integration into the city's strategic long-term plan. Without integration, public expenditures are more likely to be subsidies to wealthy owners of franchises or mega events than justifiable investments. It has been observed, "Too many critics did more 'hoping' than they did planning a strategy or establishing partnerships with private capital to achieve success" (p. 3).[8]

> It matters if the city has developed a plan for integrating the stadium in its overall strategy for the downtown area or for the region. Too often there is virtually no planning but a good deal of hoping that the stadium or arena will "jump-start" the economy or region. By itself, a stadium or arena cannot jump-start even the small economy of a part of downtown. But as part of an overall plan or strategy, a stadium could be helpful and useful. Does such a plan exist, and what is expected or anticipated from the development of the stadium or arena? (p. 205)[24]

The differing extents to which integration of sport facilities has been carefully planned and executed as part of a holistic approach explains most of the variability in their effectiveness in accomplishing their catalyst role.

In the past, focus was on building a sport facility. Now the vision is typically broader, and the broader vision is likely to provide more justification for public subsidy if it can successfully facilitate additional urban redevelopment. This broader vision has design implications. A facility cannot be a catalyst for development if it is an island built in the middle of a sea of surrounding concrete parking lots.[25] This isolates fans from other development, rather than integrating them. If the stadium is intended to stimulate other development, then fans should be channeled to it through carefully planned corridors to maximize secondary economic activity.[26] Further, the design should build upon and assimilate the character of surrounding structures; otherwise, the facility becomes an ugly intrusion on the urban fabric instead of an indigenous component of it. Thus, at Camden Yards in Baltimore, Indianapolis, San Diego, and Columbus, Ohio, all viewed as successes, the sports facilities were carefully crafted in terms of their scale (height) and construction materials to ensure they fitted into the neighborhoods.[8]

There is not necessarily a natural symbiotic relationship between a sport facility and other kinds of economic activity. Their use is episodic and is interspersed with prolonged "dead time" when the area around them may be deserted. Thus, facilities have to complement daily life in the district. This is why Wrigley Field on the north side of Chicago has been extolled as a prime example of how communities can interact effectively and a model that new major facilities should seek to emulate.

> There's eighty-one baseball games a year there, and it certainly is a natural draw; people all over the world come to go to Wrigley Field, to that neighborhood, but the neighborhood functions quite well the other 280 days of the year when there is not a game there. Within a five-minute walk from the pitcher's mound at Wrigley Field, you've got businesses, restaurants, schools, churches, convents, and public transportation. There's a daily life to the neighborhood that exists independently of the ballpark. The ballpark enhances, and vice versa, but the notion of the city is the notion of a place where people live and work and hang out all the time. (p. 147)[27]

Many new stadiums do not foster surrounding development because they are not physically interwoven with other components of the urban fabric. Rather, these stadiums are designed for quick entry and exit of suburban fans with automobiles. Even though they are technically inner-city parks, often their urban integration is limited to supplying parking facilities close to the downtown business district.

The Conflicting Goals of Public and Private Interests

It has been pointed out that an integrated plan allows "the public and private investors to clearly understand a city's redevelopment goals and what the completed projects will produce [which] helps to create confidence that the dream can become a reality . . . [It] enables private investors to determine how a related project that they would create would complement and benefit from the overall strategy and interconnections among all the planned assets" (p. 254).[8] However, while a primary public rationale for investing in major league facilities is for them to stimulate rejuvenation of an area, team owners are not in the urban redevelopment business.

Traditionally, it was anticipated that complementary development to service the facilities would emerge in the form of restaurants, bars and souvenir stores. Coors Field, the home of the Colorado Rockies, is sometimes cited as an example of this type of catalyst role. It is credited with aiding the revitalization of Denver's Lower Downtown or "LoDo" district. Restaurants, sports bars, and sports memorabilia stores opened with Coors Field to serve the fans who make over three million visits to attend Rockies games. However, the new generation of fully loaded facilities means there is now little opportunity for businesses to flourish in a parasitic relationship with major facilities. The owners' intent is to capture all discretionary spending by their visitors on food, beverages, merchandise and the like within the facility and to minimize the amount spent at businesses in the proximate area outside the facility's gates. It has been suggested that these new facilities are analogous to European walled cities seeking to enclose all commercial activities and revenue flows within their confines,[28] and has been termed the "Disneyfication" of sport:

> When Walt Disney saw that his Disneyland theme park in Anaheim, California, stimulated numerous hotels, restaurants and other recreational values in the proximate area, he determined that in future developments he would capture those revenue streams. This he accomplished when Disney World was developed in Florida. This incorporated all those elements and captured the complete range of spending associated with the park visit experience. New "fully loaded" sport facilities embraced this strategy.[5]

Thus, the pioneering Orioles Park at Camden Yards stadium features an outdoor walkway lined with souvenir shops and fast food outlets, but it is within the stadium. As one critic observed, "These guys are supposed to be capitalists and for the free market, but that's the last thing they want! They want to have a monopoly" (p. 144).[27] Given this reality, it is possible that in some contexts a major sport facility may deter redevelopment of an area, since periodically full parking lots and game-day traffic gridlock might have an adverse effect on people's willingness to visit the area. This point is illustrated in Exhibit 7.4, where the isolation of Millennium Stadium in Cardiff[29] contrasts markedly with the integration of the SportCity facilities in Manchester described in Exhibit 7.3.

Public investment in sport facilities can create a platform for private sector activity, but success is dependent on leadership and investment from the private sector. Integration into a development plan is a necessary condition, but it is not sufficient. It must be accompanied by large-scale private sector investment. The experiences of the large number of cities that have contributed to fully loaded facilities in the past two decades confirm that the likelihood of their successfully anchoring downtown rejuvenation is relatively low. It is only the exceptional city that has accomplished this. A business and civic

---

Exhibit 7.4

The Impact of Millennium Stadium on the Surrounding Community[29]

The primary legacy from Wales hosting the Rugby World Cup was the construction of Millennium Stadium in the city center of Cardiff, the capital city of Wales. It was built as a replacement for Cardiff Arms Park which was steeped in Welsh rugby tradition, but was a very basic spectator facility with primitive toilets, and no restaurants, bars, corporate suites or boxes. An economic impact study undertaken shortly before it was replaced, showed that the 14 events it hosted in that year, four rugby games, three soccer matches, two boxing contests, three concerts, and two religious gatherings contributed approximately $55 million to the Cardiff economy.

The Millennium Stadium was built essentially in isolation from surrounding developments and was not directly connected to other regeneration initiatives in the city. It has 125 hospitality boxes, two full service restaurants, five banqueting areas, 22 public bars, 16 food and beverage outlets, and 18 retail outlets. After it opened, the Cardiff County Council commissioned a review to ascertain its economic impact on the city. It drew the following conclusions:

1. Far from supporting the regeneration of the neighboring city center, the construction of a stadium in such a location might actually have a negative economic impact if it permanently depressed retail expenditure.

2. Especially in this regard, the timing and frequency of matches was important; games staged for example on consecutive Saturday afternoons in the run-up to Christmas had the potential to cripple the city's retail trade.

3. There was a further need for a transport plan that could empty the stadium and clear people away from it without bringing the city center to a standstill. The gridlock which exiting spectators caused had an adverse effect on people's willingness to visit the city center on match-days and therefore also on the retail trade within the vicinity.

4. There was a further need for a long-term strategy to integrate the stadium within the city's day-to-day activities, rather than focusing upon its position as an extraordinary part of the city.

In short, the Welsh Rugby Union's drive to bring corporate customers within the stadium had been achieved at the cost of the conference and banqueting trade within the vicinity. Furthermore, the sheer density of traffic and crowds in the city center on match-days deterred shoppers from also traveling in and spending their money. The benefits that accrued during the construction phase and the World Cup itself were one-off, and non-repeatable.

leader in Minneapolis who was instrumental in bringing professional sports to that city observed the following:

> The argument about economic development has been attempted here, but it's never proven to be true. I don't think it is a strong argument. Do businesses open up because they want to be near a stadium? I don't think so. People go to a stadium for one single purpose, to go to a game. They are not going shopping. There has been no economic development around the Metrodome. (p. 240)[3]

He was acknowledging that when the Metrodome was constructed promises of economic development and selling lucrative development rights to the parcels of land around the dome were made, but there was no economic spin-off in the surrounding area.

The ideal situation is to secure this commitment during initial negotiations with private partners seeking public funds. The potential of this strategy was demonstrated in San Diego's negotiations with the Padres regarding the city's investment in PETCO Park:

> The team were appointed master developer of a dilapidated twenty-six block area around the stadium. They guaranteed to generate a sufficient level of private investment from this area to yield the property taxes needed to pay the annual payment on the bonds the city issued to pay its share of the facility. The formal agreement stated, "The Padres and its Master Developer will have an additional 24-month period of time after Opening Day to have on the tax-rolls projects with an assessed valuation of at least $311 million." They also promised to develop 850 hotel rooms to generate hotel taxes that the city would use to pay off some of the bonds.
>
> When the ball park opened, 744 hotel rooms had been completed and the Padres claimed that higher than planned room rates would compensate for the tax lost on the 106 uncompleted rooms. Six months after the park opened, there had been $1.2 billion in private investment in the twenty-six block area; and the Padres arranged at least $600 million of it. Thus, development exceeded the guarantee by 400%. The team owner personally benefited from the associated development, as his development agency purchased much of the land in the area that was built on. Nevertheless, there is universal recognition that redevelopment of the downtown area anchored by the ballpark has been an impressive success, generating a positive cash flow for the city.[30]

SUMMARY

As it has become apparent that public investment in major league and mega event sport facilities rarely can be justified in terms of direct net economic impact, attention has turned to the structural and social capital benefits these facilities may provide to communities. Structural capital refers to the built sport facilities, complementary development associated with them, and physical infrastructure improvements that they stimulate.

Major sport facilities have become ubiquitous anchors in the downtown redevelopment efforts of many US cities, based on a belief that they will stimulate economic development around them. This will not occur unless there is a threshold level of cumulative attraction beyond an isolated sport facility. The facility will not generate sufficient traffic for it to be viable for businesses to locate around it; there must be a critical mass of complementary attractions.

Clustering is a form of cumulative attraction that occurs at a regional rather than a local level. Businesses in all industries tend to cluster in a particular region, because of the symbiotic and complementary relationships among them. In the sport industry, this is especially prominent in motor racing, horse racing, and sailing.

The rejuvenation legacy of mega events is likely to comprise three elements—first, rehabilitation of derelict land, decaying industrial sites or contaminated areas. In most large cities, the large acreages required for new sport facilities and ancillary parking are most readily available at these deteriorated sites. A second legacy is the facilities, and if they are designed with future utilization as the primary consideration, then they can be an ongoing source of both positive economic impact and social capital. Third, mega events invariably expedite infrastructure improvements, since the time constraints, media focus, and large number of visitors create a sense of urgency and priority.

The differing extent to which sport facilities are integrated as part of a carefully planned and executed holistic approach explains most of the variability in their effectiveness as catalysts for stimulating surrounding economic development. The integration challenge is exacerbated by the conflicting goals of public and private interests. While the public sector seeks rejuvenation, major sport team owners are not in the urban development business. Rather than encouraging other businesses to locate close by, the owners' goal with the new generation of fully loaded facilities is to capture all discretionary spending by visitors to their facilities and to minimize spending outside the facility.

References

1. Misener, L., & Mason, D. S. (2006). Creating community networks: Can sporting events offer meaningful sources of social capital? *Managing Leisure, 11*(1), 39–56.

2. Rosentraub, M. S., & Ijla, A. (2008). Sport and social capital. In M. Nicholson & R. Hoyle (Eds.), *Sport and social capital* (pp. 339–358). Oxford, UK: Elsevier.

3. Eckstein, R., & Delaney, K. (2002). New sports stadiums, community self-esteem, and community collective conscience. *Journal of Sport & Social Issues, 26*(3), 235–247.

4. White, A. (2001). Sporting a new image? Sport-based regeneration strategies as a means of enhancing the image of the city tourist destination. In C. Gratton & I. P. Henry (Eds.), *Sport in the city* (pp. 127–148). New York, NY: Routledge.

5. Rosentraub, M. S. (2008). Sports facilities and urban redevelopment: Private and public benefits and a prescription for a healthier future. In

B. R. Humphries & D. R. Howard (Eds.), *The business of sports vol. 3* (pp. 57–80). Westbrook, CT: Praeger.

6. Hannigan, J. (1998). *Fantasy city: Pleasure and profit in the post modern metropolis.* London, UK: Routledge.

7. Hamilton, B. W., & Kahn, P. (1997). Baltimore's Camden Yards ballparks. In R. G. Noll & A. Zimbalist (Eds.), *Sports, jobs and taxes.* (pp. 245–281). Washington, DC: Brookings Institution.

8. Rosentraub, M. S. (2010). *Major league winners: Using sports and cultural centers as tools for economic development.* Boca Raton, FL: CRC Press.

9. Schimmel, K. S. (1995). Growth politics, urban development, and sports stadium construction in the United States: A case study. In J. Bale & O. Moen (Eds.), *The stadium and the city* (pp. 111–155). Keele, Staffordshire, UK: Keele University Press.

10. Seewer, J. (2006, July 17). Baseball fans flocking to minor-league parks. *The Eagle*, B1.

11. Henry, N., & Pinch, S. (2000). Spatializing knowledge; placing the knowledge community of Motor Sport Valley. *Geoforum, 31*(2), 191–208.

12. Connaughton, J. E., & Madsen, R. A. (2007). The economic impacts of the North Carolina motorsports industry. *Economic Development Quarterly, 21*(2), 185–197.

13. Newman, P. W. G. (1989). The impact of the America's Cup on Freemantle—an insider's view. In G. S. Syme, B. J. Shaw, D. M. Fenton, & W. S. Mueller (Eds.), *The planning and evaluation of hallmark events* (pp. 46–58). Aldershot, UK: Avebury.

14. Klacik, D., & Cook, T. (2004). *Motorsports industry in the Indianapolis region.* Indianapolis, IL: Indiana University—Purdue University Indianapolis, School of Public and Environmental Affairs.

15. Spanberg, E. (2001, May 21). Airport took off when stock cars did. *SportsBusiness Journal.* Retrieved from http://www.sportsbusinessdaily.com/Journal/Issues/2001/05/20010521/Special-Report/Airport-Took-Off-When-Stock-Cars-Did.aspx?hl=Special%20Report&sc=0

16. Spanberg, E. (2001, May 21–27). Entire region hears NASCAR's roar. *SportsBusiness Journal,* pp. 25, 30.

16a. Davies, L. E. (2012, July). Beyond the Games: Regeneration legacies and London 2012. *Leisure Studies, 31*(3), 309–337.

16b. Brooke, J. (2002, June 2). Soccer: Legacy of World Cup may be the stadiums left behind. *New York Times.*

17. Searle, G. (2002). Uncertain legacy: Sydney's Olympic stadiums. *European Planning Studies, 10*, 845–873.

18. Woods, R. (2005, July 3). Get set, spend! *The Sunday Times*, p. 21.

19. Tookey, K., & Veal, A. J. (2000). *The Olympic Games: A social science perspective.* New York, NY: CABI Publishing.

20. Daly, E., & Fickling, D. (2002, December 6). Barcelona and Sydney: The hosts who got the most. *The Observer.* Retrieved from http://www.guardian.co.uk/politics/2002/dec/08/athletics.olympics2012

21. Cushman, R. (2006). *The bitter-sweet awakening: The legacy of the Sydney 2000 Olympic Games.* Sydney, Australia: Walla Walla Press.

22. Department for Culture, Media and Sport. (2002). *Game plan: A strategy for delivering government's sport and physical activity objectives.* London, UK: DCMS Strategy Unit.

23. Bullard, S. (1998, March 23). Gateway draws businesses to once-dismal district. *Crain's Cleveland Business*, 6–8.

24. Rosentraub, M. S. (1997). *Major league losers: The real cost of sports and who's paying for it.* New York, NY: Basic Books.

25. Baade, R. A., & Dye, R. F. (1988, July). An analysis of economic rationale for public subsidation of sport stadiums. *The Annals of Regional Science, 22*(2), 37–47.

26. Schaffer, W. A., & Davidson, L. S. (1984). *Economic impact of the Falcons on Atlanta.* Atlanta, GA: Georgia Institute of Technology.

27. DeMause, N., & Cagan, J. (2008). *Field of schemes: How the great stadium swindle turns public money into private profit.* Lincoln, NW: University of Nebraska Press.

28. Siegfried, J., & Zimbalist, A. (2000). The economics of sports facilities and their communities. *Journal of Economic Perspectives, 14*(3), 95–114.

29. Tunnicliffe, N. (2001, September). Regeneration: Stadium projects. *Leisure Manager*, 19–20.

30. Hitchcock, M. (n.d.). Welcome to PETCO Park: Home of your Enron-by-the-sea Padres. *Berkeley Law.* Retrieved from www.law.berkeley.edu

8

The Alternate Justifications for Public Subsidy: Social Capital

SOCIAL CAPITAL

Social capital refers to relationships, norms and connections that bind people together and contribute to accomplishing collective goals. In the context of this chapter, the term relates to enhancing a community's brand equity—that is, awareness of its identity and its desired image; attracting businesses and tourists to give residents improved employment opportunities and income levels; building community pride and self-esteem; and strengthening community bonding and social cohesion.

Brand equity and attracting businesses and tourists may be categorized as *external* or indirect dimensions of social capital in that the sport facilities are intended to positively influence the impressions and actions of those who reside outside the community. In contrast, community pride and social cohesion are *internal* dimensions, since these anticipated emotional and psychological benefit outcomes directly impact a community's residents.[1]

ENHANCING A COMMUNITY'S BRAND EQUITY

Cities seek to highlight those of their attributes that cause them to stand out from the crowd and differentiate them from other cities. Thus, a city's *brand equity* comprises the strong and distinctive favorable attributes that people associate with the city in their memories. If a city has strong brand equity, then that should translate into the tangible social capital benefits of new jobs and more development from attracting more businesses and more tourists than other cities. Brand equity is dependent on people's knowledge of a city and is defined by two elements: awareness and image.[2] Each of these is discussed in the following sections.

Awareness

Awareness has two roles. First, there is a suggestion that repeated exposure to a city's name may lead to an increased affinity for it.[3] Second and more importantly, awareness is a prerequisite to image, since if there is no awareness of a city then there can be no image of it. This prerequisite role of awareness was a primary justification for the city of Adelaide's investment in its Grand Prix event:

> This is the first step in marketing Adelaide to international markets. Any promotion to create market knowledge of what Adelaide has to offer as an international visitor destination can only be effective after potential visitors know it exists and where it is. Achieving this prerequisite awareness is a considerable hurdle to be overcome. The cost and effort in doing so for a new long haul destination is quite high. Therefore the Grand Prix influence (of which the first year is only part of a cumulative process) is quite valuable in that it would be difficult to achieve by alternative means. (p. 54)[4]

A professional sport franchise guarantees a substantial amount of media coverage for the city in which it is located. It keeps the community's name in front of a national audience. The importance of this exposure was recognized by an official in Washington, D.C. when the Redskins were considering a move from that city to Arlington, Virginia: "Officials in Washington could only fear that getting Skinned meant the town would be rubbed off the map, 'Brooklyn has never been the same since the Dodgers left,' said the D.C. council chairman whose own city lost two baseball clubs in the 1950s. 'You don't even think about Brooklyn'" (p. 51).[5]

A baseball owner noted to a reporter, "Tonight, on every single television and radio station in the USA, Seattle will be mentioned because of the Mariners game, and tomorrow night and the next night and on and on. You'd pay millions in public-relations fees for that" (p. 103).[6] Further, sports teams usually generate favorable publicity plugging troubled cities into "the good news network . . . We're OK say the sports pages" (p. 103).[7] The city will likely hold an all-star game once every twenty years or so, and enjoy all of the national attention associated with it. Exposure will be further enhanced when it makes the play-offs and especially when it appears in a championship final. In the case of these latter events, the exposure is accompanied by the luster of success.[7]

Efforts often are made to attribute an economic value to this exposure. For example, the organizers of the Sydney Olympics claimed that at one point or another, 3.7 billion people saw or listened to the Games and that an equivalent advertising campaign for Australia would cost $2.4 billion.[8] Certainly, this linkage between community exposure and team visibility is widely articulated. Proponents of public subsidies for sport facilities imply that the relationship will aid recruitment of relocating businesses and tourists and, thus, lead to enhancement of a city's economic base. Hence, when Jacksonville was awarded an NFL franchise, a city leader commented, "T.V. sets in division rivals Cleveland, Pittsburgh and Cincinnati will be showing Jacksonville's sunshine in the dead of winter, luring future tourists" (p. B8).[9]

The desire to generate awareness for the community sometimes creates friction between public entities. Most commonly, cities may resent losing the awareness identity of "their" team to a regional or state entity. Thus, for example, after Denver invested substantial effort to acquire a MLB franchise, the team was named the Colorado Rockies instead of the Denver whatevers. The loss of city identity to state or regional names has occurred in the case of approximately 20 major league teams. On the other hand, there are cities that receive visibility from teams who play elsewhere and are subsidized by other communities. For example, the New York Giants play in East Rutherford, New Jersey, while Detroit benefits from being identified with the Pistons even though the team plays in Auburn Hills, and Dallas still "owns" the Cowboys even though they play in the city of Arlington.

Image

Awareness is an important element in building a city's brand equity, but it is not sufficient to impact external audiences because the image of a city is the defining element. Image is the mental reconstruction of a place composed of beliefs, ideas and impressions residing in an individual's memory. It is an ordered whole built from scraps of information, much of which is inferred rather than directly experienced.

The pervasive popularity of sport in the media has persuaded many cities that sport may be a useful vehicle through which to enhance their image. Thus, some believe that major sports events and teams are the new "image builders" for communities.[10] The central idea in positioning a city is to identify the attributes or "unique selling proposition" that give people a compelling reason for engaging in business or tourism there. In the construction years after World War II, this role was performed by tall building tower skylines, large span bridges, or manufacturing industries (for example, Motor City or Steel City). As the economy has switched to a service orientation, major sports events and teams capture the imagination and help establish a city's image in people's minds. Perhaps the earliest manifestation of this shift was the construction of the Houston Astrodome, which was the self-proclaimed "eighth wonder of the world," and was an important element in the city's effort to recast its image from "sleepy bayou town to space-age Sunbelt dynamo" (p. 104).[6] Thus, in the debate over the spending of public money on a new stadium for the NFL's Minnesota Vikings, a letter writer observed:

> Tell me how many Fortune 500 businesses want to have their headquarters in a state known for Siberian-style winters and collapsing bridges. Probably not many. But if we lose the Vikings, we lose a marketing and advertising tool that continuously keeps our state in the eyes of the world for more than just cold weather and crumbling infrastructure. In my experience, when you ask people from elsewhere to name things that they equate with our state, Vikings football is usually one of the first things they cite. (p. A12)[11]

Since television created global audiences for mega events, hosting these events has been used as a vehicle through which countries and cities seek to position or reposition themselves in the consciousness of the world's publics. Their intent is to recreate their personalities by using the event as a platform from which their image can be leveraged, and the "positive vibes" created during the event used to present a new image of themselves. This is most vividly illustrated by the Olympic Games:

- The Tokyo Games served as a stage to affirm Japan's claims to First World status and demonstrate its leadership in technologies. The later Seoul Games served the same goal for Korea.
- The Mexico Games were intended to project that nation onto the international stage as a modern country and pre-empt the prevailing image held by many of it being an apathetic, lazy and backward country.[12]
- The Munich Games were used to celebrate West Germany's economic and political rehabilitation in the quarter century following WWII.[13]
- The Moscow Games were intended to demonstrate the superiority of the socialist path to development, while the following Los Angeles Games featured the virtues of free enterprise and capitalism.
- The Barcelona Games sought to restore Catalan cultural, economic and political identity, which had been suppressed by the Franco regime, in the emerging transition to democracy.[14]
- London's position as a center for finance, business and creative services, culture and tourism, and as a home for both government and corporate headquarters has almost no parallel in the world. The goals of its Games were to emphasize that it is special and set it apart from all other European cities, and to demonstrate the competence of its government and business communities in managing huge, complicated undertakings.

International sport events have become brand equity opportunities for rising powers like China, Brazil, South Africa and India that are rapidly moving into the top echelon of the global economic order:

> China has cities of 10–15 million people but you can't even pronounce their names, so why would you go there? They need to brand themselves and that is where sports events can help. Internationally, if you asked people, I would say 80% can only name two major cities in China—Beijing and Shanghai. Not many can name the third city, so Shenzhen wanted to use the University Games as a platform, as a branding initiative to bring the world's youth to the city and give them an understanding of what it has to offer.

> The calendar of GAISF, the General Association of International Sports Federations, underlines the scale of the phenomenon, listing 23 major international events as being staged in Chinese cities other than Beijing and Shanghai during 2007 and 2008.

Kazakhstan wants to host the Olympic Winter Games; of course it should. Our perception of it would change immediately; at the moment we only know it from *Borat*.

> The same goes for Africa; there are some countries in Africa now doing quite well yet we still see them as poor countries. That could change and South Africa will take the lead in that. Central and South America could also be next. (p. 23)[15]

Exhibit 8.1

The Role of the Grand Prix in Changing the Image of Adelaide

Promotion of the Grand Prix by both the organizers and the sponsors focuses on the action and the glamour aspects that dominate the image of the event. The event becomes recognized as part of the Adelaide tourism product and hence strongly associated with the city's image. The Grand Prix has made an immediate impact on the state's tourism image. People now associate the Grand Prix with South Australia, and South Australia with the Grand Prix. Recent market research conducted in Melbourne supports this. Among Melbourne residents who said it was either extremely or highly likely that they would visit Adelaide during the next twelve months, 22% said the Grand Prix was a very important factor in their decision to visit South Australia. The perceived excitement and action of the Grand Prix,

aptly captured in the Grand Prix marketing slogan, "Adelaide Alive," contrasts markedly with Adelaide's longstanding image in interstate markets as being "quiet," "boring," "City of Churches," etc. The existing image has acted to inhibit consideration of Adelaide as a travel destination for many would-be visitors. The Grand Prix influence in changing that image thus creates a greater market receptiveness to promotion of Adelaide as a travel destination.

The resources required to achieve such an impact on Adelaide's image by alternative means would be substantial, and hence the value of this tourism benefit is considerable. However, this is only a potential tourism benefit, since if the opportunity thus created is not effectively exploited then no tourism benefit is gained.

In addition to using sport events to present a community's attributes to a wide audience, a host community also seeks to appropriate or "borrow" some of the attributes of the sport event and transfer them to itself. When that process is successful, an *image transfer* occurs. Those attributes are such things as technological or organizational excellence, excitement, emotional strength, "big-league" status, etc. In crude terms, the host is saying, "We want our community to have this set of image attributes," while the event property says, "We will convey those attributes to you for a price." An example of this process is given in Exhibit 8.1, which describes how a Grand Prix Formula 1 motor race was used to spearhead the "Adelaide Alive" image that was intended to reposition the Australian city's traditional, rather unexciting image.[4]

The Adelaide event provided a platform for leveraging an image change, but the description cautions that if it is an isolated, one-off event, rather than an integrated element in a long-term holistic strategic plan, then it will likely fail. It seems likely that image enhancements based on a sporting event will decay over time. If the catalyst for change impetus initiated by an event is to be fully capitalized upon, there needs to be a coherent plan in place to sustain the initial momentum. This was the key to the success of Indianapolis (Exhibit 7.1) and Manchester (Exhibit 7.3) in changing their images.

The Role of Major League Status in Image Creation

Being seen as a major league city is symbolically powerful. There is much public sympathy for the adage that no community really can be considered a major league city or "first-tier" city if it does not have a major league sports team. The team is positioned as being symptomatic of a city's character, and as defining external perceptions of the city. Proponents of public subsidy for facilities frequently manipulate community self esteem by framing the issues so that another urban area is socially constructed as being inferior:

> People in Cleveland warned that without new professional sports stadiums the city would be "just like Akron." Ballpark proponents in Minneapolis and Denver seemed worried that without new stadiums the cities would be just "a colder version of Omaha." Phoenix elites insisted that major-league baseball would prevent Phoenix from turning into "another Tucson." (p. 240)[1]

Consider the following comments made by an advocate imploring voters to support a referendum requesting $125 million for a new arena in Dallas:

> Do we want our community to be considered Major League or Minor League? Do we want to be a community of vision or a community that lacks vision? A great step toward becoming a visionary community would be the construction of a state-of-the-art arena and focusing on maintaining and enhancing our existing sports and entertainment infrastructure . . . Our greatest obstacle is our reputation as a "Can't Do Community" rather than a "Can Do Community" . . . In the past few years we have lost the World Special Olympic Games to Connecticut; major sport status and prestige for the Cotton Bowl; and bids for the Goodwill Games, U.S. Soccer Federation and Women's Sports Foundation headquarters. Our lack of vision and leadership have become the brunt of jokes and ridicule among many prominent sports leaders and organizations throughout the world. (p. J1)[16]

Proponents of the new sports stadiums in Cincinnati developed similar arguments: "There is a whole bunch of . . . second-tier cities creeping up on our heels. Unless we continue to provide a viable exciting community, we're going to wake up and wonder how Nashville, Charlotte, even Albuquerque outran us. Cleveland's already done it" (p. 229).[17] The Cincinnati Chamber of Commerce warned the city's residents that it was on the verge "of becoming another Memphis" (p. 229).[17] The campaign to build public support for a sales tax increase to fund new facilities adopted the tagline "Keep Cincinnati a major league city." A politician central to the initiative explained:

> We played off that, saying it means more than major-league sports but major-league schools, parks, arts, and entertainment. Do we really want to be like Louisville, Kentucky? Columbus is a great place, but it's struggling to get an NHL team there. We've got an NFL and major-league [baseball] team. Do we really want to risk that? Do we want to be a city on the move or a city that's spiraling down? (p. 240)[1]

Similarly, a journalist who covered the city's stadium debates for many years commented:

> For me, as someone who grew up in northern Kentucky, Cincinnati had always had a sort of superiority complex. The sales tax campaign played on those fears,

which were already there. The thought was what distinguishes us from these other towns is that we have two major-league teams in such a small market. We need to hang on to this so we don't become another one of those podunk towns that doesn't have football. (p. 240)[13]

Despite these claims, the legitimacy of the premise that a major league team equates to a major league city is challengeable. "Do people view Charlotte, Jacksonville and Nashville to be big-time locations and Los Angeles an also-ran place because the former have NFL teams, while the latter does not?" (p. 103).[18] Large cities receive constant media attention. Their size ensures that a disproportionate number of newsworthy events occur there, both positive and negative. Hence, their image is molded by a host of symbols, events, people and behaviors, so the incremental contribution of a sports event, facility or team to the image of those cities is likely to be relatively small. Their contribution to the image of smaller cities is likely to be proportionately more substantial:

> While the largest cities viewed sports teams as an important piece of their overall cultural package, in many less populous cities the teams have become inextricably linked with the city's image. Cities such as Oakland, St. Louis, Kansas City and Cincinnati—none of them among the top 25 cities in population—all have proved to be great sports towns; in many cases, their sports franchises constitute validation that these cities were in the 'big leagues.' "Sports means more to Oakland" says the former city manager. It makes less of a difference to New York, San Francisco, or Chicago." (p. 36)[19]

Before the NFL awarded a franchise to Jacksonville, many people had never heard of the city, while others had no idea where it was located. Similarly, few would have heard of Green Bay if it did not have an NFL franchise. When the NBA's Super Sonics left Seattle to become the Oklahoma Thunder, it meant that Oklahoma City was listed in the league standings along with Dallas, New York, and Los Angeles. Oklahoma's governor said, "It will enhance public perception of the entire state. We'll be on Sports Center every night" (p. 62).[20]

There is a belief that mega sports events can have a similar role on elevating host communities to major league or world class status. Again, the potential for such elevation is likely to be a function of the extent to which the event is part of an integrated plan rather than a one-off occurrence, and the size and existing reputation of the community. Thus, London did not need the Olympics to boost it to world class status, but for smaller cities like Munich, Barcelona, and Atlanta, the Olympics were an opportunity to launch onto the international stage.

Competency and Excellence Transfer

People frequently make judgments about the competence and excellence of a community from snippets of information or from symbols. This "image of competence and excellence transfer" may occur in the context of professional sport franchises, high-profile college sport teams, and mega events. These teams and events are highly visible symbols that may be considered by some to be a symbolic embodiment of the city/college/country as a whole.[21] This means that their presence, administrative competence and level of performance may be regarded as surrogate indicators of the competence and quality of life in their host communities.

Thus, a successful professional sport franchise, or the acquisition of a new franchise after competition with other communities, may be portrayed as being symptomatic of a community's economic and social health. For example, a leader in the campaign to attract the NFL Colts to Indianapolis from Baltimore stated, "If Indianapolis lands the Colts or any NFL team, it's going to do some amazing things for the city in terms of prestige, economic development, and in terms of enticing companies to locate to Indianapolis" (p. 144).[22] If a city successfully negotiates and implements a major sports event or franchise agreement, then the inherent complexity of the task and the extensive publicity these actions generate are likely to convey an aura of high competency upon the city's leadership.

Conversely, if a city loses a sports franchise, it may create the impression that local businessmen and politicians are incompetent, that the community is a "loser" and in decline, and that its residents lack civic pride. Indeed, it may be worse for a city's image to lose a major event or major league team than to never have had one at all. When the Colts left Baltimore, city officials stated that it "inflicted a painful blow to the city's renaissance image that would slow economic development" (p. 144).[22] A case could be made that Indianapolis absconded with Baltimore's "major league city" status along with its football team. Seattle had several professional franchises; nevertheless, the movement of the city's NBA Super Sonics to become the Oklahoma Thunder aroused considerable acrimony:

> The emotions invested in keeping the Sonics appeared to be less about a consuming interest in professional basketball than the humiliation of a smart, sophisticated city losing a franchise to a perceived cow town. A fifth year player on the team observed, "There wasn't much excitement about the Sonics to be honest. But the idea of the Sonics moving to Oklahoma City said something about Seattle that people there didn't want to believe." (p. 62)[20]

Those in leadership positions in cities where franchises leave—for example, the Sonics, Raiders , Colts, and Cardinals—may forever be stigmatized in the eyes of many, irrespective of the intrinsic merits of their decisions. This may account for the reaction of the Governor of Illinois when the White Sox threatened to leave Chicago, who said, "I'll bleed and die before I let the Sox leave Chicago" (p. 11).[23]

While association with sport teams generally is perceived to enhance a city's image, there is some risk that if a team performs poorly then it could create, or at least reinforce, a negative image: "Cleveland's image as a failed city was reinforced by a long string of losing seasons by the Indians, who played in a dingy stadium tabbed the 'mistake by the lake.' Even the local media took to calling Atlanta 'Loserville, U.S.A.' during the years when the Braves, Falcons, and Hawks were going nowhere" (p. 107).[6]

The powerful impact of franchise movements on image in some communities was described by an urban economist reporting on his experience at a radio call-in talk show. The caller wanted him to discuss the decline of St. Louis that took place after the Cardinals left for Arizona. The economist had analyzed the St. Louis economy and found it had not suffered, indeed it had improved after the Cardinals left, but the caller had the distinct impression that the city was in decline. The economist went on to report:

> It was not only the caller who believed St Louis's image had declined. When we interviewed civic officials in St. Louis regarding the investments they made to attract the Rams from Los Angeles to the new domed stadium, each told us they supported the concept because most people in America believed that "St. Louis's best days were behind her." So, image matters to people even if those of us who study the economic effects of stadia and teams conclude there is no real benefit from the presence of a team. (p. 205)[7]

Given the potential positive impact of a franchise on a city's image, those cities with the most to gain from it are probably those that are in decline. They are most desperate to communicate signs of economic and social rejuvenation and, as the Indianapolis case shows, it can be a successful strategy. Unfortunately, these struggling cities are also likely to be the least able to make the major investments necessary for this strategy to succeed.

The discussions of awareness and image enhancement have focused on professional sports franchises, but most of the suggested outcomes also apply to the college context. Many colleges view their high-profile sport teams as important image builders and promotional vehicles for the school, and as a focal point with which students and alumni can identify. Sport teams are commonalities that cross disciplines and represent the school as a whole. All alumni cannot get excited about the excellence of the English or chemistry departments, because most of them have no relationship with those entities. However, all can unite and bond in support of "the team" since it is a common element—a beacon to rally around. The team characteristics of spirit, success, and camaraderie are metaphors and exemplars with which alumni and students identify. Sport teams also constitute the image of the college and its level of excellence held by most of the population who know nothing else about the school.

When a *mega event* is staged successfully, it is widely recognized as a substantial political and organizational accomplishment indicating both an ambitious corporate sector and business-oriented political leadership: "Important signals are sent to outside investors about wealth and organizational competence, and about governments that work effectively with the private sector" (p. 83).[24] Thus, in the context of a Super Bowl it was suggested, "Probably the best thing that came out of the Super Bowl is that Houston demonstrated its ability to handle big events, big conventions, and handle it very well" (p. 8D).[25]

In some circles, even among its own citizens, the UK government had an unfortunate reputation for poor commitment and poor delivery on major projects, and for poor coordination among the various branches of government. The perception was of a socialist, bureaucratic state so circumscribed by layers of government and their rules that it was difficult to do business there. This image had been reinforced by three high-profile mega projects in the decade preceding the London Olympics that were widely viewed as expensive failures and indicators of incompetence: the building of Wembley Stadium, construction of the Millennium Dome, and withdrawal of the UK from hosting the 2005 track and field championships because of its failure to build the promised stadium for them. The hugely successful London Olympics demonstrated that both London and the UK were capable of delivering and moving forward. The event demonstrated that branches of government could work well together and could partner effectively with the private and nonprofit sectors. The Games delivered a strong legacy, the facilities were built on time, planning was inclusive and implementation was innovative, creative and imaginative. The event effectively nullified the prevailing negative image and provided powerful momentum upon which to build a positive "can-do" position in the minds of the world's publics.

The Mediating Role of the Media

A city's image is primarily determined by the mediating filter of media stories. It was pointed out in Chapter 4 that local media often join a community's power elite in supporting major sport facilities and events because they provide a wellspring of news, opinions and interest that garners widespread public attention. However, the community does not have control over the image projected, and this transfer of control from the producers of images to the transmitters of images means there is no guarantee that media coverage will be favorable. This raises four major concerns.

First, the media sometimes focus on creating news rather than merely reporting it. To this end, there is a tendency to report the unusual, bizarre and negative even though these may be minor issues or trivial failings in the overall context because, by definition, such stories are likely to arouse more public interest than "ordinary," mainstream, or positive events. Thus, for example, any bad behavior by a team's players or fans, no matter how trivial, is likely to receive extensive coverage, detracting from the positive brand equity transfer emanating from association with the sport property.

Major criminal activity will not only destroy any positive image transfer, but will create or reaffirm long-term negative associations with a community. A prime example is the riots in Miami when it hosted a Super Bowl, which reinforced the city's reputation as a violent and dangerous place with many thousands of the world's media present, rather than reflecting, as its leaders hoped, "the changed reality and the changed image of Miami" (p. 104).[6] Similarly, riots occurred during the NBA finals in Detroit, where "the city's national image baked in the glow of car fires and burning buildings rather than the goodwill associated with an NBA championship" (p. 112).[26] Other examples include the Mexico Olympics, where the lingering memory is the massacre of 500 Mexican students just 10 days before the opening ceremonies took place; and the Munich Olympic Games, where the abiding images are of the carnage created by the terrorist group Black September that murdered Israeli athletes—a nightmare for the Germans because this happened to Jewish people. Also, the bomb explosion at the Atlanta Games tarnished that city's image: "Despite some outstanding athletic performances, and a generally positive response from both the local populace and actual spectators . . . the Atlanta Games were often presented in the world's media as something approaching a disaster" (p. 808).[27] When the Super Bowl was held in Houston, it was observed that

> the showcase factor can be a two-edged sword that highlights the city's warts as well as its beauty marks. Several out-of-town reporters were working on news stories about Houston's high-profile topless nightclubs. "I got called by three or four different reporters working on stories suggesting Houston was the sleaze capital of the world," a local economist stated. (p. 8D)[25]

To counter negative media stories, the hosts of major sport events often sponsor "familiarization trips" for groups of out-of-town journalists, paying all their bills and escorting them through a planned itinerary designed to display a community's positive attributes. The unstated *quid pro quo* is that in return for being wined and dined, the journalists will produce positive stories—for example, at the Sydney Olympics:

> In tourist trade jargon, it was important to assist these journalists "to find and file stories that are consistent with the destination positioning that Australia seeks to achieve . . . This particular selling job was, in fact, a long-term project, having had its beginnings during the early stages of the bid, with the Australian Tourist Commission's wooing of international journalists through the Visiting Journalists' Program. Its aim was to produce "favorable publicity on Australia as a tourist destination," and in the three years leading up to the Games over 3,000 media writers and broadcasters were invited to Australia under the program, and almost $2.3 billion worth of publicity was generated.[8]

A second media-related concern in seeking image benefits is that despite the zeal with which cities compete with each other for mega events, the exposure a city receives during the broadcasting of an event may be minimal. The media focus will be on the event itself, not on the city that is hosting it. Hence, it is likely that there will be only a few incidental visual images and mentions during the broadcast. Further, since they are embedded as peripheral context in the event actions and activities, and last only a few seconds, it seems improbable that they will register in many viewers' memories. This lack of resonance is reinforced by the lack of distinctive icons in most cityscapes, so the views of one city look very much like those of another and there is nothing distinctive to anchor the visual in viewers' memories.[28]

Third, the broadcasts of outdoor sport events explicitly communicate vivid messages about the weather in those locations. Thus, while televised PGA tour events in Hawaii's sunshine in January may positively reinforce interest in vacationing in that state, the broadcasting of an NFL game in Buffalo in the same month being played in blizzards and Arctic cold is likely to reinforce negative perceptions of that city.

A final frustration with media is the selectivity of what they elect to report. For example, WNBA and MLS teams receive minimal coverage, as do the international accomplishments of the U.S. women's basketball and volleyball teams, and male and female track and field teams, despite their dominance. This means there is little image gain for host communities as a result of their investments in facilities for these franchises and events.

ATTRACTING BUSINESSES

One of the sources of social capital often claimed as likely to emerge from public investments in sport facilities is that they are an economic development aid in attracting new businesses to a community, which enhances job opportunities and income for residents. The probability of there being immediate and direct business gains is remote. There may be occasional instances when people are attracted to an event at, for example, a resort area and are sufficiently enthralled by the community that they promptly decide to invest in it. This is an unlikely scenario. The more probable scenario is that if any investment is forthcoming there will be substantial time delays before it is evident, and disentangling the role of the sport event or facility in facilitating it vis-à-vis all the other factors that go into such decisions may be impossible.

Nevertheless, there are four conduits through which sport facilities may induce positive business outcomes: 1) attraction from increased awareness; 2) attracting talent; 3) facilitated networking at sport facilities; and 4) facilitated networking at mega sport events.

Attraction From Increased Awareness

It is sometimes suggested that views of a city and its skyline that appear on television as part of a sports program, or the presence of a major league franchise, aid in economic development. Thus, advocates for public subsidy of facilities are likely to state, "The team's presence on national television is the best advertising the city has. You never know who is watching an NFL game. Viewers may include convention planners, business CEOs, and relocation consultants, so the team's presence is a real benefit for the city." This type of optimistic statement exemplifies the belief that the big-league image will serve as a magnet and attract businesses to the city. Such a positive outcome seems improbable since the publicity or the winning image of a team does not change any of the cost and market factors that influence business relocation decisions, and economic development and growth.[7]

Attracting Talent

The strength of a community's economy will be determined primarily by its ability to expand the number of "high-end" jobs, especially in the high technology, research and development, company headquarters, and information- and knowledge-based service sectors. These are the engines that stimulate lower-paid jobs and the housing and retail that follow jobs. There is fierce competition among cities to nurture and attract these businesses. Essentially, they are "information factories" whose viability and vitality is dependent on their ability to attract and retain highly qualified educated knowledge workers.

Knowledge workers are highly compensated, but of at least equal importance to them is the quality of life in the city. For many people, once they obtain a threshold level of income, improvements in quality of lifestyle become more important than increases in salary. It is argued that professional sport franchises and mega events are elements in quality of life that contribute to attracting talented people to a community. A business leader explained:

> What's the greatest problem a business has today? Workforce. If you interview 50 businesses at random, I'll bet 49 would say that my biggest problem is getting qualified workers. To get workers, you have to get people who want to be in your community because they love the community, it's got things to offer. As the incoming CEO of [one local] company said, I got 80 people making over $100,000 in this operation. Every one of them are young, aggressive, highly compensated people. They go to the best schools in the country, they can go anywhere they want, they are the A players in the business world. I need things that A players want. (p. 241)[1]

On the same theme, another proponent of a new stadium observed:

> You are in Cleveland, Ohio, and you have 23 or 24 Fortune 500 companies headquartered here, and these guys are competing for CFOs and CCOs, and all these key players with cities all over the world, and they are trying to get the same talent you get in New York and Philadelphia and San Francisco and Los Angeles. So what are you going to sell? You sell the city's amenities. We have a great art museum, a great orchestra, and major league sports. Nice suburbs? There are nice suburbs everywhere. (p. 241)[1]

Facilitated Networking at Sport Facilities

Professional and major college sport facilities may be a catalyst for new business by offering companies the opportunity to invest in hospitality through the use of boxes, suites, and similar options. The objective of offering hospitality to existing or prospective customers is not to conduct business, but rather to use a relaxed informal context outside the normal business environment to create a personal interactive chemistry that will be conducive to doing business later. Indeed, a crucial tenet of hospitality is not to do anything that makes guests feel uncomfortable or that makes them feel that they are being sold to. It offers access to valued stakeholders that would not be possible without the sport event as a backdrop. The role of hospitality opportunities in facilitating new businesses has been articulated in these terms:

> An invitation to discuss trade is often counter-productive because the target audience is wary that acceptance of the invitation to discuss trade will be interpreted as a commitment to actually trade. Moreover, in the case of a meeting which has as its sole objective the investigation of opportunities for trade, embarrassment is the only result where one party wishes to trade but the other does not. This contrasts with a situation where any non-professional common interest—stamp collecting, social drinking or sporting event—is either the pretext for a meeting, the real object of which is to investigate opportunities for trade, or is the main attraction where trade is discussed only incidentally. In these cases both parties can

avoid loss of dignity in the event that they are unable to reach agreement about prospects for trade, and can meet again in the future to discuss other projects without rancor. (p. 176)[29]

There needs to be a strategic approach with deliberate intent beyond "Let's invite friends, and existing and prospective customers to a big party." This will involve such issues as who in a host community or company is best placed to influence positive outcomes, and whether entertaining those people at this sport event will favorably influence them.

Facilitated Networking at Mega Events

The justification used by leaders in host communities for spending large amounts to attract mega events invariably includes their potential for creating subsequent new business. While the aspirational rhetoric is convincing to many, results were rarely apparent because there was no intentional organizational vehicle in place to facilitate realization of the aspiration. Without such a vehicle, any positive business outcomes were serendipitous, relying on unplanned ad hoc interactions among executives in attendance, or private meetings between interested parties who were already networked.

This changed at the Sydney Olympic Games with the establishment of Business Club Australia (BCA).[30] This model has subsequently been adopted by host communities for all mega events. The genesis of the idea sprang from Sydney representatives who attended the preceding Atlanta Olympics. They observed that while a large number of international business decision-makers were there, there was no established vehicle through which the hosts could relate to them. One of those representatives commented:

> The origin of the club actually lies in lessons out of Atlanta. There were all these business people floating around—we wondered how we could actually make a connection. How could we question them? What sort of vehicle could we use? And the concept of a "club" seemed like a good vehicle because of the nature of the networking venture. (p. 246)[30]

The BCA comprised representatives from the federal government, state governments, major corporations, industry trade associations, and from the Sydney Organising Committee for the Olympic Games (SOCOG) and the International Olympic Committee (IOC). Official sanction from the SOCOG and IOC allowed the BCA to use the Olympic Rings in its promotional materials, which bestowed legitimacy on the initiative, and it brought the network of Olympic sponsors into its membership. This bundling of BCA memberships with Olympic sponsors and suppliers served to increase the number of people present in the BCA Center, adding to its euphoria, sense of excitement, and general atmospherics.[30] The downside of this was that it precluded some companies from participating because they were competitors of Olympic sponsors.

The BCA was positioned as a club since it was designed to develop interpersonal relationships among members. It was launched at 90 Australian Consulates around the globe, two years before the Games commenced. They identified international business leaders intending to visit Sydney for the Games. Membership was on an individual rather than an organizational basis, and members were linked online in a database called the BCA Virtual Club. Over 1,000 members from the Australian business community and over 10,000 internationals were signed up.

During the Games, the BCA was centrally located in a building on Sydney Harbour and included a 98-meter catamaran berthed alongside the wharf. Facilities inside the center included venues for meetings and informal networking, computer terminals, office equipment, and multilingual trade assistance from Austrade. The catamaran had a large function room for hosting breakfasts, lunches, dinners, and cocktail receptions, as well as a VIP suite for more-private meetings. BCA was designed as "kind of like a dating agency for business" where, using specifically programmed networking functions, visiting internationals were "matched" with potential Australian business partners.[30]

The BCA Center drew over 17,000 attendees during the Games. By one month after the Games, it had generated $260 million in committed investments and was "well on track" to achieve its target of $577 million.[30] The sophistication and effectiveness of the BCA model has subsequently led to its becoming an integral ingredient of host community programs at mega events.

An obvious target group for using a mega event to showcase a community is meeting planners. They are the "gatekeepers" who provide access to groups planning large conventions. Thus, for example, the Houston Super Bowl was used by the city's convention bureau to host 15 meeting planners and their spouses, with the intent of persuading them to schedule future conventions in the city. Their expenses were fully paid; they stayed in the best hotel; and they were wined and dined, taken on tours of the city's downtown nightlife and convention facilities, and given prime seats for the Super Bowl. One of the immediate returns was a commitment from the American Medical Association to hold its interim annual meeting there, attended by 4,500. Their planner stated, "A lot of people will look a lot harder at Houston than in the past. It has become a major player since the revitalization of downtown" (p. 8D).[25] In the previous decade, Houston spent close to $1 billion in building three new stadiums/arenas for professional franchises.

ATTRACTING TOURISTS

When cities bid to host mega events, one of the arguments used to justify the expense to taxpayers is that the events will provide a boost to tourism. In Chapter 6, it was noted that much of the visitation at such events is displacement in that visitors who would normally come to the host community are displaced by event goers, so there is little net gain. However, there is often a belief that there will be a legacy effect, so future visitor numbers will increase as a result of the visibility stemming from the mega event.

This rationale derives from recognition that sport events create a platform that cities can use for showcasing and communicating to extensive media audiences the attractions, features, and benefits they offer as tourism destinations. This showcasing role has long been the goal of cities hosting winter sport events. Skiing and snowboarding are so central to the winter tourism industry that opportunities for resorts to show the excellence of their facilities to a large television audience by hosting events are highly prized. The reputation and image benefits from hosting such events may be enduring and can be used as defining positional and differential elements in promoting a winter tourism destination. For example, Albertville, France, and Lillehammer, Sweden, both received long-term benefits from holding the Winter Olympic Games. The Games better positioned them to compete with the more well-known ski resorts in the Austrian and Swiss Alps.

Beyond the specific case of winter sports, the contention that some visitors to sport events may be sufficiently impressed with the location that they will return in the future as regular tourists may have merit in some limited contexts. For example, a survey of international visitors to the Soccer World Cup held in South Africa reported the following: "75% said they were visiting the country for the first time, 83% said they would return to the country, and a whopping 94% said they would happily recommend the country to friends and family to visit the country" (p. 41).[31] Given that word-of-mouth promotion is the most effective persuasive tool, this suggests the event had marketing value for South Africa and would lead to additional tourism visitation in the future.

However, this kind of positive result is likely to be an exception rather than the rule. The positive impact of sport events on tourism is frequently negligible, and they are likely to have much less impact than advocates claim: "It is a mirage to think that a substantial tourism economy can be constructed on the back of such events alone" (p. 288).[13] If the events are one-offs, then it seems likely their influence on tourism will be at best ephemeral and will quickly decay. Certainly, they will have less impact than recurring major events held annually in a city, which provide consistent reinforcement of the tourism platform. Again, it seems likely that positive tourism spin-off from a mega event will only occur if the event is part of a broader and longer-range tourism plan.

Thus, Calgary received minimal tourism legacy gains from its hosting of the Winter Games, as did Los Angeles and Atlanta from the Summer Games. In these instances, there was no long-term strategy. In contrast, after the Barcelona Games, which were an integral part of a long-term plan, the Director of the Catalan Tourist Board said, "After the Olympics, the city was put on the map. From that moment we have been a successful tourist city" (p. 14).[32] This statement was made seven years after the Games, so it was not merely a short-term phenomenon. Similarly, after the America's Cup races were held in Freemantle, Western Australia, it was observed, "Based on the crowds which continue to come to Freemantle day and night, the town has become a major destination for tourists and local visitors in the years since it was 'discovered' by the Cup" (p. 55).[33]

In a few instances, for example, Indianapolis in the US and Manchester and Sheffield in the UK, sport events have been central to establishing the city as a tourism destination. At a national level, sport events are a significant part of the UK's tourism industry: Britain has, partly by historical accident rather than by design, become the global market leader in the staging of major sport events because its annual domestic sporting competitions such as the FA Cup Final, the British Open Golf Championship, Premier League soccer and the Wimbledon Tennis Championships attract a large number of overseas visitors and a global television audience. Major sports events held in Britain are a crucial ingredient in both the tourism economy and in the creation of the tourist image of Britain (p. 27).[34]

COMMUNITY PRIDE

Many people receive personal psychic income from their emotional attachment to a sport entity. Their emotional involvement transposes them from the dreary routine of their lives to a mode of escapism that sees them identify with and personalize a team's successes, and feel better about themselves. Life is about experiences and sport teams create them—albeit vicariously. When these personal gains are aggregated, they constitute social capital manifested in the form of community pride.

Thus, sport teams and mega events are cultural assets with the potential to enhance residents' personal wellbeing and community pride. The relationship between sport teams and their fans is often referred to as "a love affair."[35] When a team leaves a community, it is the end of a "marriage." These are nuptial-like analogies. The pervasive influence of sports is exemplified by the extensive use of sports metaphors in everyday life. Knowing how to keep a straight bat; respond to a googly; bat on a sticky wicket; keep your end up; avoid being stumped; avoid being put on the backfoot; protesting that "it's just not cricket"; recognizing "it's a different ballgame"; responding with a dead bat; or ducking a bouncer or a beamer, are cricketing phrases that are endemic in the English language of many countries. Indeed, it has been suggested that "the language of sports is the symbolic glue that holds together the entire social life world" (p. 67).[35] This might be hyperbole, but sport is a central topic of conversation in many social contexts. Another commentator noted, "Holiday celebrations include sporting events; political statements are made through sporting events; even dating is tied to the high school sports scene. Fathers and their children develop relationships through sports, and increasingly women are also involved in team sports, building for them a cherished set of memories" (p. 449).[7]

The social capital associated with professional soccer clubs in English culture was described in the following terms: "Clubs do not exist to make money. Rather, their job

Teams and mega events can enhance community pride. Courtesy of 123RF

is to make people happy. Football clubs fill a peculiar hole in British emotional life. Many people get ritual and community chiefly from football. For some, their club's stadium is more a home than the house they live in" (p 37).[36] The sense of community engendered by the team extends far beyond those who attend the games, as a commentator of the Baltimore Orioles observed:

> The identification of a sports team like the Orioles with a city surely generates some pleasure for its citizens beyond that reflected in ticket sales. In this respect the economics of sports is much different from the economics of, say, apples. A fan can derive substantial pleasure from the Orioles and identify with them as "his" team without ever attending a game, but he gets no such pleasure from knowing that somebody is eating apples in Baltimore." (p. 269)[37]

If a new computer chip plant opens up in a city, elected officials and business leaders may get excited, but ordinary residents do not because the economic benefits appear intangible and impersonal to them. When a sports team comes to a city, a much broader segment of the population becomes excited and identifies with it. A corollary of successful sport teams is that they invite residents of their host communities to share the positive "vibes," which enhances collective civic pride and self-esteem. A sports team is an investment in the emotional infrastructure of a community. Sports has been eloquently described as "the 'magic elixir' that feeds personal identity while it nourishes the bonds of communal solidarity" (p. 5).[38]

In the past two decades, 40 of England's 92 professional soccer clubs have been involved in insolvency proceedings, some more than once.[36] Yet, no club has disappeared because they are too beloved. Creditors and bank managers do not want to incur the wrath of tens of thousands of a city's residents and be stigmatized forever, which is what would happen if they sold the team's ground and other assets as they would do with any other business.

The role of teams as a central part of a community's social fabric has been consistently affirmed by the courts. It was prominent in a court's decision to approve an injunction preventing the dissolution of the Minnesota Twins described in Exhibit 8.2.[39] Similarly, the Florida Supreme Court stated there was a "paramount public purpose" and that benefits to the franchise owners were "incidental" when it rejected a suit filed by taxpayers who argued it was illegal to use public funds to construct a stadium for an NFL franchise in Tampa:

> The Court finds that the Buccaneers install civic pride and camaraderie into the community and that the Buccaneer games and other stadium events also serve a commendable public purpose by enhancing the community image on a nationwide basis and providing recreation, entertainment and cultural activities to its citizens.[40]

This view was further endorsed by the Washington Supreme Court. In a case protesting the use of public tax funds to construct a new stadium for the MLB Seattle Mariners franchise, the court ruled, "The construction of a major league baseball stadium in

Exhibit 8.2

The Minnesota Twins as Part of the Community Fabric

In 2001, MLB sought to reduce the number of teams by two and selected the Montreal Expos and Minnesota Twins for dissolution. A prime reason for their selection was the refusal of their cities to provide these franchises with new, fully loaded stadiums. There was public outrage over this decision in Minnesota. A financial analysis by the city showed that in the period since the Metrodome opened in 1982, the team received $216 million in public aid, while the owner originally paid $34 million and subsequently invested a further $130 million during this period. Hence, the public had a larger financial stake in the team than the franchise. Further, their lease required the Twins to play the 2002 season at the Metrodome.

When the city's agency, the Metropolitan Sports Facilities Commission, applied to the courts for an injunction prohibiting the proposed dissolution, it was granted. The judge in his ruling placed great emphasis on the team's contribution to the community fabric, stating:

> The relationship between the Twins and the Commission is not a typical landlord tenant relationship. The relationship provides the State's citizenry and fans with substantial non-monetary benefits. . . .

> Baseball is as American as turkey and apple pie. Baseball is a tradition that passes from generation to generation. Baseball crosses social barriers, creates community spirit, and is much more than

a private enterprise. Baseball is a national pastime. Locally, the Twins have been part of Minnesota history and tradition for forty years. The Twins have given Minnesota two World Series Championships, one in 1987, and one in 1991. The Twins have also given Minnesota legends such as Rod Carew, Tony Oliva, Harmon Killebrew, Kent Hrbek, and Kirby Puckett; some of whom streets are named after. These legends have bettered the community. Most memorably, these legends volunteered their time to encourage and motivate children to succeed in all challenges of life. Clearly, more than money is at stake. The welfare, recreation, prestige, prosperity, trade and commerce of the people of the community are at stake. The Twins brought the community together with Homer Hankies and bobblehead dolls. The Twins are one of the few professional sport teams in town where a family can afford to take their children to enjoy a hot dog and peanuts at a stadium. The vital public interest, or trust, of the Twins substantially outweighs any private interest. Private businesses were condemned to build the Metrodome. In condemnation proceedings, the building of the Metrodome was deemed to be in the interest of the public. The Commission, the State, citizenry and fans will suffer irreparable harm if the Twins do not play the 2002 baseball games at the Metrodome.

King County confers a benefit of reasonably general character to a significant part of King County" and went on to say that the benefit to the Mariners as principal tenants of the building was incidental to the broader public purpose the stadium provided.[41]

The city-wide community pride associated with a team may be accentuated at the local neighborhood scale by pride in the presence of a team's facility in the locale. For example, construction of the main Commonwealth Games stadium in Manchester, which was later transferred to English Premier League team Manchester City, had a transformative influence on local residents' perceptions of their neighborhood:

> It certainly has transformed the image of the area—not only in terms of the images that were portrayed of the stadium in use as far as the region and the national

audience is concerned but I think it has also started to transform the local population's view of their own area as being a dynamic and happening place and in that regard it has been an outstanding success. (p. 233)[42]

A similar effect was noted among the people of Cardiff, the capital of Wales, when the highly regarded national Millennium Stadium was constructed there: "It is something which the (local) people are very proud of and that generates confidence and people are proud of the capital city" (p. 233).[42]

The intangible social capital associated with community pride may have a tangible manifestation in the form of increased property values: "If people are proud of the area in which they live, they are more likely to invest in their property and this in turn is likely to enhance the desirability of the area and stimulate increased demand for property" (p. 234).[42]

The book and movie *Friday Night Lights* illustrated the prominent role played by football in generating social capital in some communities. The author documented how the featured community's morale and emotions ebbed and flowed with the fortune of its high school football team. He quoted a long-time resident of the city as saying, "When somebody talks about West Texas, they talk about football. There is nothing to replace it. It's an integral part of what makes the community strong. You take it away and its almost like you strip the identity of the people" (p. 43).[43] Another resident observed, "Life really wouldn't be worth livin' if you didn't have a high school football team to support" (p. 20).[43]

The author concluded, "The town drank deeply from the chalice of high school football" (p. 63).[43] Later he noted that "football stood at the very core of what the town was about, not on the outskirts, not on the periphery. It had nothing to do with entertainment and everything to do with how people felt about themselves" (p. 236).[43] Presumably, the intense sense of community pride and identity linked to high school football explains the decision of voters in another Texas city to approve a $60 million referendum to construct a new high school football stadium.[44] It also likely explains the "celebrity" status often conferred on high school and college athletes. Education is a personal experience, but athletic teams' accomplishments take on the persona of a collective experience. Approbation from collective success is showered on the individuals who are responsible for it. This contrasts with the recognition for excellence in education achievement, which is usually confined to a small circle of family and friends.

The use of facilities to create civic pride may be particularly important in communities where there has been a long period of decline that has demoralized residents. It has been suggested that the success of the Dallas Cowboys was instrumental in redeeming the collective self-esteem of the residents of Dallas:

It is widely believed that the city's redemption from its darkest day—Nov. 22, 1963—came with the rise of the Cowboys, their glamour and their glory sprinkling stardust upon the discredited city. Once it was blithely assumed that Dallas had somehow killed President Kennedy. Now, no matter who else may be accused of that crime—the CIA, the Mafia, Cuba, aliens—Dallas is no longer impeached.

And J.R. is gone, too. Dallas is just the home of the Cowboys, a franchise that has never seen its equal. *You know who I am.* I am Dallas; I am the Cowboys. (p. 62)[45]

The social capital emanating from community pride is likely to be proportionately greater in small or mid-sized cities. Such communities cannot compete with New York City, Chicago or Los Angeles in economic or cultural terms, but their residents can derive at least a temporary aura of superiority and civic pride whenever their team defeats a big city team.

Perhaps the most famous illustration of a sport event restoring community pride occurred in the final of the 1954 soccer World Cup held in Berne, Switzerland. Germany played Hungary, which was widely recognized as the world's dominant team, having been unbeaten in over 30 games in the previous five years. This was Germany's first venture into international competition after World War II, and in the earlier group stages of the competition they had lost to Hungary by 8 goals to 3.

Hungary established a 2–0 lead, but Germany came back to win the game 3–2. The win evoked euphoria throughout Germany. It was the first time the German national anthem was played in public since the war. The unexpected triumph was a psychological turnaround from the country's decade of post-war trauma. It is known as "The game that made a nation" and credited by historians as sparking the national energy and sense of pride that were needed to build a new country. It led to the rejuvenation of West Germany in the late 1950s and 1960s. The game is referred to as "Das Wunder von Bern" (The Miracle of Berne), and 50 years later in 2004 its anniversary was marked by huge national celebrations.[46]

Cricket played a central role in uniting the West Indian islands when they were transitioning from colonialism to independence. The West Indies team's dominance in the 1960s and 1970s fostered a sense of identity and self-esteem. The appointment of Frank Wornell as the first Black West Indies captain to preside over the team's decade of excellence played a vital part in confirming the process of self-determination.[47]

In contemporary times, perhaps the most vivid illustration of the extraordinary influence of sport on community self-esteem is the impact of cricket games on the nations of the sub-continent, where the national pride of well over a billion people is at stake. This is described in Exhibit 8.3.[47,48,49]

It has been suggested that when this community pride "feel-good" factor is advocated as justification for the public expense of hosting a sport mega event, then it becomes less convincing than when it is linked to sports teams. Would residents be any prouder or feel any better if the success at the event took place in a distant city rather than at a home city?[50] It seems unlikely that the feel-good factor would be less because the accomplishments were not at a home arena. Indeed, it is possible to argue that away-from-home success would confer greater civic pride because it is more difficult to achieve. However, it is probable that the home-field advantage would inspire a greater level of success, and thus greater community pride, than if the event were held elsewhere.

A further dimension of the use of community pride to justify the cost of hosting a mega event is the boost to community self-esteem that may be associated with hosting

Exhibit 8.3

The Role of Cricket in Creating National Pride on the Sub-Continent

When India plays Pakistan in one-day World Cup cricket matches, everyday life in the sub-continent comes to a halt. Businesses, banks and offices close for the day and tens of millions of workers stay home. The roads are empty. Every television set, from the huge screens set up especially for the games in every five-star hotel to the battered black and white set flickering at the back of the tea shop, draws its crowd like bees round a hive. One billion people watch the games on television. A management consultant in Bombay calculates that on these days India is over $6 billion poorer due to World Cup cricket-inspired absenteeism.

While the score may be measured in wickets and runs, few supporters in either country have any illusions about the real stakes. In this cricket-mad region every match is important, but the India vs. Pakistan games are no less than a surrogate battle between bitter enemies who have fought three wars in 50 years. No other institution provides such a visible convenient vehicle through which to exhibit patriotism and embrace community pride.

In India, Pakistan and Bangladesh, there are over 500 million people who live in abject poverty. For many of these people, cricket offers a sense of pride, a route of escapism, a vicarious notion of achievement. Most of them will never have the opportunity to be educated or to overcome the poverty they've been born into. They can afford merely a community television on which to watch the matches. Exulting in the success of 11 men on a green field is as close as they will ever get to success. Cricket provides rich nourishment in a diet that is low on self-esteem.

The qualities of cricket that make it riveting to the sub-continent are its valor, elegance, charisma, defiance, team spirit, and the tantalizing flukes and freaks of fortune. For India and Pakistan, cricket is vicarious warfare: "IT'S WAR NOW" screamed the headline in Bombay's weekly *Blitz* when India's star batsman was hurt by a Pakistani bowler in a game between the two countries played in Calcutta. The crowd rioted, the stadium had to be emptied, and the match was finished in front of empty stands. The association of cricketing fortunes with national fortunes is logically absurd, especially given the fluky nature of the abbreviated one-day game (traditional international cricket games are five days long). But in a part of the world where national passions burn like cordite, it is unavoidable.

When Bangladesh went home early after having been knocked out of the World Cup, they still received a rapturous welcome because they defeated Pakistan, their historical enemies, in an early game. The government declared a national holiday and Dhaka, the capital, a city not known for its joyfulness, came alive with thousands of revelers dancing and singing. "The jubilation today" said the Prime Minister, at the grand civic reception "reminds me of 16 December 1971 when men, women, and children came out of their homes to celebrate the victory of our independence war. Again, the whole nation has awakened for another victory."

the event, independent of any home successes at it. For example, when Brisbane, Australia, hosted the Commonwealth Games, some suggested that the most important outcome was not associated with economic gains or external image: "It was the people of Brisbane themselves who were the primary targets of messages about the kind of city they could become" (p. 83).[24]

What is going on here . . . is that a regional population who have traditionally been thought of as provincial—*and have thought of themselves as provincial*—are

encouraged to become more ambitious and outward-looking in their aspirations
. . . A mega-event, therefore, is not only about showing the city off to the world, it
is also about putting the global on show for the locals, and inviting them to take
on new identities as citizens of the world. (p. 83)[24]

Some believed that South Africa would prove inadequate to the task of hosting the soccer World Cup. When the doubters were proved wrong, "this success registered where
it matters most. The psyche of the people. Never have we seen South Africa so pleased
with themselves" (p. 40).[31]

SOCIAL COHESION

Social cohesion refers to the tangible focus that sport teams can provide for building
community consciousness, identity, and social bonding. Often, it is a corollary of community pride. Members of contemporary communities are atomized, alienated and dis-
connected from each other with few opportunities to interact, relate, and bind. A sport
team or mega event can be an important component in the collective experience of
communities that ties residents together across race, gender, and economic lines. Indeed, sport has become one of the few vehicles available for developing a sense of community cohesion which is defined by shared values, beliefs, and experiences.

In the past, religion provided this social glue, but, since there is no longer a single
dominant religion providing shared values and beliefs, high-profile sport has at least
partially filled the social void.[1] Thus, the mayor of Baltimore proclaimed, "We have to
have things that create a sense of community and sports is the glue to help hold the
community together" (p 110).[6] Similarly, the mayor of Philadelphia when lobbying the
public to support funding a new stadium said, "These Phillies, if we give them our full
support, will bring us together; solidify a sense of community with civic pride as they
drive toward the pennant" (p. 26).[51] The potential for sport to foster social cohesion
crosses cultures:

> That is the thing with cricket in India. In a chance encounter between Indians
> who have different mother tongues, come from different social classes and live in
> different parts of the country, you will see the disparities begin to dissolve no
> sooner has the topic of the latest Sachin Tendulkar [India's most renowned player]
> innings come up.[52]

Sports is a theater where Kipling's twin imposters of triumph and disaster run side by
side and impact large numbers of people. It provides a theater of emotions to fantasize
about and to casually share.[53] Sports are not like other businesses. They are about "triumphs of the human spirit, community bonding, and family memories. They're about
taking a break from the pettiness that divides us. They're about celebrating some of the
things that make society whole: competition, victory, redemption" (p. 309).[54] Cities
wracked by social and racial tensions can find moments of release through their collective identification with the successes of sport teams. They engage a wide spectrum of
society and can be particularly effective in connecting with those who feel marginalized

in communities. The euphoria emanating from a team's success can raise the collective morale of all residents and generate a communal "electricity" that, at least temporarily, binds people together.

"Fans who chant 'we're number one' are trumpeting the superiority of both their team and their town. In rallying around the home team, people identify more closely with a broader framework in the spatially, socially, and politically fragmented metropolis" (p. 9).[6] A substantial proportion of a community emotionally identifies with "their" team and feels elation, anxiety, despondency, optimism and an array of other emotions according to how the team performs. Some of these people may not understand the nature of the event or the nuances of the sport. Nevertheless, the team constitutes "a common identification symbol, something that brings the citizens of the city together, especially during those exhilarating times when the city has a World Series champion, or a Super Bowl winner" (p. 176).[55] Thus, when the Arizona Diamondbacks beat the New York Yankees in Game 7 of the World Series, the senior senator from Arizona proclaimed it "the most unifying event in Arizona since statehood was granted to us in 1912 . . . It was pride in the state of Arizona that I think was without precedent" (p. 35).[56]

The social cohesion emanating from community pride is intangible, but more tangible cohesion may be manifested through the social mixing that may occur when stadiums attract people from the suburbs to the downtown area who might otherwise avoid the city center. If there is a large degree of economic or racial segregation between downtown and suburban populations, then this creates opportunities for people who might otherwise not visit a downtown area to "see how the other half live."[57]

The potential of mega events to foster social cohesion was illustrated by the emotional response of Atlanta residents to the news that the Olympic Games would be coming to their city:

> Karen Twait was weaving her way to work through heavy eastbound traffic on Interstate 20 when the announcement came over the radio. "Suddenly horns started honking, and fists came out of car windows. Everywhere I looked people were screaming. It was incredible. I started screaming too. And tears just started streaming down my face. It was so dramatic. I never expected so much emotion to come over me." On the other side of the city, Robert Clark, 52, an Atlanta native and downtown businessman, was watching TV, getting ready for work. "I was startled," Mr. Clark said. "I just broke down and cried when the guy said, 'Atlanta.' I don't know why. It's been more than 30 years since I cried. But I know I'll remember that day for a long, long time." The instant the Olympic announcement was made Tuesday morning, a change swept through the city. The town rose up, rearranging a collective psyche that some say has long been subject to a Southern inferiority complex. Winning the Games seems to have finally ripened a town that's forever been on the edge of maturity. (p. R12)[58]

The London Olympic Games took place one year after riots and looting spread from London to other British cities, shocking the country. The Olympics changed the public mood: "We have seen ourselves for a while in our best light; glittering and happy, belonging to something bigger than all of us. Here we are, all in it together just for a while."[59] The British medalists embraced a spectrum of skin tones, speech patterns and class accents ranging from the queen's granddaughter to a Black, boxing gold medal lady-boxer from an under-privileged, inner-city neighborhood. All were similarly feted without equivocation.

It has long been recognized that the emotional identification with sport teams has an extraordinary impact on the morale of many people. In recent years, a biological explanation for this has emerged.[60] Winning and losing have a direct effect on the chemical composition of our brains, particularly on levels of a neurotransmitter called serotonin. The social environment, not heredity, has been shown to be the critical determinant in serotonin levels. Winning raises levels and losing lowers them. This at least partially explains the observation, "Every time we win, we're like a different country. Everybody's happy. Football (soccer) can bring peace" (p. 56).[61] People with low levels of seratonin are more depressed and aggressive than people with high levels. When individuals identify with the fortunes of their team and it loses an important game, subconsciously, they lose. They are more likely to feel depressed or become violent afterward because their serotonin levels dropped. Anti-depressant drugs, such as Prozac, work by raising serotonin levels.

Another dimension of social cohesion that may emerge from hosting mega events springs from the requirement that multiple political, non-profit, and community organizations have to cooperate to bring an event to fruition. By working together over a prolonged period of time, personal chemistry among individuals may be nurtured, relationships established, and trust created as they learn to rely upon and to appreciate the contributions of other entities. As a result, a reservoir of goodwill and expertise from these strengthened networks is established. This can be the fertile ground from which the seeds of future partnerships and collaborations can grow.

Professional teams contribute to building a community's "sense of place."[9] In the context of Minneapolis, one commentator believed that:

> the Twins or Vikings or North Stars or Timberwolves have provided each of us and all of us with exquisite memories that attach us to our grandparents, our parents, our neighbors, our siblings, our children . . . Pro sports in a metropolitan area the size of the Twin Cities can especially become the collective memory of a diverse citizenry constantly seeking common ground. (pp. 451–452)[62]

The warmth derived from these kinds of connections is difficult to quantify in dollars; sounds sort of hokey; and gets lost in the endless cynical wrangling between millionaire players and billionaire owners and public bodies. Nevertheless, it may resonate as a justification for investing public money into professional sports.

When Jacksonville was awarded a franchise to become the NFL's thirtieth team, it became a catalyst for unifying diverse groups in the city: "Linked by a mighty passion for football, the citizenry overcame the town's diverse history and pulled together—white bankers and black preachers on the same team—to sell out the 73,000 seat stadium in record time and grab the NFL's admiration" (p. B8).[9]

The social cohesion justification for sport facility expenditures invariably incorporates a level of wishful thinking and hyperbole. Consider the following claim from a senior executive of the Minnesota Twins: "I think sports can bring people together across social and economic lines. Those lines are obliterated. You can have a CEO of a major corporation sitting next to a homeless person and they both are there for a baseball game; they are both there for the same reason. So, it has tremendous social value" (p. 242).[1] The vision of CEOs sitting next to homeless people in a new stadium seems improbable. The wholesome image of everyone coming together behind the home team glosses over the reality of separating sports fans along class, income, ethnic, and racial lines:

> Luxury boxes and other premium seating arrangements physically divide the well-off from ordinary fans, and rising ticket prices prevent lower income groups from attending most major league games . . . [It] ignores the fact that the new stadiums are sought, in large part, because they will provide more luxury boxes and club seating, which is likely to separate social classes in the ballpark rather than integrate them. (p. 112)[6]

Sport offers cathartic moments in which diverse groups can come together, but the euphoria usually evaporates so that the resultant social cohesion does not endure. Thus, it has been suggested that "stadium supporters may only want others to believe that sports provide this social glue because it obfuscates the important [and enduring] class, race, and gender differences in the community" (p. 239).[1] Some extension of cohesion may be encouraged through the use of memory prompts such as tangible buildings, statues, museums, banners, or other totems recalling past triumphs. Even though this may have some limited effect, the cohesion is likely to be ephemeral. Nevertheless, it is often real for that short time period, which makes it compelling when advocates use it to justify spending on sport facilities.

MEASURING SOCIAL CAPITAL BENEFITS

This chapter has highlighted the benefits that may accrue to a community, beyond economic impact, in the form of social capital. Clearly, these have value. The benefits derive from two sources. First, *private consumption benefits* are enjoyed by those who attend a sports event, but perceive they receive more benefits from it than they pay for in the admission price. Economists call this *consumer surplus*, recognizing it is the surplus benefit that event attendees receive which is not captured in revenues by the event's property owners. Second, *public consumption benefits*, which refers to the "free riders" who benefit from social capital emanating from a sports team or mega event, but do not compensate the property owners for the satisfaction and enjoyment they receive. The uncaptured economic value of social capital from public consumption benefits is likely to be much greater than the consumer surplus from event goers:

> The problem facing soccer teams in the English Premier League is what economists call appropriability. Clubs cannot make money out of [cannot appropriate]

more than a tiny share of the population's love of soccer. A poll found that 45% of British adults are interested in professional soccer, but on any given weekend only about 1.5% of Britons go to a stadium to watch a professional game. In other words, most football fans rarely go near a stadium. They watch football only on TV, sometimes for the price of a subscription, or for the price for some pints in the pub. It's a cheap way to have fun.

And watching games is only a tiny part of the fans' engagement with football. Fans read newspapers, trawl internet sites, and play computer games. Then there is the football banter that passes time at work and school. All this entertainment is made possible by football clubs, but they cannot appropriate a penny of the value people attach to it. (p 37)[36]

Entire sections of daily newspapers are devoted to covering sports, the sports network ESPN is available in approximately 100 million homes, and during the evening rush hour drive home, the radio stations will be replete with experts and non-experts alike heatedly debating the sports issues of the day.

Since a property cannot directly charge for its contributions to civic pride derived from the enhanced community visibly, image, status and identity; social cohesion; and employment and income opportunities, it seems reasonable that its owners should be reimbursed by tax funds. If a substantial proportion of a community perceive that they receive benefits for which they do not pay, then the tax system is the appropriate mechanism for rectifying this inequity.

Exhibit 4.5 described the financial gains secured by the owners of the Dodgers when they left Brooklyn for Los Angeles, but consider the following scenario:

The Dodgers left Brooklyn for Los Angeles because they could make greater profits in California than in New York. But if the Dodgers had had a way to charge Brooklynites for the pleasure received when they discussed the team, read about it, or exulted in the civic pride it brought to the borough of Brooklyn, the Dodgers may well have stayed in Flatbush. (p. 209)[63]

It is possible that if the social capital value of the team had been considered, then its total value may have been greater if it had stayed in Brooklyn, since many residents of that community still felt betrayed 50 years after the move was consummated. Because the team owners could not capture that social capital value, they opted for Los Angeles, where the franchise's profits would be greater.

Elected officials increasingly use social capital arguments to justify the spending of tax dollars on sport facilities as investments rather than subsidies. As increased skepticism greets advocates' arguments relating to economic development, their focus has shifted to claims regarding social capital. Conveniently for proponents, it is more difficult to verify social capital claims, so they are more challenging to refute. While there is widespread acceptance that they exist, there is rarely agreement on the magnitude of tax support that is commensurate with them. The key question is: How much public funding should be provided to teams and/or facilities to fairly compensate them for the positive experiences they offer to residents in a host community, beyond what residents pay for that experience? The Gateway complex of sport facilities in downtown Cleveland has created civic pride, excitement generated by the teams' presence, and many more people visiting an area that was previously avoided. How much is this worth to the residents of Cleveland and Cuyahoga County?

> Will this new recreational nexus create a great many jobs? No. Will the sports facilities encourage a substantial or significant change in development patterns? No. Is downtown Cleveland a more exciting place? Is there a greater sense of excitement and civic pride? Are people who long ago gave up on downtown returning for recreation? The answer to each of those questions is yes . . . Are these benefits or returns worth the hundreds of millions of dollars spent by taxpayers to subsidize sports? . . . The investment in sports amounts to less than $10 per person per year . . . Did Cleveland and Cuyahoga County get good or adequate value for their investment? In a city with a full set of urban challenges, is the new image created by these public investments worth the commitments if there is no direct economic impact? (pp. 26–27)[7]

The Contingent Valuation Method

For many decades, a number of techniques have been proposed for measuring social capital. This work has been spearheaded by resource economists who seek to establish an economic value for natural amenities such as parks, open space, wetlands, wildlife preserves, wilderness areas, and coastal habitats. Many taxpayers may never visit such resources but, nevertheless, derive satisfaction from knowing they exist and, thus, are supportive of expending tax dollars on them (public consumption benefits). Further, among those who do visit them, there are some whose commitment to the environmental cause is so strong that they would be willing to pay more than they are charged for admission (consumer surplus).

The preferred approach for measuring these uncaptured economic gains is contingent valuation method (CVM). CVM places dollar values on goods and services not exchanged in the marketplace. The method is referred to as *contingent valuation* because people are asked their willingness to pay (WTP), contingent on a specified scenario and description of the service. There is an emerging awareness that CVM is potentially a useful tool for measuring social capital associated with sport teams and events. It is a survey-based approach to eliciting the level of subsidy that individuals would be prepared to pay to support a new facility for a sports team. To obtain valid and reliable results, the implementation of CVM requires technical expertise, but the general approach is easily understood. Typically, the survey comprises three elements: the scenario, a discrete choice (sometimes called *dichotomous choice*) question, and a payment-card (sometimes called *continuous*) question. These are shown in Exhibit 8.4. The estimates provided by the two questions should be similar, so their reliability can be checked. If they are not, people were either confused or not taking the survey seriously. The study referenced in Exhibit 8.4 was designed to find out how much the residents of Jack-

---

Exhibit 8.4

Key Elements of a Contingent Valuation Survey

The Scenario

Professional football teams often move to new cities. Since 1984, National Football League teams have left Baltimore, St. Louis, Oakland, Houston, Cleveland, and Los Angeles (twice).

Consider the following situation. Within the next 10 years the owners of the Jaguars decide to sell the team. The new owners want to move the team to another city, such as Los Angeles, where they could make higher profits.

Suppose the city of Jacksonville was able to buy a majority of the team. If the city owned a majority of the team, the Jaguars would never leave Jacksonville. Large sums of money from Duval County taxpayers would be needed to buy a majority of the team. It has been estimated that it would take annual tax payments of $40 for the next 20 years from all Duval County households to buy a majority of the team. Your total payment would be $800.

The Discrete Choice Question

"Would you be willing to pay the annual payments of TAX for the next T years out of your own household budget so the city of Jacksonville could buy a majority of the Jaguars?" TAX could take any one of several randomly assigned values; in the Jacksonville survey, the values were $5, $10, $20, or $40. The number of years T was 10 in half the surveys, 20 in the other half. Respondents were given three choices: "Yes," "No," and "I don't know."

The Payment-Card Question

"What is the highest annual tax payment you would be willing to pay for the next T years out of your own household budget to keep the Jaguars in Jacksonville?" Respondents were given the following choices: "zero," "between $0.01 and $4.99," "between $5 and $9.99," "between $10 and $19.99," "between $20 and $39.99," between $40 and $75," and "more than $75."

---

sonville, Florida, were willing to pay in higher taxes to keep their NFL team from moving away.[63]

Respondents to those surveys can be categorized into those who attend games and provide an estimate of the private consumption benefits (consumer surplus), and those who do not attend, whose values constitute an estimate of the public consumption benefits. The total economic value is calculated by multiplying the willingness to pay of attendees and non-attendees in the sample by the total number of residents in each of those categories in the community.

Results From CVM Studies

An early commentary that provided an important stimulus for undertaking CVM studies posed a hypothetical investment situation of a stadium receiving a subsidy of $250 million in a metropolitan area of 5 million residents. The annual cost of servicing the debt to finance such a stadium would be equivalent to approximately $5 per resident. The authors commented: "It does not vastly stretch credulity to suppose that, say, a quarter of the population of a metropolitan area derives $20 per person in consumption benefits annually from following a local sports team. If so, the consumption benefits of acquiring and keeping a team exceed the costs" (p. 58).[64]

A similar line of argument was used in an analysis of the tax support provided for the building of Oriole Park at Camden Yards: "The state and its subdivisions lose approxi-

Exhibit 8.5

Social Capital Value of the Pittsburgh Penguins

In October 1998, the Pittsburgh Penguins of the National Hockey League (NHL) declared Chapter 11 bankruptcy. The NHL considered two options—disbanding the franchise, or selling it to the higher bidder which meant it likely would be moved to another city. The bankruptcy judge issued a permanent injunction against moving the Penguins to another city, stating:

> The Penguins are as much a part of the warp and woof [sic] of this community as are its other professional sports teams, museums, parks, theaters and ethnic neighborhoods. As important as [the creditors'] interests are, they may have to give way when the interest of the community at large so dictates. In this case, it so dictates.

In essence, the judge ruled that when social capital was included in the valuation, the team's value in Pittsburgh exceeded its likely value in another city. Soon after the judge's ruling, the NHL sold the Penguins to a group of local investors for less than they were worth on the open market.

This situation provided a good context in which to undertake a CVM analysis of the value of the team to the community. There was no suggestion that a new arena be built for the Penguins, so the study focused exclusively on what the Penguins were worth to Pittsburgh. If new owners could not be found who would agree to keep the team in Pittsburgh, then an alternate scenario was that the Penguins could become publicly owned by the taxpayers. It was this scenario which was presented to a random sample of households in Pittsburgh. The mail survey posed the following questions:

> If the city of Pittsburgh were to buy the team, it would never leave Pittsburgh. But in order for the city to buy the team, pay off its debts, and challenge for the Stanley Cup, taxpayer money will be needed. One estimate is that each Pittsburgh household would have to pay $TAX each year in higher city taxes.

Four $TAX amounts ($1, $5, $10, and $25) were randomly assigned.

Then respondents were asked the discrete-choice willingness-to-pay question—"Would you be willing to pay $TAX each year out of your own household budget in higher city taxes to help keep the Penguins in Pittsburgh?"—and were given three response categories: "Yes," "No," and "I don't know." All respondents were then asked the open-ended willingness-to-pay question: "What is the most you would be willing to pay out of your own household budget each year in higher city taxes to keep the Penguins in Pittsburgh?" They were presented with the following "payment card" categories to choose in response in the question: "Zero," "Between $0.01 and $4.99," "between $5 and $9.99," "between $10 and $19.99," "between $20 and $39.99," between $40 and $75," and "more than $75."

Although 72% identified themselves as fans, only 51.5% were willing to pay higher taxes to keep the Penguins in town. Among those willing to pay, people who went to games were willing to pay more than non-attendees. While some households were willing to pay a lot and others were willing to pay nothing, the average Pittsburgh household was willing to pay a total of $5.57 per year to keep the Penguins in town. For the 947,500 households in metropolitan Pittsburgh, the total willingness to pay for the Penguins as a public good came to $3.87 million per year. At an interest rate of 8%, $3.87 million per year could finance a lump sum payment of $48.3 million. This is the maximum subsidy that could be justified.

Prior to administration of the survey, a consortium of local investors bought the team for $85 million, so the CVM values represented 57% of the team's market value. However, their purchase of the team alleviated the immediate threat of losing it, which is likely to have persuaded respondents to indicate a lower willingness to pay than when the threat was "live." The cost of building a new arena averages $223 million (Table 4.3). If these social capital values are transferred to that context, then it suggests Pittsburgh residents would be prepared to subsidize 21% of a new arena's cost in return for the social capital benefits they would receive. While this is far below the 48% average of public contributions to new arenas, there are some examples of public subsidies at or below this level (Table 4.3).

Exhibit 8.6

A Community's Willingness to Pay
for A New University Basketball Facility

Although it would be built with private money, a new arena for the University of Kentucky would have imposed large costs on taxpayers in Lexington, the team's host city. They own UK's current arena, subsidize its operating costs, and will be paying off construction debt for the next 16 years. The loss of their major tenant would have increased the tax revenue needed to pay debt and operating costs. Also, Lexington was one of the largest metro areas in the United States without a professional baseball team. The Southern League said it would move a team to Lexington if the city built a stadium for $10 to $12 million.

A survey was mailed to a random sample of households in Lexington who were asked: "What is the most you would be willing to pay out of your own household budget per year to make a new arena possible?" The results showed respondents had a relatively high level of enthusiasm for the basketball team, but that did not translate into support for a large subsidy. It suggested Lexington residents would support a subsidy of $610,000 a year, which would service a capital cost of $7.28 million—far below the envisaged $100 million cost.

Respondents, however, even those who described themselves as fans, had little incentive to support the new arena because the UK team would stay in the community irrespective of whether a new arena was built. This is not the case when professional franchises are involved.

The community's subsidy tolerance for the baseball stadium was $592,000, which would service a capital cost of $7.6 million. Again, this was much lower than the $10–12 million projected cost of the stadium.

---

mately $9 million a year on [Oriole Park at] Camden Yards. This is approximately $12 per Baltimore household per year; the public subsidy to the stadium is justified only if the public consumption benefits of the Orioles are at least this large" (p. 274).[37]

The first empirical CVM study relating to sport was stimulated by the threat of the NHL Pittsburgh Pirates franchise leaving the city. The study is described in Exhibit 8.5.[65] It provided a basic model upon which others have subsequently built.

CVM was used to identify the level of subsidy that would be acceptable to residents of Lexington, Kentucky, to support a proposed new $100 million basketball arena for the University of Kentucky team and a $10–12 million baseball stadium, which was intended to attract a minor league team to the community. The results are described in Exhibit 8.6.[66]

Civic, business and political leaders in Portland, Oregon, have long had aspirations to attract an MLB franchise to the community which would require construction of a new stadium. When MLB relocated the Montreal Expos, Portland—along with Washington, D.C. and Las Vegas—was a contender for the franchise, but it went to Washington, D.C. The city is currently the largest market in the US with only one major franchise (NBA's Portland Trailblazers). A telephone sample of area residents were asked both a discrete-choice and a payment-card question designed to ascertain how much they would pay annually in taxes to construct a new stadium that would ensure the relocation of an MLB team to Portland. The results are shown in Table 8.1.[67] The stadium that Washington D.C. agreed to build cost $693 million in public funds.

Table 8.1. Public Investment Supported by Total Willingness-to-Pay for a New MLB Stadium in Portland			
	Mean annual household WTP	Aggregate annual WTP	Net present value over 30 years
Payment-card Estimate	$14.35	$8,179,500	$109,640,603
Discrete-choice Estimate	$12.88	$7,341,600	$98,409,126

Clearly, the willingness of Portland taxpayers to provide only approximately $100 million fell far short of the amount needed for their bid for the franchise to be competitive.

Exhbit 8.4 showed the elements of a CVM survey undertaken in Jacksonville. Results from that study showed that the average household was willing to pay $148 spread over twenty years to keep the NFL Jaguars in the city. When discounted at 7% per year, this meant the 427,000 households in the Jacksonville metropolitan area were willing to pay $35.8 million. The city spent $207 million in tax funds upgrading its stadium, which is much more than the CVM suggested its residents would support.[63] It suggests that the social capital generated did not justify the large expenditures on the stadium.

CVM studies were undertaken to ascertain the perceived social capital emanating from a proposed new stadium for the Minnesota Vikings[68] and that derived from each of the seven major league franchises in Michigan and Minnesota.[69] Both concluded that aggregate willingness-to-pay values were nowhere near large enough to support the level of public tax funding that was provided for those facilities.

Although the number of CVM studies measuring the value of social capital is small, they are unanimous in revealing that the social capital that residents perceive to accrue does not justify the magnitude of public tax expenditures on major league facilities and franchises. Its value falls far short of the subsidies granted, which led one commentator to conclude, "These results suggest that most cities would be better off bidding farewell to their teams rather than bidding for new stadiums" (p. 215).[63] However, the same commentator recognizes a puzzling inconsistency in that "sizeable percentages regularly read about and discuss their local teams [and] consider themselves fans, and believe their team improves the quality of life" (p. 215)[63] and observes:

> The CVM results represent something of a mystery. Sports dominate the nation's attention as few other things do—almost every major daily newspaper has a sports section, local newscasts devote 25 or 30% of their time to sports, and with the exception of a papal visit, it's hard to think of anything else besides a World Series or Super Bowl championship that can attract millions to a parade. So why are the estimated values of sports public goods so low? Why, if people care so much about sports, are they not willing to pay more for the civic pride, the thrill of victory, and the pleasure of reading about and discussing the home team? (p. 228)[63]

One consistent finding among the studies is that most of the social capital value comes from non-user free riders, rather than consumer surplus associated with users. The results shown in Table 8.2 referring to the proposed MLB Stadium in Portland are illus-

Table 8.2. Level of Public Investment for a MLB Stadium in Portland Supported by Social Capital			
	Mean annual household value	Aggregated annual household value	Net present value
Non-user "free-riders"	$7.22	$4,115,400	$55,164,122
User consumer surplus	$2.46	$1,402,200	$18,795,532
			$73,959,654

trative of this pattern. Given this pattern, the benefit principle of taxation directs that the bulk of public funds should be generated from broad-based, non-user, general taxes for new facilities, rather than on selective taxes such as surcharges on tickets.[67]

The CVM approach is equally applicable to a collegiate context. There is an ongoing debate as to whether college athletic programs should be self-sufficient, operating independent of a university's operating budget, or whether they should be subsidized by student fees. Many students do receive social capital from the successes of an athletic program, even if they do not attend the games. This suggests that they may be prepared to subsidize those programs. The CVM approach could identify how much per student they would be prepared to pay, and this would give an indication of the level of subsidy that was appropriate.

When London was contending for the Summer Olympic Games along with multiple other cities, a CVM study was undertaken with respondents in three British cities: London, Manchester and Glasgow. The averages of willingness to pay in the three cities were £22, £12, and £11 per household per year, respectively, for ten years.[70] Aggregating over all London households and discounting at 5% yields a total willingness to pay in London of £480 million. Extrapolating the Manchester and Glasgow willingness to pay estimates to the rest of the United Kingdom yields an aggregate discounted total willingness to pay of £1,952 million, or approximately $3.5 billion.[70] The most important social capital benefits identified by respondents were the uniting of people, creation of a feel-good factor, enhanced national pride, motivating/inspiring children, and the legacy of sports facilities.

The size of the perceived social capital gains reflects the widespread popular appeal of the world's largest mega event; the national, rather than regional or local, identification with it; and the international attention it attracts not only for the two-week period of competitions, but also for a period of many years before and after the event. Nevertheless, the $3.5 billion aggregate CVM amount was far short of the $16 billion cost of hosting the Games.

Direct Payment: An Alternate Approach to Paying for Social Capital

While subsidizing major league facilities may be viewed as a way to compensate property owners for the social capital their franchises generate, an alternative approach would be to make a direct payment to them each year out of tax funds. This parallels the collegiate situation in that in those instances where general student fee support is forthcoming, the funds usually go to athletic programs rather than facilities.

When the New York Yankees suggested that the city play a major role in financing a new stadium for them, one respected commentator suggested that instead of subsidizing a new stadium, the city could just hand the Yankees $10 million each year. Or even better, the city could pay a fixed incentive sum for each game won, with a million-dollar bonus for winning the pennant.[71] This latter proposal would tie the subsidy directly to winning, which is an important dimension of social capital.

Direct payments to franchises, beyond subsidies for new facilities, are a feature of many stadium lease contracts. These payments may be for facility maintenance costs, to purchase unsold tickets, or to guarantee the franchise a given annual gross revenue. For example, to retain its NFL franchise in the 1990s, the city of Indianapolis agreed to guarantee that the Colts' gross revenues would be at the average of all the NFL teams. To escape this subsidy payment, Indianapolis paid $620 million, or 86%, of the $720 million cost of the Colts' new Lucas Oil Stadium. The new lease for that stadium provided for no guaranteed revenue from the city and tied the franchise to it for 30 years with no "escape clause." Without the stadium, the city's annual direct payments to the team in 2010 would have been approximately $20 million with the prospect that this subsidy would continue to increase, and the ongoing threat that the team would relocate elsewhere.[7]

The preferred alternative in professional sports is to subsidize construction of a facility rather than pay an annual subsidy. There are at least five reasons for this:

- As the Indianapolis case illustrates, more of the financial risk is moved to the franchise. Instead of a guaranteed payment from the city, the franchise has to generate those revenues, which in a very small market like Indianapolis is challenging.
- Constructing a facility may help to secure political support from labor unions, contractors, property owners, and other members of the community elite who will benefit from developing a facility.
- Facility leases are for 20 to 30 years, so facilities are likely to be more successful than direct subsidy in tying a team to the city.
- A facility provides a team with potential rather than realized revenue, creating an ongoing incentive for the team to perform well and keep attendance high. Cash transfers from the city to the team would provide no incentive for team improvement.
- If subsidies come only in the form of facilities, then they do not establish precedents for other potential subsidy recipients who do not need a facility for their activity.

As was noted in Chapter 4, direct cash subsidies to wealthy team owners is more likely to fuel resentment from voters against politicians.[18]

SUMMARY

In Chapters 5, 7, and 8, it has been suggested that public investment in major sport facilities is consistent with their status as merit goods which was described in Chapter 4. Given that they are merit goods, such facilities should be subsidized to the extent that equates to the benefits from them which are perceived to accrue to the whole community. In Chapters 5, 7 and 8, nine potential community benefits have been identified: 1) direct economic impact; a legacy of structural capital from 2) built facilities, 3) complementary development associated with them, and 4) physical infrastructure improvements that they stimulate; and social capital from 5) enhancing a community's brand image, 6) attracting businesses, 7) attracting tourists, 8) community pride, and 9) social cohesion.

The discussion in Chapters 5 and 6 indicated that justifications for public subsidy that rely on direct economic impact from a facility are now viewed with skepticism by media, taxpayers, and elected officials. This has required advocates to redirect their arguments for public subsidy away from direct economic impact, and toward structural capital and social capital. This is the new frontier. If such justifications are valid, then they offer decision makers a way of retaining their integrity while supporting public subsidy of a facility. By shamelessly using flawed direct economic impact rationales to justify subsidies, elected officials and other community elites position themselves as being untrustworthy, manipulative charlatans with an agenda to sell. If physical and social capital are used as justification, and scientific measurement is commissioned to appraise their value and, hence, the appropriate subsidy to invest, then these proponents could reposition themselves as responsible keepers of the public purse.

Structural capital as represented by major sport facilities may serve as a catalyst for economic development, but its primary community benefit role is likely to be that it enables and facilitates social capital. Social capital refers to relationships, norms, and connections that bind people together and contribute to accomplishing collective goals. Its potential contributions may be manifested in five forms.

First, sport facilities may enhance a city's/country's brand equity, which is defined as the strong and distinctive favorable attributes that people associate with the place in their memories. Brand equity has two dimensions: awareness and image. Awareness has two roles. First, repeated exposure to a city's name may lead to increased affinity towards it. Second and more importantly, awareness is a prerequisite to image, since if there is no awareness of a city then there can be no image of it.

Image is the mental reconstruction of a place composed of beliefs, ideas, and impressions residing in an individual's mind. It is the defining element in establishing a city's brand equity. Since television created global audiences for mega events, hosting them has been used as a vehicle through which countries and cities seek to position or reposition themselves in the consciousness of the world's publics. A host community seeks to appropriate or "borrow" some of the attributes of the sport event and transfer them to itself.

A central role of sport in enhancing image is to establish a community (or college) as a "major league city." Even though this premise has obvious flaws, there is much public sympathy for the adage that a place cannot be a major league city if it does not have a major league franchise. The team or event is positioned as being symptomatic of a city's status, and as defining external perceptions of it. Some are likely to consider a sport team as a symbolic emblem, bell weather, or embodiment of the city as a whole. Thus, if a city successfully negotiates and implements a major sports event or franchise agreement, it may convey an aura of competency upon the city's leadership. Conversely, if a city loses a franchise, it may create the impression that its business and political leadership is incompetent; that the community is a "loser" and in decline; and that its residents lack civic pride.

A community's image is primarily determined by the mediating filter of media stories. There are four major concerns when a community has to cede control of its image to media. First, the media sometimes focus on creating news rather than merely reporting it, so there is a tendency to report the unusual, bizarre and negative even though these may be minor failings in the overall context. Second, the exposure a city receives during the broadcasting of an event may be minimal, because media focus will be on the event itself, not on the city that is hosting it. Third, the broadcasts of outdoor sport events explicitly communicate vivid messages about the weather in those locations, so if it is bad then negative perceptions are conveyed. Fourth, media are selective in what they elect to report, and if only minimal reporting occurs then there can be little image gain to host communities.

A second claimed social capital contribution is that major sport facilities will aid in attracting new businesses to a community. There are three conduits through which this may occur. First, major sport teams or events generate substantial media coverage. Some claim that exposure of a city's name or skyline that appear on television as an incidental by-product of a broadcast may arouse interest among businesses considering expansion or relocation. That is an optimistic and improbable scenario. Second, professional sport franchises and mega events are elements in quality of lifestyle that may contribute to attracting talented people to a community, and many "high-end" footloose businesses locate where talented people want to live. Third, professional and college sport facilities and mega events may be a catalyst for new business by offering companies the opportunity to network through the use of hospitality boxes, suites, and similar options.

Sport events create a platform that communities can use to showcase and communicate to extensive media audiences their attractions, features and benefits that may be appealing to tourists. However, gains in social capital from tourism are only likely if the event is part of a broader, long-range plan.

Many people receive personal psychic income from their emotional attachment to a sport entity even though they do not physically attend sport events. Such people may follow "their" team through the media and take pride in it. In this sense, a sport facility or event is an investment in the emotional infrastructure of a community. When these personal gains are aggregated, they constitute a fourth source of social capital manifested in the form of community pride and collective self-esteem. This role of teams as central components of a community's social fabric has been consistently affirmed by the courts.

A fifth source of social capital is the social cohesion that sport teams can provide, which refers to building community consciousness, identity and social bonding. It is defined by shared values, beliefs and experiences. Sport events can create collective experiences for communities that tie residents together across race, gender, and economic lines. The social cohesion justification for sport facility expenditures invariably incorporates a level of wishful thinking because the euphoria and community ecstasy usually evaporate, so the resultant social cohesion does not endure. Nevertheless, even though the cohesion is likely to be ephemeral, it is often real for that short time period, which makes it compelling when advocates use it to justify spending on sport facilities.

Efforts to measure social capital benefits are emerging. They seek to measure both private consumption benefits of those who attend sport events that exceed what they pay for in the admission price, and public consumption benefits which refers to the "free riders" who do not attend events but receive benefits from them. The preferred approach for measuring these uncaptured economic gains is contingent valuation method. This is a survey-based approach to eliciting the level of subsidy that individuals would be prepared to pay to support a new facility for a sports team or event. Although the number of these studies is small, they are unanimous in revealing that the social capital that residents perceive to accrue does not justify the magnitude of public tax expenditures on major league facilities and franchises, and mega sports events.

References

1. Eckstein, R., & Delaney, K. (2002). New sports stadiums; community self-esteem, and community collective conscience. *Journal of Sport and Social Issues, 26*(3), 235–247.

2. Keller, K. L. (1993). Conceptualizing, measuring and managing customer-based brand equity. *Journal of Marketing, 57*(1), 1–22.

3. Cornwell, T. B., Weeks, C. B., & Roy, D. P. (2005). Sponsorship-linked marketing: Opening the black box. *Journal of Advertising, 34*(2), 21–42.

4. Van der Lee, P., & Williams, J. (1986). The Grand Prix and tourism. In J. P. A. Burns, J. H. Hatch, & T. J. Mules (Eds.), *The Adelaide Grand Prix: The impact of a special event.* Adelaide, Australia: The Centre for South Australian Economic Studies.

5. Corliss, R. (1992, August 24). Build it and they will might come. *Time,* 50–52.

6. Danielson, M. N. (1997). *Home team: Professional sports and the American metropolis.* Princeton, NJ: Princeton University Press.

7. Rosentraub, M. S. (1997). *Major league losers: The net cost of sports and who's paying for it.* New York, NY: Basic Books.

8. Lenskyi, H. J. (2002). *The best Olympics ever? Social impacts of Sydney 2000.* Albany, NY: State University of New York Press.

9. Thurow, R. (1995, August 18). NFL's arrival stirs Jacksonville's conscience. *The Wall Street Journal,* B8.

10. Burns, J. P. A., & Mules, T. J. (1986). A framework for the analysis of major special events. In J. P. A. Burns, J. H. Hatch, & T. J. Mules (Eds.), *The Adelaide Grand Prix: The impact of a special event.* Adelaide, Australia: The Centre for South Australian Economic Studies.

11. Brown, C. (2011, October 21). Don't be so eager to see the team go. *Minneapolis Star Tribune,* A12.

12. Brewster, C., & Brewster, K. (2006). Mexico City 1968: Sombreros and skyscrapers. In A. Tomlinson & C. Young (Eds.), *National identity and global sports events* (pp. 99–116). Albany, NY: State University of New York Press.

13. Whitson, D., & Macintosh, D. (1996, August). The global circus: International sport, tourism, and the marketing of cities. *Journal of Sport and Social Issues,* 278–295.

14. Kennett, C., & deMoragas, M. (2006). Barcelona 1992: Evaluating the Olympic legacy. In A. Tomlinson and C. Young (Eds.), *National identity and global sports events* (pp. 177–196). Albany, NY: State University of New York Press.

15. Walmsley, D. (2008, May 22–24). The brand new strategy. *SportBusiness International,* 134.

16. Lavalle, N. (1995, July 23). Go for the win. *The Dallas Morning News,* 1J, 10J.

17. Brown, C., & Paul, D. M. (1999). Local organized interests and the 1996 Cincinnati sports stadia tax referendum. *Journal of Sport and Social Issues, 23*(2), 218–237.

18. Siegfried, J., & Zimbalist, A. (2000). The economics of sports facilities and their communities. *Journal of Economic Perspectives, 14*(3), 95–114.

19. Fulton, W. (1988, March). Politicians who chase after sports franchises may get less than they pay for. *Governing,* 34–40.

20. Schoenfeld, B. (2008, October 26). Where the

Thunder comes dribbling down the plain. *New York Times Magazine*, 60–65.

21. Euchner, C. C. (1993). *Playing the field: Why sports teams move and cities fight to keep them.* Baltimore, MD: The Johns Hopkins University Press.

22. Schimmel, K. S. (1995). Growth, politics, urban development, and sports stadium construction in the United States: A case study. In J. Bale & O. Moen (Eds.), *The stadium and the city* (pp. 111–155). Keele, Staffordshire, England: Keele University Press.

23. Shropshire, K. L. (1995). *The sports franchise game.* Philadelphia, PA: University of Pennsylvania Press.

24. Whitson, D., & Horne, J. (2006, December). The global politics of sports mega events: Underestimated costs and overestimated benefits? Comparing the outcomes of sports mega-events in Canada and Japan. *The Sociological Review*, *54*(2) , 71–89.

25. Feser, K. (2004, February 8). City hopes Super Bowl partyers return. *Houston Chronicle*, 1D, 8D.

26. Baumann, R. W., Matheson, V. A., & Muroi, C. (2009). Bowling in Hawaii: Examining the effect of sports-based tourism strategies. *Journal of Sports Economics*, *10*(1), 107–123.

27. Whitelegg, D. (2000). Going for gold: Atlanta's bid for fame. *International Journal of Urban and Regional Research*, *24*(4), 801–817.

28. Green, B. C., Costa, C., & Fitzgerald, M. (2003). Marketing the host city: Analyzing exposure generated by a sport event. *International Journal of Sport Marketing and Sponsorship*, *4*(4), 335–353.

29. Bentick, B. L. (1986). The role of the Grand Prix in promoting South Australian entrepreneurship, exports and the terms of trade. In J. P. A. Burns, J. H. Hatch, & T. J. Mules (Eds.), *The Adelaide Grand Prix: The impact of a special event* (pp. 169–185). Adelaide, Australia: The Centre for South Australian Economic Studies.

30. O'Brien, D. (2006). Event business leveraging: The Sydney 2000 Olympic Games. *Annals of Tourism Research*, *33*(1), 240–261.

31. More, C. (2011, January). South Africa the legacy: The world beyond football. *SportBusiness International*, 40–41.

32. Steiner, S. (1999, March 18). Olympic leap into the heart of tourists. *The Times*, 14.

32. Newman, P.W.G. (1989). The impact of the America's Cup on Freemantle—an insider's view. In G. S. Syme, B. J. Shaw, D. M. Fenton,

& W. S. Mueller (Eds.), *The planning and evaluation of hallmark events* (pp. 46–58). Aldershot, England: Avebury.

33. Gratton, C., Dobson, N., & Shibi, S. (2000). The economic importance of major sports events: A case study of six events. *Managing Leisure*, *5*(1), 17–28.

34. Schimmel, K. S. (2001). Sport matters: Urban regime theory and urban regeneration in the late-capitalist era. In C. Gratton and I. P. Henry (Eds.), *Sport in the city* (pp. 259–277). New York, NY: Routledge.

35. Lipsky, R. (1979). Political implications of sports team symbolism. *Politics & Society*, *9*(1), 61–88.

36. Kuper, S. (2010, February 28). Football is not about corporations, it's about clubs and communities. *The Observer*, 37.

37. Hamilton, B. W., & Kahn, P. (1997). Baltimore's Camden Yards ballparks In R. G. Noll & A. Zimbalist (Eds.), *Sports, jobs and taxes* (pp. 245–281). Washington, DC: Brookings Institute.

38. Lipsky, R. (1981). *How we play the game: Why sports dominate American life.* Boston, IL: Beacon.

39. Metropolitan Sports Facilities Commission v. Minnesota Twins Partnership. Hennepin County District Court, November 25, 2001 and MN. Court of Appeals C2-01-2010, January 22, 2002.

40. Poe v. Hillsborough County, 695 So.2d 672 (1997).

41. Clean v. Washington State, 130 Wash.2d 782, 928 P. 2d 1058 (1997).

42. Davies, L. E. (2006). Sporting a new role? Stadium and the real estate market. *Managing Leisure*, *11*(4), 231–244.

43. Bissinger, H. G. (2000). *Friday night lights: A town, a team, and a dream.* DaCapo Press.

44. Cook, B. (2012, August 13). Why Allen, Texas, built a $60 million high school football stadium. *Forbes.* Retrieved from http://www.forbes.com/sites/bobcook/2012/08/13/why-allen-texas-built-a-60-million-high-school-football-stadium/

45. Deford, F. (1996, September 9). Why cowboys became kings. *Newsweek*, 62.

46. Smit, B. (2004, July 25). Miracle men. *The Observer.* Retrieved from http://www.guardian.co.uk/football/2004/jul/25/sport.comment1

47. Atherton, M. (2010, March). Poverty turns defeat into priceless gift. *The Times*, 29.

48. Popham, P. (1999, June 7). Bats replace guns in war for heart of Asian sub-continent. *The Independent*, 6.

49. Philip, C. (2003, February 28). Nuclear rivals

take cricket tensions to fever pitch. *The Times*. Retrieved from http://www.thetimes.co.uk/tto/news/world/article1970393.ece

50. Houlihan, B. M. J. (2003, January 26). The risks of an Olympic bid. *The Observer*. Retrieved from http://www.guardian.co.uk/uk/2003/jan/26/olympics2012.olympicgames

51. Carlino, G., & Coulson, N. E. (2004). Compensating differentials and the social benefits of the NFL. *Journal of Urban Economics, 56*, 25–50.

52. Bhattacharya, S. (2006, November 26). Saints and spinners. *The Observer*. Retrieved from http://www.guardian.co.uk/sport/2006/nov/26/cricket.features1

53. Weiner, J. (1999). Stadium games: *Fifty years of big league greed and bush league boondoggles*. Minneapolis, MN: University of Minnesota Press.

54. Morgan, J. (1997). *Glory for sale*. Baltimore, MD: Bancroft Press.

55. Quirk, J. P., & Fort, R. D. (1992). *Pay dirt: The business of professional team sports*. Princeton, NJ: Princeton University Press.

56. McCain, J. (2004, January 26). The title that binds. *Newsweek*, 35.

57. Rosentraub, M. S. (2006). The local context of a sports strategy for economic development. *Economic Development Quarterly, 20*(3), 278–291.

58. Bronstein, S. (1990, September 23). World recognition gives Atlantans a new sense of pride in their city. *The Atlanta Journal and Constitution*, R12.

59. Cowell, A. (2012, August). Britain basks in a golden afterglow. *New York Times*, 14.

60. James, O. (1997, June 8). The serotonin society. *The Observer*, 18.

61. Price, S. L. (2001, April 16). A good man in Africa. *Sports Illustrated, 94*, 56–59.

62. Weiner, J. (2000). *Stadium game: 50 years of big league greed and bush league boondoggles*. Minneapolis, MN: University of Minnesota Press.

63. Johnson, B. K. (2008). The valuation of non-market benefits in sport. In B. R. Humphries & D. R. Howard (Eds.), *The business of sports vol. 2* (pp. 227–233). Westport, CT: Praegar.

64. Noll, R. G., & Zimbalist, A. (1997). The economic impact of sports teams and facilities. In R. G. Noll & A. Zimbalist (Eds.), *Sports, jobs and taxes* (pp. 55–91). Washington, DC: Brookings Institution.

65. Johnson, B. K., Groothus, P. A., & Whitehead, J. C. (2001). The value of public goods generated by a Major League sports team. *Journal of Sports Economies, 2*(1), 6–21.

66. Johnson, B. K.b & Whitehead, J. C. (2000). Value of public goods from sports stadiums: The CVM approach. *Contemporary Economics Policy, 18*(1), 48–58.

67. Santo, C. A. (2007). Beyond the economic catalyst debate: Can public consumption benefits justify a municipal stadium investment? *Journal of Urban Affairs, 29*(5), 455–479.

68. Fenn, A., & Crooker, J. R. (2005). "The willingness to pay for a new Vikings stadium under threat of relocation or sale," working paper, Colorado College.

69. Owen, F. G. (2006). The intangible benefits of sports teams. *Public Finance and Management, 6*(3), 321–345.

70. Atkinson, G., Mourato, S., Szymanski, S., & Ozdemiroglu, E. (2008). Are we willing to pay enough to "back the bid"?: Valuing the intangible impacts of London's bid to host the 2012 Olympic Games. *Urban Studies, 45*(2), 419–444.

71. Noll, R. G. (1996, April 11). Wild pitch. *New York Times*, A25.

Section III
Primary Sources of Capital Funding

9

Sources of Public Sector Funding

Over the last half-century, local governments, and to a lesser extent state governments, have played a major role in building and operating sport facilities from big-league ballparks and arenas to community golf courses. Chapter 6 showed that public financing may be used to subsidize some combination of land acquisition, facility construction, infrastructure development, maintenance, and operations of these sport facilities.

The money used by government jurisdictions for these subsidies comes from a variety of different taxes. The chapter begins with a discussion of the property tax and the sales tax because these are the traditional sources of revenue used by local and state governments to fund sport amenities. These two forms of taxation are called *general taxes* because the burden of payment falls on all, or a significant proportion of, taxpayers in a jurisdiction. These taxes are relatively difficult to impose because they usually require voter approval. The more general the tax proposed for a sport project, the broader the potential opposition is likely to be. Thus, the second section of the chapter discusses *selective taxes*. These include tourist taxes on hotel rooms and rental cars; cigarette, liquor and gambling, or "sin" taxes; a tax on players' incomes; and ticket surcharges. These are borne by a relatively small proportion of taxpayers and are, therefore, potentially easier to levy. These selective taxes have grown in importance in response to increased voter resistance to approving broad-based general taxes for sport facilities.

These taxes provide the revenues necessary to pay the public's share of costs, but the financial instruments commonly used by jurisdictions to actually finance new sport facilities are called *bonds*. The final section of the chapter provides a discussion of the types of bonds most commonly used for sport facility construction. Bonds are long-term debt instruments that allow governments to borrow the money needed to underwrite land acquisition, infrastructure, and construction costs. The revenues subsequently collected from the imposition of various taxes are pledged to repay the bonds over an extended period of time, typically from 15 to 30 years. The long-term repayment arrangement allows governments issuing the bonds to pay off the debt in annual installments, thereby avoiding the need for large tax increases.

GENERAL TAXES

General Property Tax

For generations, the general property tax has been the backbone of local government finance. More than 96% of property tax revenues go to local governments (e.g., cities, counties, school districts). There has been some decline in its dominance, but it remains the preeminent source of finance at the local level. In 1932, property taxes provided local governments with 92.5% of their total revenues.[1] Today, the aggregate figure has declined, but it still remains at approximately 64% of all local government tax revenue, with the specific percentage varying quite substantially across jurisdictions.[2]

The dependence of local governments on the property tax stems from their lack of alternative revenue-generating options. The potential of other taxes is limited. Local taxation of income, sales, or business could deter new business expansion and ultimately bring about shrinkage of the tax base. However, real property is immobile. Only a very substantial tax on land and buildings would induce people to move from their homes and places of work. Retail businesses must locate close to customers and, once committed, manufacturing establishments tend to stay because even severe property taxes represent only a small part of their overall operating costs. In short, real property offers a dependable base upon which local governments can safely levy taxes.

Theoretically, the property tax is consistent with both the ability-to-pay and the benefit principles of taxation. To the extent that the value of property owned increases with income, those with greater ability to pay will pay higher taxes. Property tax serves as a benefit tax because its revenues are used to finance local government expenditures on services that benefit property owners and increase the value of their properties.

All property owners are required to pay the property tax; but churches, charitable organizations, educational institutions, and other government entities such as state and federal institutions are excluded from paying the tax in almost every state. Classes of exempt property also may include cemeteries (42 states), hospitals (40 states), and historic properties (13 states).[3] These exemptions can inflict substantial financial problems on some jurisdictions. For example, a major state university located in a small city requires extensive support services from the city but provides no taxes to pay for those services.

Figure 9.1 shows a taxonomy of the types of property that may be subjected to taxation. The fundamental distinction is the difference between real property and personal property. Real property means real estate, i.e., land, and improvements on that land. It encompasses soil and things fixed to it by nature (trees, crops, grass, water, minerals, etc.) or by people (buildings, fences, etc.).[4] Most variation across jurisdictions as to which of the property elements shown in Figure 9.1 are taxed occurs in the personal property category. This includes everything that can be owned but that is not real property, for example, machinery and equipment, jewelry, household furnishings, stocks and bonds, automobiles, and boats. It is difficult and requires a complex administrative system for appraisers to locate, inventory, validate, and value personal property. The tax is highly unpopular with voters and is relatively easy for people to circumvent. For these reasons, a tax on personal property survives in only a few states.

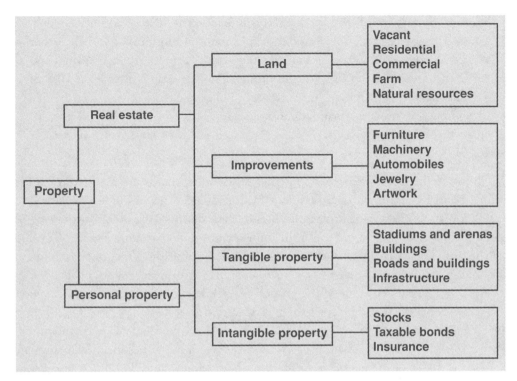

Figure 9.1. Types of property that may be subjected to taxation.

Estimates of the value of real property are called *assessments*. The task of determining the value of properties is assigned to an assessor, who is either appointed or elected. In most states, responsibility for assessing and collecting local property taxes falls to the county tax assessor. It is the responsibility of the assessor's office to list on the tax rolls each parcel of taxable property within the jurisdiction and, on a specified date each year (often January 1), to place a value on each parcel in conformity with assessment rules. Current market value is defined as:

> The most probable price at which the property would be transferred in a competitive and open market under all conditions requisite to a fair sale between a willing buyer and a willing seller, neither of whom is under any compulsion to buy or sell and both having knowledge of relevant facts at the time of sale. (p. 16)[5]

A state's tax law may or may not require that property be assessed at the current market rate. Indeed, in only 19 states is assessed value supposed to reflect 100% of market value. In the other states, the practice is to use fractional assessment, whereby property is assessed at below market value. Some of the states define assessed value as a fixed percentage of market value. Examples range from 70% in Connecticut to 10% in Louisiana. In some states (New York, New Jersey, Delaware, and Maine), the ratio is allowed to vary by local taxing unit. In 19 other states and the District of Columbia, the assessment ratio varies by property class. Such tax systems are usually referred to as *classified*. For example, in Alabama:

Class I property (public utility property) is assessed at 30% of appraised value; Class II property (real and personal property not falling into any of the other classes) is assessed at 20% of appraised value; Class III property (agricultural and forest, historic buildings and sites, and residential property) is assessed at 10% of appraised value; and Class IV (private automobiles and trucks) is assessed at 15% of appraised value. Note that agricultural and residential properties end up with most favorable assessments. That is the usual result in classification systems (p. 517).[4]

To illustrate the consequence of using an assessed value that is different from market value, consider a city whose assessment ratio is 30%. Thus, if a home is valued at $200,000, its assessed value for tax purposes in that county is $60,000. A tax rate of $2 per $100 assessed value would mean the homeowner would pay annual taxes of $1,200 to the city. The intent of this practice is to create an illusion. Fractional assessment makes it much less likely that an assessor's valuation of a property will be challenged.

Because the assessed value of the property is below market value, unwary property owners may believe that they are getting a concession and, therefore, be less inclined to challenge the assessor's judgment. In fact, the actual tax payment made by the homeowner is likely to be the same irrespective of whether all properties in a jurisdiction are assessed at 100% or some lesser percentage of their market value. This is because assessment levels can be counteracted by differences in the tax rate. For instance, suppose a municipality seeks $20 million from its property tax and the market value of taxable property is $800 million. If the assessment ratio is 100%, a property tax rate of $2.50 per $100 assessed value will yield the desired amount of money. If the assessment ratio is 50%, a property tax rate of $5.00 per $100 assessed value will produce the desired revenue. Thus, low assessment ratios will be compensated for by higher tax rates.

The aggregate value of all the assessed property within a particular jurisdiction is referred to as the *tax base*. Once the tax base has been determined by assessment, the local government sets a *tax rate* to meet its revenue needs. Tax rates are usually expressed in terms of dollars and cents per $100 assessed value. The function of the property tax is to fill in the gap between the revenues that an agency's budget requires and the amount that the agency expects to derive from other local, state, and federal sources. Thus, tax rates are established by dividing the local government's budget (projected expenditures for one year), less anticipated income from non-property sources (e.g., sales taxes, fees, fines, federal and state funds), by the total assessed value of property. For example, assume that the total assessed value of property in a community is $400,000,000 and the tax revenue needed by a government unit amounts to $5,000,000:

(a) tax rate = $5,000,000 / $400,000,000 = 0.0125

This may be expressed as a tax rate of $1.25 per $100 assessed value. The relationship between the budget needed and total assessed value always determines the tax rate. For example, if a city increases its budget expenditures and the assessed value total remains stable, the tax rate goes up:

(b) tax rate = $6,000,000 / $400,000,000 = 0.0150

Exhibit 9.1
Tax Calculation Examples

Assume that to pay for a sport facility, a community establishes an annual tax rate of 1 mill per dollar on a homeowner's property that is assessed at $150,000. The amount the homeowner must pay is figured by multiplying the assessed value by the dollar amount of the tax rate:	$150,000 \times $0.001 = $150
	
	 The same tax rate may be expressed as 10¢ per $100 assessed valuation:
	
	 A. Divide the assessed value by $100
	    $150,000 \div $100 = $1500
	
	 B. Multiply the result by 10¢
	    $1500 x .10 = $150

Conversely, if the assessed value or tax base goes up and the city budget remains the same, the tax rate will go down:

$$\text{(c) tax rate} = \$5,000,000 \ / \ \$500,000,000 = 0.0100$$

When the tax rate has been established, it is a simple matter to determine the amount of tax that will be collected from individual homeowners. The calculation involves multiplying the approved tax rate by the assessed value of taxable property:

$$\text{Tax Rate} \times \text{Assessed Value} = \text{Tax Revenue due from property}$$

Thus, if a property has an assessed value of $100,000 and the tax rate is set by elected officials at $1.25 per $100 of assessed value, then the annual tax to be paid by the property owner would be $1,250. Although the tax rate most frequently is expressed in terms of dollars and cents per $100 assessed value, it is expressed in some states as a millage rate in terms of mills per dollar of assessed value. A *mill* is $0.001. Thus, a millage tax of 1 mill per $1 assessed value is equivalent to a tax of 10¢ per $100 assessed value or $1 per $1,000 assessed value. Tax calculations using both of these approaches are shown in Exhibit 9.1.

Property owners are obligated to pay their annual tax bill. If they fail to do so, then a tax lien can be attached to the property. This gives a jurisdiction the power to have the property sold and the proceeds applied to delinquent taxes, penalties, and accrued interest. However, if they believe the tax is too high, property owners have the right to protest and appeal the value at which their property is appraised for tax purposes. Each state establishes appeal procedures that jurisdictions must follow, and these are publicly announced. The procedures that property owners in Brazos County, Texas, must follow, for example, are specified in the announcement reproduced in Exhibit 9.2, which appeared in the local newspaper.

The newspaper headline in Exhibit 9.3 announces that the city council of College Station, Texas, decided not to raise the property tax in the coming year. Most residents in the community are likely to interpret this as meaning that the council is exercising tight cost controls and that residents' annual property tax payments will be the same next year as they were for this year. Claims of this nature are frequently made or implied by local elected officials and supportive media. However, such claims are likely to be

Exhibit 9.2

Property Tax Protest and Appeals Procedures

The law gives property owners the right to protest actions concerning their property tax appraisals. You may follow these appeal procedures if you have a concern about:

- the value placed on your property;
- any exemptions that may apply to you;
- the cancellation of an agricultural appraisal;
- the taxable status of your property;
- the local governments which should be taxing your property; or
- any action taken by the appraisal district that adversely affected you.

Informal Review

Call or meet with staff appraisers at 1421 Waterfield #A101 (409-555-8731) Monday–Friday 8 a.m.–5 p.m. Appraisal Review Board policy requires that you meet with a staff appraiser before the date of your hearing.

Review by the Appraisal Review Board

If you can't resolve your problem informally with the appraisal district staff, you may have your case heard by the appraisal review board (ARB). You must file a timely notice of protest by June 12th. The ARB is an independent board of citizens that reviews problems with appraisal or other concerns listed above. It has the power to order the appraisal district to make the necessary changes to solve problems. If you file a written request for an ARB hearing (called a Notice of Protest) before the deadline, the ARB will set your case for a hearing. You'll receive written notice of the time, date and place of the hearing. The hearing will be informal. You and the appraisal district representative will be asked to present evidence about your case. The ARB will make its decision based on the evidence presented. You can get a copy of a protect form from the appraisal district office at 1421 Waterfield #Al01, Bryan, TX, or call 409-555-8731.

Note: You shouldn't try to contact ARB members outside of the hearing. The law requires ARB members to sign an affidavit saying that they haven't talked about your case before the ARB hears it.

Review by the District Court

After it decides your case, the ARB must send you a copy of its order by certified mail. If you're not satisfied with the decision, you have the right to appeal to district court. If you choose to go to court, you must start the process by filing a petition within 45 days of the date you **receive** the ARB's order. If the appraisal district has appraised your property at $1,000,000 or more, you must file a notice of appeal with the chief appraiser within 15 days of the date on which you receive the ARB's order.

More Information

You can get more information by contacting your appraisal district at 1421 Waterfield #Al01, Bryan, TX (409-555-8731). You can also get a pamphlet describing how to prepare a protest from the appraisal district **or** from the State Comptroller's Property Tax Division at P.O. Box 13528, Austin, TX 78711–3528.

Deadline for Filing Protests with the ADD

Usual Deadline

On or before May 31st (or 30 days after a notice of appraised value was mailed to you, whichever is later). THE DEADLINE FOR FILING A PROTEST IS JUNE 12th FOR BRAZOS COUNTY APPRAISAL DISTRICT. Late protests are allowed if you miss the usual deadline for good cause. Good cause is some reason beyond your control, like a medical emergency. The ARB decides whether you have good cause.

Late protests are due the day before the appraisal review board approves records for the year. Contact your appraisal district for more information.

THE BRAZOS COUNTY APPRAISAL REVIEW BOARD EXPECTS TO APPROVE THE RECORDS BY JULY 18th.

Special Deadlines

For change of use (the appraisal district informed you that you are losing agricultural appraisal because you changed the use of your land), the deadline is before the 30th day after the notice of the determination was mailed to you.

For ARB changes (the ARB has informed you of a change that increases your tax liability and the change didn't result from a protest you filed), the deadline is before the 30th day after notice of the determination was mailed to you.

If you believe the appraisal district or ARB should have sent you a notice and did not, you may file a protest until the day before taxes become delinquent (usually February 1st). The ARB decides whether it will hear your case based on evidence about whether a required notice was mailed to you.

Exhibit 9.3

Property Taxes May Increase Without Raising the Tax Rate

Budget leaves property tax alone

By YVONNE SALCE, Eagle staff writer

CS plan won't raise property tax rate

College Station residents won't see a property tax increase in the proposed budget thanks to the enormous amount of growth in the city, said the assistant finance director.

The College Station City Council received the city's proposed budget at Wednesday's workshop meeting. The $60.5 million proposal, which includes a number of additional staff members, is about $5.2 million more than the city budgeted last year. Charles Cryan, assistant city finance director, said the property tax rate of 44.50 cents per $100 property value will probably remain the same.

But because that rate is 5% above the effective tax rate of 42.38 cents per $100 property value, a public hearing must be called, he said. If the proposed tax rate of 44.50 cents is approved, Cryan said, it would mean higher property taxes for residents whose homes have increased in value.

The effective tax rate is the rate that, using current property values, will generate the same amount of tax revenues as last year's tax rate.

Under Texas law, any increase of 3% or more above the effective tax rate requires a public hearing. The council voted to hold a public hearing Aug. 25 on the proposed budget. At that time, the council is expected to schedule a public hearing for the proposed tax rate, also called the ad valorem tax rate.

"There's no ad valorem tax increase because other revenue streams are growing fast enough," Cryan said, listing sales taxes as the big revenue maker. He said sales tax revenues are up $150,000 more than expected. For the coming year, Cryan estimates $9 million will be made from sales tax.

---

grossly misleading because they ignore increases in the tax base. Later, in the body of the text in Exhibit 9.3, the reporter notes that the city budget is actually $5.2 million higher (9.6%) for the next year. Further, a city official acknowledges that if the unchanged proposed tax rate is approved, it would mean higher property taxes for residents whose homes have increased in value.

Exhibit 9.3 and the earlier tax rate example (c) illustrate how it is possible in communities where land values are escalating for a government body to announce, rather magnanimously, its plan to reduce the tax rate. Actually, its claim often is based on the value of the property base having grown so much that the council can afford to reduce the tax rate substantially without losing any property tax revenue. Hence, even when reductions in the tax rate are announced, it is probable that the actual tax the property owner is required to pay will increase.

To counter the possibility that taxpayers may be misled in this way, some states require all taxing jurisdictions to announce publicly their proposed *effective* tax for the coming year and to hold public hearings to discuss it before approving it. The effective tax rate enables the public to evaluate the relationship between taxes for the preceding year and current taxes that a proposed tax rate would produce if applied to the same properties taxed in both years.

Table 9.1 describes how the effective tax rate is calculated. It shows that if the city collected the same amount of property tax revenue from the same properties as it did

Table 9.1. Calculating the "Effective" Tax Rate

Last year's tax rate	$
• Last year's total property tax	20,010,500
• Last year's tax base	4,554,050,979
• Last year's tax rate	0.439400/$100
This year's effective tax rate	**$**
• Last year's adjusted taxes	19,693,182 (after subtracting taxes on lost property)[1]
• This year's adjusted tax base (after subtracting value of new property)[2]	4,654,356,349
• This year's effective tax rate[3]	0.423112/$100

1. This is the actual amount of property tax revenue collected last year, recognizing that for various reasons some small proportion invariably is not collectable.

2. By removing new property that has been added since last year, the comparison is with identical tax bases. It shows a small increase (from $4.554 billion to $4.654 billion)

3. To raise the same amount of property tax this year as last year ($19.693 million) a tax rate of 42.3112 cents per $100 assessed valuation would be levied. This is lower than the previous years 43.94 cents tax rate because the tax base has increased.

last year, then the tax rate (the "effective" tax rate) would be slightly lower this year because the assessed value of properties has slightly increased.

Revenues collected from the taxes that cities and counties levy usually are placed into the general fund of the respective government units. The general fund consists of revenue from multiple sources including property tax, sales tax, user fees, fines, and intergovernmental transfers. The general fund finances almost all government services including sport facilities and programs.

Property taxes are considered general taxes because the burden of payment falls on all of the property owners of the jurisdiction. These taxes are challenging to use for financing new sport projects because before they can be adopted to finance capital projects, a public referendum granting approval is almost always required. Voters are asked if they want to pay additional property taxes to support capital projects for schools, fire protection, new stadiums, athletic fields, or whatever.

The potential for using property taxes for sport projects has been made more challenging by laws enacted in almost all states that restrict the amount of revenue that can be derived from property taxes. These restrictions take the form of (a) limits on tax rate for overall local spending, (b) limits on property tax revenue growth, or (c) limits on the growth in property assessment values, which have been imposed in 20 states and range from a low of 2% per year maximum increase in assessed values of property in California, through 3, 5, 6, 8, or 10% in other states, to the highest cap of 15% in Minnesota.[6] These limits restrict the amount of property taxes that are available to meet cities' operating costs as well as their capital investments. However, many states do have an override option in their legislation that authorizes the limits to be discarded if voters approve increases beyond those limits in a referendum. In most states, an override requires a simple majority of the votes cast, but in a few instances, more onerous criteria have to be met. In the state of Washington, for example, a *super majority*, or 60%, is necessary to pass a property tax measure. Given these constraints, it is not surprising to find that in the last 10 to 15 years, property-tax-financed major league sport facilities have been rare.

General Sales Tax

Sales taxes are the largest single source of state tax revenues and the second largest source of tax revenues for municipalities after the property tax. Indeed, in some cities with large retail centers, sales tax receipts exceed revenues received from the property tax. All but five states (Alaska, Delaware, Montana, New Hampshire, and Oregon) impose a general sales tax at the state level. Thirty-five states authorize local retail sales taxes. Thus, local sales taxes tend to ride piggyback on taxes that the states levy, but the local rates are generally much lower than the state sales tax rates. The combined local-state general sales tax rates generally range from 4% to 9%, but the portion most commonly collected by cities and/or counties usually ranges from 1% to 2%.

Local governments can only tax those items that the state allows them to tax. Most sales taxes are imposed on nearly all transactions involving tangible products at the retail level, but often are not applied to the sale of services. Typically, food for at-home consumption and prescription drugs are exempted, and in some states this exemption has been expanded to include clothing. Purchase of these essential items constitutes a higher percentage of the income of low-income families than of high-income families. Thus, if these items remained taxable, the sales tax would be regressive. In some situations, sales taxes have particular appeal to local residents because a large proportion of such taxes may be paid by visitors from outside the jurisdiction who, thus, ostensibly subsidize the sport amenities constructed mainly for residents' use. This rationale extends to selective taxes on tourists and to the player income tax, which are discussed in the following sections of this chapter. It follows the popular political maxim: "Don't tax you; don't tax me; tax that person behind the tree." However, while this perception is promoted by project advocates, it is fallacious because it ignores opportunity cost, since the sales tax could be designated to support a host of other public services or to reduce property taxes rather than be earmarked for sport.

The general sales tax has been used to finance a number of major sport facilities over the past decade. Typically, a fraction of a percentage point of the existing rate is earmarked toward retiring a facility's debt. Often, these increases are introduced to a geographic area that is larger than a single municipality, recognizing that benefits from the facility extend beyond its jurisdiction's boundaries. For example, to finance the MLB Colorado Rockies stadium, the state legislature created the Denver Metropolitan Major League Baseball Stadium District and authorized it to impose a .1% increase in the sales tax over a six-county area to pay for the new stadium. When a general sales tax is imposed over a broader area, the magnitude of the tax needed to produce necessary revenues is substantially smaller than a tax applied in a single municipality. In these situations, an important corollary for advocates is that the individual incremental tax burdens are likely to be too small to encourage active resistance.

The broader geographical area may reduce the inequity that occurs when inner-city taxpayers finance a facility which primarily benefits wealthy suburbanites. In some instances, broadening the geographical area may increase the proportion of those impacted by the sales tax who support the sport project. Thus, opposition to sport tax proposals in Cleveland and Denver was offset by support from the beyond the city limits. However, the converse may also occur. For example, efforts by Cincinnati's political and business leaders to involve a broader area in financing new stadiums for the Bengals and Reds were rebuffed by outlying suburban counties, which were not supportive of their residents' tax dollars being spent in downtown Cincinnati.[7]

The sales tax is consistently identified in opinion polls as the least objectionable tax to voters. Hence, if a general tax source of funds is used for a sport project, it is more likely to be a sales than a property tax. As with the property tax, voter approval is generally necessary for a jurisdiction to levy a general sales tax because its burden is borne by all residents. Other facilities that have been at least partially funded by a general sales tax include:

- The city of Carbondale, Illinois, which approved a half-cent sales tax increase to help pay for building a new football stadium for Southern Illinois University and renovating the basketball arena.
- Southeast Wisconsin Professional Baseball District levied a .1% increase in sales tax over a five-county area to partially finance Miller Park for the Milwaukee Brewers.
- King County, Washington; Maricopa County, Arizona; Arlington, Texas; and Hamilton County, Ohio imposed sales tax increases of .5% for Safeco Field, .25% for Chase Field, .5% for the Ballpark in Arlington, and .5% for Great American Ball Park, respectively.

SELECTIVE TAXES

Selective taxes are borne by a relatively small proportion of residents. Selective sales taxes target non-residents and consumers of cigarettes, alcohol, and gambling because there is likely to be relatively little political resistance to raising taxes on these target groups. For example, the Governor of Illinois, speaking of the hotel-motel tax that partially underwrote a new ball park in Chicago, stated, "It's financed largely by out-of-towners. You can't get a better deal than that" (p. 277).[7] Similarly, when the Mayor of Chicago supported a $370 million public investment in refurbishing Soldier Field, he claimed the deal "won't cost the people of Chicago a penny" because it relies on the city's hotel bill tax. It should be pointed out that these types of observation conveniently ignore opportunity cost. The funds raised from all of these selective sales taxes could be earmarked for other public projects, which may yield "a better deal."

A limitation of selective taxes is that they are regarded by the bond market as being less reliable than taxes based on general property or sales taxes. This means that interest rates will be higher or the market may require the public entity to incur the additional cost of purchasing insurance to guarantee against there being insufficient revenues to make the annual debt payments.[8]

In this section, the most common of these selective sales taxes used to fund venues are discussed: tourist taxes, sin taxes, a jersey tax, player income tax, and ticket surcharges.

Tourist Taxes

Unlike the general sales tax, which is levied on a broad spectrum of sales transactions, tourist taxes are imposed on occupancy of a hotel/motel room and car rentals. They generally earmark a surcharge on existing taxes for a sport project, rather than impose these taxes for the first time, which would be a more difficult political challenge. Tourist taxes are thought to be relatively price insensitive because they are often business related, and hence tax deductible, so their imposition does not adversely impact demand.

The justification for levying these taxes is that tourist visitors will be the likely beneficiaries of sport events, stadiums and arenas, so it is appropriate to finance them from these tax gains. This assumes they serve as attractions that lead to out-of-town visitors occupying hotel rooms and renting automobiles as a part of their desire to experience a major league sporting event. However, it was noted in Chapter 6 that spectators at most major facilities and events are locals, so the assumption of a nexus between sport facilities and tourists is often attacked by the tourist industry. A Tourist Industry Association spokeswoman said, "It is really becoming ridiculous any way you look at it. It's nothing short of political cowardice. Cities are ready to tax people who won't be there to utilize it" (p. 1).[9] Examples of major league facilities funded mainly from tourist taxes include:

- At Houston's Minute Maid Park, tourist taxes were used to pay for 84% of the public's $215 million contribution.
- At Seattle's Safeco Field, tourist taxes accounted for 60% of the public's $372 million share.
- In Dallas, tourist taxes paid 50% of the public sector's $125 million toward the American Airlines Arena.
- The NHL Florida Panthers Arena cost $185 million, which was fully funded by Broward County earmarking a 2% tourist tax for this purpose.[10]

Tourist taxes are politically attractive for two reasons. First, in most states they do not require voter approval, whereas this is often required at the local level for general sales tax increases. Second, it transfers costs to many nonresident visitors who do not vote on tax increases and are unlikely even to realize that the tax is underwriting sport facilities and events.

The hotel-motel tax is levied on room accommodations or occupancy, charged either per night or as a percentage of the room rate. Frequently, it is imposed by both state and local governments. Usually, it is mandated that revenues from the tax have to be used for tourism development and promotion. Since many sport events attract visitors from outside the host community who are likely to stay overnight, their costs often are eligible to be underwritten by hotel-motel tax revenues. Ostensibly, those who appear most likely to oppose the tax are a community's hoteliers because they are required to add it to their guests' bills and collect it. However, sport events are likely to help fill rooms; therefore, hoteliers may support such taxes.

A tax on car rentals has become an increasingly popular mechanism for financing sport facilities. For example, in Dallas, Houston, Tampa, and San Antonio a 5% tax is added to every car rental charge, while in King County (Seattle) and Detroit a 2% car rental tax is collected, and the funds are earmarked to retire bonds for new arenas or stadiums in those communities. Thus, an individual paying a weekly car rental rate of $350 in Dallas would be charged an extra $17.50 tax, all of which goes to retiring the debt of the American Airlines Center. The two counties in which the Atlanta Hartsfield International Airport is located agreed to impose a 3% car rental tax to repay $72.5 million in bond funding for public off-site improvements associated with the $184 million Philips Arena, which hosts the NBA Hawks.

One prominent public official in Houston commented, "Fair or unfair, it's the easiest thing to do. Of course, the team ought to pay. But, the average citizen in Houston doesn't face the [car] rental tax every day, and the attitude toward the tax is very favorable" (p. 9).[11] Although advocates argue that a car rental tax is paid primarily by out-of-town visitors, the car rental industry in San Antonio stated that approximately half of all car rentals were booked by local residents.[12] Because half of the $120 million gross revenue in San Antonio is paid by locals, residents paid $3 million a year in new taxes to fund the NBA Spurs' arena. These arguments were used by a coalition of car rental agencies to fight against the imposition of new taxes on them in Kansas City to build a new arena designed to attract an NBA franchise.[13]

Sin Taxes

Cuyahoga County applied a tax on cigarettes and alcohol sales to finance the construction of three major league sports venues in downtown Cleveland. Courtesy of Wikimedia Commons

The so-called sin taxes are those imposed on the sale of cigarettes, alcohol, and lotteries. Taxes on these items for sport projects are likely to be supported by segments of the population who have no interest in sport, because they are perceived to encourage changes in undesirable behavior, especially among youth. There is a belief that increasing the price of these items through a tax will reduce their use among young people, because this group has relatively little disposable income to spend. The conceptual flaw in using sin taxes as a funding source is that if the incremental increase in price does succeed in changing behavior, then the revenue stream for redeeming the debt will be lower than anticipated. The reality is that the increases in tax increment are likely to be too small to discourage the "sinful" behavior.

Nevertheless, the reservoir of public support for sin taxes makes them a politically attractive source of income for sport project advocates. Thus, for example, Cuyahoga County approved tax increases on alcohol ($3 a gallon on liquor and $0.16 a gallon on beer) and tobacco ($0.045 per pack) for 15 years to service $117 million in bonds for Cleveland's Progressive Field and Quicken Loans Arena. An overwhelming majority of voters (72%) subsequently approved extending these taxes for additional years to finance the Cleveland Browns stadium.

There is no reason to believe that sports fans are more "sinful" than other segments of the community, so there is no reason that smokers, drinkers, and gamblers should be expected to pay for sport facilities.[13] Indeed, critics point out that sin taxes are notoriously regressive. Not only do those with lower incomes pay a disproportionate amount of their income to purchase them, but the high price of admission to the major league facilities they often are used to finance makes it unlikely that these people will be direct beneficiaries of their tax payments. Thus, a previous owner of the Baltimore Orioles commented on the use of lottery funds to build their new stadium: "It's awful. Using it ought to be condemned. They won't even be able to afford the buck that it takes to get there on the subway. The underclass that plays the lottery so significantly, they are not the people who buy season tickets to baseball games." (p. 99)[14]

Gambling in one form or another is now legal in every state with the exception of Hawaii and Utah, and 42 states have state-run lotteries. The lottery tax is built into the price of the tickets, and these are disproportionately purchased by low-income people. However, this inverse income redistribution makes lotteries an appealing funding choice for advocates because the poor and uneducated are less likely either to organize against a sport project or to vote in a referendum on it, than other segments of the community. Among the major league facilities partially supported by lottery funds are the Baltimore Orioles Park and PSINet Stadium at Camden Yards, and SafeCo Field and Seahawk Stadium in Seattle.

While sin taxes are more attractive political options than general sales or property taxes, debates around designating them for sport projects rarely discuss their opportunity costs. The cost of the sport facility is not paid for by the "sinner!"[8] It is paid for by the whole community who could have benefitted from the sin taxes being designated for other pressing public needs or to reduce their property or general sales taxes. This point was made in the public debate over the use of sin taxes to fund the Cleveland Gateway Complex. Some were outraged that it was "decided that the most appropriate use of those taxes was for a stadium complex, rather than for either dealing with social service problems or dealing directly with the capital problem of the Cleveland public schools falling apart physically." The business community in Cleveland had a chance "to fix up those broken buildings, or hire social workers to deal with the kids' problems, or open up the schools at night so they could become stabilized institutions in a totally destabilized community." (p. 154) Instead, those business leaders backed the using of the sin taxes to fund Gateway.[15]

Jersey Tax

The notion of creating a tax on licensed sports apparel and memorabilia to fund professional sport facilities was introduced by the governor of Washington State in 1997. He
proposed a 10% tax on these items to fund the public's share of Seattle's proposed new
football stadium. He abandoned this proposal in the face of vigorous opposition, perhaps reinforced by the proximate presence of Nike across the state's border in Oregon,
and settled on less controversial sources which had plenty of precedent (i.e., an
extension of the state's bed tax and taxes on Seahawks tickets and parking).[15]

The idea of taxing licensed sport products was subsequently considered in Minnesota, where legislators considered a "Jersey tax" as one of the revenue sources that
could be used to pay for reconstruction of the Metrodome, where the Minnesota Vikings
play.[16] The tax would have provided funds to improve all four major league venues in
the Twin Cities: the Twins, Wild, and Timberwolves, as well as the Vikings. The proposal was to impose a wholesale tax on all licensed merchandise sold in Minnesota and
would have raised approximately $17 million. Minnesota did not have a tax on cloth-
ing, but as the proposal's main advocate noted, "You don't have to buy that Brett Favre
Jersey if you don't want to. It's not like we would be taxing a necessity." The idea was
not adopted, but it was an imaginative attempt to create a new user tax without affecting the general population, many of whom have no interest in supporting professional
sport teams.

Player Income Tax

After the Chicago Bulls beat the Los Angeles Lakers in the 1991 NBA Finals, California decided to extend its state income tax to Michael Jordan and the rest of the Chicago
team. Inevitably, the following year Illinois retaliated by imposing its own tax on players
from states that taxed visiting athletes. Thus was born the "Jock tax." Today, 20 of the
24 states that have a franchise in at least one of the four major leagues impose this tax.
Texas, Florida, Tennessee and Washington are the exceptions. Because these four states
do not levy an income tax on their residents, they are legally prohibited from imposing
the tax on nonresidents by the interstate commerce clause.[17] Table 9.2 identifies 12 major league cities that also impose a tax on income earned by visiting players. Thus, for
example, when playing games in New York City, players will pay 10.50% of their
income in tax (3.65 + 6.85). In many cases, this has been extended to those professional
athletes playing on the home team whose year-round residences are in other states.

The player income tax is based on a well-established legal principle that states and
cities may tax nonresidents on income earned for services performed within their
boundaries. It is a convenient tax for elected officials because it shifts the tax burden to
people who do not vote. Further, their schedules and salaries are easily publicly accessible so it makes tax evasion unlikely. It is a highly concentrated pool of wealth that can
be taxed with little enforcement.

Taxing visiting athletes has proved to be a fairly simple way to raise money, as it does
not take much to figure out what is owed. Players' salaries are published, as are team

Table 9.2. Player Income Tax Rates in U.S. Cities		
City	**Local tax**	**State tax**
Philadelphia	3.54%	3.07%
New York	3.65%	6.85%
Cincinnati	2.10%	5.92%
Columbus	2.50%	5.42%
Detroit	1.25%	4.35%
Kansas City	1.00%	6.45%
Pittsburgh	1.00%	3.07%
St. Louis	1.00%	6.00%
Pontiac, MI	1.00%	4.35%
Baltimore	3.05%	6.75%
Indianapolis	0.97%	3.40%

schedules. These schedules allow tax auditors to calculate the number of days athletes worked in their states or cities. The athletes are then taxed on the portion of their total salary earned in that jurisdiction. Auditors can run the numbers and send the bills. As a result, athletes may be paying taxes in twenty or more cities and states. The tax is payable irrespective of whether the player sets foot on the field or even if he does not make the trip with the team.

State laws differ somewhat. Illinois does not tax residents of states that do not have an income tax. However, Illinois also taxes the entire salary of their athletes and does not allow credits for taxes paid to other states. Most states allow athletes credits for taxes paid to other states.

The tax used to be based either on the *games played method* or the *duty days method*. The games played method can be illustrated using MLB's 162 game season. If three games are played in a given state, then the taxable income would be 3/162 of the athlete's salary. However, this has been abandoned and now the duty days method is used exclusively.[17] This refers to the number of duty days a professional athlete spends working in a state or municipality. For example, in Maryland duty days are defined explicitly as "game days, practice days, days spent in team meetings, promotional caravans and preseason training camps."[18] The total number of duty days is used to calculate that portion of a player's overall salary that was earned in a particular state or locale. The tax is then assessed on that portion of total salary earned in that taxing jurisdiction. Thus, in baseball there are typically 210 duty days, so if a player earned $2.1 million he would make $10,000 each duty day. If the player's team had three games in California, he would be responsible for that state's taxes on $30,000 of income.

Given the soaring salaries of professional athletes, player income taxes can result in a useful revenue windfall for state and local governments. For example, California, which has 15 major professional teams, receives over $100 million annually in taxes from visiting athletes. Michigan imposes a 4.35% tax on nonresident athletes and the city of Detroit an additional 1.25% tax. This means that a typical NFL quarterback will pay out around $10,000 of his salary each time he plays in Detroit to a city and state where he has no residence and no affiliation. Thus, MLB franchises favor Florida for spring training not only because of its weather, but also because the players are able to increase the number of duty days that are allocable to a state that imposes no income tax.

In most instances, these tax revenues are placed in the jurisdiction's general fund, recognizing that municipal expenses associated with staging games—traffic management, security, waste management, etc.—can be substantial, and these are paid out of the general fund. In some instances, the tax has been used to pay part of a public entity's share of a facility cost. For example, the city of Pittsburgh levies a 1% tax on that portion of players' wages related to their play in Pittsburgh. All revenues collected from the tax, estimated at approximately $800,000 a year, are dedicated to helping the City retire its debt obligations on PNC Park (Pirates) and Heinz Stadium (Steelers).

Critics of the player income tax, which is sometimes a separate law but more often is seen by states as a simple extension of an income tax to nonresidents, claim that it is deceptive, arbitrary, and unfair. The deception derives from the levy being seen by the public as a tax on multimillionaires who can afford to pay more taxes, but it is actually a tax that hits not only all players regardless of their salary but also the support staff of teams in the four professional leagues (scouts, trainers, broadcasters, logistical staff, equipment personnel, etc.). It is arbitrary because it targets only those athletes who play in the major leagues and not in the minor leagues or less remunerative sports. It is unfair because it targets a specific occupation, while those in other occupations who also travel for business do not have to pay taxes in each state where they work. Thus, it is rarely if ever applied to other entertainers such as pop singers, dancers and comedians, or to performers in orchestras, ballets or opera. More generically, critics ask: Is it fair they are taxed differently from investment bankers, corporate lawyers, airline pilots, truck drivers or any of the other professions who work in multiple states? Since President Obama threw out the first pitch and Sheryl Crow sang the national anthem at the MLB All-Star Game, should their "duty day" be similarly taxed? Legally, every worker who crosses a state's boundaries could be taxed, but only athletes and other employees of teams in the four major professional leagues are being systematically tracked down.

For the athlete, it is administratively complex since he is required to file upward of 20 state and city tax forms each year. Each of these has different tax rates; different definitions of what constitutes a "duty day"; and different rates on what is taxed (salary, per diem, complimentary tickets given to friends, etc).

There is a rationale for taxing player incomes to support the public sector's contributions to a team's operational costs or venue financing. It stems from the benefit principle of taxation, which states that taxes are justified to the extent to which those paying the tax receive direct benefit. Proponents of the player's income tax argue that because their states/cities are providing a market for visiting teams' personnel to earn money, tax on their income should go to them and not to the team's home state.[19] Clearly, a case can be made that players are significant beneficiaries of an improved venue. The rationale is strongest for those players in leagues with strong revenue-sharing agreements such as the NFL and NBA. Players in both of these leagues, by virtue of their collective bargaining agreements, are entitled to approximately half of the gross revenues generated by each league. In Chapter 4, it was noted that the new generation of sports facilities produces abundantly greater revenues than the stadiums or arenas they replaced. Hence, an argument can be made that players, particularly those in the NFL and NBA, are major beneficiaries of new facilities. More facility revenues ultimately translate into higher salaries. Thus, it would seem that proponents of a new sport facility could make a compelling case, based on the benefit principle, that a player income tax is a fair and appropriate source for venue capital.

Ticket Surcharges

Ticket surcharges may take the form of a dollar amount, usually between $1 and $3 a ticket, or a percentage of the ticket cost, usually between 5 and 10%. The surcharge is collected by the team and then paid to the public entity that owns the facility. Examples of dollar amount surcharges are the $1 surcharge at the Ballpark at Arlington, and the sliding scale at the Phoenix Chase Field where the surcharges are $0 on attendances under 2 million; 50 cents on those between 2–2.5 million; $1 between 2.5–3 million; and $1.50 between 3–3.5 million. The percentage formula is used, for example, at the Baltimore Orioles Ballpark (10%), and the Portland Rose Garden (6%). In some cases, the total amount from ticket surcharges is capped. For example, at the Ballpark in Arlington any amounts over $1 million remain with the team.

A surcharge is levied at approximately a third of facilities in the four major leagues.[10] Sometimes the surcharge is captured by the public entity taking all or a portion of car parking revenues, or by imposing an additional increment of tax on food and beverage sales inside the stadium. Surcharges have the politically important virtue of being paid by the fans who benefit from these facilities, which is more palatable than levying a general tax on the whole community or resorting to selective taxes on tourists or "sinners," many of whom have no interest in the facility. The revenues from the surcharge usually are designated either to service part of the debt charges, or to pay for maintenance expenses if the lease directs that these are the responsibility of the public partner.

While surcharges are equitable in that those who pay the surcharge directly benefit from it, unfortunately the amounts they raise are too small to make a major contribution to debt charges:

> This type of direct financing of new stadiums rarely raises a sufficient amount of revenue to cover the expense of building a new stadium. The average size of the public subsidy for the 31 stadiums and arenas built with public money for teams in the big four American professional sports since 2000 is just under $250 million. The average gross level of public funding for NFL stadiums alone since 2000 is similar. Finance charges on such an expense might exceed $20 million per year (assuming a 30-year, fixed rate, fixed payment loan at 7% interest rate). The average annual attendance for a team in the NFL in 2004 was roughly 539,000. If a new stadium is to be paid for exclusively through ticket taxes, the average ticket tax would need to be roughly $37 per ticket, a figure that would represent an extraordinary high 67% tax rate based on an average NFL per ticket price of $55. (p. 312)[13]

Small variations in the surcharge when combined with variations in attendance can result in wide variations in the total revenues collected:

> At Baltimore Oriole Park, for example, a 10% ticket surcharge on an average ticket price of $19.82, over the average season attendance of 3.554 million results

in $6.4 million annual cash flow to the Maryland Stadium Authority, or $79 million over 30 years. Conversely, the $0.25 ticket charge at Cincinnati's Paul Brown Stadium over the average regular season attendance of 47,000 yields $118,000 per year for the public, or $1.5 million over 30 years. (p. 108)[10]

While this funding mechanism is politically popular, it is resented by team owners. They consider it to be a loss of revenue to them because, in theory, tickets are already priced at the marginal demand level prior to imposing the tax. Indeed, if new facilities were fully financed by ticket surcharges, from the team's perspective this would be the same as the team paying for the facility itself.

DEBT FINANCING

The ability of cities and counties to finance the construction of sport facilities has depended on their ability to borrow substantial amounts of money over extended periods of time. Most public agencies finance major capital development projects in the same way individuals purchase new homes or cars. Rather than paying the entire purchase price in advance, or up front, government agencies pay for the cost of a new facility over several years. The needed capital for home construction is borrowed from a lending institution, typically a bank, which then requires the borrower to repay or retire the debt in a series of scheduled payments that typically stretch out over 20 to 30 years. In the case of publicly funded sport facilities, the revenues pledged to repay the debt obligation are derived from either general or selective taxes imposed by government agencies that were discussed in the previous sections of this chapter.

The downside to spreading out payments over a 20- to 30-year period is that substantial interest costs are incurred. For example, the city of San Antonio adopted an upfront payment approach to financing its Alamodome, which cost $174 million to build. Most of the money was raised by a 5-year surcharge of an additional 0.5¢ on the local sales tax, which was approved by the city's voters in a referendum.[20] The project director estimated that if long-term, 30-year, general obligation bonds had been used to finance the project, taxpayers would have paid a total of $435 million in principal and interest payments over the years of the bond issue. This would have required annual debt service payments of $17 million, which would have been equivalent to a 15% increase in the property tax.

Using taxes collected over a period of years to pay the debt charges emanating from major capital projects like stadiums and arenas is usually preferred for several reasons. First, by spreading the payments over an extended period, the tax burden borne by taxpayers in any single year is less onerous. For example, in a county that imposed a half-cent general sales tax increase to fund a new stadium, a household that spent $15,000 a year on taxable goods and services in the county would pay an additional $75 in taxes. Hypothetically, if 200,000 households were to spend at the same level on average, the general sales tax would produce $15 million in new revenues. That amount, if perceived by lending institutions to be a stable stream of revenue, could secure a construction loan for as much as $150 million. This approach is likely to be more palatable than asking each of those 200,000 households to pay $750 in additional taxes in one year to pay for the facility, the amount that would be required if the $150 million facility were funded by a one-time, up-front payment. When the Colorado Rockies' ballpark was being financed by residents of the Denver metropolitan area, the following comment was made: "We're not talking about big dollars. It's a twelve-pack of Coca-Cola per taxpayer in the district, it's not a big deal. Is that worth the price of having major league baseball in Denver? I think your average person would say yes, that's worth it." (p. 279)[7]

Second, from a political perspective, debt financing is a desirable approach. For many elected officials, guided by their preeminent goal to be reelected, financing that shifts the cost of a new facility as far into the future as possible is an attractive option. This extended-payment approach pushes most of the potential political penalties associated with increased taxes well into the future, so they become problems for political successors. Meanwhile, politicians responsible for the facility reap the benefits of creating a new community asset.

Third, from an equity perspective, the use of long-term debt financing makes good sense, particularly when general property or sales taxes are used to retire the debt. When the burden is placed on local residents, a system that defrays taxpayer payments over many years accommodates the reality that population turnover is a constant. If cities used alternatives to borrowing such as making a one-time payment in full, then some present residents would pay the full cost of the facility, but if they later left the community they would receive only partial benefit from their investment. Conversely, others moving into the community would receive benefits from an asset to which they had made no financial contribution. With debt financing, some measure of equity is achieved, because all residents contribute tax dollars and pay their share of the amenity to which they have access.

The method by which government agencies borrow money to finance major capital development projects like stadiums and arenas is through the sale of bonds. Formally, bonds are defined as a promise by the borrower (the public jurisdiction) to pay back to the lender (the financial institution) a specified amount of money, with interest, within a specified period of time.

Bonds are issued as formal certificates on which three primary elements are commonly engraved: a) the face value or principal amount of the bond, typically $5,000; b) the rate of interest, fixed at a specified percentage for the life of the bonds; and c) the date of maturity, which identifies the specific date on which the face value of the bond must be repaid in full. The dollar amount of the interest owed by the borrower is easy to calculate. The annual interest payment is determined by multiplying the rate of interest, often referred to as the *coupon rate*, by the face amount of the bond. For example, a bond with a face value of $5,000 and an interest rate of 7% would pay the lender $350 per year. Commonly, the interest is paid in two semiannual installments, which in the case of this example would be $175 per payment.

In a bond transaction, where a city borrows $10 million, it would issue two thousand $5,000 bond certificates to the lender. The lender would then hold the bond certificates until their maturity. In effect, the certificates represent interest-bearing IOUs. In most transactions, the maturity dates on the bonds are sequenced so that a prespecified number of certificates will mature or be payable each year. Under this arrangement, the public agency pays off a small portion of the total debt obligation each year. This gradual, sequenced payment is referred to as a *serial retirement schedule.*

Table 9.3 demonstrates two approaches commonly used by government agencies to repay long-term debt obligations. The left side of the table shows a *straight serial retirement* schedule, and the right side shows a *graduated serial* schedule. In both hypothetical examples, a $10 million bond to pay for a sport facility is being repaid over 20 years at a fixed rate of interest of 6.5%. The major difference between the payback schedules is the manner in which the principal amount borrowed is repaid on an annual basis. The straight serial approach retires the $10 million over 20 years in equal annual principal payments of $500,000. In addition to the one yearly principal payment of $500,000, the borrower (e.g., city or county) must pay interest (split between two semiannual payments at a coupon rate of 6.5%). The interest costs are based on the amount of debt obligation still outstanding. Consequently, in a straight serial arrangement, as the borrower pays off an equal portion of the outstanding principal year after year, the annual interest payments decline correspondingly. In the example, the agency pays $650,000 in interest costs in Year 1 (.065 coupon rate × $10 million total outstanding principal = $650,000). When the interest payments are added to the principal payment ($650,000 + $500,000), the total debt service payment in the initial year of the repayment schedule comes to $1,150,000. Under the straight serial arrangement, by Year 20 (2029) interest payments have fallen to a total of only $32,500 (two semiannual payments at $16,250 each) because the agency only has to pay interest on the final one hundred $5,000 certificates that remain to be paid.

In contrast, with the *graduated serial retirement* schedule, annual principal payments increase progressively over the duration of the borrowing period. In the hypothetical example shown in Table 9.3, the principal payments grow from $200,000 in years 1 and 2 to $900,000 in the final 2 years. Two differences are evident from comparing the alternative approaches to debt retirement. First, the graduated schedule is considerably more expensive than the straight serial option. Even though the basic lending terms are exactly the same, $10 million for 20 years at 6.5% interest, an agency using the straight serial method would have "saved" over $2 million. Using the equal principal payment approach, the entire debt service totaled $16.8 million. In comparison, the total cost of borrowing the $10 million comes to almost $18.9 million using the graduated payoff approach. Clearly, the more rapidly the agency can pay down the principal, the less interest it has to pay.

Given the significant cost savings of the straight serial method, why would an agency use the more expensive graduated retirement schedule? The primary reason for its adoption is that the graduated approach allows the agency more flexibility in managing its debt retirement obligation. This greater flexibility may be necessary when an agency is concerned about how much revenue will be available to meet its annual debt requirements. As shown in the far right column of Table 9.3, the total yearly payments under the graduated schedule are relatively stable over the duration of the lending period. The annual debt service payment does not exceed $1,000,000 in any given year of the retirement schedule. In contrast, due to the heavy interest costs on the front end of the straight serial schedule, the first five annual payments all top $1,000,000. In the example used here, an agency using the straight serial option would pay $5.43 million in principal and interest costs over the first 5 years. On the other hand, if the public jurisdiction were to use the graduated schedule, its total costs over the same period would be considerably lower at $4.31 million.

For an agency faced with some uncertainty about the amount of revenue that a new selective tax (e.g., players' income tax or car rental tax) may produce, the more conservative, albeit more expensive, graduated schedule would be the more prudent choice. On the other hand, when an agency has obtained voter approval to secure a bond through a general tax source (e.g., property tax or broad-based sales tax), virtually guaranteeing sufficient revenues, the least expensive borrowing option (in this case, the straight serial approach) would be appropriate.

A fundamental guideline associated with issuing long-term debt instruments is to not issue them for a period longer than the project's useful life. People should not be paying for a major sport facility after it is no longer in use: "If the debt life exceeds useful life, the project's true annual cost has been understated and people will continue to pay for the project after it has gone. If the useful life exceeds the debt period, the annual cost has been overstated and people will receive benefits without payment" (p. 408).[4] In the context of major sport facilities, if a facility is being built to accommodate a franchise, then *useful life* effectively may be defined as the period of time for which a franchise occupies the structure. Thus, this guideline counsels that the length of a bond's maturity should coincide with duration of the municipality's lease agreement with the franchise.

The main types of bonds that are issued to finance the acquisition or development of a sport facility are shown in Figure 9.2. The figure shows that the most fundamental differentiating quality among the various types of bonds is whether they are tax-exempt or taxable. Among those that are tax-exempt, a key differentiating quality is whether they constitute a *full-faith and credit* obligation of the government jurisdiction issuing them, which means that all taxpayers are responsible for their redemption; or whether their repayment is *nonguaranteed* by taxpayers, which means repayment is dependent only on revenues accruing from designated income sources. This section commences with a discussion of the differences between tax-exempt and taxable bonds and then proceeds to describe the characteristics of each type of bond shown in Figure 9.2.

The Use of Tax-exempt Bonds

Tax-exempt bonds can be issued only by governmental entities or by public benefit corporations serving as surrogates for government entities. The tax-exempt feature of these bonds means that the interest payments made to bondholders are free from all federal income taxes and usually from those in the state in which they are issued (if the state

Table 9.3. A Comparison of Two Common Types of Bond Retirement Schedules: Straight Serial Method

Maturity Date	Principal	Coupon Rate	Interest Payment	Total Annual Payment
6/1/10 12/1/10	$500,000	6.5%	$325,000 $325,000	$1,150,000
6/1/11 12/1/11	$500,000	6.5%	$308,750 $308,750	$1,117,500
6/1/12 12/1/12	$500,000	6.5%	$292,500 $292,500	$1,085,000
6/1/13 12/1/13	$500,000	6.5%	$276,250 $276,250	$1,052,500
6/1/14 12/1/14	$500,000	6.5%	$260,000 $260,000	$1,020,000
6/1/15 12/1/15	$500,000	6.5%	$243,750 $243,750	$987,500
6/1/16 12/1/16	$500,000	6.5%	$227,500 $227,500	$955,000
6/1/17 12/1/17	$500,000	6.5%	$211,250 $211,250	$922,500
6/1/18 12/1/18	$500,000	6.5%	$195,000 $195,000	$890,000
6/1/19 12/1/19	$500,000	6.5%	$178,750 $178,500	$857,500
6/1/20 12//20	$500,000	6.5%	$162,500 $162,500	$825,000
6/1/21 12/1/21	$500,000	6.5%	$146,250 $146,250	$792,500
6/1/22 12/1/22	$500,000	6.5%	$130,000 $130,000	$760,000
6/1/23 12/1/23	$500,000	6.5%	$113,750 $113,750	$727,500
6/1/24 12/1/24	$500,000	6.5%	$ 97,500 $ 97,500	$695,000
6/1/25 12/1/25	$500,000	6.5%	$ 81,250 $ 81,250	$662,500
6/1/26 12/1/26	$500,000	6.5%	$ 65,000 $ 65,000	$630,000
6/1/27 12/1/27	$500,000	6.5%	$ 48,750 $ 48,750	$597,500
6/1/28 12/1/28	$500,000	6.5%	$ 32,500 $ 32,500	$565,000
6/1/29 12/1/29	$500,000	6.5%	$ 16,250 $ 16,250	$532,000
TOTALS	$10,000,000		$6,825,500	$16,824,500

Table 9.3. A Comparison of Two Common Types of Bond Retirement Schedules: Graduated Serial Method

Maturity Date	Principal	Coupon Rate	Interest Payment	Total Annual Paymen
6/1/00 12/1/00	$200,000	6.5%	$325,000 $325,000	$850,000
6/1/01 12/1/01	$200,000	6.5%	$318,500 $318,500	$837,000
6/1/02 12/1/02	$250,000	6.5%	$312,000 $312,000	$874,000
6/1/03 12/1/03	$250,000	6.5%	$303,875 $303,875	$857,750
6/1/04 12/1/04	$300,000	6.5%	$295,750 $295,750	$891,500
6/1/05 12/1/05	$300,000	6.5%	$286,000 $286,000	$872,000
6/1/06 12/1/06	$350,000	6.5%	$276,450 $276,450	$902,500
6/1/07 12/1/07	$350,000	6.5%	$264,875 $264,875	$879,750
6/1/08 12/1/08	$400,000	6.5%	$253,500 $253,500	$907,000
6/1/09 12/1/09	$400,000	6.5%	$240,500 $240,500	$881,000
6/1/10 12/1/10	$500,000	6.5%	$227,500 $227,500	$955,000
6/1/11 12/1/11	$500,000	6.5%	$211,250 $211,250	$922,500
6/1/12 12/1/12	$600,000	6.5%	$195,000 $195,000	$990,000
6/1/13 12/1/13	$600,000	6.5%	$156,000 $156,000	$912,000
6/1/14 12/1/14	$700,000	6.5%	$132,250 $132,250	$966,500
6/1/15 12/1/15	$700,000	6.5%	$110,500 $110,250	$921,000
6/1/16 12/1/16	$800,000	6.5%	$ 84,500 $ 84,500	$969,000
6/1/17 12/1/17	$800,000	6.5%	$ 58,500 $ 58,500	$917,000
6/1/18 12/1/18	$900,000	6.5%	$ 29,250 $ 29,250	$958,000
6/1/19 12/1/19	$900,000	6.5%	$ 0	$ 0
	$10,000,000		$8,904,250	$18,904,250

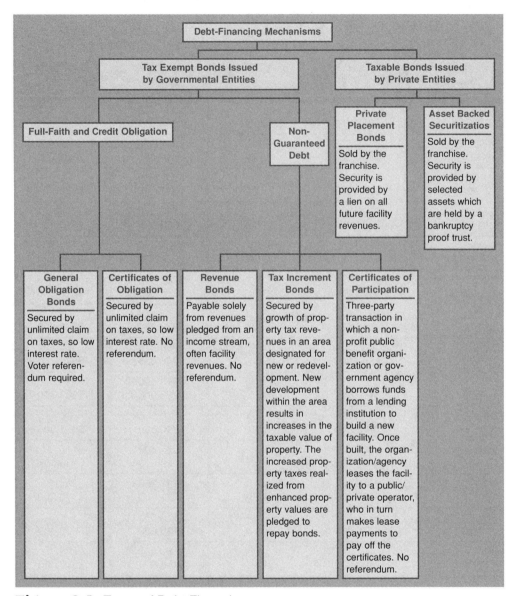

Figure 9.2. Types of Debt Financing.

has an income tax). This results in substantial tax advantages for those in the highest income brackets. Thus, Table 9.4 indicates that an investor whose marginal tax rate is 35% (that is the rate on the last dollar earned, and this was the highest level of taxation paid to the federal government at the time this book was written) should be as willing to purchase a municipal bond offering 5% interest as to purchase a corporate bond offering 7.7%. Taking away the 35% federal income tax that would have to be paid on the 7.7% return would leave a taxable yield to the bond investor of 5%.

Table 9.4 illustrates that the higher a bondholder's tax rate, the more attractive tax-exempt bonds become. The taxable equivalent yield of a tax-exempt bond is calculated by using the following formula:

Table 9.4. The Yield Required on a Taxable Investment Equal to the Yield on a Tax-Exempt Investment for Four Different Tax Rates					
	Equivalent taxable yields in these marginal tax brackets				
Tax-exempt yield	15%	25%	28%	33%	35%
3.0%	3.5	4.0	4.2	4.5	4.6
3.5%	4.1	4.7	4.9	5.3	5.4
4.0%	4.7	5.3	5.6	6.0	6.2
4.5%	5.3	6.0	6.3	6.8	6.9
5.0%	5.9	6.7	6.9	7.5	7.7
5.5%	6.5	7.3	7.6	8.3	8.5

$$\text{Taxable equivalent yield} = \left| \frac{\text{tax-free yield}}{100\% - \text{tax bracket }\%} \right|$$

For example, an investor in the 28% tax bracket who invests in a 5.5% tax-exempt bond would receive a taxable equivalent yield of 7.6%:

$$\text{Tax equivalent yield} = \left| \frac{5.5\%}{1-28} \right| = \left| 7.64\% \right|$$

The tax-exempt provision allows governments to offer their bonds more cheaply than private firms and to provide lenders with equivalent after-tax returns on their investment. In effect, this means that state and local public facilities funded by tax-exempt bonds receive a federal subsidy because their interest income is exempt from federal income taxes. Although the cost of borrowing differs depending on the fiscal strength of a public agency and its credit rating, that cost invariably will be lower than the cost that a private, for-profit organization would be required to pay.

Conceptually, the *equivalence theorem* states that it makes no difference whether governments fund projects through raising taxes or by issuing bonds. Since bonds are loans, they must eventually be repaid by raising taxes in the future. The choice is, therefore, "tax now or tax later." However, when a jurisdiction uses bonds to finance a sport facility, their tax-exempt status means all other American taxpayers share in its cost, whereas if it is funded by raising taxes rather than borrowing the money, the costs are fully borne by local residents.

If a government entity uses taxable bonds to finance sport facilities, its costs will be substantially higher. Similarly, if a government entity can be persuaded to make its relatively inexpensive money available to a franchise or commercial operator, the private operator will receive a considerable subsidy. For example, over the past quarter-century, the interest-rate differential between long-term taxable corporate bonds and long-term tax-exempt state and local bonds has ranged between 2 and 4%. Assuming $\frac{1}{30}$ of the bond principal is retired at the end of each year, it has been calculated that the savings (present value) as a percentage of construction cost at the 2% and 4% differential levels amount to 16.8% and 33.5%, respectively. Thus, on an arena costing $225 million, the savings at the 2% and 4% differential levels would be $37.7 million and $75.4 million, respectively.[21] This latter subsidy is $2.5 million per year over the life of the project.

From the outset of the first income tax law passed in the United States in 1913, the interest income of government bondholders was not taxable.[21] This enabled state and local government entities to issue bonds and use the proceeds to make loans to private businesses and individuals for any and every purpose. Typically, these bond issues were structured so that revenue in the form of lease fees from the private facility was used to fully pay the annual debt service, so state and local taxpayers saw no reason to oppose these arrangements. The government entity and private partner would sign an agreement under which the public agency built a facility with its capital to the commercial operator's specifications and leased it to the operator at a price that enabled bond repayments to be met. Leaseback arrangements of this type offered the lessee at least four advantages:

- The lessee was freed from providing capital financing for the development.
- The rental was tax deductible as an operating cost.
- The rental amount was reduced because of the government owner's ability to finance the development with tax-exempt bonds.
- The lessee did not have to pay property taxes on the development because it was municipally owned.

The tax-exempt status represents a subsidy by federal taxpayers. They have foregone the federal tax revenues which would have been paid on the interest income that would have been forthcoming if taxable bonds had been used. Thus, in allowing these kinds of arrangements, the federal treasury was annually foregoing billions of dollars through an inability to tax investors' interest from these bonds. In 1968, Congress addressed this issue and imposed stringent conditions that tax-exempt bonds had to meet before they could be issued. However, sport facilities were among a limited number of uses that were exempted from most of these conditions.

Despite these conditions, these bonds continued to flourish. By the 1980s, they accounted for almost 80% of all government bonds issued and attracted so much capital from investors that there was relatively little left over for genuine public interest projects.[15] From 1984 onward, it became obvious from Congressional hearings that there was strong sentiment among legislators to curtail the use of public tax-exempt bonds to develop facilities for private interests. Thus, many cities hustled either for their potential projects to be grandfathered into the legislation or to sell their bonds before such legislation was enacted. Some of the multitude of new sports buildings that were initiated in the 1980s (Chapter 4) were the result of deals put together when the threat of changes in the federal tax law became apparent.

When the 1986 Tax Reform Act was passed, it was intended to terminate all tax-exempt funding of arenas and stadiums for franchise owners. It imposed more rigorous restrictions, but it contained some loopholes that were subsequently exploited. This act stated that states and local governments no longer had the right to issue tax-exempt bonds to finance the construction of sport facilities IF (a) more than 10% of the stadium's useful service was consumed by a private business entity OR (b) more than 10% of the principal and interest payments came directly or indirectly from sport franchise revenues. The first provision is called the *business use test*. This standard is difficult for most professional sport teams to meet because most clubs use or occupy more than 10% of a facility's schedule capacity over the course of a year. The intent of this test was to ensure that the primary beneficiary of the exemption is the general public, not a private entity such as a sport team. If one organization has preferential treatment that exceeds 10% of the facility's use, then the business use test is violated and the bonds do not qualify for an exemption.

However, the Tax Reform Act stipulated that government agencies could still issue tax-exempt bonds by meeting only one of the two tests. As a result, those attempting to secure tax-free bonds concentrated on meeting the second provision, called the *private payment test*. To avoid exceeding the restriction imposed by this test, the bond repayment must be structured so that no more than 10% of the debt service is paid from revenues generated from stadium or arena operations. This precludes paying off the bonds from standard contractually obligated sources such as luxury suite leases, naming rights, and ticket-tax revenues. Dollars generated from parking, signage, premium seating, and concession sales or sales tax on them also count as private payment revenues. In general, any form of rent paid by private tenants such as teams to use the facility is applied to the 10% limit.

One potentially important source of facility-generated revenue, however, is not subject to the 10% limitation. The act allows monies derived from permanent seat license (PSL) sales to secure the issuance of tax-exempt bonds (a discussion of PSLs follows in Chapter 11). Despite the controversy over the sale of these seat reservation programs, the government agency and/or team attempting to build a new stadium or arena may find the interest cost savings realized from their sale a compelling reason to use PSLs. Hence, it has been pointed out that "cities prefer to use PSLs in order to preserve [their] tax exemption" (p. 23).[22]

The 1986 Tax Reform Act had an unanticipated effect. If a facility is leased to a team that contributes less than 10% of revenues toward the debt payments, then the private payments test is met and tax-exempt bonds can be used. There was no anticipation among the sponsors of the act that local officials would capitulate to team owners by signing agreements that repaid *less than* 10% of the debt charges. However, that is what has happened! In essence, this provision has resulted in many government entities' providing highly favorable leases to franchises and has palpably weakened their bargaining position. The result of these unanticipated effects has been that "the owners reap a windfall as they rent the stadium for a minimal sum, collect the ticket and concession revenues, and are relieved of having to pay any of the interest on the construction debt" (p. 150).[23]

The situation appeared to change dramatically when the Internal Revenue Service (IRS) issued rulings that said stadium-related revenues from two proposed New York City stadiums *could* be used to pay the debt charges on government bonds. The case is described in Exhibit 9.4. Widespread condemnation of the convoluted rationale used by the IRS in this ruling, which is described in Exhibit 9.4, led to its subsequent rescission in 2008 so the 1986 act's limitations continue to apply. However, this temporary aberration allowed New York City to issue tax-exempt bonds to finance new facilities for the Yankees, Mets and Nets, saving each of those teams hundreds of millions of dollars.

The nuances surrounding tax-exempt bonds in public-private partnership situations make it imperative that operating responsibilities relating to a facility are determined before it is constructed. For example:

> If tax-free instruments issued by the municipality are used to finance development expenses, it can be difficult to structure a lease without prejudicing the tax-exempt nature of the bonds. Similarly, although management contracts can be signed with a facility financed with tax-free bonds, they can be no longer than five years in duration if the incentive component of the manager's compensation exceeds five percent of its total compensation. Management contracts can last up to 15 years provided the incentive component of total compensation doesn't exceed five percent of total compensation. Your tax advisor and bond counsel can further advise you on the details of these IRS guidelines. (p. 58)[26]

Full-faith and Credit Obligations

Debts that are full-faith and credit obligations of a government entity have an unlimited claim on the taxes and other revenues of the jurisdiction borrowing the funds. The burden of paying these debts is spread over all taxable property within the issuing government's geographical boundaries. Table 9.5 identifies the two most common forms of full-faith and credit obligations: general obligation bonds and certificates of obligation. They are discussed in this section.

General Obligation Bonds

When it issues general obligation bonds, a government unit makes an unconditional promise to the bondholder (usually a commercial bank) to pay back the principal and interest it owes through its authority to levy taxes. When general obligation bonds are issued by local governments, payment is usually secured by property taxes. State governments, which rely on non-property tax sources, usually pledge revenue streams from sales or income taxes to repay general obligation bonds.

State statutes impose limits on the total amount of general obligation debt a local government agency can assume. These limits vary from one state to another. This restriction is generally referred to as the *statutory debt ceiling*. In almost all cases, the debt ceiling is expressed as a percentage of the total assessed value of property within a jurisdiction. For example, in the State of Oregon, local governments cannot issue general obligation debt that exceeds 3% of the aggregate value of taxable property within their jurisdictions.

Exhibit 9.4

The New York City Tax-exempt Bond Loophole

The 1986 Tax Reform Act said that if private sport facility revenue was used to pay for more than 10% of the debt service on private bonds, then this would make the bonds taxable and not tax exempt. In 2006, New York City found a creative way to end-run this rule. The city wanted to issue $943 million and $547 million in tax-exempt bonds to build new baseball stadiums for the Yankees and Mets, respectively, and to have the debt fully serviced by stadium revenues. This was ostensibly prohibited by the 1986 Act.

However, New York City claimed that although the Yankees and Mets were to use 100% private money to fully service the bonds, these payments technically were not being used for this purpose; rather, the funds were payments in lieu of taxes (PILOT). They were made because the city owned the stadiums and, thus, the franchises were not liable to pay property taxes.

The regulations pertaining to the 1986 Act specifically stated that PILOT payments which were limited to a property benefitting from an improvement (such as the two stadiums) were not a generally applicable tax but rather were a special charge. Elsewhere the regulations stated that a PILOT should be treated as a special charge if it is "made in consideration for the use of property financed with tax-exempt bonds" which was the case here.

The distinction between a special charge and a generally applicable tax is important because generally applicable taxes, such as property or sales taxes are not considered to be part of the 10% private payment limit that would disqualify the bonds as being tax exempt. Generally applicable taxes are defined as those that are collected for the general purpose of raising revenue to be used for government purposes.

The wording of the IRS regulation appeared to be specific in refuting New York City's claim: "For example, a payment in lieu of taxes made in consideration for the use of property financed with tax exempt bonds is treated as a special charge" (Section 1.141–4(a)(5)ii of the IRS code). Despite this wording and even though it was clear that the PILOT funds for the stadiums were not allocated for general governmental purposes in the same manner as property taxes with which they were being compared, the IRS agreed with the City's position and eliminated this clause. Even the City's own independent budget office called this "a very, very aggressive interpretation of the tax code" (p. 312)[15] The impact of this ruling was far-reaching:

> Suddenly, private-activity bonds, as they have been understood since 1986, can be used to finance stadiums because the 10% debt service rule has been eviscerated. In effect, taxable private-activity bonds have been reclassified as tax-exempt governmental bonds. (p. 105)[24]

Nevertheless, the IRS characterized this ruling as "a technical clarification rather than a substantive change."

Since PILOT payments are based on property tax assessments critics alleged that New York City overvalued the stadium properties so the PILOT payments would be sufficient to pay the annual debt charges. They valued the land on the Yankees site at $204 million whereas two other independent appraisers valued it as $26.8 million and $40 million. If $40 million was the correct valuation, then the tax-exempt bonds would have been limited to $40 million and the other $164 million would have to be taxable bonds.[25]

The Yankees' annual PILOT payments to service the debt are $57 million a year. Their annual savings attributable to the tax-exempt status in reduced borrowing costs on the $934 million ranged from $7.7 million to $15.7 million for a period of 30 years totaling between $231 and $471 million.

After the IRS issued this ruling, Congressional hearings were held and the agency was strongly criticized for it. In response, the IRS subsequently in 2008 approved a regulation prohibiting such shell games, so it appears this loophole will not be available to other sports projects in the future.

However, there was one final wrinkle. The New York Nets commenced building a new arena for the basketball team at the Atlantic Yards site in 2010 to open in 2012 using the same PILOT mechanism to service the annual debt payments on $511 million in tax-exempt bonds. The IRS ruled in 2008 that the project's planning was sufficiently far along based on the agency's earlier PILOT ruling that it should be "grandfathered" and excluded from the new more rigorous regulation.

Table 9.5. Summary of the Pros and Cons of General Obligation Bonds	
Advantages	**Disadvantages**
1. Lower interest rates then nonguaranteed debt options.	1. Obtaining voter approval is required.
2. Full-faith and credit backing virtually eliminating risk of default.	2. All taxpayers pay regardless of any direct benefits they may receive.
	3. Borrowing capacity constrained by debt ceiling.

General obligation bonds offer a number of advantages. Because of their full-faith and credit backing, they are the most secure of any of the available long-term debt instruments. Consequently, the borrowing costs associated with general obligation debt are considerably cheaper than any of the other debt financing options. The difference in interest rates between general obligation bonds and nonguaranteed tax-exempt bonds may be as much as 1% or 2%. In other words, it may cost 7% to finance a project using nonguaranteed bonds as opposed to 5% if general obligation bonds are used. The additional interest cost over the full period of the loan may be substantial. The difference between paying 5% and 7% on a 20-year, $5 million dollar issue is almost $1.5 million.

Because the sale of general obligation bonds represents an obligation that all taxpayers must meet, the government body desiring to issue them must first obtain voter approval. This has become increasingly difficult for financing sport facilities. The growing unwillingness of taxpayers to fund expensive sport projects from general taxes was discussed earlier in this chapter. As a result, there has been a pronounced shift toward the issuance of bonds redeemed by selective taxes that do not require voter approval, such as revenue bonds redeemed by tourist taxes, or bonds secured by sin taxes where voter approval has been easier to obtain. The pros and cons of general obligation bonds are summarized in Table 9.5.

Conducting a Bond Campaign

Although the challenge of convincing voters to raise their property taxes in support of new sport facilities may be daunting, a well-orchestrated campaign to educate residents as to the actual costs and benefits associated with a project can lead to a favorable outcome. This is particularly true for smaller projects that are perceived to provide widespread public benefit. Sport facilities that are good prospects for general obligation bond support include youth sport complexes, community swimming pools, and action or skate parks (e.g., skateboarding, inline skating).

Confronted with a multimillion-dollar bond proposal for the acquisition and development of sport facilities is likely to be intimidating to many voters and result in a negative reaction from them. Such large aggregate figures are misleading because they represent the amount that all taxpayers are being asked to contribute. Thus, it is important to present bond costs in terms of their impact on an individual taxpayer. Table 9.6

Table 9.6. The Effect of a $4 Million Bond Issue on Individual Homeowners' Taxes in a Hypothetical Jurisdiction

Property Value	Annual Tax Increase	Monthly Approximate Tax Increase
$100,000	$7.00	$0.585
$150,000	$10.50	$0.875
$200,000	$14.00	$1.17
$250,000	$17.50	$1.46

illustrates how this may be done. The owners of property assessed by this particular jurisdiction at $100,000 will be required to pay an additional $7.00 per year, or approximately 58 cents per month, to pay the debt charges on a $4 million bond for an athletic complex.

In addition to the cost of servicing the bond repayments, residents also need to be informed of how operating and maintaining the new facilities will affect their taxes. Thus, if it is estimated that operating expenses are $200,000, then residents should be informed that the ongoing tax implication for a home assessed at $100,000 is likely to be (for example) 35 cents per month. Presenting costs in terms of their implications for individual taxpayers gives voters a perspective that for "less than the equivalent of a cup of coffee a week," they can enjoy the benefits of the athletic complex.

Marketing theory offers three key concepts that are central for an effective campaign to pass a bond referendum. The first is *market segmentation*, which recognizes that residents are likely to have heterogeneous perceptions, attitudes, and interests toward sport facilities. Thus, there will be some residents who will not support any proposals that they are asked to consider because, as a matter of principle, they are opposed to increases in taxation. Investment of resources directed at changing their mind is likely to be wasted. Rather, efforts should be targeted at those segments of the population likely to be most supportive—that is, those who are likely to benefit most from the proposal.

In Dubuque, Iowa, authors of a bond referendum for a softball and baseball complex compared voter registration lists with softball rosters and determined that a large number of softball players were not registered to vote. A small group of softball players established voter registration booths at all softball fields. Finally, they mailed postcards to softball players prior to the election indicating the negative impact on softball should the referendum fail.[27]

In Waterloo, Iowa, volunteers staffed a bank of 14 telephones from 10:00 a.m. until 9:00 p.m. for four weeks before the bond referendum. They called individuals who had participated in the city's sports programs and activities. Using a prepared script and asking if people knew about the bond election and if they would vote *yes*, the volunteers spent less than 1 minute on average for each call. They also answered questions that were later compiled and distributed as most frequently asked questions and answers. A second call made on election day reminded individuals to vote and arranged for rides. The bond election passed with an 85% *yes* vote.[27]

The second central marketing idea focuses on the *benefit principle*. This involves addressing the question "What's in it for them?" This question is relatively easy to answer for the groups who will use the proposed facilities, but there is also a need to identify benefits that may accrue to nonusers. Some of these nonusers may not recognize that they are beneficiaries, and identifying the benefits they would receive may persuade them to support the proposal. Those nonuser benefits were discussed in detail in Chapters 5, 7 and 8 and may include:

- economic impact on the community created by nonresidents using the new facilities and spending money in the area while doing so;
- increased community visibility;
- enhanced community image;
- stimulation of other development; and
- psychic income and civic pride.

The third central marketing idea is *development of a strategic plan*. Passing a referendum requires much more than developing some promotional pieces and then hoping that enough sympathetic residents will turn out to vote on election day. It calls for a carefully organized campaign. Formulation of the plan should be based on research that identifies which segments of the community are likely to be responsive and unresponsive, which facets of the bond proposal are controversial, and which benefit appeals are likely to be most effective. The plan should address issues such as how to disseminate information, how to contact prospective voters, how to involve the media, how to raise funds to support the campaign, and how to organize the bond's supporters to maximize their effectiveness.

The campaign should build momentum steadily toward reaching a peak in the week of the actual referendum. It should begin 6 to 8 weeks before the referendum day. This allows sufficient time to generate the necessary support and still maintain the enthusiastic commitment of campaign volunteers. A good way to start the campaign is to hold a press conference to which representatives from all media are invited. Press packets containing prepared articles about the bond issue, illustrations, statistical data, and fact sheets would be made available to the media at this meeting. Media support is likely to be critical in the bond referendum, and close liaison should be maintained with the media throughout the campaign.

Websites, Facebook, Twitter and other electronic media, telephone calls, door-to door solicitations, television and radio shows, media advertisements and bumper stickers may all play a role in disseminating information. Jurisdictions are likely to provide details of the bond on their websites, and they may also directly mail literature to every resident or taxpayer, and pay for an insert in local newspapers.

Every civic and community organization should be contacted and an offer made to present information about the bond issue at their meetings. Some of the individuals in these groups are likely to be important opinion leaders in the community. For this purpose, presentations of 5, 10, and 20 minutes should be prepared so that different time slots can be accommodated. Endorsements from these groups and from prominent community residents should be solicited and then publicized. When these endorsements are publicly disseminated, many voters are likely to be reassured that the bond proposal has merit.

Convincing more people to vote *yes* than *no* in a bond referendum is likely to be a substantial undertaking. When the referendum outcome is known, it is important that all of the people who were involved in supporting it be recognized and publicly thanked for their efforts.

Certificates of Obligation

In contrast to general obligation bonds, certificates of obligation do not require voter approval from a referendum, but they are still backed by the full faith and credit of a jurisdiction's tax base. The legislative body is required to publish a legal notice announcing a public hearing of their proposed use. Like general obligation bonds, the debt is retired over a given period of years with property tax revenues. In the context of sport facilities, these instruments typically are used in one of the following circumstances:

- If the capital investment is not made quickly, then the opportunity will be lost. For example, if land suitable for an athletic complex comes on the market, there may be insufficient time to go through the lengthy process of obtaining voter approval for the investment.
- The legislative body has doubts that voters would approve the purchase, but its members are convinced strongly that the project is in the community's best long-term interest.
- They can be redeemed by designated income streams without recourse to property tax revenues.

By using this approach, elected officials commit their residents to paying for a facility with tax revenues without asking them. Such an action may be controversial and result in them being criticized and vulnerable to defeat in a future election. Hence, this vehicle may involve substantial political risks.

Nonguaranteed Debt

The resistance to full-faith and credit obligations has resulted in more public sector investment in sport facilities in recent years using nonguaranteed funding mechanisms. These are not backed by the full faith and credit of the government entity. Rather, they are sold on the basis that repayment will be forthcoming from designated revenue sources other than property taxes. If revenue from the designated sources falls short of what is required to make the debt payments, the government entity is not obligated to make up the difference.

Nonguaranteed debt instruments have three major advantages. First, in most states, direct voter approval is not required because the general taxpayers are not being asked to pay these debts. Second, they are not considered statutory debts, so they do not count against the government entity's debt ceiling capacity. Third, if the revenue accrues directly from the project, then the people who most benefit from the facility pay for it.

Investors who buy these nonguaranteed instruments incur more risk, which means that the government borrowers have to pay higher interest rates to lenders than they would pay on full-faith and credit obligations. However, cities often seek to reduce this risk either by purchasing insurance that guarantees the lender will be reimbursed by the insurer if the revenue stream is insufficient to meet the debt requirements, or by accepting either a real or a moral obligation to secure the loan. Accepting this obligation requires the jurisdiction to pledge either legally or orally that it will appropriate money from its annual revenues to meet full debt service on the bonds if the designated revenue source does not provide it. Jurisdictions take these actions for two reasons. First, they reduce risk and, hence, rate of interest that lenders charge for the bonds. Second, even though a jurisdiction has no legal obligation to support nonguaranteed debt, a default would damage a jurisdiction's reputation in the investment markets and make securing capital funds in the future more difficult and expensive.

A wide array of nonguaranteed funding mechanisms have been created, but the three that are likely to be most pertinent for development of major sport facilities are revenue bonds, tax-increment bonds, and certificates of participation (see Figure 9.5).

Revenue Bonds

Revenue bonds are particularly appropriate when a new facility is capable of generating enough revenue to pay for its own operations and any debt obligations incurred in its construction. Because revenue bonds are repaid from income produced by the facility and not from property or sales taxes, no referendum is required. They are secured by the revenues of the project being financed.

Revenue bonds have become a popular approach to financing the construction of a range of revenue-generating sports facilities, including golf courses, indoor tennis centers, athletic fields, and marinas. For these kinds of facilities, the revenue usually is generated from a variety of non-contractually obligated sources such as admission fees, concession income, and user fees. The fundamental requirement for the use of revenue bonds is that the facility has the means to generate sufficient income to cover both operating and maintenance costs as well as annual principal and interest payments. An illustration of how a softball complex was funded through the use of revenue bonds is provided in Exhibit 9.5. The example shows how the imposition of a modest user surcharge resulted in the development of an 80-acre sports park.

The financial feasibility analysis shown in Exhibit 9.5 demonstrates that over the 16-year borrowing period, the revenues available from fees charged to teams using the complex would almost double the amount needed to repay annual debt service costs. By Year 16, aggregate user-fee revenues total $905,020, whereas the total principal and interest costs amount to $463,562. The relationship between revenues available for debt service and the total cost of the debt obligation is expressed as the *coverage rate*. The far right column of the table in Table 9A lists the coverage rates for each year of the lending agreement. In no single year is there less than $1.55 of available revenue for every $1 of debt obligation owed. The average annual debt coverage for the issue is a substantial 1.95. Most financial institutions will require a minimum coverage rate of 1.5 for revenue bonds.

Exhibit 9.5

Developing a Softball Complex With Revenue Bonds

Johnson County, Kansas, used revenue bonds to develop an 80-acre, seven-field softball complex with three additional multi-purpose fields for soccer and for flag and touch football (all irrigated) and with a 2.5-acre lake for fishing and ice skating, a jogging trail, a playground area, a concession stand, a restroom area, picnic shelters, and a parking lot. A federal Land and Water Conservation Fund grant of $246,000 was matched with $260,000 of revenue bonds to develop the complex. The county already owned the land but they had no capital money with which to develop it. They would not back the bonds with a cross-pledge of tax revenues, so the revenue bonds had to be sold at full risk on the commercial market.

The Johnson County Softball Players Association was approached. They contacted their 4,500 members who agreed to pay a surcharge of $5 per player to provide the funds needed to repay the revenue bonds. This surcharge was in addition to the normal fee paid to Johnson County that covered all operating, maintenance, utility, minor improvement, and overhead costs. The athletic associations were pleased to cooperate because it meant that they would have additional facilities available for their use. The district had turned away more than 240 softball teams, and the park and recreation agencies in the Kansas metropolitan area had turned away 1,000 teams due to a lack of facilities. This was evidence of a substantial demand for new ball fields.

The bonds were redeemable from the revenues received from players and teams playing in the softball and soccer leagues and tournaments scheduled through John-son County. Table 9A illustrates that revenues from this source were projected on a yearly average of 1.95 times the necessary income to cover the average yearly principal and interest payments required along with operation and maintenance costs. This income was derived from the approximately 6,000 players (3,000 in each of two seasons) whom the county projected were likely to use the facility. A second source of security was unencumbered recreation fees derived from other recreational programs scheduled through the Johnson County Park and Recreation District. Because these had historically exceeded $100,000, this latter provision enabled the bonds to be rated AA instead of A.

The surcharge was imposed for one year before the county sold the bonds in order to demonstrate to the banks that the scheme was feasible. In that year, officials collected $36,000 from the $5 surcharge. This convinced a consortium of local banks to buy the bonds, which had a 15-year payback period at 8.5% interest. The park and recreation district agreed to place the $36,000 in a special reserve account as an additional source of security to the lending banks. This amount exceeded the highest yearly payment for interest and principal (see Table 9A on the next page) and was meant to be used only to prevent default of payment of principal and interest on the bond.

The complex proved to be a financial and recreational success. It generated substantial surplus revenues that the county reinvested in further capital improvements on the project.

(see table 9A on overleaf)

In addition to substantial coverage rates, lenders usually require that borrowers create a debt-service reserve fund as additional security. The size of the debt-service reserve fund is usually equal to the maximum annual debt payment. The fund may be established from the proceeds of the bond when it is issued or as an up-front capital contribution from another source. In Table 9A, the reserve fund consisted of $36,000 derived from a one-year collection of a $5 surcharge fee on softball players before the revenue

Table 9A. Financial Feasibility of Revenue Bonds

Year	# Annual seasonal softball teams	# Annual seasonal soccer/football teams	Total teams	Team annual special assessment maintenance fee	Total gross revenue	Annual (1) facility maintenance expenses	Available for debt service	Bond issuance debt service	Annual (2) debt coverage
1	470	77	547	$84	$45,948	$5,000	$40,948	—	—
2	800	77	877	85	74,545	15,000	59,545	31,212.50	1.90
3	800	77	877	86	75,422	16,500	58,922	30,387.50	1.93
4	800	77	877	87	76,299	18,150	58,149	29,562.50	1.96
5	800	77	877	88	77,176	19,965	57,211	28,737.50	1.99
6	800	77	877	102	89,454	21,961	67,493	27,912.50	2.41
7	800	77	877	103	90,331	24,157	66,174	32,112.50	2.06
8	800	77	877	103	90,331	26,572	63,759	30,912.50	2.06
9	800	77	877	103	90,331	29,229	61,102	29,712.50	2.05
10	800	77	877	103	90,331	32,151	58,180	33,512.50	1.73
11	800	77	877	111	97,734	35,366	62,368	31,912.50	1.95
12	800	77	877	111	97,734	38,902	58,832	30,312.50	1.94
13	800	77	877	11	97,734	42,792	54,942	33,662.50	1.63
14	800	77	877	111	97,734	47,071	50,663	31,600.00	1.60
15	800	77	877	111	97,734	51,778	45,956	29,537.50	1.55
16	800	77	877	111	97,734	56,955	40,779	32,475.00	2.27*
							$905,020	$463,562.50	

Average annual debt coverage 1.95

(1) Total gross revenues and annual facility maintenance expenses require an increase in annual team assessments to cover anticipated increased in annual costs.

(2) Actual debt service.

*Coverage for Year 16 includes $36,000 in Bond Reserve

Exhibit 9.6

Financing Golf Facilities with Revenue Bonds

The Fairfax County Park Authority (FCPA) in Virginia financed a substantial expansion of their golf facilities with a revenue bond issue of $13,870,000. The bond funds were used to develop new golf facilities at the Authority's existing Twin Lakes Golf Course and Oak Marr Park, as well as the renovation of the clubhouse at its Greendale Golf Course.

The Twin Lakes Golf Course was an existing 18-hole course, which was 28 years old. Other than a small clubhouse (2000 square feet), there were no practice facilities or other amenities associated with the existing golf course. A portion of the bond funds were used to construct a new 18-hole regulation-length golf course, a new 4,000–5,000 square foot clubhouse, a 50-station practice range, croquet courts, and entrance road and parking improvements. There were also extensive renovations to the existing golf club, the removal of the existing maintenance facility, and the construction of a new maintenance facility. The cost of these improvements at Twin Lakes was $7,995,715.

The 137 acres of Oak Marr Park contained a recreation center, two soccer fields, a baseball field, and parking facilities. A portion of the bond funds was used to develop a golf teaching and practice center, with a 60-station driving range, a par-3 golf course, practice greens, a small clubhouse/control building, a maintenance building, a miniature golf course, and parking. Also included was improvement of the two existing soccer fields and elimination of the baseball field. These improvements cost $3,101,000.

The Greendale Golf Course was an existing 18-hole regulation-length course with an 1,800 square foot clubhouse. The bond funds were used to remodel and enlarge the existing clubhouse to include an array of new amenities such as pro shop, snack bar, dining area, and secured storage area for 60 golf carts. The cost was $490,000.

The total investment at these three facilities was $11.586 million. Revenue bonds were sold to the value of $13.870 million and total funding for the project consisted of:

Revenue bonds	$13,870,000
Investment earnings on the bonds	$1,394,000
Total available funding	$15,264,000

This available funding was spent in the following ways:

Capital investment in the three golf facilities	$11,586,000
Capitalized interest	$2,145,000
Debt service reserve fund	$1,166,000
Costs of insurance	$367,000

Capitalized interest is the funds used to pay the interest on the revenue bonds in the first three years. During this period, the improvements in the three facilities are being constructed, and the revenue stream from them that is used to cover the bond's principal and interest payments cannot start until construction is finished.

Debt service reserve fund will be used to make the principal and interest payments in any year in which the revenue stream from the golf project is inadequate to cover these payments. As an alternative to establishing this fund that gives some added protection to the buyer of the bonds, FCPA could have provided them with an insurance policy guaranteeing that deficits would be covered or a letter of credit guaranteeing to meet any deficit out of the FCPA's general fund.

Costs of insurance include legal fees, underwriters' discount, and other fees and costs of issuing the bonds. The bond schedule showing yearly payments of principal and interest is set forth in Table 9B. The coverage ratio projections shown in Table 9C (on page 366) were not extended beyond Year 14 for two reasons. First, the consistent upward trend line from Year 3 to Year 14 of the coverage ratio was likely to continue because net revenues continued to increase whereas total debt service remained constant. Second, projection of what demand and prices are likely to be become increasingly speculative as the time frame of the projection is extended, so such projections serve little purpose.

FCPA already operated five courses (including Twin Lakes and Greendale) and the average ratio of revenues to expenditures across these facilities was 1.55. Thus, the agency had a strong track record of profitably operating golf courses, experience that would give prospective investors added confidence in purchasing the bonds.

The debt service on the bonds was to be repaid from fees and charges generated by the facilities they funded. The operational revenues and expenditures of the facilities were

Exhibit 9.6 *(Continued)*

Financing Golf Facilities with Revenue Bonds

derived from a feasibility study that FCPA commissioned from a respected outside consultancy firm. Their complete feasibility study was incorporated as part of the bond prospectus, so prospective investors in the bonds could see how these protections were derived and evaluate their likely level of accuracy. The bond prospectus stated in bold, capital letters:

"POTENTIAL PURCHASERS OF THE BONDS SHOULD READ THE FEASIBILITY STUDY IN ITS ENTIRETY."

The bond prospectus also carefully identified the risk factors associated with investment in the bonds. These included that (a) the construction bids for the projects may substantially exceed the amounts available from the bonds; (b) completion data of the projects may be delayed substantially by the uncertainties inherent in construction; (c) demand for golf in the area may decline; (d) other new courses may provide competition that reduces the expected demand at these facilities; and (e) prolonged periods of inclement weather could adversely affect the demand and revenue projections.

This example is based on a Fairfax County Park Authority bond issue. It has been adapted here for illustrative purposes. The authors have omitted and changed some details in order to facilitate an easier understanding of the general procedure that was used.

TABLE 9B. Annual Principal and Interest Payments

Year[1]	Principal	Interest	Total Debt Services	Year[1]	Principal	Interest	Total Debt Services
1	00	$375,000	$375,000	14	$505,000	$658,000	$1,163,000
2	00	$900,000	$900,000	15	$540,000	$625,000	$1,165,000
3	$265,000	$900,000	$1,165,000	16	$575,000	$589,000	$1,164,000
4	$280,000	$886,000	$1,166,000	17	$610,000	$551,000	$1,161,000
5	$295,000	$870,000	$1,165,000	18	$655,000	$510,000	$1,165,000
6	$310,000	$852,000	$1,162,000	19	$695,000	$467,000	$1,162,000
7	$330,000	$834,000	$1,164,000	20	$745,000	$421,000	$1,166,000
8	$350,000	$814,000	$1,164,000	21	$790,000	$372,000	$1,162,000
9	$370,000	$793,000	$1,163,000	22	$845,000	$319,000	$1,164,000
10	$395,000	$770,000	$1,165,000	23	$900,000	$263,000	$1,163,000
11	$420,000	$745,000	$1,165,000	24	$960,000	$204,000	$1,164,000
12	$445,000	$719,000	$1,164,000	25	$1,025,000	$140,000	$1,165,000
13	$475,000	$690,000	$1,165,000	26	$1,090,000	$72,000	$1,162,000

1) The FCPA Bond Years end on July 15. Hence, Years 1 and 26 are approximate half years.

bonds were issued. A more complex example of the use of revenue bonds is described in Exhibit 9.6. The pros and cons of revenue bonds are summarized in Table 9.7.

A popular strategy used by governments to reduce the risk associated with revenue bonds and, hence, the interest paid on them, is for the jurisdiction to accept the risk by issuing certificates of obligation in lieu of revenue bonds. These do not require a referendum; the legislative body authorizes them based on a business plan that shows no

Table 9C. Coverage Ratios

Year	Projected Excess of Ratio Revenues	Operating Revenues	Coverage	Expenses Over Expenditure
1	—	—	—	—
2	—	—	—	—
3	$1,515,000	$1,077,000	$438,000	—
4	$2,976,000	$1,759,000	$1,217,000	1.04
5	$4,174,000	$1,869,000	$2,305,000	1.99
6	$4,379,000	$1,927,000	$2,452,000	2.11
7	$4,576,000	$1,984,000	$2,592,000	2.23
8	$4,645,000	$2,042,000	$2,603,000	2.24
9	$4,846,000	$2,102,000	$2,744,000	2.36
10	$4,920,000	$2,164,000	$2,756,000	2.36
11	$5,134,000	$2,229,000	$2,905,000	2.49
12	$5,211,000	$2,295,000	$2,916,000	2.50
13	$5,422,000	$2,363,000	$3,059,000	2.62
14	$5,505,000	$2,431,000	$3,092,000	2.66

Table 9.7. Summary of the Pros and Cons of Revenue Bonds

Advantages	Disadvantages
1. Reflects a "user pay" philosophy.	1. Higher interest rates due to their nonguaranteed status
2. Voter approval not required.	2. Restricted to facilities with "profit-making" ability
3. Do not count against the statutory debt ceiling	3. High coverage rate requirements
	4. May restrict participation because of higher user fees.

cost to the jurisdiction, which provides political cover for their use; but the interest rate is lower because if the business plan is flawed and there is a shortfall in revenues, this becomes an obligation of the jurisdiction.

Certificates of Participation

Certificates of Participation (COPs) are lease financing arrangements. Four entities are involved in the COP process. Their roles and the relationships between them are described in Figure 9.3. The process starts with an *intermediary organization*, which may be a governmental agency or a public-benefit nonprofit organization, selling COPs to a financial institution to raise the money to build the facility (flow 1, Figure 9.3). The

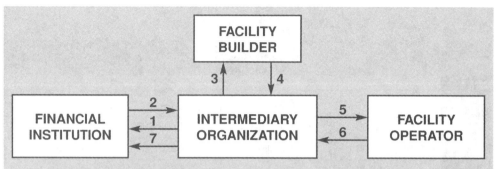

1. Intermediary sells COPs to a Financial Institution to raise the money to build the facility.

2. The Financial Institution delivers the funds to the Intermediary.

3. Intermediary pays a builder to construct the facility using the COP funds.

4. Builder delivers the facility to the Intermediary who holds title to it for the benefits of the investors.

5. Intermediary signs an annual renewable lease with a Facility Operator to run the facility.

6. Facility Operator pays a lease fee to the Intermediary that is sufficient to meet the annual debt charges on the COPs.

7. Intermediary pays the annual debt charges on the COPs to the Financial Institution.

Figure 9.3. Steps in the Issuance of Certificates of Participation.

financial institution holds title to the facility as security for its loan, but confers possessory interest rights to the intermediary through a long-term agreement. After receiving funds from the financial institution (flow 2), the intermediary contracts with a *builder* (flow 3), who constructs the facility (flow 4). The intermediary leases the facility to a *facility operator* (flow 5), for a lease fee (flow 6) that is sufficient to pay the annual debt charges on the COPs (flow 7). When the COPs are paid off, the title for the facility passes to the facility operator. The COPs are tax exempt because the lease payments (passed through the intermediary) are tax exempt since the project serves a government purpose.

The use of COPs is growing rapidly, and the increase appears likely to continue. A legislative body can issue COPs without a referendum, so they are a means of surmounting legal and political impediments to the use of traditional bonds. Hence, their growth has been particularly prominent in states severely constrained in their ability to borrow funds by tax or expenditure limitation statutes.

> For instance, California local governments can borrow only after receiving approval from two-thirds of special referendum voters. In that environment, one vote over a one-third minority could prevent projects from having the support, including the willingness to pay a tax to finance the project, of the remaining voters. The COPs provide easier access to capital markets without the referendum test; given the size of the state, the pressures on state and local governments there to provide services, and the rigidity of the debt constraint, it is no surprise that California has the largest share of the COP market. (p. 42)[28]

The ability to enter into these arrangements without voter approval is a controversial feature of COPs.[29] In some jurisdictions, voters have opposed their use because they are not subject to citizen review and they dilute the government's general resources. This concern is particularly relevant in relation to the public trust model (described below) because under this arrangement, the city assumes the role of facility operator, so lease payments are likely to come from the jurisdiction's general operating fund.

A referendum is not required because the lease agreement is not backed by the full faith and credit of the city, and certificates of participation do not count against the jurisdiction's debt ceiling. Payments of the lease are dependent upon an annual appropriation by the governing body. This differentiates the lease from regular debt because the present-year legislative body's action does not bind succeeding legislative bodies to pay the obligation. There is a moral, rather than a legal, obligation for the jurisdiction to pay the lease fee to the lender annually either from appropriations from the general fund or from a designated income stream. Hence, certificates of participation tend to be viewed as higher risk than traditional bonds and so tend to have higher interest rates. If the government entity fails to make the required payments, the financial institution has the right to take possession of the property and can operate or sell it. Typically, COPs are rated approximately one letter grade lower than general obligation bonds (the meaning of these ratings in discussed later in this chapter). As a result, interest rates on COPs commonly run as much as 1% higher than borrowing rates for general obligation bonds, reflecting the potential added risk that a government may not appropriate the annual lease fee.

Two models of COPs have emerged: the *public trust model* and the *public-private partnership model*. The essential difference between them is that in the former arrangement the facility operator is a public entity, whereas in the latter model the intermediary leases the facility to a private company.

The Public Trust Model

In the public trust model, if the lease fees are a revenue stream from a facility such as a sport arena or golf course and revenues that accrue are smaller than anticipated, then the public agency's general fund guarantees the debt service. The intermediary is usually a nonprofit organization acting as a public-benefit corporation, but in some circumstances it may be a different government entity. If a public-benefit corporation is used, its directors are likely to be publicly spirited citizens deemed acceptable to the government entity. When the debt is paid in full, then the sport facility becomes the jurisdiction's property. COPs tend to be used as alternatives to bonds and, thus, possess relatively long maturities (more than 20 years).

In the city of North Augusta, South Carolina, for example, the Riverview Park Activity Center was funded by $2.4 million from the city's capital projects fund and $3.12 million in COPs. A corporation named Riverview Park Facilities Incorporated was established, and its directors constituted the five members of the North Augusta Parks and Recreation Advisory Board. The North Augusta City Ordinance No. 92-02 stated:

Whereas, in order to finance the cost of the project, the City has determined to enter into a Base Lease Agreement whereby the City will lease the existing site whereon the Project will be constructed (the "Land") to RIVERVIEW PARK FACILITIES, INC. (the "Corporation"), and contemporaneously with the execution of such Base Lease, the city will enter into a Project Lease Agreement whereby the Corporation will lease back the Project together with the land, as improved in the manner discussed above (the "Facilities") to the City; and WHEREAS, the Corporation will assign its interest in the Project Lease Agreement to FIRST UNION NATIONAL BANK OF SOUTH CAROLINA, as Trustee for holders of Certificates of Participation in the Project Lease Agreement, which will provide the financing source for the project. (p. 1) [30]

The Public-Private Partnership Model

In this alternative approach to using COPs, the local government agency assumes the role of intermediary. Rather than taking direct operational responsibility for the new facility as in the previous model, under this arrangement the city or county engages a private company to manage the day-to-day operation of a new building. Using the services of a private operator is most appropriate when the project requires specialized knowledge beyond the customary expertise of the local government unit. In the context of sport facilities, such amenities as golf courses, marinas, ice rinks, and stadiums are good candidates for this type of public-private collaboration. A particularly innovative use of COPs is demonstrated in Exhibit 9.7, which describes the financing of Anaheim's Arrowhead Pond Arena[31] (now named the Honda Center).

In its role as broker of the development project, the city or county first procures the services of a qualified operator with a successful track record of managing the kind of facility the agency believes would be a community asset, such as a new ice rink, baseball stadium, or municipal golf course. The intent is to create a needed resource for the community. The inducement for the private operator, such as a hotel management company or owner of a minor league baseball team, is that the city can borrow the construction capital to build the new asset at a much more favorable rate of interest through the use of COPs. Because of their tax-exempt status, COPs can be issued at significantly lower rates, as much as 3% lower, than the cost charged to private companies for standard commercial bank loans. Access to such relatively inexpensive development capital by partnering with a government agency is a powerful inducement for a private company to seek collaboration.

Tax Increment Financing (TIF) Bonds

Tax increment financing (TIF) bonds are local tax-exempt bonds issued for special improvement districts where the benefit from the project being financed is specifically manifested through higher property values. The tax increment financing generates revenue for bond repayment from the incremental change in property values caused by the financed improvement. After creating a special district, two sets of tax records are maintained—one that reflects the property's value before the enhancement, and a second

Exhibit 9.7

Anaheim's Arrowhead Pond*

The Arrowhead Pond arena was a joint venture between the City of Anaheim and Ogden Facility Management Corporation. The project to construct the Arrowhead Pond was funded by Certificates of Participation. However, all of the debt service payments associated with the COPs are paid by Ogden Management Corporation in return for which Ogden received a 30-year contract to manage the arena during which period the company retained all arena revenues excluding those associated with the Mighty Ducks. Ogden also received 7.5% of gross gate revenues from the Mighty Ducks. At the end of the 30-year period when the bonds are paid off, the arena will be turned over to the City of Anaheim. The city paid for the land, infrastructure improvements, and legal documentation, whereas Ogden's total cost was $126 million (including cost of debt service). Ogden anticipated losses in the first 12 years of operation, but projected the profits in the last 18 years would be more than the first 12 years of losses. Apart from the naming rights to the facility and approval of the annual budget, the City gave Ogden almost complete autonomy to operate the arena. The financing arrangement is unique in that Ogden is solely responsible for guaranteeing payment of the facility's debt service. Ogden's facility manager at Arrowhead Pond observed:

> As far as the way this was financed, you'll probably never see one like it again. When you're a publicly traded company, everybody's looking for an immediate return. On the other hand, 15 years from now, when the people who put this deal together no longer work for the company, someone else is going to see the fruit of their labor. (Cohen, 1995, p. 59)

In addition to the Mighty Ducks, the arena is the home of the Anaheim Bullfrogs, a franchise of the Roller Hockey International League. Arrowhead Pond also hosts indoor soccer, tennis events and many concerts. The aggregate number of annual visitors exceeds 2 million.

*In October 2006, the name of the arena was changed to the Honda Center when the Honda Motor Company became the new title sponsor of the building.

which is the increment that reflects growing assessed values (and tax payments) after the enhancement and serves as the source of bond repayment.

In 1952, California became the first state to authorize tax-increment financing. Today, all states except Arizona have passed enabling legislation authorizing TIFs, and they are used by over 5,000 agencies. The original intent was that a TIF should be used to stop the growth of urban decay and blight, but in many states its use has been broadened so that it is now perceived as a tool for facilitating economic development in any context rather than only in decaying urban areas. It has become especially appealing in greenfields' contexts because they have very low base-value property tax assessments and no sales tax values at all, and so offer very large increments.

Although specific regulations for administering TIF programs vary from state to state, the basic concept in all of them allows cities and other local jurisdictions to create TIF districts to subsidize the cost of developing or redeveloping designated areas in a community. Typically, the tax-increment process involves two phases. The first stage requires designating the area to be developed or revitalized as a TIF district. Usually, a specific agency is established to plan and oversee the redevelopment process. For example, in Florida the administrative designation of TIF districts is *redevelopment agencies*, while in Oregon they are referred to as *urban renewal agencies*. In the second stage, the

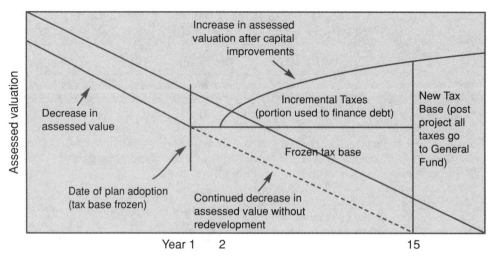

Figure 9.4. Tax increment Financing to Stop Urban Decay.

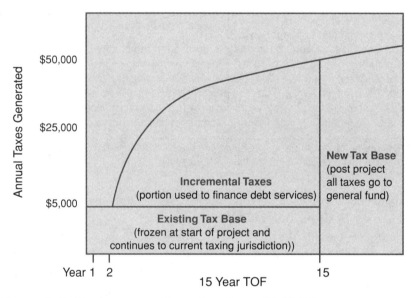

Figure 9.5. Tax increment Financing Green Field: TIF.

local development authority issues tax-increment bonds and uses the proceeds to demolish substandard buildings, clear land, or prepare land for development by installing infrastructure improvements such as utilities or roads.

Although TIF is usually based on property taxes, some states allow TIF that is based on sales taxes. A sales tax version of a TIF, for example, was passed by the Pennsylvania state legislature to pay for new facilities for the Pittsburgh Pirates and Steelers, and the Philadelphia Phillies and Eagles. The baseline was the amount of sales tax received by the state from the existing facilities, and the increment was the additional sales taxes received from the new facilities. The increment was passed back to the teams to repay their contributions to these projects.[15]

Figures 9.4 and 9.5 illustrate how TIF works. The tax revenue collected in the designated TIF district is divided into two parts: the base-year tax amount and the tax increment. Base-year taxes are the taxes collected on the property assessments in the year when the TIF district is established. They continue to be paid to all the normal taxing jurisdictions (e.g., city, county, and school districts), but the assessments upon which these base-year taxes are collected are frozen for the life of the TIF district. Incremental tax revenues are the taxes collected in any increase in the assessed property values. This increment includes taxes from three sources: 1) growth in existing property assessments from higher market values over time; 2) assessment increases from new investment in existing properties; and 3) new property development. Incremental tax revenue is diverted from the normal taxing jurisdictions and instead is used to redeem the bonds.

The scenario in Figure 9.4 illustrates the use of TIF to rejuvenate a decaying area. The property tax base valuation has been consistently falling for a number of years. To arrest this downward spiral, the community negotiates a partnership with a major anchor development such as an athletic stadium, arena, hotel, or supermarket. As its part of the agreement, the community provides substantial infrastructure and/or landscaping to complement and assist the development using TIF bonds.

Figure 9.4 shows no increment in property tax in year 1 because the anchor development is still being built, but in year 2 the tax revenue from it becomes available. In subsequent years, this amount continues to increase as other smaller businesses attracted by the anchor's traffic are built around it. The longevity of TIF districts varies, but in Figure 9.4, it is assumed to be 15 years. At that time the district is dissolved, so taxes levied on both the increment and the base go into the community's general fund, just like those of all other properties in the community.

In Figure 9.5, a "green fields" illustration is given. The area is undeveloped, so the tax base is minimal. Thus, in this case the focus is on using TIF funds to stimulate development of a new site, rather than in rejuvenating an existing urban area.

Most state laws require all taxing entities affected by the formation of the TIF district, such as cities, schools, and counties, to agree to its establishment. Each taxing unit can choose to dedicate all, a portion of, or none of the tax revenue that is attributable to the increase in property values due to the improvements within the TIF zone. Most taxing entities agree to dedicate the revenues to the TIF because in the short term, TIF districts assure continued tax collections, while in the long term, they promise significant future gains.

To fund infrastructure improvements associated with its bid for the Olympic Games, New York City proposed a TIF district. However, it needed approval from the state legislature to do this. When their approval was not forthcoming, the city created the innovative strategy described in Exhibit 9.8.[15] This adopted the principles of a TIF, but used an alternative legal mechanism to implement them.

TIF appeals to sport facility advocates and is politically popular because ostensibly it addresses the opportunity cost criticism associated with many sport projects in that this revenue would not exist without the sport project. It finances projects from increased tax revenues that the projects generate, rather than from new taxes or tax increases, so

Exhibit 9.8

A New York City Variation of a TIF District

New York City needed to raise $2.8 billion to pay for a new subway line, new streets and other infrastructure costs associated with construction of a new stadium at the Hudson Railyards site as part of their bid for the 2012 Olympic Games. The facility subsequently would be used by the New York Jets. The city proposed to pay for it by creating a huge TIF of 59 city blocks on the West side from 28th to 41st Streets and from Ninth Avenue to the Hudson River. Clearly, this prime area would develop extensively without a TIF and a stadium. The TIF was merely a mechanism to pay for the stadium infrastructure.

Under New York law, the state legislature had to authorize the TIF and there was reason to believe that it would not do so because polls showed that a large majority of New Yorkers were opposed to spending money on a stadium unless it paid for itself. Thus, the TIF was replaced by a payment in lieu of taxes (PILOTS) mechanism. This adopted the principles of a TIF, but since it was not a TIF it did not require state authorization.

The mechanism authorized the mayor to single-handedly grant property tax exemptions to developers of new property, and in return they paid an equivalent amount in fees to the newly created Hudson Yards Infrastructure Corporation which used them to pay off bonds for the new infrastructure projects. The entire project was authorized by a single rezoning vote by the city council which approved it by a majority of 46 to 1 and at the same time authorized the $2.8 billion in city backed bonds.

The city and the state subsequently still had to raise $600 million as the public's share of the stadium's cost. Neither entity was able to persuade its legislative body to appropriate its $300 million share for the project so the stadium was not built and the Olympic bid was stalled, but the infrastructure projects were completed.

the money could not have been spent on other projects. There are two fallacies in this argument. First is the assumption that no new development would occur at that site without TIF. If other taxable property was constructed there, then clearly the TIF would have a negative impact on the tax revenues that a city collects. Indeed, TIF has been criticized for subsidizing developments that would occur anyway. By using it to finance road and infrastructure improvements at locations that are likely to attract new private development without TIF funding, then tax revenue is simply being diverted to benefit a specific company or developer.

A second fallacy is that there is widespread perception that under TIF, property owners pay the normal tax burden, so there is no real loss to the community from using the incremental tax dollars for infrastructure financing.[32] However, because all property taxes accruing from the enhanced property tax base go into the TIF, none are available to pay for the increased services that the new development has created. Thus, additional operating funds for police and fire services, schools, etc. have to be forthcoming from outside the TIF, which means, in effect, that other taxpayers subsidize these services until the TIF is dissolved. This issue is less contentious if the use of TIF generates non-property tax revenues, for example, a sales tax that flows into the general fund and can be used for these purposes. TIF districts exist for a fixed amount of time, which typically ranges from 10 to 25 years. Once the TIF bonds are repaid in full and the district is dissolved, the frozen tax base is lifted, and all the enhanced property tax revenues go directly to the taxing jurisdictions.

A challenge with TIF projects is the uncertainty of the future increments of revenue because it is dependent on the pace and growth of future real estate development. Thus, lenders seek protection either through insurance or by a commitment by the city to meet any shortfalls in the amount of incremental revenues needed to meet the debt repayments. The situation is exacerbated by the inevitability of a time lag of several years between the gradual growth in property values and the immediacy of debt service payments that become due in the first year. If TIF revenues are insufficient to make interest payments in the initial years, then an alternative source of cash flow is needed. For example, the city of Fort Myers in Florida issued TIF bonds totaling approximately $22 million to fund a new spring training facility for the Boston Red Sox. Unfortunately, the TIF area lacked the economic capacity to support the bond repayment because the new stadium had relatively little impact in stimulating development around it, so the city had to underwrite much of the debt service from its annual budget.

An alternative strategy to the city being liable for a shortfall in revenues from the project is to shift this liability to the developer. The developer would then agree to reimburse the city for any shortfall in the tax increments.

In most cases, stadium projects using TIF have been part of downtown redevelopment plans. In Memphis, Fresno, and Peoria, for example, new minor league ballparks were the centerpieces of each community's efforts to revitalize declining city centers. In each case, the TIF redevelopment plan viewed the new stadium as the catalyst for bringing residents back to the downtown areas on a regular basis, which was anticipated, in turn, to stimulate other commercial activity proximate to the new ballpark.

However, the real issue in using TIF for a sport facility is the extent to which the additional taxes are actually an increment. If the project was not undertaken and people spent the same amount of money for recreation and the associated spin-off developments in the project elsewhere in the community, then there is no real increment.[8] In short, the key question is: Does growth in the TIF area come at the expense of other areas in the host community?

In sport facility projects where TIF financing has been used, the contribution of tax-increment dollars has been relatively modest. For example, TIF contributed $10 million toward the development of Pac Bell Park in San Francisco, while in Los Angeles TIF bonds accounted for the $12 million contribution to the Staples Center paid by the city of Los Angeles. A more substantive example was the city of Fort Worth's establishment of a TIF district as part of the plan to develop Texas Motor Speedway. A city-created nonprofit organization, the Fort Worth Sports Authority owns the Speedway, which is exempt from property taxes. While the Speedway does not pay property taxes, the surrounding properties within the 1,489-acre TIF district are subject to taxation. Speedway Motorsports built and operates the Speedway. The Fort Worth Sports Authority is paying $20 million from the TIF fund to Speedway Motorsports in order to buy the stadium back and cover the cost of acquiring the site.

Despite their often modest contribution, tax-increment funds can be vital to a sport project's ultimate success. For example, in Peoria, the city spent approximately $3 million in tax-increment funds to acquire and prepare the site (including demolition of old

Exhibit 9.9

Using TIF to Fund an Arena

A 192-acre site of rolling farmland and scattered trees was designated a TIF district. The undeveloped land was located on the edge of the city. It was owned by two developers who petitioned the city to designate the area a TIF district. The developers planned a 315-bedroom, up-market hotel and a 250,000 square foot office development, whereas the remaining acreage was designated for office, high-density residential, and commercial use. The projected value of the development was $153.35 million.

The city saw an opportunity to capture the property tax revenues from this development to build a 60,000 square foot arena and encouraged the developers to submit their petition to the city council. The TIF district was established for 20 years. It was also approved by the county commissioners who, like the city, authorized the incremental tax the county would have received from the development to be used for constructing the arena. A board of directors to oversee the TIF district was established comprising six representatives appointed by the city council and three by the county commissioners. All the appointees by state law either must own property in the TIF district or be an employee or agent of a person who owns property in the district.

A schedule showing the annual tax increments that were projected to accrue from the development is given in Table 9D. The Base Value shown in column 2 is the total appraised value of all property in the TIF district at the time it was created; that is, $3.444 mil-

TABLE 9D. Schedule of Annual Tax Increments from the Development

1	2	3	4	5	6	7
Year	Base	Annual Capture	Cumulative Captured	Tax Rate	Annual Tax Increment Generated	Cumulative Tax Increment Generated
2002	$3,444,610	$0	$0	.9021	$0	$0
2003	$3,444,610	$0	$0	.9021	$0	$0
2004	$3,444,610	$0	$0	.9021	$0	$0
2005	$3,444,610	$31,675,000	$31,675,000	.9021	$285,741	$285,741
2006	$3,444,610	$36,675,000	$68,350,000	.9021	$616,585	$902,326
2007	$3,444,610	$10,000,000	$78,350,000	.9021	$706,795	$1,609,121
2008	$3,444,610	$10,000,000	$88,350,000	.9021	$797,005	$2,406,126
2009	$3,444,610	$10,000,000	$98,350,000	.9021	$887,215	$3,293,341
2010	$3,444,610	$10,000,000	$108,350,000	.9021	$977,425	$4,270,766
2011	$3,444,610	$10,000,000	$118,350,000	.9021	$1,067,635	$5,338,401
2012	$3,444,610	$10,000,000	$128,350,000	.9021	$1,157,845	$6,496,246
2013	$3,444,610	$10,000,000	$138,350,000	.9021	$1,248,055	$7,744,301
2014	$3,444,610	$10,000,000	$148,350,000	.9021	$1,338,265	$9,082,566
2015	$3,444,610	$5,000,000	$153,350,000	9021	$1,383,370	$10,465,936
2016–2022	$3,444,610	$0	$153,350,000	.9021	$1,383,370	$20,149,526

Exhibit 9.9 *(Continued)*

Using TIF to Fund an Arena

lion. The table indicates that the first increment from development was to accrue in 2005 with the completion of the hotel, which was valued at $31.675 million (column 3). In the first 3 years of the district, the plans would be produced and construction initiated, but no development would be completed in this period, so there is no annual capture of property taxes in those years. The 2005 hotel development was followed by the large office development in the following year ($36.675 million). By year 2015, the development would be completed and its cumulative value was estimated at $153.35 million (column 4).

The city and county tax rates were 0.4777 and 0.4244, respectively, per $100 assessed valuation. Thus, the total tax rate available was 0.9021 (column 5). In 2005, when the tax rate of 0.9021 is levied on new value of $31.675 million it generates $285,741 in property taxes towards redeeming the TIF debt (column 6). Column 7 shows that during the life of the district, the cumulative amount of property taxes accruing is $20.149 million (column 7).

To pay for the arena, the city issued $18 million of certificates of obligation (COs). In this case, they served as the tax-increment financing bond mechanism. These were a full-faith and credit obligation of the city. Thus, their redemption was not solely dependent on project revenues. If the projections were wrong, the city was required to pay the annual debt charges to redeem the COs.

The schedule of debt repayments is shown in Table 9E on the following page. The annual debt payments on the COs are shown in column 2. The city and county used three revenue streams to pay the annual debt. First, hotel/motel taxes generated by the 315-bedroom hotel were pledged to the TIF and were estimated at $550,000 per year when the hotel was fully operational (column 3). Property taxes from the development increments are shown in column 4. Because these were inadequate in the first few years, the city also loaned the TIF $300,000 in 2004 and a total of $1.175 million in the

first 6 years from its existing hotel-motel tax fund. This was to be repaid after the year 2015 when the TIF started showing positive cumulative balances. Column 6 shows the aggregate funds from these three sources to meet the debt charges (column 2). Column 7 shows that in every year up to 2009, the annual revenue streams are inadequate to meet the debt charges, but after 2009 the development reaches a threshold level generating sufficient resources to make the annual cash flow positive. By the end of the 20-year life of the district, a cumulative positive balance of over $4 million is projected.

If all debts of the TIF district are paid off before the end of its 20-year life, then the district will be dissolved at that point and its pledged tax revenues will revert to the general funds of the city and the county. The tables assume no increase in either the tax rate or the tax base beyond their 2002 values. It would be politically unwise for an elected official to suggest that these will increase in the future—tantamount to acknowledging that an increase in taxes is inevitable! However, such increases are inevitable. The result is that, if the development occurs as projected, then the annual tax increments will be bigger than shown so the COs will be redeemed in a shorter period than shown in Table 9E.

The biggest winner from this arrangement is likely to be the school district. It did not contribute to the TIF district, so revenues from the development started flowing into the school district's general fund in 2005. The school district will receive $1 million in tax revenues in 2007, increasing to $2.5 million annually when the development is built-out in 2015.

There are two other upsides for the community. First, the city receives a "free" arena from the development, in the sense that existing taxpayers do not have to pay for it through higher property taxes. Second, when the TIF district is dissolved, the city and county will receive an additional $1.383 million per year (column 6, Table 9D) in tax revenue from the developments.

Exhibit 9.9 *(Continued)*

Using TIF to Fund an Arena

The major downside to the community is that because all the property tax funds in the new development are designated to retire the capital debt, the development contributes nothing to pay for the city services it will require until the TIF district is dissolved. Roads, water, wastewater, and utility improvements were not funded through the TIF, and no property taxes are available from it to pay for police, fire, street repair, public transportation, park maintenance, or any of the other services the area will require. The rest of the community will effectively be subsidiz-

ing the development with these until the district is dissolved.

Another downside is the risk that the development will not be built-out in the time frame shown in the schedule or that its appraised value will be lower than that anticipated in the schedule. If either of these situations occurs, it would adversely affect the revenue flow from the development, and the city's taxpayers would be required to provide the compensatory funding necessary to meet the debt payments.

TABLE 9E. Schedule of Debt Repayments

1	2	3	4	5	6	7
Year	Annual Debt Payments	Hotel-Motel Tax Revenues	TIF Revenues	Hotel-Motel Tax Transfer	Total Available Revenues	Cumulative Balance
2002	$0	$0	$0	$0	$0	$0
2003	$0	$0	$0	$0	$0	$0
2004	$465,055	$62,500	$0	$300,000	$362,500	($102,555)
2005	$1,719,790	$400,000	$285,741	$250,000	$935,740	($886,605)
2006	$1,513,123	$450,000	$616,585	$250,000	$1,316,585	($1,083,142)
2007	$1,515,680	$500,000	$706,795	$150,000	$1,356,795	($1,242,027)
2008	$1,517,258	$550,000	$797,005	$150,000	$1,497,005	($1,262,280)
2009	$1,512,948	$550,000	$887,215	$75,000	$1,512,215	($1,263,012)
2010	$1,517,598	$550,000	$977,425	$0	$1,527,425	($1,253,185)
2011	$1,516,139	$550,000	$1,067,635	$0	$1,617,635	($1,151,689)
2012	$1,513,755	$550,000	$1,157,845	$0	$1,707,845	($957,598)
2013	$1,515,395	$550,000	$1,248,055	$0	$1,798,055	($674,938)
2014	$1,515,918	$550,000	$1,338,265	$0	$1,888,265	($302,591)
2015	$1,653,618	$550,000	$1,383,370	$0	$1,933,370	($22,838)
2016	$1,688,580	$550,000	$1,383,370	$0	$1,933,370	$221,952
2017	$1,686,630	$550,000	$1,383,370	$0	$1,933,370	$468,692
2018	$1,222,641	$550,000	$1,383,370	$0	$1,933,370	$1,179,423
2019	$1,224,940	$550,000	$1,383,370	$0	$1,933,370	$1,887,853
2020	$1,226,690	$550,000	$1,383,370	$0	$1,933,370	$2,594,533
2021	$1,227,890	$550,000	$1,383,370	$0	$1,933,370	$3,300,014
2022	$1,223,680	$550,000	$1,383,370	$0	$1,933,370	$4,009,704

buildings and environmental cleanup) for a new $20 million downtown ballpark for the Peoria Chiefs, the city's privately owned minor league baseball team. These publicly financed improvements proved to be crucial to inducing 41 private investors to commit $17 million to the construction of O'Brien Field. The new ballpark was located in a part of the city's redevelopment district, which the local newspaper had declared prior to the project's initiation as "a hardcore hangout for the city's underclass, a gathering place for the homeless and the hopelessly addicted."[33] Within the first year of the park's opening, significant benefits for the neighborhood were apparent. Capacity crowds consistently filled the 7,500-seat stadium stimulating new business activity in the area that locals were beginning to refer to as "O'Brienville." A detailed case study describing the central role of TIF in the financing of an arena is shown in Exhibit 9.9.

The absurdity of elected officials advocating the widespread use of TIF for sport projects was effectively lampooned by the following whimsical anecdote:

> My wife and I have often talked about a small addition that would extend the back porch the full width of the house . . . It would be nice if the government would give us the money to do this. The value of the house would increase and so would our taxes. The higher taxes would pay the government back eventually, so it wouldn't cost taxpayers anything . . . It seems like a great idea, but for some reason the government is not willing to step up to our plate. We threatened to move to Portland or Charlotte if we don't get help, but officials just laughed. (p. 6)[34]

Taxable Private Activity Bonds

When the modern era of fully loaded sport facilities emerged in the mid 1990s, lenders recognized that the cost structure of these facilities was relatively fixed and highly predictable, and that their revenue streams represented a diversified basket of predictable, multi-year cash flows. These two conditions made these facilities relatively attractive candidates for long-term (25 year) loans, which led to the emergence of private activity bonds and asset-backed revenue bonds.

Under the 1986 Tax Reform Act, if a bond is to be tax exempt, then either at least 90% of its proceeds have to be used by a state or local government, or no more than 10% of the debt service must be derived from stadium or arena operations. If a bond does not meet one of these criteria, then it is classified as a taxable private activity bond, and the revenue to service it emanates from the for-profit private-partner's resources. Long-term naming rights, luxury-suite lease contracts and multi-year sponsorship rights fees are particularly attractive collateral assets for private activity bonds.

Portland's Rose Garden provides an illustration of how private activity bonds are arranged. The arena was one of the first major sport facilities to be almost entirely privately financed, and it has served as a model for subsequent private bond issues. The Portland Trailblazers basketball team (NBA) established the Oregon Arena Corporation for the purpose of raising private capital to fund the construction of a 20,350-seat multipurpose sports and entertainment center. The Oregon Arena Corporation enlisted the services of a national firm experienced in underwriting large bond transactions to first advise the team on how to structure the private debt offering, and then to place the bonds with institutional investors. The firm received more than $215 million in orders for the $155 million arena debt offering. Nine insurance companies bought the taxable private-placement bonds at 8.99% interest for 27 years. As security, the Oregon Arena Corporation pledged almost all of the new facility's contract-guaranteed revenues such as suite sales, rent from the Trailblazers' 30-year lease, advertising, and rent by the team and other tenants of an adjacent office building.[35]

Although borrowing at 8.99%, when compared to tax-exempt bond rates, was expensive, the arrangement was the Trailblazers only option because substantial support from public agencies for building the arena was not available. The city of Portland had already committed a substantial portion of the local hotel-motel tax to building a new convention center. Thus, the city's financial contribution was limited to $34.5 million for the provision of plazas, improved access, and some parking around the arena.

Following the successful Rose Garden financing, the Boston Bruins (NHL) and Celtics (NBA) sold $160 million of private activity bonds to build the Fleet Center. The owner of the NHL Philadelphia Flyers used a $142 million private placement to finance a new arena that opened as the new home of the Flyers and NBA 76ers. According to a spokesperson, "the deal worked out because the 22-year life of the bonds frees up more cash each year to go towards the teams . . . of an estimated $35 million in annual revenues coming from premium seating, advertising, and concessions, $14.5 million goes to debt service" (p. 59).[36]

Asset-backed Revenue Bonds

Asset-backed bonds (ABB) are taxable revenue bonds backed by a pledge of collateral in the form of future revenue flows from specified assets. The assets may be physical such as buildings, facilities, or land and the income attached to these; gate revenues; contractually obligated income sources such as naming rights, luxury suite leases, club seats, broadcast revenues, concession contracts, or sponsorship agreements; or the market value of professional players. Typically, when private activity bonds are used, the team or facility operator is required to commit all future venue income as collateral, but in the case of asset-backed bonds, the bondholders do not have claim on all the assets, only on those specified in the legal bond covenants. Thus, their attraction is that only a portion of a facility's revenues must be pledged as security, and teams do not have to open their books to creditors as they do when securing other kinds of loans.

ABB financing was first used to finance the Pepsi Center Arena in Denver. These bonds produced $139.8 million of the $175.5 million construction cost. The interest rate of 6.94% over the 21-year life of the bonds was only 1% above the 10-year U.S. Treasury note rate at the time of the transaction. The bond covenants required that only four of the ten multiyear revenue streams: sponsorships, naming rights, concession contracts, and the facility's luxury suite lease revenues, be pledged as security for the bonds, leaving the facility operators and its principal tenants (the Nuggets and Avalanche) with unrestricted rights to all other revenues.[37] The principles of ABB are easy to understand, but they are complex to implement. For example, the law firm handling the Pepsi Center transaction produced fifteen two-inch-thick bound notebooks containing the materials needed to complete the Denver arena arrangement. Indeed, because of their inherent complexity and rigorous documentation requirements, it is widely acknowledged that they need to be issued in amounts of $50 million or greater to be cost effective.

ABBs have emerged as a viable funding source for new arenas because of their long-term contracted streams of revenue. The Staples Center in Los Angeles is a prime example. It followed Denver's pioneering role by funding much of its $312 million construction with ABBs. Its major revenue streams made this possible. The facility contains 160 suites which at that time were leased from $197,500 to $307,500 annually. Their ten "founding" corporate sponsorship agreements generated $50 million annually, while Staples paid $100 million over 20 years for the naming rights. The magnitude of these guaranteed revenue streams meant ABBs were perceived by investors to be relatively low risk. After Denver and Los Angeles had demonstrated the potential of ABBs, at least a dozen other arenas adopted them.[38]

The commitment of renewal rights is an important feature of ABB transactions because it means that investors have a long-term claim on revenue sources that are often short term in nature. For example, the initial contract term for some luxury suites and corporate sponsorships does not extend beyond 3 to 5 years. By conveying the right to access revenues from subsequent contract renewals of suite leases, concession contracts, and so on, investors have greater assurance of timely repayment.

The Spanish soccer club, Real Madrid, one of the world's elite teams, sold $70 million worth of bonds secured solely by its membership fees (Real has 75,000 fans who pay to be official club members) and ticket sales that typically amount to $40 million a year. The team used the proceeds to acquire top players. The ABB funding was perceived to initiate a positive cycle of events; that is, the club uses the money to buy players who help the club become more successful. This, in turn, means that the team gets more people in the stadium and more television revenue, so there is additional income to pay the bonds. Previously, Real Madrid had committed the team's $10 million annual footwear and apparel sponsorship agreement with adidas as the revenue stream that enabled the club to sell $50 million of bonds to investors.[39] While ABB funding allowed Real Madrid to flourish, the case described in Exhibit 9.10 shows that injudicious use of ABB has the potential to result in financial catastrophe.[40]

In ABB transactions, the future cash flow from facility assets is sold to investors. In this respect, ABB is similar to traditional revenue bond and private activity bonds. What makes ABB financings different and more complex is that the contractual ownership of the pledged revenues is first sold into a trust that, in turn, issues notes to investors. The independent trust acts as the transaction agent. The trust first collects the promised facility revenues pledged by the facility operator and then redistributes them to each investor on a pro rata basis to meet guaranteed principal and interest payment obligations. The trust structure is created to make the possibility of bankruptcy more remote, so that if the arena or stadium owner should declare bankruptcy, the assets of the trust remain inviolable. This "bankruptcy remote" feature of the ABB transaction

Exhibit 9.10

The Asset-backed Revenue Bond Route to Bankruptcy

Leeds United Football Club was one of the English Premier League's elite clubs with an exciting young team playing in the semi-final of the European Cup, which identified them as one of the top four soccer teams in Europe. The euphoria associated with their success led to aspirations for even greater success. This could be attained by acquiring even better players. As a result, the club boldly made large investments in a cadre of top players, including Rio Ferdinand whom they purchased for a then British record price.

To buy the new players, the club needed a new source of finance since its existing resources were fully stretched. They used ABB, with the players serving as the asset. Thus, when Leeds bought a player for say, £10 million, they would immediately sell him to a finance house for the same amount before buying him back. Thus, a financial institution would loan the money to Leeds United which would be paid back with interest, over the length of the player's contract—typically four years. If the club failed to make the quarterly payments, then the lender's security was the mandate to require the club to sell the player and hand over the proceeds. If the player's value had declined, the bank could claim the difference from the club. The club was required to insure the whole arrangement so if it went bankrupt, the insurer would cover the lender's loss.

The loans were short-term and relatively high interest. In addition, the insurance was expensive and had to be paid up front. Although the quarterly payments proved onerous for Leeds, player values in the Premier League were rising at an unprecedented rate, so the book value of the assets was increasing. Given these increases in the assets value, the lenders were amenable to Leeds' request to restructure the loans so that only half of the original cost would be paid over the contract period, with the remaining 50% in a lump sum at the end.

Nevertheless, the magnitude of the debt payments combined with the very large salaries the players received resulted in substantial annual operating losses that were not sustainable making Leeds' finances precarious. Thus, Leeds sought another restructuring of the debt using an alternative asset. Leeds is the biggest city in England with only one professional soccer club and its fans are unusually dedicated. These fans were the new asset. The arrangement worked as follows.

A loan was arranged with major financial institutions that would be repaid over 25 years and the once-a-year repayments were guaranteed through a special 'locked box' account. Every summer, when Leeds put season tickets and corporate hospitality boxes up for sale, all the revenue would be paid into the locked box, so that a substantial sum had built up by 1 September. On that date the lenders would withdraw the payments due to them from the locked box and only then was the club allowed access to the residue. Thus, the multitude of short-term loans for each player were shifted into a single long term loan to be serviced with an annual payment from the locked box.

The long-term loan was for £60 million ($100 million) which not only enabled the loan to be restructured, but also provided additional funds to buy more top quality players. With the depth and quality of their squad, the expectation was that Leeds United would reign supreme. But it did not work out that way.

Several of the team's key players were injured. Star players did not get along with each other or with the manager. The team's manager and the board chairman's relationship deteriorated. The fans became angry when their high expectations dissipated and vociferously dammed the players, manager, and board of directors. The team's performance plummeted and with it the club's reve-

---

Exhibit 9.10 *(Continued)*

The Asset-backed Revenue Bond Route to Bankruptcy

nue streams that were servicing the debt payments and high wage bill.

All was not lost, however, because the players' asset book value was £200 million, so the debt could be wiped out at any time through the judicious sale of some players. Unfortunately, four factors came together to undermine this "safety value" back-up plan:

• Markets go down as well as up. At the time Leeds began to sell, the transfer market as a whole was in decline and, barring a few exceptional cases (such as Ferdinand, for whom a desperate Manchester United paid £26m), most transfers were being done at notably lower prices than previously.

• Players who are playing badly lose value. A bad run for the club doesn't make the player worthless, but if he is a defender leaking goals or a striker not scoring them it is bound to depress his price.

• Sell in distress and you sell at discount. Rival clubs know you need to do the deal and they will exploit that. The introduction of the transfer windows made the worse,

as Leeds became exposed to end-of-window brinkmanship. Players are not slaves. If you want to break a player's contract he may refuse to go, or he may demand compensation.

• And sales are closely related to confidence. Just as buying players boosts a team's ability, resources and morale—so selling them sucks those things out. Not only is the team weaker but it is less willing, less positive, and so more matches are likely to be lost.

The end result was a disaster for Leeds United who went into a free fall. They were relegated from the Premier League to the Championship League, and subsequently from the Championship League to League I. In a six year period, from being one of the top four clubs in Europe, they dropped to being ranked lower than 60 in England. They went into bankruptcy, narrowly avoided liquidation, and were required to sell both their stadium and training ground to make debtor payments.

---

makes it more attractive to prospective institutional investors. Typically, an established financial institution such as a bank will establish and administer the trust.

MECHANICS OF SELLING BONDS

After a sport facility bond proposal has been developed, bond specialist lawyers and consultants are hired to develop the financial, legal, and technical details that are required before bonds can be offered for sale. Three tasks must be accomplished when preparing bonds for sale: 1) obtain a bond rating, 2) ensure the financial transactions are completed efficiently, and 3) ensure that the legal contractual language in the bond sale agreement is accurate.

Bond Ratings

The level of risk that investors incur strongly influences the interest rate for bonds. Full-faith and credit bonds remain among the safest investments available; however, very occasionally, defaults do occur. To provide potential investors with information regarding the degree of risk involved in a bond issue, two major rating agencies—Moody's

Table 9.8. Credit Ratings by Moody's and Standard & Poor's

Moody's Ratings Compared to other US municipal or tax-exempt bond issuers the grade. . . .	Symbol	Symbol	Standard & Poor's Ratings
INVESTMENT GRADE Demonstrates the strongest creditworthiness	Aaa	AAA	The highest rating. Capacity to meet debt payments is extremely strong.
High quality; smaller margin of protection or larger fluctuation of protective elements than Aaa	Aa	AA	Strong capacity to meet debt payments; differ from the highest rated issues only in small degree.
Upper medium grade, many favorable investment attributes; but elements may be present which suggest some susceptibility to future risk	A	A	Strong, but more susceptible to adverse effects in circumstances and economic conditions than in debt in higher rated categories.
Medium grade: neither highly protected nor poorly secured; adequate present security that debt payments will be met but may be unreliable over any great length of time.	Baa	BBB	Adequate capacity to meet debt payments, but adverse economic conditions or changing circumstances are more likely to weaken this capacity than in higher rated categories.
SPECULATIVE GRADE Judged to have speculative elements; not well safeguarded; very moderate protection of principal and interest, payments over both good and bad times. Element of uncertainty.	Ba	BB	Less near-term vulnerability to default than other speculative issues, but faces major ongoing uncertainties or exposure to adverse economic conditions which could lead to inadequate capacity to meet debt payments.
Lack characteristics of desirable investment. Assurance of debt payments over the long term may be small.	B	B	Greater vulnerability to default, but currently has the capacity to meet payments.
Poor standing; may be in default or may be elements of danger to meeting debt payments	Caa	CCC	Is currently vulnerable to default. Is dependent on favorable economic conditions to meet debt payments. If these conditions deteriorate, it is not likely to have the capacity to meet debt payments.
Speculative in high degree; in default or other marked shortcomings.	Ca	CC	Highly vulnerable to nonpayment.
Lowest rated class; extremely poor prospects of ever attaining any real investment standing.	C	C	Bankruptcy petition has been filed, but debt service payments are continuing.
		D	Default. Debt payments are not made on the date due.

Moody's rating may be modified by the addition of a plus or minus sign to show relative standing within the major rating categories. In Standard & Poor's ratings, numerical modifiers 1, 2, and 3 are added to letter ratings.

Investor Service, Inc., and Standard & Poor's—analyze an issue's risk of default and assign a credit rating to the bonds. The bond issuer pays for the rating. The rating agencies prepare an opinion of the borrower's credit quality, or of the revenue stream supporting non-guaranteed bonds. Credit quality depends on the ability of the tax base or revenue source to generate the required debt service payments while financing regular

Table 9.9. Bond Ratings for Selected Cities With Sports Franchises

City	Standard & Poor's	Moody's
New York	AA	Aa3
Los Angeles	AA-	Aa2
Chicago	A+	Aa3
Houston	AA	Aa3
Philadelphia	BBB	Baa1
San Diego	A	A2
Phoenix	AAA	Aa1
Dallas	AA+	Aa1
Washington, D.C.	A+	A1
New Orleans	BBB	Baa3
Atlanta	A	A1
Denver	AAA	Aa1
Cleveland	A	A2

Source: "Bond Ratings for City Governments by Largest Cities: 2010," in *Statistical Abstract of the United States*, by U.S. Census Bureau, 2012, Washington, DC: Superintendent of Documents.

current expenditures. The agencies' ratings are distributed widely to the investment community and have a major influence on borrowing costs. An issue without a rating is unlikely to sell on national markets, but issues may not be rated if banks in local markets will buy them, such as in the Johnson County, Kansas, sports complex example in Exhibit 9.5.

The alphabetical rating systems used by the two agencies are generally considered to be equivalent. An issue is assigned one of the ratings shown in Table 9.8. To illustrate the impact of these ratings in one community, the difference between AA and AA+ ratings, which are only marginally differentiated for a bond of $11.8 million over 20 years, was 0.5%, which amounted to over $850,000 over the life of the bond.[41] Table 9.9 shows bond ratings for selected cities in which sport franchises are located.

In recent years, the influence of ratings on borrowing costs has been altered with the evolution of insurance for new municipal bond issues. In the early 1980s, fewer than 4% of new municipal bond issues were insured, but this percentage now has increased to more than 50%. Typically, an insurer agrees to guarantee the timely payment of principal and interest to investors in return for a one-time premium paid on the issue date of the bonds. The insurance enables a lower-rated issue to be sold at the level of a AAA rating. Fees for insurance fall somewhere between the interest payment that would be due on a bond issued with the jurisdiction's credit rating, and the interest payments on a bond with the insurance company guaranteeing it as a AAA rating. The insurance allows the jurisdiction to harvest some of the interest-rate savings that the higher credit rating may confer. Typically, borrowers seek competitive bids on the insurance premium and have investors interested in their bond offerings bid on both an insured and uninsured basis. This allows the market to determine the cheaper way to borrow.

Financial and Legal Advisors

If employed, financial advisors serve as a jurisdiction's impartial consultants on structuring and selling the bonds. Their primary responsibilities are to advise on the most feasible timetable for retiring the debt (this includes a maturity schedule and interest payment dates), the fee structure and methods necessary for supplying enough money to pay the principal and interest, and the relative acceptability of the sealed bids when they are opened. All states have laws that require general obligation bonds to be sold to the bidder offering the lowest net-interest cost at an advertised public sale. The bond consultants also assist in distributing the official notice of sale to potential lenders. Financial periodicals generally are used to ensure broad exposure. Prospective lenders (e.g., banks, investment houses, insurance companies) are invited to submit bids to the government entity detailing the terms under which they will lend the money.

Bond counsel play a critical role in attracting the interest of potential investors in a bond issue. Bond buyers place great confidence in nationally recognized bond counsel. They are lawyers who have extensive experience in working with bonds, and investors expect the bond counsel to screen out unacceptable risks. Legal restrictions are prone to new interpretations and tests. It is the job of bond counsel to monitor and incorporate these changes in the advice and documents prepared for their clients. Bond counsel will be called on to make numerous interpretations of federal laws and regulations, state constitutions and statutes, and local charters and ordinances. Even the smallest technical or legal error may result in invalidating an entire issue.

SUMMARY

State and local governments play a major role in financing and operating a wide spectrum of sport facilities. Property and general sales taxes have been the traditional revenue sources used by government entities to fund sport venues. In recent years, there has been a pronounced shift away from these general taxes where the burden of payment falls on all taxpayers, toward selective taxes. These include tourist taxes on hotel-motel rooms and car rentals, sin taxes on cigarettes, alcohol and lotteries, and income taxes on players' earnings, where the burden of payment is borne only by particular segments of the community.

Cities and counties often rely on property taxes to finance projects. Property tax values are determined by an assessor, and the aggregate value of all the assessed values within a particular jurisdiction is referred to as the tax base. After the tax base has been determined by assessment, the government entity sets a tax rate to meet its revenue needs. Property taxes may be increased annually by raising the value of the tax base, by increasing the tax rate, or by raising both elements. Although property taxes are a stable source of revenues, most states and/or local governments require at least a simple majority of voters to use property tax monies to construct sport facilities. Some states now require super majorities to pass a property tax increase. As a result, property tax-financed sport facilities have become less common.

The second largest source of revenues for state and local governments is the general sales tax. When it has been used to fund major sport facilities, the sales tax has usually been adopted over a regional or county-wide area. Imposing a sales tax on selected purchases has become a favored approach in the field. Thus, most of the major sport venues built in recent years have been financed at least in part by either a bed tax and/or a car rental tax. Another selective tax imposed by most states and a growing number of cities is on the portion of a visiting player's salary earned in their jurisdictions. Typically, the tax is determined by calculating the number of "duty days" a player accumulates in a particular state or city. A ticket surcharge is perhaps the most equitable of the selective taxes, since it enables fans who benefit from a facility to make a contribution to its debt charges or maintenance expenses.

Debt financing is the most common way local governments raise money to pay for major capital development projects like sport complexes and stadiums. Cities and counties borrow money from lending institutions and private investors through the sale of bonds. Bonds are defined as a promise by the entity borrowing the money to pay back the principal and interest amount within a specified period of time. The source of funds used to repay or "secure" the debt comes from either tax sources (e.g., property, sales) or from revenues produced by the facility itself. The major types of bonds are named by the source of revenue used to repay them.

The 1986 Tax Reform Act was intended to severely curtail the issuance of tax-exempt bonds for the construction of stadiums and arenas. The loss of the tax exemption can result in an increase in debt service costs of as much as 2–3%. Under the act, a city or county cannot issue tax-exempt bonds if (a) more than 10% of the debt service is paid from stadium or arena revenues or (b) more than 10% of the stadium or arena's utilization is consumed by a single private tenant such as a professional sports team. Revenue derived from the sale of personal seat licenses (PSLs) still qualified as tax exempt under the act. Given the difficulty of meeting the 10% limits and growing taxpayer resistance to any form of general tax support for sport facility construction, teams and owners pursued other borrowing alternatives.

General obligation bonds are full-faith and credit obligations backed by the local government's authority to levy taxes. Typically, they are secured by an increase in either property or general sales taxes. These bonds are very secure, and as a result the interest rates charged by lenders are relatively low compared to other bond options. Before state and local governments are authorized to issue general obligation bonds, they must have voter approval.

In contrast, revenue bonds rely on revenue produced by a facility, or other designated revenue streams, to redeem them. With revenue bonds, the burden of facility financing shifts from general taxpayers to users who receive direct benefit. Admission fees and concession and parking revenues are user-generated revenues that are typically used to secure revenue bonds.

Certificates of Participation (COPs) use the leasing power of local governments to secure long-term debt financing. COPs require a third party to act as an intermediary. With the public trust model, a public benefit corporation borrows money through the issuance of COPs to build the facility and then leases it back to the city. The public corporation repays the debt obligation from the lease fees it receives from the government entity. In the public-private participation model, the city acts as the intermediary by recruiting a private operator for the proposed facility. The city issues COPs to a local bank to raise money to build the new facility. The city then leases the facility to a private operator and uses the lease payments to repay the debt. No referendum is necessary with COPs.

Tax increment financing bonds (TIFs) are repaid usually by incremental property taxes but sometimes also by sales taxes resulting from infrastructure and amenity improvements paid for by the bonds. Originally TIF was intended to facilitate urban renewal in blighted areas, but in many states it has been broadened and is especially politically appealing in greenfields contexts.

Two private debt-financing options have become prominent: private activity bonds and asset-backed revenue bonds. Both are taxable, so the interest rates associated with their issue are higher than the rates charged for tax-exempt bonds. Both types of bonds are sold by a private entity, commonly the team, its owner, or a development corporation representing the team's interests. In each case, the bonds are secured by revenues generated by the facility being financed. With private activity bonds, security for the bonds is provided by a lien on all of the future facility revenues. Asset-backed revenue bonds have emerged as an attractive alternative to private activity bonds because they impose less stringent collateral requirements. With asset-backed transactions, the revenues of only selected assets (naming rights, luxury suites, etc.) are bundled into a financial security and sold to a "bankruptcy-proof" trust, which in turn issues the notes to private investors.

The selection of the most appropriate debt-financing mechanism among those discussed in this chapter is determined by the situational context of a proposed facility. For example, replacement of a city swimming pool that has long been perceived as a well-used community resource might be best achieved by using straight serial general obligation bond financing. Obtaining voter support for such a project may have a high probability of success. On the other hand, the user-pay philosophy demonstrated in the Johnson County, Kansas, sports complex and Fairfax County golf course examples was the optimal financing decision for developing those facilities. Using revenue bonds, paid for by those who directly benefited from the creation of the softball and golf amenities, to finance the projects made a great deal of sense. In a growing number of communities, taxpayer support for major sport facilities is not widespread. Under such circumstances, tourist and sin taxes, which are more likely to win support than general taxes, are likely to be the best options for public investment. Finally, for those projects that have the capability of generating substantial amounts of income, private activity bonds and, more recently, asset-backed bonds may be legitimate alternatives.

Entities selling bonds must procure the expertise of a number of specialized consultants. The process is likely to involve retaining a bond counsel to ensure that all aspects of the bond process, including the contractual language in the bond documents, are legal and accurate; and hiring a financial consultant to structure the debt retirement schedule, sell the bonds, and in some cases, obtain a bond rating.

References

1. U.S. Bureau of Census. (1935). *Financial statistics of state and local governments 1932.* Washington, DC: Government Printing Office.

2. U.S. Bureau of Census (2012). *Annual finances of government.* Washington, DC: Superintendent of Documents.

3. O'Sullivan, A., & Sheffrin, S. M. (1995). *Property taxes and tax revolts: The legacy of Proposition 13.* Cambridge, UK: Cambridge University Press.

4. Mikesell, J. L. (2011). *Fiscal administration: Analysis and applications for the public sector.* Boston, MA: Wadsworth.

5. Kozlowski, J. C. (1995). Private property bill more demanding than Constitution. *Parks and Recreation, 30*(5), 16–24.

6. Haveman, M., & Sexton, T. A. (2008). *Property tax assessment limits: lessons from thirty years of experience.* Cambridge, MA: Lincoln Institute of Land Policy.

7. Danielson, M. N. (1997). *Hometeam: Professional sports and the American metropolis.* Princeton, NJ: Princeton University Press.

8. Sandy, R., Sloane, P. S., & Rosentraub, M. (2004). *The economics of sport: An international perspective.* New York, NY: Palgrave, McMillan.

9. Mukherjee, S. (1997, April 25). U.S. cities are taxing tourists to fund new stadiums. *Boston Business Journal,* 1–4.

10. Long, J. G. (2002). *The real cost of public subsidies for major league sports facilities.* Cambridge, MA: Harvard University PhD dissertation.

11. Sanders, L. (1997, September 23). To subsidize or not subsidize? First ask who benefits. *Stadium & Arena Financing,* p. 9.

12. Weiss, S. (1999, October 18–24). Car-rental tax for Spurs' home is drawing fire. *Sports Business,* p. 8.

13. Baade, R. A., & Matheson V. A. (2006). Have public finance principles been shut out in financing new stadiums for the NFL? *Public Finance and Management, 6*(3), 284–320.

14. Richmond, P. (1993). *Ballpark: Camden Yards and the building of an American dream.* New York, NY: Simon and Schuster.

15. DeMause, N., & Cagan, J. (2008). *Field of schemes: How the great stadium swindle turns public money into private profit.* Lincoln, NE: University of Nebraska Press.

16. Muret, D. (2010, May 24–30). Could a jersey tax become fashionable for facility financing? *SportsBusiness Journal,* p. 18.

17. DiMascio, J. (2007). The "jock tax": Fair play or unsportsmanlike conduct. *University of Pittsburgh Law Review, 68,* 953–973.

18. Comptroller of Maryland. (2001) *Nonresident professional athletes and entertainers* [Administrative release No. 24]. Retrieved from www.marylandtaxes.com/publications/bulletins/it/ar_it24.pdf

19. Hoffman, D. K., & Hodge, S. A. (2004). *Nonresidents state and local income taxes in the United States: The continuing spread of "jock taxes."* Washington, DC: Tax Foundation.

20. Kormon, R. (1989, February 20). A matter of pride. *Sports Inc.,* 34.

21. Zimmerman, D. (1997). Subsidizing stadiums: Who benefits, who pays? In R. Noll & A. Zimbalist (Eds.), *Sports, jobs and taxes* (pp. 119–145). Washington, DC: The Brookings Institution.

22. Noll, R., & Zimbalist, A. (1997). Build the stadium—create the jobs! In R. Noll & A. Zimbalist (Eds.), *Sports, jobs and taxes* (pp. 1–54). Washington, DC: The Brookings Institution.

23. Burke, D. (1997). The Stop Tax-Exempt Arena Debt Issuance Act. *Journal of Legislation, 23,* 149–157.

24. Zimmerman, D. (2008). New developments in stadium financing. In B. R. Humphreys & D. R. Howard (Eds.), *The business of sports,* vol. 3 (pp. 99–110). Westpoint, CT: Praeger.

25. Greaves, T., & Henchman, J. (2009). *From the house that Ruth built to the house the IRS built.* Washington, D.C.: Tax Foundation Fiscal Fact #167.

26. Phillips, H. (1998, June). The municipal development game. *Parks & Recreation,* 50–59.

27. McLean, D. D., & Martin, W. D. (1991). Blueprints for successful bond referendums. *Journal of Physical Education, Recreation and Dance, 62*(10), 40–44.

28. Johnson, C. L., & Mikesell, J. (1994). Certificates of participation and capital markets: Lessons from Brevard County and Richmond Unified School District. *Public Budgeting and Finance, 14*(3), 41–54.

29. Joseph, J. (1994). *Debt issuance and management: A guide for smaller governments.* Chicago, IL: Government Finance Officers Association.

30. Gladwell, N., Sellers, J., & Brooks, J. (1997).

Certificates of participation as an alternative funding source for capital projects: A case study. *Journal of Park and Recreation Administration, 15*(4), 23–37.

31. Cohen, A. (1995, April) Webbed feet first. *Atlantic Business*, 57–59.

32. Man, J. Y. (2001). Determinants of the municipal decision to adopt tax increment financing. In C. Jackson & J. Y. Man (Eds), *Tax increment financing and economic development* (pp. 87– 100). Albany, NY: State University of New York Press.

33. Reynolds, D. (2002, May 22). Stadium might be neighborhood's springboard [Electronic version]. *Peoria Journal Star*, Special section ("Guide to O'Brien Field"). Retrieved from www.pjstar .com/services/special/2002obrien field/stories.html

34. Lotterman, E. (2004, March 18). My Tiff with TIF: It's misleading. *St. Paul Pioneer Press*, p. 6.

35. Stephens, K. (1994, June 24). The new arena. *Dallas Morning News*, D5.

36. Fischl, J. (1997, June 17). Private parts. *Financial World*, 58–60.

37. Kaplan, D. (1999, February 22–28). Rating agency backs private arena bonds. *SportsBusiness Journal*, p. 26.

38. Kaplan, D. (1998, November 2–8). New strategy creates a buzz around bear. *SportsBusiness Journal*, p. 8.

39. Kaplan, D. (1998, May 3–9). Real Madrid soccer team will sell $70 million in bonds. *SportsBusiness Journal*, p. 10.

40. Cathcart, B. (2004, March 6). Money to burn. *Observer Sport Monthly*.

41. Lee, R., & Johnson, R. W. (1989). *Public budgeting systems*. Rockville, MD: Aspen Publications.

10

Implementation of Public-Private Partnerships

INTRODUCTION

Understandably, but incorrectly, the popular perception of government is that it is what it does, rather than what it decides. Fortunately, there is a growing recognition that the provision (policy) decision and the production (implementation of service delivery) decision should be made independently. It is remarkable how infrequently separation of this duality of roles is overtly discussed and how powerful the implications are once their independence is recognized. Public entities make policy decisions about what should be provided and retain the functions of planning, coordination, regulatory control, and monitoring of performance outcomes. After a policy decision has been made, the key question is: How can a project be best made to work in the public interest? The emergent contemporary approach is that it is more effective and efficient to solicit private sector partners with expertise, technological innovation, and business acumen to implement service delivery, and that a public entity should take responsibility for delivery only if such private partners are not available.

A partnership is a collaboration among business, non-profit and government organizations, in which risks, resources and skills are shared in projects that benefit each partner as well as the community.[1] Collaboration refers to the process of two or more stakeholders pooling resources to achieve a goal that neither can or will do alone, or that they can accomplish more efficiently and effectively by working together. In essence, the partners leverage their resources to accomplish something beyond what they could do alone. They seek synergy so the sum is greater than the parts. The collaborators share a mutual vision, aspirations and a commitment to work with their partners over time.

This chapter discusses the challenges in facilitating public-private partnerships; reviews the complementary assets that public agencies and sport businesses potentially could pool in collaborations; and gives examples of different types of partnership collaborations.

CHALLENGES IN FACILITATING PUBLIC PRIVATE PARTNERSHIPS

The initial challenge for both parties in a proposed public-private collaboration is to create a climate that is conducive to the partnership's being successful. The two most impor-

Collaboration is an essential component of successful Public-Private Partnerships. Courtesy of Dreamstime

tant facets in nurturing this climate are reconciling value systems and removing sources of unfair competition.

The spheres of business and government often are viewed as distinct in terms of philosophies, objectives, reward structures, and codes of conduct. Relations between the two spheres may not always have been cordial. If antipathy prevails, then partnerships are unlikely. Hence, the first challenge is for both parties to understand, reconcile, and accept as legitimate the different value systems and constituent expectations that prevail in the two sectors.

It is self defeating to laud the benefits of partnerships if public agencies engage in activities that engender distrust and alienation among potential private-sector partners. Thus, a second task is to remove any suspicion that the public agency is competing unfairly with sport organizations in the services it delivers. A perception of unfair competition is likely to result in animosity from the sport community and to negate the possibility of partnerships with it.

Reconciling Value Systems

Agencies are mandated to serve the whole community, especially its most disadvantaged members. Hence, their traditional value systems are concerned with social outcomes, equity, and benefits that are relatively intangible and difficult to measure. In contrast, the value systems of private sport organizations focus on the tangible, easily measured outcomes of financial return on investment, and their mandate is to maximize return to owners or stockholders. This means that their services tend to be targeted narrowly at those segments from which the sport business perceives the highest return on investment is likely to be realized. Clearly, there is inherent potential for frustration, friction, and conflict between those focusing only on responsive market segments with a willingness and ability to pay, and those concerned with equity and social outcomes. For example, in the context of golf courses the objective of a public sector partner is likely to be to provide low or moderately priced golf for residents, which may compromise the private sector partner's ability to generate an acceptable return on investment.

Tensions are heightened by the different environmental milieus in which the two sectors operate. Public agencies are constrained by bureaucratic procedures that are necessary to ensure accountability for their expenditure of public funds. Thus, although a sport organization may want to proceed with a project immediately, a public agency may be required to engage in an extensive planning process involving broad public participation, lengthy legislative approval procedures, extended budgetary hearings, and frequent consultation with elected officials. These checks and balances, which accountability necessitates, cause delays and may cause potential sport business partners who do not understand how government works to perceive a public agency as lacking commitment to the project, being slow moving, or being indecisive.

Indeed, there is a central conundrum. In many cases, a primary reason for a public entity to seek a private partner is to break away from the political and bureaucratic processes inherent in purely public projects. However, at the same time a public entity has to incorporate checks and balances to ensure transparent accountability for its stewardship of taxpayer resources.

Synchronization of budgets may be a particularly frustrating problem when capital for constructing facilities is involved. A sport business probably can borrow funds quickly for a promising investment, but an agency interested in partnering with it may have to wait much longer for resources to be authorized by a legislative body or a bond referendum. If more than one public agency is involved in a partnership, the problem is compounded because city, county, state, and federal agencies may all have different fiscal years and budget-planning cycles.

These distinctive differences between the two sectors sometimes lead to negative, stereotypical attitudes that impede the development of partnerships. In the authors' experience, the popular perceptions of government inefficiency and private sector efficiency are exaggerated grossly.

There is a segment of the population, including some managers in the private sport sector, who perceive public agencies as being wasteful, unresponsive, tradition-bound, incompetent, and inefficient bureaucracies staffed by people who have never had to meet a payroll and who sometimes seek to frustrate the legitimate goals of business. Much of this perception is derived from public agencies' being required to operate openly and to give the media full access to all of their actions. Freedom of information acts and government-in-the-sunshine laws are deliberately written to guarantee public and media access to whatever is done by officials who act on the public's behalf. These laws are designed to ensure that public agencies are fully accountable to their taxpayer bosses for their actions. The requirement that government decisions be transparent means that actions taken by public managers or elected officials that fail to achieve the projected positive outcome are likely to result in those responsible being subjected to public criticism, scorn, and ridicule when the failure is extensively reported in the media.

In contrast, private organizations are, for the most part, entitled to keep their decision processes and actions confidential. Hence, media focus most of their investigative reporting efforts on public organizations, because the rights of privacy that prevail in the private sector preclude public access. Thus, the general public remain unaware when projected outcomes of projects in the private sector are not met.

An inherent corollary of collaborating with a private partner is that a public agency has to compromise the degree of control it can exercise over the service delivered. The partner who takes the financial risk expects to exercise control over the operations of a facility. Private sport organizations have to be able to demonstrate to investors and bankers that they have sufficient control to operate the venture successfully before they can acquire the capital necessary to develop it. A key factor in control is the length of a contract or lease. When the length is short—for example, less than 5 years—control is retained largely by the public entity because the arrangement is periodically evaluated to ensure that it remains in the public interest. In contrast, long leases mean surrendering control of a public resource often for 25 to 30 years. Such long leases are needed when a commercial firm invests substantially in capital assets in order for it to have time to successfully amortize all of the capital improvements and secure an acceptable return on its investment.

One manager who is widely experienced in developing partnerships observed that financial necessity alone does not ensure that successful partnerships will ensue:

> Partnerships can fail because the parties become too eager to close a deal before they have squared their visions (Why are we building a new facility?) and missions (Once we build it, what are we going to stand for?). Some people partner just because of financial reasons, but that is not the only reason to do it. The real reason is that you want to solve a community problem and create a better quality of life, and you want to find a partner who can complement your strengths and improve on your weaknesses—and everybody has both. (p. 35)[2]

The success of partnerships depends on how the parties work together, but each partner also has to ensure that its own organization's objectives are met in the arrangement. Each entity's negotiators are responsible for meeting the expectations of its stakeholders about the outcome. The different outcome objectives of the cooperating parties frequently cause friction in partnership negotiations. A consequence is that partnerships often take longer than anticipated to come to fruition. The probability of acceptable compromise positions being agreed upon is likely to depend on the extent to which there is mutual trust and understanding, and the effectiveness of communication. While there are no generalizable formulas for forging partnerships because personalities, local conditions, state and local enabling laws, community values, and other factors vary widely, the two elements of mutual trust and effective communication are common principles that underlie successful partnerships.

Ultimately, the personalities of individuals and the personal relationships they forge determine the effectiveness of the partnership. If attempts are made to consummate partnership arrangements without a genuine commitment from those who will be responsible for executing them, then the arrangements will be undermined and fail. Mutual trust and understanding usually grow over time. They stem from familiarity and successful experiences of working together. This suggests that partnerships are most likely to flourish in jurisdictions where leadership in key organizations in the public, nonprofit, and private sport sectors is relatively stable, enabling networks of trusting interpersonal relationships to evolve.

With multiple parties involved, confusion and misunderstanding can easily emerge over goals, funding, timing, division of responsibilities, and a host of other issues. Effective communication alleviates these problems. Communication should start with clear articulation of the outcomes each partner seeks from an arrangement and the common vision and purpose the partners share for it. Sometimes this initial step is overlooked because it is assumed that each partner is aware of the others' goals and aspirations. Overlooking the first step may lead, for example, to a public agency's interpreting a partner's expectations in a manner which is consistent with the outcomes that the agency seeks even though this interpretation may be incorrect. Written documentation is essential because points throughout the negotiation process that were initially clear and agreed upon may not be recalled accurately 12 months later.

The Unfair Competition Issue

Let's say you own a small, neighborhood grocery store. You have owned your store for many years, dutifully paying taxes and contributing to the community in a variety of ways. Suddenly, you find out that you will have new competition in six months. Another grocery store will open just down the road.

"Fair enough," you say. "My customers like my store because the prices are fair, the store is clean, and my employees are friendly. I may lose a few customers, but having good, clean competition is part of doing business. Besides, this may help me find new ways to appeal to my loyal customers." But wait a minute. . . . You find out that the new store will look exactly like yours (only newer). The new store claims that selling food is a service to the community and that it will sell healthy food which promotes a sound mind and body. Since the store will "benefit the community as a whole" and "promote health," the money to buy the land and build the store will come from tax-exempt bonds redeemed by public tax dollars. You pay thousands of dollars every year in interest on the money you borrowed to buy the land and build your store. The competition won't be paying for anything.

Not only does the new store avoid paying debt charges but because it "promotes health" and wants to encourage as many residents as possible to take advantage of its healthy foods, its annual operating costs are subsidized by taxpayers—it is not required to break even. Further, since it is owned and operated by the public sector, it does not have to pay property, sales or income taxes which you are required to do. Finally, it receives free advertising and promotion from agency brochures, literature and articles, and is signed on all the surrounding highways informing travelers of its existence and location. In contrast, you have to pay for all your promotional vehicles.[3]

Given these advantages, the new grocery store is able to price its food products at half the prices you are charging. How can you compete with it? This scenario occurs repeatedly in the world of sport when public sector and nonprofit organizations offer similar services in the same geographic area to those offered by commercial sport operators. Consider the following example:

> I operate two clubs, 4 swimming. The other club is a 16,000 square foot facility including a $500,000 addition for a swimming pool, also occupying 4,000 square feet of the total. The North Clackamas Parks and Recreation District will locate its 80-acre Regional Park complex costing $16 million, precisely between my two clubs. The new indoor complex will be a 60,000 square foot aquatic center with five pools under one roof. My combined square footage for swimming is only

8,000 square feet. The projected costs to users of the huge regional complex who purchase monthly passes will be one-third to one-half the cost that my business charges. My business caters to middle class families, not upper-income wealthy individuals. The regional complex will market their facility to this same group. Clackamas County orchestrated a sophisticated marketing and advertising campaign in order to sell this idea to the voters, with the assistance of three highly compensated full-time staff who worked on this project for 18 months prior to advancing the concept to the voters.[4]

The advantages of the public sector include paying no property, sales, or income taxes; being self insured; financing improvements with tax-exempt funds rather than borrowing money at commercial rates; not being required to cover debt charges with operating revenues; not being required to cover operating expenses with revenues; being exempted from many regulations; and receiving free advertising from the agency. The potentially devastating impact of this competition is illustrated by the following examples:

- Lafayette, Colorado, has a population of 15,000. The city built a $4 million sports and fitness facility with three pools, steam rooms, a whirlpool, dry saunas, racquetball courts, a gymnasium, an indoor track, a fitness center with free weights and cardiovascular equipment, and babysitting services. When it opened, three private fitness clubs operated in Lafayette. After one year, one had gone out of business; a second saw its membership decline from 500 to 250; and the third, which was an aerobics studio, was unable to maintain the numbers it needed to justify proceeding with an expansion to which it had previously committed.[5]
- Gore Mountain Ski Center, a public facility operated by the state of New York, received an annual tax subsidy of $50,000 each year and was constructed with tax-free bonds. It applied for $246,000 in federal grants to help fund a $2.87 million capital extension that involved installing snowmaking machinery and other equipment. The balance of the capital was raised by issuing tax-free bonds. With these advantages, Gore Mountain charged $400 for a family season pass. The four commercial resorts in the area charged an average of $1,125 for the same pass because they had to pay commercial prices for investment capital and received no assistance from federal grants. They also had to show a reasonable return on their investment. Thus, the publicly operated state project gradually forced the commercial operations out of business. An editorial in the *Wall Street Journal* commented: "By a sort of Gresham's law of competition, we have noticed that state enterprises in the mixed economy tend to drive out private enterprise." (p. 4)[6]

Table 10.1 documents the financial disadvantages faced by a private athletic club operator who is in competition with a public or nonprofit organization in the same area. The example assumes that the club invested $3 million in acquiring five acres of land and is building the facility. In this example, the club has to pass an additional $502,203 in annual costs on to its customers. If the club had 1,800 members, then each would pay $279 per year, or $23.25 extra per month. Because the public or nonprofit facility

Table 10.1. A Comparison of Costs Incurred by a Public Agency or Non-Profit Organization and a Private Athletic Club on a $3 Million Facility		
Venue Name	**Public/ Nonprofit**	**Private Club**
Annual Land Carrying Costs (assuming a land value of $100,000 per acre and a 15-year loan on $500,000 at 9% interest)	0	$60,856
Annual Building Mortgage (assuming a $2 million,15-year loan at 9% interest)	0	$243,424
Furnishings and Equipment ($300,000 borrowed for five years at 11%)	0	$78,273
Postage (tax-exempt or public sector entitled to a 33% discount)	$13,400	$20,000
Real Estate Taxes (assuming a property value of $3,000,000 at 50% taxation rate of $4 per $100)	0	$37,800
Personal Property Taxes: State In- come Taxes (state tax rate of 7% on profit of $200,000)	0	$14,000
Federal Income Taxes (federal rate of 22.25% on first $100,000 and 39% on next $100,000)	0	$61,250
Total Annual Costs	**$13,400**	**$515,603**
ANNUAL COST ADVANTAGE TO PUBLIC/TAX EXEMPT SECTOR		$502,203

Prepared by Roger Ralph, President, Bel Air Athletic Club and Chairman, Harford County Coalition for Fair Competition. Reproduced in International Health. Racquet & Sportsclub Association (nd). *The Case for Fair Competition in the Fitness Industry.*Boston, MA: IHRSA

does not bear these costs, it can provide identical services at a substantially lower price than that of the private club. This egregious situation is exacerbated if the public agency's annual operations are also subsidized by tax funds.

Many private sport club managers allege that new public or nonprofit centers are often indistinguishable from their existing facilities and services and serve only to drive private clubs out of the marketplace. Some of their more extreme spokespeople ask: "Why should government build public sport facilities, when they don't build public food stores or pharmacies?" Others more reasonably ask: "Is the city going to build and operate its own movie theaters and bowling centers as well as sport facilities, since they are also recreation amenities?"

Public agencies argue that because community sport facilities usually are financed with general obligation bonds that have to be approved by a referendum, the public's willingness to finance them indicates that citizens do not perceive the private sector as meeting their demands. Further, they note that municipalities, colleges, and YMCAs have had gyms, pools, weight rooms, and playing fields that predate the first commercial sports clubs by 75 years or more.[7] Finally, competing public sport amenities generally are defended on the grounds that they aim at target markets in the community that do not have access to commercial facilities, such as families, seniors, and children, whereas commercial operators primarily target young adults ranging from 16 to 30 years of age. For example, a spokesman defending the decision of the city of North Richland Hills, Texas, to build a $7.8 million fun water park stated: "The park is not meant to compete with the large commercial water parks that target teens with their high-adventure rides, but is for families, particularly those with young children. We wanted elements that mom and dad would get out with the kids and interact together."[8]

It has been suggested that the opposition of private sports and fitness club owners is short-sighted because:

> It hurts facility owners—if not now, then later. Today's 14-year-old who is intro-duced to weights and stationary bikes in the community recreation center may well become an 18-year-old habitué of the college recreation center and then a 22-year-old—or 30-, or 40-, or 50-year-old—enthusiastic health- or racquet-club member. Killing opportunities for recreation in an industry that knows it is not even reaching 20% of the country—well, that's just bad business (p. 11).[7]

In Boise, Idaho, the West Family YMCA/Boise City Aquatic Center was the result of a three-way partnership between the city, which paid $5 million of the $9.4 million con-struction costs; the YMCA, which paid the rest of the construction cost and operates both the city's aquatic center portion and its own fitness center portion of the facility; and a research park, which donated the land. The facility's manager stated: "Part of the Y's mission is to help provide for those who would otherwise not be able to afford it." That closely conforms to what the city wanted to do by making sport facilities very affordable. However, the project was perceived differently by community health and fit-ness club owners in the area. One of them described it as "one of the most lavish health clubs in the area which has been responsible for putting four clubs out of business since it opened." Another club owner stated:

> It was presented as a place for our youth to learn solid values and strengthen body, mind and spirit, as a way to counteract the influence of gangs. Who can complain about that? . . . But in actual fact, they're catering to middle- and upper-class adults. From our point of view, what they are doing is using their special treat-ment through their tax exemptions, and the fact that they don't have a mortgage to pay. They were given this facility by the community, and are using these advan-tages to unfairly compete with the non-paying businesses in the fitness industry here in Boise. (p. 34)[2]

The funding for most public-agency sports facilities has to be approved by a public ref-erendum. Because in most parts of the country there is no legal mechanism for stopping public agencies from constructing competing facilities if they wish to do so, some pri-vate sport managers have mounted campaigns to stop facilities at the voting booth.

Exhibit 10.1 reports the response of sport and fitness club owners who led a success-ful campaign to defeat a $25 million bond proposal for a family recreational center in Southfield, Michigan. A similar campaign in Fairfax County, Virginia, was not success-

Exhibit 10.1

Defeat of a $25 Million Bond Proposal for a Family Recreational Center

Proposal A on the ballot in Southfield, Michigan, sought a 20-year bond issue of up to $25 million to expand the existing civic center sports arena, which contained a 30-year-old ice rink, into a family recreational center and to renovate the existing space. This would have added a 1.09 mill tax to taxpayers' bills, so the owner of a $92,000 home (average for Southfield) would pay $50.14 each year. The proposed facilities included

- a three-court gymnasium;
- an elevated jogging track;
- an indoor-outdoor aquatic center with a leisure pool and a second pool for lap swimming;
- a second full-sized ice arena with 1,500 spectator seats and a studio ice facility for figure skating;
- a senior citizen center;
- a teen center; and
- meeting rooms, kitchen facilities, food services, and locker rooms.

Fitness businesses in the community quickly organized to oppose it. "We pay a lot of taxes and pay a lot of people and we will be hurt by this," said the general manager of Franklin Fitness & Racquet Club. "We've been a solid business operation in this community for 25 years," he said. "You don't want to start competing with the city which is using donated land and doesn't pay taxes to itself. If the measure passes, we and other clubs through the increased taxes we'd be paying, in effect, would be subsidizing a competitor. Is there a need to tax 100% of the people for what 5, 10, or even 15% are going to use?"

The city authorities argued that they had an obligation to provide recreational facilities for their citizens, to which the fitness club general managers responded, "Maybe, but to what degree? When does it stop? Sure cities provide recreational facilities, but at what level? Would they want to provide bowling? Should they build a movie house?"

"There's a misunderstanding that may be there," said the assistant parks and recreation director. "They feel we're being competitive, but we're not. We have a family atmosphere, not a club atmosphere. We feel we can bring in fun for young people, toddlers, and adults. There would be no full-blown fitness program or body-building facility . . . We don't think we compete for the same clientele. We offer an introduction to people to the things they do at the private clubs. In that regard, we may actually be helping them because people try something out and if they find out they like it, they might want to sign up with a club."

Franklin Racquet Club celebrated its 25th anniversary that year by dedicating a new $1 million basketball- volleyball floor. "Basketball leagues are flourishing here on weekends and in the evenings," the club's manager said, "but volleyball hasn't yet gotten so popular here. And if the city winds up with a new basketball/volleyball gym, what will that mean to places like Franklin? It definitely will affect our business. We can't grow like we want to. If someone could afford a league over here and get it at halfprice over there—even if they could afford the higher price—why wouldn't they go there? We may not have made that $1 million investment if we knew we'd have been competing with the city."

At approximately the same time that this proposal was announced, the city, in conjunction with Providence Hospital, opened a new wellness center at its Beach Woods Recreation Center. They filled an existing 12,000 sq. ft. room with equipment. They charged $250 per year for membership and hoped to attract from 300 to 350 members. Four physiologists, who were not employed by the hospital, were available to members, each working 20 hours per week in the center. The fitness clubs developed a brochure that emphasize reasons the bond proposal should be rejected (see figure 8-1A). This brochure gave no indication that the fitness clubs planned and funded the campaign. The group registered itself as Friends Opposed to Proposal A. This strategy was designed to ensure that the residents objectively reviewed the points raised. If this had not been done, some recipients may have dismissed the campaign as merely the disgruntled efforts of a narrowly vested commercial interest.

The fitness group invested approximately $20,000 in their opposition campaign that included the following:

- A brochure mailed to each household in Southfield (see figure 8-1A)—printing, postage, and mailing cost $6,500
- Brochure inserts in the *Detroit Free Press and News* for Southfield—$3,000
- A full-page advertisement in the *Free Press and News*—$4,200
- A full-page advertisement in the *Southfield Observer*—$2,500
- Individuals handing out a brochure outside voting areas on the day of balloting—$2,000

As a result of their efforts, Proposal A was defeated overwhelmingly by 5,582 votes to 2,055 votes.

ful, but it emphasized the convincing arguments that can be made by the sport and fitness industry against new public recreational centers. In the Fairfax County case, the private-sector recreation suppliers authored a 16-page report documenting their belief that the county park authority was directly and unfairly competing with them when it proposed to build four new recreational centers. The report was entitled *Unfair, Unfair, Unfair Competition: How the Fairfax County Government and Fairfax County Park Authority Directly Compete Against Private Recreation*. The first paragraph of the report stated:

> We are optimistic this document will make governmental agencies aware of the unfair situation that occurs when non-taxpaying public facilities compete directly against private taxpaying facilities, and will encourage responsible public officials to pass legislation that would prohibit any government recreation facility from locating within a specific distance of an existing private facility. This type of legislation would give the Fairfax County Park Authority a clear guideline and prohibit the park system from competing unfairly or duplicating recreation that is already provided by a tax paying business. In Fairfax County there are numerous privately owned recreational facilities. . . . Competition in the leisure/recreation field has become increasingly fierce due to many factors; however, when you consider normal business expenses and the additional burden created by trying to compete with the very government you pay taxes to, it is difficult to understand why any new recreational businesses would enter the market. It should be noted that hundreds of privately owned recreation/leisure facilities are competing for the same recreation/leisure dollar. A large general public is needed to support and patronize these businesses for them to succeed. As the County continues to expand into the revenue-producing recreation field, the recreational dollar is further diluted, which eventually will bankrupt some businesses and certainly discourage others that hope to build additional facilities.[9]

Regardless of the legal and ethical issues raised by unfair competition, there are two pragmatic reasons that public agencies should avoid it. First, the presence of fair competition by private suppliers may stimulate the agency to improve performance in terms both of responding to user demands and of minimizing costs. Second, most public agencies are unable to fully satisfy all of the demands expected of them. If some of these demands can be met by the private sector, then agency resources can be redirected to meet other needs.

Legal Principles Relating to Unfair Competition by the Public Sector

While competition with commercial sport operators may present significant philosophical, ethical, and political problems, agencies are not required legally to refrain from such competition. Under the general power authorizing them to provide park and recreational opportunities for citizens, agencies (if they choose to do so) legally can provide facilities and programs similar to those that private businesses offer.[10]

The courts have consistently rejected arguments by commercial operators that municipal competition would cause a loss of profits and thus effect an unconstitutional taking of property without compensation. They have confirmed that municipalities have no duty or obligation toward private competitors whose businesses suffer from competition by public enterprises. In a typical ruling, one court stated:

> We know of no principle of law which would require a city to reimburse private business for loss of profits suffered as a result of lawful competing municipal activity, at least in the absence of statutory requirements. Nor is the fact that an operation that act may tend to lessen the profits of a few private dealers or even force them from business, a matter of consideration for the court. It is for the legislature to determine from time to time what laws and regulations are necessary or expedient for the defense and benefit of the people. (p. 23)[11]

The courts recognize that providing fitness and health opportunities falls within the public purpose mandate of municipalities to preserve and promote the general public health, safety and welfare of their residents. These are the broad powers generally given by state laws to local entities. These powers authorize municipalities to offer a wide array of public recreation facilities and programs that may compete with the private sector. The courts recognize the nexus between providing recreation opportunities and the government function of promoting public health.

A state supreme court noted that as a general rule, governmentally "owned and operated enterprises have been permitted to engage in head-to-head competition with privately owned companies," (p. 34)[12] while another court noted, "Whether the City is engaged in a proper activity is not determined by whether it competes with private business, but whether it is an authorized public purpose" (p. 40).[12]

Legal Principles Relating to Unfair Competition by Nonprofit Organizations

In contrast to their lack of success in challenging public sector facilities and programs, commercial operators have had success in the courts in challenging non-profit organizations. Most of their efforts have been directed at YMCAs and non-profit hospitals whose tax-exempt status is perceived to give them an unfair advantage.

In their formative nineteenth century years, the religious mission of the YMCAs was to provide young men with a place to escape the temptation and evils of the cities and to convert them to Christianity which meant "saving the whole man, body, soul and spirit" (p. 78).[13] Inevitably, this led to fitness programs becoming a central element of YMCA offerings. Revenue-producing programs were necessary to fund programs that lost money and to pay for free memberships for those who could not afford to join the YMCA. However, over time, revenue-producing programs took precedent in many YMCAs and in some cases programs for the underprivileged were eliminated.

This shift in mission has led operators of commercial sport and fitness clubs to contest the tax-exempt status of some YMCAs. Their legal case has been articulated in the following terms:

We argue that YMCA recreation and fitness centers are not tax-exempt by reason of what they do (providing such facilities), but rather by reason of whom they are serving. YMCA facilities, whose services are focused primarily on taking care of youth, the elderly, the poor, the handicapped, etc., deserve every tax break they receive. On the other hand, YMCA facilities whose services are primarily focused on providing recreational fitness services to affluent suburban communities or an upscale business and professional clientele are not public charities and ought not to be tax exempt.[14]

This fundamental principle has been accepted as the key factor by courts that have ruled in these cases. The commercial operators support their argument with the following data:

- 37% of YMCA member households have income of $75,000-plus and 74% pay full fees—very similar to the membership profiles of tax-paying health clubs.
- Nearly 33% of local YMCAs offer no fee discounts for needy residents of their community.
- The YMCA is the largest non-profit institution in the United States, with nearly 2,600 local clubs with 20 million members. Its annual revenues, including user fees, exceed $4.75 billion.
- Just like a taxpaying fitness club, the majority of the YMCA's revenue comes from membership sales. Fully 78% of YMCA revenues come from selling memberships, not from donations.
- About 65% of YMCA members pay to use the YMCA exclusively for fitness services—just like the customers of tax-paying health clubs.[15]

While hundreds of YMCAs continue to serve the poor, aged, underprivileged, those with disabilities, and youth and are clearly public charities, others have moved away from this model and constructed modern fitness centers that cater to downtown businessmen or middle-class suburbanites. These are physically and operationally indistinguishable from commercially operated fitness and sports clubs. These new facilities use commercial advertising that focuses on selling memberships and not on appealing for volunteer and financial help for the needy. In form and format, their advertisements are often no different from those of commercial facility operators.

When the YMCA built a $2 million facility in Salisbury, Maryland, the existing Merritt Athletic Club lost 33% of its members to the YMCA. In Saco, Maine, the New England Health and Racquet Club saw its sales fall 50% when the $2.6 million North York County Family YMCA opened within three miles. Executive Athletic Club had been in Oakland, California, for 50 years when the YMCA opened a $10 million facility around the corner and drove the taxpaying club out of business.[16]

The unfair competitive advantage that the YMCAs enjoy stems from a myriad of special privileges granted under federal, state, and local laws and regulations governing them. These include:

Exemption from federal income taxation under Section 501 of the Internal Revenue Code. Nonprofits also enjoy exemption from state and local income and

---

Exhibit 10.2

Tax Concessions Granted to a Sport Business

Genesis Health Club operated four fitness centers in Wichita, Kansas. It planned to open two more facilities and to renovate one of their existing facilities. The Wichita City Council agreed to assist in two ways. First, it provided a 50% property tax abatement for 10 years. This exempted Genesis from paying an estimated $1.73 million over that time period. Second, it agreed to issue $11.85 million in industrial revenue bonds which Genesis could use to fund both construction and equipment purchases. The club owner argued that this access to tax abatements and cheap money enabled Genesis to compete on more equal terms with the city's YMCAs:

> The industrial revenue bonds and tax abatement afford Genesis the opportunity to offer its current and future members better facilities while keeping its expenses—and, thus, member and non-member costs—as low as possible. In small measure this allows Genesis to operate on the same playing field with

the YMCA, which pays no taxes and has a financial competitive advantage compared to a tax-paying, private business such as ours.[18]

Others in the community disagreed with this logic: "The YMCA should not be used to justify the Genesis tax break unless Genesis is willing to provide the same community services. It is comparing apples to oranges."[18] The CEO of the Greater Wichita YMCA denied that the non-profit, 75,000 member YMCA competed with Genesis which had approximately 30,000 members: "I feel we earn our tax exemption every day. Regarding the question of fair or unfair competition, saying it's unfair implies that Genesis is doing the same things we are," he says. "We have 20,000 kids in youth sports, 20,000 kids on scholarship, 1,300 kids in swim lessons, 6,000 kids in free after-school day care. If Genesis is doing these kinds of things, then it ought to become a 501(c)(3)."[18]

---

property taxes, and many are exempt from state unemployment compensation regulations. They benefit from significantly lower nonprofit postal rates. In addition, a nonprofit organization enjoys a special status in the marketplace; tax-exempt status makes an organization especially attractive to prospective customers. (p. 57)[17]

In addition, having 2,600 YMCAs in the U.S. facilitates benefits from economies of scale including learning curve benefits, training programs, marketing and purchasing.

Exhibit 10.2 offers an example of how the alleged tax advantages of a YMCA were used by a sport business to successfully win major tax concessions from a city council.[18] A description of industrial revenue bonds and tax abatements is given in the next section of this chapter, together with discussion of the broader implications associated with them.

The conceptual rationale for tax exemptions for YMCAs, as the debate in Exhibit 10.2 suggests, is that they provide social services that would otherwise have to be provided by government, so it is appropriate that they be subsidized in this way. However, sport and fitness club owners argue that these new YMCAs render few, if any, charitable services; allocate only small proportions of their revenue toward financial assistance or subsidized programs targeted at low-income groups; and target their services at those who can pay substantive fees. The YMCA points out that it needs to have some profitable programs, even if such programs compete with private businesses, because they are a major revenue source for providing services to the needy. However, it is illegal for a tax-exempt organization to use profits to subsidize other services. If a charity makes money from a source unrelated to its exempt purpose, it is required to pay taxes on that revenue. In this context, the IRS has made it clear that colleges are required to pay taxes on income they receive from fees paid by the general public to use college recreation and sport facilities. For example, the IRS demanded that the University of Michigan pay $7.6 million in taxes for income received from the university's ice-rink, golf, and other sports facilities.[19] In the view of the IRS, this income falls outside the school's nonprofit exemption.

The focus of the court cases has been the legitimacy of the YMCA's exemption from local property taxes. The most prominent case concerned the Columbia—Willamette YMCA's Metro Fitness Center located in Portland.[20] The Oregon Supreme Court ruled that this 4,400-member YMCA club should be placed on the tax rolls because too few of its services could be defined as charitable. Indeed, only 5% of its revenue went toward financial assistance. This ruling required the YMCA to pay $150,000 in annual property taxes from which it had previously been exempt. However, two years later, its property-tax exemption status was restored when it changed its name to Metro Family YMCA, expanded beyond its adult fitness focus by adding 20 new programs for youth including drug and alcohol rehabilitation and alternative education, and increased the level of financial assistance so it was extended to 33% of its members.

Commercial operators continue to lobby for more rigorous enforcement of the tax laws requiring that YMCAs are consistently required to verify and justify their tax-exempt status. As a result of this pressure and court rulings, YMCAs recognize they must be accessible to all regardless of ability to pay. They also now link mission to programs, including fitness, with more than "lip service":

> Ys now articulate a service component in many of their adult fitness programs and facilities and keep increasingly rich and detailed records of their costs, income, and subsidies to those in need. "We do health and fitness programs for persons of all ages and abilities" not to subsidize the needy, explained the chair of the Y's Public Policy Committee, but "because programs that build 'spirit, mind and body' are at the core of our charitable mission." (p. 15)[21]

Similar court rulings have been made against hospital health clubs that have claimed tax-exempt status. For example, the Supreme Court of South Dakota found that Sioux Valley Hospital's $6 million wellness center was not a charitable organization since only 0.5% of the club's 2,600 memberships were subsidized by the hospital. It rejected the argument that wellness centers are exempt as health care facilities:

> The Court noted that if it adopted such a broad definition of health care, all physical activity and all healthy activities would be exempt so that if the cafeteria provided health foods related to maintaining a state of soundness of the mind and

body, the cafeteria would be tax exempt. Again, if the pro shop sold items used for general fitness; which related to maintain a state of soundness of the mind and body, the pro shop would be tax exempt.[22]

A similar decision was reached in *Middle Tennessee Medical Center v. Assessment of Appeals Commission of the State of Tennessee.*[23] In that case, the court found that the hospital fitness center was not exempt from state taxes for non-patient use. The Court noted, "The great majority of those who use the . . . Center are not under a doctor's care. They have chosen the Center over competing health spas for reasons of their own, and it is not the role of this court to encourage that choice by according the . . . Center a more favorable tax treatment than that permitted by its competitors." The court added, "We feel it would be a misuse of the tax exemption granted to charitable hospitals if every revenue-generating venture they embarked upon automatically benefited from the exemption, so long as that venture could be characterized as in some way promoting health."

THE COMPLEMENTARY ASSETS OF PUBLIC AGENCIES AND PRIVATE SPORTS ENTERPRISES

Governments have always been active investors in the private economy, routinely using their assets to seed new businesses. For example, the federal government gave 9.3% of all land in the continental United States to the railroads as an inducement to build a transcontinental system.[24] Public jurisdictions have assets that they can use as incentives to stimulate investment by sport businesses that otherwise might not be forthcoming. These public assets can be used to prime the pump and leverage commercial investment by encouraging businesses to enter partnerships.

Critical to understanding the potential of partnerships is a recognition that each sector has financial, expertise, or regulatory resources of value to offer the other. The essence of forging a collaborative agreement is finding a way to fuse the complementary resources of each sector to the mutual advantage of all parties involved. A financially driven partnership generally seeks capital from the private sector partner and, in exchange, allows that partner to control most, if not all, of the facility's cash flow. This is necessary since the private sector partner will require a market-based return for its investment. In contrast, an expertise-driven partnership doesn't necessarily require a financial contribution from the private sector partner but capitalizes on that partner's experience in development and operations.

Public sector organizations have access to a range of resources that can act as powerful enticements to private businesses. These resources include a substantial land bank, the ability to access low-cost developmental capital, the capacity to confer a number of tax incentives, and control over zoning and permit applications. On the other hand, the private sector offers an array of resources that have proven to be attractive stimulants for public sector cooperation. These inducements include specialized management expertise, reduced labor costs, adaptability to scale of service, and reduced liability risks. The complementary resources that serve as the basis for public-private sector collaboration are summarized in Table 10.2.

Table 10.2. Complementary Assets that the Public and Private Sectors Can Contribute to Joint-Venture Collaborations	
Public Sector Assets	**Private Sector Assets**
Land Bank	Management Expertise
Low-Cost Capital	Reduced Labor Costs
Tax Waivers	Adaptability to Scale of Service
Control Over Permit and Zoning Processes	Reduced Liability Risks

Public Sector Assets

Land Bank

Among the valuable assets that a public agency possesses are the land it owns and the mechanisms and vehicles it is authorized to use to acquire land for public purposes. It is not easy to find sites in urban areas for sports facilities, and the challenge from residents in proximate urban neighborhoods has intensified as sport facilities have become larger, with higher capacities, more exclusive concessions areas, and more ancillary areas such as restaurants and hotels:

> Additional land is needed for parking lots, access roads, and expressway connections to accommodate the automobiles that bring most customers to games. Their size and nature make sports facilities unwelcome neighbors for most urban dwellers. Sports facilities bring crowds, litter, noise, and crime to an area, along with more traffic, air pollution, and parking problems. Residents fear that sports facilities, like other large developments, will inalterably change the character of their communities and reduce their property values, worries that are reinforced by the scheduling of most sporting events at night. (p. 280)[25]

It is common to find a substantial portion of a community's existing open space under the jurisdiction of a county or municipal park and recreation agency. Often, this inventory includes not only the largest tracts of potentially developable property, but also some of the most attractive parcels with respect to location, access, and commercial value. If such land is not available, then a public jurisdiction can use its extensive regulatory and financing powers to assemble a site. It is much more difficult for a private entity to do this, and it is inconceivable that a private entity would attempt it without support from a public agency.

From a developer's perspective, land is an unproductive cost. It is not depreciable, it adds to property taxes, and it yields no revenue flow. It is a prerequisite for building projects, but is merely a cost center. If its cost can be removed from a sport project, then it may make a project viable that otherwise would be unfeasible.

Once land has been deemed by a public jurisdiction to be available for a sport project to use, the jurisdiction may be prepared to offer a nominal lease (for example, $1 a year) in order to encourage development of a sport amenity that the public agency lacks the resources to develop on its own. Without this incentive, the high cost of land would make the project economically unfeasible for a private organization. Before considering arrangements of this type, there should be a careful review of local and state enabling legislation to ensure that the agency has the authority and power to proceed in this way. In a few cases, passage of new legislation at the state level may be required to create the necessary authority. In addition, each piece of land considered for use in this way should be reviewed to ensure that it is free of restraints and covenants imposed when it was obtained because these could prevent such use. This is especially important if the agency land was purchased with federal funds, which often prohibit any change of use.

In order to attract private investment funds, it is likely that an agency will be required to offer a long lease of 15 to 30 years on the land to allow a developer sufficient time to obtain a reasonable return on the investment. Normally, these leases provide optional permit-renewal clauses allowing continued private operation for one or two additional 5-year periods, after which time the entire facility usually becomes the property of the public agency.

Development of the Joe Robbie Stadium (currently named Sun Life Stadium) in Miami provides an example of how land can be used to prime the pump. The 73,000-seat, open-air stadium on the northern edge of Dade County was financed almost entirely by Joe Robbie, owner of the Miami Dolphins. The project became financially feasible when the land was offered at no cost to Mr. Robbie, the owner at that time of the NFL team. The developer who owned the 100-acre parcel of land on which the stadium was built leased it to Dade County for 99 years at $1.00 per year. Dade County then offered it on a similar lease to the Dolphins. Freed from site acquisition costs that would have run into the millions and from paying sales taxes because it was on county property, the owner of the Dolphins was able to apply all of the revenues raised through the successful sale of luxury suites and club seats prior to construction. The revenue was used as security on a 30-year, revenue-bond issue by Dade County. Robbie pledged income from the leasing of 234 luxury boxes and 10,000 club seats. Leases on the luxury boxes averaged $45,000 to $50,000 per year for a period of 10 years. Club seats, also leased for 10 years, were rented from $600 to $1,400 per year. Most of these exclusive seats were sold by the first year of the stadium's operation. The leases generated over $13 million a year, exceeding the $10 million annual debt charges on the stadium.

Similarly, the contribution of land by the city of Anaheim Redevelopment Agency was a key element in the partnership collaboration that led to the development of Disney Ice, a community ice-skating center adjacent to the Arrowhead Pond Arena (now named the Honda Center), which is described in Exhibit 10.3.

Although land is a powerful pump-priming asset, any proposal to change the use of existing park land to accommodate sport activities is likely to stimulate vigorous opposition. This opposition is likely to be especially pronounced if the activities are offered by a private business. An illustration of the backlash that may occur when park land is used to encourage private investment is given in Exhibit 10.4.[26]

There are multiple examples of public agencies contributing land to jointly develop

Exhibit 10.3

Development of Disney Ice

The city of Anaheim joined with Disney to develop Disney Ice as a community ice skating center, which was a complementary facility to the Arrowhead Pond amenity described in Figure 7-5. There were three parties involved in the development:

1) The Anaheim Redevelopment Agency, which is charged by the city with leading its downtown redevelopment efforts;
2) DSCR Inc., which is a wholly owned subsidiary of The Walt Disney Corporation; and
3) Disney GOALS, Inc., a 501(c) (iii) organization.

The genesis for Disney Ice occurred when the Walt Disney Company purchased a National Hockey League franchise, the Mighty Ducks. City officials were enthusiastic about the idea of partnering with Disney to develop a high profile sports venue in Downtown Anaheim. Designed by architect Frank Ghery, the City envisaged this would create another focal point in Downtown Anaheim, which was only minutes away from Disneyland and the Anaheim Convention Center.

The project's four objectives were to provide:

1. a fully equipped training center for the Mighty Ducks of Anaheim, a National Hockey League franchise, which committed to use the ice-rink as its primary practice facility;
2. a focal point for local and regional hockey leagues and exhibition games;
3. community programs that offered free skating and other activities for seniors and youth; and
4. a resource for under-served youth in the area through the Disney GOALS program (Growth Opportunities through Athletics, Learning and Service).

The Redevelopment Agency conveyed the 3.2 acre site for Disney Ice to Disney GOALS. This land was valued at $4.3 million. Disney GOALS and DSCR Inc., constructed the facility. The glass enclosed entrance fronts a large plaza designed for community functions and activities and painted in the Mighty Ducks' colors. A 3,000 square foot pro shop and Mighty Ducks superstore (where visitors can purchase top-of-the-line figure skating, ice hockey, and in-line hockey equipment and National Hockey League merchandise) are located to the right of the entrance. Rental skates are located on the left with plenty of seating room throughout the area. As visitors walk through the entrance hall, they see an 85 foot × 200 foot National Hockey League-size rink to the left, and a 100 foot × 200 foot Olympic-sized rink to the right.

The facility was leased by Disney GOALS to DSCR Inc. Thus, GOALS has income from the property, which is used for its ongoing programs. The primary purpose of the community programs provided through Disney GOALS and through DSCR's operation of the ice rink is to address the city's gang/drug problem by focusing on youth and families. The programs are required to provide a mix of activities that will attract Anaheim citizens of all ages; however, an emphasis will be on youth activities, ranging in age from preschool to senior high school; involving both boys and girls; and discouraging drug, alcohol, and tobacco use.

The agreement required Disney GOALS to provide services in the form of ice time, equipment, instruction, and services to the community on an annual basis for 30 years. The financial arrangements required the value of the public programs and services offered by Disney GOALS to be $375,000 annually. These contributions are made in lieu of cash payments for the land. The value of the annual services over the 30 years term of the agreement is $11.25 million. The net present value is $4.35 million. Thus, the services provided by Disney GOALS exceeded the cost to the city of providing the land by $50,000. In addition, the new property tax income derived from the facility was projected to provide $1.15 million (net present value) over the 30-year life of the contract.

The $375,000 annual in-kind contribution consists of 500 hours of ice-time, valued at $115,000; services, equipment rental, and/or vouchers/coupons to be redeemed at the Ice Rink, valued at $85,000; and the Disney GOALS program agreed to expend no less than $125,000 annually on salaries and services to the youth of Anaheim located in targeted neighborhoods. The GOALS programs include youth hockey, "learn to skate," and figure skating lessons, and their implementation is monitored and evaluated by the Anaheim Community Services Department.

Exhibit 10.4

A Backlash to the Commercialization of Parks

The Metropolitan Dade County Parks and Recreation Department is widely recognized as one of the nation's outstanding agencies. Like many others, it has been required to accept substantial additional responsibilities but has not been provided with additional tax funds commensurate with fulfilling those responsibilities. In the past decade, the land that the department managed increased more than 50%, from 8,700 to 13,500 acres, while its tax revenues actually shrunk when adjusted for inflation from $27 million to $24 million. Hence, the agency's managers had no alternative except to raise additional funds by encouraging private businesses to operate in some of the agency's parks.

This created a passionate backlash from park lovers and stimulated a campaign for a charter amendment that would have required county voters' specific approval before any commercial structure larger than a snack stand was placed in a park. The leader of this movement called what was happening to Dade parks an "ecological Chernobyl. This is a nightmare. I don't think the public has realized how much of this is going on." One of his associates observed:

> The county sees park property as a way to steal from the parks budget and invest in the tourism budget. They're leasing out our birthright. The tennis stadium may be the biggest example, and you know they've even rented space so used cars could be sold in a park, but my personal favorite is Santa's Enchanted Forest at Christmastime. This is in Tropical Park. They charge you $8 so you can see a drunken spider weaving up and down stringing the lights. This gaudy display is the tackiest thing I've ever seen in my life. The county has been shameless in this. Every time there's been the slightest bit of land available, they've had this urge to make money on it.

The agency's director responded that his department desperately needs the $165,000 that the Christmas attraction poured into the county coffers just as it needs the other concessions to help keep the parks going as the budgets continued to be squeezed. "I need money to pay for cutting the grass," he said.

JIM MORIN'S VIEW

The director pointed out that throughout the county, neighborhoods were crying out for more services in their parks from tot lots to ballfields. With no tax money available, new ways of securing financing had to be found. These included inviting bids from private companies to build ballfields on west Dade County park land. The selected company would get its money back by charging the teams that use the fields.

Working arrangements with private businesses that allowed them to operate in the parks resulted in substantial revenues accruing to the agency. For example, the Sundays on Key Biscayne, which was an expansion of what was once a little snack shop on park land, generated $350,000 each year to the agency. The restaurant at Haulover Beach in north Dade County netted the county $157,000. The beach grill managed by Christy's at Matheson Hammock earned the department $84,000.

From John Dorshner. Keep off the grass: Must Dade's parks be paved to be saved? *The Miami Herald.* July 29, 1992, pages 8–12. Reprinted with permission of *The Miami Herald.*

golf courses. Typically, the private developer/operator leases the land for a nominal rent of $1 per year and pays a rent to the public agency. The rent usually includes a fixed minimum guarantee and a percentage of gross revenues from the course's operations. When the lease expires, ownership of the course reverts in its entirety to the public

Exhibit 10.5

Using Land to Pump Prime a Golf Development

The Mile Square Golf Course was constructed on land owned by Orange County and leased to the developer/operator for 30 years. Orange County has been one of the fastest growing regions in the United States for many years, and there was a substantial demand for a new golf course. Mile Square is an 18-hole, par-72, 6400-yard course. It accommodates over 100,000 rounds annually and generates gross revenues in excess of $2 million. Orange County receives over $250,000 in lease payments over the 30 year period, which were based on the following schedule:

Year	Minimum Rent ($)	Percentage Rent	
		Green Fees Golf Car Rentals Range Fees (%)	Food & Beverage Sales Retail Sales (%)
1	12,000	7	3–4
2	12,000	8	3–4
3	12,000	9	3–4
4	12,000	10	3–4
5–10	12,000	12	3–4
11–30	12,000	14	3–4

agency. An example of this type of arrangement is the Mile Square Golf Course in Orange County, California, which was one of the earliest public-private joint ventures in the sports field.[27] This is described in Exhibit 10.5.

Low-cost Capital

It was pointed out in Chapter 9 that the interest investors receive on bonds issued by state and local governments is exempt from federal income taxation. This exemption causes the interest rate on these bonds to be lower than that on taxable bonds of equivalent risk and maturity issued by corporations. This is because a potential bond purchaser focuses on the after-tax interest return received from the investment. If a public partner can make this relatively inexpensive money available to a business enterprise, it can contribute a substantial financial incentive. It has been calculated that "a $225 million stadium built today and financed 100% with tax exempt bonds might receive a lifetime federal tax subsidy as high as $75 million, 34% of construction costs" (p. 398).[28] The lifetime federal subsidy represents the amount the federal treasury foregoes by allowing the business to benefit from tax-exempt bonds rather than requiring it to finance the venture with nonexempt bonds.

The 1986 Tax Reform Act made it more difficult for local jurisdictions to directly assist private sport facility developers with access to their low-cost capital. More frequently, governments now use their low-cost capital to assist projects by developing infrastructure such as roads, sewers, water, and utilities, which reduces the developer's total costs. Examples of this were given in Chapter 7.

Tax Waivers

The ability of the public sector to substantially reduce the property tax payments of private investors can encourage their participation in a partnership. These incentives most commonly take the form of tax abatements. A tax abatement is an agreement between a public jurisdiction and a commercial operator that the jurisdiction will waive at least some of the property taxes on a proposed new development for a given period of time. This incentive is used as a competitive strategy to encourage a business to locate in a community.

The terms of a tax abatement are negotiable and may range from a waiver of some proportion of taxes for a short period to absolution of all property taxes for an extended period. Abatement programs exist in almost all states. Typically, if a community has a policy to grant abatements, then abatements are awarded whenever they are requested and they routinely constitute part of a community's incentive package in negotiations with commercial enterprises. The length of the time period varies according to state-enabling legislation. For example, the usual period in New York is 10 years, whereas the period in Ohio is 20 years. The extent and magnitude of these abatements in professional sport stadium and arena projects was discussed in Chapter 6.

Tax abatements can be viewed as tax expenditures since giving a business a tax abatement is comparable to taxing it at the full tax rate and then appropriating money to expend as a gift to the private entity. Tax abatements are used widely even though the conventional wisdom of economists is that they are not very effective. Conceptually, if tax abatements are not given then a city saves the subsidy expenditure, enabling it to reduce its taxation levels, which encourages companies to locate in the community.

In Chapter 6, it was noted that the use of tax abatements is widespread, but in recent years some jurisdictions have discontinued them because they were perceived to discriminate unfairly against established businesses in the community. The unfair competition issue was discussed earlier in the chapter, and this is another dimension of it. Consider the following example:

> A new, $3 million health and fitness club is granted a tax abatement for 10 years, meaning that it does not have to pay the property taxes of $50,000 each year for which it normally would be liable. Similar clubs that have been operating in the city for many years pay property taxes. The new facility is able to offer its services at a lower price than the long-established clubs, which threatens their survival because the new facility pays no property taxes, making its costs of operation substantially lower.

While public agencies' advantage of paying no property taxes may enable them to unfairly undercut the prices charged by sport businesses, tax abatements offered to new businesses constitute a similar threat.

Control Over Permit and Zoning Processes

Nowhere is the adage *time is money* more relevant than with respect to development projects. Invariably, one of the most challenging, and often time-consuming, aspects of the development process is meeting the various preconstruction permit requirements.

The ability to expedite permit applications has become increasingly important. The impact of government legislation and regulations is felt by the private sector from the initial planning of a project through to its development and operation phases. The development of a sport facility by a private company is subject to myriad regulations and requirements that a great number of government agencies administer. The complexity of the situation for a large project is illustrated in Figure 10.1. It shows the steps that would have confronted the San Francisco Giants professional baseball franchise if it had proceeded with a proposal to build a new baseball stadium in the China Basin. The site was owned by two public agencies: the state of California and the San Francisco Port Commission.[28]

Imagine a private firm setting out to build a ballpark in China Basin on its own. Starting in the upper left corner, Figure 10.1 describes the steps with which the firm would be confronted in simply acquiring a site. Initially, a tract of land (large by any measure) would have to be assembled. As Figure 10.1 indicates, once a site has been selected, elected government officials would be required to act. The colossal height of a coliseum would require a zoning variance by the zoning board, by the San Francisco Board of Supervisors, or by an initiative. Because the building of stadiums is controversial, local politicians prefer an initiative that provides approval by the voters through a referendum. Therefore, site assembly would probably involve a referendum.

If the ballot measure were approved, as Figure 10.1 illustrates, a host of further approvals from the city would be required to meet environmental remediation and traffic mitigation requirements, culminating once again with a vote of the Board of Supervisors. If that hurdle were passed, Figure 10.1 imagines what would have to happen next if this very large site were acquired. Many agencies would have to sign off, and once again the Board of Supervisors would have to give its assent.

Getting environmental, safety, and traffic approvals and the acquisition of the state land definitely would be easier if an organ of government, for example, the Port of San Francisco, were the agency applying. Government agencies have credibility before other public agencies, and probably before the press and public also, that private firms do not have. It is hard to imagine a private firm working through the 28 steps indicated in Figure 10.1 without the prior agreement of the mayor and a majority of the Board of Supervisors (p. 328).[28]

Obtaining all of the necessary permits and permissions to proceed is frequently a frustrating process that discourages many developers. A public jurisdiction is likely to be able to assist in expediting this process. The public agency working from within the government system can push much more effectively for rapid permit approval than can private firms operating outside the structure of government.

Some segments of the general public are always likely to be suspicious that while projects result in profits for developers, they inflict unacceptable costs on other stakeholders. If a public agency's elected representatives take responsibility for facilitating the necessary permits and zoning authority, then some of the angst may be removed from the situation because, by definition, those elected officials represent the public interest.

Control over land use through zoning is a basic asset that most local governments

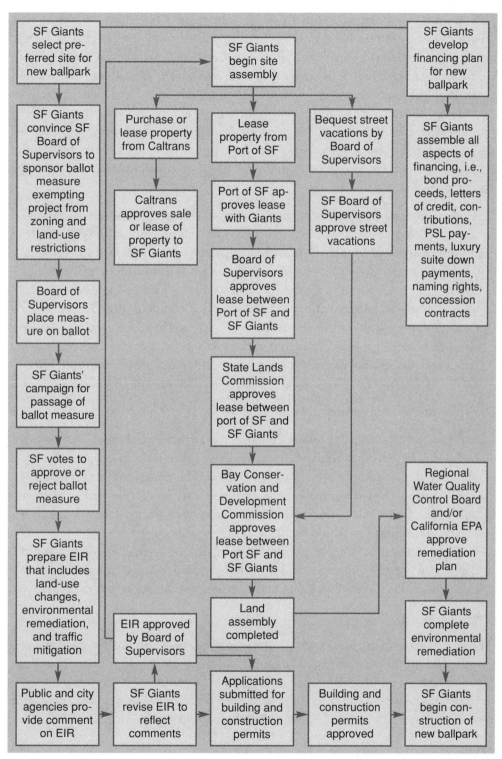

Figure 10.1. Steps toward Private Construction of a Ballpark at China Basin in San Francisco. SF, San Francisco; PSL, personal seat license; EIR, engineering investigation report; EPA, Environmental Protection Agency.

possess. Land-use zoning substantially impacts the value of land, and changes in it can greatly amend a project's viability. If a business purchases land that is zoned for agricultural purposes, then the land's cost and its value are likely to be much lower than if it were zoned for development because the income potential of agricultural land is significantly lower. If the zoning is changed after the land has been purchased at a price reflecting agricultural use and if the land is then used to develop a sport project (so the operator does not use land already zoned for development), then the cost to the business will be much lower, making the purchase potentially more profitable. Hence, changes in zoning that increase the amount of development allowed on a piece of land are likely to increase its value:

> After Sacramento voters rejected an initiative to construct a stadium on county land, private developers acquired 510 acres of rice farm land on the edge of the city that was zoned for agricultural use. In making this purchase, the developers gambled they could convince the city to rezone the site for commercial development. The developers purchased the Kansas City Kings NBA franchise and brought it to Sacramento. This mobilized eager basketball fans, who helped lobby for the rezoning so that a new arena could be built for the team on this land. The rezoning was granted, which meant that the value of the rice farm land and hence the developers' assets increased dramatically. The sports project was used effectively to leverage the zoning change, which otherwise was unlikely to occur.[29]

The trade-out was described in the following terms:

> Sometimes the cost of obtaining a team may not be money (which may be put up by business leaders, not taxpayers), but rather the sacrifice of a long term policy objective. This is what happened in Sacramento. The rapidly growing state capital of California had all the makings of a major-league town (it was the 21st largest television market in the country). But when local developer Gregg Lukenbill bought the Kansas City Kings basketball team, he and a few other landowners effectively traded their promise to bring the team to Sacramento for permission to develop an area the city voters had previously set aside for agriculture. The City Council—hungering for big-league status—eagerly went along with the deal.[30]

Private Sector Assets

The most obvious contribution of the private sector to joint partnerships is an ability to provide funds for operation, maintenance, and/or capital development of a venture. However, there are four additional aspects of private sector involvement that may also be attractive to the public sector: management expertise, reduced labor costs, adaptability to scale of service, and reduced liability risks. Each of these is discussed in this section.

Management Expertise

Often, government agencies do not have personnel with the necessary training, experience, and/or equipment to effectively operate specialized sport facilities such as ice rinks, indoor tennis centers, skateboard parks, arenas, golf courses, and ski areas. On the other hand, established private firms draw upon a depth of technical expertise that provides many advantages. These benefits include the ability to focus their work force and equipment more intensively to perform a specific function, coupled with the likelihood of owning more up-to-date, specialized equipment.

Commercial companies that specialize in a particular service area can often lower operating costs because of superior purchasing power with suppliers, especially if they operate a network of similar facilities. For example, a company managing several arenas is likely to be more successful at attracting top entertainment talent than an agency manager responsible for only one facility would be. A large company may also have an array of marketing skills, cost controls, and other systems that have proven effective at similar facilities, whereas an agency manager of a single facility may have to reinvent the wheel. An experienced sports manager in charge of food and beverages at a facility highlighted the importance of such systems:

> I am not for one moment suggesting that people who work in food and beverage are one iota more dishonest than anyone else in this imperfect world. But these staff, and anyone who comes into contact with them in the course of their work, from delivery drivers to the customers, are dealing in cash, food and drinks. I can't think of three more temptingly tradable or consumable commodities handled together!

It is for very good reasons that the best commercial vendors spend an enormous amount of time and money establishing effective and efficient control systems. When these are well monitored they ensure a tight grip on the business. I have looked at food and beverage operations where a 10% royalty from a good contractor would have far exceeded a presumed 30% profit from "our own people" for reasons of control alone.[31]

A large business with specialized expertise in a given service area may be better able to attract good managers to be responsible for the service than public agencies. Such an organization can offer that manager a career path with promotion to larger facilities and more responsibility, whereas a public agency frequently can offer promotion only to a relatively restricted level unless other duties outside the area of expertise are included. Further, the organization will have other trained managers with new ideas to replace the current manager when he or she resigns or is promoted, whereas an agency will have to invest effort and resources in recruiting from outside or will have to promote an assistant who may not be as able.

The specialized expertise needed to operate golf courses optimally has resulted in several companies' emerging to meet this need. They include American Golf Corporation, which operates 116 courses in the U.S.; Troon Golf with 200 courses; Billy Casper Golf Company with 140 courses; and ClubCorp with more than 150 facilities.

The American Golf Corporation provides a good example of how one firm has parlayed its management expertise into becoming a leader in public golf course management. Exhibit 10.6 indicates that the company offers a public agency a range of specialist services designed to enhance both operating efficiencies and the quality of the golf

---

Exhibit 10.6

The American Golf Edge

American Golf has been the world's leader in public golf course management for the past 20 years. We have provided excellence in every facet of our operations and continually strive to stay on the leading edge of all developments in the golf industry.

We are able to provide services like no other management company because of the expertise found in our corporate personnel and our management and operations techniques.

Some of our unique human resources are

- *the construction department.* This department supervises all designs and construction of new site facilities and renovation of existing buildings.
- *landfill construction.* One example is Mountain Gate Country Club, a 27-hole private country club located in Los Angeles.
- *drainage reconstruction.* Inadequate draining is a problem on many courses. We have had experience with every type of drainage problem across the country. One

example of our redesign and construction can be found at Fullerton Golf Course in Fullerton, California.

- *agronomy expertise.* Our in-house agronomy expert supervises and advises all regional and course superintendents nationwide in the proper care of trees and turf.
- *training.* This department ensures that all new employees are thoroughly trained in American Golf procedures, policies, and philosophy.
- *employment opportunities.* Career opportunities and competitive wages are offered nationwide (based on nationally collected salary survey information).
- *the marketing department.* All corporate marketing, advertising, promotion, and public relations direction, as well as pro-shop merchandise coordination, falls under this umbrella. Where possible, central buying results in tremendous price savings for all American Golf pro shops.

Adapted from The American Golf Edge. Produced by American Golf Corporation, 1633 26th Street, Santa Monica, CA 90404.

---

experience. Rarely does a public agency responsible for operating a golf course have the resources or expertise to furnish such a complete array of specialized services. The company specializes in revitalizing golf courses for which governments do not have capital funds. American Golf's approach involves initial investment (sometimes reaching $1 million) to improve the course and related infrastructure, dramatically increasing rounds of play through enhanced service quality and vigorous marketing, and reducing costs largely through more flexible and cost-effective use of personnel. The company's takeover of four municipally owned golf courses in Detroit illustrates the benefits of private sector expertise:

American Golf Corporation entered into a 20-year lease agreement with the city of Detroit Recreation Department to operate four of the six city golf courses. The courses consistently had lost money for the city. Operating losses of close to $600,000 had to be covered by monies from Detroit's general fund. The contract required American Golf to spend close to $2 million for improvements, including clubhouse renovations, new irrigation systems, landscaping, bunker restoration, and drainage work. In addition, the terms of the agreement stipulated that Ameri-

Exhibit 10.7

The Emergence of Skateboard Park Management Companies

In the past decade, skateboard parks have been built in many communities. To address cities' liability concerns associated with these facilities, many states have passed laws exempting cities from liability for accidents resulting from use of the parks if they enact ordinances requiring safety gear, post the law at the park and don't supervise activities there. The result is that a preponderance of city attorneys and risk managers discourage any kind of continuous skatepark supervision.

This development has created a real dilemma for communities that have discovered the potential skateparks have as youth development centers. A park supervised by trained staff opens up all sorts of opportunities for sports training programs and special events. But the fear is that it also makes the city vulnerable to liability for injuries occurring there.

Some publicly built parks have addressed this dilemma by partnering with the Action Park Alliance (APA). The APA is a private organization that operates parks designed and built by cities for sports such as skateboarding, BMX biking and inline skating-activities once termed extreme sports by the media and now more commonly referred to as action sports.

APA carries comprehensive public liability insurance covering all activities at the park. As the primary insured, it serves as a layer of liability insulation for the city. Their staff are responsible for monitoring park activities, conducting programs, undertaking regular safety inspections and maintenance, keeping a database of users and their contact information for parents or significant others, constructing a pro shop, developing special events and regional competitions, and promoting the park.

can Golf pay the city $50,000 in the first year of the lease, increasing to $200,000 by the fifth year. In return, the possessory lease provided American Golf with exclusive operating rights to the four courses. American Golf's regional director acknowledged the risks for his firm: "We'll lose money for six years." However, American Golf's strategy was to recoup losses as the dramatic changes in the courses drew people back. The company's goal was to attract 10,000 more golfers per year to each of the courses. The use of its own employees, who were paid considerably less than unionized city workers; sales from concessions; and equipment rentals also helped create efficiencies.[32]

It is important to note that the city of Detroit excluded two of its six golf courses from the management agreement with the American Golf Corporation. Jurisdictions that encourage some level of competition among service providers produce substantial savings from contractors. In this case, the city induced competition between the courses that American Golf Corporation operated and those that the city maintained in-house; this action gave both service providers incentive to produce high levels of service.

A plethora of skateboard parks has emerged in recent years. For reasons explained in Exhibit 10.7, public agencies frequently not only lack expertise in this area, but also face legal constraints that inhibit their ability to provide supervision or programming at these parks. This vacuum has spawned a number of management companies that offer the services described in Exhibit 10.7.[33]

Reduced Labor Costs

The labor-intensive nature of many sporting opportunities offered by governments makes the cost of personnel a major element in the cost of service delivery. The bargaining agreements that public employee unions negotiate, the longevity of many agency personnel, and the protection that civil service regulations afford the employees frequently mean that their wages are substantially higher than those that businesses pay. For example, when Indianapolis contracted out its 12 golf courses, the contractors hired staff at an average of $7 per hour, whereas the city's average cost for the same positions was $18 per hour plus an incremental amount per hour for overtime when employees worked more than 40 hours each week.

Agencies typically pay from 30% to 35% in fringe benefits to employees for things such as health insurance, retirement, sick leave, and maternity leave. Many businesses, in contrast, are not required to maintain such a high level of overhead. Federal and state laws require commercial operators to pay Social Security and payroll taxes, but not employee medical or pension benefits. As a result, payroll overhead costs for private firms may only be 12% to 15%. The substantial savings advantage in benefit costs that many businesses enjoy allows them to provide the same level of service much more economically than a public organization. In addition, their exemption from civil service requirements provides them with greater flexibility in determining level of pay, fringe-benefit payments, and a mix of full- and part-time personnel.

Exhibit 10.8 illustrates the cost advantage of private sector companies in low-skilled activities such as mowing athletic fields. It shows that the private sector's cost is only 43% of the public agency's cost. The example in Exhibit 10.9 illustrates how one government agency overcame a staffing cost problem by partnering with a private business.

Exhibit 10.8

Who Are You Going to Hire to Mow Athletic Fields?

The mowing of athletic fields is now commonly contracted out to private sector businesses. Consider the comparative costs of the two entities.

Public Agency

Pays salary averaging $12 an hour for a 40-hour work week to mowing crew staff, i.e. Pays a benefit package of	$25,000 a year
	$10,000 a year
Total Cost	$35,000

Private Business

Pays an hourly rate of $8, but does not pay when the weather conditions prohibit mowing and offers no paid vacation. Thus, the contractor pays labor for the equivalent of 40 weeks only, i.e.Pays a benefit package of	$12,800 a year
	$2,200 a year
Total Cost	$15,000

Exhibit 10.9

Public Agency Savings From Contracting Out a Golf Course

A publicly managed golf course in Alameda County, California, operated on a 13-hour summer schedule, opening at 6:00 a.m. and closing at 7:00 p.m. All maintenance activities were performed by public employees of a regional park and recreation agency. The employees formed a bargaining unit, affiliating with the American Federation of State, County, and Municipal Employees, which is a public-employee labor union. The labor contract established between the federation and the park agency stipulated a standard workday of 8 hours for full-time employees. Compliance with the contract required the park agency to commit two separate 8-hour shifts of maintenance and operations personnel to the golf course. The park and recreation agency estimated that under this agreement, staffing costs at the golf course would increase as much as 21%.

Faced with an intractable situation, the agency made the decision to contract out the operation of the golf course to a specialized management firm. An advertisement placed in the *Wall Street Journal* produced several legitimate bidders. A long-term lease (5 years with four 5-year renewable options) was awarded to a private firm with a successful track record in operating and maintaining golf courses. The agreement called for the management company to provide more than $600,000 in capital improvements over the first 5 years of the lease. By applying a more flexible personnel schedule to accommodate actual work demands and, at the same time, not being obligated to pay as high an overhead (e.g., retirement, vacation, and hospitalization benefits), the park agency estimated that the private firm reduced labor expenses at the golf course by as much as 50%. The result was that the golfing public benefited from an enhanced resource. At the same time, the park agency freed approximately $400,000 each year in public monies, which previously were committed to paying golf course personnel, to apply to other service areas of concern.

Even when businesses pay their employees as much as public agencies both in salary and fringe benefits, they are able to save in labor costs. One empirical study reported that these savings emerged because businesses

- used less labor,
- had about 5% less absenteeism,
- made managers responsible for equipment as well as labor,
- used younger workers (who tend to cost less),
- used more part-time labor,
- terminated more employees (which is probably why there was less absenteeism), and
- used more capital equipment (which may be why less labor was needed).[32]

Adaptability to Scale of Service

The commercial sector is often better equipped to deliver services that require large numbers of part-time employees for short time periods. The bureaucratic procedures required of government agencies to hire and pay part-time employees is sometimes lengthy, cumbersome, and onerous, whereas it is generally easy for businesses. Thus, it may be efficient for an agency to partner with businesses for producing special events or highly seasonal services.

Partnerships with a commercial entity are also likely to be beneficial when an agency cannot take advantage of economies of scale. A business serving multiple organizations is likely to be able to purchase state-of-the-art equipment and materials at a lower price and is likely to be able to use them more efficiently than a single government agency can because the business services a larger number of units. An agency may not be able to justify purchasing equipment that will sit idle for much of the year. An example of gains accruing to public agencies as a result of partnering with businesses is illustrated by the economies of scale available to large companies like American Golf Corporation.

Each year, American Golf Corporation may purchase more than 2,000 golf carts for the 116 golf courses it operates, and this volume enables the company to negotiate a substantially lower purchase price per cart than any single public agency can. This scenario is repeated for its purchase of all other types of golf course maintenance equipment and of clothing and supplies sold in pro shops.

A related advantage that sometimes accrues to large commercial companies is that they may be able to take advantage of federal business tax laws, which may permit rapid depreciation of new equipment and offer investment tax credits for its purchase. These types of regulations make it advantageous for companies to acquire new equipment, and this translates into greater operating efficiency (although some of this advantage is mitigated because unlike public agencies, they are required to pay sales tax on equipment).

Reduced Liability Risks

An increasingly attractive incentive for public agencies to enter working partnerships with private organizations is that such a collaboration can substantially reduce the liability risks borne by government organizations. Most liability suits arise from careless or reckless acts (negligence) that result in unintentional harm to an injured party. The decline in the doctrine of sovereign immunity, which historically prohibited units of government from being sued, has resulted in cities, counties, and school districts being more vulnerable to negligence claims. Now there are many examples of multimillion-dollar liability awards that government agencies have paid. The increased threat of such catastrophic claims has necessitated that agencies purchase expensive insurance premiums.

A key question for agency managers, then, is how they can minimize the possibility of a financially catastrophic claim being made against their agency. Because liability insurance premiums are largely based on the estimated degree of risk facing an agency, any actions that it can take to reduce level of exposure to risk should lead to reduced premium costs. Government agencies have found joint ventures to be an effective strategy for minimizing their liability risks and, therefore, the costs associated with insurance protection. Increasingly, agencies are structuring partnership agreements in order to transfer as much of the risk and responsibility for liability as possible to the commercial or private operator. Typically, the transfer of liability risk is conferred in the lease agreement establishing a public-private partnership. The following example is drawn from a lease agreement established between a municipality and a commercial operator for the maintenance and operation of a sport complex:

CLAIMS. The contractor shall hold harmless the city and all of its agents, employees and officers from any and all damages or claims of any kind or nature, that may be made or may arise directly or indirectly from the performance of duties by the contractor, its agents and employees, including but not limited to any claims which may arise either directly or indirectly from the use of any equipment or tools which the city may lease or sell to the contractor. The contractor shall appeal and defend any action or suit instituted against the city arising in any manner out of the acts or omissions defined herein above. The contractor's duty to indemnify hereunder shall include all costs or expenses arising out of all claims specified herein, including all court, and/or arbitration costs, filing fees, and attorney's fees and costs of settlement.

The example identifies two provisions key to effective transfer of liability risks. The first element establishes that the public agency will be held harmless in the event of a negligence claim. The intent is to release the agency from all liability risks. However, although crucial, the hold-harmless clause alone may not provide ironclad protection. A standard provision is to add an indemnification clause stipulating that if the hold-harmless agreement is not completely adequate—for example, if the government agency is found liable of contributory negligence—the commercial operator would pay any damages that the agency owed. Thus, the private contractor exclusively bears responsibility and costs related to liability concerns.

PUBLIC-PRIVATE PARTNERSHIP MODELS

It is evident that each sector has resources that could be of significant value to the other. In public-private partnership arrangements, public and private sector organizations agree from the outset to share responsibility for development and/or expansion of a sport resource. Impetus for forming the working relationship can come from either sector. To provide a framework for understanding how these assets can be forged into effective public-private partnerships, examples of partnership arrangements are presented in this section. They have been classified into seven categories: public sector leasing; leaseback from the private sector; public sector takeovers; private sector takeovers; private sector pump-priming; expansion of existing public facilities; and multiparty arrangements. The latter category is a catchall classification that presents an array of different joint-funding models that have been used. There is no common thread among them except the desire on the part of multiple stakeholders to see a sport project come to fruition. The partnership examples described in this section illustrate the remarkably imaginative and creative funding arrangements that have characterized the financing of sport developments over the last decade.

Public Sector Leasing

The most common form of public-private sport partnership is the leasing of facilities to private entities in which public funds have been invested. Leases establish the fee that a private entity will pay to a landlord (lessor) to use a facility over a given time period. The example in Exhibit 10.10 is illustrative of public sector leasing agreements. The city gains the private partner's expertise, frees itself from maintenance and liability obligations, and may be fully reimbursed for the cost of the facility's construction (as in the case of Cathedral City, which was rewarded for agreeing to pioneer the concept of a public-private partnership). But, subsequent Big League Dreams' partnerships did not include the company paying facility construction costs.[34]

Exhibit 10.10

Leasing to Big League Dreams

Big League Dreams USA (BLD) is a private corporation launched in the late 1990s that operates athletic complexes on public land. Its first project was at Cathedral City in California where the city leased a 20 acre site to the company for 30 years. At Cathedral City, BLD featured replicas of Yankee stadium with white arched facades trimming the outfield and elongated power alleys; Fenway Park with a 30-foot high "Green Monster" wall in left and an odd-angled pocket in the wall in right-center; and Wrigley Field with the brick-look outfield wall adorned with ivy. The fields are scaled down to regulation size for Little League and adult softball.

It is the only amateur park in the country which has fans and mist cooling systems in the dugouts. Those who want to warm their posteriors on the "real" thing can sit in rows of seats purchased from Angel Stadium when it was renovated. There is a 20,000-square foot arena for roller hockey and basketball that doubles as a stage for entertainment. There is also a children's play area, volleyball courts, and batting cages. The nucleus of the playing fields is a large restaurant with windows for spectator viewing. It serves the usual fan fare of hot dogs, pizza, popcorn and beer. Selected games are videotaped and shown in the Sports Club bar and restaurant, along with network TV sports events. Game heroes and seasonal home-run leaders are recognized over the public address system and on a leaderboard. Player-of-the-game honorees also are recognized on local TV sportscasts.

Cathedral City agreed to use its bonding capacity to obtain the $6.3 million to build the project. These were 30-year taxable lease bonds backed by the city. As a new company with an unproven product BLD was unlikely to be able to borrow these funds from a lending source. BLD are obligated to pay the quarterly debt service payments for the 30-year period. Thus, if BLD's revenue projections are met, there will be no cost to the city for the facility. In addition, BLD agreed to pay the city 3% of its gross over $2 million, 5% over $2.5 million, and 7% over $3 million.

The facility was built for less money than if the city had constructed it because the private company was not impacted by the state's requirement that public entities are required to pay prevailing wages. This allowed the developer to invest about 20% more into improving the features of the project, which the city would not have done.

Based on 35,000 out of town visitors attending tournaments, pop concerts, and other sporting events, the facility has an economic impact of over $10 million a year on the region.

Subsequently, BLD has developed projects elsewhere in California at Redding, Colton and Redlands. However, for these projects, BLD is not paying the debt charges. The cities are building the sites to BLD's designs, but at their cost and then leasing them to BLD. In these cases, the appeal to the cities is no longer having responsibility for the maintenance costs, and receiving a share of the gross revenues.

	Table 10.3. Types of Lease Structures
1	Fixed rent
2	Fixed rent plus additional stadium related payments
3	Per game rent
4	Minimum per game payment, percentage rent and seat use charge
5	Minimum rent plus attendance based rent
6	Straight percentage-based formula
7	Fixed minimum rent combined with a percentage based formula
8	Fixed rent minus rental credits, plus additional rents
9	Initial per-game rent followed by percentage rent
10	Percentage rent, but if less than a specified amount, then a minimum rental
11	Either a minimum rental or a percentage, whichever is greater
12	A floor and cap provision: where the rental is stated in a maximum amount and a minimum amount
13	Attendance based rent
14	Percentage rent, attendance based rent, and revenue from hockey
15	Base rent or fluctuating attendance based payments, whichever is greater
16	Rent as operating and maintenance costs
17	Payments in regard to luxury boxes with a rental off-set
18	Combination of fee payments
19	Nominal or rent free structure

Public entities sometimes use a lease arrangement to facilitate renovation or an upgrade of an existing facility. This means the agency does not have to use its own money or borrowing authority to make the capital improvements. In exchange for the rights to the cash flow for a defined period, the private sector partner makes an initial capital investment to improve the facility. Usually, the public partner also shares part of the revenue stream.

Most lease agreements involve much more than negotiating a fixed rent for use of a facility. Some indication of their complexity, versatility, and variety can be gleaned from the list of lease structure formats shown in Table 10.3. These nineteen different structures were identified as being used in the four major professional sport leagues.[35] The array of revenue streams whose disposition may be negotiated in these leases is described in Exhibit 10.11.[35a, 35b]

Leaseback From the Private Sector

It is not unusual for public agencies to use facilities leased from the commercial sector. Indeed, it is standard federal government practice to lease commercial office space

Exhibit 10.11

Sources of Revenues Used as Lease Payments to Public Partners at Major League Facilities

The lease agreements that public agencies have negotiated with sport teams in the five professional sports leagues which they have assisted with land or facility construction may include payment from one or more of eleven revenue streams: base rent, ticket surcharges, total facility revenues, ticket sales, premium seating, concessions, advertising, naming rights, parking, other major league-related revenues, and non-major league revenues.

The number of major league facilities (n = 121) whose leases required them to share each of these revenue sources with public partners is shown in the following bar chart.

The chart shows that it is common for the public sector to participate in facility revenues through base rent (59 cases), ticket surcharges (38 cases), parking (22 cases), and non-major league revenues (46 cases). For all other revenue streams, the rate of participation is one-sixth or fewer of all the cases.

The most widely used vehicle is a *base*

or *fixed rent*. In some cases, the public partner receives only a token rent of $1 per season, for example, at Chicago's New Comiskey and Detroit's Comerica Park. However, the Houston Astros pay $4.6 million for their facility and land leases, the Texas Rangers base rent to the city of Arlington is $3.5 million a year, while Minneapolis receives $6 million annually from the Xcel Energy Center.

Ticket Surcharges are fees added to the ticket price collected by the team and passed along to the public jurisdiction. Typically, they are between 5 and 10% of the price of a ticket. For example, the surcharge on Pittsburgh Pirates' tickets is 5%, while the Baltimore Orioles pay a 10% ticket surcharge to the Maryland Stadium Authority. A relatively rare arrangement is for the public entity to share in the *total revenues earned* at the facility. Thus, the Seattle Mariners pay 10% of net facility operating revenues to their public sector landlord. The public share of non-premium seat *ticket sales* is usually set at between 5 and 10% when it is part of the

Number of Faclity Deals

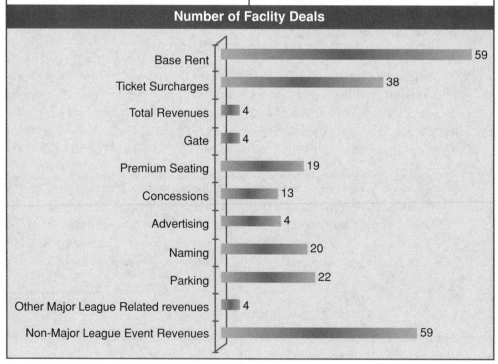

Revenue Source	Number of Facility Deals
Base Rent	59
Ticket Surcharges	38
Total Revenues	4
Gate	4
Premium Seating	19
Concessions	13
Advertising	4
Naming	20
Parking	22
Other Major League Related revenues	4
Non-Major League Event Revenues	59

Exhibit 10.11 *(Continued)*

Sources of Revenues Used as Lease Payments to Public

lease fee, and in some cases the lease includes a guaranteed minimum. For example, the NFL Detroit Lions pay the city of Detroit the greater of $1.44 million per year or 7% of ticket sales.

Premium seating refers to luxury suits and club seats. Public sector partners seek to negotiate a share of this revenue because creating premium seating is a primary driver of new facility construction and has substantially increased construction costs, and league rules minimize sharing of premium seating revenues among teams so it can be a large stream to tap. Typically, any lease payments will be tied to a percentage of the rent. For example, the Cincinnati Reds pay 7.5% of luxury suite rental revenues to the city of Cincinnati in addition to the 7.5% of non-premium ticket sales over $2.3 million.

It is not common in the major leagues for the public lessor to share in *concession revenues* which comprise food, beverage and novelty item sales, such arrangements are widely used in other sport contexts. Typically a percentage of gross, rather than net, revenues is negotiated. There are two reasons for this. First, there is incentive for the private partner to maximize the costs attributed to concessions if net revenues is used in order to reduce the amount they have to pay to the public partner, and these costs can be complex and difficult to audit. Second, private partners are generally reluctant to allow external entities to audit their costs of operation which they regard as valuable proprietory information.

Advertising revenues are those derived from interior signage and it is rare for public partners to share in them. However, the NFL St. Louis Rams, for example, pay 25% of the first $6 million in advertising revenue to its public landlord the St. Louis Regional Convention and Visitors Commission, and 10% of revenues above $6 million. In approximately one-sixth of major league faciltites, *naming rights revenues* are shared. For example, in Denver, the public sector received 50% of the $120 million paid by Invesco over 20 years i.e. $3 million per year. When the Sports Authority negotiated purchase of the naming rights from Invesco in 2011, for $150 million over 25 years, this revenue sharing arrangement continued. This is used to offset the cost of building the stadium.

Parking revenues from game days are widely shared by lessors. For example, the NHL Calgary Flames give 100% of game day parking revenues to their public landlord, while the NBA Indiana Pacers pay a $3.4 million annual fee to rent parking spaces at their facility from their public landlord. Teams are relatively sanguine about sharing parking revenue because it is a small portion of total facility revenue. Further, if the public partner controls parking, it may smooth the project approval process if local traffic impacts are a contentious issue.

Other major league-related revenues is a catchall category for other types of lease payments. For example, the New York Yankees pay the city of New York 10% of their local broadcast revenues net of expenses. *Non-major league revenues* refer to those associated with other events at a facility, including rock concerts and ice shows. Politically, retaining public control of these revenues may be important, as such events and the profits from them can be perceived as a strong supplementary argument to support public investment in a facility.

rather than to encourage agencies to purchase their own office space. The same principle can be used to extend the range of sport opportunities that a public agency can offer its clientele. Leaseback arrangements offer communities a way to fulfill equipment or facility needs without paying out large sums up front.

In broad terms, leasebacks can be classified into two categories: either build and transfer (BT) or build, own and operate (BOO). Both arrangements require the public and private partner to enter into a long-term contract. In both cases, the cost of construction is borne entirely by the private partner and the building is leased to the public agency at the previously negotiated, fixed or graduated annual rent for an extended period of time (usually 20–30 years). The difference between the two approaches is that in the BT model, the private sector partner's responsibility ends with the construction of the facility, whereas the more comprehensive BOO agreement requires the private partner not only to design, build and finance a facility, but also to operate, maintain and renovate it for the lease period.

Since the private partner in BOO arrangements is committed for the long term, its focus shifts to costs for the whole of the facility's life cycle, rather than only initial development costs. This encourages the private partner to build in such things as energy-reducing features, and more durable and high-standard materials and equipment which may cost more initially but result in lower operation and maintenance costs. Hence, the BOO model is likely to be most useful in projects where there are substantial maintenance costs, so that whole-life costing becomes a primary concern, such as aquatic and ice-rink facilities. In essence, the public agency is not buying an asset, rather it is purchasing a stream of services under specified terms and conditions. This is a crucial difference since procurement of a facility is not the goal, rather it is securing the flow of services that emanates from the facility.

In BOO arrangements, the public agency specifies the outputs it requires (not the inputs) in its request for proposals and the basis of payments for these outputs. The outputs may be restricted to the availability of the facility or may extend to include the personnel staffing it. If performance standards are not met, then deductions are made from the annual payments. This means that the private partner is responsible for cost overruns on construction of the facility; timely completion of the project, since the private partner does not get paid until the service is provided; and future costs associated with the asset. For example, if pipes in a pool break, the mechanical plant fails, or the pool's pH level is wrong, then the private partner is not paid while the pool is closed.

Leaseback partnerships mean that a public jurisdiction does not have to pay large sums initially or seek a bond issue for capital development costs. This type of arrangement was used by the Dallas Stars and the city of Euless in the construction of the Star Center Ice Arena, which is described in Exhibit 10.12.

Another example of this approach was the leaseback agreement established between the City of Dublin, Ohio, and Columbus Hockey, Inc., owners of the East Coast Hockey League franchise, the Columbus Chill. This example is explored in the following paragraphs.

The city and the hockey team agreed to collaborate on development of a $3.3 million indoor ice rink. The 60,000-square foot facility included two ice surfaces (one NHL size—190' × 85'—and one Olympic size—200' × 100'), a pro shop, skate rental area, video game room, public locker room, and a concession area. In addition, the ice

Exbibit 10.12

The Euless Dr. Pepper Star Center

The Dallas Stars are one of several franchises that have located in the Sun Belt in the past decade. With the exception of some migrants from the north, the four million residents of the Dallas-Fort Worth Metroplex area have no long-standing heritage or tradition of playing or watching ice hockey. Thus, a major challenge confronting the franchise was to create a market for ice hockey. The Stars' strategy for doing this was comprised of two elements.

First, there was recognition of the importance of a winning team in arousing local interest, and the Stars experienced success relatively soon after locating in Dallas. In 1999 they won the NHL's Stanley Cup, and in 2000 they were defeated in the Stanley Cup finals in the last match of a seven game series.

The second element in the strategy was to stimulate long-term grassroots involvement in ice hockey by encouraging youth to play the game. The key to this being successful was the availability of ice hockey facilities. The Stars long-term goal was to cooperate with cities to build and operate ten ice hockey facilities across the Metroplex area. The case study presented here describes the public-private partnership between the Stars and the city of Euless. This was the second of the Stars' facilities to be opened. The first was the Star Center in Valley Ranch. A third facility is being constructed in Duncanville, and the Stars are negotiating for a fourth and fifth with the cities of Southlake and Plano.

The partnership arrangement between the Stars and the city of Euless is typical of the model the Stars are pursuing in the other communities. Euless has a population of approximately 50,000. The Euless Dr. Pepper Star Center stands on six acres of land owned by the city, which was leased to the Stars. The Stars built the facility, which is approximately 95,000 square feet and contains two NHL size ice-rinks, a proshop, skate rental service; a self-service grill, a number of meeting rooms, and 125 parking spaces. When construction was completed, the city bought the facility from the Stars for $10.29 million, which was the cost of construction. The city sold Certificates of Obligation to raise the needed capital. The city then leased the facility to the Stars for a 25-year period. The annual lease fee is equal to the amount of the annual amortization of the city's principal and interest payments on the Certificates of Obligation and other expenses incurred by the city in obtaining financing. The lease fee is paid to the city in monthly installments. The Stars have the option to extend the 25-year agreement for two successive five-year periods if they wish to do so. The city agreed not to assist or become involved in any other ice-skating facility during the term of the lease without the consent of the Stars. If the Stars withdraw from the agreement before the end of the 25-year period, they are required to give the city one year's notice, so the city can find another operator or organizer to operate the facility itself.

The Stars pay no property taxes because the city owns the land on which the building is situated, but they do pay all utility bills. The Stars have full and exclusive control of the management and operation of the leased facility. They own all revenues from all sources generated in the building, and have all sponsorship rights including those associated with naming the building. The Stars pay for all maintenance and repairs of the building, but the city pays for all maintenance and repairs to the parking areas adjacent to the building and for all landscaping maintenance. The city has 24 hours per year of free use of the meeting rooms at the facility and 24 hours of free ice time.

When the city initiated discussions with the Stars, it considered forming a quasi-public benefit company as an intermediary with authority to issue tax free bonds. However, their bond consultants subsequently reported this would be in breach of the 1986 Tax Reform Act, so the facility was paid for by the Stars using the more expensive tax-

Exhibit 10.12 *(Continued)*

The Euless Dr. Pepper Star Center

able bonds. If the city had issued the bonds under the terms of the 1986 Act, the city would have had to operate it or to accept lease payments of no more than 10% of the facility's annual debt service.

The involvement of the Dallas Stars in the public-private partnership was a key factor in the city agreeing to participate because of the Stars' reputation for excellence. The Euless city manager said, "This is not just another ice arena run by some private group. It's an ice arena run by the Dallas Stars. If it had not been with the Dallas Stars, I don't think it would have occurred in our city."

It would be reasonable to ask: Why didn't the Stars organization borrow the money to build the facility from a financial institution and make annual repayments to that institution, which is the normal way businesses finance their capital development? Why did the Stars want to partner with the city when there was no "cheap money" from tax free bonds available? There were two reasons for involving the city:

1) The city's ownership of the building and the land means that the Stars do not pay property taxes.

2) The venture is too risky for a traditional financial institution to finance over 25 years. Recreation interests change, demand may wane, and the project may become non-viable. The partnership contract enables the Stars to withdraw from the agreement if they give one year's notice. These conditions would be unacceptable to financial institutions. Thus, the city of Euless essentially acts as guarantor and banker. The city carries the risk. If the Stars exercise their right to give one year's notice, then the city has to take over the facility and pay the annual amortization payments. This is not an untenable position for the city since many public recreation facilities are subsidized. Hence, the city can legitimately reposition the ice hockey facility as a Public Amenity rather than a private good, whereas a traditional financial institution has to evaluate the project's financial feasibility on its merits as a private facility.

arena housed offices for the Chill's management staff and a team locker room and training facility.

Impetus for establishing a new ice rink came from the Chill, who were finding it increasingly difficult to reserve adequate ice time for team practices at the one ice rink in the metropolitan area of 1.4 million residents. So great was the demand for ice at the single arena owned and operated by the local state university that the Chill were limited to one-hour practices, often at 5:00 or 6:00 a.m. Analysis of the area's imbalance between supply and demand led management of the hockey team to develop a proposal for creation of a permanent facility, which could be utilized beyond the team's practice needs to accommodate the apparent demand for youth and adult hockey, figure skating, and speed skating in central Ohio. The Chill approached the City of Dublin with a joint development proposal in which the hockey team would build and operate the ice arena but lease back initially up to 20% of the facility's ice time to the city. In return for utilization privileges, the city agreed to lease an eight-acre parcel of land (market value $400,000) to the Chill for 25 years at $1.00 per year. The reciprocal benefits from this partial leaseback arrangement are extensive. The city received (a) a state-of-the-art community resource that will serve the ice-skating needs of its residents year-round at minimal taxpayer expense, and (b) a regional attraction that will lure thousands of overnight and day-use visitors each year to the city to attend tournaments and annual events.

It was noted in Chapter 9 that tax-free bonds can no longer be used for many of these types of projects, which means that leaseback partnerships now effectively substitute private credit for public credit. Thus, a major disadvantage arising from this mechanism is that it is more expensive for commercial developers to borrow money than it is for public agencies. In addition, the costs to an agency have to include the investor's profit margin. Hence, in many cases this method of financing projects is likely to be more expensive than the direct use of public bond issues. However, in some situations this difference may be regarded as an acceptable "risk" premium, especially in BOO arrangements, since the risk associated with unanticipated increases in capital costs, project delays, and future maintenance is transferred to the private partner.

Perhaps the most common type of leaseback is lease/purchase financing involving a leasehold contract between a private developer and a public entity. The public entity will usually solicit bids for the project. Golf courses are particularly good candidates for this approach because the installment on lease payments may be funded from a course's net revenues. However, the public agency's general fund remains the ultimate guarantee if projected revenues are inadequate to meet the payments. Usually, revenue bonds are a superior option for public agencies for the reasons cited in the previous paragraph. However, if the revenue bonds are too high risk or the political climate makes their use unadvisable, lease/purchase offers an alternative.

Public Sector Takeovers

The takeover of a faltering private sport facility should not necessarily be viewed as a public bailout. There are occasions when it should be viewed as an opportunity to retain an existing sport asset that will otherwise disappear. Takeovers may be an appropriate strategy if a private entity closes and the type of sport opportunity that it offers either is not offered by another supplier in the area, or can be used to service a market segment that is presently not being reached with that opportunity. However, sometimes takeover opportunities have to be foregone because a public agency cannot respond quickly to market forces, and the business or lending institution is unable to wait for the time-consuming referendum process necessary to authorize bonds for capital investment.

The Minnesota Timberwolves contemplated moving to New Orleans because although the team itself was profitable, the Target Center, which was built with private funds, was costing the owners $6.25 million per year in debt charges. The owners could not see how the overall venture could be profitable while they were encumbered with these debt charges. The Minnesota community mobilized and forestalled the move; another local partnership group agreed to purchase the franchise and, most important, a city agency agreed to buy the Target Center. The facility purchase was undertaken with general obligation bonds backed by property taxes, tax-increment financing, dedicated revenues from the city's parking fund, a 3% citywide entertainment tax, and a $750,000 annual appropriation from the state.

The takeover of facilities such as golf courses, ski facilities, softball complexes, or ice rinks is likely to be much less controversial than taking over a facility for a professional sports franchise, because the former facilities are more consistent with the public's image of the types of facilities that are appropriate for government to provide. For example, the town of Eastchester on Long Island purchased the financially ailing Lake Isle Country Club with its 18-hole golf course, five pools, eight tennis courts, and large banquet hall. The wording of the referendum that approved the town's purchasing the facility required it to be a self-sufficient operation. It could not look to local tax revenues to support its $2.4 million budget. However, the complex did not have to yield a return on equity or meet debt charges associated with the purchase cost, so it was easier for the complex to be self-sufficient than for the previous private operator, who had to recover capital debt and equity costs.[36]

A further financial advantage that accrues to a public agency when it takes over a facility is that the facility may be eligible for grants for capital improvements from federal or state programs that are not available when the facility is operated privately. Thus, the Lake Isle complex received more than $750,000 in capital grants from the federal Land and Water Conservation Fund's matching grant program. The grant funds and the low interest rate of public debt meant that these improvements cost substantially less than half of what they would have cost a private operator.

In Euless, Texas, which is centrally located between Dallas and Fort Worth, the city of Euless purchased Softball World from a private operator who could not pay the debt charges on the facility. The city renamed the park Softball World at Texas Star. It is a state-of-the art facility with plush, bermuda-grass outfields, finely groomed infields, 30-foot electronic scoreboards, professional lighting, the largest softball pro shop in Texas, and a full-line concession stand with sales that include alcohol. Annually, over 2,000 league and tournament teams played at the facility, and it was too important to the city's economy to allow it to fold and be used for other purposes.

A public agency may be able to operate a facility that commercially fails because the purchase price that an agency pays for a takeover may be substantially less than the original cost or the asset value of the operation as a going concern. Consider the situation confronting a bank that is forced to foreclose on a specialized sport facility such as a ski lift because the operator is unable to make contributions toward the loan payments. The equipment has minimal resale value, and the bank is unlikely to have either the expertise or the inclination to operate the ski lift. Thus, the bank may be receptive to an offer from a public agency to purchase it for (say) 50% of its cost because this would enable the bank to recoup at least some of the capital it lent the operator to build the facility. In addition, by enabling the facility to continue to operate, the bank is contributing to maintenance of the area's economic health and quality of life, both of which are important to the bank's long-term profitability.

Private-sector Takeovers

This category of partnerships refers to situations in which a private organization takes over responsibility for operation of a facility or service owned by the public sector. Toronto's Rogers Centre (formerly known as the Sky Dome) offers an example of this principle. It was built with a combination of public and private funding. Thirty Canadian companies contributed $5 million each toward construction of the stadium, with city and provincial government paying the rest of the bill. The project ended up costing approximately $600 million, more than 2 ½ times the original projected cost. The debt charges on the then-Sky Dome were 60,000 dollars a day. The Blue Jays MLB team attracted 4 million baseball fans in a year and sold out consistently, so the franchise made impressive annual operating profits of $30 to $35 million. However, the stadium's onerous debt charges and business taxes resulted in annual net losses of over $30 million a year. This persuaded the provincial government to cut its losses and sell the Sky Dome for $151 million to a consortium of private investors.

Given the escalating costs of renovating sport facilities, some cities are effectively giving their stadiums to franchises without going through the controversial process of handing over the title to a facility. For example, the city of Anaheim's arrangement with Disney Corporation, when the company purchased the MLB Anaheim Angels in 1996 (the team changed its name to the Los Angeles Angels of Anaheim in 2005) effectively handed over the stadium to Disney:

> Anaheim stadium required a $100 million renovation. In exchange for financing $70 million of the restoration cost, Disney was allowed to retain all revenues derived from ticket sales below 2.6 million people and any revenues from stadium naming rights, concessions, and inside-stadium advertising. Disney was allowed to keep all baseball parking revenues below $4 million and all outside advertising revenues above $800,000.

In return for its $30 million, the city of Anaheim had the team renamed the Anaheim Angels and received any revenues not retained by Disney. Because the Angels had only exceeded an attendance of 2.6 million four times in their history, these revenues seemed likely to be minimal. However, the city's mayor, in defense of what seemed a one-sided agreement, noted, "No longer will the citizens of Anaheim have to worry about the burden of overhead required to operate the stadium. For the past 30 years, it has been a burden to Anaheim. It is right and proper to shift the burden to the private sector" (p. 29).[35]

Most older cities throughout the United States and Canada have a large number of decaying, underutilized sport facilities desperately in need of rehabilitation. Given the fiscal constraints confronting most local governments, public funds are invariably inadequate or nonexistent for refurbishing tennis courts, athletic fields, ice rinks, and golf courses that have fallen into disrepair, so governments are often receptive to overtures from private sector investors.

Private-sector Pump Priming

A business may use some of its assets to induce a public agency to make a major investment in a facility from which the enterprise also will gain. This type of partnership has occurred most frequently in golf course provision. Developers offer land and perhaps other resources such as cash, equipment, infrastructure preparation, or in-kind assistance to encourage a public agency to build and operate a public golf course. They do this because such a facility substantially increases the value of the property that the developer sells around the course, it releases the developer from an obligation to operate the golf course, and it removes the developer's liability for property taxes from the course acreage. Often, the land dedicated to the public sector is unsuited for construction of buildings because it is flood plain or environmentally sensitive land.

From a public agency's perspective, the cost of land is a major element in building a golf course. If this is removed, then often it becomes feasible for a public course to be self-sufficient, including covering its debt charges. This enables revenue bonds to be issued to pay for course construction; therefore, a service can be provided to the community at no cost to the taxpayer.

- As part of a 1,600-unit residential development called Rancho Solano in Fairfield, California, the developer dedicated 200 acres for development of an 18-hole, par-72, 7,000-yard golf course. As part of the development agreement, the city built a championship golf course and provided partial funding for a clubhouse with restaurant, cocktail lounge, and pro shop. The city invested $1.25 million for one-quarter ownership of the clubhouse, with the developer putting up the remaining portion. The clubhouse was dedicated to the city, with food and beverage operations leased to an operator. The city shared 25% of the profit or loss from all operations. The city retained a specialist golf management company to operate the course and clubhouse and contracted with Rancho Solano Country Club and Resort, Inc., to operate the food and beverage services. It issued $7 million in bonds to cover the construction of the course and one-fourth of the clubhouse.[27]
- Richmond Bay Development Company developed Meadow Lakes, a master-planned residential community in North Richland Hills, a suburb located about 10 miles north of Forth Worth. The developer, electing not to enter the golf-course development business, was unsuccessful in attracting a private firm to develop the course. A number of apparent issues concerned these firms, including the tree cover, the terrain and other land features, cost and availability of water, and the limited amount of land area (the 120 acres available would not allow construction of a regulation golf course).

Subsequently, the city of North Richland Hills reached an agreement with the developer to construct a golf course, with the understanding that the course would be high-quality design. The city assembled three parcels—the 120 acres dedicated at no cost by the developer, a 35-acre parcel acquired for the nominal price of $1.00 from the Federal Savings and Loan Insurance Corporation, and a five-acre parcel leased from an adjoining city—for construction of a regulation course. Most of the land was in a flood plain. The city retained a designer and an operator and acted as developer, coordinating design and construction.

Construction cost of the golf course was $2 million; total turnkey cost was $4.5 million. Tax-exempt bonds totaling $4.25 million were sold to finance the course. The developer contributed $100,000 toward construction, in addition to dedicating the land. The developer designed a subdivision with approximately 65 lots fronting on the golf course.[37]

- Lee County, Florida, solicited a donation of 150 acres of land from developers and land speculators. The county intended to build a championship, 18-hole golf course on the land. Six offers were received. All of the proposals observed that a quality golf course could enhance residential developments being considered. For example, one corporation proposed that the city build its course on 150 acres of a 340-acre residential community that it was planning to build. Another corporation offered to contribute $100,000 for the planning and design of the course, in addition to the land, if it were built on its 1,800-acre residential area site.[37]

There are many examples of this strategy along the Front Range in Colorado. Developers in Westminster donated land to the city for a golf course, and the developers then built expensive homes overlooking the course. In the Denver suburb of Commerce City, land for an 18-hole golf course built close to the new Denver International Airport was donated by landowners who planned to develop around it. Other golf examples are the Coal Creek course in Louisville, Mariana Butte in Loveland, West Woods in Arvada, and Indian Peaks in Lafayette. A golf course architect in the area who was involved in designing several of these courses states: "The biggest rationale on all the courses is upscale housing. Developers are coming in and saying, 'I know the value of homes on golf courses. I'm willing to give the land to the tax entity so I can build around it'" (p. 42).[38] He added that many times the developer is giving up land that could not be built on anyway. Coal Creek, Indian Peaks, and Mariana Butte are on flood plains. Also located on flood plains is Fox Hollow, which is a prime championship course built in the Denver suburb, of Lakewood on land leased from the Corps of Engineers. Under the lease agreement, no homes can be built on the course.[38]

The pump-priming principle was used by a commercial developer in the context of the Salt Lake City Winter Olympic Games:

A real estate developer gave 386 acres of his mountainous tract to a Utah state agency as a site for a winter sports park that would include ski jumps and a bobsled and luge run. This became Utah Olympic Park—a central facility for the 2002 Salt Lake City Winter Olympic Games. In exchange, the agency agreed to build an access road to the sports park that would run through the remaining 750 acres of the developer's land, opening the area to the development of single-family homes and condos. In addition, the agency pledged to install "all necessary utilities including electrical power, natural gas, telephone, water system and sewer" to serve both the sports park and the 700 residences built on the remaining 750 acres. When the land was acquired, it was valued at $5 million. Ten years later, the land alone—excluding houses that had been built—was valued at $48 million, a 16-fold increase.[39]

Expansion of Existing Public Facilities

Expansion of an existing public facility may be achieved with the assistance of a sport business that is prepared to invest in improvements, renovations, or expansion of the facility in exchange for the authority to lease the facility or to operate it at off-peak

Exhibit 10.13

Expanding a Velodrome to Include Go-Carts

Indianapolis Parks and Recreation Department constructed and operated the Taylor Velodrome at the city's Lake Sullivan Recreational Area. The annual net operating loss for the Velodrome was more than $50,000, and its losses meant that it was in danger of being closed. The department entered into a partnership with Fast Masters, Inc., by which the company constructed, at its own expense of approximately $250,000, a permanent track for go-cart racing inside the velodrome. Go-cart racing was becoming popular in the area, and there was a shortage of facilities. The stands for spectators, concession areas, parking, and infrastructure at the velodrome were used only occasionally for bike racing, so go-cart racing was a complementary use. The partnership was for a three-year period, after which ownership of the track reverted to the city.

Before Fast Masters entered the partnership, the company and a television network, ESPN2, agreed that the network would transmit 12 races per year with each session lasting 3 hours. ESPN required Fast Masters to raise $75,000 in advertising for the network to pay for these transmissions. The television coverage was key to the company's ability to attract sponsors. Any sponsorship fees in excess of $75,000 remained with Fast Masters. Other revenue sources for Fast Masters were entry fees received from the go-cart racers (from 125 to 150 people raced at each meet) and admission fees received from spectators.

The city's return from the agreement comprised $25 from the entry fee of each go-cart, one-eighth of the gross receipts from spectator admissions, and all revenues from concessions that the city operated. Fast Masters paid utility and cleanup costs associated with the 12 events.

times. Exhibit 10.13 illustrates how an existing facility may be adapted by additional investment to accommodate new activities. In this case, a velodrome was adapted so that go-cart racing could also take place there.

More commonly, this type of joint venture has occurred in northern states and has involved the commercial developer in converting an existing facility for winter use.

> The city of Oak Park, Michigan, leased land to a commercial operator for a 10-year period, with the lessee having an additional two successive 5-year options to extend the lease. The lessee paid 5% of gross sales to the city for rent. The developer constructed and operated a five-court indoor tennis facility, including a permanent support building, five asphalt courts, and a five-court air-supported structure. The city provided all utilities to the site and prepared the site for contractors.

The operator had exclusive use of the courts for a 32-week winter season and erected and dismantled the air-supported structure at the beginning and end of each season. The city had exclusive rights to the courts in the 20-week summer season without the air structure. At the end of the agreement, ownership of all facilities, with the exception of the air-supported structure, passed to the city. To the satisfaction of both parties, the agreement worked successfully, and it was extended to cover an additional five courts. To safeguard the operator's investment, the city agreed not to construct, operate, or allow the construction or operation of any other indoor tennis facility on municipal property in Oak Park without first offering the rights for construction and operation to the lessee.

Similar partnerships to the tennis joint venture described at Oak Park have been forged for a wide range of activities. For example, a golf driving range under an inflatable dome was operated by a developer between November and May on a 2.5-acre park site in Oakland County, Michigan. A similar structure was used in Madison Heights, Michigan, for winter softball games. These structures were removed in the summer months. The agencies received an agreed percentage of the gross receipts and access for constituents to a facility that otherwise would not be available without incurring capital costs.

In this type of arrangement, it is important that the developer should build facilities that meet the public agency's specifications. This is the only way in which quality control can be exerted. Without this condition, the developer may use lower-quality materials that need replacement in a shorter period of time. Hence, when the public agency takes over the development at the end of the lease, which typically is negotiated in the contract, it may be faced with substantial renovation costs.

Multiparty Arrangements

It is increasingly common for large-scale public-private sport partnerships to be complex arrangements involving multiple financial partners. Often they are spearheaded by an independent quasi-governmental body to facilitate collaborative exchange between the various public and private entities involved with the project.

Pilot Field in Buffalo is the home of the AAA Buffalo Bisons, which is one of the most successful minor league baseball teams. It is example of a complex multiparty agreement with a host of different organizations contributing to its financing. The stadium has been called "a minor league stadium with all the major league amenities," "the best ballpark in the minor leagues," and "the city's ticket to Glory Days."[40] The principal objectives of the project were to develop a facility designed to attract a major league baseball franchise and to act as a catalyst for downtown redevelopment. The arrangement is described in Exhibit 10.14.

The Hubert Humphrey Metrodome, AAA baseball in Colorado Springs, a golf academy in Indianapolis, and adaptations of the principles of time-sharing to build a sports center are all examples of multiparty arrangements.

In the case of the Metrodome in Minneapolis, the Metro Sports Facilities Commission (the Commission), a special authority created by the state legislature, was established to assemble the necessary financing from various private and public sources and to oversee the operation of the facility.

The Commission negotiated with a group of Minneapolis land developers to have a 20-acre stadium site, valued at $9 million, donated to the Commission in return for the right to develop the surrounding real estate, which the developers owned. The key to the success of the project was the Commission's ability to broker an agreement between the City of Minneapolis and the downtown business community for the sale of $55 million of revenue bonds. The tax-exempt bonds issued by the City were purchased by five local corporations. To secure bond repayment, the Commission entered an agreement with the City of Minneapolis to collect an annual hotel-motel tax (2%) and liquor

Exhibit 10.14

The Financing of Pilot Field in Buffalo

Contributions of the financial partners in the construction of Pilot Field are shown below:

Contributions	Amount (in millions)
City of Buffalo	
General improvement serial bonds	5.32
Downpayment on bonds	0.28
Three-year operation and maintenance budget	2.10
TOTAL	7.70
New York State	
State Urban Development Corporation funds	22.50
ECIDA	
Revenue bonds	4.20
Other Contributions	
Buffalo Development Companies	4.00
Buffalo Bisons	3.00
Buffalo Urban Renewal Agency (land credit)	2.00
Erie County legislature	0.75
TOTAL	9.75
Total Cost of Pilot Field	44.15

The largest contributor to Pilot Field was the New York State legislature, which appropriated $22.5 million in state Urban Development Corporation funds for the project. When these funds were approved, tripartite agreements were signed that delineated the responsibilities of the state, the city, and the Erie County Industrial Development Agency (ECIDA), which was the developer of the project. The ECIDA was a public-benefit corporation created to foster economic prosperity in Buffalo and Erie County. Under these agreements, the state was repaid from any profits that may be realized after a maintenance reserve fund of up to $75,000 annually was established and after the debt service was paid on bonds issued by the ECIDA and the city. The agreements also required the city government to pay for all cost overruns. Under the terms of the tripartite agreement, the ECIDA was the owner of Pilot

Field, and the city had a noncancelling, 15-year agreement with the agency. At the end of the lease, title to the stadium passes to the city.

The city was responsible for operation and maintenance of the facility. Its major source of revenue was a contract with the Buffalo Bisons, the principal tenant. The lease agreement was critical because it was the city's guarantee that it could operate and maintain the stadium without having to subsidize the operation with additional tax dollars. Since the project involved the construction of an expandable stadium so that it could accommodate major league baseball in the future, the council wanted an expandable lease to ensure the city would benefit from the future growth.

To forge this partnership, a lease was developed that linked the rent to paid admissions. That is, the percentage of ticket reve-

Exhibit 10.14 *(Continued)*

The Financing of Pilot Field in Buffalo

nues that the Bisons paid to the city increased as gross receipts increased. Any profit the city realized from the operation of Pilot Field was to be applied toward the $800,135 it paid annually for principal and interest on the bonds issued by the ECIDA and the city for stadium construction. The term of these bonds was 15 years, corresponding to the term of the lease agreement the city had with the ECIDA. ECIDA's participation as project director was important because it had the ability to establish a construction price ceiling that the contractor was required to meet for the entire project. If the city had served as the developer, it would have been compelled by the city charter to bid each of the various aspects of the project and face the cost overruns that would occur with the inevitable change orders.

The city council authorized the sale of city bonds in the amount of $5.32 million to cover the city's share of the project. As Table 10.2 reports, several other groups also contributed. The Buffalo Development Companies, a consortium of local development agencies, contributed $4 million, including $150,000 in Urban Development Corporation handicapped-access funds. The Buffalo Urban Renewal Agency, an ancillary agency of city government, contributed the land. The Bisons contributed $3 million towards the purchase of the scoreboard and the construction of the concession areas, the restaurant, and team offices.

The project also was aided by being included as a "grandfathered" project in the 1986 Tax Reform Act, enabling construction to be financed by tax-exempt bonds. This inclusion saved the project an estimated $17 million in interest payments over the 15-year life of the bonds.

This figure is adapted from Johnson, A.T. (1993). Minor league baseball and local economic development. Urbana, Illinois: University of Illinois Press.

tax (2%). The revenues collected from these taxes were used to pay all the debt-service costs (principal and interest) on the revenue bonds. In addition, the Commission assessed a 10% admission tax on all events held at the Metrodome. Monies realized from this surcharge were used to cover annual operating expenses. The remaining $20 million was raised from $13 million in interest earned on the revenue bonds and $7 million from two of the Metrodome's principal tenants, the Minnesota Vikings football team and the Minnesota Twins baseball team. The latter revenue came principally from the lease of luxury box suites.

Crucial to establishing financial stability was the Commission's effort to negotiate long-term tenant lease agreements with the Twins, the Vikings, and the University of Minnesota. These agreements confirmed a minimum of 100 dates per year for the next 20 to 30 years. The 30-year lease arrangement with the Vikings provided the Commission with 10% of the gross ticket sales. For 81 regular season games played in the Metrodome, the Twins surrendered 7.5% of their gross gate receipts. To date, these revenues, along with admission tax proceeds from other events, have allowed the Commission to operate the Metrodome free from public subsidy of any kind.

The owner of the AAA Pacific Coast League Hawaii Baseball team was interested in relocating the team to Colorado Springs. The city needed a stadium for the team, but voters had previously rejected proposals to spend public money for a stadium. The owner was referred to a major real estate development company that was developing a 2,000-acre site, 8.5 miles from downtown. Believing it would give visibility to their development, the company agreed to donate the land for a stadium. The city agreed to pay the owner who was developing the new stadium $500,000 as its share of the project. This pump-priming contribution was crucial to bringing the stadium to fruition: "City financial participation was critical to the owner and was perceived by city officials as a potential deal-breaker" (p. 238).[40] Because the state's constitution forbade the use of public money for private interests, the city was required to receive something of value for its $500,000. Thus, a joint use agreement called for the stadium to be used by the city 180 days of each year. However, given the weather conditions in Colorado Springs outside baseball season, this use was much less generous than it may at first appear to be.[40]

One of the most common approaches to developing tourism real estate has been time-sharing. Time-sharing enables individuals who desire to own property at a resort area to purchase a selected number of weeks per year at a condominium rather than having to purchase a whole condominium unit. This enables the purchase price to be shared by a number of buyers (52 of them if each buys one week), and maintenance of the unit is the responsibility of a management company. A county agency planned to use the time-sharing principle to finance the building of an indoor sport center that would have provided a new facility for residents at no cost to the sponsoring county agency.

Seven of a number of corporations who were invited to participate agreed to buy exclusive use of part or all of a proposed sport center for their employees at selected times on weekdays from 11:00 a.m. to 1:00 p.m. and from 5:00 p.m. to 8:00 p.m. At other weekday times and on weekends, the facility would be available for use by all residents of the county. The facility would be operated and managed by the county at all times.

The capital cost of the facility was approximately $3 million. Each corporation agreed to pay $100 per day per hour for the exclusive use of the facility's space. This space and time was purchased in advance for a 5-year period with an option under which it could be renewed for a further 5-year period. The pre-sold space and time allocations from the seven corporations provided all of the initial finance needed to construct the building. The county had negotiated with a private developer to lease a park site to him for a 15-year period, and he agreed to build the facility. He would then lease it back to the county in order to take advantage of depreciation on the structure. The county agreed to pay him a lease fee based on the debt charges on the building that were covered by the pre-sold time shares purchased by the seven corporations.

Although the county commissioners were informed fully of the progress of the intended development, they refused to support it in the end because they were reluctant to grant the developer an exclusive 15-year lease on county property. The developer required an exclusive lease because, if for some reason the scheme failed, he had to be able to use the building for some other purpose in order to generate revenue to pay the annual debt charges on the building for which he would be liable. After being rebuffed by the commissioners, the developer took the feasibility data that the county staff had assembled and proceeded to build the facility elsewhere and manage it himself as a private venture.

Exhibit 10.15

Establishing a Golf Academy Through Multiple Partnerships

Indianapolis had no public facility for teaching golf and no course on which learners could practice. Thus, the Indianapolis Parks and Recreation Department envisaged creating a golf academy, which was to be a teaching facility incorporating six elements:

1. A clubhouse approximately 14,400 square foot in size that included a pro-shop, concession area, a covered 80 foot × 20 foot training area with 18 tee positions, a training video viewing area, a club fitting and repair area, a classroom, and two golf simulators.
2. An outdoor, lighted driving range with 40 outdoor tee positions.
3. A practice putting green.
4. A pitching practice area.
5. A sand-trap practice area.
6. A nine-hole, par three training golf course with greens built to Professional Golf Association standards but with holes not exceeding 150 yards in length. Regular courses intimidate learners because of the level of difficulty and their tendency to slow play, frustrating experienced golfers behind them. The nine-hole facility would alleviate this problem.

The golf academy's mission was to expand the exposure of golf to Indianapolis residents, particularly to young people. Total projected cost of the project was $1,750,000. To bring it to fruition, resources were pooled from four partners: the park department, a private golf course operator (R. N. Thompson & Associates), the United States Golf Association, and the Indianapolis corporate community.

The park department issued a request for proposals, inviting private operators to lease a 35-acre site for 15 years for the purpose of funding, constructing, and operating the golf academy. The site was located in Riverside Regional Park, which was a 680-acre park incorporating both a wide range of recreational facilities and extensive passive areas. The site was highly visible from major traffic arteries, and it was situated in a lower-income, racially diverse area with moderate gang activity. Within 1.5 miles of the site were three golf courses. There was no other driving range in the area, and this component of the academy was seen as the cash cow undergirding the financial viability of the venture.

The park department established a 501(c)(iii) organization, the Indianapolis Junior Golf Foundation, to own and govern the project for two reasons. First, the academy was intended to be a self-sufficient, but nonprofit, venture with any surplus funds being reinvested to fund capital improvements, improve promotion, and offer additional training opportunities for youth. To operate in this manner, it needed to be free of political interference from the city council. Second, if the city directly operated the academy, the city would likely have more difficulty persuading corporations to contribute to its construction.

In response to the request for proposals, R. N. Thompson & Associates were selected. The company was a major real estate developer in the Indianapolis area, had developed four residential golf courses, and owned and operated four other daily-fee golf courses and a private golf academy in the area. Thompson agreed to pay a lease fee to the park department of 10% of the first $500,000 gross receipts; 7%, between $500,000 and $750,000; and 5%, in excess of $750,000. This lease fee went into the park's golf enterprise fund and was reinvested in golf. Thompson also agreed to contribute $450,000 toward design and construction of the academy and to operate it for a management fee set at an amount necessary to reimburse actual maintenance and management expenses. R. N. Thompson & Associates were entitled to additional compensation if specified performance goals were exceeded.

R.N. Thompson & Associates were required to maintain a capital improvement fund of at least $40,000 each year to reinvest in the academy's operation and to appoint a full-time experienced general manager, who was acceptable to the park

Exhibit 10.15 *(Continued)*

Establishing a Golf Academy Through Multiple Partnerships

department and was a licensed, Class A, Professional Golf Association golf professional. The lessee could not sublet or assign the lease to anyone else under the contract terms because the city's long relationship and shared vision with Thompson were viewed as key to the venture's success.

The United States Golf Association contributed a grant of $300,000 to the golf academy. Additionally, it provided technical assistance with the design, construction, and operation of it. The Association recognized that much of the current boom in golf was attributable to the baby boomer cohort reaching the prime age for golfers. They believed that 7% of adults played golf. Given the smaller numbers of people in age cohorts following the baby boomers, a larger proportion of them would have to be players if the demand for golf was not to fall. The Association saw minority groups as a main target market because minorities were substantially under-represented among golfers and were the fastest growing demographic segments.

The golf academy site was easily accessible to minorities in Indianapolis. Prices and quality standards were controlled by the park department through the contract with Thompson, and a variety of measures were used to permit economically disadvan-

taged youth to earn green fee credit as an alternative to paying the academy's fees. The academy was available to all youth regardless of their access to funds. The United States Golf Association invested in similar programs targeted at minority youth in San Diego, Dallas, and New Orleans. If these pilot projects were successful in expanding the number of minority golfers, the Association was likely to increase substantially its investment by extending the program to other cities.

The final partner was the corporate community in Indianapolis from whom the park department solicited $1 million to raise the balance of the funds. The department did this by working with the Indianapolis Corporate Community Council, comprising major businesses that annually selected quality-of-life projects to support. Appeals to the corporate community were based on the belief that if golf is made available to inner-city youth, then acquisition of the skill to play golf and participation in junior tournaments will assist in building self-esteem, confidence, and good social characteristics. This involvement would provide an alternative to joining local gangs. The golf academy's development was phased so that the clubhouse's indoor components were constructed while corporate donations were solicited to complete the project.

A 501(c)(iii) organization is a non-profit, non-government corporation organized and operated for the benefit of the general public. The number refers to a paragraph in the IRS Code that defines this type of nonprofit organization.

A more complex joint development involved the city of Indianapolis, a commercial operator, the United States Golf Association, and philanthropic donations from civic-minded major businesses, coming together to establish a public golf academy. It is described in Exhibit 10.15.

SUMMARY

Before entities from the public and private sectors enter into direct partnership and pool their resources to deliver a service or build a facility, a favorable supportive environment for such partnerships has to be present. The first challenge is for the potential partners to recognize and accept as legitimate their different value systems. Public agencies are mandated to serve the whole community, especially its disadvantaged members;

are concerned with social outcomes, equity and benefits that are relatively intangible and difficult to measure; and are constrained by bureaucratic procedures that are necessary to ensure accountability for their expenditure of public funds. Private organizations are mandated to serve stockholders by maximizing their return on investment, which is frequently obtained by focusing on narrowly defined, responsive target markets, and they are relatively flexible with the ability to respond quickly to new opportunities. The different value systems may result in negative stereotypes and attitudes between those working in the different sectors. Removing these stereotypes and attitudes and building the mutual respect needed for partnerships to succeed requires the establishment of forums to facilitate communication and liaison.

A second factor that may inhibit the formation of partnerships is allegations that the public sector is engaging in unfair competition with businesses. Public agencies have advantages that enable them to deliver services at a lower price than commercial enterprises. The advantages include paying no property, sales, or income taxes; not being required to cover operating expenses with revenues; being exempt from many regulations; being self-insured; financing improvements with tax-exempt bonds; not being required to cover debt charges with operating revenues; and receiving free advertising and promotion.

Since there is no legal mechanism for stopping public agencies from constructing competing facilities if they wish to do so, private sport managers have to mount campaigns at the ballot box to stop facilities from being built. In the case of unfair competition from nonprofit organizations such as YMCAs, private sport organizations have had some success in seeking legal redress to remove the tax-exempt status of those nonprofits that are serving affluent clienteles rather than underprivileged groups.

The potential for public-private partnerships stems from a recognition that each sector has resources of value to offer the other. A successful collaboration requires finding a way to fuse the complementary resources of each sector to the mutual advantage of all parties involved. Public sector organizations have four major assets to which the private sector is likely to seek access. They are: (i) a substantial land bank and the regulatory authority to assemble land needed for a project; (ii) ability to borrow money at a lower interest rate than a private organization; (iii) authorization to waive a proportion of, or all, property and other local and/or state tax payments; and (iv) control over permit and zoning processes enabling those processes to be expedited and, in some cases, even changed or waived. Public officials can often use these assets to negotiate with private sport organizations without being subjected to the scale of controversy and criticism that invariably surrounds proposals to use tax dollars for this purpose.

The private sector has five types of assets that it can contribute to a partnership arrangement with a public agency. First, it has the capacity to raise capital quickly and easily, provided it can be demonstrated that a project is likely to generate a satisfactory return on the investment. Second, it has management expertise in specialized areas that it may not be efficient for a public agency to acquire through hiring personnel with these skills. Third, labor costs often are lower in terms of both salaries and fringe benefits. Fourth, it is often much easier for a business than for an agency to hire and pay part-time workers who may be required to handle one-time services or short peak seasons. Further, businesses serving multiple organizations may be better able to take advantage of efficiencies associated with economies of scale. Fifth, the involvement of sport businesses may enable public agencies to substantially reduce their vulnerability to liability claims by passing such risks along to their business partners.

A remarkable array of imaginative and creative public-private partnerships has emerged in the financing of sport projects over the last decade. Their creativity and, in some cases, complexity make their classification into a comprehensive taxonomy somewhat arbitrary. Nevertheless, seven broad categories of partnerships have been identified: (i) public sector leasing. where a private sports business pays a fee to lease a public facility; (ii) leaseback from the private sector, where a private developer constructs a facility and in some cases operates and/or staffs it, and leases it to the public agency at a previously negotiated rent; (iii) public sector takeover of a private sport business to preserve a sport opportunity that would otherwise become unavailable to a jurisdiction's residents; (iv) private sector takeover of facilities whose ongoing costs have become an unacceptable burden to public agencies; (v) private sector pump-priming, whereby a business uses some of its assets to induce a public agency to make a major investment in a sport facility from which the enterprise will also gain; (vi) expansion of an existing public sport facility by an infusion of funds from a private organization; and (vii) multiparty arrangements that involve multiple financial partners making contributions to a project.

References

1. McQuaid, R. W. (2000). The theory of partnerships: Why have partnerships? In S. P. Osborne (Ed.), *Public-private partnerships* (pp. 9–35). New York, NY: Routledge.
2. Cohen, A. (1996). Togetherness. *Athletic Business, 20*(10), 31–37.
3. IHRSA. (n.d.). *The case for fair competition.* Boston, MA: IHRSA.
4. Testimony of M. Jennifer Harding to the Oregon House of Representatives concerning HB 3513. The Unfair Competition Bill, which would have prohibited public sector organizations from providing goods and services that are already provided by private businesses.
5. Martinsons, J. (1994, May 20–26). The new kids on the block: Parks and rec departments. *Club Industry.*
6. "Mike Brandt's competitors." (1975, September 12). *Wall Street Journal.*
7. Cohen, A. (2002, June 11). Good business. *Athletic Business.*
8. Schmid, S. (1995). Water world: It's water, water everywhere at a Texas water park. *Athletic Business, 19*(10), 24.
9. Weisiger, H. (1983, October). *Unfair, unfair, unfair competition: How the Fairfax County government and Fairfax County Park Authority directly compete against private recreation.* Distributed to members of the Fairfax County Park Authority, Va.
10. Kozlowski, J. C. (1993). Authorized public recreation may legally compete with private facilities. *Park and Recreation, 28*(9), 36–44.
11. Kozlowski, J. C. (1982). Municipal competition with private enterprise must satisfy public purpose test. *Parks and Recreation, 17*(12), 21–26.
12. Kozlowski, J. C., (2003). State bills would ban public competition with private business. *Parks and Recreation, 38*(8), 34–40.
13. Miller, L. K., & Fielding, L. W. (1995, February). The battle between the for-profit health club and the commercial YMCA. *Journal of Sport and Social Issues, 19*, 76–109
14. McCarthy, J. (1990, February). Competition for the sports dollar—A response to Mr. Cousins. *Non-Profit Times*, 20–21.
15. American Sports Data, Inc. (2003). *IHRSA/ASD health club trend report.* Hartsdale, NY: ASD.

16. ISRSA. (n.d.). *Non-profit expansion of impact* [Information sheet]. Boston, MA: IHRSA.

17. DeMarcus, R. (1985, November). Non-profit commercialism: A growing problem. *Club Business*, 57–58.

18. Bynum, M. (2004, October). Spot me? A Wichita health club asks for and gets public financial aid, but not without controversy. *Athletic Business*, 46–50.

19. Cohen, A. (1996, April). Audited: IRS forces university recreation departments to limit public access. *Athletic Business*, 18–20.

20. Young Men's Christian Association of Columbia—Willamette v. Department of Revenue, 308 Or. 644, 784 P.2d. 1086. (1990).

21. Stern, M. (2011). Real or rogue charity? Private health clubs vs. the YMCA, 1970–2010. *Business and Economic History On-Line*, *9*, 1–17.

22. Sioux Valley Hospital Association v. South Dakota State Board of Equalization, 513 N.W. 2d 562 (1994).

23. Middle Tennessee Medical Center v. Assessment of Appeals Commission of the State of Tennessee, 1994 Tennessee App. LEXIS 43.

24. Osborne, D., & Gaebler, T. (1992). *Reinventing government*. Reading, PA: Addison-Wesley.

25. Danielson, M. N. (1997). *Hometeam: Professional sports and the American Metropolis*. Princeton, NJ: Princeton University Press.

26. Dorshner, J. (1992, July 8–12). Keep off the grass: Must Dade's parks be paved to be saved? *The Miami Herald*.

27. Muirhead, D., & Rando, G. L. (1994). *Golf course development and real estate*. Washington, DC: The Urban Land Institute.

28. Agostini, S. J., Quigley, J. M., & Smolensky, E. (1997). Stickball in San Francisco. In R. G. Noll & A. Zimbalist (Eds.), *Sports, jobs & taxes* (pp. 385–426). Washington, DC: Brookings Institution.

29. Korman, R. (1989, February 20). A matter of pride. *Sports, Inc.*, 32–37.

30. Fulton, W. (1988, March). Politicians who chase after sports franchises may get less than they pay for. *Governing*, 34–40.

31. Urquhart, J. (1986). Catering: To contract or not? *Leisure Management*, *16*(5), 21–22.

32. Stevens, B. (1984). Delivering municipal services efficiently: A comparison of municipal and private service delivery. Summary. *U.S. Department of Housing and Urban Development*. New York, NY: Ecodata.

33. Lee, E. (2003, August). The supervision solution: A public-private approach to skatepark management. *Parks and Recreation*, 39–41.

34. Truppelli, G. F. (2001, September/October). Dreaming of the big leagues. *Government West*.

35. Greenberg, M. J., & Gray J. T. (1996). *The stadium game*. Milwaukee, WI: National Sports Law Institute of Marquette University.

35a. Long, J.G. (2002). *Full count: The real costs of public funding for major league sports facilities*. PhD. Dissertation, Harvard University, Cambridge, Massachusetts.

35b. Long, J.G. (2013). *Public/private partnerships for major league sports*. New York, NY: Routledge.

36. Steinborg, J. (1993, August 13). Public park is too private to suit the government. *New York Times*, B1.

37. Winton, P. (1994, August 3). Developers scramble for shot at public golf course. *Fort Myers News-Press*, pp. 1, 16.

38. Marchant, W. (1995). Open range: Municipalities and developers coordinate their respective interest to fuel a public golf boom in Colorado. *Golf Course Management*, *63*(7), 41–42.

39. Bartlett, D. L., & Steele, J. B. (2001, December 10). Salt Lake money. *Sports Illustrated*, 79–98.

40. Johnson, A. T. (1993). *Minor league baseball and local economic development*. Urbana, IL: University of Illinois Press.

Section IV

Revenue from Enterprise Sources

11

Revenue Sources
From Sports Venues

INTRODUCTION

Over the past two decades, the revenue model for sports organizations at all levels of professional sport, and at a growing number of colleges, has changed dramatically. With the advent of fully loaded sport facilities that characterized the construction boom of the 1990s and 2000s, sport managers have developed a number of new sources of revenue. More recently, especially in those facilities built within the past five years, new sports venues "have begun to showcase premium amenities, features, finishes and services that are competing for discretionary dollars by focusing on non-game elements" (p. 1).[1] New arenas and stadiums in New York City; Arlington, TX; and Miami and Orlando, FL, have become entertainment destinations, offering a wide spectrum of non-traditional options such as high-end restaurants, night clubs, and penthouse suites. Fans are being offered more premium seating options than ever before. Over the last decade, the latest generation of sports venues has moved from two principal premium seating options (luxury suites and club seats) to a much more diverse mixture of choices, including terrace and loge seating, and party and bunker suites. These new seating options have given teams and facility operators greater flexibility in offering individual fans and corporations attractive seating options that match the client's needs in terms of location, amenities, and willingness to pay. The first part of this chapter will focus on the current state of premium seating and the changes occurring in the both the design and sale of luxury suites, clubs and other high-end seating options.

The second part of the chapter will examine the current state of, and practices related to, the sale of personal seat licenses, or PSLs. Selling seat licenses has been a common practice of professional sports teams since the mid-1990s and has more recently become a widespread feature of major college athletic programs. As recently demonstrated by the Dallas Cowboys, under the right circumstances PSLs can be an abundant source of revenue for teams and owners who are building new venues. The Cowboys generated over $700 million from the sale of seat licenses prior to or during the construction of their $1.2 billion stadium in Arlington, Texas.

Finally, the chapter will examine trends in the sale of venue naming rights. Operators of sports enterprises have been able to grow their operational revenues to unprecedented levels by exploiting the desire of corporations to use new, state-of-the-art facilities to increase their visibility and create new business opportunities. Companies have committed over $6 billion to place their company (or brand) names on an arena or stadium. Currently, over three-fourths of major league sports teams play in corporately named facilities. Naming rights in some sports and countries have been extended from facilities to jerseys, and the potential of this revenue source is illustrated. The chapter explores the reasons companies are willing to pay so much for the naming rights to sports facilities and jerseys, and identifies the key provisions in naming rights partnerships that ensure corporations receive a fair return on their investment.

While teams continue to attempt to fully exploit the potential of all three of these venue income-producing opportunities, the impact of the Great Recession is still evident. Since the economic downturn, many teams and facility operators have struggled to sell a significant portion of their traditional high-priced premium seating inventory and seat licenses. A substantial number of major sports facilities remain corporately unnamed after, in some cases, years of searching for a corporate naming rights partner. The changing economic circumstances have required teams to become more innovative, flexible and price sensitive in order to meet the changing market conditions. This chapter will examine the many new innovations in the types of premium seating inventory now available in sports venues and the new approaches teams are using in the marketing and selling of seat licenses and naming rights opportunities.

PREMIUM SEATING

Perhaps no single development in the last several decades has had more of a transformational effect on major team sports than premium seating. Luxury suites, loge boxes and various forms of club seating have become an almost universal feature of modern arenas and stadiums. The introduction of this type of high revenue yielding seating inventory is a fairly recent phenomenon. As discussed in Chapter 4, the first facilities to incorporate a significant number of luxury suites and club seats were the Palace at Auburn Hills and Job Robbie Stadium (now, Sun Life Stadium). Both of these venues were built in the late 1980s. The Detroit Pistons' then-owner self financed the construction of the Palace by pre-selling 180 luxury suites and 3,000 club seats. Similarly, the then-owner of the NFL Miami Dolphins also privately financed his new state-of-the art stadium through the sale of an unprecedented number of luxury suites (216) and club seats (10,302).

Both of these new facilities broke the mold. Up to that time, sports venues were built in relatively uniform fashion with few amenities. Most seating was bench or bleacher style, often with just 16 to 18 inches allocated per seat, with no seat backs. Food and beverage options were few and lines were long at both concession stands and bathrooms. Customer service was limited largely to ushers whose primary role was directing foot traffic. The introduction of premium seating, and the opportunity to sit in comfortable seats with access to more readily available services (in some cases, semi-private or restricted-use restrooms and in-seat food service)—even if it meant paying considerably more for these benefits—was received with enthusiasm both by many individual fans and by companies.

Table 11.1. Number and Prices of Suites and Club Seats Across Major Leagues		
League	Number Suites (Avg./venue) Price range	Number of Club Seats (Avg./venue) Price range
MLB	1,890 (63) $119,010–$233,666	102,927 (3,431) $4,949–$14,801
NBA	2,667 (89) $135,538–$291,461	56,244 (1,875) $6,031–$11,372
NFL	4,917 (154) $69,281–$ 223,250	262,804 (8,216) $1,781–3,386*
NHL	2,850 (95) $129,500–$283,166	54,212 (1,807) $5,917–$8,722
Totals	12,324	476,187

*Many teams require club seat holders to pay a seat license fee in addition to the cost of the club seats

Sources: 2011 Revenues From Sports Venues: Pro Edition; Mediaventures (2011), Association of Luxury Suite Directors, 2011–12 Reference Manual

As shown in Table 11.1, the venues in which teams in the four major leagues play contain over 12,000 luxury suites and close to 500,000 club seats. The purchase price of this inventory is substantial, with luxury suites ranging from an average low of $100,000 per season to an average high of $250,000. In large, high-demand markets like New York City, suite sales for the New York Knicks start at $400,000 per season in Madison Square Garden, while at the Staples Center in Los Angeles they go for as much as $380,000. The Dallas Cowboys charge $500,000, the single highest fee, for exclusive rights to their most expensive suites in Cowboy Stadium. Club seats, which offer a number of premium amenities to individual seat purchasers, are also sold at substantially higher price points than regular (non-premium) seating. As shown in Table 11.1, even at the low average end of the price continuum, full season club seats range from almost $1,800 per seat per season in the NFL to around $6,000 in an NBA arena. The very best club seats offered by major league teams average close to $15,000.

The NFL has several advantages in offering premium seating opportunities to their fans. Strong consumer demand, based on the league's popularity, coupled with its teams playing in substantially larger venues (average seating capacity for an NFL stadium is 70,000 compared to 18,000 for an NBA arena), has allowed the league's teams to offer on average more than twice the number of suites and three to four times more club seating than any other major league. In 2012, the average NFL stadium contained 157 suites and 8,200 club seats.

The following section highlights the extraordinary revenue produced by suites and club seats and new forms of premium seating recently introduced in sports venues. The high per capita yield ensures that premium seating will be an increasingly prominent feature in stadiums and arenas in the years ahead.

High-yield Inventory

The primary reason that premium seating has become so popular is that the sale of this inventory yields such abundant revenues. As shown in Table 11.2, in both the NFL and MLB, club seats are sold on average for more than three times the price of a regular (non-premium) game ticket and for more than double the price of a regular ticket in the NHL. Given that the average premium customer spends considerably more on food and beverages during a game, the average "per cap" yield for someone purchasing a club or loge seat, including parking, exceeds $300 at an NFL game and well over $100 at an MLB game. With teams generating three times as much on a per capita or per-seat basis from premium customers, it is not surprising that sports facilities built over the past 10 to 15 years have emphasized the inclusion of this high-priced seating inventory.

Table 11.3 illustrates the disproportionate contribution of premium seating on a team's annual operating income. Prior to the opening of their new ballpark in April 2012, the Miami Marlins baseball club offered a diverse range of highly exclusive—and expensive—premium seating opportunities. The combination of suites and club seats listed in Table 11.3 provide seating for approximately 1,250*—accounting for less than 4% of the stadium's overall seating capacity of 37,000. As shown in the table, this relatively small number of seats generated an enormous revenue return of more than $20 million in the ballpark's first year of operation. The income realized by the sale of 675 Diamond (379) and Dugout (296) Club seats grossed an estimated $12.8 million, producing a per capita yield of $18,962. This expensive inventory was sold out months before the stadium opened.

The Miami Marlins' success in selling this high-priced inventory demonstrates the willingness of a segment of fans to pay a high price for the privilege of sitting in the very best seats and receiving VIP treatment. As discussed in Chapter 1, sports fans with the financial wherewithal to afford these special privileges account for a narrowing portion of American households (about 15% of all US households report total incomes exceeding $100,000). It is not surprising, then, that the Marlins offered a very limited supply of this high-priced inventory and emphasized their exclusivity to create a sense of urgency among high-income prospects.

The revenue-generating potential of premium seating was fully exploited by the NFL's Dallas Cowboys. In 2009, the Cowboys built a lavish $1.2 billion stadium in Arlington, Texas, which included 320 luxury suites and over 16,000 club seats. A detailed breakdown of the premium seating inventory and the initial sale price for each seating option is provided in Table 11.4. Despite prices that doubled or tripled the cost of a non-premium reserved seat, 90% of the Cowboys' premium seating inventory was sold prior to the team's first game in their new venue. It is estimated that the Cowboys realized $33,750,000 from the sale of 16,200 club and loge seats, for an average per capita yield of $2,080. The team also pre-sold 288 of the 320 suites offered in the new stadium for an estimated gross of $72,500,000. The average sale price per suite

---

*This estimates the full capacity of the 40 luxury suites at 480 (12 per suite). The three other premium seating options (Diamond and Dugout Clubs and Champion Suite) accommodate an estimated total of 777 seats.

Table 11.2. Cost of Premium Seating 2011–12 Major Leagues

	Avg. Regular Ticket	Avg. Premium Ticket
NFL	$77.34	$242.35
MLB	$26.98	$88.18
NBA	$48.48	NA
NHL	$57.39	$133.62

Source: Team Marketing Report (2012)

Table 11.3. Miami Marlins High-Priced Premium Seating Inventory in New Stadium

Seating Inventory	Number and Price (Average Cost for Full Season)	Status of Inventory*	Estimated Revenues
Diamond Club	379 seats @ $210–$395/game (avg. $113,700 FSE*)	SOLD OUT	$9.2M
Dugout Club	296 seats @ $135–$175/game (avg. $44,400 FSE)	SOLD OUT	$3.6M
Champion Suites	2 Suites, 103 seats @ $150/game** (avg. $12, 250 FSE)	SOLD OUT	$1.2M
Luxury Suites	40 @ $150,000–$250,000 per season	30 Sold to date	$6.0M
		Total Est. Revenues $20.4M	

*FSE refers to Full Season Equivalent or full season ticket package (every game)

**Total price for Champions Suite includes cost of food, beer, wine and soft drink

Source: Muret, D. & Fisher, E. (2011, April 4). Marlins hook premium seat buyers. *Sports Business Daily*.

exceeded $250,000. The estimated total revenue generated by the Cowboys from the sale of their premium seating inventory alone exceeded $106 million.[2]

Luxury suites have been particularly attractive to corporations who have found sports venues to be a unique and highly effective place to entertain key clients. Although the physical features of suites may vary from one venue to another, they are likely to include amenities such as carpeting, wet bars, lavish furnishings, and seating for 12 to 14 patrons. Private restrooms used to be commonly built into luxury suites, but many new facilities have provided easily accessible restrooms outside of the suites. These generally up-scale restrooms are available exclusively to suite holders and their guests. Suite prices vary according to location, size and number of amenity features. The average cost of the best or most expensive suites across all four major leagues ranges from a low of $225,000 to almost $300,000 per season. The gross income produced by the more than 12,000 luxury suites in major league venues exceeded $2.5 billion in 2012.

Table 11.4. Estimated Revenue from Sale of Premium Seating Inventory at Dallas Cowboys Stadium

Seating Option (Price Range)	# Seats	Average Price	Ticket Revenue
Loge Seats ($1,250)	1,200	$1,250	$1,500,000
Club Seats ($1,250/$3,400)	14,000	$1,250	$17,500,000
Founders All Access ($1,250/$3,400)	1,000	$1,250	$1,250,000
Suite Seats (90%) ($1,250)	12,000	$1,250	$13,500,000
Suite Leases (90%) ($100,000–$500,000)	288 Suites	$250,000	$72,500,000
		TOTAL REVENUES	$106,250,000

Source: John Vrooman (2010, April 4). Dallas Cowboys Stadium analysis. Retrieved from http://www.vanderbilt.edu/econ/faculty/Vrooman/cowboys-estimate.pd

Many professional teams offer suites on an extended contract basis. Rather than selling the entire inventory on an annual basis, prospects are offered the opportunity to lease or rent a suite for 3, 5, 7, or 10 years. Often, payment terms are designed to encourage clients to select long lease agreements. Thus, suite holders who elect a 7-year lease would pay less on an annual basis than those choosing a 3-year term. Staggering the length of the contracts over different time periods also ensures that the school or team does not have to deal with the challenge of renewing or replacing all current suite holders every year.

Due to the considerable investment required of those purchasing private suites, the prospect pool is generally limited to large corporations. Companies find suites an ideal place to entertain key clients and/or reward high-performing employees. In addition, as was noted in Chapter 6, corporations can mitigate the higher cost of leasing suites by writing off a considerable portion of the investment. Direct payments for game tickets, food, parking and other goods may be written off as a business expense if used to entertain clients. In addition, companies can deduct most of the lease fee from their taxable income.

Traditionally, club seats have been considered one step removed in status from luxury suites. Over the past 10 to 15 years, club seats have become the preferred option for smaller businesses and a growing numbers of individual fans who are willing to pay a premium for the special benefits provided by this seating arrangement. Not only are most club seats located close to the action, but they also provide fans with superior comfort. Typically fans sit in chair-back, wide-bottom, cushioned seats. In addition, individuals purchasing club seats receive access to a variety of specialty services and amenities. These special services may range from in-seat wait service during games, to offering club seat holders exclusive access to a club lounge for pre- and post-game food and beverage.

While club seats are most often sold on an annual basis, several professional sports teams sell them on an extended lease basis, ranging from 3 to 10 years. Under this arrangement, the purchaser prepays the entire amount upfront or contracts to make several payments over a stipulated period of time, typically 2 to 5 years, depending on the length of the lease agreement. At the other extreme, the Great Recession has caused some facilities to sell some club seats on a per-event basis.

Fans enjoying *Royal Box* experience at Charlotte Bobcats game.

Family viewing Charlotte Bobcats game from *Terrace Table* seats.

Illustrations of the Most Recent Premium Seating Options

The most recently built sports venues provide fans with a much more diversified range of premium seating options. Contemporary arenas and stadiums, such as the Amway Center in Orlando, the Barclays Center in Brooklyn and the Cowboys Stadium in Arlington offer a varied menu of premium accommodations from luxuriously appointed suites to intimate, courtside or field level loge seating, complete with top-flight cuisine, concierge services and access to VIP lounges. Modern venues have moved from providing one kind of suite, characterized by their standardized size, amenities and location (many of the original suites were called *skyboxes* because of their location in the upper reaches of the arena or stadium), to a mix of suite options differentiated by location, size, amenity features, and price.

Currently, the most popular premium seating innovation is the emergence of loge box or terrace table seating.[3] This recent seating alternative takes the traditional box seat concept to a completely different level. It combines the special vantage point benefit of traditional box seats with the ultimate VIP experience. The Charlotte Bobcats offer two versions of this more intimate seating option. Both Royal Box and Terrace Tables as shown provide private, opera-styled, open-air boxes with accommodations for 4 to 6 people. Further differentiating the experience are benefits, such as a flat-screen television monitor in each box with access to live-game and instant replays, bench tables, comfortable seating, in-box wait service, and immediate access to semi-private bathrooms. In addition, Royal Box and Terrace Table patrons have access to an exclusive hospitality area before, during and after games where they can enjoy upscale food and beverages.

Figure 11.1 shows the diverse range of premium seating options provided in the Amway Center. The state-of-the-art arena was built in 2010 for $380 million as the new home for the NBA Orlando Magic. The venue showcases the versatile array of

Founders Suite

Located mere 19 rows from the floor. Each suite provides plush lounge area and theater seating for 12 and 4 bar rail stools.

MVP Table Seating

Unique viewing experiences with access to premium club level amenities.

Presidents Suite

Just 27 rows from the floor and in close proximity to upscale restaurant with fixed seating for 12.

Legends Suite

Enjoy first-class perks of a luxury suite with immediate access to premium club.

Loge Seating

Center court setaing, as close as 24 rows from floor. Plush seating in 4- and 6-seat loges provide in-seat food service and access to club-level amenities.

Figure 11.1. Premium Seating Options in the Amway Center. Photos courtesy Fernando Medina/Orlando Magic

Southwest Airlines Flight Deck
Private seating space on terrace level councourse with seating for 4.

Hardwood Suites
Located 19 rows from floor. Six suites with capacity 30 each, with capability of expanding to 60 in three suites.

Figure 11.2. Group Hospitality Decks and Suites.

exclusive, premium seating in modern sports venues. Magic fans are presented with a broad range of opportunities, ranging from traditional suites and club seats to more intimate terrace and loge seating options.

In addition to the range of premium seating options offered to individual fans, modern venues offer premium spaces targeting private groups such as companies or organizations for hospitality events. Figure 11.2 displays two of the group hospitality spaces designed to accommodate from 32 to 60 attendees. These areas are sold as individual game inventory to organizations seeking an opportunity to host special events for staff and employees or key stakeholders. The branded Southwest Airlines Flight Deck provides a unique hospitality experience for 32 guests. The space contains a private bar and a deck view of the court. The Hardwood Suites pictured in Figure 11.2 are also rented on an individual game basis. These larger hospitality areas, located only 19 rows from the court, offer a broader range of amenities suitable for off-site business gatherings.

The Boston Bruins and Celtics offer a similar more casual group experience for their fans. Rather than targeting companies and organizations, the AT&T SportsDeck in the TD Garden focuses on providing a unique viewing opportunity for individuals and small groups. The space offers 160 reserved seats and standing room for 75. Access to individual reserved seats are sold in 10 and 22 game packages, and standing-room only (SRO) tickets are sold only as 10-game packages. SRO purchasers are offered the opportunity to "mingle while watching the game" in the bar or lounge area. Fans purchasing 10 or 22-game packages are given the option to choose all Bruins, all Celtics or a combination of both teams. As shown in Figure 11.3, the starting price for packages range from $1,200 (SRO) to $5,434 (22-games), with costs varying by seating location.* For these premium prices, fans receive a number of exclusive "membership" privileges, including complimentary food ("all you can eat appetizers"), access to a private cash bar, in-seat wait service and use of semi-private restroom facilities. While expensive, the cost

---

*The prices for the AT&T SportsDeck were drawn from the TD Garden website for the 2012–13 season

AT&T SportsDesk
More casual and affordable premium viewing experience.

Figure 11.3. TD Garden's Unique Premium Options for Small Groups and Individuals.

for the privileges of the SportsDeck provides fans with a considerably more affordable opportunity to enjoy a premium seating experience when compared to the more exclusive options in the TD Garden such as executive suites, the Heineken Boardroom, and The Lofts (see Figure 11.3). For example, the price for one of the 12 Lofts, offering opera-style boxes seating four to six, run as high as $17,000 for a 10-game package. While considerably more expensive, the Lofts offer a uniquely elegant and more intimate setting for entertaining either clients or family members. The "all-inclusive" price for the experience includes a three-course menu, game tickets and parking. Loft bene-

The Lofts
More exclusive, high-end hospitality premium options.

fits even extend beyond the arena to include access to three of the top golf courses in New England.

Figure 11.4 showcases the elegant club areas found in the new Barclays Center. The arena built in 2012 is the home of the NBA Brooklyn Nets. Similar to the Amway Center, the $637 million venue is loaded with elegant premium seating options. The Courtside Club sets a new standard in elegance for fans who have purchased courtside seating to Brooklyn Nets games. The large club area is located directly outside the Nets locker room, so fans can have intimate access to players as they enter and exit the court. When not watching the game, fans using the Courtside Club are offered a fine dining experience in a luxurious setting.

Courtside Club
Elegant, spacious club areais exclusive to fans in courtside seats. Located on event level, directly outside Net locker room.

North/South Clubs
Twin clubs on opposite sides of the arena. Club seat holders are provided full-service bar, lavish food offerings, and access to semi-private restrooms.

Figure 11.4. Barclay's Center Club Area.

In addition to providing the finest in fan accommodations, the Nets have teamed with the world-renowned Disney Institute to ensure that guests visiting the Barclays Center will be provided with "unmatched 'Street-to-Seat' service" and hospitality. Fans will receive the same level of preeminent customer service upon which Disney has built a world-wide reputation. According to the CEO of the Barclays Center, "Through our alliance with Disney Institute, we will employ the Disney approach to guest services to create a truly unique fan experience in one of the most stunningly designed venues in the world."[4]

Challenges in Premium Seating

While suites and club seats remain key features of modern sports facilities, the rapid growth that characterized premium seating inventory before the Great Recession has generally flattened and in some instances the inventory has declined. As teams struggled to sell this high-priced inventory in a difficult economy, some arenas and stadiums drastically reduced the number (and price) of both suites and club seats. Prior to the recession, in 2006, the average number of suites in an NBA arena was 93 and the average number of club seats had reached an all-time high of 1,974. As shown in Table 11.1 earlier in the chapter, the average NBA arena now contains 89 luxury suites and 1,875 club seats. Given the reduced demand in many markets, particularly for traditional luxury suites, many NBA arenas are converting a significant number of private suites into "party" suites or "lofts." These are discussed in the next section of this chapter.

In 2011, a leading industry analyst proclaimed that unsold premium seating inventory remained a major problem in the sports industry.[5] He identified several "financial and cultural" factors that would likely depress demand for traditional suite and club seat sales for an extended period of time:

1. *A prevailing culture of austerity*—Given the economy's slow recovery and persistent high unemployment rates, many companies will be reluctant to "associate their brands" with expensive premium seating products, like *luxury* suites, fearing a negative public perception: "Companies don't want to be seen spending lavishly on entertainment, when so many people are hurting."[6]

2. *The rising cost of attending a game*—Many companies have slashed their entertainment budgets, making it increasingly difficult to pay not only for the expensive seating inventory ($200,000 for a suite), but for the additional costs related to entertaining guests, such as gourmet food and beverage service over the course of a full season: "Traditionally, suite holders spend as much in ancillary dollars as they do on the suite itself . . . costs can easily escalate in the mid-seven-figure range."[6]

3. *Advanced technology has made it more appealing to stay at home*—This addresses the increased quality of in-home entertainment options and their adverse impact on live attendance. As discussed in Chapter 1, the growth of HD television, and the proliferation of sports programming on TV has made it easier for price-conscious consumers to stay at home. Rather than committing to expensive, and in some cases, long-term contracts for a club seat (3- to 7-year lease agreements), the increased quality of home entertainment allows fans to enjoy the event in their own homes.

4. *A surplus of single-event inventory cannibalizes long-term demand*—In the tough economy, many teams have struggled to sell or lease all of their premium seating inventory, particularly luxury suites. Unable to sell this expensive inventory to clients for a full season, teams have offered unsold inventory on an individual-game basis. However, moving to a single-game sales approach can have a devastating impact on the ability of a team to resell the inventory on a long-term basis: "If you know that discounted club seats are on sale for just about any game, why would you commit to an expensive full-season package? Or if you see another company occasionally renting the suite next door on a per-game basis, why would you renew your long-term suite lease?"[5]

All of these factors have created significant challenges for teams or venue operators in almost every market in the US. One immediate consequence of the depressed demand for traditional premium options has been a widespread reduction in the amount of inventory, particularly of luxury suites, in a growing number of arenas and stadiums.

Early in 2012, the Detroit Pistons announced their intentions to eliminate nearly half of their 178 suites. Their president stated, "We just have too much [suite] inventory."[7] The team found that even offering deep discounts on unleased suites on a game-by-game basis had been a tough sell. The proposed plan called for the team to convert 80 suites into "more profitable spaces." Potential conversion options under consideration included a restaurant, a sports hall of fame, and social media gathering sites.

As part of a $975 million renovation, Madison Square Garden eliminated 71 suites at the historic arena. The removed suites originated in a 1989 remodel and were located at the very top of the arena (literally on the 10th floor). They were classic examples of the "sky suite" era in which suites were located far above the playing surface. While providing luxury amenities, their distance from the court left many guests feeling disconnected or isolated from the action of the event. Most modern venues have addressed this concern by placing suites closer to the field of play. The Seattle Seahawks offer 12 "Red Zone" suites a mere 52 feet from the playing field. While not as proximate to action as the suites at CenturyLink Field in Seattle, Madison Square Garden is relocating 58 suites much closer to the floor, moving the new "lower-level" suites to the middle of the arena. In addition, the revamped arena will include 20 "event-level" suites which will be located below courtside, complete with "amenities nicer than most apartments in Manhattan."[7] These suites provide direct access to the courtside seating.

The Staples Center, operated by the Anschultz Entertainment Group (AEG), converted eight upper-level skyboxes into a 175-person lounge called the Hyde Lounge. The membership club is modeled after a club on the Sunset Strip by the same name. The 4,000 square foot space features two salons, three bars, a dance hall and private great room with strategically positioned "floating" LCD TV screens. The lounge includes a spectator viewing area with ledge seating overlooking the floor from the arena's stage end, offering members intimate views of concerts and shows in addition to sporting events (e.g., Lakers, Clippers, and Kings). The former skyboxes had proven to be hard to sell on a single-game rental basis, particularly for the Clippers and Kings games. AEG entered into a partnership with Entertainment Group, the leading provider of night-life venues in the Los Angeles area, to transform the former suites into an exclusive, VIP space for *very* important people. The Entertainment Group reputedly spent $1.3 million creating the entertainment area, which by one account rates "an 11 . . . on the difficulty meter" in terms of celebrity access."[8] According to the Staples Center General Manager, the suite conversion has been a "home run" for all major tenants in the venue.[8] Annual membership fees to the popular club cost $5,000. For special events, the front row ledge tables in the Hyde Lounge are offered to the general public for $600 minimum (seating for 6), with food and beverage, not including the price of tickets.

A prominent feature of the suite conversion trend has been the creation of party suites. In the face of declining demand from single tenant lease partners, teams and venue operators have converted suites into group spaces designed to appeal to companies or organizations interested in renting the suites for special occasions. These are often referred to as super suites, because the renovated space typically consolidates two or more single suites into an expanded entertainment space that can accommodate anywhere from 20 to 120 guests.

Many teams have found a very solid market for offering these suites on a per-game basis. They have proven to be very popular with companies and organizations looking to provide clients and/or members with exclusive perks at reasonable prices. The United Center, home of the NBA Chicago Bulls and NHL Black Hawks, consolidated several skyboxes into six 20- and 80-person suites, which they rent on a game-by-game basis. Both teams offer prospective customers a variable pricing menu is based on several factors, including size (20 v. 80 capacity), menu quality (classic v. premium) and attractiveness of the game opponent (silver v. platinum). The difference in rental rates across all of these options can be considerable. A company planning to rent a 40-person penthouse suite can spend as much as $11,500 for a premium package (Platinum opponent and Premium menu) and as little as $7,750 for the least expensive option (Silver opponent and Classic menu). The per capita expenditure difference amounts to around $93 for each invited guest, with the most expensive package costing $287 per guest and the least expensive about $194, for food and beverage and a game ticket. Note that the day-of-event rates also include a number of parking passes depending on the size of the suite rented. These super or party suites have sold well for both the Bulls and Blackhawks.[7]

The Arizona Diamonbacks are one of a growing number of MLB teams that rent suites on a game-by-game basis. As shown in Figure 11.5, along with exclusive use of the premium space, the Diamondbacks also incorporate a number of complimentary benefits, most notably, food, drink and parking, as part of the suite rental fee. This "all-inclusive" pricing arrangement has become very popular. For an up-front payment of $2,300 to $2,500 (price varies by location), a company renting a suite can provide its guests (up to 18) with access to an "all-you-can-eat" buffet and premium parking. From the individual guest's standpoint, all of these benefits are free.

In addition to converting suites originally leased to single

Figure 11.5. Arizona Diamondbacks Per Game Suite Rental Program.

tenants on an extended contract basis to party suites offered to multiple tenants on a game-by-game rental arrangement, many teams have adopted more flexible sales tactics to fill suites in the face of soft demand. *Suite sharing* has become a common sales approach since the economic downturn. It is analogous to *time-sharing* at resort properties. The arrangement allows multiple companies to share the same suite. Over the course of the season, depending on the size of the share, each company is provided access to a certain number of games. The most common practice is for teams to offer half or quarter shares. In the case of the NBA and NHL, this would amount to 21 or 10 regular season games, respectively. Some NBA teams offer 1/8 shares or the opportunity for a suite tenant to attend as few as 5 regular season games. Suite shopping provides companies with the ability to enjoy the benefits of guaranteed suite access without having to pay full price. The following example describes how a suite share arrangement might work for two tenants:

> Company A and B enter a time-share agreement for a suite at an NBA arena. They each get the suite for three high-value games (based on opponent), then they each choose which of the remaining games they want. Finally, they might have to take turns at having the first right of refusal for playoffs, championships and special events (p. 132).[9]

An additional benefit to teams from suite sharing is that they can charge a total price that is higher than if the suite were occupied by a single tenant. This enables them to cover their additional costs related to scheduling and servicing multiple clients.

PERSONAL SEATING LICENSES (PSLs)

The Growth and Magnitude of Seat License Programs

The concept of selling seat licenses was first introduced in 1993 by the Carolina Panthers. The then-expansion team's innovative plan was to finance a new stadium by selling personal seat licenses (PSLs) that guaranteed the holder a lifetime's right to purchase season tickets to that seat. The program was hugely successful as the new NFL franchise sold 62,000 seat licenses, ranging from $600 to $5,000, allowing the team to contribute $125 million to the construction of the new football stadium in downtown Charlotte.[10]

The idea of selling seat licenses was attributed to the practice in the south whereby the best seats in the churches used to be reserved for the leading members of the congregation.[11] Those families making a large donation were accorded the privilege of sitting in the same "named" pew for every Sunday service. The belief was that avid NFL football fans would be willing to make a similar investment to guarantee access to the best seats in the new Panthers stadium every Sunday. This successful pioneering effort spurred many other teams to initiate seat license programs. To date, over 40 professional teams and a number of major collegiate football programs have adopted the concept. The scope and magnitude of some of the most successful PSL programs are illustrated in Table 11.5.

Table 11.5. Size, Price and Financial Impact of PSL Programs			
Team (League)	Total (# of PSLs/capacity)	Price Range	Total Revenue
Dallas Cowboys (NFL)	34,000/50,000	$2,000–$150,000	$720,000,000
San Francisco 49ers (NFL)	68,500/68,500	$2,000–$80,000	$500,000,000
New York Giants (NFL)	82,500/82,500	$1,000–$20,000	$170,000,000
New York Jets (NFL)	55,000/82,500	$2,500–$30,000	$120,000,000–$140,000,000
Houston Texans (NFL)	50,000/69,500	$600–$3,900	$74,000,000
Cleveland Browns (NFL)	64,000/71,5000	$250–$1,500	$74,000,000
Philadelphia Eagles (NFL)	29,000/66,000	$1,760–$3,617	$50,000,000–$60,000,000
San Francisco Giants (MLB)	13,400/40,930	$1,500–$7,500	$40,000,000–$50,000,000
Pittsburgh Steelers (NFL)	48,000/65,000	$250–$2,700	$35,000,000–$40,000,000
Seattle Seahawks (NFL)	8,300/67,000	$2,000–$3,000	$16,000,000–$17,000,000
Minnesota Twin (MLB)	3,000/55,000	$1,000–$2,000	$4,000,000–$5,000,000

The seat license concept depends on the willingness of core fans to make a substantial, up-front payment to secure the rights to a particular seat or seats in a venue. Often, that particular seat may be a club seat. Buyers make a one-time payment that allows them to purchase the season ticket to that designated seat for a specified period of time. The seat license provides the buyer with an exclusive claim to that seat as long as he/she continues to purchase season tickets.

Seat licenses are often referred to as PSLs, but there is no common agreement to what the "P" means in the term PSL. Over the last 20 years, PSL programs have been alternatively called personal, private, and/or permanent seat licenses. The most recent PSL sales programs have tended to use the term *permanent*, because the teams selling the licenses wanted to convey that the advance payment gave the fan lifetime control over seat or seats being purchased. This approach was in contrast to early programs in which *personal* or *private* seat licenses were sold for a fixed period of time. Examples include the Oakland Raiders' disastrous seat license program, which limited seat guarantees to a 10-year period, at which time seat license owners were expected to pay an extravagant renewal price. The Raiders abandoned their seat license program before the renewal period because of their fans' angry reaction to the prospect of paying another high premium for the privilege of buying season tickets to seats they had occupied for an extended period of time.

Seat license programs have proven to be an effective mechanism for teams to raise capital *in advance* of the construction of a new sport facility. The Pittsburgh Steelers were the first team to use the name *seat builder licenses* (SBLs) when they introduced seat licenses to cover a significant share of the team's capital construction contribution to a new stadium in 2001. The intention of labeling the licenses as SBLs was to convey to prospective buyers that the seat license revenues would be used exclusively for stadium construction costs and would "in no way be used to enrich the team or the owner."[12] The Steelers were required to contribute about $70 million to the construction of a new stadium in downtown Pittsburgh. They imposed a seat license requirement on 35,000 of the 65,000 seats in what became Heinz Field, ranging from $250 for seats in the upper deck to $2,700 for the choicest seats. The SBL program proved to be very successful, selling out in a short period of time, resulting in the team raising close to $40 million.

Other NFL teams have followed the Steelers' approach to marketing seat licenses, emphasizing that by purchasing licenses, fans are investing in the team's future success (not the owner's). The San Francisco 49ers are the latest team to offer SBLs, but at a level well beyond the Steelers' original conception. The 49ers' plan was to raise $500 million in seat license sales to cover a significant share of the team's $850 million construction debt for their new MetLife Stadium in Santa Clara, a suburban community south of San Francisco.[13] The full cost of the stadium, due to open in late 2013, is expected to exceed $1 billion. The team began offering seat licenses in early 2012, with the one-time fees priced as high as $80,000 for the 1,000 most expensive seats in their new stadium. Rather than requiring a seat license for just a portion of the seats, as in Pittsburgh, the 49ers plan to sell close to 65,000 SBLs, which will represent 91% of the stadium's capacity.[14]

While the 49ers' goal to raise $500 million in seat license sales is audacious, even if successful, it would still rank second behind the Dallas Cowboys in terms of total monies generated from a seat license program. It was estimated that the Cowboys' total PSL sales exceeded $700 million.[13] The owner of the team agreed to pay for half the anticipated $650 million construction costs. Soon after breaking ground for the new 85,000-seat domed stadium, it became apparent that the pre-construction estimate was well below the actual building costs, which grew to $1.2 billion. Thus, the owner's share of the construction costs jumped from the original projection of $325 million to close to $900 million. Fortunately for the Cowboys, the team pre-sold 50,000 PSLs to Cowboys fans. The 1,000 Founder Seats, the choicest seats in the spectacular new venue, required a seat license fee of $150,000. License fees imposed on 15,000 club seats ranged from $16,000 to $50,000 per seat. Prior to the opening of Cowboys Stadium, nearly the entire seat license inventory was sold, grossing an estimated $720.4 million for the Cowboys. Thus, 80% of the owner's total investment in the new stadium was offset from seat license revenues.

A high level of demand is the key ingredient to achieving success with seat license programs. Thus, PSL sales have been most successful in those markets with pent-up demand for professional sports, such as when the NFL rewarded Charlotte with an expansion franchise, or in existing markets with particularly fervent fan bases. For example, the Cleveland Browns and Pittsburgh Steelers, two franchises with storied histories, both sold more seat licenses than they had originally placed on the market. The Browns sold 64,000 licenses, raising more than $74 million. In the case of the Steelers, the original plan to sell 35,000 seat licenses had to be quickly adjusted up to 48,000 to more fully accommodate local interest.[15]

Many franchises do not maximize their PSLs because they want to ensure there is a reasonably sized inventory of seats available for people who cannot afford PSLs or who choose not to invest in them. This enables people other than PSL and season ticket holders to sample the game experience and for the team to continue to develop the size of its fan base.

Of the 23 NFL teams that moved into new or substantially renovated venues between 1995 and 2010, 20 sold seat licenses. Other leagues have approached PSLs more conservatively because they have a much greater inventory of games to sell. For example, Major League Baseball teams have 81 games to sell each season (versus the NFL's 10 home dates). Fans, therefore, have many more opportunities to buy tickets and the necessity of paying a premium to *guarantee* the right to purchase a ticket is not nearly as compelling. Consequently, the small number of MLB teams that have implemented seat license programs have offered only a limited inventory. The San Francisco Giants offered 13,700 seat licenses (approximately one third of the total seating capacity in their new ballpark) priced from $1,500 for an upper box seat location to $7,500 for a premium field seat. The one-time, upfront payment provided purchasers with a lifetime guarantee to buy season tickets to the Charter Seats they purchased. The Giants' entire seat license allocation sold out in less than six months. The club attributed the program's success to its ability to convince the public that all revenues raised would be used to finance the construction of the new ballpark and, according to a team representative, "not line the pockets of team owners."[16]

How PSLs Work

Although the prices and lengths of PSL programs vary widely from one team to another, the basic conditions and administration of seat license programs are similar. Fundamental to all PSL programs is that after the seat holder has been awarded a seat license, he or she must purchase an annual season ticket to the assigned seat. Failure to renew season tickets results in forfeiture of the PSL. The guaranteed right of purchase is good only for as long as the rights holder continues to buy tickets.

Most PSL programs offer substantial price discounts to current season ticket holders. The seat license discounts have proven to be effective in those cities where an existing team is moving to a new venue and a PSL charge is being imposed for the first time. Clubs offer price discounts in an effort to reduce negative fan reaction to the prospect of having to pay substantially more to continue buying tickets. Some teams offer simple, straightforward discount rewards to their existing ticket holders. For example, the NFL Philadelphia Eagles extended an across-the-board 13% discount to all current ticket accounts. The Cleveland Browns, however, created a much more elaborate dis-

Exhibit 11.1	
Cleveland Browns PSL Loyalty Program	
• No PSL—10,000 Dawg Pound section seats and 5,580 other seats (21.0%) • $250 PSL—5,159 seats (7.3%) • $500 PSL—18,050 seats (25.5%)	• $750 PSL—11,175 seats (15.8%) • $1,000 PSL—17,100 seats (24.1%) • $1,500 PSL—3,800 seats (5.4%)
Loyalty Discounts: Season ticket holders 1–3 years (10%); 4–6 years (15%); 7–9 years (20%); 10–19 years (30%); 20–29 years (40%); 30 or more years (50%)	

count program targeted at rewarding current fans on the basis of their longstanding loyalty. Exhibit 11.1 shows that the Browns' graduated discount program was based on the length of continuous season ticket ownership. Those fans who had demonstrated the greatest loyalty were rewarded the deepest discounts, up to 50% off for those who had maintained season tickets for thirty or more consecutive years.

As an additional effort to reduce price resistance, teams typically allow fans the opportunity to pay for PSLs over time. The Houston Texans' PSL advertisement reproduced in Figure 11.6 shows that purchasers were extended the option of paying for their seat licenses at Reliant Stadium over three installment payments, interest-free. The Texans sold $48 million worth of PSLs in three weeks, with one third of these being nternet sales. Before the stadium opened, the Texans sold their full complement of $74 million of PSLs. These PSLs were for 30 years (i.e., the projected life of the stadium) and were fully transferable.

In addition to discounts, most programs allow the rights holder to transfer the PSL by gift, bequest, or sale to any third party. The transfer feature is attractive in that it

Figure 11.6. The Houston Texan's Advertisement Soliciting the Purchase of PSL's.

provides seat holders with the ability to pass their seats on to family members. In addition to establishing a family legacy, PSLs also have proven to be reasonable investments. In Charlotte, for example, the Carolina Panthers' fully transferable PSLs, which originally sold for between $600 to $5,400, are now being resold for as much as $975 to $12,000 in what is called the PSL aftermarket. Baltimore Ravens' PSLs, which sold from $250 to $3,000 when the new Ravens stadium opened in 1998, are selling for approximately triple their original cost (from $750 to $8,000). As shown in Figure 11.6, the Houston Texans, in their PSL promotional advertisement, highlight the rights transfer feature as one of the important benefits of owning a PSL.

Like any investment vehicle, the secondary market for PSLs is likely to rise and fall:

> In circumstances where the team has continuously performed poorly, the market may not be buoyant, forcing the PSL owner to continue purchasing season tickets to a poorly performing team or sacrifice his or her right to the license. In such a situation, a PSL owner may decide to ride out the poor seasons the team is having, much as an investor might ride out a tough time on the stock market. In contrast, the secondary market for licenses to teams that are doing well will inevitably be good, allowing the licensee, at the very least, to recoup his or her investment (p. 42).[17]

Seat licenses have provided multiple benefits to teams. They provide a sizable amount of money and the one-time, upfront payment means those dollars are immediately available to the sports property. The ability to pre-sell seat licenses in advance of construction ensures that the team and/or government authorities responsible for financing the construction will not have to borrow as much money. Thus, PSLs reduce the financial requirements of teams and governments by pushing more of the financial burden onto sports fans who buy the licenses. For those subscribing to the benefit principle of taxation discussed in Chapters 4, 5 and 9, placing more of the cost onto those who receive the most direct benefit is an eminently fair and supportable arrangement. With seat licenses, those who benefit the most, pay the most. This rationale gains greater credence when the "user pays" orientation of PSLs is compared against selective taxes, discussed in Chapter 9, where the primary burden of venue financing often is carried by tourist or business visitors paying higher hotel and/or car rental taxes.

While PSLs are justifiable from the perspective of the taxation benefit principle, their added cost per seat increases the probability that for many fans, the cost of the PSL plus payment of season tickets may be prohibitive. A serious question facing sports properties using PSLs is: How much of a direct burden is it fair for their fans to assume? For example, for an existing Chicago Bears season ticket holder to gain access to one of the approximately 20,000 "non-club" PSL seats offered in the newly-renovated Soldier Field, the fan was required to pay at least $2,500 (the PSLs average $2,000 and season tickets range from $450 to $650). Thus, for a family of four with plans to renew season tickets, the total cost in the first year of the PSL program approximated $10,000.

A financial commitment of that magnitude places even the most loyal fans in a difficult position. Some might be forced to give up their tickets because they simply cannot afford to pay for one or more seat licenses. Others who may be financially able to afford the payment might harbor substantial resentment at being required to pay so much more for the privilege of buying tickets to seats they had held for many years. Further, the PSLs are useful only for as long as a franchise is in the facility. If the team moves, PSL owners are not compensated.

Therefore, it is imperative that teams planning to implement PSL programs give careful consideration to many of the features designed to reduce price barriers, such as installment payment plans and graduated discounts similar to the Cleveland Browns' successful fan loyalty initiative (shown in Exhbit 11.1). In addition, PSL purchasers must be convinced that their payment is making a direct and meaningful contribution to facility construction. They need to believe they are being offered the "thrill of participating" in either attracting a new team to their city or enhancing the fortunes (literally and figuratively!) of their beloved sports team.

From a team standpoint, seat license programs are valuable not only as a source of revenue for capital construction but also as a strong incentive for season ticket renewals. The only way a fan can maintain the benefits of a seat license "permanently" is by renewing his or her season ticket package annually. Since the purchase of a PSL requires a substantial upfront investment, it provides a built-in incentive for the license holder to continuously renew.

Exhibit 11.2 provides a description of how two teams, the New York Giants and Jets, sharing the same venue took very different approaches to marketing their PSL programs to their respective fan bases. While the introduction of PSLs into an established market invariably provokes a negative reaction from existing season ticket holders—after all, they are being asked to pay a steep price for something that has always been free—it's clear that the Giants' approach was received much more favorably.

When PSLs have been used in contexts outside the four US major sports leagues, they have had mixed success. Sydney tried to use them as the primary funding source

Exhibit 11.2

Tale of Two Teams

In 2010, the New York Giants and New York Jets moved into the Met Life Stadium. The cost of the new, state-of-the-art facility topped $1.6 billion, making it the most expensive sports facility ever built in North America. Since the new building was entirely privately financed (although assisted by the tax exempt loophole explained in Exhbit 9.5), each team implemented a personal seat license program designed to help defray their share of the construction costs. The teams took a very different approach to the sale of PSLs to their respective fan bases.	The Giants imposed a seat license on all seats, requiring every season-ticket holder to pay for the right to retain their season ticket privilege. However, they set a relatively modest license fee of $1,000 for 27,000 seats in the upper bowl of the 82,500 seat stadium. The Giants also took a more conservative approach to pricing the preferred (and more expensive) seats in the lower bowl, imposing a $20,000 PSL fee on only the approximately 5,000 seats in the club section of the stadium. In contrast, the Jets made the decision not to require a

Exhibit 11.2 *(Continued)*

Tale of Two Teams

license fee for all 27,000 seats in the upper deck. However, in order to compensate for the "lost" revenue (as much as $27 million when compared to the Giants), the team imposed substantially higher prices for seats in the lower bowl of the stadium. The least expensive PSL was $4,000 for seats located in the end zone sections, with seats in the club section requiring a license fee as high as $30,000. In addition to paying a PSL fee of $30,000 for the right to buy seats in the area referred to as the Coaches Club Seat section, the cost of a ticket in that premium seating area was $700 per game (or $7,000 for the season). The PSL price for other sideline club seats ranged from $16,000 to $25,000 per seat. In order to moderate the immediate impact of purchasing a seat license, the Jets provided buyers with two extended payment plans. Fans were given the option of paying the PSL off in either 5 or 15 years. Using figures provided by the Jets, an individual purchasing two Coaches Club seats would be required to pay a total license fee of $60,000. If this buyer elected the 15-year payment plan, he or she would first have to put down a upfront deposit of 10% or $6,000. Over the next 15 years, the Jets fan would have make an annual payment of $5,842 (including an annual interest charge of 8%), for a total investment of $93,615—this does not include the cost of season tickets. (The cost to a fan purchasing two PSLs in the corner of the mezzanine section of the endzone for $8,000 under the same 15 year payment plan would pay an $800 deposit and make annual payments of $779 for a total investment of $12,485).

While the Giants received some criticism from fans about the requirement that every season ticket holder must pay a seat license fee, the program was very successful with almost all 82,500 seats being sold prior to the start of the 2010 season. In contrast, fan reaction to the Jets PSL was decidedly more negative. Just three months prior to the opening game of the season, the *New York Post* reported 17,000 seats remained unsold, prompting serious concerns about the NFL imposing its local market television "blackout" rule on a Jets game for the first time since 1977. In the face of poor sales and the potential imposition of TV blackouts, the Jets were forced to slash prices for both PSLs and season tickets. The team reduced prices for most of their unsold PSLs, cutting license fees in half for 10 endzone sections from $5,000 to $2,500 and from $15,000 to $10,000 for four sections of lower bowl sideline seats. The dramatic price reductions resulted in the Jets moving a significant amount of its unsold PSL inventory, allowing the team to avoid the embarrassment of TV blackouts. One news source reported the team was at least 5,000 PSLs short of selling out the new stadium at the season opener.

One tactic that may have had a positive influence on the attitude of Giants' fans toward PSLs was a letter sent by the owners, John Mara and Steve Tisch, to all Giant season ticket holders prior to the announcement of the team's seat license program. In the letter, the owners provided an explanation and rationale for why the team was initiating PSLs, stating: "At a cost of over $1.6 billion, the new stadium development is the largest 100% privately-financed stadium project in the U.S. . . . We cannot build these new facilities without the sale of "PSLs" (Personal Seat Licenses) to Giants' season ticket holders. The net proceeds from the sale of the PSLs will be used to pay for the construction of the new stadium." The owners also expressed their desire to offer a broad range of choices and affirmed that over 90% of the upper level seats would be priced at $1,000. The direct outreach approach was well received and from several reports had a moderating effect on fans' initial aversion to mandatory PSLs.

for its main Olympic stadium. The goal was to raise $344 million by offering 34,400 PSLs at $10,000 each that entitled the purchasers to buy tickets both to Olympic events at the stadium and to subsequent events held there for the next 30 years. However, only 10,800 were sold, mainly because no contracts for sporting events after the Games had been signed.[18]

Colleges have been using a variation of the PSL concept referred to as priority seating ever since Clemson University initiated its IPTAY (I Pay Ten [Dollars] a Year) Club in 1933. Virtually all major college athletics programs now require those seeking prime seats to make an annual donation to the athletic department. Those fans contributing the largest sums of money, over the longest period of time, are allocated the best seats.

One major athletic program found that while fans may be willing to pay more for the right to sit in the best seats, imposing the requirement of a large *up-front* payment for access to those seats may be asking too much of even the most avid college fans. Thus, fans resisted when Louisiana State University (LSU) sought to use PSLs to raise $115 million to build and renovate five major athletic facilities, the Louisiana Legislature intervened and made it clear to LSU officials that they would not allow it.[19]

Inevitably, high schools are now using PSLs. For example in Ohio, Ravenna High School used PSLs priced at $1,000 and $1,500 to cover some of the cost of a new football/soccer stadium, while Napoleon High School sold almost 800 of them at $300 each. The athletic director at Ravenna said that not all license holders come to the games: "They just want to contribute. Some people who brought them didn't even live in the community" (p. 36).[20]

NAMING RIGHTS

Professional Sports Venues

The corporate naming of major sports facilities is a relatively recent phenomenon, even though the Chicago Cubs Wrigley Field has had a corporate name since 1926. However, it was named after the team's owner rather than the chewing gum company that his family also owned, and no payments for the naming rights were made. A similar situation characterized Busch Memorial Stadium—home of the St. Louis Cardinals that opened in 1956. The team was owned by the Anheuser-Busch Company. Thus, the first real naming rights agreement dates back to 1971 when Schaefer Brewing Company paid $150,000 to rename the then-Boston Patriots stadium as Schaefer Field. Two years later, the Buffalo Bills renamed War Memorial Stadium as Rich Stadium, after signing a $1.5 million, 20-year agreement with Rich Products, a local frozen food supplier.[21]

These early naming rights agreements did not stimulate a widespread trend. From the early 1970s through the mid-1980s, few sports facilities were corporately named. During this period, major sports venues, all of which were publicly financed, typically maintained the tradition of being named either for prominent civic leaders such as the Hubert H. Humphrey Dome in Minneapolis (1982) and Brandon Bryne Arena (1981) in New Jersey, or to provide local or civic identity such as the Louisiana Superdome (1975) and Pontiac Stadium (1978).

The naming rights of the Los Angeles Forum were sold to Great Western Bank in 1987, Arco Arena was named in Sacramento in 1988, and the Target Center in Minneapolis in 1990, but it was not until the last half of the 1990s that naming rights agreements became prominent. From 1995 through 2000, the number and financial magnitude of venue sponsorships grew significantly. By 1997, one third (41 of 113) of the venues used by teams in the four major leagues had been named for corporations.[21] Within five years, that percentage doubled. By 2002, the proportion of corporately named venues had increased to almost 70%, with 80 of 121 teams playing in facilities named after major companies.[22] In part, this growth was stimulated by the large number of new sports facilities that were constructed in the late 1990s. The availability of these new facilities created an unprecedented inventory of entitlement opportunities for corporations seeking to exploit the commercial benefit of placing their names on prominent sports venues. Currently, over 77%, or 94 of 122 professional teams in the "big four" major leagues in North America play in corporately-named venues. At the start of the 2012 season, 13 of 19 Major League Soccer teams were also playing in stadiums named for a company or brand.

The Growing Value of Naming Rights Agreements

The growth in entitlement opportunities over the past two decades has been accompanied by substantial increases in the amounts paid by corporations for these rights. Staples, an office products company, set a record in 1998 by agreeing to pay $100 million for the rights to the new downtown arena in Los Angeles. Within a year, FedEx eclipsed the $200 million barrier when the package delivery company paid $205 million ($7.6 million per year on average for 25 years) to the Washington Redskins to name the NFL team's new football stadium FedEx Field. Shortly thereafter, the $300 million barrier was broken when Reliant Energy purchased the rights to the Houston Texans new football stadium in 2000 at $10 million per year.

Substantial naming rights activity occurred until the Great Recession. Between 2001 and 2007, 13 naming rights deals in excess of $100 million were signed. Two of the largest were signed in early 2007. When Citigroup, Inc. agreed to pay $400 million ($20 million per year over 20 years) for the naming rights to the new New York Mets ballpark, it was the most expensive sports-stadium rights deal ever, superseding the previous record agreement at Reliant Stadium by a substantial margin. Shortly after the Citi Field announcement, Barclays Bank announced it would become the new naming rights partner with the Brooklyn Nets and would pay between $300 and $400 million over 20 years for the naming rights to a new arena, which opened in 2012.*

Tables 11.6 and 11.7 identify the 20 largest stadium and arena naming rights deals in North America, respectively. Leading the way by a substantial margin is the Farmers Insurance naming-rights deal worth $600 million. Early in 2011, AEG, the entertainment company that owns and manages many prominent venues, including the Staples

*In 2011, the *SportsBusiness Journal* reported the actual worth of the Barclays Center naming rights agreement at $200 million. The authoritative publication reduced the original value announced by the Nets after reviewing the official 2009 prospectus for the issuance of the arena bonds.

Table 11.6. 20 Largest *Stadium* Naming Rights Deals

Name, City, Team (League)	Total Price (millions)	Length (Years)	Avg. Annual Payment (millions)	Expiration Year
Farmers Field, Los Angeles, (NFL)	$600–$700	30	$20–$23	TBD
MetLife Field, New York, Giants/Jets (NFL)	$425–$625	25	$17–$20	2036
Citi Field, NewYork, Mets (MLB)	$400	20	$20.0	2028
Reliant Stadium, Houston, Texans (NFL)	$310	31	$10	2032
Gillette Stadium, New England, Patriots (NFL)	$240	15	$8.0	2031
FedEx Field, Washington D.C., Redskins (NFL)	$205	27	$7.59	2025
Minute Maid Park, Houston, Astros (MLB)	$178	28	$6.36	2029
University of Phoenix, Arizona, Cardinals (NFL)	$154.5	20	$7.72	2026
Bank of America Stadium, Charlotte, Panthers (NFL)	$140	20	$7.0	2023
Lincoln Financial Field,, Philadelphia, Eagles (NFL)	$139.6	20	$6.98	2022
Lucas Oil Stadium, Indianapolis, Colts (NFL)	$121.5	20	$6.07	2027
Citizens Bank Park, Philadelphia, Phillies (MLB)	$95	25	$3.8	2029
M&T Bank, Baltimore, Ravens (NFL)	$79	15	$5.0	2017
Great American Ball Park, Cincinnati, Reds (MLB)	$75	30	$2.5	2032
Home Depot Center, Los Angeles, Galaxy (MLS)	$70	10	$7.0	2013
U.S. Cellular Field, Chicago, White Sox (MLB)	$68	23	$2.96	2025
Chase Field, Arizona, Diamondbacks (MLB)	$66.4	30	$2.2	2028
Comerica Park, Detroit, Tigers (MLB)	$66	30	$2.2	2030
Petco Park, San Diego, Padres (MLB)	$60	22	$2.73	2025
Sports Authority Field at Mile High Stadium, Denve,r Broncos (NFL)	$60	10	$6.0	2021
CenturyLink Field, Seattle, Seahawks (NFL)	$60– $100	15–20	$4.0–$5.0	2019–2024

Source: *SportsBusiness Journal*, In-Depth: Naming Rights, September 19–25, 2011

Name, City Team (League)	Total Price (millions)	Length (Years)	Avg. Annual Payment (millions)	Expiration Year
Table 11.7. 20 Largest Arena Naming Rights Deals				
Barclays Center Brooklyn Nets (NBA)	$200	20	$10.0	2032
American Airlines Center Dallas Stars (NHL), Mavericks (NBA)	$195	30	$6.5	2030
Philips Arena Atlanta Hawks (NBA)	$185	20	$9.25	2019
Nationwide Arena Columbus Blue Jackets (NHL)	$135	Indef.	NA	Indef.
TD Garden Boston Bruins (NHL), Celtics (NBA)	$119.1	20	$5.95	2025
Staples Center Los Angeles Kings (NHL), Lakers (NBA), Clippers (NBA)	$116	20	$5.8	NA
Prudential Center New Jersey Devils (NHL)	$105.3	20	$5.26	2027
Toyota Center Houston Rockets (NBA)	$95	20	$4.75	2023
FedExForum Memphis Grizzlies (NBA)	$90	22	$4.09	2024
Consol Energy Center Pittsburgh Penguins (NHL)	$84–105	21	$4.0–$5.0	2031
RBC Center Carolina Hurricanes (NHL)	$80	20	$4.0	2022
Excel Center Minnesota Wild (NHL)	$75	25	$3.0	2024
Pepsi Center Denver Avalanche (NHL), Nuggets (NBA)	$68	20	$3.4	2019
Bell Center Montreal Canadiens (NHL)	$63.94	20	$3.2	2023
Honda Center Anaheim Ducks (NHL)	$60.45	15	$4.03	2020
HP Pavilion at San Jose San Jose Sharks (NHL)	$47	15	$3.13	2016
Verizon Center Washington Capitols (NHL), Wizards (NBA)	$44	20	$2.2	2017
American Airlines Center Miami Heat (NBA)	$42	20	$2.1	2019
AT&T Center San Antonio Spurs (NBA)	$41	20	$2.05	2022
Amway Center Orlando Magic	$40	10	$4.0	2020

Center, announced a 30-year agreement with Farmers which would name a proposed stadium in Los Angeles "Farmers Field." The deal is unique in that it is completely speculative. At the time of the signing there was no stadium—a site had not even been approved—and no team!

There has not been an NFL franchise in Los Angeles since the Rams abandoned the market for a new stadium in St. Louis in 1994. Crucial to the return of the NFL to Los Angeles was the construction of a modern, fully loaded stadium. For more than a decade, a number of alternatives were proposed, including the renovation of both the LA Coliseum and Rose Bowl sites, building new state-of-the-art venues in suburban communities, and AEG's most recent proposal to build a new stadium as part of their existing downtown entertainment district, L.A. Live. While Los Angeles was working on building a new stadium, NFL Commissioner Roger Goodell, in his 2012 State of the League address, reiterated the league's intent to bring NFL football back to the city, adding that "the league would add two teams if it ever decided to expand."[26] The intent of the AEG-Farmers partnership was to provide momentum for AEG's plan to build a new, $1 billion stadium. AEG believed that the announcement of the record-breaking naming rights deal with Farmers would expedite approval by the city for its stadium proposal. AEG's president stated that it ". . . doesn't mean football is back (in L.A.) tomorrow. But it means we took probably the most significant step in the last 15 years to getting football back here soon."[26] The naming rights agreement between AEG and Farmers is conditional on the new downtown stadium's being built and occupied by an NFL franchise. At that point, the conditional agreement would be activated and Farmers would start making payments of no less than $20 million per year, providing AEG with a crucial source of contractually obligated income (COI) for 30 years.

The Indianapolis Colts sold new stadium naming rights to Lucas Oil for $121.5 million. Courtesy of BigStockPhoto

While by far the largest, the Farmer's deal was one of several major naming rights agreements announced in 2011. In August 2011, another insurance company, MetLife, became the naming rights partner for the new $1.6 billion stadium jointly occupied by the New York Giants and Jets. The total value of MetLife's commitment is estimated at between $425 to $625 million,* with the company making annual payments of between $17 and $20 million over 25 years. Other major naming rights deals consummated in 2011 include: Mercedes-Benz USA taking the rights to the New Orleans Superdome for an estimated $100 to $125 million,[27] CenturyLink investing $60 million to extend an existing naming rights deal with the NFL Seattle Seahawks, and the Sports Authority purchasing the naming rights to the NFL Broncos stadium in Denver for $60 million.

A number of analysts believed these agreements signaled the resurgence of the naming rights market, which had suffered through several difficult years following the Great Recession. Given the difficult economic climate of 2008 and 2009, most companies were reluctant to commit millions of dollars to naming rights deals. In 2009, when the economy was at its lowest point, the only major agreement completed was the naming of the Orlando Magic's new arena. The $40 million, 10-year deal to name the venue the Amway Center was signed by team owner, and co-owner of Amway Global, Richard DeVos. The otherwise depressed market prompted a leading sports economist to declare the post-recession period of 2008–2010 as "the worst time in the last 20 years to sell naming rights."[28]

Challenges Ahead

While there are signs that the naming rights market is rebounding, many teams are still having a difficult time finding naming rights partners. Several high-profile teams have struggled for years to find a venue title sponsor. Among them is perhaps the most well known sports property in North America, the NFL Dallas Cowboys. For many years, this iconic sports brand was ranked by *Forbes* as the world's most valuable sports franchise. In 2009, the Cowboys moved into the then-most expensive stadium and many would argue, the most spectacular sports venue ever built in the United States. As a result, many analysts believed the Cowboys would achieve the biggest naming rights deal in sports history.[28] Almost four years *after* opening the new venue, the team was still searching for a naming rights partner. The story described in Exhibit 11.3 of the MLB Washington Nationals' unsuccessful effort to sell the naming rights to "Nationals Park"—five years *after* the team opened the new ballpark—illustrates the challenges facing teams in a post-recession economy. Prior to moving into the $693 million venue to start the 2008 season, the Nationals had hoped to create a naming relationship with a national brand worth $8 to $12 million annually for 10 to 20 years. Like the Dallas Cowboys, the Nationals were still seeking a naming rights partner when this book went to press in late 2013.

---

*Estimates of the value of the MetLife naming rights deal have ranged from a high of $23 million to a low of $17 million per year. The most commonly reported annual payout is a range between $17 and $20 million over 25 years. Using these figures, the total value of the MetLife Stadium deal would range between $425 million and $500 million.

Exhibit 11.3

Washington Nationals' Naming Rights are Still Marketable

Whatever happened to [Insert Corporate Name Here] Park? When the Washington Nationals opened their new stadium on the Anacostia River four years ago, "Nationals Park" was widely understood to be a placeholder, to be used only until the team sold naming rights to some corporate brand for upward of $10 million a year.

But on April 12, the Nationals started their fifth season in none other than Nationals Park. And to experts in the sports marketing world, the stadium remains one of the great unrealized marketing assets in America.

"It's sort of a mystery why it's not sold yet," said Dean Bonham, CEO of French sports marketing firm Bonham/Wills & Associates and negotiator of 12 major stadium naming rights deals. "It's a prominent market. The team—it's not a World Series team, but it's an interesting team. I can't see any reason why that deal hasn't been done."

The Nationals aren't talking. There's little outward evidence of an active sales effort, industry insiders say. One potential deal bubbled up late last year, but that was the only activity since the ballpark's earliest days, said Lisa Delpy Neirotti, a sports management and tourism professor at George Washington University who speaks with club sources regularly.

But that doesn't mean a deal isn't out there, waiting for the right blend of creativity, opportunity, salesmanship and shrewd strategizing to take hold. While it might have been much easier to strike a deal before the recession hit corporate America, experts say the market hasn't dried up entirely, as evidenced by recent deals in Los Angeles and New York. Major stadiums in Dallas, Miami and Kansas City, however, remain without a sponsor.

To be sure, some experts acknowledge the Nationals' best chance to make a deal may have been before the stadium opened. According to one industry analyst, "They were in the marketplace at a time when you would have thought it would have been a good window of opportunity to sell. But, by the middle of 2008, we realized we were in serious trouble economically and the markets just shut down."

Experts say the naming rights' value has eroded only modestly—perhaps justifying a conservative approach from team owner Ted Lerner and his son, Mark Lerner. The closest avatar for Washington might be the Philadelphia Phillies, which have a $57.5 million, 25-year deal with Citizens Bank, along with a $37.5 million advertising package—less than $4 million a year. But unrealistic expectations may be to blame for the lack of a deal prior to 2008. Before the recession, Rob Prazmark, CEO of 21 Sports and Entertainment Marketing Group, Inc. said, "Everybody involved believed the Nationals could lure top dollar in the heyday of naming rights." Dean Bonham also felt the Nationals' expectations exceeded market reality, "If I had to offer a guess on why it hasn't been sold, I would guess it's related to an inaccurate analysis of the value of the property as opposed to the lack of marketability." Skepticism rests in a widely held belief that in a struggling economy there simply aren't many companies with the wherewithal, political freedom and positive brand identity to strike a deal amenable to the Nationals.

By far, the industry best represented on the marquees of major venues are financial services providers, followed by the automobile industry. Since the federal bailouts and Troubled Asset Relief Program, however, those companies have been closely scrutinized by lawmakers and regulators. Citibank, for instance, drew ire from several on Capitol Hill when it struck a $400 million, 20-year deal to name the New York Mets' new stadium in 2008. Others may hesitate to follow in their footsteps, particularly in Congress' backyard.

Local corporate partners have emerged as trendy buyers of naming rights now, case in point being Baltimore's M&T Bank Stadium or San Diego's PetCo Park. But one obvious local candidate, Capital One Financial Corp., is working on an acquisition of

Exhibit 11.3

Washington Nationals' Naming Rights are Still Marketable

ING Direct's U.S. business, and companies with major strategic moves in play often don't agree to such ancillary, high-dollar deals.

Multiple experts said the buyer could be a complete dark horse, a company that wouldn't generally consider a naming rights deal, but could be swayed with the right package of unique benefits only offered by the Nationals— for instance, signs literally visible from the U.S. House offices or the U.S. Department of Transportation. Prazmark said the Nationals may find the most promise in expanding a relationship with an existing marketing partner.

For now, the Lerners appear to be willing to sit on that potential value, just as Dallas Cowboys owner Jerry Jones has done with the crown jewel of stadium naming rights, Cowboys Stadium.

Source: This article written by Ben Fisher, Staff Reporter, appeared in the *Washington Business Journal* on April 13, 2012.

Another challenge facing teams and venues hoping to sell naming rights is the limited prospect pool. With more than three-fourths of major league teams playing in corporately named buildings, a substantial share of major companies with national brands have already entered into long-term naming partnerships with existing facilities. As shown in Table 11.8, some of the largest companies in a wide range of consumer product and service categories have committed millions of dollars annually to place their company name or brand on a sports facility. A few prominent consumer service firms have purchased the naming rights to multiple venues (e.g., American Airlines, AT&T and Wells Fargo). The result is that many of the major national brands, companies with both the capability and willingness to invest the substantial financial resources necessary to buy and sustain naming rights partnerships, are no longer available as potential prospects.

Table 11.8. National Brands with Sports Facility Naming Rights by Product or Service Category

Product or Service	Major Companies
Airlines	Air Canada, American, United, US Airways
Automobile	Ford, Honda, Toyota
Banking	Bank of America, Citizens, Wells Fargo
Energy	Consol Energy, Chesapeake Energy, Reliant, Xcel
Financial Services	Citi, Edward Jones, PNC, Raymond James, Scottrade
Insurance	Farmers, MetLife, Progressive, Prudential, Safeco
Telecommunications	AT&T, Bell Centre, U.S. Cellular, Verizon

Consequently, most of the recent naming rights agreements have been with companies with a more "local" association or connection to the market or city in which they purchase the naming rights. Teams seeking venue naming partners have found a more receptive client pool within their own region or market area. In fact, a significant number of naming agreements established over the last decade have been with firms whose company headquarters are located in the same city or metropolitan area as the venue they name. Examples include: Farmers Insurance (Farmers Field, Los Angeles), Petco Animal Supplies (Petco Park, San Diego Padres), Sports Authority (Sports Authority Field at Mile High, Denver Broncos), H.J. Heinz (Heinz Field, Pittsburgh Steelers), Target Corporation (Target Field, Minnesota Twins), Consol Energy, Inc. (Consol Energy Center, Pittsburgh Penguins), FedEx Corporation (FedEx Forum, Memphis Grizzlies), EverBank (EverBank Field, Jacksonville Jaguars) and BMO Harris Bank (BMHO Harris Bradley Center, Milwaukee Bucks). The executive vice president of BMHO Harris, in explaining his bank's decision to purchase the naming rights to the Bradley Center in downtown Milwaukee, stated, "Sponsorship of a community treasure like the Bradley Center is a great opportunity for us to deepen our local commitment and strengthen our relationship with customers in Milwaukee and across Wisconsin."[29] Expanding the firm's visibility and connection to the local and regional market is a common theme, as expressed by Sports Authority's chief marketing director in announcing the sporting goods firm's decision to purchase the naming rights to the Denver Broncos stadium: "We're the third largest private company in Colorado, yet people don't know that our headquarters are in Colorado. We don't look at this as a corporate partnership. We look at this as a Colorado sponsorship."[30]

While the shift from national to more local or regional companies has allowed teams and venues, particularly in smaller markets, to successfully sell their naming rights, it has meant that many teams have had to settle for less money and for shorter-length partnerships. The limited prospect pool and poor economy have made it difficult for teams to negotiate deals comparable to those established prior to the Great Recession. Two recent naming rights deals illustrate this broadening trend. The Miami Dolphins and Sun Life Financial signed a five-year, $25 million deal in 2012, and the Jacksonville Jaguars reached a five-year, $16.6 million agreement with EverBank in 2010. After signing the agreement, the Jaguars Chief Financial Officer confirmed that that terms were as good as the team could negotiate in the current market, commenting, "From our standpoint, the term was shorter than we would have liked, [and] the dollars were less than we would have liked."[31] Other teams or venues signing shorter-term agreements at the start of this decade include: Oakland Raiders ($7.6 million for 6 years with Over stock.com), Houston Dynamos MLS team ($20 million for 10 years with BBVA Compass), New Orleans Saints ($100–$120 million for 10 years with Mercedes-Benz USA), Denver Broncos ($60 million for 10 years with Sports Authority) and the Calgary Flames (10-year deal with ScotiaBank to rename the Saddledome; financial terms were not disclosed).

A primary reason companies are increasingly reluctant to enter into extended naming rights contracts is that the uncertain economic climate makes it difficult to justify long-term agreements of 20 years or more. Firms have become more cautious and circumspect. As one experienced naming rights dealmaker asserted:

> In a world that's changing so rapidly as the one we live in, does it make sense to commit that much money for that much time? It's a tactic that limits your flexibility to move dollars from one investment area to another because they are committed for years. So here's the thing: Companies need to be nimble. They need to be able to change direction quickly. If they conduct any media mix modeling, they can evaluate pulling the plug on less effective marketing investments in favor of new tactics or current tactics proving to be more effective.[27]

While there are challenges to professional teams and venues attempting to find naming rights partners, the market still remains viable. The Farmers Stadium and Mercedes-Benz Superdome arrangements are recent examples of successful transactions. However, the reality for many teams playing in smaller markets or in older venues is that there are not as many available prospects who will be willing to commit as much money for as many years as in the past.

Shirt and Team Naming Rights

Jersey and facility naming rights offer different types of exposure. Companies associated with facilities benefit from their association being routinely referenced in external media. This benefit does not accrue to companies that appear on jerseys. But they become the focus of fans throughout the event whether viewed live or on television. Given the active focus of fans on the players and their jerseys, it seems likely that this association will resonate more strongly than facility naming rights.

While facility naming rights are widely accepted by the four major professional leagues, this has not been extended to shirt or apparel naming rights. The NFL does permit the manufacturer's name or logo to be discretely featured on footwear, apparel, and helmets. Similarly, an NBA uniform has the maker's insignia on it. Their regulations require manufacturers to pay the leagues a fee for the right to display these logos. The NCAA uniform rules limit the size and number of manufacturers' logos on game jerseys to "a single manufacturer's logo not to exceed 2¼"." A similar limitation is imposed on socks, headbands and wristbands.

Major League Soccer (MLS) teams do sell shirt ("kit") sponsorships. The back of club jerseys are reserved for league-wide sponsors, but the front is available for individual club shirt sponsors. The league established a floor of $500,000 per year for this. Unlike the English Premier League, MLS prohibits online gambling companies. The MLS shirt sponsors are listed in Table 11.9.

The amount companies are willing to pay to use MLS teams as a platform for connecting their brands to team supporters has increased substantially in recent years. A decade ago, the league charged $2.5 million annually to place a company logo on a team uniform as well as on sideline boards and television scoreboards. By 2012, many MLS kit sponsorships were being sold for more than $4 million. Vitamin manufacturer

Table 11.9. MLS Club Shirt Naming Rights		
Team	**Sponsor**	**Annual Value**
Chicago Fire	Quaker	Undisclosed
Chivas USA	Corona	Undisclosed
Columbus Crew	Barbasol	Undisclosed
FC Dallas	AdvoCare	Undisclosed
D.C. United	Volkswagon	$3.1 million–$3.7 million
Houston Dynamo	Greenstar Recycling	$2.54 million
Los Angeles Galaxy	Herbalife	$4.4 million
Montreal Impact	Bank of Montreal	Undisclosed
New England Revolution	UnitedHealthcare	Undisclosed
Philadelphia Union	Bimbo	$3 million
Portland Timbers	Alaska Airlines	Undisclosed
Real Salt Lake	XanGo	$1 million
Seattle Sounders FC	Xbox	$4 million
Toronto FC	Bank of Montreal	C$4 million+
Vancouver Whitecaps FC	Bell Canada	C$4 million+

The New York Red Bull jersey sponsor is Red Bull, which owns the club. Teams without jersey sponsor: Colorado, Kansas City, San Jose.

Herbalife paid the Los Angeles Galaxy $4.4 million for shirt and team naming rights for the 2012 season.

The reticence of the American major leagues in embracing shirt sponsorship was shared by the European soccer leagues a few decades ago. Club uniforms were perceived to be an integral part of a team's heritage and of the heritage of the sport. Thus, shirt sponsorship was banned by the English soccer authorities until 1977. Liverpool became the first club to endorse shirt sponsorship when they signed an agreement with Japanese electronics giant Hitachi. Others quickly followed, so within a decade it had become an accepted, noncontroversial practice. As global interest in the EPL has grown exponentially, it has driven huge increases in shirt naming right fees. Thus, foreign broadcast rates for EPL games increased by over 400% between 2006 and 2011, which led to commensurate increases in shirt sponsorship fees.

Kit sponsorships for preeminent English Premier League (EPL) teams are now extraordinarily lucrative. In 2012, Manchester United reached an agreement with US automobile manufacturer General Motors to put the Chevrolet brand on its uniform shirt. Starting in 2014, the record rights deal will cost General Motors $420 to $490 million over the seven-year contract period.[32] In effect, General Motors is paying $60 to $70 million per year for the Chevrolet brand to receive 90 minutes of guaranteed exposure in matches that attract huge global audiences. Manchester United, owned by the American Glazer family, is reputed to be the most popular sports team in the world, with 659 million followers.

While Manchester United is the pre-eminent brand in the EPL, other teams also have impressive shirt sponsorship arrangements. United's cross-town rivals, Manchester City, negotiated a 10-year agreement with Abu Dhabi's Etihad Airways for $56 million a year, which includes naming rights to the team's stadium and practice ground as well as shirt sponsorship. Similarly, Liverpool signed a six-year agreement with Warrior Sports, owned by New Balance, to sponsor the club's shirts at $40 million a year. Liverpool's replica shirts sales reached nearly 900,000 a year, making it the fourth largest selling kit in the world behind Manchester United, Barcelona and Real Madrid. Top European soccer clubs in other countries have negotiated similar amounts. For example, the Qatar Foundation's logo will appear on the front of Barcelona's shirts in return for $200 million over five years from the nonprofit.

The escalation in EPL shirt naming fees was vividly illustrated by Chelsea. The club had signed a deal with Umbro, a sport apparel supplier, in 2001 for $8 million a year for 10 years. In a move which is perhaps unprecedented in professional sports, five years later the club paid Umbro almost $40 million to terminate the contract (which resulted in Umbro's shares falling by 6% when it was announced).[33] This freed the club to sign a shirt naming rights agreement with Samsung at $30 million a year for 10 years.

From a corporate sponsor's perspective, shirt naming rights are likely to be preferable to facility naming rights because they have the added value not only of appearing in front of live crowds but also on television and in press action photographs. In addition, they appear on the replica uniforms purchased and worn by fans of the teams. Thus, shirt sponsorship creates thousands of "mobile billboards" displaying a company's name in every park and open space in countries where children seek to emulate the skills of their team idols, and these shirts are also worn by older people as casual leisure wear. In their ongoing search for new revenue sources, it seems likely that the US major leagues ultimately will follow the European soccer precedent and embrace shirt naming rights.

Perhaps the ultimate naming rights agreement from a corporate perspective is to have the franchise branded with the corporate name. Red Bull pioneered this strategy and subsequently the company has continued to exploit it extensively.

Red Bull, a company that essentially created the energy drink market and continues to dominate it with a 70% market share, has specialized in creating its own sport properties. One of the company's fundamental tenets has been that a successful sport property can be built and not simply bought. Typically, it has invested in comparatively small sport properties before building them and molding them to fit the Red Bull image. Today, Red Bull has an arguably unrivaled international sporting empire, including, among others: EC Red Bull Salzburg (Erste Bank Hockey League, Austria), FC Red Bull Salzburg (Austrian Bundesliga), F1 teams Red Bull Racing and Scuderia Toro Rosso, Major League Soccer's New York Red Bulls, NASCAR's Team Red Bull, Red Bull Brasil FC (Segunda Divisão Paulista, Brazilian second division) and fifth division German football club SSV Markranstädt, to be renamed RB Leipzig.

Red Bull has strict criteria for any sports property it creates or buys. The team or event must bear the Red Bull name in some way and be branded or rebranded to meet the company's color scheme and identity. With its soccer teams, however small, Red Bull insists on blanket exposure for the brand. Wherever possible, the team's stadiums have all been renamed the "Red Bull Arena." Playing in Red Bull-named arenas and stadia, hosting new and unrivaled sporting events, and branding everything with Red Bull's colors and logo, the company has succeeded in building one of the most visible sporting empires in the world.[34]

An alternative to owning the property is to purchase the right to change a property's name to the corporate name without owning the team. This was the strategy adopted by Tau Ceramica, which is one of the best basketball teams in Europe but is also one of Spain's top producers of floor and wall tile.[35] The company bought the team name in exchange for an infusion of money and changed the team's existing name to the corporate name. The company does not own the team. If it did so, then it would be unable to withdraw its name if the team were chronic losers and would have to invest company funds in players and basketball, which is not its business. The team's name resonates among the young active, sports-minded consumers who make up the company's desired demographic target market. A similar model was adopted by a Welsh company. Total Network Solutions (TNS) was a full-time professional soccer team playing in the Welsh Premier League based in the village of Llansantffraid. The company, TNS, was based in the area and agreed to provide the team $400,000 over four years in exchange for it changing from its village name to TNS. The company's managing director commented: "Immediately we had our name being read out on the national radio, then on Sky Television, then on the BBC. We reckon about 8 million people hear the name each Saturday when the football results are reported." The arrangement worked so well for TNS that the company increased its sponsorship to $800,000 a year, which enabled the club to become more successful and generate additional visibility for TNS. The arrangement ended when TNS was taken over by British Telecom.[36]

There are other examples of this in Europe. For example, Caja San Fernando and Unicafa are named after Spanish banks. In the US, major league franchises have remained linked to geography, not corporate entities. When Federal Express Corporation tried to buy the team name of the Vancouver Grizzlies franchise when it moved to Memphis, the NBA refused to allow it, but it seems likely they will revisit this in the future since it is a potentially lucrative revenue source.

College Sports Venue Naming Rights

Table 11.10 shows that a growing number of colleges and universities also have sold naming rights to stadiums and arenas on their campuses. Most of the collegiate naming rights agreements are modest in comparison to those negotiated by major league teams. However, the number and financial magnitude of deals have grown substantially over the past ten years, with several agreements approaching the values realized by big league venues. The single largest agreement was the $40 million agreement Pepsi signed with Fresno State University. After acquiring the naming rights to the university's proposed

Table 11.10. Top 10 College Naming Rights Deals					
Facility	School	Total Price (millions)	Length (Years)	Avg. Annual Value	Year Expires
Save Mart Center	Fresno State	$40	20	$2,000,000	2023
TCF Bank	Minnesota	$35	25	$1,400,000	2034
Comcast Center	Maryland	$25	25	$1,000,000	2026
Apogee Center	North Texas	$20	20	$1,000,000	2030
AT&T Stadium	Texas Tech	$20	25	$800,000	2019
Chevy Chase Bank Field at Byrd Stadium	Maryland	$20	25	$800,000	2030
Bright House Stadium	Central Florida	$15	15	$1,000,000	2022
Summa Field at InfoCision Stadium	Akron	$15	20	$750,000	2029
TD Ameritrade Park	Creighton/ College World Series	$15	20	$750,000	2030
Papa John's Cardinal Stadium	Louisville	$15	32	$468,750	2040
Source: *SportsBusiness Journal*, In-Depth: Naming Rights, September 19–25, 2011					

sports and entertainment center, the soft drink company "passed through" the naming opportunity to one of its key retail suppliers in central California, Save Mart Supermarkets. The joint sponsorship agreement resulted in the new facility being called the Save Mart Center, with PepsiCo retaining exclusive pouring rights across the entire Fresno State campus as well as preferred aisle and shelf space placement for Pepsi products in all Save Mart outlets.

Colleges frequently name sports facilities after major donors. The requirement at most universities to qualify for naming status is that the lead donor contribute 50% of the cost of the construction or renovation.[37] However, this is not a rigid criterion and in some cases it may be as low as 30%. In addition, an increasing number of colleges are requiring a maintenance endowment to accompany the 30% to 50% capital contribution before they will offer naming rights. The magnitude of the maintenance endowment varies, but an endowment sufficient to generate 30% of the total maintenance costs appears to be a fairly typical figure.

Naming rights extend beyond the building to particular facilities within the building.[38] These may include plazas, auditoriums, halls of fame, natatoriums, gymnasiums, weight rooms, and locker rooms. Thus, Ohio State University sold the naming rights to the gymnasium inside its event center to Value City Department Stores for $12.5 million, so the university's basketball and hockey teams play in the Value City Arena at the

Jerome Schottenstein Center. The late Mr. Schottenstein was founder of Schottenstein Stores Corp., which at the time of the naming rights agreement owned Value City, a discount department store chain. The naming rights agreement pays tribute to his many contributions to the city of Columbus and Ohio State University and, at the same time, provides broad exposure for the Value City brand. Georgia Institute of Technology signed a six-year agreement with McDonald's restaurants. In return for $5.5 million and a percentage of gross revenues, McDonald's received the rights to operate restaurants at two campus locations, and Georgia Tech agreed to rename a square-block area of the campus containing its basketball arena and other athletics facilities as the McDonald's Center at Alexander Memorial Coliseum.[39]

When dealing with donors, naming rights are made in perpetuity. This is an important difference from naming rights at professional facilities which are in force only for as long as they are paid for or until the agreement terminates. When a college needs to renovate a facility 20 years after its construction, it cannot jettison the original owner's name and replace it with the name of the lead donor of the renovation. A way has to be found to incorporate both donors' names. For example, the original Smith Pool when renovated may become the Smith Pool in the Jones Natatorium to accommodate both the original and the renovation lead donors.

Although the number and value of agreements has increased, there is resistance among some schools that are wary of increasing commercialism on campuses. Some on college campuses view the selling of corporate exposure as "an invasion of the sacred realm of academe," arguing that educational programs "should not be in the business of promoting commercial products" (p. 13).[40]

Thus, the athletic department at Stanford University reacted to criticism of growing commercialism by removing all large corporate signs and banners from its football, basketballb and baseball venues. This corporate "cleansing" cost the athletic department approximately $2.5 million per year.[41] The athletic director at Stanford commented, "I see this as the right decision for Stanford, but I'm not sure we're a national model for anybody else. Only the rich can afford to be moral. If the choice had been either to have advertising or drop sports, we might have come to another decision." (p. 3).[42] While few schools may follow Stanford's lead, it is clear that many will struggle with finding an appropriate balance between maintaining the ideals of amateurism and academic integrity and the ever-increasing expense of sustaining big-time collegiate athletic programs.

Perhaps the compromise reached by the University of Iowa offers a model for future collegiate naming rights agreements. To address both institutional concerns regarding academic mission and the athletic department's pragmatic need for financial support, Iowa named its on-campus arena "Carver-Hawkeye Arena." Roy J. Carver, chair and founder of a tire manufacturing company, gave $25 million to the university. The university "insisted that Hawkeye be part of the name so you'd know where the thing is." (p. C12).[43]

Given the growing sensitivity about the commercialization of college sports, negotiations involving the sale of naming rights are especially complicated in the college sector. One experienced naming rights negotiator commented, "There are many more folks in the mix on the college-side than on the professional side. On the pro side, you're dealing with single ownership. But, on the college side you're dealing with an athletic director, a president, a board of regents or trustees, and then sometimes there's also a state public works division involved. There are just more hoops to go through." (p. 14).[44]

Despite these challenges, the potential financial benefits of selling naming rights for stadium and arena development will continue to incentivize many colleges and universities to pursue corporate naming partnerships because "the money available is hard to ignore."[45] With so many collegiate athletic programs facing severe budget pressures, it is likely that corporately named sports venues will increasingly become a common part of the collegiate sports landscape.

High School Venue Naming Rights

Like other innovative revenue strategies, facility naming rights has percolated down so numerous high schools have sold stadium and field naming rights. Like colleges, many high schools are constrained in pursuing such agreements by their stadiums' already being named after prominent local residents. Attempts to replace those names would invariably result in community outrage. However, where the existing facilities bear generic names, or where new facilities are being built, the sale of naming rights is increasingly being considered.

The movement is perhaps most prominent in Texas, where an early pioneer was Midland ISD. They partnered with Grande Communications to put the company's name on its stadium in return for $1.2 million over 25 years. This was quickly surpassed in 2003 by Forney ISD whose new $4.4 million stadium was named City Bank Stadium, replacing the previous Jackrabbit stadium named after the school's beloved mascot. In return for the naming rights, City Bank agreed to purchase the bonds used to finance the stadium at a discounted interest rate that saved the ISD one million dollars over the 15-year life of the bonds. The revenues escalated yet again in the state in 2004 when Tyler ISD partnered with Trinity Mother Frances Health System, renaming its Rose Stadium Trinity Mother Frances Rose Stadium in return for $1.92 million over 12 years.

As funding for state schools continues to get tighter and more high school varsity athletic programs are forced to move to "pay to play" funding, it seems likely that the sale of naming rights at high school stadiums will continue to grow.

Why Companies Buy Naming Rights

There are three fundamental reasons corporations are willing to pay for naming rights. Initially, the principal reason companies found naming rights so attractive was the exposure opportunities provided by taking the name of a conspicuous public attraction. From an exposure perspective, naming rights agreements offer companies significant advantages over traditional advertising alternatives:

> You can't bypass a name on a stadium the way you zap through a commercial—it's tougher to ignore. While each sponsorship needs to be measured for its effec-

tiveness, a lot of marketers are looking for a less cluttered, high impact way to get a brand in front of the public eye. Associating with marquee properties is one great way to accomplish this. (p. 14)[46]

The scarcity of supply enhances the chances of escaping clutter. Because there are only a limited number of such opportunities, competitors find it more difficult to duplicate a naming rights communication platform.

The unique "24–7" exposure afforded by naming rights agreements is an appealing benefit, particularly for companies with little or no brand recognition. Swedish telecommunications giant Ericsson, Inc. was virtually unknown in the United States before it paid $20 million in 1995 for the naming rights to the NFL Carolina Panthers' new stadium in Charlotte, North Carolina. Market research conducted in 1998 found that in less than three years, the Ericsson brand grew from almost no public presence to being recognized by 50% of the adults in the Carolinas and by 44% nationally. The owner of the Carolina Panthers observed that "the naming rights deal all but eliminated the 'Who is Ericsson?' question" (p. 14).[46] In 2004, Ericsson decided not to renew the original 10-year agreement after achieving the brand awareness benefits they sought.

In addition to rapidly enhancing the recognition of a new product or company in a cluttered marketplace, established consumer product companies have been attracted to naming rights deals because of the long-term, national exposure benefits they offer. Why was Farmers Insurance willing to commit over $20 million a year for 30 years to name the proposed NFL stadium in Los Angeles? According to Farmers's chief marketing officer, the answer was simple: "You go to where the people are." During the year they signed the agreement with the Anschultz Entertainment Group, 18 of the 20 most-watched television shows in the US were NFL broadcasts.[47]

While enhancing a company's awareness is an important benefit of naming rights agreements, the most important reason companies are willing to pay so much for the association with sport venues is the company's desire to use the facility as a platform for increasing sales. In fact, the amount of the rights fee is often based largely on the company's estimate of the amount of incremental sales that will be realized from the partnership. The incremental sales benefits are most apparent in naming rights transactions that convey exclusive selling rights to the entitled company. For example, the Pepsi Center in Denver, Colorado, home to the NBA Nuggets and NHL Avalanche, provides Pepsi USA with exclusive pouring rights in the building, allowing the company to recapture a significant portion of the $3.4 million they pay in rights fees annually. Philips Electronics paid $185 million for the naming rights to Atlanta's 20,000-seat arena, which is home to the NBA Hawks and NHL Thrashers. The 20-year agreement provides Philips with a 10,000 square foot consumer products display area, The Philips Experience, where the company can showcase its latest consumer entertainment products. In addition, the agreement required the $213 million venue to be fitted exclusively with Philips equipment and products from the state-of-the-art turnstiles to the hundreds of big screen monitors located throughout the arena.[15] Banks may place their ATMs in the building and airlines their ticket booths. Companies also use their affiliation with a popular sports team to create traffic-driving promotions, such as player appearances at retail outlets, to derive tangible benefits from their naming rights agreements.

The final benefit, closely related to increasing sales, is the entertainment opportunities provided to companies through naming rights partnerships. An almost universal element of every naming rights contract is that the corporate partner receives access to at least one luxury suite in the sports venue. This allows the company to create indirect selling opportunities with key customers by hosting them in premium surroundings at games or concerts. The goodwill engendered through these kinds of hospitality efforts is intended to strengthen business relationships that translate into increased or renewed sales opportunities. Some teams have extended hospitality benefits to their corporate partners beyond the venue itself. These extended benefits may include: providing the company with the right to designate a number of guests to travel on the team charter to away games during the regular season, making retired players or "legends" available for company events, and making "star" players available for personal appearances at company events on non-game days.

The summary of benefits received by Scotiabank in its agreement with the NHL Ottawa Senators illustrates the range of tangible rights commonly extended as part of the naming sponsor's deal (see Figure 11.7). In 2007, Scotiabank, Canada's third-largest bank, signed a 15-year, $26 million (Canadian) contract for exclusive entitlement rights

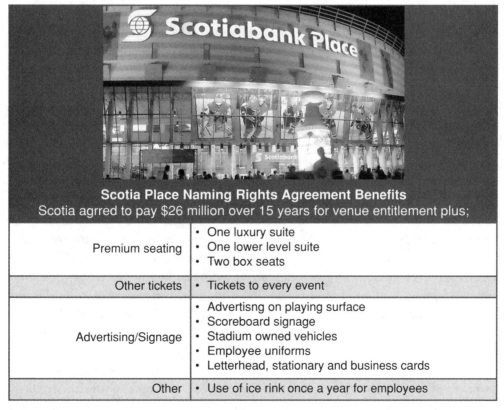

Scotia Place Naming Rights Agreement Benefits
Scotia agrred to pay $26 million over 15 years for venue entitlement plus;

Premium seating	• One luxury suite • One lower level suite • Two box seats
Other tickets	• Tickets to every event
Advertising/Signage	• Advertisng on playing surface • Scoreboard signage • Stadium owned vehicles • Employee uniforms • Letterhead, stationary and business cards
Other	• Use of ice rink once a year for employees

Figure 11.7. Benefits received by Scotiabank from Naming Rights Agreement.

to the arena. In addition to the arena's being named Scotiabank Place, the bank also received premium seating inventory (two suites and two box seats), exclusive access to the facility for an annual trade show, and a day on the ice for company employees.

Ultimately, all of these corporate rationales for investing in naming rights are expected to increase companies' profitability. If investors believed naming rights contributed to this end, then there should be a boost in a company's stock price when such agreements are announced. A study of the naming rights holders at 49 stadiums and arenas reported that on average, the companies' stock prices increased 1.65% at the time the agreements were first announced. This was a net-of-market increase; it was strongly statistically significant, and was considerably in excess of the returns associated with other major marketing programs such as the signing of the Olympic sponsorships or celebrity endorsers.[48]

The Potential for Controversy

What's in a name? that which we call a rose

By any other word would smell as sweet

With these words, Juliet Capulet tells Romeo Montague that a name is an artificial and meaningless convention, and that she loves the person who is called "Montague," not the Montague name. In some contexts, however, Shakespeare got it wrong because names do matter. They have power and meaning. A name is not merely a label; it is shorthand for describing who or what someone or something is. If the entity bearing the name is important to people, then it follows that the name matters.

Changing a name also changes the relationship with the object being renamed. When a facility has a long-established, beloved heritage name, it is likely to be associated with fond memories stretching back across generations. If it is changed, many will feel a loss of ownership, continuity, and history. As a result, those involved in making such a change are like to be subject to opprobrium and ridicule, and regarded with contempt by many. When the storied New York Yankees moved their new stadium in 2009, their management recognized the power of the stadium's cultural meaning. Consequently, they avoided upsetting fans by retaining the "Yankee Stadium" moniker.

Others have not been so wise. Consider the case of Newcastle United, which has one of the most renowned, largest and most passionate fan bases in the English Premier League. When Newcastle was purchased by a new owner, he changed the team's stadium 119-year old name from St. James' Park to sportsdirect.com@ St. James' Park so it incorporated the name of his sports equipment company. This was greeted with massive outrage from all sections of the city. While no additional revenue accrued to the club for this naming right, the owner's intent was to showcase the potential of the naming rights to other companies that might purchase them. His expectation was that the naming rights would sell for around $15 million annually. There was no interest. Indeed, the name became fodder for comedians' jokes and was subjected to national ridicule. The owner persevered. He attributed the lack of interest to companies wanting the opportunity to fully rebrand the stadium, rather than only to attach their name to St. James'

Park. Accordingly, he changed the name to SportsDirect Arena as a temporary measure to "showcase the sponsorship opportunity to interested parties." The fans were even more intensely affronted, and were scathing in their criticism. The end result was fan alienation and contempt for the owner; extended national and local negative publicity for his company; and creation of a toxic environment that destroyed any interest among potential naming rights purchasers.

In addition to being sensitive to fan sentiments, companies considering naming rights also have to scan the broader political environment. The challenge was illustrated by Citigroup's conundrum relating to its $400 million investment of $20 million a year for 20 years for the naming rights to the Citi Field, which was intended to make the company's name synonymous with New York baseball.

The agreement was signed in 2006, but when the Great Recession arrived in late 2007, Citigroup received a $306 billion bailout in 2008 from the U.S. Treasury to insure loans and asset-backed securities, and laid off 52,000 employees. Many in the media and the U.S. Congress urged the company to "Scrap the deal with the stadium and make sure you take care of those mortgages."[24] It was pointed out: "Even in the flush times during which it was signed, the deal seemed questionable. With high name recognition and a place among the world's banking leaders, Citigroup hardly needed the Citi name plastered on a ballpark to enhance itself" (p. 3).[25]

The firm's rationale for retaining the naming rights agreement was that it "provides an incredible platform to promote our world-class brand, enhance our relationship with current clients, attract new clients and expand our considerable community efforts" (p. 2).[25] It was pointed out that "for a company as big as Citigroup, $20 million a year is pocket change. Still the spending is symbolic. It's on a baseball stadium in a gloomy economy, an investment that seems to thumb its nose at laid off workers (p. 3).[25] In spite of the criticism, the naming rights remains in place.

Key Elements of Naming Rights Agreements

The standard naming rights agreement is typically a 15- to 25-page contract that stipulates the terms and conditions in explicit terms. Typically, the primary elements of a naming rights agreement address:

1. *Term or length of contract*
2. *Consideration* (amount and schedule of payments)
3. *Signage rights and limitations* (number, size, placement and type of signs, and design approval process)
4. *Installation costs* (responsibility for expenses related to preparation, installation and maintenance of signage)
5. *Marketing rights* (number and location of luxury suites, boxes, club seats, and on-site exhibit space, ATMs, etc.)
6. *Termination upon default* (provision to terminate contract if either party fails to perform obligations of the agreement with no more than 90 days notice)

7. *Reimbursement* (naming sponsor compensation in event of incomplete season due to strike, lockout, weather)
8. *Renewal option* (current sponsor given First Right of Refusal to extend agreement, generally 30 days to six months prior to expiration of contract)

The specific terms and conditions related to each of the major provisions vary, reflecting the negotiation process between the naming rights partners. Two central aspects of the agreement, which are discussed in the following subsections, are the manner in which the corporate sponsor will pay consideration for receiving the benefits of the title sponsorship and the length of the agreement.

Method of Payment

Historically, naming rights fees have been paid either as an upfront cash payment, or as annual payments over the length of the agreement. While annual installment payments have been the most commonly used approach, a number of agreements have been consummated that have required a single, upfront payment. When Marine Midland Bank purchased naming rights for 20 years to Buffalo's downtown arena in 1995, the financial institution made a single payment to the NHL-Sabers of $6.73 million. When interest and inflation were taken into account, that figure was estimated to be equivalent to approximately $15 million over 20 years.[49]

The one-time, upfront payment provides the team or venue operator with an immediate infusion of cash. That approach is likely to be especially advantageous to a team having to make an upfront contribution to the construction of a new venue. By applying the rights fee to the team's share of financing the new facility, the team will reduce the amount of debt obligation it would otherwise incur. At the same time, the corporation paying the rights fee will pay considerably less in "actual" dollars. Further, unlike naming rights agreements based on annual payments, the company knows the exact cost of its investment. In contrast, estimating the present value of a stream of annual payments for as long as 30 years is difficult because the rates used to equate present values, such as the cost of capital and interest rates, are unpredictable.

Despite the benefits of greater certainty to the corporation buying the rights, and immediate cash to the team, few naming rights transactions are paid in this way. It was noted in Chapter 9 that almost all new facilities are debt financed. Typically, bonds are sold by either a government authority or privately, by the team, with the contractual obligation to repay the borrowed amount, with interest, over a specified period of time. A prominent potential source of debt repayment revenues is the money realized from the sale of naming rights. Lenders require projects they finance to produce significant and stable amounts of contractually obligated income (or COI). Naming rights transactions have been an excellent source of COI because of their financial magnitude and the long-term nature of the agreements. Thus, lenders have determined that naming rights contracts, along with luxury suite leases, club seat licenses, and concessionaire contracts, are acceptable security for venue financing.

Table 11.11. Indianapolis Colts—Lucas Oil Products Naming Rights Payment Schedule

Year 1	$5,000,000	Year 11	$6,094,971
Year 2	$5,100,000	Year 12	$6,216,871
Year 3	$5,202,000	Year 13	$6,341,208
Year 4	$5,305,040	Year 14	$6,498,032
Year 5	$5,412,160	Year 15	$6,597,393
Year 6	$5,520,404	Year 16	$6,597,393
Year 7	$5,630,812	Year 17	$6,597,393
Year 8	$5,743,428	Year 18	$6,597,393
Year 9	$5,858,296	Year 19	$6,597,393
Year 10	$5,975,462	Year 20	$6,597,393

Under such an arrangement, the team pledges the annual payment it receives from its naming rights partner (e.g., Bank of America, PepsiCo, Lucas Oil Products) to the lender or bondholder. Thus, the agreement between the team and the naming rights holder must include a specific payment schedule spread over the length of the naming rights sponsorship. Typically, naming rights agreements are structured with an initial rights fee payment, followed by annual cash payments that increase by a pre-determined percentage every year, usually between 2 and 5%.[21] The annual percentage increase, commonly referred to as an "escalator clause," is used as a hedge against rising operating costs and inflation.

In addition, the gradual annual increases reduce the potential "sticker shock" effect when the agreement is up for renewal. "Slight increases each year in the value of the deal are easier for sponsors to digest," said one team executive. "The idea is to avoid a major jump in price when it comes time for renewal" (p. 47).[21]

The naming rights agreement between the NFL Indianapolis Colts and Lucas Oil Products provides an example of a typical annual payment schedule. The 20-year agreement calls for an initial payment of $5,000,000 in the first year and the escalator clause increases the annual payment at a rate of 2% annually for the first 14 years of the contract. The remaining six years are paid at a fixed rate of $6,597,393 per annum. The actual payment schedule is detailed in Table 11.11.

In addition, the agreement required Lucas Oil to pay the Colts $2,000,000 on the day the naming rights contract was signed. This down payment, commonly referred to as a *preliminary rights fee*, is a common feature of contemporary rights deals. When the full rights fees are tallied over the full length of the agreement, Lucas Oil will invest a total of $121,454,012 as the Indianapolis Colts naming rights partner.

Teams have used naming rights revenues to meet their contribution to the upfront costs of a new facility. Thus, when the Seattle Mariners were lobbying the state legislature to fund a new stadium with public money, it was repeatedly pointed out that the team was investing $45 million of its "own" money into the stadium. However, in the stadium lease agreement, the team was given the naming rights to the stadium, that is, the rights to sell the name of the stadium to the highest bidder. These naming rights were the source of the team's contribution.[50]

In some cases, the value received by the team from the corporate naming partner comes in the form of in-kind benefits rather than cash. A good example was the arrangement Continental Airlines established with the New Jersey Sports & Exposition Authority when it purchased the naming rights to the Brendan Byrne Arena in 1996. In lieu of cash, the airline agreed to provide $700,000 annually in complimentary air service as a part of its agreement to name the arena the Continental Airlines Arena (currently named the Izod Arena). The arrangement enabled the two anchor tenants of the multi-purpose arena, the NHL Devils and NBA Nets, to substantially reduce their annual travel expenses.

Sometimes, naming rights are acquired as part of a larger business package. For example, Coors made an equity investment of $30 million for an ownership stake in the Colorado Rockies, but it is estimated that $7 to $8 million of this investment was attributable to naming rights.[51]

Length of Agreement

Most naming rights agreements established prior to the 2008 Great Recession are long-term in nature, with a majority extending 20 to 30 years. The prevailing attitude of both parties from the 1990s throughout most of the first decade of the 2000s was that longer contracts benefited both the corporate sponsor and the team. Teams favored long-term agreements because they ensured a stable income stream over an extended period of time. At the same time, the long-term relationship enabled the naming rights partner to develop an enduring identity with the sports facility and provided the opportunity to develop marketing programs to realize an acceptable return on their investment. Further, with a long-term contract the corporation eliminates the risk of being outbid and replaced in a short period of time by a competitor, and receives price stability and certainty over a long time period.

As discussed earlier in the chapter, recently some corporate and team executives have questioned the desirability of committing to 20- or 30-year naming rights deals. Companies are concerned about committing major dollars so far into the future, while sports teams are also more cautious. Their caution is the result of several agreements that failed. The economic downturn and accounting scandals in 2001–02 which were especially severe in the high-tech, communication, and airline sectors, led seven companies with major facility naming rights deals to file for bankruptcy: Enron Corp (Houston Astros); ANC Rental Group, parent company of National Rental Car (Florida Panthers); Adelphia (Tennessee Titans); Fruit of the Loom, Ltd., parent company of Pro Player (Miami Dolphins); Trans World Airlines (St. Louis Rams); WorldCom, parent company of MCI (Washington Capitals and Washington Wizards); and PSINet Inc. (Baltimore Ravens). It seems likely that future agreements will be much shorter in length. Rather than a 31-year agreement with no renewal option (e.g., Reliant Stadium in Houston), increasingly contracts will be structured with shorter terms, say 5 to 10 years, with subsequent options to the agreement for 3 to 5 year increments. This kind of arrangement provides both parties with greater flexibility in managing their relationship over time.

The Impact of Naming Rights' Partner Failings

In some cases, the bankruptcy of corporate partners that prematurely terminate a naming rights contract may be a blessing if the franchise entered into a long-term agreement in the early 1990s when naming rights prices were relatively low. For example, in 1995, TWA agreed to pay the St. Louis Rams $15 million over 20 years to put its name on the new domed stadium. When TWA declared bankruptcy, the Rams were able to negotiate a new agreement with Edward Jones company, a financial services firm headquartered in St. Louis. In return for naming the facility the Edward Jones Dome, the firm paid the Rams $31.8 million over 12 years ($2.85 million per year), with an option to extend the agreement another 11 years for an additional $35.2 million. Thus, the bankruptcy enabled the Rams to almost double their revenues from naming rights.

In other situations, bankruptcy can create a major public relations and image problem. Enron Corporation was America's seventh largest company when it signed a 30-year, $100 million agreement with the Houston Astros to name their new ballpark Enron Field. The name was on all exterior and interior signage, uniforms worn by game-day staff, cups, plates, napkins, and tickets. When Enron collapsed at the end of 2001 as a result of unethical accounting practices, tens of thousands of people experienced financial hardship through the loss of their jobs, pension funds, or stock. To the Houston and broader American public, Enron quickly became a pariah. The name became synonymous with unethical behavior, shame and failure. The continued use of the name Enron Field stigmatized the Astros. Their spokesperson noted, "The Enron logo displayed on the stadium wrongly suggests to the public that the Astros are associated with the alleged bad business practices of Enron . . . The current perception of Enron is incompatible with the honesty and integrity embodied in baseball as America's pastime and espoused by the Houston Astros" (p. A5).[52] The trustees acting for Enron's creditors refused to surrender the naming rights because they regarded them as an asset that had value. Ultimately, the Astros paid $2.1 million to Enron to remove the company's name from the stadium. The team then regained this revenue stream by reselling the naming rights to Houston-based Minute Maid, the fruit-juice subsidiary of the Coca-Cola Company, for $100 million over 28 years, so the ballpark became Minute Maid Park.

Similar challenges may also confront colleges that accept naming rights. For example, John E. DuPont gave Villanova University $5 million to build a recreation center which was named the DuPont Pavilion. However, in a high-profile court case some years later, DuPont was convicted of murder.[37] Fortunately for Villanova, there was no formal written agreement requiring the school to retain the name and it was able to simply call the center "The Pavilion."

The potential of corporate partners' names becoming an embarrassment at some time in the future suggests that contracts should contain a clause that provides a disassociation option if a donor or corporate partner embarrasses a college or franchise, respectively. Companies commonly include such clauses in contracts with celebrity endorsers, and this appears to be an analogous situation.[39]

The corporate sponsor can also be a loser in naming rights deals. For example, in the 16 months after Lowe's home improvements chain invested $35 million for the naming rights to Charlotte Motor Speedway, the company became associated with a series of accidents and tragedies that took place at the track. First, during an event at the speedway, debris from a wreck flew into the crowd and killed three fans. Four months later, two Lowe's stores were pipe-bombed in apparent retaliation for the accident. Next, a pedestrian bridge at the speedway collapsed injuring over 100 people, some seriously. Finally, an explosion staged as part of a Memorial Day observance before a major race sent plywood into the crowd and injured four people. Lowe's misfortune has caused companies to add clauses to naming rights contracts enabling them to terminate if anything occurs that has a negative impact on the company's image or reputation. One commentator noted, "When you pay to name a facility and then your name and image are part of such negative situations, it's almost like turning lemonade back into lemons" (p. 80).[53]

SUMMARY

Many teams and venue operators have been able to exploit the abundant revenue-generating potential of modern sports facilities. The development of three sources of income—premium seating, seat licenses and the sale of naming rights—have had a dramatic impact on the financial growth and viability of professional sport franchises. Premium seating options, seat licenses and long-term naming rights agreements will all continue to be prominent elements of the professional sports landscape in the foreseeable future.

Premium seating has become an increasingly prominent feature of modern sports venues. Ever since the Palace at Auburn Hills demonstrated the abundant yield from the provision of premium seating options, teams have clamored to build new facilities loaded with luxury suites, club seats and, most recently, loge boxes, terrace seating, and luxurious night clubs. The primary reason premium seating has become so popular with team and venue operators is that the sale of this inventory generates abundant revenues. The per cap yield for fans purchasing a club or loge seat is three to four times that of what a team realizes from the sale of non-premium or regular seating options. The Miami Marlins baseball team generated close to $13 million through the sale of less than 4% of its total seating capacity. The 675 club seats located close to the field of play produced a per capita yield of nearly $19,000 per seat. The entire inventory was sold out prior to the start of the season.

Suites have proven to be highly attractive to corporations interested in finding impactful opportunities to entertain important clients. However, in recent years, many teams have struggled to sell all of their luxury suites. The poor economy has depressed demand for suite sales, which depend primarily on corporate clients. Many companies have slashed their entertainment budgets and, as a result, have not been able to afford the expense of leasing suites that might cost upward of $1 million per season. Declining demand for suites in particular has resulted in many venues reducing their suite inventory over the past several years. One prominent trend has been to convert luxury suites originally designed for single tenants into super or party suites. Rather than offering the space to a single client for the entire season, the enlarged suites, typically capable of accommodating from 20 to 100 guests, are rented to companies and other organizations on a game-by-game basis. Another prevalent trend is selling suites on a time-share basis. Multiple companies share a suite over the course of a season. Typically each of the tenants purchases a $\frac{1}{2}$ to $\frac{1}{4}$ share, each paying for only the number or proportion of games in which they occupy the suite. Suite sharing has proven to be a popular option for many companies unwilling or unable to lease a suite for the entire season. "Less is more" has become a common theme in premium seating. Since only a finite number of companies or individual households can afford or are willing to pay for premium seating options, teams have begun to reduce the number of suites and club seats while substantially raising the price on the remaining premium inventory. The scarcity can stimulate demand for the limited opportunities to sit in the "best seats in the house" and enjoy VIP amenities and services. Given the magnitude of revenue return, the creation and sale of premium seating options will continue to be a priority for professional teams into the foreseeable future.

Personal seat license (PSL) programs provide teams with the ability to raise an abundant amount of development capital for new facility construction. PSLs require purchasers to make a one-time payment, which provides the seat license holder with the right to purchase a ticket to that seat usually for the lifetime of that facility (thus, PSLs have also commonly been called *permanent* seat licenses). Although PSL programs have been largely successful, they have also been controversial. They require fans to purchase the license as a precondition of being able to buy season tickets to the most desirable seats in a stadium. The substantial upfront fee (the new 49er stadium requires a "one-time" license fee from $2,000 to $12,000 per seat) has made it increasingly difficult for many fans to afford the cost of attending regular season games. The NFL New York Jets were forced to slash PSL prices when more than 15,000 seat licenses remained unsold shortly before their first game in the then-new MetLife Stadium. Jet fans had balked at paying what they believed to be a much too expensive seat license requirement.

Some teams, including the 49ers, have attempted to alter negative perceptions by assuring fans that all income derived from the sale of seat licenses will be applied to stadium construction. The Pittsburgh Steelers coined the phrase "stadium builder licenses" to convey the clear message that by purchasing an SBL, fans were making a meaningful contribution to building a new home for the Steelers. This tactic has been successfully replicated by other franchises, most notably by the Dallas Cowboys, who raised $700 million from seat license sales to offset a significant portion of the $1.2 billion construction cost of their new stadium. Another attractive feature of seat license programs is that most teams allow the rights holder to sell or transfer the PSL to any interested party. As a result, in many NFL markets, PSLs have proven to be good investments, with the value of fully transferable licenses increasing as much as three times their original cost.

At this time, three-fourths of major league sports facilities in North America have been corporately named, with the aggregate investment exceeding $6 billion. The sports venue naming rights market has rebounded recently following a slow post-recession period. Several major agreements were announced after 2010, led by the record-breaking Farmers Insurance company's $700 million, 30-year agreement with AEG to name a proposed football stadium in downtown Los Angeles. The deal announced in 2011 is conditional upon the stadium being built and occupied by an NFL franchise.

While the four major US sport leagues have not yet authorized naming rights on team jerseys, these are sold by MLS teams and are widely used in other countries. In the EPL, for example, Manchester United, Manchester City, Liverpool and Chelsea have multi-year jersey naming rights for annual amounts of $65 million, $56 million, $40 million and $40 million, respectively.

Although the brand equity and sales benefits provided by naming partnerships continue to make them attractive investment opportunities, teams hoping to sell venue rights in the current market face challenges. One major challenge is the diminishing prospect pool. With over 75% of major venues already corporately named, a significant share of those companies with both the interest and financial capacity have already committed to partnerships. Consequently, in recent years teams have increasingly shifted their focus from national brands to finding naming partners with a more local association. This has meant that many have had to settle for less-generous terms, with respect to both the total financial payment and the length of the agreement. Most deals established in the recent years have been for a far shorter duration than those prior to the Great Recession. Given the tumult of the Great Recession and the still uncertain financial climate, companies have been increasingly reluctant to enter into extended naming rights contracts. Instead of 20- or 30-year agreements, most naming rights deals are now no longer than 10 years in length.

Colleges have become active participants in selling the naming rights to their stadiums and arenas. While the financial terms are modest compared to those negotiated by major league franchises, the incremental revenues (often in excess of $15 million) make selling naming rights increasingly attractive to cash-strapped collegiate programs. Like other innovative revenue strategies, facility naming rights is percolating down to high schools.

Corporations seek three major benefits from becoming naming rights partners: (a) 24/7 exposure, (b) the ability to use the venue relationship as a marketing platform to increase sales, and (c) the entertainment and hospitality opportunities provided by the partnership. The visibility provided to corporations through their alignment with prominent sport venues is especially attractive to companies with little or no brand recognition, such as Ericsson Inc., which was a virtually unknown brand until it purchased the naming rights to the NFL Carolina Panthers' new stadium in the early1990s. Increasingly, however, corporations have been attracted to naming rights agreements because of the substantial business-building opportunities they provide. Many agreements now include provisions that guarantee corporate naming rights partners opportunities to sell their products inside "their" venues.

Naming rights can be controversial, especially if they are being imposed on a facility that has a long-established, beloved heritage name. The loss of such a name translates to a loss of ownership, continuity and history to many fans and is likely to alienate them. Naming rights sales are much less controversial when they are attracted to new facilities.

References

1. Lambeth, C. (2005). Trends in stadium design: A whole new game. *Implications, 4*(6). Retrieved from http://www.informdesign.umn.edu

2. Vrooman, J. (2010, April 4). *Dallas Cowboys Stadium analysis.* Retrieved from http://www.vanderbilt.edu/econ/facility/vrooman/cowboys-estimate.pdf

3. Why the big deal about premium seating? (2007, Winter). *SEAT Magazine*, p. 13.

4. Barclays Center. Retrieved from http://www.view.barclayscenter.com/premiumseating/suites/

5. Connolly, B. (2011, August 9). Unsold premium seating is becoming a structural problem. *Facilities.* Retrieved from http://www.thebusinessofsports.com/2011/08/09/unsold-premium-seating-is-becoming-a-structural-problem/

6. Schoettle, A. (2009, October 17). Sales of luxury suites slow at most Indianapolis sports venues. *Indianapolis Business Journal.* Retrieved from http://www.ibj.com/pro-teams-endure-notso suite-time/PARAMS/article/10587

7. Lombardo, J. (2012, July 12). Piston renovations at Palace of Auburn Hills include cutting 16 suites, upgrading 40. *SportsBusiness Journal.* Retrieved from http://www.sportsbusinessdaily.com/Daily/Issues/2012/07/11/Facilities/aspx

8. LeTellier, A., & Shatkin, E. (2009, December 11). Hyde Lounge at Staples Center. *Los Angeles Times.* Retrieved from http://www.latimes.com/2009/dec/11/entertainment/la-et-night/

9. Titlebaum, P., & Lawrence, H. (2011, March). The reinvention of the luxury suite in North America. *Journal of Sponsorship, 4*(2), 124–136.

10. Noll, R., & Zimbalist, A. (1997). Build the stadium—create the jobs! In R. Noll & A. Zimbalist (Eds.), *Sports, jobs, and taxes: The economic impact of sports teams and stadiums.* Washington, DC: Brookings Institution Press.

11. Personal communication with Max Muhleman, January 11, 2000.

12. Eagles to charge stadium builder license fees. (2001, July 10). *Philadelphia Business Journal.* Retrieved from http://www.bizjournals.com/philadelphia/stories/2001/07/09/daily18.html

13. Kaplan, D. (2012, February 27–March 4). Niners estimate seat licenses will bring in $500M. *SportsBusiness Journal*, pp. 1, 32.

14. NFL teams sold an average of 48,200 personal seat licenses last season. (2011, September 8). *SportsBusiness Daily.* Retrieved from http://www.sportsbusinessdaily.com/Daily/Issues/2011/09/08/NFL-Season-Preview/PSLs.aspx

15. Howard, D., & Crompton, J. (2004). *Financing sport* (2nd ed.). Morgantown, WV: Fitness Information Technology.

16. Feurstein, A. (1996, October 13). Giants take the early lead in seat sales. *San Francisco Business Times*, p. 12.

17. McCarthy, L. M., & Irwin, R. (1998). Permanent seat licenses (PSLs) as an emerging source of revenue production. *Sport Marketing Quarterly, 7*(3), 41–46.

18. Searle, G. (2002). Uncertain legacy: Sydney's Olympic Stadiums. *European Planning Studies, 10*(7), 845–860.

19. Steinbach, P. (2003, September). Suspended licenses. *Athletic Business*, p. 34.

20. Popke, M. (2005, December). Is this seat taken? *Athletic Business*, p. 36.

21. Naming rights deals. (1997). *Team Marketing Report.* Chicago, IL: Team Marketing Report.

22. Mahony, D., & Howard, D. (2001). Sports business in the next decade. *Journal of Sport Management, 15*(4), 275–296.

23. Weiner, J. (1999). *Stadium games: Fifty years of big league greed and bush league boondoggles.* Minneapolis, MN: University of Minnesota Press.

24. Nasaw, D. (2008, November 25). Baseball stadium named for Citigroup faces scrutiny. *The Guardian.* Retrieved from http://www.guardian.co.uk/world/2008/nov/25/citigroup-new-york-mets-stadium

25. Sandomir, R. (2008, July 20). Citigroup puts its money where its name will be. *New York Times*, p. 3.

26. Farmer, S. (2011, January 31). AEG, Farmers Insurance in naming rights deal for proposed NFL stadium. *Latimes.com.* Retrieved from http://www.latimes.com/sports/la-sp-0s01-la-nfl-20110201,0,867951,print.story

27. Levy, K. (2011, October 19). Mercedes-Benz Superdome—worth it? Or worthless? *Forbes.com.* Retrieved from http://www.forbes.com

/sites/keithlevy/2011/10/19/mercedes-benz-su
perdome-worth-it-or-worthless/

28. Why Cowboys can't sell naming rights. *Fan Nation.* Retrieved from http://www.fannation.com/truth_and_rumors/view/102674-why-cowboys-cant-sell-naming-rights

29. Kass, M. (2012, May 21). BMO Harris secures Bradley Center naming rights. *The Business Journal.* Retrieved from http://www.bizjournals.com/milwaukee/news/2012/05/21/Bmo-harris-secures-bradley-center-naming-rights.hmtl?page=all

30. Kils, M. (2012, August 10). Sports authority makes a play to have its name on Broncos Stadium. *Denverpost.com.* Retrieved from http://www.denverpost.com/broncos/cl_18658353

31. Mitchell, T. (2010, July 28). How the Ever-Bank–Jaguars deal was reached. *The Florida Times Union.* Retrieved from http://www.jacksonville.com/sports/football/jaguars/2010=0-07-28/story/

32. Man Utd deal takes shirt sponsorships to new heights. (2012, August 3). *IBN Live.* Retrieved from http://ibnlive.in.com/news/man-utd-deal-takes-shirt-sponsorships-to-new-heights/278195-5-21.html

33. Day, J. (2005, January 20). Chelsea pays £24 million to drop Umbro. *The Guardian.* Retrieved from http://www.guardian.co.uk

34. Gorse, S., Chadwick, S., & Barton, N. (2010) Entrepreneurship through sports marketing: A case analysis of Red Bull in sport. *Journal of Sponsorship, 3*(4), 348–357.

35. Schoenfeld, B. (2001, May 28–June 3). No city name, just a happy sponsor. *SportsBusiness Journal,* pp. 1, 38.

36. Rae, R. (2003, August 14). Villagers go in unlikely search of big city solutions. *The Guardian.* Retrieved from http://www.guardian.co.uk/football/2003/aug/14/sport.comment

37. Cohen, A. (1999, July). The naming game. *Athletic Business,* pp. 37–43.

38. Teams search and fund new avenues of revenue from the naming rights of stadiums and arenas sections. (2001, January). *Team Marketing Report, 13*(4), pp. 1–2.

39. Blumenstyk, G. (1995). Georgia Tech and Mc-Donald's sign $5.5 million deal. *Chronicle of Higher Education, XLI*(21), p. A44.

40. Tucker, J. (2000, December 26). Schools for sale? *Oakland Tribune,* p. 1, 13.

41. Workman, B. (1998). Stanford seeks way to reverse trend of commercial sponsors. *San Francisco Chronicle,* p. 1C.

42. Post no billboards. (2000, September/October). *Stanford Magazine,* p. 3.

43. Miller, A. (1995, November 17). It pays to play name game. *Columbus Dispatch,* p. C12.

44. Lee, J. (2001, August 8–13). Colleges feature fewer chances, more hassle. *SportsBusiness Journal,* p. 14.

45. Tanner, J. (2001, Fall). Corporations go back to school: Colleges attract naming rights deals. *Marquette National Sports Law Institute.* Retrieved from https://law.marquette.edu/national-sports-law-institute/corporations-go-back-school-colleges-attract-naming-rights-deals

46. Zoghby, J. (1999, November 1–7). Ericsson makes name with N.C. stadium. *SportsBusiness Journal,* p. 14.

47. Bertoni, S. (2011, February 4). Why did Farmers commit $700 Million to an NFL team that doesn't exist? *Forbes.com.* http://www.bogs.forbes/stevebertoni/2011/02/04/why-did-farmers-commit-700-million-to-an-nfl-team-that-doesn't-Exist?

48. Clark, J. M., Cornwell, T. B., & Pruitt, S. W. (2002, November/December). Corporate stadium sponsorships, signaling theory, agency conflicts, and shareholder wealth. *Journal of Advertising Research,* pp. 16–32.

49. Bernstein, A. (2000, July 3–9). Arenas wrangle over new names. *SportsBusiness Journal,* p. 23.

50. Quirk, J., & Fort, R. (1999). *Hard ball: The abuse of power in pro sports teams.* Princeton, NJ: Princeton University Press.

51. Greenberg, M., & Gray, J. (1996). *The stadium game.* Marquette University Law School: National Sports Law Institute.

52. Easton, P. (2002, February 8). Astros want Enron name off stadium. *The Bryan-College Station Eagle,* A1, A5.

53. Fleming, D. (2000, June 22). Lowe's can't catch a break. *Sports Illustrated,* p. 80.

12

Ticket Sales and Operation

~ Gregg Olson ~

Regional Vice President, Stadiums and Arenas SMG Managed Facilities

INTRODUCTION

This chapter examines a number of issues facing sport managers with respect to the selling and pricing of tickets for sporting events. First, the chapter provides a perspective on attendance trends for collegiate and professional sport and their implications for increasing revenues from charged admissions. Attention is given to the major impacts that emerging technology is having on the sale and distribution of tickets, including Web-based ticketing applications. The chapter concludes with an in-depth discussion of the organization and administration of ticket sales. Accounting procedures as well as current ticketing systems are described.

It is estimated that U.S. consumers spend almost $15.9 billion on admissions to spectator sporting events.[1] As shown in Chapter 3, the importance of ticket sale revenue to professional sports varies considerably from one league to another. The media-rich NFL depends far less on live gate than the other leagues. The typical NFL team receives less than 20% of its total operating revenues from ticket sales. In contrast, gate receipts represent the most significant share of overall revenues for most all other MLB, NHL and NBA teams.[2] Ticket sales constitute between 23% and 42% of total income for MLB and NBA teams. The prominence of admissions is particularly evident for hockey, where over half the franchises in the NHL rely on ticket sales for at least 50% of their annual earnings.

Gate receipts are the lifeblood of minor league baseball. A former general manager with the Class A Everett Giants notes, "The core of a (minor league) team's existence is the admission ticket" (p. 27).[3] Approximately half the total revenues generated by minor league teams comes from ticket sales, and it has been pointed out that

> high attendance is desirable not only for the ticket revenue, but also for the revenue from the sale of concessions and novelties. The size of the concession revenues greatly influences whether a team is profitable. In many cases, concessions account for more than 25% of a team's revenues. (p. 25)[3]

Table 12.1. Ticket Sales as Percentage of Total Revenues for Big Ten Conference Athletic Programs, 2010

School	Ticket Sales	% of Total Revenues
Pennsylvania State Univ.	$41,836,815	39%
Univ. of Michigan	$41,715,138	39%
Ohio State Univ.	$39,515,387	32%
Univ. of Wisconsin	$25,732,357	27%
Michigan State Univ.	$23,504,865	28%
Univ. of Iowa	$21,815,895	25%
University of Minnesota	$21,514,964	27%
Univ. of Illinois	$17,861,359	24%
Purdue Univ.	$16,587,166	27%
Indiana Univ.	$13,346,437	19%

Note: Northwestern University's ticket sales numbers are not included because as a private institution it is not required to comply with open records requests.

Source: Dosh, K. (2011, April 20). Big Ten ticket revenue. *The Business of College Sports*. Retrieved from http://businessofcollegesports.com/2011/04/20/big-ten-ticket-revenue/

At the collegiate level, ticket sales are also a prominent source of revenue. At the Division I-A level, 27% of athletic departments' annual revenues are derived from ticket sales, the single largest revenue category. Table 12.1 provides insights into the relative importance of ticket sales to overall revenues for one of the nation's premier conferences. The table lists the gate receipts of each athletic program in the Big Ten and the percentage of total athletic department revenue accounted for by ticket sales. The revenue figures are driven largely by football attendance. Three of the conference's most prominent programs, Pennsylvania State, Michigan and Ohio State, led the NCAA FBS division in attendance in 2010, all averaging more than 104,000 per game. Conversely, Indiana and Purdue were at the bottom of football attendance, both averaging fewer than 42,000 per home game. It is not surprising, then, to find such a large gap, more than $25 million, between those schools at the top and those at the bottom of the conference in total ticket sale revenues.

As shown earlier in Chapter 2 (Table 2.6), the significance of ticket sales to overall revenue varies considerably among Division I-A level programs. The largest athletic departments, those in the upper or 1st quartile, generate on average more than $24 million annually in gate revenues; those in the bottom or 4th quartile barely generate $1 million on average from ticket sales—accounting for about 5% of total revenues. Similar to FCS (Division I-AA) and Division II and III athletic programs, these smaller FBS level schools rely more on direct subsidies from the institution or student activity fees than on gate receipts as their most important source of revenue.

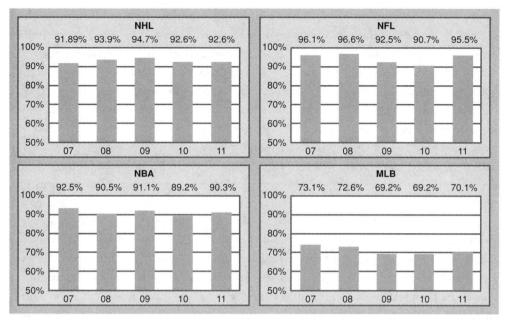

Figure 12.1. Percentage of Seating Capacity by Major Leagues from 2007–2011/12.

Figure 12.1 shows the percentage of available seating capacity actually sold across the four major North American sports leagues from 2007 to 2011–12. Three of the four major leagues sold more than 90% of their available capacity during 2011–12, with the NFL leading the way at 95.3%. It is interesting to note that the NHL sold a higher percentage of its ticket inventory than the NBA over the last three years. MLB remained relatively flat, selling around 70% of its available capacity each year. Major League Baseball's substantially reduced performance is largely a function of the fact that teams play far more home games (81) during the course of a regular season and, therefore, have significantly greater inventory of available seating. A typical MLB team playing in a 35,000-seat ballpark has almost 3 million seats to sell over the course of a season—five times more than an NFL team playing in a 65,000-seat stadium with only eight home games. Close inspection of the attendance patterns of individual MLB teams shows significant variation in the amount of seating inventory actually sold. In 2011, the top third of MLB teams sold over 85% of their seating, while the bottom third sold 60% or less of their available seating inventory.

THE CHALLENGE

The 5-year profiles of all four leagues show a generally flat or stagnant attendance pattern. The struggling economy is still the biggest factor. Attendance across all of the leagues has still not recovered to pre-Great Recession levels. Affordability remains a challenge for an increasing number of families. Five years *after* the massive recession, household income fell to its lowest level in more than two decades. Middle-class families have sustained the largest losses in disposable income, limiting both their ability and willingness to spend on entertainment options.[4] As discussed at length in Chapter 1, flat or declining attendance over this period is a function of a number of factors. There is some evidence that the explosive growth of televised sport is having an adverse impact on live game attendance. With more content than ever before and with the quality of the viewing experience enhanced by high-definition and emerging 3D technologies, watching televised sports provides an affordable option to live game experience. And, as discussed in Chapter 1, the growing cost of attending professional and collegiate sporting events is a severe impediment to a growing number of households. The cost of a ticket to a major league game has more than doubled since 1990 in real dollar terms. In 2012, the average price of a ticket to an NFL game was $77, followed by the NHL at $54.25, NBA at $47.66 and the MLB at $27. However, purchasing a ticket is only part of the cost of attending a major sporting event. When you add parking, food and beverage, etc., the full cost grows substantially. According to *Team Marketing Report*, the complete price of attending a single major league game for a family of four on average exceeded $300 in 2011–12.[5] The relatively high price makes it likely that potential spectators will substitute a host of other less-expensive entertainment options for attending games. Although there is little empirical evidence on the type and extent of switching behavior that occurs among entertainment options (such as renting a movie instead of attending an NBA game), the potential for cost-saving substitution is considerable and deserving of careful examination by sport managers. At the very least, teams need to offer more flexible, affordable opportunities to increasingly price-conscious fans. A number of more price-sensitive approaches recently adopted by sports teams are discussed later in this chapter.

THE EVOLUTION OF TICKETING

The practice of ticket sales and operations has changed dramatically over the past two decades. This section provides a brief historical perspective of the transition from the era of preprinted "hard ticket" sales that persisted into the early 1990s to the modern era of computerized ticketing, electronic turnstiles, and smart cards. The application of new technologies and development of specialized software has transformed ticket sales from a process focused on distribution and audit control to a much more dynamic customer-service oriented process.

Before the advent of computer systems in the mid- to late 1980s, tickets for sporting events were preprinted. These hard tickets, as they were called, had to be ordered from a specialty printer well in advance of each season to assure the availability of tickets for advanced ticket sales. Ticket sales and operations departments worked together to estimate the number of tickets that would likely be sold for each event from every possible sales channel. In this way, the franchise could avoid the cost of printing a ticket for all of the seats in the entire house for a game that was likely to draw significantly fewer fans than a sellout. As an example, a team whose on-field performance had suffered for long periods of time that played in a stadium which held 74,000 seats might often draw only 5,000 or fewer fans. The box office usually ordered 10,000 ducats for such events with the expectation that there would be more than enough inventory to satisfy the sales demand.

Because circumstances could change quickly, every team's box office, however, maintained a full set of preprinted, undated tickets in stock in case the number of tickets ordered for an individual game proved insufficient to cover the sales need for a surprise "hot" game. Such a game could be created by the confluence of a number of factors including an unexpected winning streak, a special promotion, a player on either team approaching a milestone statistical event (e.g., home run record or consecutive games played) or simply great weather on a spring day that drew business people to the park in droves. Care was required in selecting tickets from this preprinted stock to avoid selling seats in the same section twice. In the event this backup set of tickets was used, the team ordered replacements only for the sections it used from the preprinted set.

One of the drawbacks of the preprinted ticket system was that in stadiums where the team didn't sell out, its building breaks were readily apparent between the various price categories. In baseball, for example, the best seats are generally defined as those being closest to home plate and closest to the field. As tickets in the lower box seat area were sold, sections filled down each of the first and third base lines. If not enough tickets were sold to fill each lower box seat section, parts or even whole sections that were deemed to be box seats would remain empty, and a line of filled seats would start at the first lower reserved seat section. This phenomenon would occur between each of the three main price sections: box seats, reserved seats, and general admission. For the fourth price section, the bleachers, this condition was not as readily visible because there was a physical break created by those seats being separated by the construction of the building.

This preprinted system created a host of operational issues for the home team. First, it opened opportunities for people who had paid a lower price for a less desirable section the opportunity to move into seats where they did not belong. Naturally, this created conflict between guest services attendants (ushers in those days) who tried to enforce the seating rules and customers who couldn't understand why sitting in an empty seat was a problem. This made it necessary to have a greater number of staff at each game to monitor and enforce these rules, which drove up staffing costs. Additionally, because virtually every section ended up being used by at least some fans, the entire building needed to be cleaned after each event even though far fewer than half of the seats were actually sold, again creating a much greater cost than was truly necessary.

Managing the inventory of tickets was a challenge under the preprinted ticket system. Each ticket was printed with a unique, sequential number. The ticket printer would provide a certified manifest that reflected the number of tickets printed in each price category in the stadium, including the number sequence printed on those tickets, so that an inventory of all tickets available for each game could be maintained in order to support the sales records of the franchise. The beginning and ending sequences of each batch of tickets were closely monitored.

Preprinted tickets were as good as cash, and treated as such, usually kept locked in heavy walk-in vaults similar to those found in most banks. Meticulous records were kept by hand of the number and type (seasons, groups, etc.) of tickets sold in each price category and the amount of payments that were received to pay for those tickets. Cash receipts were deposited to the franchise bank account via armored car after having been locked in a safe inside the vault until the arrival of armed guards from the transport service. Records of the deposits were maintained both by the box office and the accounting department, and those records were frequently compared to assure that there was no discrepancy in receipts.

Each game-day window ticket seller was closely checked to assure that sales were properly accounted for each day. At check-in, each seller was issued a change till along with a batch of preprinted tickets for each price category. It was the seller's responsibility to count the cash and verify both the starting and ending numbers in the sequence of tickets for each price category. Each sequence was counted as well to assure that every ticket in the sequence was present. Ticket counting was done using a machine referred to as a "tickometer," which saved countless hours of counting tickets by hand. At the conclusion of each night, each seller would return to the box office and complete the process again, counting and recording all the cash in his or her till, and recording the preprinted number on the ending ticket inventory. The number of tickets sold was verified by the number of tickets in each price category remaining as counted by the tickometer. The unused tickets were referred to as "deadwood." Each seller would prepare a four-part deposit slip for the amount of their sales and seal three copies of it in a special bag along with the cash to be deposited. The fourth copy they kept for themselves to prove what they deposited. The bags were placed into a safe inside the vault using a special roll-top device that allowed the bags to be dropped in without opening the safe. The key to the roll-top safe was often held only by the armored car service, which would pick up the bags the next day and deliver them to the cash vault at the team's bank, where the deposits would be verified and credited to the team's account. The verified deposit slips were returned with one copy to the box office and one copy to the accounting department.

Turnstiles were used at every gate to count the number of fans who entered into the stadium for the event. The beginning count of each turnstile was recorded prior to the opening of the gates for each game. As each guest presented a ticket, the ticket was torn in two, referred to as being "stubbed," with half given to the guest and half deposited into a bin for counting later. The guest then passed through the turnstile, which recorded one entry. As entry gates were closed, the ending counts of each turnstile were recorded and the number of attendees was determined based upon the total number of "clicks" on all the turnstiles combined. As a measure to assure that patrons were not allowed to enter without a ticket, all the stubs collected at each turnstile were taken to a room where they were counted and compared to the turnstile count. Significant variances were investigated because they represented the potential for lost revenue if a ticket taker allowed guests to enter without having paid.

The day after each event, the box office staff would gather all of the deadwood from the previous day's event together to be re-counted. This process was known as auditing the game's sales. It entailed counting all the deadwood for each price category, summarizing all of the ticket sellers' game-day worksheets into a master, accounting for all the sales of tickets for each category that occurred prior to game day whether as a season

Exhibit 12.1

An Auditor's Perspective Before Computerized Ticketing

The ticket sales process represents a significant portion of a team's revenue and was quite complex. Further, ticket sales involved many transactions frequently paid for with cash. This environment created great opportunity for error or out-and-out fraud, so many controls needed to be put in place.

Among those controls were regular audits of the procedures and processes used by teams in its ticket sales. Auditors were engaged to do surprise visits to the stadium to test these processes and observe the behaviors of box office employees, ticket sellers, ticket takers and security personnel.

In the days of hard, preprinted tickets, auditors still wore dresses, suits and ties to their clients every day, including those days when their work consisted of an audit at the ballpark in the dead of summer. Auditors would show up to the box office prior to the arrival of any ticket sellers, randomly select several cash tills to test and then go off to observe the opening turnstile recording, watch ticket sellers at work in their booths and stand watch over patrons passing through the turnstiles prior to returning to the box office to watch their selected sellers count back in at the end of the night.

They would return to the box office the following day to observe the deadwood count. Later, the auditors would trace all the deposits to bank statements and trace all the ticket counts to the printer's manifest.

Despite the long hours and tedious work, drawing the sports team engagement was considered to be a great prize in the auditor's office.

ticket, a group ticket or an individual ticket sold at the box office window, and comparing the total sold plus the deadwood to the number of tickets printed for that game as reported on the certified manifest provided by the printer.

TICKETING MOVES INTO THE ELECTRONICS AGE

By the late 1960s, computers began their surge into the realm of event ticketing when a major data processing company offered services through a subsidiary known as Ticketron that were primarily used by teams and venues to sell tickets in remote locations away from their primary box offices. These outlets, as they were called, were often placed in large public businesses like banks, department stores and even grocery stores.

In the earliest days of computerized ticketing, Ticketron was given allocations of tickets that were limited to certain sections scattered across price categories throughout the stadium. In baseball, for example, the outlet agency would have box and reserve seat locations on each of the first and third base sides of the field, as well as some in both the lower and upper deck. General admission and bleacher seats without a seat assignment were also made available.

The box office manager would determine which sections would be allocated to the outside ticketing agency for its outlet sales, and pull or "kill" the hard printed tickets for box and reserved seats from each game to avoid selling the same seats twice. Outlets stopped selling tickets on game days several hours before the game so that any unsold allocation could be returned to the box office to be sold at the venue if needed.

The ticketing company assumed the cost of establishing the network of outlets including the hardware, which consisted of a CRT (computer monitor), a special ticket printer and modem, plus telephone lines to support the communications to its central computer system. The computerized ticketing company made the arrangements with outlet locations, such as a major retailer like Sears, to place its equipment in their stores, usually in locations like the customer service or credit and catalog centers. The ticketing company provided training and ongoing support for the store staff charged with selling tickets through its system.

Customers were charged a convenience fee for using the outlet location to purchase tickets. These fees were originally split between the ticketing company and the outlet location whose employees used part of their time selling tickets on the system. Retailers and bankers agreed to the arrangement because the additional foot traffic generated by ticket sales often helped drive customers to their locations, who they then tried to convert to customers of their core business, especially when large or very popular events brought in many ticket buyers.

Outlets faced some risks as well. Because each outlet was given only an allocation of seats in select locations, customers were frequently unhappy with the seats they were able to purchase. Additionally, for high-demand events like major rock concerts at sporting venues, would-be ticket buyers often lined up outside outlet locations hours, or even days before tickets went on sale, creating difficulties for the major retailers that hosted ticket outlets. Occasionally, any number of ticket buyers who had waited in line for hours or days never got to buy tickets because that particular outlet sold through its entire allocation before satisfying the ticket needs of all the buyers in line. There are stories of violence and damage to store locations from disappointed and irate ticket buyers in such circumstances.

Eventually, computerized ticketing companies increased their sales presence by adding telephone sales as an optional sales channel in addition to the outlets. The phone sales functioned similarly to outlets; the ticketing company created its own central telephone sales room to receive calls from ticket buyers. They could achieve economies of scale by funneling calls from many team and venue customers to the same room. In the earliest days, callers to such phone rooms were not even told their seat locations but were simply sold the "best available" seat at the time of sale. The fact that phone sales were also made from allocated seats in limited sections was never really discussed with buyers. Convenience fees for this service were charged on a per ticket basis, plus a handling and mailing fee was added to each order.

As computers became more prevalent and widespread, ticketing system companies like Ticketron developed software to manage the full range of ticketing requirements. As the computerized ticketing business grew, competitors to Ticketron emerged. One such company, TicketMaster, grew quickly and eventually acquired Ticketron. These software programs were created to help manage the "back office" requirements of ticketing, including ticket inventory management that allowed access to every seat in a venue from every ticket sales location such as the primary box office, day of game window sellers, phone rooms, and remote outlets. This unprecedented access to virtually every seat spawned a new era of improved customer service offered by teams and venues. Fans no longer had to go to a particular outlet, or a particular gate at a venue to get a specific seat or section they wanted.

Other key improvements brought about by computerized ticketing include the management of season passes or subscriptions. Imagine no longer having to open each of 81 boxes of hard tickets to pull out a season ticket from the preprinted ticket stock in order to build a full season ticket package. And counting the deadwood for each game became a thing of the past as only tickets that were needed were printed on demand as and where they were sold.

Starting in the mid-1990s, teams began printing bar codes on each ticket as the system created them. These bar codes would eventually be used by electronic turnstiles to tell gate attendants that the ticket presented by the guest was valid and had not yet been used to enter the venue. The data provided by scanning the bar codes on these tickets helped venue managers become more efficient at getting patrons into their buildings by recording and summarizing entry patterns that identified when and where additional staff were needed. By reducing gate attendants or delaying their start times, venue managers also learned to save money.

Since the earliest days of electronic turnstiles, many venues have now gone to wireless handheld scanning devices. The latest generations of these scanning devices have the ability to scan a printed bar code or a magnetic stripe, or to read data from a microchip (sometimes referred to as *smartcards*) embedded in a card or ticket. Smartcards offer teams the ability to provide customers with special incentives by downloading extras like food and beverage or merchandise credits directly to the card that can be redeemed only in the venue- or team-controlled stores.

Exhibit 12.2 describes the MLS Seattle Sounders' efforts to replace traditional paper tickets with smartcards. In 2012, season ticket holders were given the option to go paperless. Rather than issuing game tickets, fans were offered smartcards. Not only would card holders be allowed admission, they could also use the card to purchase food, beverage and merchandise at 625 points of sale throughout the stadium. Fans are provided a completely cashless game experience and the team is able to use the card technology to monitor the spending behavior of card users. As described in Exhibit 12.2, the Sounders are planning to take further advantage of the customer service benefits of the smartcard technology by designing a full-scale rewards program for card holders. Given the advantages smartcards provide consumers and teams, it is very likely that the transactional aspects of the fan experience in sports venues (gate admission, purchasing food, etc.) will become increasingly paperless as the card replaces the need for carrying both a ticket and cash.

The players in the computerized ticketing market have changed dramatically over time, but probably never more rapidly than over the period from 2009 to the present. TicketMaster (which merged with Live Nation, the largest talent promoter in the world) remains a major force but now faces competition from Paciolan/New Era (owned by Comcast-Spectacor), Tickets.com (owned by Major League Baseball), Veritix (owned by Dan Gilbert, owner of the Cleveland Cavaliers), AXS Ticketing/Outbox (owned by

Exhibit 12.2

Sounders Using Smart Cards for Season Ticket Holders; Seahawks Next

The Seattle Sounders are using smart cards for season tickets at CenturyLink Field, new technology that the Seahawks plan to adopt next year ,according to officials representing both teams.

The Sounders and Seahawks are owned by Paul Allen, co-founder of Microsoft. The paperless technology is tied to a Microsoft Dynamics CRM system installed last year to track data from gate admissions and food and retail concession sales.

About 11,000 of the Sounders' 32,000 season-ticket holders use the cards. All season-ticket holders were given the option to go paperless during the renewal process in September, said Bart Wiley, director of business development. The Sounders pitched paperless in part as a green initiative.

The cards have two stored-value functions. The bar code on the front is scanned at the stadium gate for admission. The magnetic stripe on the back is used to pay for food and merchandise at 625 points of sale throughout the stadium and CenturyLink Field Event Center next door.

Early in the season, the Sounders are testing the magnetic stripe by providing groups of 15 card holders with $10 in complimentary credits to spend on food, drink and retail at four home games in May, Wiley said.

The goal is to make the cashless piece available for all card holders by midsummer, he said. To add value, card holders log into their Ticketmaster Account Manager program to link a credit card number. They can also transfer their tickets by email for games they cannot attend.

To further track fans' spending habits, the Sounders are encouraging all card holders to have their cards swiped every time they make a food, beverage or retail purchase. During the month of May, card holders receive a 30% discount on all food and drink, excluding alcohol, and a 20% discount on Sounders polo shirts. The discounts are in effect for 90 minutes, from the time the gates open through the first kick.

In addition, the Sounders activated a promotion called "Swipe. Save. Win." tied to an opportunity for one fan to watch the final minutes of the match on the field and participate in a meet-and-greet with a Sounders player after each game.

After the season, the Sounders will analyze all smart card data to create a full-scale rewards program for next season, Wiley said.

The Sounders are not the first MLS team to use paperless ticketing. The New York Red Bulls installed a similar system at their new stadium when it opened in 2010. In the NBA, about a half-dozen teams have used smart cards as season tickets and for concessions.

In the NFL, the San Francisco 49ers and Tampa Bay Buccaneers have used paperless technology for season-ticket holders, said league spokesman Brian McCarthy.

In Seattle, the Seahawks plan to activate smart cards for the 2013 season after the technology is fully developed, Wiley said. As it stands now, the Seahawks would be the first NFL club to store all ticketing, food and merchandise data in one card, McCarthy said.

Anschutz Entertainment Group, owner of several sports franchises, venues and the second largest touring talent promoter in the world) along with others. Ticketing platforms have been significantly upgraded with special attention to improved customer service that in turn offers fans the ability to self-serve in many areas of the ticket buying experience. For example, the on-sale process for special events at sports venues like major concerts are now done almost exclusively online, and often sellouts are achieved in a matter of minutes, selling as many as 20,000 to 50,000 tickets in a very narrow window, sometimes as small as mere minutes. These systems have eliminated ticket buyers sleeping outside stadiums and outlet locations hoping to snap up the best seats. Sports teams have gone to online renewal of season tickets to reduce transaction costs and speed the process of signing-up their best customers for another year of events.

TICKET SALES DEPARTMENT ORGANIZATION

The ticket sales process generally consists of three primary functions: sales, service, and operations. The sales organization is charged with the responsibility of filling all the seats in the venue for each event. While there is no exact standard for how these sales teams are built and organized, one common approach segments the department's sales staff into divisions that focus on specific inventory and sales channels. See Figure 12.2 for a typical ticket sales and service organization structure. Sellers each have a specialty, but are usually permitted the ability to do "full-menu selling," which allows them to sell products outside their specialty if a lead they are working wishes to buy something outside that specialty. Product groups are often organized into the following categories:

- **Season tickets**—Season passes range from full season tickets that include the same seat for every event in a team's season all the way down to packages that can include as few as two or three events in a single season. It is not uncommon for teams to offer half or quarter season packages to help fulfill demand for partial season products, especially in sports with 41 or 81 home games.
- **Groups**—Tickets sold in large blocks, usually for single events and often at a discount, are considered group sales. Teams view these as sampling opportunities to get otherwise casual or first-time buyers to try their product in the hopes they can later convert them to customers who buy tickets for future events.
- **Premium sales**—Seats in high-demand locations like courtside, private clubs and suites are often categorized as premium seats. Teams have discovered that sales of this level of inventory require the long-term development and maintenance of personal connections with customers and prospects, which in turn requires a dedicated sales force. The inventory in these areas often comes with a varying array of special amenities such as private clubs, exclusive access to special team events, all-

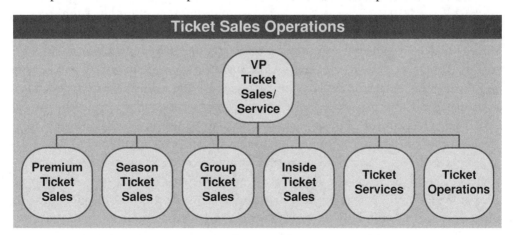

Figure 12.2. Example of a Team Ticket Sales Organizational Structure.

inclusive food and beverage arrangements, and other perks not offered to other season ticket customers.

- **Inside sales**—This group of sellers is sometimes considered the triple—A development team among ticket sales departments. Often these sellers are recruited directly from college to fill these entry level positions. Inside sales people have access to the full range of products to sell, but are usually focused by management on smaller packages as they develop their sales skills and gain proficiency at closing transactions. Sometimes inside sellers staff the telephones for in-game ticket promotions as they learn to upsell callers into bigger packages. Accomplished inside sales staffers are usually the first to be offered regular sales roles in the other divisions when a vacancy occurs or additional sales capacity is added by a franchise.

Once a season ticket purchase is made, the account is assigned to a dedicated service representative who is responsible for handling many of the day-to-day needs or requests of the customer. Examples of matters handled by the service manager include selling additional tickets for specific events onto a customer's account when requested, reprinting lost or forgotten tickets for individual events, enrolling the customer in fan programs that grant things like special access to the field or court, and fulfilling any special benefits that came with that customer's level of ticket purchase. Additionally, service managers maintain an ongoing relationship with each of their accounts, which can number up to 450–500. Service managers are generally the first point of contact for a customer during the process of renewing their tickets for the subsequent season. Research conducted by the NBA's Team Marketing and Business Operations group indicates that customers who have a strong relationship with their service manager throughout the year, with multiple interactions, are most likely to renew.

Walk-up ticket windows at a stadium. Courtesy of Dreamstime

The ticket operations department is charged with control over the seating inventory and the physical distribution of tickets sold by each of the various sales divisions or channels. This group assures that seats to be sold as season tickets are available for every game in the series of events included in a particular package, for example, full season, half season or quarter season. Once a season ticket is sold, the operations group assures that the seat involved is removed from the inventory of each of the games in the subscription. They often interact with sales and service staff to assure that payments are properly collected and posted to each customer's account. Some operations departments participate in creating and approving each of the group flyers to assure that inventory is available, and that the group pricing offered is correct and authorized. Ticket operations departments often handle the printing and mailing of super group tickets, and even other types of ticket orders. Some operations groups also oversee management of the facility box office that maintains regular retail-like hours, and handles walk-up sales on the days of events.

THE TICKET SALES PROCESS

Season Tickets

The basis of team ticket sales success starts with selling season tickets. These subscriptions help assure some minimum level of ticket sales for every event regardless of the team's performance on the field, court or ice since most season ticket sales are made prior to the start of each season. This base of tickets provides a solid financial footing on which to build the remaining sales strategies.

In offering full-season ticket packages—commonly referred to as FSEs or full-season equivalents—ticket sales staff are asking prospective purchasers to commit to buying a seat (or seats) for every home game. The extent of the commitment in terms of time alone varies tremendously from one major league to another. An FSE for the NFL consists of 10 games (2 preseason and 8 regular season), whereas a full season package for MLB includes 81 home season games during the regular season. FSE packages for the NBA and NHL typically consist of 43 games (2 preseason and 41 regular season). In the case of Major League Baseball, a FSE package commits a fan for 81 games over a 7-month period (April through early October) with games alternately played on different days of the week, with variable start times. When you add the actual monetary costs (often thousands of dollars) to purchasing a full season package to the considerable non-monetary costs (travel time and in-venue attendance), unsurprisingly in most markets selling FSEs is a major challenge. Finding fans with both the time and monetary resources is very difficult.

For this reason, teams have devised a number of tactics to induce prospects to purchase full season ticket packages. One approach to overcoming concerns related to both the time and financial commitment required of FSEs is to offer full season holders the opportunity to share their tickets with a partner, even going as far as including the share-partner in the account record, granting them some rights and benefits such as invitations to ticketholder-only events and renewal priority continuation should the primary account holder decide that he or she no longer wishes to continue as a customer of the team. Some teams even offer a partner program that helps share-partners find each other. One final strategy involves offering their season ticket customers the opportunity to resell their tickets on a team-controlled (or ticketing vendor controlled) online marketplace.

Teams can also build packages of benefits that season ticket holders enjoy in addition to having guaranteed access to the same seat or seats for every game. These benefits range from things like the right of first refusal on their seat location from year to year and discounts on merchandise in the team store, all the way up to opportunities to attend a road game or trip with the team on the team plane.

The priority number assigned to season ticket holders at their time of purchase can be an important and valuable element of owning seats. This priority number translates into the date and even the time a customer made their first purchase commitment to the franchise, thereby setting the customer's place in the pecking order among ticket buyers. This number is used by teams in a variety of ways, but among the most important is establishing the order in which ticket holders have the opportunity to move into prized seating locations when they become available. While every fan's definition of the perfect seat for the events they love most can be different, it is generally accepted that those seats closest to the action are the most sought-after locations. As such, there tends to be much greater demand for those particular seats than there are seats, and further, these prime locations do not frequently become available because the accounts that hold them recognize and value what they have. A long-time season ticket holder will have a much lower priority number, and therefore have the earliest right to relocate into prime seats should they become available. Priority numbers can also be used by teams for determining seating locations in a new venue should the team get a new building.

Different teams manage the ownership of full-season ticket accounts differently, but the rules around this can create value for the account holder as well as the team. Some teams establish rules that prevent transfer of the ownership of an account from a long-time owner to a new one without the permission of the team. In this way, the team retains the opportunity to control the transfer and dictate the rules around any discounts or other perks that have accrued to the long-time holder, but might not be granted to a new buyer. It also allows the team to take back inventory it might need to package with high-value sponsorships or to recapture key seating inventory for other club purposes. However, some teams allow account holders to have permanent benefits in their accounts with the ability to pass those rights to family members, or even sell those rights to a third party for cash. In franchises that allow this practice, it is not unheard of for seating locations to be passed along to family members for decades.

Mini-season Ticket Plans

Recognizing that many prospective customers, even ardent fans with the financial capability, are unable to purchase full-season packages, many teams are now offering partial season ticketing plans. Often called mini-plans, they offer guaranteed seating for a prescribed, often customized, number of games. They offer an attractive alternative to those fans who do not have the time or monetary resources to purchase a full season package. The MLB Milwaukee Brewers achieved an all-time franchise season-ticket sales record the first season they offered a new "product line" of 13- and 16-game mini packages. According to the Brewers' Vice President for Ticket Sales and Operations, "The revamped approach to our mini season plans attracted many new customers, both business and individual, who would have otherwise spent little or no money with us" (p. 9).[6]

Following the demonstrated success of teams like the Brewers, most major and minor league teams and a growing number of colleges offer partial or mini-ticket plans as a way of creating more flexible and affordable ticketing options for their fans. Mini-plans require tickets to be purchased for a specific number of games. One type of plan specifies exactly which games are being offered. Generally, when these "set" plans are being used the organization will present a few different options from which the fan may choose. Figure 12.3 provides an example of a menu of fixed game partial plans offered

AT&T Wireless Big Ten Packs

Maximize your free time and entertainment dollar with a flexible, affordable AT&T Wireless Big Ten Suns ticket package. Packages start at just $100 and you get an extra preseason game FREE!

- Same great seats for all 10 games!
- Save up to $50 off single-game prices!
- Buy playoff tickets BEFORE they go on sale to general public! **PICK THE PACK THAT FITS YOUR STYLE.**

EAST COAST		
DAY	DATE	OPPONENT
Monday	Nov. 4	Cleveland Cavaliers
Monday	Nov. 25	Milwaukee Bucks
Weds.	Nov. 27	New Jersey Nets
Monday	Dec. 16	Orlando Magic
Thurs.	Jan. 2	Philadelphia 76ers
Monday	Feb. 3	Chicago Bulls
Friday	Feb. 14	New York Knicks
Sunday	Feb. 16	Boston Celtics
Monday	March 17	Toronto Raptors
Friday	March 21	Washington Wizards

WEST COAST		
DAY	DATE	OPPONENT
Friday	Nov. 8	Portland Trailblazers
Friday	Nov. 15	Houston Rockets
Monday	Dec. 23	Seattle Sonics
Sunday	Jan. 12	Utah Jazz
Weds.	Jan. 29	Los Angeles Lakers
Tues.	Feb. 11	Los Angeles Clippers
Sunday	March 9	Minnesota Timberwolves
Thurs.	March 13	Sacramento Kings
Weds.	April 9	Dallas Mavericks
Sunday	April 13	San Antonio Spurs

WEEKEND		
DAY	DATE	OPPONENT
Friday	Nov. 1	Cleveland Cavaliers
Friday	Nov. 29	San Antonio Spurs
Friday	Dec. 6	Indiana Pacers
Saturday	Dec. 21	Sacramento Kings
Friday	Dec. 27	Los Angeles Clippers
Saturday	Jan. 4	Los Angeles Lakers
Friday	Jan. 17	Dallas Mavericks
Saturday	Feb. 1	Golden State Warriors
Saturday	March 1	New Orleans Hornets
Saturday	April 5	Minnesota Timberwolves

Figure 12.3. Sample of Phoenix Sun's Mini-Ticket Package.

by the NBA Phoenix Suns (p. 9).[7] The Suns created several six-ticket packages that allow fans, for $100, the opportunity to sample NBA games throughout the season. They also offered three 10-packs that focused on weekends, Western Conference ("West Coast") and Eastern Conference ("East Coast") games, respectively. The team created a 20-game (half-season) package and a "family night" package that included, along with four Suns game tickets, four vouchers to a local movie theater chain, four sandwiches, and four sodas. The family package was offered at $75, with a face value of $125. The Suns found corporate sponsors for several of their partial ticket programs, such as the "Budweiser 6 Packs" and the "AT&T Wireless Big 10 Packs." Not only did the team benefit from extending greater branding opportunities to its corporate partners, but the sponsors in turn helped to promote the ticket plans through company TV, radio, and print advertisements throughout the season.

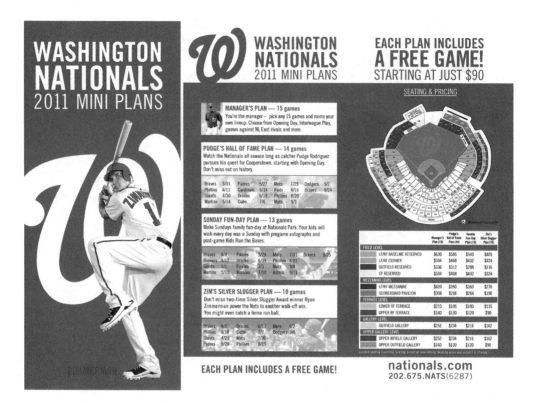

Figure 12.4. Washington Nationals Flexible Mini Plans.

The MLB Washington Nationals provide an example of a much more flexible partial ticketing plan, which allows fans a combination of a number of themed packages that specify a fixed number of games and opponents, as well as a customizable option in which fans can pick any 15 games (see Figure 12.4). One of the themed mini plans feature a mix of traditional National League teams and nearby "Beltway Rival" rival, the Baltimore Orioles. The Sunday Fun-Day Plan focused on attracting families to the ballpark. The "Manager's Plan" provided fans the opportunity to build their own lineup of 15 games, including Opening Day as part of the package. For each of the plans, fans were allowed the opportunity to reserve a preferred seating location from field level to upper deck. In addition to guaranteeing seating at a preferred location, fans purchasing the mini plans were offered one additional "free" game as part of the package.

Although teams would rather sell full- and half-season packages, it has become evident that many fans look for more flexible and affordable ticketing options. A senior vice-president of an NBA franchise noted, "Teams can no longer rely on a handful of traditional ticket plans as before." He stated that the future will be in "creating packages for distinct demographic groups and marketing them in a targeted way to appeal to those particular audiences" (p. 9).[6]

Group Tickets

Sales of group tickets often help fill the seats in venues. Group ticket buyers often purchase tickets to these events in order to attend a social event with their group more so than because they are die-hard fans. Teams then use these group ticket sales to create a sampling opportunity to attract casual or first-time buyers in the hopes that these customers will find the product appealing and attend a future event on their own, and perhaps eventually even become a season ticket buyer.

Groups are usually offered volume discounts based upon the number of tickets purchased for the entire group. Some teams even offer groups a rebate per ticket sold to help the group with fundraising. In these cases, the group ticket prices can range from their normal gate price to some discounted price that still includes the rebate if the volume is large enough. These groups leverage their buyers' affinity for the social or charitable purpose of their group to both raise money and simultaneously create an opportunity for social interaction with their supporters.

In order to enhance the social experience for groups, most teams offer special pre-event catering packages that can be combined with the tickets and allow the group to have a meal before the game, or possibly dessert and coffee at halftime. The team usually arranges these catering activities through its on-site food and beverage vendor, which naturally brings some incremental revenue to the team while providing a convenient solution for the group organizer. Newer buildings, and those that have undergone upgrades in recent years, usually include areas designed specifically to capture the group all-inclusive business that provides a bundle of benefits including admission, catering, merchandise and even meet-and-greets with team celebrities like broadcasters, alumni, executives, cheerleaders and mascots.

Traditional group sales consist of the ticket seller working with a single contact who makes all the group arrangements, collects payment from the individual members of the group or group sponsor (e.g., a corporate employer), and distributes the tickets to the attendees. As technology has improved, the "super group" has evolved, in which the ticket seller works with one individual or group sponsor, the team produces a flyer that includes special group pricing for a specific date, which is then distributed to the group either directly as a piece of paper or online either as an email or by posting on a group website or intranet. Individual buyers who are part of the group submit individual orders directly to the team that include their payment information for their particular order. The individual orders are processed from the block of tickets set aside for the group, and tickets are sent directly to the individual group buyer. Most computerized ticketing systems now offer a feature called the "group window" that offers this functionality. Super groups require more direct processing and order handling, but often result in much larger group sales than traditional groups because they offer the group organizer a turnkey method of delivering the group experience without as much effort.

Single Tickets

Seats not sold as part of either a season ticket package or as part of a group, are made available as individual tickets. Tickets sold in this manner are often priced at the highest rate for tickets in similar areas in order to recognize the investment made by season and group buyers. Individual event tickets are usually not made available by teams until a

concerted effort to sell season subscriptions and groups has been completed so that locations are protected for these package sales across all the events in each subscription.

Teams have increasingly begun to recognize that not all games have the same value to
the general public. For example, opponent teams that feature one or more superstars or
that occur on specific days will experience significantly higher demand than games
without such draws. With ticketing systems that now include nearly unlimited comput-
ing capabilities, teams have started using variable pricing to capture the potential revenue upside in these sought-after games. While other industries like airlines and hotels
have used variable pricing models that adjust prices based upon demand, sports have
been slower to adopt this model because of fear that season ticket customers might react negatively to the notion that while packages are generally priced on a standard price
per seat, some games are not as valuable as others. As teams have become more comfortable with the concept of variable pricing, a few teams have started using computerized price adjustment programs that are truly dynamic and automatically change prices
on the fly (the same way that airlines and hotels have for years) based upon moment-to-
moment changes in the variables of supply and demand for tickets in specific locations.
Most teams, however, still maintain a limited number of price levels and periodically
adjust the price level of games depending upon factors like team play, including that of
opponents, the potential for achievement of some specific milestone by a team or player,
or other factors. Most teams using this more manual variable pricing structure may
adjust prices upward but rarely reduce pricing based upon similar factors.

PRICING TACTICS: MOVING FROM
COST RECOVERY TO DEMAND-ORIENTED FOCUS

Historically, when establishing ticket prices, most sport managers made decisions "by
the seat of their pants." As recently as 2000, one analyst asserted that "ticket prices for
professional sport teams are the best-informed *guesses* [emphasis added] of management" (p. 144).[10] Historically, sport managers relied primarily, if not exclusively, on
their own judgment as to what ticket prices would be most acceptable to fans. The prevailing approach has been to raise prices incrementally by some arbitrary percentage or
flat rate. In fact, over most of the 1980s and 1990s, ticket prices grew annually at double-
digit rates for all four major leagues. Even during the 2001 recession, almost 7 out of
every 10 major league teams raised their ticket prices. During this period, the NFL and
MLB increased their ticket prices on average by 12.9% and 8.7%, respectively. Over the
entire two decade span, pricing decisions seemed to have been based loosely on two
considerations: either the estimated revenue needs of the organization or management's
perception of what the market would bear.

However, since the Great Recession and the resulting persistent and broad-based erosion in attendance, teams have had to approach the market with a much more customer-
oriented approach. In recent years, teams have become much more price sensitive, moving from cost-oriented to more demand-oriented pricing. Thus, we now see a growing
number of sports organizations applying variable and dynamic pricing tactics. The
accompanying inset describes the basic differences between the two differential ap-

Exhibit 12.3

What's the Difference?

Variable Pricing typically is defined as the practice of charging different prices for the same seat, depending on the game. Those prices are set before the season. With rare exception—such as the reclassification of a game because of a trade or an event that might make history, such as a record chase, they don't move. When they do move, it's to another pre-established pricing category.

Dynamic pricing is the fluid movement of ticket prices once the season is under way, typically driven by shifts in demand, the desire to change purchase behavior or both. A team might raise prices in response to a trade, then move them back down if buyers don't respond. When fully implemented, dynamic pricing provides fans a transparent view of prices to all games simultaneously, so that they can make buying decisions based, at least in part, on price.

proaches to pricing being used by teams, golf courses, and ski resorts.

As discussed previously, variable pricing has become widely adopted because of its ease of implementation and favorable fan reaction.

A growing number of teams sell tickets at different prices depending on the attractiveness of the opponent and the dates of play. The Colorado Rockies charge fans extra when the team plays the New York Yankees. The San Francisco Giants have added a surcharge for weekend games. The St. Louis Cardinals require fans to pay more for tickets in the summer months. In all three cases, teams used the pricing tactic to achieve a fuller and/or more balanced use of venue capacity. The intent is to encourage use of services at off-peak times and to maximize revenue production during peak demand times.

The St. Louis Cardinals reduced ticket prices in order to raise attendance during the traditionally slower months of the 7-month long major-league baseball season. According to a club spokesperson, ". . . We reduced prices for those times of year when we'd had trouble. Basically, we're talking about April, May, and September, when kids are in school. It's a practice we're going to continue, because there's a definite benefit to having people in the ballpark even at a lower price" (p. 50).[8] On the other hand, the Cardinals compensate for the discounted portion of the season by raising every ticket $1 for games played in the high-demand period between May 31 and September 2, which was projected to net the team $750,000 in increased revenues annually.[9]

The San Francisco Giants charge as much as $5 more for weekend games (Friday evening to Sunday afternoon). The decision produced for the team an additional $1 million in net revenue.[16] According to one baseball executive, "weekend summer games and certain matchups generate a different level of demand than other games. It only makes sense to price them differently"(p. 40).[10]

While a growing number of teams have executed variable pricing programs, it is evident that adjusting prices by demand will not work in every circumstance. Since variable prices are set well in advance, usually before the start of a season, anticipating the attractiveness of an opponent late in the season is less than perfect. For example, in 2010, the St. Louis Cardinals miscalculated on two late-season opponents. The first was a three-game series against the Cincinnati Reds over Labor Day weekend. Historically, the summer's last holiday had not been a big draw for the team, and the Reds were not viewed as a primary rival by Cardinal fans. As a result, prior to the season, the team priced the games on the low end of the variable price continuum. In fact, when the Reds came to town they were battling the Cardinals for first place in their division, and the teams were coming off a bench-clearing brawl in a recent series in Cincinnati. Ticket demand for the series turned out to be extraordinary with all three games completely sold out, leaving the club with the belief that they had underpriced the series and "left money on the table."

Later that month, the Cardinals played their historical arch rivals, the Chicago Cubs, in a three-game series. In anticipation of high demand for the bitter rivalry, the Cardinals had priced the games at the highest end of the differential price range. Unfortunately, by the time the Cubs arrived in St. Louis for the late-season series, they were playing poorly and completely out of the pennant race. Cubs fans, who generally followed the team to St. Louis, stayed at home, as did many home town fans. Consequently, attendance fell far short of what had been anticipated and with thousands of unsold seats, the team generated far less revenue than was predicted. As a result of these back-to-back miscalculations, the vice president of ticket sales for the Cardinals questioned the static nature of variable pricing. "No other business I know sets prices nine months out without the ability to change them. That's how we did it. But it's not how we should do it today."[11] He was referring to the fact that the very next season, the Cardinals implemented a dynamic pricing system for all 81 home games.

According to the team president, the move to dynamic pricing "creates a better match of supply and demand."[12] The system allows the team to reset single game prices on a daily basis. Prices can be significantly altered for different games within the same series based on such factors as the pitching match-up, special promotions (e.g., fireworks display, Bobblehead giveaway) or even the weather forecast. Exhibit 12.4 provides an in-depth description of how many teams have effectively established dynamic pricing. It is clear that the more dynamic differential pricing models described in the figure will become a predominant practice in admission pricing across the sports landscape.

One relatively recent development in ticketing that has helped drive teams into variable pricing schemes is the advent and proliferation of the secondary ticket market. The Internet has helped spawn many avenues for ticket owners and buyers to transact ticket sales after the original ticket is purchased from the team or venue. These marketplaces started as third-party arrangements that helped ticket buyers find sellers who, for whatever reason, were looking to sell their tickets. The website operators charge fees to both the seller and the buyer in order to collect the payments and transfer the tickets. Because teams have easy access to information about the value of tickets sold on the secondary market, they often use this data to help determine the pricing for their own unsold inventory by understanding what buyers are willing to pay on the open market. As discussed earlier, tickets all contain some form of digital code (a bar code, a magnetic stripe, or a smart chip) that is used to grant access to the venue. One challenge faced by these third-party resellers is the physical transfer of those tickets that preserves the valid access data. Ticketing vendors that contract with teams have now built ticket resale cen-

Exhibit 12.4

Ticket Challenge: Getting the Price Right

Dynamic Pricing Gathers Steam, but Will Consumers Push Back?

It was only three years ago that the San Francisco Giants became the first team in sports to try dynamic pricing. It wasn't until last year that three other MLB teams, including the Cardinals, joined them. This season, 17 of 30 MLB clubs will make the switch with some, if not all, of their seats. The results of those who have gone before them were too compelling to ignore.

In a study of MLB clients that fully implemented dynamic pricing last season, ticket pricing software company Qcue found that teams increased revenue by an average of $900,000 for the season by adjusting the price in each section of the ballpark one time for each game.

Demand-based dynamic pricing also has caught on to varied degrees across the NBA, where seven clubs price all their single-game seats dynamically and transparently, allowing fans to see a grid of all their games and make choices based on price, and the NHL, where two teams are doing it. Many teams in both leagues now reserve the right to tinker with prices here and there.

"What teams are realizing with dynamic pricing now is that there's really not a downside," said Barry Kahn, founder and CEO of Qcue, the Austin, Texas-based software company that pioneered dynamic pricing in sports and now works with 15 MLB clubs, as well as a smattering of teams in the NBA and NHL. "We always thought the most important thing to show people when we went in was the upside. But we found that people understood the upside. What was holding them back was the fear of what could go wrong.

"Once teams saw that they could drive more revenue and it wasn't going to cost them their season-ticket base or hurt the way they were perceived by the fans, dynamic pricing became a very easy thing to accept."

A full, dynamic pricing system typically costs teams $100,000 to $200,000 per year, said industry sources. Scaled down services that include data but not pricing advice can be had for less than $25,000 a year.

The initial hesitation with dynamic pricing, Kahn said, was tied to the dangers of an unfettered market. Teams worried that season-ticket holders might revolt if they regularly saw tickets go for less than they paid, as they sometimes do on the secondary market. They feared that ticket prices for a game might drop all the way to $1, thinking of them like a plummeting stock.

"There was a perception that what we were doing was keeping up with what the market price was," Kahn said. "There is a difference between the market price . . . and what the best price is at a given point in time for a team. And it's the latter that we're giving you."

It is a revolution riding the tails of rapid evolution in the ticketing business. Dynamic pricing is the most radical aspect of it. But there have been other sizable shifts.

"The world has changed drastically in the last two years," said Bill Sutton, a sports marketing professor who consults on ticketing matters with teams across sports. "And it's still evolving."

For many teams, dynamic pricing has come as a logical progression from the variable pricing that has beome commonplace. Analytical tools provided by vendors like Qcue, Digonex and Stratbridge, and ticketing providers such as Ticketmaster, Tickets.com, Paciolan and Veritix allow teams to more reliably predict the market for games at the start of the season and react efficiently to shifts in demand.

Chris Granger, executive vice president of the NBA's team marketing and business operations division, said that all 30 NBA teams this season are using variable pricing and most are employing some type of dynamic pricing strategies for regular-season games.

"They're both efficient in different ways," said Pete Guelli, executive vice president and chief sales and marketing officer for the Charlotte Bobcats, who, despite the worst record in the league, have managed to keep attendance from falling. "It's not about pricing around opponents but also around dates. The initial step is variable and it is critical because it defines what the revenue streams will be for the year, but dynamic pricing makes sure that you don't miss any opportunities. We have seen dramatic spikes in individual games sales, and a lot has to do with dynamic pricing."

Exhibit 12.4 *(Continued)*

Ticket Challenge: Getting the Price Right

Fred Whitfield, president and COO of the Bobcats, pointed to the team's recent game against the Los Angeles Clippers as an example of the benefits of flexibility. The Feb. 11 game between the Bobcats typically would have been a tough sell against the historically bad Clippers. But the game drew in marquee value after the Clippers landed Chris Paul in a trade at the start of the season. The Bobcats responded by upping the ticket price for his visit.

"It gave us a huge opportunity to drive more revenue for a game that we didn't anticipate being in demand," Whitfield said.

Kahn said many clients who used his company's tools to help them place games in the correct price category soon came to realize that no matter how much the data improved, they still were going to miss opportunities on some games and overshoot the mark on others.

"For me, the light bulb went off when I realized how little flexibility we really had," said Jarrod Dillon, vice president of ticket sales and services for the San Diego Padres. "Even if we're variably priced to the T, if the next Stephen Strasburg comes along or the next Barry Bonds home run chase happens, we have no way to react to that."

The Padres will implement dynamic pricing for all seats this year. That's a radical departure for a team that last year priced all 81 home games the same.

"Once you accept that not all games are created equal, the next step a club will move to typically is variable [pricing]," said John Abbamondi, vice president of strategy and business analysis for the Padres. "I'm going to look at the schedule and make some judgment calls as to which games are move or less desirable. The problem is, you're going to be wrong on those. You don't know how certain other teams are going to do. All dynamic does is give you an infrastructure that allows you to correct your mistakes."

Abbamondi is an example of a shift toward analytics that has swept front offices across sports. A graduate of MIT and Stanford business school. Abbamondi was an assistant general manager with the St. Louis Cardinals when the Padres hired him a year ago to work on both business and baseball.

A Matter of Timing

Thus far, much of the attraction to dynamic pricing has been the ability to drive more revenue from high-demand games and goose sales for tickets that aren't moving. But, increasingly, teams are considering the potential to change not only how many tickets they sell, but when they sell them.

The message the Padres crafted around their shift to dynamic pricing focuses on the fact that they set on-sale prices below what they expected fans would pay, making it likely that those who buy first will get the best deals. It's too early to tell if it's working, Dillon said, but he and Abbamondi are optimistic about its chances. If it doesn't work, they can adjust again.

That's been one of the lessons passed along by the teams that already have implemented dynamic pricing, and stressed by Qcue.

In its MLR analysis last season, Qcue found that teams that moved prices up did so at an average of $3.27 per seat. Price drops came at an average of $13.63 per seat. Both mirror Qcue's advice to teams to move up conservatively to test the market, but to drop prices precipitously in order to catch the consumer's eye. The average price move was a $1.55 increase.

Last season, the Cardinals saw attendance drop by 200,000, a dip they attribute to the soft local economy and the lack of a close pennant race. Yet ticket revenue increased by 2%.

"You are going to be surprised by some of the recommendations, both on how high the price should be on some games and how low they should be on others," Strohm said. "It counters how we've priced tickets for years now. You're going to end up pricing tickets in some locations much higher than you've ever priced tickets. But you're also going to reach a lower price point than you ever offered. You've got to trust the data that you're seeing versus going with past practices.

"Changing your habits is not easy. But you've got to trust the data."

Excerpted from an article written by Bill King for the *SportsBusiness Journal*, March 19, 2012, p. 1

ters that help team ticket holders transfer tickets within their own system. This innovation allows the ticketing vendor, and the team, to capture fees that were once the sole domain of these third-party resale entrepreneurs.

TICKET SERVICES

Building a base of repeat customers is generally critical for any business to succeed. In no other industry is this truer than in sports and venue management. Creating a culture in which season subscribers feel a real connection to the franchise is a critical component of keeping them as customers year after year. While teams utilize many different strategies to build this environment, they have increasingly turned to their service staff to create and reinforce that one-to-one relationship that keeps subscribers in the fold for the long term.

The service team is usually the group primarily charged with generating the season ticket renewal at a high level that becomes the life-blood of any franchise's ticket sales plan for the subsequent year. Retention of existing accounts is key to achieving increasing ticket revenues year to year that help support all team finances. The higher a team's season ticket renewal rate, the fewer number of accounts and seats the sales team must replace each year. Most teams pay a lower rate of commission and bonuses on ticket renewals than that paid on new sales because it is generally easier to keep these existing customers than to find and build relationships with new contacts until they become customers. In addition, the cost to gather data and mine it for potential leads for new sales adds to the cost of sales. These two factors combine to create a substantially higher cost to garner a new customer than to keep an existing one.

Ticket services representatives can carry account loads of between 250 and 500 accounts. Their responsibilities include making routine "wellness" calls to customers to assure that each account receives the level of attention that they expect from the team. These account managers are frequently charged with providing personalized invitations to season ticket holder-only events and other special perks that are offered as value-added amenities to season accounts. Service team members help customers with various needs related to their accounts like assisting them with online access, reprinting tickets for specific events, or adding additional single or package ticket plans to their accounts. The service team is important to a franchise because they help cement customer relationships that make sales from year to year less dependent upon team performance.

THE SALES ESCALATOR

The ultimate goal of every ticket sales department is to capture a first-time customer, build a relationship with that customer and then build that customer's year-over-year investment in the team. Franchises build products that include differing pricing structures and differing numbers of events so that they have a plan for every fan. This strategy supports the concept that retaining existing customers while moving them up in annual investment value is less expensive to the franchise than finding new customers. The concept is often referred to as taking the customer up the escalator (see Figure 12.5).

As an example, a team might offer an in-game promotion during its game broadcast

Figure 12.5. Escalator Model of Ticket Sales;

that calls on customers to purchase tickets by phone for a package that includes two tickets plus some food and beverage. Those calls are answered by the inside sales representatives who talk with the callers and attempt to get them to purchase an even bigger package that includes two or three games plus some amenities like food, beverage and parking. Once customers have purchased a package, their contact information is part of the team's customer relationship database. That data is later mined for known purchasers with certain characteristics: purchased for a certain day of the week, a specific opponent, or a specific amenity. The data request returns a list of prior purchasers who fit query criteria. A custom package or special offer of multiple games is designed, specifically targeted at the group because of their similar prior purchase. Purchasers of this second, larger package have now moved up to the next level on the escalator.

CUSTOMER RELATIONSHIP MANAGEMENT

As computer systems with greatly improved data collection, storage and management software have evolved, sports teams have increasingly begun to utilize their resources to capture more data about their customers that can help them better understand their patron base. What once were separate systems used to make and track individual ticket sales from those made through other sales channels, like seasons and groups, are now fully integrated data warehouses that organize and store all the customer information. Even information about corporate sponsors is now married with ticket account data to help franchises understand the 360-degree view of the value of each customer, and to unlock potential additional value hidden there. In addition to ticket and sponsorship customers, teams often collect sales leads from other sources like in-venue contests, which they use to augment the number of potential leads in their database.

The information in these data stores is often scrubbed to eliminate potential duplicates. The records are sometimes compared to public databases to help further qualify and segment each one in order to improve the potential return on lists of contacts generated from the data warehouse. Queries of these improved data records create reports to be used as call lists for season, group or inside sellers. Lists are also generated to be used in targeted mail or email campaigns. Because past purchase history can be matched to each record, teams can create special packages/offers that can be as specific as targeting all the records in a database that have attended a game against a particular opponent or group of opponents. This same set of customers can be cross-referenced to the ticket purchase records of the venue to determine their taste in music so that they might be offered a special pre-sale opportunity for an act that fits that particular genre.

In addition to data collected from the sales side of transactions, all the tickets that enter the facility are scanned by the bar code or other unique identifier on each ticket. This data can be used to determine whether season ticket customers are utilizing their tickets regularly. A team that finds a customer who has not attended several events can make that customer a special offer to get them to come to the park or arena where additional revenue from things like parking, food and beverage concessions, and merchandise can help improve a team's bottom line. History has shown that season ticket holders who regularly use their tickets, either for themselves, their customers, or their employees, are much more likely to renew their seats for subsequent seasons.

Reducing the number of anonymous attendees has become a goal of many teams. Using all the means at their disposal to capture unique identity information about each buyer, as well as each user of every ticket, the team has the ability to expand its understanding of the makeup of its full fan base, which it can use to create the targeted, relevant offers most likely to be purchased by each potential buyer. One mechanism that helps move this agenda forward is the function in ticketing systems that allows customers to send their tickets to others electronically either through email or some system website. Many of these systems require that the recipients of forwarded tickets create an account to claim the tickets sent to them by their season ticket customer friend. Once such a transfer is complete, the team has full identity information for both the buyer and the user of a particular ticket.

SUMMARY

Consumers in the U.S. spend almost $16 billion a year buying tickets to sporting events. For many sport organizations, ticket sales are a key source of revenue; the NBA and NHL depend on gate receipts as their single greatest source of income. Admission charges and fees are the lifeblood of a range of other sport organizations. In collegiate sport, ticket sales are a vital source of revenue, composing almost 30% of the total income generated by Division IA athletic departments.

The Great Recession of 2007–2008 contributed to a widespread decline in attendance and a corresponding decrease in gate receipts at many sport organizations. Erosion in ticket sales was aggravated by a sharp rise in the cost of attending many sporting events. Ticket prices for major professional league and collegiate football and basketball games more than doubled over the past decade.

Determining the cost of tickets to fall within fans' price tolerance is key to maintaining attendance. The prevailing approach has been to raise prices incrementally by an arbitrary percentage or flat rate. Historically, pricing decisions have been based on either the revenue needs of the organization or on management's perception of what the market will bear. Confronted with increased competition from other entertainment providers

for consumers' discretionary dollars, faced with a "soft" economy and widespread attendance declines, it is imperative that sport organizations adopt more price-sensitive
approaches to setting admission and service prices.

A number of teams have adopted differential pricing strategies, whereby different
prices are charged for essentially the same product (e.g., attending a game) or service
(e.g., using a ski lift). Prices are raised or lowered based on time of day or season and/or
by seat location to either increase demand at off-peak times or to maximize revenue
during peak-use times. Flexible ticket packaging or the use of mini ticket plans has
proven effective in stimulating demand by providing more flexible and affordable
options. Although money-back guarantees have been used sparingly by sport organizations, evidence suggests that a promise to refund the purchase price (e.g., season ticket
package, season pass) to customers who are not satisfied can encourage sales.

Internet ticketing has become a prominent vehicle for the sale and resale of tickets to
sporting events. The Internet's greatest contribution to the ticket distribution process
may be its ability to facilitate the resale or exchange of pre-purchased tickets. Organizations have created team websites with "secondary" ticket programs where season ticket
holders can sell tickets to games they are unable to attend. Fans are not left with expensive, unused tickets at the end of the season and are inclined to renew their season ticket
packages.

Effective ticket sales offices share sound fundamentals. First, they are proactive, not
reactive. Extensive preparation can lessen the number and severity of last-minute problems. Second, they maintain accurate and complete records, needed for the annual
audit and for investigation of any discrepancies. Third, they are focused on customer
service, crucial to building a positive image of the organization and sustaining a high
level of repeat sales.

References

1. Survey of current business. (2006, August). *U.S. Bureau of Economic Analysis*, p. 86.

2. IBISWorld. (2012, August). IBISWorld Indus-
try Report 71121a—Sport Franchises in the U.S. Retrieved from www.ibisworld.com

3. Johnson, A. (1993). Minor league baseball and local economic development. Urbana, IL: University of Illinois Press.

4. Appelbaum, B. (2012, June 11). Family net worth drops to level of early '90s. *The New York Times*, D2.

5. TMR's fan cost index for MLB, NBA, NFL, NHL. (2011, September). *Team Marketing Report*. Retrieved from http://teammarketing.com/fci.cfm

6. King, B. (2002, April 1–7) Baseball tries variable pricing. *SportsBusiness Journal*, pp. 1, 4.

7. Eisenberg, J. (1993, October). Small-market success: How the Milwaukee Brewers sold 43% more season tickets. *Team Marketing Report*, pp. 9, 11

8. McCarville, R., Crompton, J. L., & Sell, J. (1993). The influence of outcome messages on references prices. *Leisure Sciences, 15*(2): 115–130.

9. Cameron, S. (2002, March 4–10). Bruins set prices hourly. *SportsBusiness Journal*, pp. 1, 50.

10. Rovell, D. (2002, June 21). Sports fans feel pinch in seat (prices). *ESPN.com*. Retrieved from http://espn.go.com/sportsbusiness/s/2002/0621/1397693.html

11. King, B. (2012, March 19). Ticket challenge: Getting the price right. *SportsBusiness Journal*, p. 1

12. Strauss, J. (2010, November 18), How much for a Cardinals' ticket? Well that depends. *Stltoday.com*. Retrieved from http://www.stlto-day.com/sports/baseball/professional/how-much-for-a-cardinals-ticet-well-that-depends/arti cle_1898c898-f373-11df-b05300127992bc8b.html

13

Commercializing Media Rights

~ Lee H. Berke ~

President & CEO, LHB Sports, Entertainment & Media Inc.

INTRODUCTION

Electronic media form the financial foundation of the sport industry. The Internet and wireless communications are becoming more influential, but television in all of its forms, including broadcast, cable, and satellite, remains the wealthiest medium for the sports industry, and one which continues to grow. Broadcast radio, once the only form of electronic media nearly a century ago, remains influential, but rights fees have shrunk as radio faces challenges from other digital audio platforms.

Combined rights fees from television and radio broadcasts provide an important revenue source for major league and Division IA college sports teams. Publicity generated by these broadcasts is not directly measurable, but its value is undisputed, as each one is an hours-long commercial for their respective teams and sport.

Established, marketable sporting events mean guaranteed television audiences, which translate into substantial revenues. With new television agreements in place, the NFL averages over $6 billion annually from its multi-network contracts. The NBA averages $930 million annually from Time-Warner's Turner Broadcasting and from Disney's ABC and ESPN for nationally broadcast and cable television games through 2016. The NHL has a record-breaking $2 billion deal with NBC Sports, ensuring the league an average of $200 million per year through the 2020–21 season.

Despite occasional protestations from television stations, cable providers, and satellite distributors that increasing rights fees cannot continue indefinitely, the battle for sports programming and the escalation in rights fees show no signs of slowing, due to the basic economic principle of supply and demand. There are a relatively fixed number of brand-name professional and college sports properties that drive interest and usage from fans and sponsors. In the United States, these properties include the NFL, NBA, MLB, NHL, NCAA football and basketball, PGA golf, Grand Slam tennis, NASCAR, and the Olympics. While expansion leagues and other sports have been introduced over the last several decades, none have rivaled the leagues and sports listed above, or greatly expanded the overall amount of brand-name sports properties.

Yet, while the supply of these properties remains relatively fixed, demand for these sports from consumers, sponsors and media distributors has skyrocketed. In analyzing the marketplace, the *Financial Times* noted that "at the heart of this success is the American public's seemingly insatiable appetite to watch live games on TV."[1] This has led to steady and expanding ratings for the above properties even while overall television viewership has fragmented and declined due to an expanding array of media platforms and leisure-time activities. In addition, the number of media companies and technologies competing for these key sports properties has grown, both in numbers and size. Today's competitors for sports rights include Comcast-owned NBC and NBC Sports Network; Disney-owned ESPN and ABC; News Corporation-owned FOX, FX and FOX Sports Net; Viacom-owned CBS and CBS Sports Network; Time Warner-owned TNT and TBS; Liberty Media-owned satellite company DirecTV; plus an expanding array of broadband and wireless media platforms being introduced by Verizon, AT&T, and Google/YouTube.

Major league professional sports teams, leagues and properties and a growing number of college athletic programs and conferences have become reliant on the revenue streams from networks, subscription television services, and digital media. Table 13.1 summarizes the current value of television agreements for each major sports property. Major networks have committed $69 billion to the "big four" major leagues through 2022. The impact of these multi-billion dollar, long-term deals is most evident in the National Football League. Beginning in 2014, the NFL will receive more than $6 billion per year from its many broadcast partners. FOX, CBS and NBC are each paying over $1 billion per year to air NFL games, and ESPN is reportedly paying almost $1.9 billion per year for *Monday Night Football*. Add in the additional $1 billion a year paid by DirecTV for the rights to *NFL Sunday Ticket*, and the league's television rights revenues easily eclipse $6 billion each year through 2021.[2] Due to the NFL's generous revenue-sharing model in which each team receives an equal share of the annual television rights fee revenues, starting in 2014 every team will receive about $200 million. In effect, before the season starts, the television revenue will provide revenues sufficient to cover close to 75% of a team's annual operating expenses. According to one NFL analyst, "That is more than $200 million per team every year, *before* one ticket, beer or jersey is sold."[3]

The growing prominence of television revenues is also apparent at the collegiate level. This is particularly true for schools playing in major football conferences, like the Big Ten, PAC 12, SEC, and ACC. The Big Ten disbursed about $25 million in television revenues to each conference school in 2012, as the result of its "remarkably profitable" Big Ten Network.[4] This single source of revenue accounted for at least a third of the total revenues generated by many athletic programs in the Big Ten conference. In 2011, the SEC distributed a conference record $19.5 million to each of its member schools from its television contracts with CBS Sports and ESPN.[5] Fortunately for the great number of big-time athletic programs that have become increasingly dependent

Table 13.1. Major Sports Television Deals

Property/ League	Networks	Package	Terms
National Football League	ABC, CBS, FOX ESPN Direct TV	Regular season, playoffs Monday Night Football Sunday Ticket	$27.0 billion, 2014–2022 $15.2 billion, 2014–2021 $ 4.0 billion, 2011–2014
Major League Baseball	FOX ESPN TBS Direct TV MLB International	Regular season, All-Star, World Series Regular season, Sunday Night Baseball Regular season, post season Extra Innings All-Star game, post season	$4.20 billion, 2014–2021 $5.60 billion, 2014–2021 $2.60 billion, 2014–2021 $0.70 billion, 2009–2015 $0.31 billion, 2011–2013
National Basketball Association	ESPN, ABC, Turner	Regular season, playoffs, finals	$7.4 billion, 2009–2016
National Hockey League	NBC Sports	Regular season, playoffs	$2.0 billion, 2012–2021

Sources: *SportsBusiness Daily*, August 28, 2012; Bloomberg News, October 2, 2012

on television monies, rights fees for collegiate sports are trending upward. In May 2011, the Pac-12 Conference signed what was at that time a record agreement with FOX and ESPN. The 12-year deal is worth an estimated $3 billion, ensuring each conference member will receive no less than $21 million per year. Shortly after adding two new conference members, Texas A&M and Missouri, the SEC began working on a new contract with its television partners, ESPN and CBS. The talks are reputed to include the start of an SEC network, modeled after the Big Ten Network and Pac-12 Network (which launched in August 2012). While the negotiations are ongoing at the time of this publication, most analysts believe the SEC agreement will establish a new record for conference television rights fees.[6]

THE BUSINESS OF TELEVISION AND MEDIA

Like other businesses, media companies are composed of businesspeople in search of profit. A generation ago, these companies were focused solely on broadcast television, which generates only one main revenue stream: from selling commercial time to advertisers looking to reach their respective target audiences. Now, broadcast television has been overtaken in large part by multichannel subscription television services that carry cable and satellite networks. Along with advertising sales, each of these networks also generates a second revenue stream: from selling subscriptions to viewers who pay fees to watch programming. For many of these networks, particularly those that emphasize

sports programming, these subscription revenues can often far surpass the dollars generated by advertising. As one example, ESPN generates an average monthly subscription fee
of over $5.00 from each of its subscribers. With more than 100,000,000 subscribers na-
tionwide, ESPN receives over $6 billion of total subscription revenues each year.[7]

As for advertising sales, media companies offer entertainment to attract a crowd.
Once networks attract an audience, advertisers pay to make their pitch. The networks'
product, then, is not programming; it is the audience that is sold to advertisers. Programming is merely a tool used to build audiences.

Television Ratings and Shares

Because audiences are bought and sold, they must be measured. Nielsen Media Research
provides audience estimates and demographics data to both television broadcasters and
advertisers. Nielsen reports there are more than 115.9 million television households in
the United States today, and Nielsen has divided the nation into 210 distinct designated
market areas (DMAs). Television DMAs are not of equal size. The largest, New York,
covers not only New York City but also adjacent counties in New York State, New Jersey, Connecticut, and Pennsylvania, a total of over 7.38 million households. The smallest, rural Glendive, Montana, encompasses just 4,180 homes in the northeastern corner
of the state.[8] Through electronic meters, viewers' diaries and intensive surveying,
Nielsen determines what people are watching. A similar market-based system is used by
Arbitron to measure radio audiences.

Audience size in television is expressed most often in terms of ratings and shares. A
program's *rating* represents the percentage of television households within the survey
universe tuned to the program. For a network program shown in every market, then, a
nationwide rating of 10 means 10% of the nation's 115.9 million households with television sets is tuned in—nearly 16 million households. A program's *share* represents the
percentage of television households with *sets in use* tuned in to the program. As both research and common sense indicate, not every home is watching television all the time.
Viewership gradually builds during the day, peaks in the evening at an average of 61.9%
of the nation's television households, and then declines again. If 60 million households
across the country were using televisions, the program being viewed in 16 million would
have a 26.6 share—26.6% of the households using television. If only 30 million homes
were using televisions, the program would boast a 53.3 share.

Nielsen ratings are closely monitored in the industry and are published in many major newspapers, trade publications, websites and blogs. Until recently, ratings for sports
broadcasts usually trailed those of the more popular entertainment programs on television. However, in an increasingly fragmented media landscape, with a variety of screens
and electronic products eating away at overall television viewership, sports ratings have
held constant, or, in the case of premier properties like the NFL, have grown. For example, during 2011, NFL football games composed 23 of the top 25 most-watched television shows of the year.

Table 13.2 shows the ratings and size of viewing audiences for the championship
game or series for each of the four major leagues. The 2012 Super Bowl was the most

Table 13.2. TV Ratings for Major Leagues Championship Events, 2011–12		
League/Property (Event)	Avg. US HH Rating	Number of Viewers
National Football League (Super Bowl)	47.0	111.3 million
Major League Baseball (World Series)	10.0	16.6 million/avg.
National Basketball Association (Championship Finals)	10.1	17.3 million/avg.
National Hockey League (Stanley Cup Finals)	2.7	4.7 million/ avg.

watched television broadcast ever in the US, attracting an audience of over 111 million. While considerably more modest, the 2012 NBA Finals also attracted a record-breaking viewership averaging more than 17 million. Major League Baseball's Fall Classic, the World Series, followed closely behind with a 10.0 rating and an average of 16.6 million viewers per telecast.

The NFL's dominance is even more evident when comparing regular season games. During its 16-game season, NFL broadcasts average more than 17.5 million viewers. In contrast, nationally televised MLB games rarely attract more than three million viewers. While the NFL has become a "national" pastime for sports viewing, the "vast, vast majority" of baseball games are consumed on the local level.[9] Table 13.3 shows that fan avidity for baseball is much more localized, which has allowed regional sports networks to exploit fans' stronger attachment to teams in local markets. Average ratings in a number of markets are well above 6.0.

The ratings strength of sports programming is due to two key factors: avidity and exclusivity. Avidity is driven by the impact of live sports events on fans who watch each game with a higher level of interest and passion not often shown with many other programming categories. Due to avid viewers, each sports event makes news, with scores,

Table 13.3. Ratings for Selected Major League Baseball Teams in Selected Markets			
Team	Network Avg.	Rating Avg.	HHs (000)
Boston Red Sox	NESN	9.46	228
St. Louis Cardinals	FOX Midwest	7.97	100
Detroit Tigers	FOX Detroit	6.89	133
MN Twins	FOX North	6.25	108
New York Yankees	YES	4.66	346
Atlanta Braves	FOX South	3.52	81
San Francisco Giants	Comcast Bay Area	3.27	81
Source: *Sports Media Watch* (2010, April 21). Local on the Eights: Ratings for NBA, MLB and NHL Teams.			

performances and highlights that are quickly disseminated through a wide range of media outlets. From a viewership standpoint, each event has a short shelf life as viewers must watch each event live to experience it without knowing the outcome. While re-airs of games and events are popular on regional and national television networks, Video On Demand platforms, and on wireless and broadband, ratings for these re-airs are far less than for the original live airdate. Moreover, over time, as these re-airs become part of the archives of networks, leagues, teams and conferences, ratings decay as new, live sports events capture the attention of viewers.

Along with avidity, the ratings strength of live sports events is bolstered by their exclusivity. When networks obtain the rights to marquee sports properties, they effectively prevent other networks from showing the same programming. Other programming categories are often non-exclusive, as networks can offer up similar categories of entertainment programming, such as sitcoms or dramas. As an extreme example, news programming is completely non-exclusive, as any number of networks can offer up the same news event or story. However, only one media company is allowed each year to show the Super Bowl, World Series or NBA Championships.

Sports telecasts' avidity and exclusivity have served to maintain their ratings even while the ratings for other programming categories have decayed. As one example, in the 1970s, Saturday night was one of the most-watched television nights of the week for broadcast networks, with original, scripted series such as "All in the Family" and "Mary Tyler Moore" dominant in the ratings. Today, Saturday has become the least-watched night of the week for broadcast networks, which for the most part, run re-airs of scripted series and reality shows. However, ABC, CBS and FOX have begun airing sports events during Saturday night such as college football and Major League Baseball due to their proven ability to generate audiences.

Major TV networks have committed $69 billion to the "big four" major leagues through 2022. Courtesy of BigStockPhoto

As noted previously, marquee sports attractions often approach and surpass the audience levels of leading entertainment programs. Of these attractions, the Super Bowl and the Olympics provide the most dominant ratings performances. Traditionally the most-watched telecast of the year, the NFL title game constantly draws ratings in the low to mid-40s. The Olympic Games usually average in the high teens and hold special attraction to advertisers because, unlike most sporting events, they attract a high percentage of female viewers. Most other national sports broadcasts garner ratings in the single digits. Local professional and college sports events can reach double digits for key contests, which in today's fragmented media marketplace can often be the most viewed events of the day in a particular market.

Networks and sports promoters argue that the Nielsen numbers do not reveal the true size of the audience because they do not accurately count viewers at parties in private homes, in sports bars, or in college residence halls. Because local teams' broadcasts draw larger audiences than out-of-town contestants, a so-so national rating may disguise a smash hit in local ratings. When, for example, Kentucky played Massachusetts in an NCAA men's basketball semifinal game in 1996, the broadcast received a 12.3 rating and 22 share nationally. In the Boston market, however, the game drew a 23 rating and 38 share, whereas in the Cincinnati market, which includes portions of northern Kentucky, the game had a 26.2 rating and 47 share.

Ratings and shares tell only part of the story. We can determine that a program has a 10 rating and a 17.5 share—usually expressed as 10/17.5 in industry shorthand—but ratings and shares measure only households. Both advertisers and broadcasters want to know how many people are in front of those sets and, most critically, what kind of consumer those viewers may be. Are they rich or poor? Men or women? Old or young? Do they prefer to read books or ride bicycles in their free time?

Broadcasters, advertisers, and marketing research firms conduct elaborate surveys and sift through data to answer those questions in order to match the advertiser with the correct audience. Television is generally a women's medium. Nielsen studies indicate women aged 19–34 watch nearly 5 hours more television weekly than men. At any given time during the prime viewing hours of 8 to 11 p.m., when the television audience is largest, 62% of the audience is likely to be made up of women, teenagers, and children. In the morning and afternoon, the percentage of women, teens, and children exceeds 70%. In most households, women and teens decide which programs will be watched during the evening hours.[10]

Sports television offers advertisers an alternative: a predominantly male audience, one that is difficult to reach efficiently through other mass media. Although sports broadcasts often attract a smaller audience in absolute numbers than do popular prime-time entertainment shows, the demographics of the audience makes a difference. Most sporting events attract audiences dominated by adult men who, on average, are better educated and wealthier than the average television viewer or radio listener. Sports also offers a vehicle for reaching minority men, a difficult market to address through mass media. For example, while ratings surveys ranked WTEM, the all-sports radio station in Washington, D.C., 25th in total audience size among the city's stations, 80% of the station's audience was men, and 58% were men aged 25–54. The station ranked first among men aged 25–54 who had graduated from college and second among men with annual household incomes of $150,000 or more.[11] ESPN, citing Nielsen survey data, claims its typical audience is well over 60% adult men. The all-sports cable network calculated that for every 1,000 households tuned in during prime time, its audience includes 850 men over age 18.[12] The Boston Celtics' local television outlet reported that 70% of the audience for the typical game was men aged 25–54.[13] These and other instances have convinced advertisers targeting a male demographic that sports can be a highly desirable media buy.

Typically, advertisers purchase audiences by the thousand. Advertisers calculate the number of *impressions*—the number of people who will see or hear their message—and compare that number with the price of the advertisement. The calculation yields the *cost per thousand*, or CPM (M = 1,000 in Roman numerals). CPM allows advertisers to compare the efficiency of different media. Depending on the time of day, the total size and demographics of the audience, advertisers on the major television networks expect to pay about $10 to $30 for every thousand viewers they reach.[10] CPM is sometimes translated into a related concept: *cost per point*, or CPP. This compares the price of an advertisement with a program's rating to determine the cost of reaching one rating point—1.15 million homes nationally—with a sponsor's message.

Marketing and sales research is both a science and an art. Broadcasters and advertisers use advanced statistical theories and sophisticated technology to crunch the numbers, but the results then must be interpreted. Advertisers seek the most efficient means of reaching their targeted audience, whereas broadcasters look for programming that attracts the kind of audiences advertisers covet. There is no such thing as a bad audience. It is simply a question of matching the right advertiser with the desired audience.

Total Return

Although the dollar amounts involving major sports broadcasts are truly mind-boggling —NBC, for example, claimed $3.5 million for a single 30-second commercial during the 2012 Super Bowl—broadcasters and sport managers must look beyond the bottom line when they calculate the worth of sports. They need to consider the *total return* they are likely to enjoy from their partnership.[14]

Teams and leagues profit from rights payments. However, there are a variety of non-cash benefits accruing from television and radio exposure. Televised games play a critical role in establishing a fan base and the value of team, league, and conference brands. A new franchise or professional league gains credibility if its games are on television. New fans unfamiliar with the team, its players, or the sport are introduced to the game and perhaps persuaded to attend future events. Even for established sports properties, televised games and events build awareness and enhance the reputation of the in-venue experience, players, management, owners and logos with current fans, and help develop the next generation of fans. Television gives a team a platform for promoting upcoming contests and special events, selling team merchandise, and cultivating its public image. Many college television contracts, for example, explicitly include requirements that the broadcaster set aside time for promotional announcements extolling the college's academic and public service achievements. The NFL uses its network broadcasts to promote the league's charitable activities with United Way and youth fitness. The NBA promotes a similar Stay in School campaign.

Networks, too, rely on high-profile sporting events to raise their public image. ABC used its sport programming in the 1960s and 1970s, led by the groundbreaking Wide World of Sports anthology series and the introduction of Monday Night Football, to shed its image as the "Almost Broadcasting Company," a pale imitation of CBS and NBC, and become a major player in the broadcast business. The meteoric rise of the cable industry in the 1970s and the 1980s owes a great deal to ESPN, the all-sport network. ESPN's 24-hour sports coverage motivated millions of suburban viewers to sign up for cable, due to the launch of Sportscenter and an expanding roster of pro and college events. Skeptics said FOX would lose millions when it signed a $1.58 billion contract to broadcast NFC games, and subsequent write-offs by News Corporation, FOX's parent company, proved the critics right. The daring move, however, yielded a variety of indirect benefits to the then-fledgling network. FOX immediately became a major network in the eyes of viewers, advertisers, and television station owners across the country. In Detroit, Jacksonville, Dallas, Atlanta, and several other key markets, established stations signed up with FOX to gain access to the games, giving the network's entire programming lineup more viewers. The games offered FOX the opportunity to promote its prime-time programs to millions of fans who had yet to find their local FOX affiliate, resulting in larger audiences and higher advertising revenue. CBS, on the other hand, lost key affiliates and viewers when it lost the NFL to FOX and was eager to recapture NFL rights when the contract came up for renewal. During the 1990s, NBC declared that it would no longer pay exorbitant amounts for high-profile sports programming, but reversed that strategy when it became apparent that big ticket items like Sunday Night Football and the Olympics would be the most popular programming in the network's lineup. All of this reflects the increasing value of sports programming to highly competitive media companies that will bid aggressively for sports events to gain an edge over rivals.

SPORTS MEDIA OUTLET

As more media companies offer up an increasing range of platforms and devices, each one seeks programming that will appeal to larger, more valuable audiences that will commit their time, attention, and subscription dollars. Consistently, sports programming has helped drive the success of every media platform and device from broadcast and cable television to wireless and broadband. Not every sports organization can hope to land a billion-dollar contract with a national television network, but every team or league can find a viable niche somewhere in media distribution.

National Broadcast and Cable Networks

Traditionally atop the pyramid are the major national television networks: ABC, CBS, NBC, and FOX. Each boasts affiliated stations that beam the network's programming into 116 million homes with televisions. Each targets the largest possible audience, although those audiences have steadily declined over the last several decades due to the advent of cable, satellite, the Internet, and other media and leisure-time activities. Also, each is mainly fueled by one revenue stream—advertising sales—although each is now able to charge a limited amount of retransmission fees, averaging about $0.50 per subscriber per month, to subscription television services like cable and satellite. This dependence on advertising sales revenues in a fragmented market has increasingly limited the broadcast-only rights fees that broadcast networks and stations can offer up to sports properties.

National basic cable service such as ESPN, FOX Sports Network, NBC Sports Network, and Turner outlets TBS and TNT are available in households with subscription television services provided by cable, satellite, or telcos like Verizon and AT&T. About 90% of the nation's television homes subscribe to cable, satellite, or telco programming services. Therefore, ESPN and similar services reach an audience that is roughly 10% less than those audiences offered up by the national broadcast networks. Also, because subscription television homes receive scores of different television networks, the viewing audience is fragmented. Networks on these services are usually niche broadcasters that tailor their programming to tightly targeted segments of the public. Following this approach, sports networks such as ESPN and FOX Sports are willing to devote their entire programming lineup to sports coverage that major broadcast networks would not consider carrying due to their dependence on generating large, advertiser-friendly audiences that maximize their one main revenue stream.

National cable sports networks like ESPN enjoy a substantial second revenue stream denied to over-the-air broadcasters that helps offset their smaller audience numbers: subscriber fees. Each of these networks charges subscription television distributors a monthly fee for each subscriber, and in many instances, these affiliate revenues far surpass the advertising sales revenues that each can generate. ESPN, the most expensive network on subscription television, is one of the most important examples of the value of affiliate revenues. ESPN's suite of networks, including ESPN, ESPN2, ESPN News, ESPN Deportes and ESPN Classic, average over $5.00 per subscriber per month in fees, a annual windfall of over $6 billion dollars that is reflected in consumer bills, but provides substantial revenues for rights fees and cash flow for its parent company, Disney, which also owns ABC.[15]

The competitive advantage that comes with generating this level of affiliate revenues has become apparent over the past 20 years, as a number of important sports properties have migrated to ESPN from other cable and broadcast networks, including the NBA (in a combined agreement with ABC), college football's Bowl Championship Series, Monday Night Football, and the four Grand Slam tennis tournaments along with renewed agreements with Major League Baseball, the Pac-12, Big Ten and Big 12.

Reflecting the powerful economic forces driving the success of cable sports networks, every owner of a broadcast television network now owns one or more cable sports networks: News Corp. owns FOX-TV, FOX Sports, FX, and Speed. Comcast owns NBC-TV and NBC Sports Network. CBS owns CBS-TV and CBS Sports Network, and Disney owns ABC-TV and the ESPN suite of networks. In turn, each of these owners increasingly is competing for sports property media rights by structuring multi-network bids, where broadcast networks share the financial and distribution load with cable networks that can offer two revenue streams and targeted sports audiences for advertisers. For example, Comcast's recent winning bid for the US television rights for the Olympic Games includes distribution of programming on NBC-TV and NBC Sports Network as well as other Comcast-owned networks such as MSNBC, CNBC, and Bravo. In 2010, CBS joined with Turner's TNT, TBS, and TruTV cable networks to make a successful bid for the NCAA men's basketball tournament. Also, FOX and ESPN's joint agreement for Pac-12 football and basketball includes distribution on their respective broadcast and cable networks.

The growth and success of these national, media company-owned sports networks has also led to the development of professional team, league, and college conference networks. As teams, leagues and conferences profited from increasing rights fee agreements with ESPN, FOX Sports, and TNT, they began to contemplate whether they could reduce their dependency on third-party networks and maximize profitability and asset value by directly distributing their content through cable, satellite, and telcos to consumers. As compared to broadcast networks, which face a complex set of government-mandated equipment and spectrum requirements, cable and satellite networks comparatively are simple to set up and manage. As a result, during the 2000s, Major League Baseball, the NBA, NHL, NFL and the Big Ten all launched their own networks, with the Pac-12 Network launching theirs in 2012.

While each league and conference-owned network has gone through their own set of developmental issues, each has achieved substantial distribution, profitability and asset value by offering a package of live games, along with highlights, news shows, documentaries, and archived broadcasts. From a longer-term perspective, each of these networks provides their respective league or conference with a self-owned outlet that can compete with third-party networks for television rights and allows them to directly reach fans with content across a number of distribution platforms. As technology develops, these networks may provide their owners with the option down the road to reduce or eliminate the need for third-party networks so that each can become a comprehensive, multi-platform content provider.

National radio networks still offer coast-to-coast broadcasts of major sports events, but because of television, they no longer produce the audiences or the revenues they once did. Westwood One/CBS Radio Sports and ESPN Radio are the leading national sports network providers today. Westwood One carries NFL football, the NCAA basketball tournament, Notre Dame football, and the Olympics whereas ESPN offers affiliates Major League Baseball and NBA broadcasts.

Regional Sports Networks

Regional cable sports networks occupy a niche in the market between the national sports networks and local broadcast stations and traditionally specialize in covering local teams and events with strong regional appeal. The first regional sports network launched in 1969, when Madison Square Garden Network debuted, featuring the home games of MSG's teams, the New York Knicks of the NBA, and the New York Rangers of the NHL, along with other sports events taking place at the arena. The launch of MSG Network demonstrated the viability of sports owners' distributing their own content on then-nascent cable television services. Other RSNs followed, although most were owned by third parties who paid basketball and hockey teams to carry their games.

The regional sports network picture shifted radically in 1988 when MSG paid the New York Yankees $486 million dollars over twelve years to carry virtually all of their regular season games on basic cable. To make this agreement work from a financial standpoint, MSG raised its monthly subscription fee to over $1.00 per subscriber per month—an increase of over 250%. Many cable distributors fought the increase, but eventually capitulated when faced with passionate fans eager to watch their hometown team and politicians ready to pursue a settlement. As a result of the MSG/Yankees agreement, other RSNs across the country added baseball teams to their programming lineup.

The RSN marketplace was once again transformed at the turn of the century. In 1999, News Corporation, the multinational parent company of FOX, assumed full control of 21 regional sports networks and launched the FOX Sports Networks. Today, the FOX family of regional sports networks is available to 83 million households and combines regional coverage, the traditional strength of regional channels, with a nationwide platform for programming. Taken together, the FOX Sports Networks control local television rights of baseball, basketball, and hockey teams as well as numerous college sports conferences. In addition, each regional network produces highlight shows and features programs tailored to local fans. FOX also produces national highlight shows and programs shown coast to coast. The creation of FOX Sports Network marked an escalation in News Corporation's declared "ongoing effort to dominate the market in sports broadcasting."[16]

In 2002, the New York Yankees launched YES Network, one of the first times that a Major League Baseball team had owned and controlled an RSN. Due to YES's leverage in the nation's largest media market, the network achieved full basic cable distribution to over 10 million homes, along with an estimated value of over $2 billion dollars. In turn, other teams, leagues and conferences followed suit and launched their own networks, both regionally and nationally.

The evolution of regional sports networks demonstrates how conventional wisdom in the broadcasting industry changes over time. Many RSNs were launched in the 1970s and 1980s as premium services. Borrowing the business plan of HBO, which charges subscribers a monthly fee for programming not available on other channels, network managers bet that fans would pay about $10 a month over and above their basic cable bill to watch the local team. Many did, but many more did not. Today, most RSNs are included in a basic programming package available to the largest number of subscribers for a flat monthly fee. Moreover, RSNs are the second most expensive programming offered on subscription television, surpassed only by ESPN. As a result, RSNs generate substantial total revenues by reaching the largest possible audiences and maximizing both affiliate fees and advertising sales.

Digital Media: Broadband, Wireless, and Tablets

As sports properties engaged in the process of developing their own regional and national television networks, they simultaneously developed programming and production resources that can be readily adapted to digital distribution outlets. Ultimately, for viewers in general and sports fans in particular, a screen is a screen, whether it is a giant in-stadium videoboard, an in-home HD flat screen, a computer, smartphone or tablet. Over the decades, sports fans have demonstrated a readiness to follow their favorite sports and teams across screens. This readiness continues to apply today, as fans have become early adopters and consumers of sports content on various digital media screens.

In order to reach these fans regardless of the technology being viewed, sports properties need to obtain the facilities and skills required to become content providers. In-house studios, production equipment and trained personnel serve to reduce or eliminate the dependence of these properties on third parties to develop and commercialize programming. For most high-profile sports, almost every aspect of their activities generates some level of fan interest, from the games on the field to press conferences to player drafts, community events, and training camps. While not every sports activity is television network-ready, advances in media technology and the expansion of the Internet can provide a commercially-viable screen for nearly every activity. Brief profiles and highlights can work well on smartphones. Longer-form programs and roundtable discussions can be offered up on tablets and Video On Demand. Multiple live game streams can be offered up on computers. In turn, fans, sponsors, distributors and technology manufacturers can all be accessed to generate revenues associated with each form of programming.

Moreover, once programming is produced for one screen, it can be migrated over to others. Repurposed content may need to be re-edited or reformatted to fit screen sizes and ratios, but these limited expenditures allow content providers to reach additional viewers on multiple devices, and generate additional ratings, advertising sales, and fees.

Currently, every professional sports team in the NFL, MLB, NBA, and NHL along with every major college sports program offers up a range of video and audio content on their own websites. Increasingly, these properties are also introducing wireless and broadband apps that make some or all of this content available on smartphones and tablets such as the iPhone and iPad. On the league level, all four of the above leagues utilize these digital devices to offer up live video streams of games, near-instant highlights, and a range of additional video and audio programming.

Moreover, all of these sports properties are building their presence on social networks like Facebook and Twitter. As noted, anything associated with a brand-name sports property has value, from a fan-generated message to a game. By establishing official sites on social networks, these properties offer up other ways for fans to become associated with their favorites, and for sponsors to reach their target audiences. This is of increasing value since sports fans increasingly utilize networks to chat and exchange opinions and information while they simultaneously watch games on other screens. In addition, the personalized nature of social media can, when properly managed, build fan attachments and loyalties. In turn, sports leagues, teams, conferences, and colleges can utilize personalized screens to offer up fan-specific messages, programming, and promotions.

ESPN, FOX Sports, Turner, CBS, and NBC Sports are also in the process of establishing the viability of branded digital platforms for their sports content. Utilizing authentication technology to protect the subscriber fees generated by selling this content to cable, satellite, and telco distributors, each of these media companies is distributing both new and repurposed video programming to their subscribers. One of the most successful sports digital platforms to date is ESPN's ESPN3/WatchESPN. ESPN3 is a network-branded website that offers up thousands of additional sports events that can be accessed by cable, satellite, and telco subscribers whose systems pay an additional fee for this programming. WatchESPN is a section of the site and an app that provides live video streams of ESPN's suite of linear networks. ESPN estimates that ESPN3/Watch ESPN currently has 40,000,000 subscribers nationwide, a figure that they anticipate will double in the near future.

While the audiences for these digital platforms are growing, they still pale in comparison to more traditional forms of media. For example, the Super Bowl match-up between the New York Giants and New England Patriots on February 5, 2012 was the most watched program in the history of television as of that date, with over 111 million viewers. The game was also streamed on both NBCSports.com and NFL.com, and generated the largest audience ever for a streamed event on the Internet: 2.1 million unique users, a record to be sure, but an audience less than 2% of the size that watched the game on broadcast television.

The ratings performance of this game also demonstrates an emerging truth regarding sports media in the digital era—*more is more*. Many sports fans watch games on multiple screens, often simultaneously, as they multitask, check alternate camera angles, view statistics and chat with other fans and friends over social networks. If anything, distributing a sports event across multiple screens seems to enhance overall ratings and interest rather than cannibalize them. The 2012 Summer Olympics accentuated that trend, as NBC generated record television ratings for a non-US based Olympics while offering up every sports event live online and via wireless.

From a long-term perspective, both third-party sports networks and league/team/conference networks are establishing digital platforms that have limited audiences today, but may become primary viewing platforms over the next decade. Presently, authentication is utilized so that the introduction of newer, supplemental digital platforms with relatively small audiences doesn't harm larger revenue streams from established media outlets like broadcast and subscription television. However, it's possible that broadband and/or wireless may grow in usage and viewership to the point where these platforms generate audiences that rival established media audiences. At that point, sports networks may decide to abandon authentication as digital distribution and revenues increase. Over the past 50 years, much the same process occurred as televised sports events migrated from broadcast television to cable networks. Thus, sports networks with digital distribution are trying to prepare for future trends in technology, distribution, viewership, and media revenues.

Syndicators

Syndicators are independent producers who purchase the rights to events or create programs, produce the programs, and then seek to place them on stations or cable services across the country. TVS was the pioneer in the field, and it scored a major coup when it obtained national rights to the UCLA–Houston basketball game in 1968. TVS created a coast-to-coast web of affiliates that delivered a huge national audience. Raycom and other syndicators do the same today, but the growth of cable sports networks, RSNs and league and conference channels has changed the business landscape. Today, much syndicated sports programming appears on cable rather than on over-the-air television. Moreover, major sports leagues, conferences and teams are distributing an increasing amount of programming on their own, rather through third parties.

Syndication remains an important tool for sports producers, particularly those involved with second-tier or newly-launched sports properties. Whether on radio, television, or cable, a syndicator takes responsibility for producing an air-ready broadcast, then offers the complete package to the media outlet for little or no direct cost. The programs are either sold outright to interested outlets or, more frequently, bartered. In a barter arrangement, the outlet agrees to air the program in exchange for the right to sell a predetermined amount of local advertising time. The syndicator makes its money by selling the remaining advertising in the broadcast to national advertisers. Syndicators of some programs, especially popular entertainment shows, use a hybrid system called *cash-barter* in which an outlet pays a fee to air the program and also makes advertising time available to the syndicator. The size of the fee is usually determined by an auction among the stations seeking the program.

Local Television and Radio

There are 1,782 broadcast television stations and nearly 14,500 AM and FM radio stations currently on the air in the United States. Each is scrambling for an audience, and many see sports as a proven audience favorite. Because local broadcast stations by definition serve limited local audiences, they cannot generate the advertising revenue to bid on national events such as the World Series or the NCAA men's basketball tournament. Local stations can and do, however, actively pursue contracts to cover individual teams and typically establish regional networks of affiliates to broaden their audience and advertising base. However, network affiliation program requirements, audience fragmentation and competition from national and regional sports networks has led to a substantial reduction in local television broadcasts of professional sports, with most of them shifting over to regional sports networks.

In a major market, RSN rights fees can be impressive. The New York Yankees generated an annual local television and radio rights fee of over $40 million *before* creating YES, their in-house network, in hopes of generating even greater profits (according to *Forbes*, in 2011 the YES Network paid the Yankees a $90 million rights fee). In smaller markets, teams earn less. As always, the size of the potential audience and competition among potential broadcasters and networks dictates the price paid. However, as more media outlets compete for a relatively fixed number of key regional sports properties, rights fees for these properties are growing regardless of market size. In Houston, competition for the television rights of the Astros and Rockets has led to both teams leaving their longtime FOX relationship for Comcast SportsNet Houston, with the Astros receiving an estimated annual average rights fee of $80 million, which is three times their previous fee from FOX; both teams are receiving equity stakes in the network as well. Also, in Los Angeles, Time Warner Cable outbid FOX for the regional television rights to Los Angeles Lakers basketball for an estimated average annual rights fee of $150 million. In response to the competitive threat, FOX re-signed the Los Angeles Angels for an estimated annual rights fee of $150 million along with an equity stake in the FOX-managed RSN.

In smaller markets where college and minor league franchises often flourish, a team's game may generate no guaranteed rights fee at all. The team may accept a portion of the advertising revenue or help a local station or RSN meet the cost of production simply to gain the total-return benefits of having its schedule broadcast to local fans.

While still a popular outlet for local team sports, broadcast radio has become a less lucrative outlet for revenues as compared to previous decades. The growth of digital media players like iPods and satellite radio have led to declining radio audiences and advertising sales. In light of these pressures, many stations have reduced or eliminated rights fees for local team radio broadcasts. This change is most pronounced with Major League Baseball teams, which used to receive the bulk of their regional media revenues from radio. Today, only about half of all MLB clubs receive radio rights fees, with the rest involved in various forms of barter or revenue-sharing relationships with local stations.

MARKETING AND MANAGING BROADCAST RIGHTS

Sports properties and media outlets are partners. The relationship between a team and a radio or television station or network can survive and prosper only if both parties are satisfied they are receiving a fair return, either in immediate profit or in long-term gains such as promotions, competitive advantage, or improved public image.

Media rights may be assigned in several ways, but in all cases, the sports property and outlet work together, and nearly everything is negotiable. For example, a sports organization may want to reserve advertising time during a broadcast to promote upcoming games and season-ticket packages. This request reduces the outlet's inventory of commercial air time and limits potential profit. Therefore, the outlet may utilize this deal point to seek advantages such as free tickets, venue signage, advertising space in the team's game program, personal appearances by players, or similar benefits.

Media contracts routinely reveal tradeoffs. Rather than simply maximizing the amount of cash they can realize through rights fees, many sports teams also ask for commercial time to promote themselves or their corporate sponsors, authority to determine the announcers for the game, time for a weekly coaches' show, or use of the outlet's production facilities to produce advertisements or promotional videos. Outlets will agree to pay more for rights to a team's game if they can freely use the team's marks (e.g., name, logo) and personnel for on-air or in-person promotions, if they can be guaranteed choice seats for clients, or if they can have a say in the team's scheduling to ensure the game fits in the outlet's broadcast lineup. In order to accommodate television schedules and pre-game coverage, for example, many major athletic contests are scheduled to start 8 minutes after the hour or half-hour. Many major college basketball and football teams willingly agree to schedule certain opponents and adjust game times in accordance to their media partners' wishes.

Within this partnership framework, however, sports media deals are almost always arranged in one of three ways: (a) direct sales of rights from a property to a network or distributor for a guaranteed right fee, (b) in-house production of games by the team or league that then syndicates the broadcast, or (c) a cooperative or revenue-sharing agreement in which both the teams or league share the potential profit and, in some cases, the loss with the media partner.

Direct Sales of Rights

If a sports property's product is a proven commodity in the marketplace, networks will be eager to bid for rights. Major professional leagues and teams and major colleges frequently choose between rival stations or networks seeking the rights to broadcast their games.

Both rights holders and networks consider many variables as they bargain over rights fees. Networks look at production and distribution costs, but they also consider audience demographics and how the games will affect their overall broadcast schedule, and they frequently agree to carry less attractive games to gain access to key events. Traditionally, regular-season MLB games of the week attract small viewing audiences because fans follow their local franchises and show little interest in battles between out-of-town clubs. FOX agreed to baseball's demands for regular-season coverage in order to gain the rights to the All-Star Game, League Championship Series, and World Series.

On the other hand, sports organizations will sometimes leave money on the bargaining table to ensure greater exposure and broadcast services. The NCAA's original 1989 contract with CBS for men's basketball tournament telecasts required CBS to air selected games from the women's basketball tournament as well as NCAA championships in baseball, track, swimming, and a dozen other low-profile sports. CBS executives actually offered to pay the NCAA a higher rights fee if they did not have to carry the additional telecasts, but the NCAA accepted less money in order to get the additional exposure. When the tournament contract was renegotiated in 1994, the NCAA was able to sell the women's basketball tournament to ESPN as part of a separate contract. The value of the women's tournament had been increased significantly by the network exposure on CBS.

When a sports organization sells rights to a network, it should maintain as much control over the product as possible to protect its branding and image for fans and sponsors. Teams and leagues regularly demand and receive permission to veto a station or network's choice of announcers. Rights holders may also negotiate advertising restrictions that can benefit corporate sponsors by keeping the competition off the air. These points are, of course, negotiable and will usually require give and take with the network.

In-house Production

Despite the proliferation of outlets for televising sporting events, it is difficult for many new and second-tier sports properties to succeed in having their games or events aired regularly on broadcast or cable outlets in return for rights fees. In deciding to air sporting events, networks consider a range of factors, including the size of the potential audience, the cost of producing the event, and the attractiveness of the event to commercial sponsors. The demand for many sporting events in terms of both audience and commercial appeal may be insufficient initially to attract a media partner, particularly one eager to pay a rights fee to the sports organization to air the event and absorb all production costs. Sports managers who hope to benefit from television exposure may be able to change the calculus by producing their own broadcasts and distributing the finished programs.

World Wrestling Entertainment (WWE) is the classic example of the benefit of in-house production. Pro wrestling's popularity has ebbed and flowed. Titan Sports of Stamford, Connecticut (the parent company of WWE) arranged matches, hired announcers and technical crew, and offered finished programs to stations around the country at no cost. All the WWE demanded in return was the right to sell a portion of advertising time. Station operators who would not have considered telecasting a wrestling program if they had to produce and pay for it themselves gladly accepted the offer. Broadcasters received professionally produced programs that appealed to a younger demographic, especially teens, and any advertising revenue the station's sales corps generated was theirs to keep. The WWE used the programs as promotional platforms for upcoming pay-per-view and live shows and covered the cost of production and distribution by selling its allotment of commercial time to fast food chains, video-game manufacturers, candy makers, and others who wanted to make their pitch to a teen audience.

As the WWE surged in popularity throughout the 1990s, broadcasters began to battle for the right to carry the wrestling programs. The WWE signed a national distribution deal with the USA cable network, then in 1999 struck an even better deal with Viacom networks MTV and TNN, and eventually migrated back to USA and its sister Comcast/NBC Universal network Syfy. Recently, the WWE announced plans to launch their own cable network comprised of new and archived events—the same approach utilized in developing team-owned RSNs like the New York Yankees' YES Network, and league-owned networks like NFL Network, MLB Network, NBA TV, and NHL Network.

Many college sports networks are also self produced. Brigham Young University beams coverage of BYU sports to stations throughout the mountain states on BYU TV, using staff and equipment from the school's radio and television facility. West Virginia University's Mountaineer Sports Network produces games as well as coaches' shows and a weekly sports magazine in WVU's on-campus broadcast center, and distributes the programs to stations around the state. The University of Hawaii has begun distributing their own programming within the state through a distribution partnership with Oceanic Cablevision (owned by Time Warner Cable). More individual colleges and universities have turned to production and marketing companies like IMG to package radio and television broadcasts of their games.

By controlling production themselves, sports organizations maintain complete control of their broadcasts and can ensure their product is presented and promoted in a positive manner. Because they do not have to bear the cost of production, many outlets, especially in smaller markets, find games and related programs a means of filling airtime with impressive programming they could not otherwise afford to air. Ideally, in-house networks sell enough advertising to cover the cost of production and turn a profit. Colleges and pro teams frequently include broadcast advertising on their in-house network in sponsorship packages, which can include stadium signage, game program, team yearbook and website advertising, and sponsorship of radio and television broadcasts for one price. Even if an in-house radio or television network operates at a loss, sports managers should consider the value of game broadcasts as an advertising and promotion vehicle.

Revenue Sharing

As the cost of media rights has risen and the inventory of sports advertising time has increased, many third-party sports networks have instituted revenue-sharing agreements with some properties as a means of ensuring against losses. Under revenue-sharing agreements, sports properties split revenues generated from a broadcast with their media partner.

The NHL and the NBA were among the first to incorporate revenue sharing in their national network television contracts. The NHL received a $250 million deal with FOX and ESPN by assuring the broadcasters that league sponsors such as Anheuser-Busch and VISA would purchase television advertising as part of their sponsorship. When NBC and the NBA agreed to a four-year, $868 million contract in 1994, the league agreed to forego guaranteed rights payments over a certain level in exchange for a share of advertising revenue. Eventually, both the NHL and NBA were able to strike rights fee agreements with NBC-TV/NBC Sports Network and with ESPN and TNT, respectively, which reflected greater popularity and increased media outlet competition. Today, revenue sharing agreements are increasingly being utilized for newer, second-tier sports properties and on the local level for team radio rights.

Media outlets endorse revenue sharing because it protects them from downturns in advertising sales or the team's on-field fortunes. If a team slumps and advertising sales decline, the outlet is not required to pay a lump sum. Because the team benefits if advertising sales increase, radio stations find that teams are eager to become active broadcast-time sellers rather than passive partners. Revenue sharing can be beneficial for start-up leagues and local team radio because by becoming financial partners in broadcasts with a stake in the program's success, they are incentivized to exercise more control over the production and promotion of their games. These properties also use advertising sales for game broadcasts to enhance their integrated corporate sponsorship packages.

Revenue sharing has also become a cornerstone of the multimedia relationships that major colleges have developed with third-party agencies such as IMG College and

Learfield. Due to the proliferating complexity and expense of running athletic departments that may include upward of 20 or more individual sports, colleges often sell the television, radio and digital media rights for these sports to agencies in return for a financial guarantee. In turn, the agencies commercialize these rights through a range of distribution and sponsorship agreements.

However, in order to generate additional revenues and larger audiences, several schools and conferences have begun to deal directly with media companies in distributing their programming via their own television channels. The Big Ten and Mountain West Conferences began this trend, with the Big Ten generating substantial financial success through a year-round television channel that features selected second- and third-tier football games, men's and women basketball, and a wide range of events featuring other conference sports. This channel, co-owned with FOX, provides nationwide distribution and revenues from monthly subscriber fees and advertising sales to each Big Ten school over and above pre-existing rights agreements with ABC/ESPN and FOX for marquee conference programming. In 2012, the Pac-12 took this approach one step further by launching its own channel without a media equity partner.

In addition, school-specific channels have recently been launched for The University of Texas and The University of Oklahoma. The University of Texas's channel, the Longhorn Network, is owned and operated by ESPN, with the school receiving a rights fee totaling $300 million over 20 years in return for the media rights to one to two football games per season, men's and women's basketball and other UT sports. While the agreement is lucrative for the school, the channel has faced substantial distribution challenges in its early years due to resistance from cable and satellite distributers. Oklahoma has taken a somewhat different approach, reaching agreement to distribute thousands of hours of OU sports programming on pre-existing FOX RSNs and national college sports platforms. While the fees are less than those received by Texas, OU's programming strategy avoids distribution issues. As with any new channel, these efforts face distribution and sponsorship challenges. Still, they reflect the increasing value of and receptive marketplace for college sports programming.

Barter agreements are another form of revenue sharing used most commonly by minor league teams and colleges in smaller markets. Typically, under such an arrangement the local television, RSN, or radio station that agrees to air the game pays no rights fee. Instead, the sports property offers all or a portion of the game's commercial inventory to the media outlet, who in turn sells this air time to local or regional advertisers. A good example of such a barter agreement is the manner in which the Oregon Sports Network offers University of Oregon football broadcasts to its radio affiliates. The OSN radio network includes 24 radio stations that broadcast Oregon football games and a weekly coaches' show to a regional audience in four states. Only two of the radio stations, one in Portland and one in Eugene, pay an upfront rights fee to exclusively broadcast the games in their markets. All of the other network affiliates air the broadcast through a barter agreement with the University of Oregon athletic department (represented by IMG College). For many of the radio stations in small markets, like Klamath Falls or Hood River, OR, paying a rights fee is not financially feasible. Instead, the Oregon Sports Network provides game content (and the coaches' show) to 22 affiliates for free. The arrangement allows the local radio station to sell 30% of the available commercial air time in its local markets. The OSN claims the remaining 70% of the commercial broadcast inventory, which it can sell over the entire 24 station network. The way the arrangement works is that typically each football game broadcast will contain ninety-seven 30-second commercial breaks, known as commercial units or CUs. Of this total inventory, OSN will control 70% or 68 of the CUs, and 30% or 29 CUs will be provided to the local affiliate. This arrangement is attractive to both parties. The local radio stations are provided with the opportunity to sell highly attractive air time to local advertisers without incurring any production costs, and the broadcast feed is provided free to each affiliate. OSN is able to deliver the radio broadcast to a much broader audience and use the expanded reach to induce advertisers to pay higher rates to deliver their message to a broad regional audience.

The barter-agreement approach may be well suited to a sports property trying to build fan interest in a new market. An outlet interested in finding new programming may be willing to take a chance on an unproven commodity, such as a new minor league baseball team, if the outlet does not have to make a financial commitment in advance of the first broadcast. In this circumstance, a team primarily interested in increasing its exposure to local fans may assign the entire inventory of commercials to the outlet. The goal is to achieve a win-win outcome for both the outlet and the new team. Eventually, if the broadcasts are successful in building a substantial audience, it is likely the team could renegotiate a more favorable revenue-sharing arrangement with its media partner.

SPORTS TELEVISION AND MEDIA CONTRACTS

Each major sports property is unique in the way it handles its media relationships. The following section provides an historical perspective and description of the nature and scope of each property's current media agreements.

National Football League

All regular and postseason television rights rest with the league, and revenues are divided equally among all franchises. This unique policy of all-for-one, one-for-all "league-think" was advocated by former commissioner Pete Rozelle and made legal by the Sports Broadcast Act of 1961, which granted an antitrust exemption to the four major professional sports for pooled broadcast contracts. Rozelle understood the broadcasting industry, knew the value of expanding the bidding pool, and involved as many outlets as possible for NFL games. He expanded the NFL's inventory by introducing *Monday Night Football* on ABC in 1970 and Sunday night cable games on ESPN and TNT.

The NFL's revenue-sharing policy allowed small-market teams like the Green Bay Packers to survive. Individual teams retain local radio and preseason TV rights, but earnings from these local contracts are relatively small, approximately $3–5 million per year, as opposed to the approximately $200 million per year each franchise receives from the sale of national rights to CBS, FOX, NBC, ESPN, and DirecTV. CBS handles AFC games and playoffs, FOX handles NFC games and playoffs, NBC handles *Sunday*

Night Football, and all three carry the Super Bowl on a rotating basis. ESPN offers up *Monday Night Football*, which formerly aired on ABC-TV.

The nationwide popularity of NFL football has also led to the successful creation of a number of other programming packages and media platforms. NFL out-of-market games, those games not carried by local broadcast stations in a particular market, have been packaged and sold to DirecTV, which sells them to consumers as NFL Sunday Ticket. This package has been instrumental in driving the growth of DirecTV, which is now the second largest subscription television distributor in the United States. In addition, NFL Red Zone, an offshoot of NFL Sunday Ticket which provides live cut-ins to games around the league, has been sold to various cable operators. The NFL's contract with DirecTV provides another lucrative revenue stream for the league. The existing contract calls for DirecTV to pay $1 billion a year to the NFL for the exclusive rights to sell the Sunday Ticket package.

As noted above, the NFL has launched its own network to carry a package of 13 regular season games, plus highlights, studio shows and archival material. While 13 live football games may not seem like a large number of events for a 24/7/365 channel, NFL Network capitalizes on the year-round appetite that fans have for any league- or team-related programming concerning America's most popular team sport. NFL Network is owned by the league and its team owners, who profit not only from the increasing cash flow generated by the network, but also from its increasing asset valuation.

Major League Baseball

Because baseball was a mainstay on the radio by the mid-1920s and on television by the late 1940s, local contracts were in place long before national television networks became well established in the 1950s. Major-market teams in New York and Chicago prospered under the system of "localism" and had little incentive to share the wealth with smaller-market teams. When network games of the week debuted on television in the 1950s, the contract blacked out games in the major league cities when the home team's games were on local TV. Baseball fans developed intense local loyalties and had little opportunity to become familiar with other major league teams. As a result, while known as America's national pastime, nationally televised baseball has been surpassed in ratings popularity by the NFL. Critics say baseball has suffered in television ratings because it is not a "made-for-television" sport that neatly fits network schedules or television screen proportions. Nevertheless, baseball remains a much sought-after property by national broadcast and cable networks, and generates ever-increasing rights fees for national telecasts.

On a regional level, baseball's substantial number of games per season and intense fan loyalties make the sport increasingly valuable for RSNs. The fans' fixation with their local teams has led to a sharp financial division between the media "haves" and "have-nots." Major-market teams such as the Yankees and Dodgers, and clubs that enjoy large regional fan bases such as the Rangers and Red Sox, command regional media contracts that can generate up to $1,000,000 or more per regular season game in rights fees and cash flow. Smaller-market clubs such as Milwaukee and Kansas City claim a fraction of that. However, with strengthening national media revenues, the development of new stadiums, the institution of league taxes on teams with high payrolls and the use of revenue sharing, an increasing number of smaller-market teams like St. Louis, Tampa Bay, and Milwaukee have become more competitive in recent years.

Baseball remains one of the important properties in sports media. It is the only major team sport that plays throughout the summer months and provides thousands of hours of warm-weather programming. ESPN, Turner, and FOX pay Major League Baseball a combined total of $12.4 billion for media rights to games through 2013 in order to fill those summer hours. ESPN televises Sunday Night Baseball and weeknight games throughout the regular season. Turner offers up Sunday afternoon telecasts along with Divisional and League Championship playoff games. FOX airs Saturday's Game of the Week, selected Divisional playoff games, one of the League Championship playoffs, and the World Series. Given the ongoing popularity of MLB games and the increasing number of media platforms chasing after a limited number of key brand-name sports properties like baseball, baseball's television rights will continue to rise for the foreseeable future. One indication of this trend is that ESPN's reported renewal of its MLB package in 2012 includes annual rights fees estimated at $700 million, nearly double those provided in their previous agreement.[17]

The value of baseball as a media property is also reflected in the recent sales of Major League Baseball franchises. In 2009, the Chicago Cubs were purchased by the Ricketts family for $845 million, the highest price ever paid as of that date for an MLB club, and a price that reflected in part the value of the Cubs' percentage of MLB's national media agreements and the team's co-ownership of Comcast SportsNet Chicago, an RSN launched in 2004. Then, in 2012, the Los Angeles Dodgers were sold to a group led by Mark Walters, Stan Kasten and former NBA great Magic Johnson for a record price of over $2 billion. This price tag in part reflected the substantial upside for the Dodgers in negotiating a revised or new RSN agreement with one of several competitive media companies in the marketplace.

MLB has also demonstrated substantial success in launching various league-owned media platforms. MLB Network, co-owned by the league and a number of cable and satellite companies, carries over 100 regular season games, two early round playoff games, and has substantial distribution on most major cable and satellite companies. MLB.TV is the league's broadband and wireless distribution platform for out-of-market games and has become an industry benchmark for the successful digital distribution of live events on multiple screens. The league's Extra Innings package offers up the same out-of-market games to cable and satellite subscribers.

National Basketball Association

The NBA combines aspects of football's and baseball's broadcasting policies. The NBA has a national presence with regular season and playoff games on ABC, ESPN, and Turner for which the league receives $930 million per year through 2016. However, a substantial percentage of each team's media revenues comes from regional television packages. The NBA was a pioneer in mixing over-the-air and cable television coverage, and NBA games remain a major selling point for many RSNs. Basketball fans can follow their local teams throughout the season, but because of the league's national contract, they can watch other teams dozens of times each season as well.

Played on a brightly illuminated indoor court just 30 yards long, basketball is a television-friendly sport. From the beginning, cameras gave viewers an intimate look at the action. Technological advances such as slow-motion replay and extreme close-ups emphasize the grace, physical skill, and emotion of the players.

Like other professional leagues, the NBA has become a content provider that offers up a number of programming packages and platforms directly to distributors and to fans. Over a decade ago, the league launched NBA TV, a pioneer in league networks. Today, NBA TV is run in partnership with Turner, and provides approximately 100 regular season games, several early-round playoff games, highlights, and studio shows to about 60 million subscribers. The league also offers up successful out-of-market packages along with broadband and wireless platforms.

National Hockey League

Although NFL and NBA games are particularly telegenic, often enhancing the viewing experience, hockey has not fared nearly as well as a televised sport. Network contracts with CBS, NBC, and FOX came and went because of low ratings. Critics argued that fans unfamiliar with the game could not follow the puck during telecasts. NBC tried to correct this by teaching newcomers the fine points with the cartoon icon Peter Puck, and FOX experimented with computer enhancement that turned the puck into a colorful computer streak. Although clubs in major markets with established hockey traditions flourish, the league's national television agreements have struggled in comparison to other major team sports. However, in 2012, increasing competition for brand-name sports properties led to a substantial boost in the league's national television revenues. In 2012, the NHL signed a $2.0 billion, 10-year deal with NBC-TV and NBC Sports Network. The new agreement, which pays the league an average of $200 million annually, represents a significant increase over the $77.5 million a year Versus sports network (now NBC Sports Network) had been paying the league under the previous broadcast rights contract. In addition, the league has five-year agreements in place with two Canadian media companies, the Canadian Broadcast Corporation (CBC) and TSN, worth $600 million and $240 million, respectively. While the total value of the NHL broadcast package, at about $368 million a year, is worth less than half of NBA's annual national television income, the league has made significant progress. NBC Sports reported that NHL TV ratings in the US had risen 84% since the 2007–08 season.[18]

NASCAR

Long seen as a regional sport, NASCAR has become an acknowledged leader in sports marketing and avid fan interest. In 1999, NASCAR convinced racetrack owners across the country to relinquish their television rights and then went on to sign 6-year deals worth a total of $2.4 billion with FOX, NBC, and Turner to broadcast Winston Cup (now named Sprint Cup) and Busch Series races. Then, in 2005, NASCAR signed

8-year agreements with a combination of old and new broadcast partners. The multi-network deals extend the racing circuit's partnership with FOX, TNT, and the Speed Network. In addition, NASCAR added ABC/ESPN to its multi-network lineup. Each of the networks gets exclusive rights to a selected number of Sprint Cup Series events. As part of the deal, FOX was given the broadcast rights to the Daytona 500, the most-watched NASCAR race each year, while ABC/ESPN was given the rights to air the final 17 races of the Cup series, including "the Chase," NASCAR's version of the playoffs in which the 12 best drivers compete for points over the last 10 races to determine the season's champion driver. Collectively, FOX, ABC/ESPN, Speed, and TNT television are paying NASCAR $4.48 billion through 2014 to air all 36 regular season races.

Recently, NASCAR television ratings have climbed after a 3-year downturn from 2008 through 2010. Ratings for the 2011 season averaged 5.0, with an average of 8.6 million viewers, up almost 10% from the previous season. Most importantly, males aged 18–34 have returned to watching NASCAR events, with viewership for this difficult-to-reach segment up more than 20% compared to 2010. While a few years ago, NASCAR was expected to take a "huge haircut" in its next TV agreement, its recent ratings resurgence should result in continued growth for the sport's media revenues.

National Collegiate Athletic Association

Because it is not covered by the antitrust provision of the Sports Broadcast Act, the NCAA owns rights only to its own championship events. The Universities of Georgia and Oklahoma went to court to break the longstanding NCAA football cartel in 1983. Since then, each school has the authority to make its own television deals. As a result, the airwaves have been flooded by literally thousands of football and basketball games, fragmenting the viewing audience, increasing the inventory of advertising availability, and reducing the market value of any one game.

However, in the midst of reduced ratings for other programming categories, audience and distributor interest in major college sports programs in general, and college football in particular, have led to a growing marketplace for rights fees. As with professional team sports, there are an increasing number of media companies and technological firms that are eager to carry college content. As a result, ESPN/ABC, FOX, Comcast/NBCUniversal, CBS, and Turner have all reached long-term deals with major college conferences like the SEC, Pac-12, Big Ten and Big 12 that provides each member school from $20–25 million annually in national media rights fees.

The only university with its own broadcast network-television football contract is Notre Dame, with NBC. For the rest of the collegiate sports world, conference agreements are the rule. It is not considered an antitrust violation if conference members voluntarily pool their broadcast rights, and both media outlets and advertisers find regional conference packages to be a desirable way to reach advertisers.

Because of the proliferation of college games on television, ratings and advertising revenues have declined for regular season contests, particularly for college basketball. However, these declines have stabilized in recent years, and the passion and demographics of college sports fans make them prime targets for networks, subscription television providers, and advertisers. Moreover, from a content perspective, major college sports programs often participate in 20 or more sports, which means a substantial amount of content that can be commercialized across a range of media platforms. Granted, football has a larger audience and more commercial opportunities than other collegiate sports, but in the digital era, each sport can be commercially viable on an appropriate mix of screens. Football, for example, can work on national broadcast and cable networks, while volleyball or wrestling might work best on VOD or live streamed on broadband or wireless. In light of these options, colleges increasingly see television and multimedia exposure for all their sports as an important marketing tool, a valuable asset in recruiting student-athletes and non-athlete undergraduates, for rallying alumni, and for increasing public support.

The NCAA's television "gold mine" is the Division I men's basketball tournament. The NCAA signed a 14-year, $10.8 billion contract with CBS and Turner that hiked the NCAA's March Madness revenue to an average of over $771 million per year. During the term of the agreement, all tournament games will be televised on either CBS-TV, TNT, TBS, or Turner-owned TruTV. The NCAA/CBS/Turner agreement is innovative and elevates multimedia partnerships to a new level. In exchange for $10.8 billion, CBS and Turner received exclusive rights to tournament television, radio, and Internet broadcasts as well as to most marketing, licensing, and promotional opportunities. The CBS/Turner relationship came together as CBS came to the realization that subscription television, with its two revenue streams of affiliate fees and ad sales, was needed to make the tournament financially successful going forward. Because the agreement allows the Final Four and Final games to eventually migrate to cable, the media marketplace will be watching to see how this move impacts ratings and if it creates any political concerns over the loss of marquee events on "free" television.

As for college football, the creation of a March Madness-style season-ending tournament generating billions in television revenues has been stymied by the college bowl system, where numerous organizations invite top schools to play in their games. Recently, the lure of additional media revenues led the top college conferences and bowl games to create a season-ending Bowl Championship Series culminating in a showdown between the nation's top two college football teams. FOX, and then ESPN purchased rights to this series, which has been financially successful but has fallen short of being perceived by the public as a true playoff system. Plans are for the BCS to be re-tooled into a Final Four of football, which should lead to substantial distributor interest and increased rights fees for the Series.

The Olympic Games

The Olympic Games are unique among major sporting events because they attract a predominantly female audience. As a major international event, the Olympics can command huge audiences for two consecutive weeks, and the networks will pay lavish sums for broadcast rights. NBC purchased rights for all Winter and Summer Games from 2000 through 2008 and then won a 2011 auction that extended their rights through the 2020 Games for a record amount of $4.38 billion.

The network paid $456 million for rights to the 1996 Atlanta Games and was rewarded with record ratings and public visibility. The 2000 Summer Games in Sydney, however, were a ratings disappointment, if not an outright disaster. TV ratings were down 36% from Atlanta, the lowest for any Olympics since 1968, averaging a 13.8 rating and a 24 share. Observers blamed the decline on NBC's reliance on pretaped events and a lack of compelling characters and stories, but as NBC pointed out, the Olympics allowed NBC to attract a larger audience than any of its competitors and turn a profit on the games.

Despite these ratings fluctuations, NBC, FOX and ESPN all submitted bids for two Winter Olympics and two Summer Olympics, stretching from 2014 through 2020, with NBC submitting a winning bid that was approximately $1 billion higher than FOX's bid. This increase reflects the changing landscape of the media industry. More competitors with more digital screens are bidding up proven ratings performers like the Olympics. Also, with these digital screens in place, Olympics telecasts can now include thousands of hours of programming covering every aspect of the competition, with winning media companies able to charge subscription fees and generate ad sales for Olympic programming across cable, satellite, broadband, and wireless.

Roone Arledge of ABC Sports pioneered modern coverage of the Olympics. He emphasized the stories of the athletes, bringing viewers "up close and personal" and giving them a reason to become emotionally involved in "the thrill of victory and the agony of defeat." NBC's recent coverage has been criticized for devoting too much time to the stories and not enough to the competition, but this was the network's intent in order to attract the broadest possible audience. NBC conducted exhaustive audience research and determined viewers wanted "not sports but stories about sports, stories that focused on patriotism, triumph over adversity, interesting personalities and the like, a continuing narrative which, like any drama would draw them in" (p. 27).[19] Because the Olympic audience closely resembled the typical television audience dominated by women with a large percentage of teenagers, NBC devoted many hours to sports such as gymnastics, swimming, and equestrian events, which appealed to younger, suburban women, the prototypical "soccer mom" who is seen as a key consumer and decision maker. NBC's coverage of recent Winter Olympics games made a bid for younger viewers by giving plenty of time to extreme sports such as freestyle skiing and snowboard events.

Now, with the introduction of additional digital outlets carrying Olympic programming, sports fans can now choose their own Olympics by focusing on their favorite sports. Major events are streamed live online, and not embargoed for primetime broadcast as with previous Games. As with the 2012 simulcast of the Super Bowl on multiple screens, this approach has enhanced ratings and provided additional advertising and subscription revenue opportunities. The 2012 Summer Olympics from London are a perfect example of how a multi-screen Olympics can work. Alongside the traditional taped primetime highlights shown on broadcast television, the Games were shown live across an array of cable networks, online, wireless and social media digital platforms. Rather than cannibalize primetime viewership, the so-called "Twitter Olympics" generated the largest primetime ratings for a non-US based Olympics games in decades, while

streamed events garnered some of the largest audiences to date for live events shown on
the Internet and wireless.

Golf and Tennis

Golf and tennis are regularly seen on television, but they rarely draw large audiences.
The relatively small audiences, however, include a high proportion of difficult-to-reach,
upper-income men—demographics that are highly desirable to certain advertisers. Tennis and golf tournament advertising frequently includes sports equipment chosen to
appeal to this distinct audience as well as luxury cars, business travel-related products
such as hotels, airlines and credit cards, and financial planning instruments. For example, the Masters golf tournament is presented by CBS, ESPN, and the Augusta National Golf Club as a "prestige" event with low-key, limited advertising. The Masters
sponsors are usually companies like upscale auto manufacturers and financial firms that
seek an upscale audience and sell primarily to affluent, older males. Tennis is attempting to cultivate a younger and more diverse television audience, but the sport's bedrock
viewers remain older and more affluent than the typical television audience.

Despite the demographic advantage that golf and tennis provides to advertisers, both
sports are experiencing the same trends impacting other televised properties. The majority of golf and tennis tournaments now appear on subscription television, with ESPN
covering the major tennis tournaments except for some finals airing on broadcast channels, The Tennis Channel showing most of the other professional tournaments, and
Comcast/NBCUniversal's Golf Channel showing early round coverage of most golf
tournaments. Digital coverage for major tournaments is also being offered up on websites and specialized channels covering specific golfers, golf holes, or tennis courts.

Boxing and Mixed Martial Arts

Boxing was omnipresent on television in the 1940s and 1950s, but it has largely faded
from the broadcast television scene. Boxing boasts an intensely loyal audience of older
men, and gamblers who will attend major bouts in Las Vegas and other resorts with
legalized gambling. The sport suffers from an image of violence and corruption, and
this discourages many advertisers. In recent years, younger boxing fans have been
siphoned away from boxing by professional wrestling and increasingly by mixed martial
arts, led by the UFC. Mixed martial arts competitions are shorter and more violent
than boxing, and have built substantial audiences on subscription television. UFC
events have become mainstays of Pay Per View (PPV), and the property has embarked
on an important new relationship with FOX, which airs events on FOX-TV and on its
FX cable channel.

Because boxing retains a loyal core of fans, it remains popular on cable, with bouts
airing regularly on ESPN, HBO and Showtime, and has been a leader in PPV telecasts.
Major fights are sold to viewers on a per-event basis, with the payout usually divided
equally between the promoter and the local cable system or satellite distributor. Major
boxing championships may attract pay-per-view "buy rates" of 3–4% of potential homes,
which is small in terms of mass media, but in dollar terms, the income can be enor-

mous. Important fights have grossed $40 million or more in pay-per-view revenue for cable and satellite distributors.

International Sports

On April 2, 1965, the first commercial communication satellite—Intelsat I—was launched into the Earth's orbit. Today, dozens of satellites circle the globe, orbiting in time with the Earth's rotation so they remain fixed at a constant point in the sky. These geosynchronous satellites enable television signals to be flashed to viewers around the world at the speed of light. Moreover, the Internet inexpensively connects computers and digital screens around the world. These technological advantages have led to rapid growth in the international audience for programming, with sports remaining a favorite source. ESPN, through its international services and worldwide affiliates, now has more viewers overseas than in the United States. Direct satellite services are making multi-channel television programming available to hundreds of millions of viewers in Asia, Africa, and Latin America. Channels like EUROSPORT provide 24-hour sports coverage, similar to ESPN, across Europe.

Sports with international appeal stand to profit in this new environment. The Olympics are a worldwide attraction. The 2010 FIFA Soccer World Cup in South Africa attracted a large worldwide television audience. A combined total of over 2 billion people watched the 2010 World Cup in the 18 markets measured by Nielsen Media Research. The final between Italy and the Netherlands was the most watched match, with nearly 700 million viewers tuning in.[20] Formula 1 auto racing, international test cricket, and professional soccer and rugby now play before worldwide audiences. In addition, digital distribution allows displaced fans to follow their favorite sports regardless of their location or time zone. The growing interrelation among the world's broadcast systems may also lead to plush times for some sports. For instance, Rupert Murdoch's News Corporation controls the FOX network in the United States, the Seven networks in Australia, B-Sky-B satellite television in Great Britain, and similar services around the world. Murdoch organized an international rugby league, Super League, that is telecast worldwide on his News Corporation networks. International programmers with hours of airtime to fill will continue to look to sports as a primary source of programming, and events that can travel across international borders will be at a premium.

SUMMARY

The sale of media rights is a major source of revenue for many sports properties.

The demand for sports media has only increased with the advent of subscription television and digital media platforms, each of which utilize games, events and related programming to drive ratings, subscription, retention and advertising.

Cable networks are "niche broadcasters" that target their programming to specific segments of the public. Sports cable networks are able to tap into two revenue streams: advertising sales and subscriber fees and so can attract more and better programming and generate impressive financial results.

The evolution of RSNs demonstrates how the sports media industry has adapted to the marketplace, by expanding the size of their audience, realizing greater affiliate and ad sales revenues, and also attracting the attention of teams, leagues and conferences who increasingly have established their own networks to maximize programming resources and financial results.

Local broadcast stations can and do actively pursue contracts to cover individual teams. However, most local and regional sports telecasts have migrated over to regional sports networks.

Sports producers and media companies are partners in sports media agreements. Both parties must be satisfied they are receiving a fair return on each transaction, either in immediate profit or in long-term gains such as promotions, competitive advantage, or improved public image.

Each of the major league professional sports properties manages its media contracts differently, though all are increasingly exploiting their rights across a range of traditional and digital media platforms. In the NFL, all regular and postseason television rights rest with the league, and revenues are divided equally among all franchises. With MLB, teams control the regional television rights to the majority of their regular season games, leading to wide disparities in media revenues across large and small markets. The NBA combines aspects of football's and baseball's broadcasting policies. It has a national presence with regular season and playoff games on ABC, ESPN, and Turner, but much of each team's broadcast revenues come from local television and radio packages. The NBA was a pioneer in mixing over-the-air and cable television coverage. NBA games remain a major selling point for many regional sport channels. The NHL has not fared as well as a televised sport. Although clubs in major markets with established hockey traditions flourish, the league's national television agreement is the weakest among major team sports.

NASCAR has become an acknowledged leader in sports marketing and promotion. In 2007, NASCAR signed a $2.4 billion, 6-year deal with FOX, ABC/ESPN, and Turner to broadcast Sprint Cup and Busch series races. With the NCAA, the increasing value of name-brand college sports content in the marketplace, particularly for football, has led to a substantial upswing in rights fees for major conferences, schools and the NCAA Men's Basketball Tournament

The Olympic Games are unique in that they attract a predominantly female audience, are a major international event, and are televised for two weeks. For these reasons, networks will pay huge sums for media rights, which are now being utilized across broadcast and subscription television, broadband, and wireless.

Golf and tennis are regularly seen on television, but rarely draw large audiences. The audience for these sports, however, tends to include upper-income men who are difficult for advertisers to reach and are considered a highly desirable target market.

Although boxing still boasts a loyal core of fans, primarily older men, mixed martial arts properties such as UFC are rapidly gaining fans and media revenues from an audience of younger viewers.

The international television audience is growing rapidly, and sport remains a preferred programming option. ESPN now has more viewers overseas than in the United States, and channels like EUROSPORT provide 24-hour sports coverage across Europe.

References

1. Gelles, D. (2012, May 3). Glued to the screen. *Financial Times.com.* Retrieved from http://www.ft.com/cms/s/0/dad300f8-92bf-11el-9e0a-01144feab49a.html

2. Kaplan, D. (2011, December 5). Report: New NFL TV deal worth $24 billion. *Buffalo Business First.* Retrieved from http://www.bizjournals.com/buffalo/news/2011/12/05/report-new-nfl-tv-deals-worth-24b.hmtl?5-print

3. Badenhausen, K. (2011, December 14). The NFL signs TV deal worth $27 billion. *Forbes.* Retrieved from http://www.forbes.com/sites/kurtbadenhausen/2011/12/14/the-nfl-signs-tv-deals-worth-26-billion/

4. Jacobi, A. (2012, May 22). Big Ten football: Big payout for each team shows B1G is leading the way for now. *Bleacher Report.* Retrieved from http://bleacherreport.com/articles/1191928-big-ten-football-big-payout-for-each-team-shows=b1g-is-leading-the-way-for-now

5. Pucin, D. (2011, May 4). Pac-12 to feast on new TV deal. *Los Angeles Times*, p. C4.

6. Durando, S. (2012, June 1). SEC renegotiates TV deal, own network possible. *Stltoday.com.* Retrieved from http://www.stltoday.com/sports/college/mizzou/sec-rengotiates-tv-deal-own-network-possibility/article_48of4585-6021-5c6f-84fd.print=true&cid=html?print

7. Wolfley, B. (2012, March 1). ESPN continues to lead cable by a mile in terms of subscriber fees. *Journal Sentinel.* Retrieved from http://www.jsonline.com/blogs/sports/141097593.html

8. Who we are & what we do. (2012). *Neilsen Media Research.* Retrieved from http://www.neilsenmedia.com

9. Hardball talk: For the one thousandth time: NFL and MLB TV rating are apples and oranges. (2011, February 8). *NBCSports.* Retrieved from http://hardballtalk.nbcsports.com/2011/02/08/for-the-one-thousand-time-nfl-and-mlb-tv-ratings-are-apples-and-oranges

10. Online TV facts. (2001, March 13). *Television Bureau of Advertising.* Retrieved from http://www.tvb./tvfacts/index.html

11. WTEM Washington. (1995). *Sports Talk 570.* Promotional material citing Scarborough 1995 Washington metro radio survey.

12. ESPN. (1992). *ESPN delivers the right viewers!* Unpaginated promotional material from ESPN citing 1992 Neilsen quarterly reports. In author's files.

13. WSBK Boston. (1993). *Celtics Basketball.* Promotional material citing Nov. 1992–May 1993. Nielsen survey of metro Boston.

14. Klatell, D. A., & Marcus N. (1996). *Inside big time sports: Television, money & the fans.* New York, NY: Mastermedia.

15. Weiner, J. (2002, February 11). ESPN's full court press. *Business Week, 3805*, 60–61.

16. News Corporation (1999). Annual report. Retrieved from http://www.newscorp.com/report99

17. Sandomir, R. (2012, August 29). ESPN extends MLB deal, doubling what it pays yearly. *New York Times.* Retrieved from http://www.nytimes.com/2012/08/20/sports/baseball/espn-extends-deal with-mlb-through-2021.html

18. Stableford, D., & Kenneally, T. (2011, April 19). NBC, Versus seal new 10-year TV deal with NHL. *The WRAP TV.* Retrieved from http://www.thewrap.com/tv/article/breaking-nbc-versus-ink-new-hockey-deal-nhl-26588

19. Remnick, D. (1996, August 5). Inside-out Olympics. *The New Yorker, 74*, 26–28.

20. Nielsen Media Report: Nearly 1.5 billion TV viewers watch 2002 World Cup. (2002, July 31). Retrieved from http://www.businesswire.com

14

The Sale of
Licensed Merchandise

~ Rick Van Brimmer ~

Assistant Vice President, Affinity & Trademark Management at The Ohio State University

INTRODUCTION

Few industries have experienced the growth, both in revenue and importance, that the sports licensing business has enjoyed over the past 30 years. What was once limited to a few T-shirts and sweatshirts in a college bookstore or stadium shop has ballooned into a multi-billion dollar windfall for professional sports leagues and colleges and universities. In 2010, the leading licensing industry trade association estimated sports products category sales to exceed $15 billion.* As shown in Table 14.1, sports licensing trailed only two categories: character licensing (such as Snoopy, Dora the Explorer, etc.), by far the largest at $45 billion in sales; and corporate or brand

On-site merchandise stores have become a prominent feature at major sporting events. Courtesy of BigStockPhoto

---

*Total spending on licensed sports products represents combined spending from both the "Collegiate" at $3.6 billion and "Sports" categories at $11.8 billion included in Table 14.1. The latter category includes all professional sports properties such as the NFL, NASCAR, and PGA.

Table 14.1. Historical Retail Sales of Licensed Products By Property Type (2001–2010) Estimated Retail Sales (in millions of dollars)

Property Type	2001	2002	2003	2004	2005
Art	$4,312	$4,722	$4,898	$4,986	$5,133
Characters	$48,002	$49,897	$48,389	$49,607	$50,787
Collegiate	$3,246	$3,376	$3,766	$3,729	$3,766
Fashion	$19,960	$19,544	$18,580	$17,835	$18,010
Music	$2,594	$2,638	$2,505	$2,705	$2,838
Non-Profit	$606	$844	$866	$888	$931
Sports	$12,988	$14,016	$14,825	$14,604	$14,880
Corp./Brand	$22,448	$24,242	$24,709	$25,189	$25,315
Publishing	$878	$941	$899	$857	$857
Others	$465	$211	$465	$317	$381
Total	$115,498	$120,432	$119,900	$120,725	$122,896

Source: International Licensing Industry Merchandisers' Association

licensing (e.g., Coca-Cola, John Deere) at $20 billion. Total spending on licensed sports products placed just ahead of fashion licensing (e.g., DKNY, Tommy Hilfiger).

Table 14.2 provides a breakdown of the sale of licensed goods and products across the major sports properties in North America. In 2010, consumers spent $3.64 billion on licensed products associated with close to 300 colleges and universities in North America. Major League Baseball, at $2.75 billion, nudged out the National Football League at $2.7 billion in total sales among the major professional sports properties, followed by the National Basketball Association at $1.75 billion and NASCAR at $1.6 billion. It was estimated that total retail spending on sports-based merchandise resulted in sports leagues, organizations and athletes receiving royalty income of between $800 to $900 million.[1]

Professional sports leagues commonly use revenue-sharing formulas for licensed products, with teams taking equal shares of the licensing pot, similar to the revenue shares from television contracts (the exception being the Dallas Cowboys of the NFL, who maintain their own apparel licensing rights). Universities approach licensing from a variety of models, and aside from commissions paid to agencies that may assist in operating their licensing programs, keep all licensing revenues from the sale of products that bear their indicia.

Table 14.2. Worldwide Retail Sales of Licensed Products by Major Sports Properties

Sports Property	Total Sales
Collegiate	$3.60 billion
MLB	$2.76 billion
NFL	$2.70 billion
NBA	$1.75 billion
NASCAR	$1.60 billion
NHL	$0.6 billion

Source: International Licensing Industry Merchandisers' Association

Table 14.1. Historical Retail Sales of Licensed Products By Property Type (2001–2010) Estimated Retail Sales (in millions of dollars)

2006	2007	2008	2009	2010	% of Total Sales	% Change From 2009
$5,338	$5,133	$4,517	$3,989	$3,754	2.53%	−5.8%
$51,831	$52,411	$50,381	$46,616	$45,952	6.9%	−1.0%
$3,766	$3,729	$3,858	$3,710	$3,636	3.87%	−2.0%
$18,185	$17,747	$16,980	$15,447	$15,118	13.6%	−2.1%
$2,926	$2,771	$2,594	$2,439	$2,550	2.27%	4.5%
$974	$931	$844	$758	$736	0.67%	−2.9%
$15,155	$14,972	$13,594	$12,124	$11,849	12.7%	−2.2%
$25,408	$24,709	$22,727	$20,513	$19,967	16.6%	−3.9%
$857	$857	$773	$711	$690	0.65%	−2.9%
$254	$190	$127	$106	$63	0.06%	0.06%
124,695	123,449	116,396	106,211	104,044	100.0%	−1.9%

As payrolls for professional teams have escalated, and financial support for publicly funded higher education has dropped, sales of licensed products—from T-shirts to tailgate tents—have become increasingly important revenue streams. In addition to revenue generation, trademark licensing is also an important brand building tool that helps grow core business attributes, and can often expand a brand into ancillary product categories that spur growth and enhance image. While professional sports teams and universities have different core missions, the sale of their licensed products helps create and foster loyalty, and promote a brand-immersion lifestyle. With licensed items available for newborns, and even caskets and cremation urns for true fanatics, licensed products can literally take you from cradle to grave.

Licensed products are often called non-essential or emotional purchases, since they appeal to loyalty or buyers' emotional attachment to the brand, such as their alma mater or a home town team. It is not a necessity like food or shelter, but something that satisfies an emotional want or need, or serves as an expression, like "We are No. 1" or "Proud Alum."

This chapter will explore the origins of sports licensing, the various licensing operational models and philosophies, legal considerations and trademark enforcement, growth of the industry, and current trends.

Licensing Basics

To understand the licensing process, and the legal connection between licensor and licensee, it is best to start with some of the basics. The term *licensing* commonly refers to the transaction whereby an owner of an intellectual property grants another party use of that property, typically through a license agreement or contract. In most cases, the licensor (the owner of the intellectual property) will receive some form of payment or other consideration from the licensee (typically in the form of royalties).

There are many forms of intellectual property, including trademarks, patents, designs, names, works of authorship (literary or musical), right of publicity, etc. You will hear licensing professionals or attorneys refer to intellectual property as *IP*, for short. For the purposes of this chapter, we will deal mainly with trademark licensing and the products that carry sports teams and university logos, names, and symbols.

To be able to license a trademark (or any other intellectual property), you must own it, and trademark ownership is derived from the actual use of a trademark. You cannot gather a portfolio of registered trademarks to keep others from using them. Continued use and protection of your trademarks is a condition of ownership. There are many classic examples of trademarks that have fallen into the public domain because their owners failed to control or protect their IP rights, such as Aspirin, Linoleum, Escalator, Raisin Bran and others. Those were once brand names that are now generic descriptions for their individual product categories.

Specifically, as defined by the United States Patent and Trademarks Office (USPTO), "a trademark is a word, phrase, symbol or design, or a combination of words, phrases, symbols or designs, that identifies and distinguishes the source of the goods of one party from those of others." For example, the Coca-Cola logo on the packaging identifies the origin of the soda contained in the can.

Additionally, a service mark "identifies and distinguishes the source of a service rather than a product." United Parcel Services (UPS) is an example of a service mark, since there is no physical product or packaging—the service being provided is package delivery, and the symbols or name on the trucks relate to the service being provided. You will commonly hear the terms *trademark* and *mark*, and both refer to trademarks and/or service marks. Trademark owners usually register their names, symbols, or logos with the USPTO as an additional layer of protection against those who attempt to use them without authorization.

To complicate matters even further, the USPTO has added trademarks rights for sounds and colors to the list of protectable properties listed above. The famous MGM lion's roar at the beginning or their movies has been trademarked, as has the three-second chord Intel uses to identify its Pentium processor. Owens Corning has a registration that distinguishes its insulation products by use of the color pink. The distinctive shapes of the Coca-Cola bottle or the Apple iPod are trademarks, and serve as the same indication of origin or ownership that school colors and logos do for sports teams.

The word *trademark* is often used incorrectly and interchangeably with *copyright*, and sometimes it is confused with a *patent*. In layman's terms, a copyright protects an original artistic or literary work (such as a book, picture, recording or musical score), while a patent protects an invention (such as the internal combustion engine).

Registering trademarks with the USPTO is a fairly simple process, and can even be done online. Most corporate or trademark owners with a larger cache of trademarks will use either staff attorneys or outside counsel to perform the registration process and on-going monitoring of their trademark portfolios. Registrations are renewable indefinitely (currently for 10-year periods) as long as the trademark owner can prove continued and consistent use of the marks. Registrations can also be bought and sold, or bartered as an asset. It is not uncommon that a company's equity in its brand name and logos would be more valuable that the sum total of its capital or equipment assets.

The USPTO maintains a searchable public database of registered trademarks, which trademark administrators and practitioners can search to see if any other entities are claiming rights to a particular name or design. But even marks that are not registered are protectable; you establish *common law* trademark rights upon use of a particular mark. An important part of any defense of a trademark is establishing a "first use" date—essentially when you put the mark into commerce. In a dispute over a trademark, rights are generally awarded to the entity that can prove it began using the mark prior to anyone else's use.

Trademarks are registered by product categories, referred to as a *class* of goods. Classes include metal goods, clothing, toys and sporting goods, educational and entertainment services, etc. There are currently 45 different trademark classifications, and holding rights in one classification does not necessarily extend rights into another classification—you must be involved in commerce for those goods to be awarded a trademark in that classification. Popular trademark classes for sports licensors include:

Class 25: Clothing, footwear, headgear

Class 28: Games and playthings; gymnastic and sporting articles not included in other classes; decorations for Christmas trees

Class 41: Education; providing of training; entertainment; sporting and cultural activities

The Licensing Process

Once a firm foundation of legal ownership is established, trademark owners often look to licensees to both promote their brand and create a revenue stream by entering goods into commerce. While Coca-Cola makes syrup for soft drinks, they do not make the myriad of other products—from holiday ornaments to replica vending machines—that bear its world-famous trademarks. The Ohio State University (OSU) provides educational services, but there is no T-shirt screen-printing operation hidden away in a campus building pumping out sweatshirts. Coca-Cola and OSU use licensees to manufacture, distribute and often promote the sale of those products to various distribution channels, increasing brand awareness and generating a new revenue stream separate from their core product line.

The critical component of any licensing program is the actual licensing agreement, or contract. It specifies the grant of rights, the financial considerations (guarantees, royalties, advance payments, etc.), length of contract period, termination procedures, distribution channels, etc. A sample license agreement is included as an appendix at the end of this chapter.

Exhibit 14.1

Common Licensing Terms

Trademark: A word, phrase, symbol or design, or a combination of words, phrases, symbols or designs, that identifies and distinguishes the source of the goods of one party from those of others

Service mark: Functions much like a trademark, but distinguishes the source of a service rather than a product

Copyright: Exclusive legal right to a creative work; literary, musical or artistic (photographs, paintings, drawings, etc.)

Patent: Exclusive legal right to a functional design or invention, granted by the government

Licensor: Owner of the intellectual property, who grants rights to use of the property, often in exchange for financial considerations.

Licensee: Person or entity that makes use of someone else's intellectual property, under a legally binding agreement, usually in exchange for financial or other considerations

Royalty: Considerations paid by the licensee to the licensor, usually in the form of a percentage of sales

Guaranteed minimum royalties: Amount licensee agrees to guarantee against earned royalties, offering licensor an assurance of an income stream or return; guaranteed royalties are usually specified for a defined time period

Advance: Amount licensee pays to licensor in advance of any actual earned royalties, generally credited against any specified guarantee

Promotional licensing: Use of a licensor's name and/or other IP by the licensee in the promotion of an event or other campaign

Naked licensing: Licensing a trademark to a licensee, but without oversight, restrictions or control by the licensor, such as requirements for quality standards

Indemnification: included in most licensing agreement to ensure protection by licensee or licensor, usually financial protection, against possible loss, damage, or liability

License agreements can be exclusive or non-exclusive in regard to product categories (e.g., men's or women's apparel), distribution channels (e.g., mass merchants, college bookstores, fan shops), length of time, or even territory (e.g., United States or Europe).

Promotional licensing varies from actual product licensing (where the IP appears on a product, such as a T-shirt) in that it grants the use of the marks in conjunction with a particular campaign. Promotional campaigns, such as sports sponsorships that make use of the licensed marks on promotional materials trumpeting an event, or drawing an association between the licensor and licensee, are examples of this type of licensing.

COLLEGIATE LICENSING

The University of California Los Angeles (UCLA) bookstore is credited with granting the first collegiate license in 1973 to R. Gsell, a watch manufacturer. That is often referred to as the birth of the collegiate licensing industry. Shortly thereafter, both OSU and the University of Southern California began registering their names and logos with the USPTO and started their trademark licensing programs.

OSU's program actually lost money until the early 1980s, and was viewed more in those early years as a means to protect the university from unauthorized (and often unwelcome) use of its name on commercial products. The program now generates almost $10 million annually in royalty revenue, and ranks among the top-selling universities in the nation. The University of Texas has posted similar royalty revenues over the past several years and, like OSU, has enjoyed outstanding athletic success and a broad alumni base to foster increased sales.

While the NCAA had the opportunity to oversee licensing for its member institutions in the 1970s, it did not have the resources or expertise to provide the service—or the vision to see where collegiate licensing was headed from a financial standpoint. NCAA championship properties, such as the wildly successful Final Four, have given rise to many licensing opportunities for the organization, but the opportunity to have a collective collegiate program was lost, and the industry soon fragmented into a variety of different licensing models (explained in more detail later in this chapter).

A critical junction in collegiate licensing came in 1982, when the University of Pittsburgh filed suit against Champion Products, at the time the leader in collegiate bookstore and athletic apparel. Pitt claimed trademark infringement against Champion, under common law rights, since Champion was not paying royalties and would not enter into a licensing agreement. Champion claimed Pitt had abandoned its trademarks and failed to control them, and that Champion, in fact, had created the market for the goods.[2]

Others, including OSU, DePaul and UCLA, filed similar suits against Champion. Ultimately, the parties settled, and Champion soon began signing licensing agreements with other institutions rather than continuing to file suits against its own customers, and an important precedent was set for others. Also in 1982, the NFL was successful in its suit against Wichita Falls Sportswear for the manufacture of unauthorized replica football jerseys, further strengthening sports licensors' position over infringers in a burgeoning market for sports- and collegiate-related apparel.

As sports and leisure apparel became popular in the 1980s, more universities began licensing manufacturers, and by the early 1990s, more than 250 had formal licensing programs. The International Collegiate Licensing Association (ICLA) now estimates that more than 300 colleges and universities are engaged in trademark licensing.

An interesting legal challenge appeared in recent years, when former Nebraska quarterback Sam Keller (later joined by other former collegiate players) filed suit against EA Sports, maker of the NCAA Football video game titles, in 2009. Keller's suit, which included EA Sports, the NCAA and the Collegiate Licensing Company as defendants, claimed unauthorized use of his likeness, citing that the players' height, weight, and other "distinguishable characteristics" along with jersey numbers, ethnicity, and hometowns—but not actual names—make virtual use of their likenesses.[3] An early ruling in the case dismissed EA Sports from the lawsuit in 2011 when a federal judge ruled that EA had a First Amendment right to free expression, which superseded players' right to protect their likenesses.[4] The suit against the NCAA and CLC has yet to be decided.

PROFESSIONAL SPORTS LEAGUE LICENSING

As mentioned earlier, most teams in the professional sports leagues operate under an all-for-one model that pools licensing revenues and distributes them equally to each team.

The four major professional sports leagues—NFL, NBA, MLB, and NHL—all operate a centralized properties office to manage licensing concerns.

Licensees are awarded rights to each of the league's teams, rather than the "a la carte" collegiate model. Individual players' interests, for items such as trading cards and player-identified jersey replicas, also include a license from the players association within each league.

As noted earlier in this chapter, The National Football League v. Wichita Falls Sportswear[5] was an important step forward in protecting and enforcing the growing market for NFL goods. Heard in U.S. District Court in Washington D.C., the court ruled that the use of dominant team colors, abbreviated nicknames or home cities created the likelihood of confusion. Likelihood of confusion is the standard required to prove infringement under the Lanham Act, the federal statute passed in 1944 that establishes trademark rights and provides the remedies for trademark infringement. The basic question that needs to be answered is the following: Is the customer confused as to the source or origin of the goods or services they are buying? In this case, the use of team colors and city names confused or deceived the buyer to believe the goods originated from or were licensed by the NFL.

North American retail sales of licensed products for sports leagues and individual athletes totaled $14 billion in 2010. More than half that amount, 55%, was generated in what is referred to as the mass distribution channels of retail sales—Target, Wal-Mart, K-Mart and other national value-priced chains. Apparel accounts for 20% of total sales, while video games/software make up 16%, ranking as the top two product categories.

Obtaining a license for a professional sport team or league is not an easy task, and the application process alone is enough to make many entrepreneurs shy away—the NFL licensing application alone is 35 pages long, and requires detailed marketing and distribution plans and projections, references, and experience.

The professional leagues also require substantial upfront royalty payments and guarantees against royalties that may prove as barriers to entry for many companies wishing to do licensed team business. But the leagues offer a measure of protection to applicants by granting exclusive, semi-exclusive or limited licenses within product categories, which adds value to the license.

Like team revenue, most player-driven revenues are pooled and split, based on the players' time spent in the league, or actual days in a season, not their popularity. But not all players have chosen to participate.

Michael Jordan—arguably the biggest merchandise name in NBA history—was the first athlete of note to retain rights to his name. In 1992, Jordan withdrew from the collective player agreement and assigned his licensing rights exclusively to Nike. Nike and Jordan already had an ongoing relationship for shoes (Air Jordan models were extremely popular).[6]

Until a scandal in his personal life cost him several deals, professional golfer Tiger Woods had licensing and endorsement deals worth an estimated $120 million annually, including the EA Sports top-selling "Tiger Woods Golf" title.[7] Recent releases of the game have included licensing-shy Augusta National Golf Club for inclusion of its course, site of the fabled Masters, on the game. The birthplace of golf, St. Andrews Old Course, is also now included under a licensing agreement.

Post-scandal, Woods's endorsement, sponsor, and licensing deals had dropped to $64 million in 2011, dwarfing his $1.9 million in winnings that same year—and still almost five times his *best* on-the-course earnings year to date ($11.5 million in 2007)![8]

As the Internet opened up new opportunities for marketing and exposure for all commercial properties, it also opened up a variety of legal issues that spilled over into the sports licensing marketplace. Online

Table 14.3. Average Royalty Rate By Property	
Sports Property	**Royalty Rates**
NFL	12–14%
MLB	12–14%
NBA	11%
NHL	10%
NASCAR	17–20% (combined driver and NASCAR licenses)
Brands	10–12% (e.g., Coca-Cola, Jack Daniels)
Collegiate	8–12%
Source: International Licensing Industry Merchandisers' Association	

sports fantasy leagues, where fans could draft their own teams or select athletes from a pool, became a legal battlefield. Yahoo filed suit against the National Football League Players Association (NFLPA) in June of 2009, claiming it should not have to pay royalties to use "publically available NFL player statistics, and related information."[9] Earlier that year, Yahoo's licensing agreement with the players union had expired, and Yahoo claimed that, based on other court rulings, it did not need licenses. Yahoo offered fantasy leagues in virtually every major professional sport league, including football, baseball, basketball, hockey, golf, and auto racing. The parties ended up settling the lawsuit, and terms were not disclosed.

CBS Television had won a previous lawsuit in 2009 that determined it did not have to pay royalties on the use of player names and statistics in its fantasy sport league because the information was in the public domain. A federal court ruled that player statistics were, in effect, a form of free speech and protected under First Amendment rights. CBS Interactive estimated at the time that 15 million people were participating in fantasy league sports, which generated $1 billion a year in revenue. Like Yahoo!, CBS had previously held a license with the NFLPA.

The average royalty rates charged by sports properties and brands are shown in Table 14.3. Rates generally fall into a range from 11–14% but can go as high as 18–20%, depending on product category and exclusivity or simply the value of the property itself. NFL goods are more widely marketable and appeal to a wider fan base than NHL products. Thus, the NFL is able to command a higher royalty return from its licensed vendors, from 12–14% of the wholesale sale price of goods sold, than the NHL, whose royalty rate is 10%. Television ratings for broadcasts of the different leagues and events are often a tip-off to the value of a sports property license.

The use of player names or likenesses is often negotiated separately with the NFLPA, not NFL Properties. The professional leagues do not publicly disclose royalty rates, and they negotiate many of their licensing agreements individually, unlike collegiate programs that tend to have more blanket agreements and rates across broad categories.

LICENSING ADMINISTRATION MODELS

The decision as to what type of licensing model to follow involves a number of considerations, including: financial commitment, philosophy, operational structure, and the degree of marketing and merchandising support that a licensor can offer. Very little agreement exists within the industry about what is the "best" model, but some generalities exist between the various models. Since brands within an existing industry can vary widely by scope, mission and perception, they will often choose a licensing strategy and structure that best fits their interests.

Professional Leagues

As noted earlier, most of the professional sports leagues or associations use a centralized licensing model, where a league office or association manages licensing agreements on behalf of all member teams. There is a single application, licenses are awarded for all member teams, and revenues are shared.

The leagues work closely with licensees to develop product lines and marketing campaigns to boost merchandising sales. Special programs have emerged to address niche markets and demographic segments, such as the NFL's "Throwbacks," (historical or vintage logos and/or styles) and targeted merchandising programs for women and children.

The NFL, in particular, has tried a variety of licensing models throughout the years, from granting a large number of wide-ranging licenses, to narrowing down its apparel program to a single licensee (Reebok), and now opening things back up to specific product categories and/or distribution channels. Like the character and brand licensing programs, there does not appear to be a "one size fits all" model when it comes to the number of licenses a sports property should award, and the most successful programs are the ones that seems to adapt to changing market conditions.

In general, most major properties share the less-is-more philosophy, since having fewer licensees in essence raises the value of the license and allows the licensee to avoid intense price competition; they also may choose to practice selective distribution of product—basically not flooding the market with lower-priced or lower-quality goods.

Collegiate Licensing

There are basically two traditional models employed by colleges and universities to administer their licensing programs: employing an outside agency, or running the program in-house (often referred to as *independent licensing*). The truth is that most collegiate models are a hybrid of both approaches. The choice is often a combination of both practical and philosophical considerations.

Agency Representation

Several options exist in the marketplace for agency representation, and three have emerged as major players with larger rosters of clients: The Collegiate Licensing Company (CLC), Licensing Resource Group (LRG), and Sports Marketing Affiliates (SMA). CLC, owned by global sports marketing giant IMG, has the larger market share, but all three serve a variety of clients, offer full-service representation, and have been staples in the collegiate market. CLC was established in 1984, LRG followed in 1991, and SMA was formed in 1997.

It is typical for an agency to not only handle the many administrative functions of running a licensing program—such as processing applications, managing licensing agreements, collecting royalties, conducting audits, and so on— but to actively help market the client individually or collectively with other universities. They may also include both local and national trademark enforcement efforts.

There are also various approaches to how an agency is paid by the client, but most operate on a percentage of royalties basis. Some have fixed rate contracts (a specified percentage of all royalties collected), while sliding scale contracts have emerged over the past several years as a preferred model—base percentages, with certain thresholds built in that trigger different rates as revenues increase. Commission rates can vary considerably, often based on the popularity of the university's brand and appeal and historic revenue generation, but range anywhere from 8% to 25%. Agencies traditionally have negotiated these rates individually with their clients.

Some notable universities that employ the agency-assisted model include Texas, Michigan, Notre Dame, Florida, and Nebraska. According to a 2010 industry survey compiled by the International Collegiate Licensing Association (ICLA), 76% of collegiate programs are represented by an agency. Even though a university may employ an outside agency, most have at least someone on staff in a fulltime capacity to oversee day-to-day operations. Many agency-assisted programs have more than one fulltime position dedicated to licensing, or shared responsibility positions (such as sports marketing, alumni relations, and communications).

In-house Management

Although less prevalent than agency representation, there are still a number of universities that operate their licensing programs in-house. To find a program that is truly a standalone model would be rare—whether it is contracting out accounting functions such as royalty audits, or employing outside legal counsel—since most programs have some form of outside help, but retain day-to-day management with internal staff. Universities that operate under an in-house model include OSU, Oregon, USC, Iowa and Michigan State.

Choosing a Model

The argument or whether or not to employ an agency or run the program independently is as old as the industry itself, and there is no clear cut answer. An argument can be made that if a college or university is willing to commit time, money and resources into management of the program, operating the program from the campus gives it more control, oversight and marketing opportunities by dealing directly with the licensee base.

Many universities view licensing as an auxiliary, and perhaps something that is more like parking facilities or the campus food service operations. They see cost-savings or management advantages in outsourcing a business function that they may not be familiar with or possess the expertise to do themselves. Some of the larger programs, like OSU, commit staff and resources to campus-based management, which they believe gives them a more hands-on approach and more direct contact with licensees.

There is no single approach that fits everyone's needs and, thus, the industry remains somewhat fractured in its approach. It is often debated that a league approach such as the NFL or MLB employs might better serve universities and ease the burden on licensees that must now go to multiple properties to gather a base of collegiate licensees.

But that approach would also stifle a unique aspect of collegiate licensing, and that is the involvement of local or regional companies that do not want a wide base of licensees, or gain a market foothold by growing from holding a single license to a cadre of licenses. It remains as unique as the universities themselves. Unlike professional sports teams that join a collective league for many business reasons, there is no one league of colleges and universities.

Administration and Oversight

The placement of the licensing program within a university structure is also varied. A survey conducted in 2010 by the ICLA showed that the largest share of university-run licensing programs, 27%, were housed administratively in University Relations, Public Relations, Marketing, or Communications (see Figure 14.1). Only 16% were housed in Athletics, with 14% reporting directly to central administration offices or Auxiliary Services. The survey showed 17% have dual reporting lines and answer to more than one administrative unit.

Like choosing a management model (agency v. independent), the placement of the licensing program administratively can be debated on a variety of fronts. Since a great deal of the appeal of most larger licensing programs is due to athletic exposure and fan attraction, placement in Athletics makes a lot of sense, especially if the resources most major athletic programs hold in inventory are utilized and cross-collateralized to help promote product sales.

But many administrations take a more measured and legal approach to licensing, and prefer a separation of administrative responsibility from business interests. In addition to maximizing revenues (a priority on many campuses), licensing programs are often charged with overseeing the management of the university's trademark portfolio.

The decision about where to place the licensing program is again a question of philosophy and expectations of the program by the university administration. There is no clear cut and simple answer.

The ICLA survey also shows that collegiate programs average about 300 licensees per institution, but larger programs may have 500 or more licensees. There are estimated to be about 3000 companies involved in the production of collegiate licensed goods.

Royalty rates vary from institution to institution, but most average around 10% of the wholesale cost of the goods according to ICLA. Exclusives for specific products

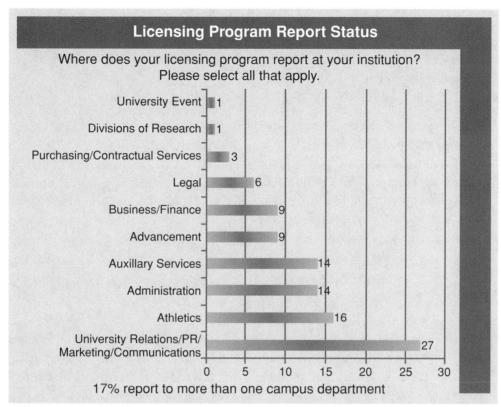

Figure 14.1. Administrative Location of University Licensing Programs.

and/or distribution channels can push that number to 18–20%, and are becoming more prevalent than in the past as universities look for ways to increase revenue streams in a maturing marketplace. Licensees are often willing to pay higher percentages to gain exclusivity to market segments or product lines.

Historically, most universities began licensing programs in the 1980s with royalty rates of 6.5% to 8%. Annual revenues have risen to over $1 million for many institutions, with Texas and OSU having reached $10 million in royalties in a single year. Universities that compete in the Bowl Championship Series (BCS) Football Bowl Subdivision (FBS) average over $2.5 million annually in royalty revenues.

The distribution of those royalties is as different as the university names, including supporting scholarships, libraries, services and many other accounts, as individual campuses decide where revenues are best spent.

Many universities have instituted licensing committees to advise or assist in policymaking or branding decisions. The scope, makeup and authority of the committees or advisory boards vary from institution to institution, and may include a combination of representatives of athletics, alumni, student organizations, communications, marketing, advancement, legal, and purchasing.

This type of group can be an effective way to manage campus branding issues, get buy-in from various stakeholders, and create a sense of community around the licensing program.

CONTRACTS

A licensing agreement is not unlike many business contracts, and serves as a consent to certain specified uses of the trademarks of the owner (the licensor) by the licensee. The agreement will spell out

- the royalty rate,
- how that rate is be to calculated and paid,
- the actual grant of rights,
- the term,
- how the contract can be terminated,
- quality control requirements,
- adherence to any specified code of conduct, and
- many other legal and functional aspects of the relationship.

One key piece of the contract is the indemnification of the licensor by the licensee, and in most instances, the amount of product liability coverage the licensee will provide, either through insurance, escrow, or bonding.

The sample licensing agreement included at the end of this chapter (Appendix 14.1) spells out the components and considerations that should go into a licensing arrangement. Many of the actual deal points are listed on Schedule A of the agreement, such as the royalty rate, any minimum guarantees and advances, and any contributions a licensee might have as an obligation to a marketing fund utilized by the licensor to promote the brand or product.

A sample code of conduct, specifying the conditions under which the products are manufactured, appears in Figure 14.2. A code of conduct is usually included in the licensing agreement, or appears as an addendum to the contract. The code spells out the specific requirements a licensor expects in regards to labor and/or environmental concerns are addressed, and add a measure of obligation to the licensee. Codes typically address such things as hours of work, harassment, safety, wages, anti-discrimination, freedom of association, etc. International labor standards are typically the models used to formulate codes of conduct, and sample codes are promoted by the Fair Labor Association (FLA), Worker Rights Consortium (WRC) and international organizations like the International Labor Organization (ILO) that have traditionally advocated for fairness and safety in labor standards.

ENFORCEMENT

As was touched upon briefly earlier in this chapter, a condition of trademark ownership is consistent and continuous use of your trademarks. If trademark owners do not use their trademarks commercially for a consecutive three-year period, they are thought to have abandoned the trademark. Additionally, trademark owners that knowingly allow others to use or trade off their trademarks may face a similar challenge of abandonment.

Trademark owners, or agents or attorneys acting on their behalf, can view applications for trademarks in the *Trademark Official Gazette*, published weekly by the United

Preamble

The FLA Workplace Code of Conduct defines labor standards that aim to achieve decent and humane working conditions. The Code's standards are based on International Labor Organization standards and internationally accepted good labor practices.

Companies affiliated with the FLA are expected to comply with all relevant and applicable laws and regulations of the country in which workers are employed and to implement the Workplace Code in their applicable facilities. When differences or conflicts in standards arise, affiliated companies are expected to apply the highest standard.

The FLA monitors compliance with the Workplace Code by carefully examining adherence to the Compliance Benchmarks and the Principles of Monitoring. The Compliance Benchmarks identify specific requirements for meeting each Code standard, while the Principles of Monitoring guide the assessment of compliance. The FLA expects affiliated companies to make improvements when Code standards are not met and to develop sustainable mechanisms to ensure ongoing compliance.

The FLA provides a model of collaboration, accountability, and transparency and serves as a catalyst for positive change in workplace conditions. As an organization that promotes continuous improvement, the FLA strives to be a global leader in establishing best practices for respectful and ethical treatment of workers, and in promoting sustainable conditions through which workers earn fair wages in safe and healthy workplaces.

CODE ELEMENT	DESCRIPTION
EMPLOYMENT RELATIONSHIP	Employers shall adopt and adhere to rules and conditions of employment that respect workers and, at a minimum, safeguard their rights under national and international labor and social security laws and regulations.
NONDISCRIMINATION	No person shall be subject to any discrimination in employment, including hiring, compensation, advancement, discipline, termination or retirement, on the basis of gender, race, religion, age, disability, sexual orientation, nationality, political opinion, social group or ethnic origin.
HARASSMENT OR ABUSE	Every employee shall be treated with respect and dignity. No employee shall be subject to any physical, sexual, psychological or verbal harassment or abuse.
FORCED LABOR	There shall be no use of forced labor, including prison labor, indentured labor, bonded labor or other forms of forced labor.
CHILD LABOR	No person shall be employed under the age of 15 or under the age for completion of compulsory education, whichever is higher.
FREEDOM OF ASSOCIATION AND COLLECTIVE BARGAINING	Employers shall recognize and respect the right of employees to freedom of association and collective bargaining.
HEALTH, SAFETY, AND ENVIRONMENT	Employers shall provide a safe and healthy workplace setting to prevent accidents and injury to health arising out of, linked with, or occurring in the course of work or as a result of the operation of employers' facilities. Employers shall adopt responsible measures to mitigate negative impacts that the workplace has on the environment.
HOURS OF WORK	Employers shall not require workers to work more than the regular and overtime hours allowed by the law of the country where the workers are employed. The regular work week shall not exceed 48 hours. Employers shall allow workers at least 24 consecutive hours of rest in every seven-day period. All overtime work shall be consensual. Employers shall not request overtime on a regular basis and shall compensate all overtime work at a premium rate. Other than in exceptional circumstances, the sum of regular and overtime hours in a week shall not exceed 60 hours.
COMPENSATION	Every worker has a right to compensation for a regular work week that is sufficient to meet the workers' basic needs and provide some discretionary income. Employers shall pay at least the minimum wage or the appropriate prevailing wage, whichever is higher, comply with all legal requirements on wages, and provide any fringe benefits required by law or contract. Where compensation does not meet workers' basic needs and provide some discretionary income, each employer shall work with the FLA to take appropriate actions that seek to progressively realize a level of compensation that does.

www. fairlabor.org

Figure 14.2. Workplace Code of Conduct.

States Patent and Trademark Office. Owners can then respond to the USPTO and challenge those applications that are confusingly similar or dilute their properties. If no oppositions are filed to trademarks published in the *Gazette*, the applications proceed to registration.

Labeling

Trademark owners will use a variety of methods to label their products, both to help identify them against counterfeited goods, and to inform the consumer that the goods are legitimate. Most major licensors require licensees to affix some sort of security tag to each piece of the licensed product.

Apparel items generally carry a hang tag that may include various security features that are difficult for bootleggers to copy, such as holograms, imbedded security markings, sequential numbering, etc. Many of the security features require a special viewing tool to verify their authenticity, and may not be visible to the naked eye. A single one inch by two inch security tag may have multiple identifiable features. Brand owners will work with law enforcement officers to help identify their goods as legitimate, either at the port of entry (via Customs) or at the retail level.

Anti-counterfeiting security tags are continually changing to keep the brand owners one step ahead of the counterfeiters, and employ an extremely high level of technology such as three-dimensional effects.

In 1992, the Coalition to Advance the Protection of Sports logos (CAPS) was formed by the Collegiate Licensing Company, MLB, the NBA, the NFL, and the NHL to coordinate enforcement efforts by major sports licensing players. They work collectively on enforcement issues and pool resources to combat counterfeiting efforts.

Customs

Since many of the licensed goods produced now for sale in the United States were manufactured overseas, they enter the U.S. through Customs. The U.S. Customs and Border Patrol (CBP) is a bureau within the Department of Homeland Security and checks trademarked goods being brought into the U.S. via a trademark recordation system. Trademark owners may register their marks with CBP to help prevent the importation of counterfeit goods.

Retail v. Swap Meet

It is rare that truly counterfeit goods make it all the way through the wholesale/retail supply chain and into legitimate retail outlets. Under trademark law, the retailer who knowingly sells counterfeit merchandise can be held liable for participating in the commission of trademark counterfeiting. Generally, the volume of the goods being sold will determine the severity of criminal charges, but laws do vary from state to state. There are a variety of statutes that speak to trademark infringement, including federal trademark law, or even fraudulent business practice statutes.

Many trademark owners spend considerable time, effort and money policing swap meets and flea markets where high volumes of counterfeit goods can be distributed, and determining the ultimate source of the goods can be difficult. Counterfeiters know bargain shoppers are attracted to brand name goods at significantly lower prices than the authentic counterparts—many times, customers being fully aware that they are not buying the "real" goods.

It is not difficult to find imitation fashion labels being counterfeited, such Rolex watches sold on the streets of major cities for $10, or fake Gucci purses and bags vended in a similar fashion or even through at-home purse parties. Trademark holders lose significant sales, and municipalities and governments lose tax revenues, to counterfeiters.

Transient vendors that move from corner to corner, venue to venue, or city to city are often harder for law enforcement officials to identify and track. Major sporting events create lucrative situations for counterfeiters, with large numbers of rabid fans descending on a small geographic area for a short period of time. Bowl games, the Super Bowl, the NCAA Final Four and many other such events continually fight against counterfeit goods being brought to market, often sold literally on the steps of or near the gates of the venue. Many event staffs now include vendor details made up of law enforcement officers to police the area. What are known as John Doe seizure orders, which allow immediate confiscation of illegal goods, are a valuable weapon in fighting back against on-the-spot vendors.

Online Counterfeiting

The growth of the Internet brought with it a wide variety of issues for trademark holders, including cyber squatters using trademarked names for URLs, as well as the ability to make, distribute or sell counterfeit goods with the click of a mouse.

From eBay to Etsy (which serves as an online marketplace primarily for handmade items), everything from counterfeit football jerseys to handcrafted items bearing team logos can be found daily on numerous websites. Many marketplace websites, such as eBay, have anti-fraud programs, where trademark holders can register and notify the site that a particular seller is making unauthorized use of trademarks. The fraudulent accounts are then shut down, and the trademark owners can pursue the seller after receiving contact information from the marketplace owner. Several Internet security firms now offer watch services to help trademark owners identify illegal online sales, and can act on the trademark owner's behalf to work with the marketplace to shut down and identify the seller.

The Department of Justice seized more than $1.5 million in proceeds from the sale of counterfeited sports apparel being sold online in May of 2012.[10] It also seized three domain names used to distribute the goods.

CORPORATE SOCIAL RESPONSIBILITY

What started as a primarily student-driven movement in the late 1990s has now become an important and controversial part of the licensing landscape. Corporate social responsibility (CSR) measures, which ensure both environmental and working condition safety and fairness, are now part of many licensing programs. The CSR agenda has gained the most traction in collegiate licensing, where both the Fair Labor Organization

(FLA) and Worker Rights Consortium (WRC) were formed to advocate for and monitor improvements in working conditions and fair wages in the thousands of factories
around the world that produce licensed products.

The FLA was formed in 1999 as part of the Clinton administration's reaction to the
discovery of sweatshop working conditions in a New York facility that produced goods
for K-Mart under the Kathie Lee Gifford label. It was one of the first such stories to
grab national headlines about sweatshop conditions, and Gifford's fame as a popular co-
host of the daytime talk show "Regis and Kathie Lee" made it even more high profile.

The FLA brought manufacturers such as Nike, Phillips Van Heusen, adidas, Patago-
nia, Eddie Bauer and others, colleges and universities, and non-governmental organizations (NGOs) concerned with labor and human rights issues to the same table to begin
addressing the complex issues surrounding global apparel supply chains.

About the same time, the United Students Against Sweatshops (USAS) was formed
as a national student movement, advocating for workers' rights primarily through freedom of association and improvement in working conditions. USAS was instrumental in
helping launch the WRC, which brought together students, college and university
administrators, and NGOs involved primarily in labor issues.

One of the primary differences between the organizations is that the FLA includes
the manufacturers in the governance of the organization, and monitors factories of its
members against a code of conduct, which addresses hours of work, wages, health and
safety issues, freedom of association, etc. The WRC, which, like USAS, has the backing
of organized labor, does not include manufacturers in its governance structure to maintain a level of independence, and rather than monitoring conditions in individual factories, reacts to workers' and third-party complaints about specific situations that may
arise in facilities used by collegiate manufacturers.

While philosophically different in their approach, both have served to raise the awareness of worldwide worker abuse, and though progress has been slow, each has a track
record of success stories in facilities that have been identified as sweatshops, although
that term is rarely defined the same way by most people within the manufacturing
industry.

The professional sports leagues require licensees to adhere to a similar code of conduct model of compliance, but have not addressed the issues as publicly as have colleges
and universities.

GROWTH AND TRENDS

The licensed products market in general, and sports licensing specifically, has grown
into more than just a logo on a shirt, which was the college bookstore model back in
the 1970s. Sports brands have become lifestyle brands, and fashionable sports leisurewear
for all ages has grown into a multi-billion dollar marketplace for team-identified goods.

As the apparel category grew, so did the need for accessories and "hard line" goods
that filled the party and tailgate categories, and new products are now being developed
for other areas of the consumer's house and workplace. Logoed goods are in ample sup-

ply for the bar and recreation areas of the house, the patio and outdoor living areas, the garage, etc.

The fans' need to show their allegiance and love for their team has caused licensed product sales to simply chase what is fashionable in other parts of the retail market—in style, color, graphic representation, and fabrication (such as performance wear), and across product lines, demographics, and distribution channels.

Licensors look for business models that will continue to grow the categories of products, and protect what have become important and lucrative revenue streams. Category and distribution channel exclusives, long practiced with high degrees of success by the character licensing industry, are now an increasing part of the sports licensing business model. The professional leagues have had similar programs in place for several years, but are now more specific and sophisticated about how they divvy up the categories or channels, all in an effort to maximize sales and not cannibalize their programs by pitting licensee against licensee for the same shelf space within the retail market. The goal is to diversify and increase shelf space with targeted products and marketing.

Licensors will continue to address narrower market niches, and at the same time will look to protect the core apparel categories that are the backbone of the industry. As revenues have grown, the dependence upon this stream has increased—but sports licensing can be one of the most volatile and unpredictable licensing categories. It's no surprise that top-selling teams are generally the most successful on the field, and licensing revenues can ride the wave up and down. In collegiate licensing, alumni can be the most loyal fan base, but even the most loyal fans get caught up in the excitement of a potential championship season or major bowl game, and bandwagon fans simply follow the winners. Scandals (on or off the field) involving players or coaches, probation or sanctions, and so on, can also negatively affect product sales.

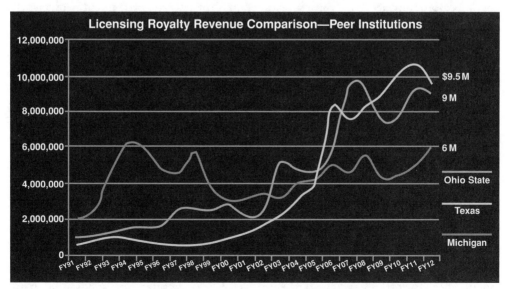

Figure 14.3. Annual Licensing Revenue Comparisons of 3 Major Universities: Michigan, Ohio State and Texas from 1991–2012.

The summary of three major licensing program royalty histories (Figure 14.3) illustrates the up-and-down nature of the sports licensing business, and how success (or lack of success) can affect sales almost immediately. Michigan rode the success of the "Fab Five" basketball phenomenon and a national championship in football through the 1980s, topping $6 million in royalties when many other programs were at $2 million or less. Texas and Ohio State saw their revenues jump as they became regular contenders on the national stage in football. Royalty revenues at Ohio State doubled, from around $2.5 million to $5 million, in 2002–2003 when the Buckeyes claimed their first football championship in more than 30 years, and revenues have continued a fairly steady growth rate since then. But even the magnitude of a perennial contender does not guard against an almost immediate downturn if fortunes change.

Exclusive and alternative licensing models are being looked at as a way to guarantee the royalty revenues streams over longer-term contracts, thus ensuring the bumpy ride is smoothed out.

SUMMARY

Sports-related product licensing dates back to the 1970s, and enjoyed a tremendous growth spurt as a "sports leisure" culture began to blossom in the 1980s. It has grown to be an important and lucrative revenue stream for colleges and universities, as well as professional sport teams, surpassing $15 billion in worldwide retail sales in 2010.

The property holder (licensor) usually receives a royalty from the licensee when the licensee manufactures products bearing the licensor's trademark. A trademark helps identify the source of the goods, and distinguishes it from those of another party. Trademarks can take the form of words, colors, sounds and shapes, and are registered by product category with the USPTO.

The basis of any licensor-licensee relationship is the licensing agreement, which spells out the specific grant of rights, including contract term, financial considerations, product categories, and channels of distribution. Licensing agreements can be exclusive or non-exclusive, with higher royalty rates generally charged for exclusive product categories or distribution channels.

There are approximately 300 colleges and universities that have licensing programs, and many are assisted by a for-profit agency, but several universities operate under an on-campus management model. The best way to operate a licensing program is often debated, and usually comes down to individual university philosophy or commitment of resources. Licensing is most often operated outside of university athletic programs.

Professional sports teams operate under a collective agreement that pools licensing revenues and operates a properties office on behalf of all teams within the league, with a few exceptions. Rights to the names and likenesses of players are often handled separately from league rights, by a players association.

Trademark counterfeiting accounts for losses in revenues for trademark holders, as popular brands or teams become targets for illegal, and often inferior, goods. Trademark owners employ several methods to slow down trafficking in counterfeit goods, including sophisticated security labeling, working with Customs, and doing sweeps of popular marketplaces for counterfeit goods.

A recent topic among trademark holders, specifically on college campuses is where and how the products are made—more emphasis is now placed on the corporate responsibility of the licensees to ensure the goods are made in safe and fair working conditions, and meet environmental standards.

As the market for licensed products continues to grow, licensors continue to look at new operating models to continue the growth trend, and to protect the valuable revenue stream royalties provide.

References

1. *Sports Licensing Report, 2010.* The Licensing Letter, July 2010, New York, NY.
2. University of Pittsburgh v. Champion Products (1982), 686F. 2d 1040, United States Court of Appeals, Third Circuit, July 7.
3. Wieberg, S. (2009, May 7). Ex-QB sues NCAA, EA Sports over use of athletes likeness, *USA Today*. http://www.usatoday.com/sports /college/2009-05-07-keller-ncaa-easports-law suit_N.htm
4. *Kotaku.com.* (2011, September 9). EA has a First Amendment right to depict real college football players, Judge Rules.
5. National Football League v. Wichita Falls Sportswear (1982), 532 F. Supp 651, No. C80–1027C, United States District Court, W. D. Washington, February 9, 1982.
6. *Footwear News* (1992, February 3). Jordan shifts rights to Nike (Michael Jordan's Exclusive Licensing Deal.
7. *The Post-Standard* (2011, July 15). Report: Tiger Wood's income is way down. http://blog.syra cuse.com/sports/2011/07/report_tiger- woodss_income_is.html
8. Kelly, B. (2012, March). Tiger Woods earnings: What is Tiger's annual income? *About.com Golf.* http://golf.abut.com/od/tigerwoods/f/tiger-woods -earnings.htm
9. *Reuters* (2009, July 7). Yahoo, NFL settle law-suit over fantasy league. http://www.reuters .com/article/2009/07/07/yahoo-sports-idUSN 0733318120090707
10. *U.S. Department of Justice* (2012, May 11). De-partment of Justice seizes more than $1.5 mil-lion from the online sale of counterfeit sports apparel manufactured in China

Appendix 14.1

SAMPLE PROVISIONS OF A LICENSE AGREEMENT

Consideration.

    A. *Royalty.* In consideration for the licenses granted hereunder, Licensee agrees to pay to Licensor during the Term of this Agreement (as defined in Schedule A attached hereto), a royalty in the amount provided in Schedule A attached hereto (the "Royalty") based on Licensee Net Sales of Licensed Products. If any amount payable to Licensor is subject to any non-US tax, charge or duty, Licensee shall furnish to Licensor official proof of such payment, including official proof of receipt of Licensee's payment from the government entity imposing such tax, charge or duty. If Licensor does not receive full and complete U.S. tax credit for any such tax, charge or duty, then the amount payable by Licensee shall be increased to provide to Licensor such amount as would be payable to Licensor in the absence of any such tax, charge, duty or impost.

    B. *Royalty Period.* The Royalty owed Licensor shall be calculated on a quarterly calendar basis (the "Royalty Period") and shall be payable no later than thirty (30) days after the termination of the preceding calendar quarter.

    C. *Marketing Fee.* During each Royalty Period on the dates specified in Schedule A, Licensee shall pay to Licensor a Marketing Fee in the amount recited in Schedule A. Licensee's obligation to pay the Marketing Fee is absolute and independent of the Royalty. Licensee shall no right to set off, compensate or make any deduction from payments of the Marketing Fee for any reason whatsoever. Any amount that Licensee may directly spend on advertising (as previously approved by Licensor) in excess of the amount required herein shall not be used to offset the required Marketing Fee for the subsequent Royalty Period. Licensor may use or expend all Marketing Fees paid by Licensee hereunder in its sole discretion.

    D. *Royalty Statement.* With each Royalty Payment, Licensee shall provide Licensor with a written Royalty Statement in a form acceptable to Licensor. Such Royalty Statement shall be certified as accurate by a duly authorized officer of Licensee, reciting: (1) gross sales of all Licensed Products for the applicable Royalty Period, itemized by SKU; (2) Net Sales on which the Royalties are based; (3) all related party sales, employee sales, parking lot, warehouse or similar sales, and any other unusual sales transactions; (4) allowed deductions or credits taken against gross sales; and (5) quantity and dollar amount of Licensed Products sold to each customer, broken down by month and each country and Channel of Distribution within the Territory, if applicable, as well as any other information relating to the Licensed Products that may be reasonably requested by Licensor. Failure to deliver statements and reports in a timely manner as provided by this Section shall constitute a material breach of this Agreement. Such statements shall be furnished to Licensor whether or not any Licensed Products were sold during the Royalty Period.

E. *Advance and Guaranteed Minimum Royalty.* Licensee agrees to pay to Licensor a Guaranteed Minimum Royalty in accordance with the terms of Schedule A attached hereto (the "Guaranteed Minimum Royalty"). As recited in Schedule A, a portion of the Guaranteed Minimum Royalty for the first year shall be payable as a nonrefundable Advance against royalties (the "Advance"). The actual royalty payments shall reflect the amount of all Guaranteed Minimum Royalty payments including any Advances made. Licensee shall only be permitted to carry forward any unused credit for the Advance or Guaranteed Minimum Royalty for the subsequent year.

F. *Net Sales Defined.* "Net Sales" shall mean Licensee gross sales (the gross invoice amount billed customers) of Licensed Products, less any *bona fide* returns (net of all returns actually made or allowed as supported by credit memoranda actually issued to the customers). In no event shall the total credits taken by Licensee for returns exceed 10% of the total gross sales for any Royalty Period. No other costs incurred in the manufacturing, selling, advertising, and distribution of the Licensed Products shall be deducted nor shall any deduction be allowed for any uncollectible accounts or allowances.

G. *Sale of a Product.* A Royalty obligation shall accrue upon the sale of the Licensed Products regardless of the time of collection by Licensee. For purposes of this Agreement, a Licensed Product shall be considered "sold" upon the date when such Licensed Product is billed, invoiced, shipped, or paid for, whichever event occurs first.

Audit.

A. *Right to Audit.* Both during and after termination or expiration of this Agreement, Licensor shall have the right, upon at least five (5) days written notice and no more than once per calendar year, to inspect the books and records of both Licensee and any of Licensee's related or affiliated entities, e.g., parents, subsidiaries, etc., and all other documents and material in the possession of or under the control of Licensee with respect to the subject matter of this Agreement at the place or places where such records are normally retained by Licensee. Licensee shall provide access to such records in electronic format, if possible, and shall fully cooperate with the Licensor or its representative in connection with such audit and Licensor and/or its representative shall have free and full access thereto for such purposes and shall be permitted to make copies thereof and extracts therefrom.

B. *Periodic Financial Statements.* Within ninety (90) calendar days after the end of each of its fiscal years Licensee shall provide Licensor (all in English) with: (1) an annual audited financial statement of Licensee (audited by an accounting firm satisfactory to Licensor); (2) an annual composite statement, certified by its chief financial officer, showing the aggregate gross sales, trade discounts, returns, allowances, payment term discounts and closeout discounts and any other deduction taken to arrive at the Net

Sales price of all Licensed Products sold by Licensee; and (3) an annual inventory reconciliation, certified by a certified public accountant, confirming actual reconciliation of the inventory to Licensee's general ledger and including computer reports summarizing inventory by SKU.

Marketing.

A. *Commercially Reasonable Efforts.* At all times during the Term, Licensee shall use commercially reasonable efforts to generate the maximum possible level of sales of the Licensed Products within the Channels of Distribution in the Territory including, without limitation, the design and development of unique retail displays to include "exclusive" styles, designs, powerful point of purchase visual display and minimum square footage requirements at each of its locations that desires to sell the Licensed Products. Licensee acknowledges that Licensor is entering into this Agreement not only in consideration of the payments to be made by Licensee, but also in consideration of the promotional value to Licensor of the widespread marketing, distribution, advertising, promotion, offer for sale and sale of the Licensed Products. Accordingly, Licensee shall use commercially reasonable efforts to seek to procure the greatest volume of sales of the Licensed Products consistent with high quality and shall diligently and continuously make and maintain timely and adequate arrangements for their manufacture, marketing, distribution, advertising, promotion, offering for sale and sale.

B. *Sufficient Inventory.* Licensee shall use commercially reasonable efforts to maintain sufficient on-hand inventory to support market demand for the Licensed Products.

C. *Marketing Plan.* No later than September 1st of each calendar year during the Term, Licensee shall provide to Licensor Licensee's proposed marketing plan and budget ("Marketing Plan") for the promotion and distribution of the Licensed Products for the ensuing calendar year.

D. *Marketing Budget.* Licensee shall establish a marketing budget, and shall expend an amount, for advertising and related sales promotion activities, for each year during the Term, equal to a percentage of all Net Sales in the amount recited in Schedule A attached hereto. Licensee shall provide Licensor within sixty (60) days after the end of each calendar year with an accounting signed and certified by an officer of Licensee, reflecting the amounts expended by Licensee on advertising the Licensed Products.

Approval of Products and Promotional Materials.

A. *Quality of the Licensed Products.* The licenses granted hereunder are conditioned upon Licensee's full and complete compliance with the marking provisions of the patent, trademark and copyright laws of the United States. The Licensed Products, as well as all promotional, packaging and advertising material relative thereto, shall include all appropriate legal notices as reasonably required by Licensor.

B. *Approval of Preliminary Material.* Licensee agrees to submit to Licensor, for final approval, sketches, prototypes and production samples of all Licensed Products and any and all advertising, promotional and packaging material related to said Licensed Products. Licensor shall provide Licensee with written approval or disapproval within ten (10) business days after receipt of such sketches, prototypes and production samples.

C. *Compliance with Standards.* The Licensed Products manufactured by or for Licensee, shall comply in all respects with Licensor's standards, specifications, directions and processes and shall be in substantial conformity with the production sample of the Licensed Product approved by Licensor. Once Licensor has approved the Production Sample(s), Licensee will manufacture Licensed Products only in accordance with such approved Production Sample(s) and will not make any changes without Licensor's prior written approval.

D. *Pre-Production Samples.* Prior to the commencement of manufacture and sale of the Licensed Products, Licensee shall submit to Licensor, at no cost to Licensor two (2) sets of samples of all Licensed Products which Licensee intends to manufacture and sell and one (1) complete set of all promotional and advertising material associated therewith.

E. *Compliance with Labor Compliance Rules.* The manufacture, packaging and storage of the Licensed Products shall be carried out only at premises approved by the Licensor or its nominee in writing from time to time. The Licensor or its nominee shall be entitled at any time on reasonable notice to the Licensee to enter, during regular business hours, any premises used by the Licensee or its manufacturers for the manufacture, packaging or storage of the Licensed Products, to inspect such premises, all plant, workforce and machinery used for manufacture, packaging or storage of Licensed Products and all other aspects of the manufacture, packaging and storage of Licensed Products. The Licensee shall, and shall insure that its manufacturers shall make any changes or improvements to its premises, plant, workforce, machinery and other aspects of the manufacture, packaging and storage of Licensed Products as the Licensor or its nominee may reasonably request. Licensee shall comply in all material respects with the LIMA Code of Business Practices attached hereto as Exhibit A.

Termination.

Licensor shall have the right to immediately terminate this Agreement by giving written notice to Licensee in the event that Licensee does any of the following:

(1) fails to meet the Product Introduction Date or the Initial Shipment Date as specified in Schedule A; or

(2) after having commenced sale of the Licensed Products, fails to continuously sell Licensed Products for three (3) consecutive Royalty Periods; or

(3) fails to obtain or maintain product liability insurance in the amount and of the type provided for herein; or

(4) files a petition in bankruptcy or is adjudicated a bankrupt or insolvent, or makes an assignment for the benefit of creditors, or an arrangement

pursuant to any bankruptcy law, or if the Licensee discontinues its business or a receiver is appointed for the Licensee or for the Licensee business and such receiver is not discharged within thirty (30) days; or

(5) fails to make timely payment of Royalties when due two or more times during any twelve-month period;

(6) fails to meet the Minimum Sales requirement in any calendar year;

(7) fails to make the Minimum Advertising Expenditure in any calendar year;

(8) fails to comply with the Marketing Requirements as provided for in Schedule A attached there; or

(9) sells Licensed Products to an unapproved customer;

A. *Inventory upon Termination.* Not less than thirty (30) days prior to the expiration of this Agreement or immediately upon termination thereof, Licensee shall provide Licensor with a complete schedule of all inventory of Licensed Products then on-hand (the "Inventory").

B. *Sell-Off Period.* Upon expiration or termination of this Agreement except for reason of a breach of Licensee duty to comply with the quality control or legal notice marking requirements, Licensee shall be entitled, for an additional period of three (3) months and on a nonexclusive basis, to continue to sell such Inventory. Such sales shall be made subject to all of the provisions of this Agreement and to an accounting for and the payment of a Royalty thereon. Such accounting and payment shall be due and paid within thirty (30) days after the close of the said three (3) month period. Licensee shall not be permitted to sell Licensed Products during this period at a price point discounted more than 50% of its traditional wholesale selling price.

C. *Discontinuance of Use of the Property.* Upon the expiration or termination of this Agreement, all of the rights of Licensee under this Agreement, except for Licensee rights under paragraph 10B., shall forthwith terminate and immediately revert to Licensor and Licensee shall immediately discontinue all use of the Trademarks, at no cost whatsoever to Licensor.

D. *Return of Materials.* Upon termination of this Agreement for any reasons whatsoever, Licensee agrees to immediately return to Licensor all material relating to the Trademarks including, but not limited to, all artwork, color separations, prototypes and the like, as well as any market studies or other tests or studies conducted by Licensee with respect to the Trademarks, at no cost whatsoever to Licensor.

E. *Continued Sale of Similar Products.* The parties understand and agree that the Licensed Products will have acquired a particular look and feel and association with the Trademarks and Property. Accordingly, Licensee recognizes and agrees that the continued use of any similar trademark, trade name, trade dress or other industrial or intellectual property has the potential to cause significant consumer confusion after termination or expiration of this Agreement should Licensee continue to use or adopt the use of any trademark, trade name, trade dress or other industrial or intellectual property that was not a "safe distance" from the Property, Trademark or any trade name or trade dress associated therewith and Licensee hereby agrees to maintain such "safe distance" upon the termination or expiration of this Agreement.

Infringements.

A. *Initiation of Infringement Actions.* Licensor shall have the right, in its discretion, to institute and prosecute lawsuits against third persons for infringement of the rights licensed in this Agreement.

B. *Cost of Litigation.* Any lawsuit shall be prosecuted solely at the cost and expense of Licensor and all sums recovered in any such lawsuits, whether by judgment, settlement or otherwise, shall be retained by Licensor.

C. *Cooperation of Parties.* Upon request of Licensor, Licensee shall execute all papers, testify on all matters, and otherwise cooperate in every way necessary and desirable for the prosecution of any such lawsuit. Licensor shall reimburse Licensee for the expenses incurred as a result of such cooperation.

Indemnification.

A. *Licensee Indemnity.* Licensee agrees to defend, indemnify and hold Licensor, and its officers, directors, employees, agents, and advisors, harmless from and against any and all costs, loses, obligations, suits, judgments, damages and costs (including reasonable attorneys' fees and costs) incurred through claims of third parties against Licensor based on the manufacture, sale, marketing, distribution, advertising or promotion of the Licensed Products including, but not limited to, actions founded on product liability or infringement of any third party intellectual property rights. Licensor shall have the right to select counsel in connection with such actions. No action may be settled or compromised without Licensor's prior express written approval.

B. *Licensor Indemnity.* Licensor agrees to defend, indemnify and hold Licensee, and its officers, directors, employees, agents and advisors, harmless from and against any and all claims, losses, obligations, suits, judgments, damages and costs (including reasonable attorneys' fees and costs) incurred through claims of third parties against Licensor based on any claim by any third party challenging Licensor's rights in the Property or its ability to enter into this Agreement including any claim for infringement of any third party rights based solely on Licensee's licensed use of the Property on the Licensed Products.

Insurance.

A. *Product Liability Insurance.* Licensee shall, throughout the Term of the Agreement, obtain and maintain at its own cost and expense from a qualified insurance company licensed to do business in [State] with a Best rating of A− or better, standard Product Liability Insurance naming Licensor as an additional named insured. Such policy shall provide protection against any and all claims, demands and causes of action arising out of any defects or failure to perform, alleged or otherwise, of the Licensed Products or any material used in connection therewith or any use thereof.

B. *Advertiser's Insurance.* Licensee shall, throughout the Term of the Agreement, obtain and maintain at its own cost and expense from a qualified insurance company licensed to do business in [State] with a Best rating of A– or better, standard Advertiser's Insurance naming Licensor as an additional named insured. Such policy shall provide protection against any and all claims, demands and causes of action arising out of any defects or failure to perform, alleged or otherwise, of the Licensed Products or any material used in connection therewith or any use thereof.

Index

About the Authors

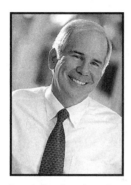

Dennis R. Howard

Dennis R. Howard is a Philip H. Knight Professor of Business at the University of Oregon's Lundquist College of Business. He served as Dean of the College from 2008 to 2010. Prior to becoming Dean, he served as Head of the Marketing Department and taught sports business classes at the Warsaw Sports Marketing Center.

Dr. Howard has authored or co-authored three books and close to 100 articles on sport and leisure industry topics. His book with John Crompton, *Financing Sport*, is the first comprehensive textbook on the many traditional and innovative revenue acquisition methods available to sports organizations. He has served as a consultant to the NFL, several major league teams, and a number of intercollegiate athletic departments on facility development projects. Dr. Howard is the founding editor of the *International Journal of Sport Finance* and has served on the editorial boards of the *Sport Marketing Quarterly* and the *Journal of Sport Management*.

Since joining the University of Oregon business faculty in 1997, Dr. Howard has received the Undergraduate Teaching Award, the Harry R. Jacobs Distinguished Teaching Award, and the James E. Reinmuth MBA Teaching Excellence Award. In 1998, he received the highest honor awarded by the North American Society for Sport Management—the Earle F. Zeigler Award for Excellence—for his contributions to the sport industry.

Dr. Howard is a graduate of the University of Oregon (BS), University of Illinois (MS), and Oregon State University (PhD). He served on the faculty at Texas A&M University, Pennsylvania State University, and Ohio State University, before returning to his alma mater in Eugene.

John L. Crompton

John L. Crompton holds the rank of University Distinguished Professor and is both a Regents Professor and a Presidential Professor for Teaching Excellence at Texas A&M University. He received his basic training in England. His undergraduate work was in physical education and geography at Loughborough College. After teaching high school for a year, he attended the University of Illinois, where he completed a MS degree in Recreation and Park Administration in 1968. In 1970, he was awarded another MS degree from Loughborough University of Technology, majoring in Business Administration.

In 1970, he joined Loughborough Recreation Planning Consultants as their first full-time employee. When he left as managing director in 1974, LRPC had developed into the largest consulting firm in the United Kingdom, specializing in recreation and tourism, with a full-time staff of 25 and supplemented by a number of part-time associate consultants.

In 1974, Dr. Crompton came to Texas A&M University. He received his doctorate in Recreation Resources Development in 1977. For some years he taught graduate and undergraduate courses in both the Department of Recreation and Parks and the Department of Marketing at Texas A&M University, but he now teaches exclusively in the Department of Recreation, Park and Tourism Sciences.

Dr. Crompton's primary interests are in the areas of marketing and financing public leisure and tourism services. He is author or co-author of 18 books and a substantial number of articles that have been published in the recreation, tourism, sport and marketing fields. He is the most published scholar in the history of both the parks and recreation, and the tourism fields.

Dr. Crompton has conducted many hundreds of workshops on Marketing and/or Financing Leisure Services. He has lectured or conducted workshops in many foreign countries and has delivered keynote addresses at the World Leisure Congress and at Annual National Park and Recreation Conferences in Australia, Canada, Great Britain, Japan, New Zealand, South Africa, and the United States.

He is a past recipient of the National Park Foundation's Cornelius Amory Pugsley award for outstanding national contributions to parks and conservation; the US Department of Agriculture's Agricultural Colleges National Teacher of the Year Award; the National Recreation and Park Association's (NRPA) Distinguished Professional award; the NRPA National Literary award; the NRPA Roosevelt award for outstanding research; the Distinguished Colleague and the Distinguished Teaching awards of the Society of Park and Recreation Educators; the Travel and Tourism Research Association's Travel Research award; the U.S. Department of Agriculture National award for Teaching Excellence; and is a Minnie Stevens Piper Professor for excellent teaching in the state of Texas.

At Texas A&M, he is Cintron University Professor for Excellence in Undergraduate Teaching. He has received the Bush Excellence Award for Public Service (presented personally by President H. W. Bush); the Vice Chancellor's Award for Excellence in Graduate Teaching; the Texas Agricultural Experiment Station's Faculty Fellow and Senior Faculty Fellow Awards for exceptional research contributions; the University Distinguished Achievement Award for Research and the University Distinguished Achievement Award for Teaching.

He was a member of the NRPA's Board of Trustees for nine years; and is a past president of four professional bodies: the Texas Recreation and Parks Society; the American Academy of Park and Recreation Administration; the Society of Park and Recreation Educators; and the Academy of Leisure Sciences. He is a Board member of the National Recreation Foundation.

In 2006, the city of College Station named a new 16-acre neighborhood park, John

Crompton Park. Dr. Crompton served four years as a city councilman for College Station from 2007–2011, and was Mayor Pro Tem in 2010–2011. The city's population is 95,000, the annual budget is $260 million, and there are approximately 900 full-time employees. The six council members and the mayor are all elected city wide.

Lee H. Berke

Lee H. Berke is the President and CEO of LHB Sports, Entertainment & Media, Inc. He founded LHB in 2001, which specializes in developing sports networks and building media rights across a range of platforms. LHB's client roster includes more than 30 teams throughout the NFL, MLB, NBA, NHL, NCAA, and NASCAR, leading venues such as Barclays Center and The Metropolitan Opera, and corporations looking to analyze the latest media and technology trends. Recent highlights include successful collaborations with the San Francisco Giants and the University of Oklahoma in developing and launching multiplatform sports networks. He is also a recurring guest lecturer at the University of Oregon's Warsaw Sports Marketing Center.

Berke's background in developing sports media businesses also includes co-authoring the original business plan for the New York Yankees' YES Network and heading up marketing for Madison Square Garden and MSG Network. He received a BA in Economics and an MBA in Marketing from the University of Michigan.

Gregg Olson

Gregg Olson currently serves as a Regional Vice President with SMG, the world's largest stadium and arena management company. Prior to overseeing the operation of a wide-range of major sports facilities, Olson spent 28 years managing the finance function of several professional sports teams. His career included stints with the Cleveland Indians, San Jose Sharks, and the Portland Trail Blazers. During his tenure he was involved with the development and building of Jacob's Field (now Progressive Park), the expansion of the Sharks to include Silicon Valley Sports and Entertainment (now Sharks Sports and Entertainment), and oversaw the finances of numerous ventures including the Trail Blazers' flagship radio stations, food service operations, and management of the City of Portland's Veterans Memorial Coliseum.

In his career, Olson has been involved with baseball (MLB, MiLB), hockey (NHL, AHL), indoor soccer, outdoor soccer (MLS), indoor roller hockey, indoor lacrosse (NLL), arena football (AFL), the Senior PGA men's golf, stadium management, and arena management. In addition to finance, Olson was the strategic partner to multiple presidents and oversaw other functions including Human Resources, Information Technology, Risk Management, Arena Management and Operations, and Administration.

He holds a BA from Baldwin–Wallace College, and was named CFO of the year by the Portland Business Journal in 2009.

Rick Van Brimmer

As an Assistant Vice President for Business Advancement, Rick Van Brimmer oversees coordination of the many affinity and sponsorship-related contracts in the Office of Trademark & Affinity Management at The Ohio State University. The position was created in response to continued innovations in outreach and business advancement activities by the university. He also oversees the university's successful international licensing program, and is responsible for coordinating Ohio State's corporate social responsibility programming for licensees.

He joined the licensing program in 1990, became director in 1999, and was named to his current post in 2012. Known for his marketing and product/idea development, licensing revenues at Ohio State have grown from $2 million to almost $10 million under his leadership, making Ohio State the leader in collegiate programs over that time period (1999–2012). Over the last 10 years, the licensing program has provided nearly $90 million in support to student scholarships and programming, and the university library system.